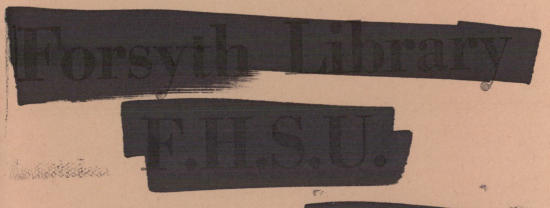

THE PAPERS OF

WOODROW WILSON

VOLUME 43
JUNE 25–AUGUST 20, 1917

SPONSORED BY THE WOODROW WILSON
FOUNDATION
AND PRINCETON UNIVERSITY

THE PAPERS OF
WOODROW WILSON

ARTHUR S. LINK, *EDITOR*

DAVID W. HIRST, *SENIOR ASSOCIATE EDITOR*

JOHN E. LITTLE, *ASSOCIATE EDITOR*

FREDRICK AANDAHL, *ASSOCIATE EDITOR*

MANFRED F. BOEMEKE, *ASSISTANT EDITOR*

PHYLLIS MARCHAND AND MARGARET D. LINK,
EDITORIAL ASSISTANTS

Volume 43
June 25–August 20, 1917

PRINCETON, NEW JERSEY
PRINCETON UNIVERSITY PRESS
1983

Note to scholars: Princeton University Press sub-
scribes to the Resolution on Permissions of the Association of American University Presses, defining what
we regard as "fair use" of copyrighted works. This
Resolution, intended to encourage scholarly use of
university press publications and to avoid unnecessary
applications for permission, is obtainable from the Press
or from the A.A.U.P. central office. Note, however, that
the scholarly apparatus, transcripts of shorthand, and
the texts of Wilson documents as they appear in this
volume are copyrighted, and the usual rules about the
use of copyrighted materials apply.

Publication of this book has been aided by a grant
from the National Historical Publications and Records
Commission.

Printed in the United States of America
by Princeton University Press
Princeton, New Jersey

INTRODUCTION

MOBILIZATION is well under way as this volume opens, and Wilson continues to maintain close control over the organization of the war effort and the conduct of American diplomacy. For example, he establishes a system to determine the prices which the United States and Allied governments will pay for basic raw materials and approves the reorganization of the General Munitions Board into the War Industries Board. He persuades the leaders of the Anti-Saloon League to relent in their campaign against the sale of beer and light wine. He suggests that the Secretary of War add sweet potatoes to the army's menu. While Congress debates the Lever food and fuel control bill, Wilson rallies his friends in Congress to defeat an amendment to that measure to establish a Joint Committee on Expenditures in the Conduct of the War. Moreover, he pardons the members of the National Woman's party who have been jailed for picketing the White House and begins a quiet campaign to get a federal suffrage amendment under way in Congress. He also publicly supports woman suffrage in a forthcoming referendum in New York State.

In many other ways, these summer months of mobilization are full of perplexities for Wilson. A vigilante group kidnaps some 1,400 copper miners on strike in Bisbee, Arizona, and sends them in boxcars into the desert of New Mexico. The War Department provides shelter and food in Columbus, New Mexico, and Wilson, outraged, sets a federal investigation in motion. Also troublesome are a strike of copper miners in Montana and the threats of strikes by the Industrial Workers of the World in the logging camps of the Northwest. Wilson sends a special envoy to confer with western governors about a plan for labor peace. Meanwhile, he works with the Secretary of Labor and the United States Board of Mediation and Conciliation to prevent or settle other strikes.

Postmaster General Burleson uses the Espionage Act to deny mailing privileges to *The Masses*, a Socialist monthly edited by Max Eastman. Wilson tries to intervene but is helpless because Eastman has taken his case to court. In all other cases of alleged violations of civil liberties, Wilson orders investigations. He refuses to permit the suppression of antidraft meetings in Wisconsin and of the People's Council, a group composed of Socialists, antiwar radicals, and pacifists. Wilson also publicly defends the loyalty of "the great body of our fellow-citizens of German blood." When a mob of whites kills many blacks in East St. Louis, Illinois, Wilson and Attorney General Gregory send federal agents to the scene.

The most nagging problem for Wilson during this summer is the continuing controversy between William Denman, head of the United

States Shipping Board, and George W. Goethals, head of the Emergency Fleet Corporation. Their constant quarreling seems to threaten the success of the entire shipbuilding program. After repeated efforts to persuade the two men to pull together, Wilson cuts the Gordian knot, "accepts" the resignations of Denman and Goethals, and gives full power to the new head of the Shipping Board, Edward N. Hurley.

The mobilization and training of the first segment of the National Army is going forward according to plan, but the crisis in shipping caused by the German submarine campaign remains acute. Wilson, who has urged the British to adopt the convoy system, sends a virtual ultimatum to London, and a full-scale convoy system is soon organized. The British government runs out of dollars in June and appeals to Washington for help. Secretary of the Treasury McAdoo drags his heels, but Wilson and Colonel House protect the pound.

A major cause of trouble abroad is the effort of the Japanese government to persuade the United States Government to agree that Japan has "paramount" interests in China, such as the United States enjoys in the western hemisphere. Wilson adamantly refuses to accept the Japanese claim, and the government in Tokyo prepares to send a special emissary to Washington to negotiate. In August, Wilson receives the members of the Root Mission, who have just returned from Russia, and makes plans to implement their recommendations.

Moderates in the Reichstag gain control of that body in mid-July and announce that Germany is ready to negotiate a peace of "no annexations, no indemnities." Two weeks later, Pope Benedict XV calls upon the belligerents to conclude peace upon a basis of the restoration of Belgium, the reconstitution of a Polish state, disarmament, freedom of the seas, and "conciliatory" settlement of territorial and other issues. Wilson, who knows that the Allies will not return a positive response, is hard at work on a reply to the Pope as this volume ends.

"VERBATIM ET LITERATIM"

In earlier volumes of this series, we have said something like the following: "All documents are reproduced *verbatim et literatim*, with typographical and spelling errors corrected in square brackets only when necessary for clarity and ease of reading." The following essay explains our textual methods and review procedures.

We have never printed and do not intend to print critical, or corrected, versions of documents. We print them exactly as they are, with a few exceptions which we always note. We never use *sic*, except to denote the repetition of words in a document; in fact, we think that a succession of *sics* defaces a page.

We usually repair words in square brackets when letters are missing. As we have said, we also repair words in square brackets for clarity and ease of reading. Our general rule is to do this when we, ourselves, cannot read the word without stopping to determine its meaning. Jumbled words and names misspelled beyond recognition of course have to be repaired. We correct the misspelling of a name in the footnote which identifies the person.

However, when an old man writes to Wilson saying that he is glad to hear that Wilson is "comming" to Newark, or a semi-literate farmer from Texas writes phonetically to complain of the low price of cotton, we see no reason to correct spellings in square brackets when the words are perfectly understandable. We do not correct Wilson's misspellings unless they are unreadable, except to supply in square brackets letters missing in words. For example, for some reason he insisted upon spelling "belligerent" as "belligerant." Nothing would be gained by correcting "belligerant" in square brackets.

We think that it is very important for several reasons to follow the rule of *verbatim et literatim*. Most important, a document has its own integrity and power, particularly when it is not written in a perfect literary form. There is something very moving in seeing a Texas dirt farmer struggling to express his feelings in words, or a semiliterate former slave doing the same thing. Second, in Wilson's case it is crucially important to reproduce his errors in letters which he typed himself, since he usually typed badly when he was in an agitated state. Third, since style is the essence of the person, we would never correct grammar or make tenses consistent, as one correspondent has urged us to do. Fourth, we think that it is obligatory to print typed documents *verbatim et literatim*. For example, we think that it is very important that we print exact transcripts of Charles L. Swem's copies of Wilson's letters. Swem made many mistakes (we correct them in footnotes from a reading of his shorthand books), and Wilson let them pass. We thus have to assume that Wilson did not read his letters before signing them, and this, we think, is a significant fact. Finally, printing typed letters and documents *verbatim et literatim* tells us a great deal about the educational level of the stenographic profession in the United States during Wilson's time.

We think that our series would be worthless if we produced unreliable texts, and we go to some effort to make certain that the texts are authentic.

Our typists are highly skilled and proofread their transcripts carefully as soon as they have typed them. The Editor sight proofreads documents once he has assembled a volume and is setting its annotation. The Editors who write the notes read through documents several times and are careful to check any anomalies. Then, once the manuscript volume has been completed and all notes checked, the Editor and Senior Associate Editor orally proofread the documents against the copy. They read every comma, dash, and character. They note every absence of punctuation. They study every nearly illegible word in written documents.

Once this process of "establishing the text" is completed, the manuscript volume goes to our editor at Princeton University Press, who checks the volume carefully and sends it to the printing plant. The volume is set by linotype by a typographer who has been working on the Wilson volumes for years. The galley proofs go to the proofroom, where they are read orally against copy. And we must say that the proofreaders at the Press are extraordinarily skilled. Some years ago, before we found a way to ease their burden, they used to query every misspelled word, absence of punctuation, or other such anomalies. Now we write "O.K." above such words or spaces on the copy.

We read the galley proofs three times. Our copyeditor gives them a sight reading against the manuscript copy to look for remaining typographical errors and to make sure that no line has been dropped. The Editor and Senior Associate Editor sight read them against documents and copy. We then get the page proofs, which have been corrected at the Press. We check all the changes three times. In addition, we get *revised* pages and check them twice.

This is not the end. Our indexer of course reads the pages word by word. Before we return the pages to the Press, she comes in with a list of queries, all of which are answered by reference to the documents.

Our rule in the Wilson Papers is that our tolerance of error is zero. No system and no person can be perfect. We are sure that there are errors in our volumes. However, we believe that we have done everything humanly possible to avoid error; the chance is remote that what looks at first glance like a typographical error is indeed an error.

We are grateful to Professors John Milton Cooper, Jr., William H. Harbaugh, and Richard W. Leopold for their careful reading of the manuscript of this volume and their comments and suggestions. We are also grateful to Judith May, our editor at Princeton University Press, for her ongoing help.

THE EDITORS

Princeton, New Jersey
December 7, 1982

CONTENTS

The Papers, June 25–August 20, 1917

Wilson Materials

Collateral Materials

ILLUSTRATIONS

Following page 294

ABBREVIATIONS

ALS	autograph letter signed
ASB	Albert Sidney Burleson
CC	carbon copy
CCL	carbon copy of letter
CCLS	carbon copy of letter signed
CLS	Charles Lee Swem
CLSsh	Charles Lee Swem shorthand
CLST	Charles Lee Swem typed
EBW	Edith Bolling Wilson
EMH	Edward Mandell House
FKL	Franklin Knight Lane
FR	*Papers Relating to the Foreign Relations of the United States*
FR-WWS 1917	*Papers Relating to the Foreign Relations of the United States, 1917, Supplement, The World War*
FR 1918, Russia	*Papers Relating to the Foreign Relations of the United States, 1918, Russia*
Hw, hw	handwriting, handwritten
HwLS	handwritten letter signed
HwS	handwritten signed
JD	Josephus Daniels
JPT	Joseph Patrick Tumulty
MS, MSS	manuscript, manuscripts
NDB	Newton Diehl Baker
RG	record group
RL	Robert Lansing
T	typed
TC	typed copy
TCL	typed copy of letter
TCLS	typed copy of letter signed
TI	typed initialed
TL	typed letter
TLI	typed letter initialed
TLS	typed letter signed
TS	typed signed
TWG	Thomas Watt Gregory
WBW	William Bauchop Wilson
WCR	William Cox Redfield
WGM	William Gibbs McAdoo
WHP	Walter Hines Page
WJB	William Jennings Bryan
WW	Woodrow Wilson
WWhw	Woodrow Wilson handwriting, handwritten
WWsh	Woodrow Wilson shorthand
WWT	Woodrow Wilson typed
WWTL	Woodrow Wilson typed letter
WWTLI	Woodrow Wilson typed letter initialed
WWTLS	Woodrow Wilson typed letter signed

ABBREVIATIONS FOR COLLECTIONS
AND REPOSITORIES

Following the National Union Catalog
of the Library of Congress

AFL-CIO-Ar	American Federation of Labor-Congress of Industrial Organizations Archives
AGO	Adjutant General's Office
CtY	Yale University
CU	University of California
DeU	University of Delaware
DLC	Library of Congress
DNA	National Archives
FFM-Ar	French Foreign Ministry Archives
FO	British Foreign Office
HPL	Hoover Presidential Library
JDR	Justice Department Records
LDR	Labor Department Records
MH	Harvard University
MH-Ar	Harvard University Archives
NjP	Princeton University
NRU	University of Rochester
PRO	Public Record Office
RSB Coll., DLC	Ray Stannard Baker Collection of Wilsoniana, Library of Congress
ScCleU	Clemson University
SDR	State Department Records
ViU	University of Virginia
WC, NjP	Woodrow Wilson Collection, Princeton University
WDR	War Department Records
WP, DLC	Woodrow Wilson Papers, Library of Congress

SYMBOLS

[July 12, 1917]	publication date of a published writing; also date of document when date is not part of text
[*July 5, 1917*]	composition date when publication date differs
[August 4, 1917]]	delivery date of speech if publication date differs
**** ***	text deleted by author of document

THE PAPERS OF

WOODROW WILSON

VOLUME 43
JUNE 25–AUGUST 20, 1917

THE PAPERS OF
WOODROW WILSON

To George Creel

My dear Creel: [The White House] 25 June, 1917

Thank you for the bound copy of the Official Bulletin,[1] May tenth to May thirty-first, 1917. I am exceedingly glad to get it in this form, and you may be sure will make any suggestions that occur to me, though the thing seems to me admirably done.

In haste   Cordially yours,   Woodrow Wilson

TLS (Letterpress Books, WP, DLC).

[1] The Committee on Public Information published the *Official Bulletin* daily except Sundays from May 10, 1917, through March 31, 1919. Edited by Edward Sudler Rochester, the *Official Bulletin* disseminated information about the American war effort at home and overseas. The *Official Bulletin* published such materials as presidential proclamations, speeches, Executive Orders, lists of casualties, and orders and regulations issued by both cabinet departments and war agencies. It was distributed free to public officials, newspapers, and other organizations equipped to spread its information. Copies were posted in military camps and in all post offices. Individuals could subscribe for $5 a year. Daily circulation varied from 60,000 in May 1917 to a high of 115,031 in October 1918 and a low of 33,000 in March 1919. The publication varied in length from eight to forty or more pages. See Stephen Vaughn, *Holding Fast the Inner Lines: Democracy, Nationalism, and the Committee on Public Information* (Chapel Hill, N. C., 1980), pp. 197-200.

Two Letters to William Bauchop Wilson

My dear Mr. Secretary: The White House 25 June, 1917

Thank you very much for your letter of June twenty-second with its enclosure, namely, your letter to Secretary Baker in reply to a letter to Secretary Lane from Mr. Walter Douglas, President of the Phelps Dodge Corporation, in reference to the labor situation in the mines of Arizona.[1]

Cordially and sincerely yours,   Woodrow Wilson

TLS (LDR, RG 174, DNA).

[1] See WBW to WW, June 22, 1917, enclosing WBW to NDB, June 22, 1917, Vol. 42.

My dear Mr. Secretary: The White House 25 June, 1917

I am very much obliged to you for sending me a copy of your reply to the memorandum from the British Embassy to the Secretary of State with regard to the desertion of seamen from British merchant vessels in United States ports,[1] and I want to say that I think your point of view is entirely justified.

Cordially and faithfully yours,   Woodrow Wilson

TLS (received from Mary A. Strohecker).
  [1] See WBW to WW, June 23, 1917, enclosing WBW to RL, June 21, 1917, Vol. 42.

To Willard Saulsbury

My dear Senator: The White House 25 June, 1917

It is a thorny business determining such matters as you refer to in your letter of June twenty-third,[1] but I hope before many days to work out a satisfactory solution, and I am very much obliged indeed for your expression of opinion in your letter.

In haste

Cordially and faithfully yours,   Woodrow Wilson

TLS (W. Saulsbury Papers, DeU).
  [1] W. Saulsbury to WW, June 23, 1917, Vol. 42.

Two Letters to Newton Diehl Baker

Personal and Private.

My dear Mr. Secretary: The White House 25 June, 1917

Senator Williams of Mississippi called my attention to a case the other day[1] which involves some serious possibilities, and I am venturing to write you a confidential letter about it.

Albert B. Dockery, First Lieutenant[2] in the Tenth U. S. Cavalry, now stationed at Fort Huachuca, Arizona, is a Southerner and finds it not only distasteful but practically impossible to serve under a colored commander. The Tenth Cavalry is temporarily in command of Lieutenant Colonel Charles Young,[3] who recently relieved Colonel D. C. Cabell,[4] and I am afraid from what I have learned that there may be some serious and perhaps even tragical insubordination on Lieutenant Dockery's part if he is left under Colonel Young, who is a colored man. Is there or is there not some way of relieving this situation by transferring Lieutenant Dockery and sending some man in his place who would not have equally intense prejudices?

Cordially and faithfully yours,   Woodrow Wilson

TLS (N. D. Baker Papers, DLC).
    [1] Wilson saw Williams at the White House on June 20.
    [2] Albert Bowdry Dockery, actually a captain at this time.
    [3] The third black graduate of the United States Military Academy (Class of 1889) and the only one still in active service at this time. He had served as military attaché in Haiti, 1904-1907, and in Liberia, 1912-1915. He had most recently been on active duty with the Punitive Expedition.
    [4] De Rosey Carroll Cabell.

My dear Mr. Secretary: [The White House] 25 June, 1917
    I am sure you will be interested in the enclosed,[1] particularly since it outlines a policy very similar to the one you were outlining to me the other day.
                Cordially and faithfully yours,   Woodrow Wilson

TLS (Letterpress Books, WP, DLC).
    [1] It is missing; however, it was a memorandum on conscientious objectors by Oswald Garrison Villard, dated June 21, 1917. Wilson commented upon it in a note to Tumulty: "Please thank Mr. Villard . . . for his memorandum. . . . It contains a great deal that is interesting and sensible, and I am sure that it will be read with as much sympathetic appreciation by the Secretary of War, to whom I am sending it, as by myself." WW to JPT, [June 25, 1917], TL (WP, DLC).

To Key Pittman

My dear Senator: [The White House] 25 June, 1917
    Of course, I understand your letter of June twenty-second[1] and I hope I may say equally of course I know that you understand that any omission such as you refer to was due to anything but my own choice as to dinner companions and those whom I would prefer to honor. You may be sure that the suggestion of your letter is well lodged and jumps with my inclination.
                Cordially and sincerely yours,   [Woodrow Wilson]

CCL (WP, DLC).
    [1] K. Pittman to WW, June 22, 1917, Vol. 42.

To Thomas Watt Gregory

                                        [The White House]
My dear Mr. Attorney General: 25 June, 1917
    Here is another item for your list of activities by the pro-Germans.[1]
                Cordially and faithfully yours,   Woodrow Wilson

TLS (Letterpress Books, WP, DLC).
    [1] The Editors have been unable to find this enclosure in any collection or file.

To William Gibbs McAdoo

My dear Mr. Secretary: [The White House] 25 June, 1917

Thank you for your letter of June twenty-third.[1] I am glad that you think there is a possibility of a satisfactory solution of the question of insurance for the men in the Army and Navy and that you are taking it up with a prospect of finding one.[2]

In haste

Cordially and faithfully yours,   Woodrow Wilson

TLS (Letterpress Books, WP, DLC).
[1] WGM to WW, June 23, 1917, Vol. 42.
[2] See WGM to WW, July 3, 1917.

Two Letters from William Byron Colver

My dear Mr. President: Washington 25 June, 1917.

I am sending you herewith the memorandum of which I spoke Saturday.[1] I asked permission to send it because a word in your talk with the Commission, gave me the impression that our argument against regulation by maximum price fixing and in favor of price fixing by government pool had not been made clear to you.

As I remember you said "Your coal plan contemplates closing down the high cost mines &c &c.

We did not mean to say that. We suggested closing only those temporary mines or "wagon-mines" which have no railroad sidings and whose product is hauled in wagons to the railroad cars. We would close them because their total output is of no importance and because the cars, held for days for loading, would enable the production of several times as much coal if sent to serve properly equipped mines where a car is loaded in four or five minutes. Also for a labor reason. These mines are non-union and bid high wages each for a few skilled miners so tending to disorganize the working force at really efficient mines by setting an unstable wage scale. Likewise they tend to draw in, as mine laborers, young men who would be far more useful in agriculture.

We would close no mine because it is high cost and our argument goes to conditions which appear to us to be fundamental.

If the memorandum shall be of the least help to you I shall be happy.   Yours very truly,   William B. Colver.

[1] W. B. Colver, "Memorandum as to Price Fixing Through Establishment of Maximum Price to Consumers as Compared with the Fixing of a Uniform Average Price by Means of a Government Pool," June 25, 1917, T MS (WP, DLC). As both the title and Colver's letter suggest, the memorandum argued against price-fixing by setting a maximum price for any given product based

upon the cost of production of the least efficient producer. Colver argued in favor of fixing a price to each producer based upon his cost of production and then passing the total product through a pool in the hands of the government, which would release it to the consumer at a fixed average price, with fixed profit margins to all middlemen. Colver asserted that the latter plan was the one which all the belligerent nations had finally worked out through trial and error. He suggested that it should apply to all vital goods and services, although he used coal as his specific example. He insisted that the control of such goods and services had to be centralized in the hands of the government but maintained that this was not "Socialism" or "government ownership."

My dear Mr. President: Washington June 25, 1917.

This tentative draft of a bill[1] has been prepared at the requests, separately made, of Senator Calder and Judge Sims of the House.

I thought perhaps you might care to see it.

Very truly yours,   William B. Colver.

TLS (WP, DLC).
[1] "Joint Resolution. To provide further for the national security and defense by regulating the production, sale, distribution and transportation of coal and coke, and for the coordination of the railroads of the United States for the efficient transportation and distribution thereof," T MS (WP, DLC). It authorized the President to create an agency which would purchase all coal and coke produced in the United States, fix the prices to producers, and then oversee the distribution of fuel to users. The agency would also set the prices and profit margins of both middlemen and the ultimate purchasers. This proposal was based on the pooling arrangement discussed in n. 1 to the preceding document. The second portion of the resolution authorized the President, if he deemed it necessary, to take over the operation of railroads, ships, and other common carriers, acting through the Interstate Commerce Commission.

Thetus W. Sims introduced this joint resolution (H.J. Res. 111) in the House on June 26. No action was taken upon it. The provisions relating to coal were incorporated in a somewhat different form in Section 25 of the Lever Food and Fuel Act enacted August 10, 1917 (40 *Statutes at Large* 276). The President, under the Army Appropriations Act approved August 29, 1916, already possessed the authority, in time of war, to take possession and assume control of any system or systems of transportation "for the transfer or transportation of troops, war material and equipment, or for such other purposes connected with the emergency as may be needful or desirable." 39 *Statutes at Large* 645.

From Robert Lansing

PERSONAL AND CONFIDENTIAL:

My dear Mr. President: Washington June 25, 1917.

I had an interview this morning with M. Paul May, the Minister of Belgium to China who is on his way to his post. Our conversation consisted mainly in his urging our Government to enter a *consortium* of the Allies on the ground that such a course was the only way to defeat the ambitious designs of Japan. He pointed out that this country and Japan would have to supply the bulk of any loans made to China, that the interests of Great Britain, France, Belgium and the United States were the same and that by an international concert there would be established a control over Japanese aggressiveness which would check political interference with China.

He said further that if loans to China were made independently by the different powers it would come down to loans by Japanese and by American houses, as other nationalities would find it impossible to enter into a competition of this sort; that Japan would at any cost or by any means obtain a preponderance of the loans because the Government would aid the Japanese bankers in order to create a situation; and that with a preponderance of the loans Japan would be in a position in case of any default on the part of China (a default almost certain to occur in view of the instability of the Chinese Government) to intervene independently in Chinese affairs with the excuse that Japanese interests were at stake and that as those interests were paramount interference by other Governments would be considered unjustified and offensive.

I told M. May that he probably was aware of the policy of this Government being opposed to a *consortium*, that we had favored independent financial relations with China because it seemed in the interests of China that there should be competition for loans and because concerted action by the powers appeared to involve political control to an extent in China. I said that at the present time I realized that policies, even when long established and based on well defined principles, might have to be modified or changed to meet the extraordinary international conditions resulting from the war, and that I was not, therefore, disposed to deny the wisdom of a *consortium* in view of the new situation or to say that this Government would reject the suggestion without carefully weighing the matter from the standpoint of expediency.

I said to him that the subject would receive thorough consideration, but that I would not indicate even my personal views as to the advisability of adopting the suggestion or express in any way the possibility of such adoption.

Baron Moncheur[1] and the Belgian Minister[2] have both talked with me about this matter during the last few days. They feel very keenly about it and very anxious to have Belgium included in a new *consortium*. My own view is that the whole question, being of so much importance to our future relations in the Far East, ought to be considered with little regard to the past.

Faithfully yours,   Robert Lansing.

TLS (WP, DLC).
    [1] Ludovic Alfred Joseph Ghislain, Baron Moncheur, former Belgian Minister

to the United States (1901-1909); at this time, 1917, chief of the political bureau of the Belgian Foreign Ministry and head of the Belgian mission to the United States, which had arrived in New York on June 16, 1917.
  2 Emile Ernest, Baron de Cartier de Marchienne.

From Sir Richard Frederick Crawford

My dear Mr. President: Washington. June 25th 1917.

In the Ambassador's absence I have the honour to transmit such information as we at present possess relative to the several points mentioned in your letter of the 23rd instant.[1] We have cabled to London for further particulars and will forward them to you as soon as received.

(1). "Great Britain's present remaining tonnage available for the sea carriage of supplies."

At the present moment the position is as follows:

Excluding vessels engaged in essential coasting employment in the Dominions there are about 3050 ocean going vessels on the United Kingdom Register (1600 tons gross or 2500 deadweight) 2400 of these being mainly cargo vessels and 650 passenger vessels. Of these about

1370 have been requisitioned for full and continuous service by the British Army and Navy, as transports, fleet auxiliaries, etc.

810 (liners) have been requisitioned on Blue book terms and are running under Government direction as to both cargoes and movements and wholly for Government account.

170 have been requisitioned for cargoes of wheat, sugar and grain.

50 (tramps) are importing miscellaneous essential articles (e.g. nitrates for explosives, oil required for munitions, etc.)

550 have been allotted to the Allies.

100 are under repair.

(2). "The present remaining tonnage available for the Allies for the same purpose."

The French and Italian ocean-going steamer fleets are each about one-tenth of the British and the Russian about one-twentieth.

The Allies as a whole, therefore, have about one quarter of the amount on the British register. The extent to which this tonnage is available for the sea-carriage of supplies in relation to the requirements is best shown by the fact that, in addition to the neutral ships the Allies have been able to charter, Great Britain has had to lend about 300 to 350 large vessels to France and 100 to 150 to Italy, while the demands of Russia would require over 200 vessels this summer.

(3). "Neutral tonnage available for that purpose."

We have not the exact corrected figures showing the result of the recent losses but have cabled for them.

The following figures show generally the size of the neutral mercantile marines (the figures include coasting as well as ocean-going craft and the tonnage is gross tonnage).

	Number of vessels	Gross tonnage
Danish	499	731,000
Dutch	894	1,400,000
Greek	233	617,000
Japanese	772	1,600,000
Norwegian	1424	2,000,000
Spanish	354	670,000
Swedish	559	652,000

It is difficult to estimate exactly how many of these may be regarded as available for sea-carriage of Allied supplies but an attempt is made in the enclosed Memorandum[2] (page 19).

(4.) "The actual tonnage destroyed by submarines since the first of January last listed month by month."

The following list gives the information required as regards over-seas tonnage of 1600 gross (2500 deadweight) and over:

Losses of British tonnage January-May 1917.

(General cargo steamers 1600 tons gross or 2500 tons d.w.)

	No. of vessels lost.	Net loss after allowing for new building etc.	Net loss of tonnage (gross tons)
January	54	45	185,047
February	61	41	137,277
March	88	53	181,874
April	112	98	384,710
May	101	70	199,076

The above figures exclude small craft under 1600 tons gross (which are not suitable for over-seas work) and vessels damaged but not lost.

Supplementary information as to the tonnage situation will be found in the enclosed Memorandum prepared by Mr. Royden,[3] Chairman of the Inter-Allied Shipping Committee, and Mr.

Salter,[4] Director of Ship Requisitioning, who have been especially sent over by the Minister of Shipping to give any information which the United States Government may require and to discuss shipping problems with them.

The Memorandum summarizes information given, and opinions expressed, at a number of discussions with the Chairman and members of the Shipping Board.

With assurances of my highest respect,

I have the honour to be, My dear Mr. President,

Yours faithfully,　Richard Crawford.

TLS (WP, DLC).
  [1] WW to C. A. Spring Rice, June 23, 1917, Vol. 42.
  [2] It is missing.
  [3] Sir Thomas Royden.
  [4] James Arthur Salter. Their report is missing.

From Domicio da Gama

Personal

My dear Mr. President,　　　　　Washington June 25, 1917

I felt (and am still feeling) some embarrassment in presenting to your Excellency with a list of names including some of men who not long ago were opposing the administration.[1]

To excuse myself I might say that I thought first of their usefulness and representativeness in the mission and then—when your Excellency called my attention to it—of their political creeds. But above all I believe that the pride of representing his own country and Government abroad is stronger than any party sentiment in the heart of an American citizen.

I am not well acquainted with the personnel of public men in the United States, but only as a suggestion and for your Excellency's personal consideration I would name the following:

Ex-President Taft
Secretary Houston
Senator Underwood
Senator Owen
Senator Phelan
John Bassett Moore
John Skelton Williams
Lewis Nixon
Lloyd Griscom
Judge Gray
John Barrett
Nicholas M. Butler

William Phillips
L. S. Rowe
Dr. Pratt
Oswald Villard
Otto Kahn

Nearly all of these men I know personally and I know also that any of them would honor his mission, but I would not dare to make a selection among them.

I trust that your Excellency will take this letter as a mere expression of my desire to help in a matter of common interest and seize the occasion to renew to your Excellency the assurances of my profound respect.   Domicio da Gama

ALS (WP, DLC).

[1] Da Gama had seen Wilson at the White House on June 22. According to the *New York Times*, July 1, 1917, Wilson was considering the dispatch of a special mission to Brazil to "arrange for a greater co-ordination of [naval] forces and the closest possible co-operation of the two Governments."

From Breckinridge Long

My dear Mr. President: Washington June 25, 1917.

The Italian Mission returns to town to-morrow afternoon. They are leaving definitely and finally the end of this week. The Italian Ambassador[1] has, this morning, requested the privilege of an interview with you for His Royal Highness the Prince of Udine, and one or two other members of Commission, for some time which will be perfectly convenient to you. I do not believe that they have anything particular to say, but they feel that they would like to say good-bye.

Will you be good enough to advise me whether it will be convenient for you to receive them on Wednesday, Thursday or Friday of this week and, if so, at what hour.[2]

Of course, the fact that they are going away is not to be known. The members of the Commission themselves do not know just when they are going or how they are going.

I am, my dear Mr. President,
            Yours very sincerely,   Breckinridge Long

TLS (WP, DLC).

[1] That is, Count Vincenzo Macchi di Cellere.
[2] Wilson saw the group on Thursday afternoon, June 28.

Robert Lansing to Joseph Patrick Tumulty,
with Enclosure

My dear Mr. Tumulty: Washington June 25, 1917.

I enclose herewith a copy of a telegram of the 21st instant from
Mr. Charles R. Crane at Petrograd for the President.
Very truly yours,   Robert Lansing

TLS (WP, DLC).

ENCLOSURE

Petrograd, June 21, 1917.

1429. For the President.

"We went into a war to free Cuba and came out of it with a
heavy responsibility in the Phillipines. The present war is vastly
greater and we may come out of it with vastly greater responsibilities for the future of Russia. The enthusiasm of the resolution [revolution] is being followed by dismay over the magnitude
of the new problems and the difficulties of firmly establishing a
new state on the wreckage. The one unified element in the empire
is the church but that in the process of Democratizing went
through more changes in the month of May than it had gone
through in two hundred years before. It has been practically
separated from the state and is now on its own responsibility. All
of the pastors have been obliged to have their positions confirmed
by election and twelve new Bishops including the Bishop of
Petrograd have been elected in the same way. The administration of the church property had passed into the hands of the Laity
and there is now sitting at Moscow the first sobor or church council since 1686 composed of 1268 members of clergy and Laity in
equal numbers selected from every parish in the empire. It is the
most truly representative assembly of the new Russia. Mr. Mott
was invited to address it; was accepted as your messenger and
made a most profound and moving discourse on the church in
itself, its relationships to the christian world, and the importance
of its position, not only in the empire but in America, and its
relation to the winning of the war. The assembly was greatly affected by the sympathy and wisdom of the address. The foremost
members of the body made most touching responses which were
followed by the whole congregation rising and singing the oldest
and most beautiful hymns as an expression of their appreciation.
One of the members in responding said, "The echo of this speech

will not die away here but within a short time will be heard in every parish in Russia." It was worth while having the commission come here if that were the one thing that it could accomplish —it certainly is the most important thing. It represented the heart of Russia and when Mr. Mott struck the war-note there was an immediate response and everyone instantly arose and applauded. It was a much more loyal, true and far reaching note than one could possibly get from any political assembly. I am sending a fuller account of the meeting to the Christian Science Monitor. Affectionate messages to the family and to the cabinet. Hope to see you all soon. Charles R. Crane."   Francis.

T telegram (SDR, RG 59, 861.00/396, DNA).

A Statement

[c. June 26, 1917]

It is important that the country should understand just what is intended in the control of exports which is about to be undertaken, and since the power is vested by the Congress in the President I can speak with authority concerning it. The Exports Council will be merely advisory to the President.

There will, of course, be no prohibition of exports. The normal course of trade will be interfered with as little as possible, and, so far as possible, only its abnormal course directed. The whole object will be to direct exports in such a way that they will go first and by preference where they are most needed and most immediately needed, and temporarily to withhold them, if necessary, where they can best be spared.

Our primary duty in the matter of foodstuffs and like necessaries is to see to it that the peoples associated with us in the war get as generous a proportion as possible of our surplus; but it will also be our wish and purpose to supply the neutral nations whose peoples depend upon us for such supplies as nearly in proportion to their need as the amount to be divided permits.

There will thus be little check put upon the volume of exports, and the prices obtained for them will not be affected by this regulation.

This policy will be carried out, not by prohibitive regulations, therefore, but by a system of licensing exports which will be as simply organized and administered as possible, so as to constitute no impediment to the normal flow of commerce. In brief, the free play of trade will not be arbitrarily interfered with; it will only be intelligently and systematically directed in the light of full information with regard to needs and market conditions throughout the world and the necessities of our peo[p]le at home and our armies and the armies of our associates abroad.

The Government is taking, or has taken, steps to ascertain, for example, just what the available present supply of wheat and corn is remaining from the crops of last year; to learn from each of the countries exporting these foodstuffs from the United States what their purchases in this country now are, where they are stored, and what their needs are, in order that we may adjust things so far as possible to our own needs and free stocks; and this information is in course of being rapidly supplied.

The case of wheat and corn will serve as an illustration of all the rest of supplies of all kinds. Our trade can be successfully and profitably conducted now, the war pushed to a victorious issue, and the needs of our own people and of the other people with whom we are still free to trade efficiently met only by systematic direction; and that is what will be attempted.[1]

Woodrow Wilson.

Printed in the *Official Bulletin*, I (June 26, 1917), 1.
[1] There is a WWsh draft of this statement in WP, DLC.

To Elihu Root

Handed me by Prest. June 26/17 RL

The President suggests that it is not advisable for members of the Commission to speak of the terms of peace or of settlement which will be insisted on by the United States.[1] The President is himself reserving all such utterances until very different circumstances arise.[2]

WWhw MS (SDR, RG 59, 763.72/5782f, DNA).
[1] As all the documents and news reports reveal, Wilson was not responding to any speech or statement by any member of the Root Mission.
[2] This was sent in the following telegram:
"FOR ROOT. The reports received of the addresses by the Commissioners and of the very favorable impression made are most gratifying and the President desires me to express his satisfaction at the success which is meeting your efforts. If there was doubt of the genuine desire of this country to see the Russian democracy achieve its aims, your convincing presentation of the sympathetic attitude of the American people has removed it.
"PARAGRAPH. The President, while extending his congratulations to the Commission on the skillful manner in which they are performing a difficult task, suggests that it is not advisable for members of the Commission to speak of the terms of peace or of settlement which will be insisted on by the United States. The President is himself reserving all such utterances until very different circumstances arise, and hopes that you will pursue the same policy.
"PARAGRAPH. The matter of establishing an efficient agency for publicity is receiving careful consideration in view of your recommendations as to its desirability." RL to D. R. Francis, June 27, 1917, T telegram (SDR, RG 59, 763.72/5782f, DNA). For the Root Mission's preliminary recommendations, see E. Root to RL, June 17, 1917, *FR 1918 Russia*, I, 120-22.

To Newton Diehl Baker

My dear Mr. Secretary: The White House 26 June, 1917

I feel as you do that the offer of troops from the Philippines is a very significant and admirable thing,[1] and I am glad you are laying the matter before the Senate Committee on Military Affairs so that the law may permit our accepting the services of these troops.

Cordially and faithfully yours,   Woodrow Wilson

TLS (N. D. Baker Papers, DLC).
  [1] See NDB to WW, June 19, 1917, Vol. 42.

From Newton Diehl Baker

My dear Mr. President: Washington. June 26, 1917.

I have received your personal and private letter of June 25th. Several Senators, curiously enough one from North Dakota, have presented cases to me of your [four] officers in the 10th Cavalry who were under the same embarrassment as Lieutenant Dockery with regard to serving under Lieutenant-Colonel Charles Young. The situation is, of course, very embarrassing, but I am endeavoring to meet it by using Colonel Young in connection with the training of colored officers for the new Army at Des Moines, Iowa. It seems likely that I will be able to tide over the difficulty in that way for at least a while.

In the meantime, Colonel Young, who is a West Point graduate and was for many years our attache in Liberia and Hayti. He is now definitely returned to the United States, but apparently is not in perfectly good health, and for the next two or three weeks he will be at the Letterman General Hospital in San Francisco under observation to determine whether his physical condition is sufficiently good to justify his return to active service. There does not seem to be any present likelihood of his early return to the 10th Cavalry so that the situation may not develop to which you refer.   Respectfully yours,   Newton D. Baker

TLS (WP, DLC).

From William Bauchop Wilson

My dear Mr. President: Washington June 26, 1917.

I have your letter of the 25th,[1] inclosing communication from Senator Weeks,[2] relative to the situation in the mining and smelting industries of the Rocky Mountain States.

On June 14th my attention was orally called to a serious situation existing in Butte, Montana, affecting the mining and smelting operations. I was advised that certain individuals, whose names were not mentioned, had come to Butte from the Pacific Coast, claiming to represent the Sinn Fein movement.[3] It afterwards developed that they were actually representatives of the I.W.W.[4] Literature of that organization was circulated in large quantities, and among other things appearing at the same time, but in an anonymous form, was a circular scattered throughout the city insisting on the shutting down of the mines in order that copper might not be furnished to the British. An unusually large number of mine accidents, principally fires, resulting in considerable loss of life, have recently occurred in the Butte District. Some of these are recognized as being of accidental origin. Others are believed to have been incendiary. The Department of Justice has been investigating these allegations.

On June 20th I was advised by telegram that a strike had occurred at Butte. In the meantime I had received from Acting Governor Bennion[5] of Utah, under date of June 16th, a telegram notifying me of a strike at Tooele, Utah, which was presumed to be in some way connected with the strike movement at Butte. The mediation fund of the Department was exhausted, but the situation seemed to me to be of such importance that on June 20th I decided to appoint two competent men to act as mediators, paying them out of the immigration fund. I sent one of them to Butte and the other to Tooele, and directed them to cooperate with each other.

Yesterday I received the following telegram from Mr. McBride,[6] the Commissioner at Tooele:

"Held several conferences with interested parties. Conditions at Tooele peaceful. Progress of a promising character being made. Telegram on Butte situation just received and am wiring Rodgers."[7] Today his report is not so encouraging. He wires:

"Repeated conferences with numerous interested parties in mining and smelting led me to hope for acceptance of compromise proposition submitted by me, but today shippers and smelters meeting refused to accept and declared for original position, which strikers had unanimously refused. Tooele strikers live three miles from smelter and everything peaceful, but companies have asked for and expect Federal troops, which, while unnecessary, will be welcomed by strikers. Tooele strike has one thousand men directly involved but fifteen thousand interested and may participate before settlement reached. Influence of unknown character interfering. Rodgers cannot locate it at Butte. Meeting Tooele tomorrow. May be policy to remain here few days but outlook for settlement anything but favorable as I view it. Advise me your judgment as to future."

I have instructed Mr. McBride to remain on the ground as long as there is a thread of hope and to wire me the substance of the proposed compromise, rejected by the employers, with the hope that I may be able to bring some influence to bear at the New York end. The information we now have seems to indicate that the strike is not likely to spread to other mining camps and smelting plants.

I am returning the letter from Senator Weeks herewith.

Faithfully yours,   W B Wilson

TLS (WP, DLC).
    [1] WW to WBW, June 25, 1917, TLS (Letterpress Books, WP, DLC): "May I have your information and judgment about the matter dealt with in the enclosed letter?"
    [2] It is missing.
    [3] That is, the Irish revolutionary nationalist party.
    [4] That is, the Industrial Workers of the World. The standard, modern study of this militant labor organization is Melvin Dubofsky, *We Shall Be All: A History of the Industrial Workers of the World* (rev. edn., New York, 1975).
    [5] Harden Bennion, Secretary of State of Utah.
    [6] John McBride, Commissioner of Conciliation employed by the Department of Labor on a *per diem* basis.
    [7] W. H. Rogers, not Rodgers, another Commissioner of Conciliation.

From Walter Hines Page

London, June 26 1917.

6543. MOST CONFIDENTIAL FOR THE PRESIDENT AND THE SECRETARY ONLY:

I have just received from the Admiralty the following startling information:

Tank steamers of sixty thousand tons capacity have been torpedoed since the first of this month. This heavy loss comes upon the top of arrangements which at best would have brought an insufficient supply. The result is stock now England for the use of British Navy will last only six weeks at the lowest conventional rate of consumption. If any special demand should be made by navy the entire supply might be used up at once. No such dangerous situation has (*) during the war. All the oil that can be carried to this country by the tankers available for naval use is only two thirds of required amount even when fleet activities are curtailed as at the present time. This perilous situation seems to me to warrant the following recommendations:

First. That ships at the present time carrying oil in bulk to neutral countries be diverted to the United Kingdom.

Second. That tank ships doing any service other than that directly aiding European military situation be taken for this purpose.

Third. That construction and conversion of oilers be hastened to the extreme limit and if necessary regardless of cost for bonuses. A failure quickly to replenish stock here may at any time cause disaster. Two hundred thousand tons must be delivered by August thirtieth and an additional by September thirtieth and the vessels which bring these quantities must be continued in the service. These quantities must be in addition to shipments already arranged for. Of course I need not (*) the necessity for absolute secrecy regarding this matter.

The Admiralty will highly appreciate an answer saying what can be done.

This message is sent after consulting the First Lord of the Admiralty[1] and Admiral Jellicoe who expressed gratitude for sending it.   Page

T telegram (SDR, RG 59, 763.72/5551, DNA).
[1] That is, Sir Edward Henry Carson.

From Joseph Patrick Tumulty

Dear Governor: The White House 26 June 1917.

A few weeks ago, Louis Seibold asked for an appointment which you did not see fit to grant. I understand your reason. Today Seibold withdrew the request, saying that he had learned you had made the statement to some one that he was a reactionary and no longer had your confidence.

I have known Louis Seibold for four years and have kept in touch with his writings. At times he has criticized various men about you, including myself, but I have never questioned his friendship or sincere admiration for you. While he is inclined to be cynical at times (for he has had misfortunes of a personal character, including the sudden death of his only son), you are the only public man in whom he has real faith and confidence, and even deep affection. I do not wish him to feel that you have withdrawn your confidence from him.

If he could serve you now in a great crisis where there is no personal reward, I am sure you would find him ready to do so, for his heart is right and it is with you. I know that you would never say anything that would cause him pain, unless it was deserved.

Could you not drop him a line, expressing your friendship for him, and tell him with what regret you were compelled to turn away from his request for an appointment?

                              Sincerely yours,   Tumulty

TLS (WP, DLC).

Sir Eric Drummond to Sir William Wiseman

                                        [London] 26.6.17

Your telegram June 20th.[1]
In view of fact that scheme seems to afford sound method of checking German and pacifist propaganda in Russia and that President is interested in it we agree to co-operate and 75,000 dollars will be placed to your credit at Morgans as soon as possible.   Drummond.

T telegram (A. J. Balfour Papers, FO 800/205, p. 155, PRO).
[1] W. Wiseman to E. Drummond, June 20, 1917, Vol. 42.

To William Charles Adamson, with Enclosure

My dear Judge: [The White House] 27 June, 1917
    I am sure you will be willing to read the enclosed letter for me and give me your impressions. I had supposed when I heard of the proviso added by the Senate that it expressed our policy any way and that its insertion would neither add nor subtract anything.
    In haste   Faithfully yours,   Woodrow Wilson

TLS (Letterpress Books, WP, DLC).

E N C L O S U R E

From Samuel Gompers

Sir: Washington, D. C. June 27, 1917.
    There was introduced in the United States Senate and passed by that body a bill known as S. 2356. This bill deals with Interstate and Foreign Commerce, and clothes the President of the United States with large powers in the conduct or movement of Interstate and Foreign Commerce in any part of the United States, or of any train, locomotive, car or other vehicle upon any railroad in the United States engaged in Interstate or Foreign Commerce.

This bill was so phrased that in the event it became a law and the provisions thereof strictly enforced, it would be a repeal of the labor provisions of the Clayton Law.

In view of the announced policy of yourself and the Council of National Defense, to maintain existing law until such time as a great emergency made necessary the suspension of any law relating to workers in industry, the representatives of the four great Railroad Brotherhoods requested those in charge of the bill in the United States Senate to incorporate an amendment. Agreeable to the request, the following amendmend [amendment] was adopted by the Senate, unanimously, as part of S. 2356:

"Provided that nothing in this section shall be construed to repeal, modify or affect either Section 6 or Section 20 of an act entitled An Act to Supplement Existing laws against Unlawful Restraints and Monopolies and for other purposes. Approved October 15, 1914."

Upon the unanimous passage by the Senate of the bill referred to with the amendment attached, it went to the House of Representatives where it was referred to the Interstate and Foreign Commerce Committee. This committee, on Monday, June 25, met to consider S. 2356. A majority of the members of the committee present eliminated from the Senate bill the provision that nothing in section one of the bill should be construed to repeal, modify or affect section 6 or section 20 of the Clayton Law. The striking out of this provision from the bill is clearly an effort to repeal the salient sections of the Clayton Law.

Your attention is respectfully called to the fact that during the period when the Sherman Antitrust Law was in the making by Congress, assurances of the most positive character were given that under no strained construction of the provisions of the proposed legislation could the normal activities of the wage-workers of our country regulating hours, wages and conditions of employment be construed by the courts as applicable to such activities. And yet, despite that assurance, the Sherman Antitrust Law, as you well know, has been so construed, much to the injury of a large number of workers, and relief was only secured after twenty-four years of hard work, sacrifice and suffering, by the enactment of the Clayton Law, to which you gave your approval.

Having in mind your clear and concise declaration with reference to the repeal of labor laws, especially a sentence included in your letter to Governor Brumbaugh of Pennsylvania relative to the repeal of the Full Crew Law of that state, I quote one of your forceful statements,

"I take pleasure in replying to your letter of June 1. I think it would be most unfortunate for any of the states to relax laws by which safeguards have been thrown about labor. I feel that there is no necessity for such action and that it would lead to a slackening of the energy of the nation rather than to an increase of it, besides being very unfair to the laboring people themselves."[1]

And, Sir, while addressing you upon this subject your attention is also respectfully called to the fact that the Lever Bill[2] as introduced in the House contained provisions which in effect would repeal the protective features of the Clayton Law by declaring that the ordinary organized activities of the workers engaged in an effort to maintain standards of work and life could be construed and stigmatized as conspiracies, thus laying the workers liable to the charge of treason. To overcome this feature of the bill, Representative Keating of Colorado prepared the following amendment:

"Provided that nothing in this section shall be construed to repeal, modify or affect either Section 6 or Section 20 of an act entitled An Act to Supplement Existing Laws Against Unlawful Restraints and Monopolies and for other purposes, approved October 15, 1914."

Under the spur of zeal or mistaken patriotism, the amendment was defeated.

Now that the House of Representatives has rejected an amendment that would guarantee to all of the workers the right to carry on their necessary organized activities, and the House Committee on Interstate and Foreign Commerce has rejected an amendment that would guarantee the same right to railroad employes, despite the fact that attention was called to the danger that this course would impose upon the workers of the country, there is no assurance that every right which the millions of workers of our country now possess will not be taken from them by Congressional action and by judicial interpretation. The courts of our country will have the right to take cognizance in any case before them that the House of Representatives put their seal of disapproval of [on] the proposed amendments and to place the workers of our country in a position of hazard so far as their rights and their freedom are concerned.

The people of our country are giving and will give wholehearted support to the great enterprise upon which our republic has entered to make the world safe for democracy. Surely in the prosecution of the contest for the establishment of that great principle the toilers of America should not be permitted to lose their rights and their freedom.

It may be additionally interesting to say that there has been no element or group of people in all our country who have done more to clarify the minds of all of the immediate necessity for the enactment of the fundamental principles of the Lever Bill than the organized wage-earners.

We are exceedingly concerned with the present status of these bills, and while we shall made [make] an earnest endeavor to prevent the repeal of the labor provisions of the Clayton Law by indirection, we feel justified in seeking whatever assistance you may be able to render to keep intact and in full force the Clayton Law which you approved on October 15, 1914.

Respectfully,   Samuel Gompers.

TLS (WP, DLC).

[1] WW to M. G. Brumbaugh, June 4, 1917, Vol. 42.
[2] About this bill, see D. F. Houston to WW, May 14, 1917, n. 2, and the White House Staff to WW, June 16, 1917, n. 1, both in Vol. 42.

To Louis Seibold

My dear Seibold: The White House 27 June, 1917

I have been beyond measure distressed to hear that someone told you that I had said that I regarded you as a reactionary and that you no longer had my confidence. Of course, that is absolutely false. My feeling towards you has never changed in the least or my confidence in your character and your principles. I have from time to time been distressed when you have seemed in your articles to be opposed to measures I thought essential for the defense and safety of the country, but I am not the sort to change my opinion of a man I know because he opposed me, and the only reason I did not arrange for the appointment you asked for was a reason which you will readily understand. The fact is I am so desperately pressed that unless an appointment is absolutely necessary I postpone it from day to day in the vain hope of finding a free interval. You know, besides, how awkward it is for me to arrange one such interview, no matter what my feeling for the man involved may be, without creating the expectation that I will see other newspaper men of unusual importance when they are in Washington.

Please, my dear Seibold, believe things only that are credible, and whenever you hear anything such as I have alluded to please let me know immediately.

With the warmest cordiality,

Your sincere friend,   Woodrow Wilson

TLS (WP, DLC).

From Edward Mandell House

Dear Governor: Magnolia, Massachusetts. June 27, 1917.

I am glad you were so gracious to Sir William last night.[1] You have made him very happy. It is important that he should be able to say that he has met you because he goes to England in about two weeks.

Spring-Rice and Sir William were here Friday and Saturday. Spring-Rice came to discuss his difficulties with Northcliffe. We persuaded him to forget them for the moment and to work harmoniously. The fact that both Northcliffe and Spring-Rice make Sir William their confident [confidant] is a tribute to his good sense and diplomacy.

Sir William is going to England in order to lay the actual situation before his government. There is a party in England determined to get rid of Sir Cecil, and Sir Cecil is aiding them in every way possible.

His first meeting with Northcliffe was at the Embassy where he had invited him to dinner. Strangely enough, he chose this place and occasion to insult him. He had asked Northcliffe to come a few minutes in advance of the other guests, in order that he might express his opinion of him. Northcliffe started to leave before the dinner, and if it had not been for the opportune arrival of the French Ambassador, who was also one of the guests, he would have done so.

Sir Cecil has lost confidence in himself, and I believe would go home without much protest provided his government will recall him in a way to save his face. I expressed the hope to Balfour and Drummond that they would pin some badges on Sir Cecil and they promised to do so. A peerage and a good part of the alphabet after his name is contemplated.

Drummond would like to succeed him. Northcliffe says he (N) was offered the place and refused it. Drummond would be an acceptable man, but he is needed in the Foreign Office and should be given Hardinge's place who is now Under Secretary of State for Foreign Affairs. Sir William is and has been the real Ambassador over here for sometime. However, I suppose his youth would prevent consideration of his name.

Northcliffe is coming up the latter part of next week. We are all working to keep him from doing the things we expected. Up to now, he has been willing to be guided. He is finding his duties irksome, and it is thought that he will feel he is needed at home before long. Affectionately yours, E. M. House

TLS (WP, DLC).

¹ For two brief reports of Wiseman's meeting with Wilson on June 26, see Wilton B. Fowler, *British-American Relations, 1917-1918: The Role of Sir William Wiseman* (Princeton, N. J., 1969), pp. 51-52.

From Newton Diehl Baker

Dear Mr. President: Washington. June 27, 1917

I beg leave to submit for your consideration the naming of the following civilian members to constitute the reorganized War Industries Board:[1]

Mr. F. A. Scott, at present Chairman of the General Munitions Board, Mr. Robert S. Brookings of St. Louis, Mr. H. A. Garfield of Williams College, and Mr. Hugh Frayne[2] of New York.

Mr. Scott has been the Chairman of the Munitions Board since the organization of the Council of National Defense. He is an extremely able man and is so familiar with the entire work that his present separation would seem to be undesirable, although he is anxious to be relieved, and in view of the fact that his company, the Warner & Swasey Company of Cleveland, manufacture some optical instruments for both the Army and the Navy, it may be desirable for him to retire after the formation of the board and after he has transferred to the other members the information and experience which he has been accumulating. I should personally regret to see Mr. Scott retire and do not believe that the relations of his company to the Government require it, as his company is the only maker of the optical instruments in question in this country and has long made them for the Government under exactly similar conditions to the contracts now in force and is always an unwilling contractor, since the company's principal business is in the manufacture of machine tools, and it is so busily employed that the work it does for the Government is admittedly its least profitable business. In addition to this, Mr. Scott does not himself participate in the making of any contracts with the Government, and is only incidentally profited by them.

Mr. Brookings is one of the foremost citizens of St. Louis, a man of large fortune, completely removed from all active business occupations, and yet of so large experience as to be an exceedingly able advisor for the Government.

Mr. Garfield is, of course, known to you. I personally know of his successful business career in Cleveland, his fineness of spirit, and his legal ability. As, however, he is intimately known to you, his suitableness for this work will be better known to you than it is to me.

Mr. Frayne is a suggestion of Secretary Wilson and would, in his opinion, satisfy labor that its interests were being properly considered.

All of these suggestions have been canvassed by the Council of National Defense and met with their approval, subject, of course, to yours.

It is the further judgment of the Council that it would be wiser to constitute this Board first and to allow them to cooperate with us in selecting for recommendation to you the names of the three yet to be chosen who are to act on behalf of the Government as Chief of Raw Materials, Chief of Finished Products, and Chief of Priorities.   Respectfully yours,   Newton D. Baker

TLS (N. D. Baker Papers, DLC).
  [1] The immediate predecessor of the War Industries Board was the General Munitions Board. For earlier discussions of the proposed reorganization, see NDB to WW, May 28, 1917, and its Enclosures, and NDB to WW, June 13, 1917, all in Vol. 42. See also Daniel R. Beaver, *Newton D. Baker and the American War Effort, 1917-1919* (Lincoln, Neb., 1966), pp. 71-72, and Robert D. Cuff, *The War Industries Board: Business-Government Relations During World War I* (Baltimore, 1973), pp. 100-102.
  [2] General organizer of the American Federation of Labor.

From Walter Hines Page

London, June 27, 1917.

6544. MOST CONFIDENTIAL. For the Secretary of State and President only. My 6503, June 20th[1] and 6543, June 26th. Sims sends me by special messenger from Queenstown the most alarming reports of the submarine situation which are confirmed by the Admiralty here. He says that the war will be won or lost in this submarine zone within a few months. Time is the essence of the problem and anti submarine craft which cannot be assembled in the submarine zone almost immediately may come too late. There is therefore a possibility that this war may become a war between Germany and the United States alone. Help is far more urgently and quickly needed in this submarine zone than anywhere else in the whole war area.   Page.

T telegram (SDR, RG 59, 763.72/5552, DNA).
  [1] WHP to WW, June 20, 1917, Vol. 42.

From Thomas Nelson Page

CONFIDENTIAL.

My dear Mr. President:　　　　　　Rome June 27, 1917.

Even at this long distance the thrill of what is going on just around where you sit, or at least, are—for I fancy that you have little time for sitting still—stirs us deeply. I wonder if it is known how tremendous the effect of the moral movement which you have headed through these long months has been here in Europe. A man said to me today—it is true he is an American, but he prefaced the remark by saying he was a Republican—"Mr. Wilson has become the spokesman of the moral conscience of the World."

Where a short time ago it was hardly a corporal's guard that stood here in Rome for you and that which you represented,—though it was a pretty intrepid guard which never yielded an inch and made some captures—everybody is now for what you have done. It has even become fashionable. But irrespective of the question of sudden conversion, the effect of America's coming in in the way in which she came in under your guidance has been something incalculable. About ten days ago the King, who was in Rome to help settle the troubles in the Ministry which threatened a Ministerial crisis, sent me a message asking me to come to see him—a thing which he had never done before. And the next morning when I called the first thing he said was that he had asked me to come to see him in order to thank us for all our kindness. A little later he spoke of the enormous relief that was felt here in all hearts when America came in and of his confidence in the outcome. He has always treated me with great consideration and cordiality and I have never talked to him without feeling that he is a man of not only a high order of intellect, but of character. I am not sure that—taking him altogether—he has not impressed me as the man of the broadest knowledge and clearest intelligence whom I have met in Italy. To say that (in my judgment) he is the best King in Europe might not be thought, in view of the intelligence ordinarily accredited to kings in Europe, very high praise. He is, however, a King who, taking into consideration all conditions, has in my judgment had no superior in any country or in any time; for he is the leader of his people according to the new dispensation of Democracy. A clever Englishman said in my house the other day that he believed that in ten years there would be but one king in Europe: The King of Italy.

In our conversation he alluded to his hope that the Italian Mission sent to America would result in making it clear what need there is in Italy for certain things, particularly coal, iron, and tonnage for the conveyance of these things. He also referred to the needs of more guns and ammunition. He said that it was owing to the want of guns and ammunition that the progress made was apparently so small, mentioning that after a bombardment of two or three days, which required millions of shells, it was necessary to wait always to replenish the stock; whereas if they had double as many they could keep on and could advance on a front much longer than at present. He said that he believed that in the latter case an advance could be made which would overwhelm Austria, and with the crumbling of Austria, Germany also would crumble.

We talked a little of the sending of a military mission (of observers) to Italy and I asked if it would be acceptable to Italy. He said he felt sure that it would be welcomed and suggested my taking the matter up with the Ministry, which I have since done with the most satisfactory results of which I have today notified the Secretary of State by cable. I feel sure that the sending of a good mission here—that is, one composed of first class men—will have an admirable effect here, not only from the military standpoint, but from a political standpoint also. It would be bad policy not to send first class men, as our Mission should measure up—I do not mean in rank, but in quality—with the others. I have written a despatch to the Department today giving a list of the several Missions already at the Italian front.

The Swiss situation[1] has caused much comment here and I think some little anxiety. But the appointment of M. Ador as head of the political section of the Federal Council has quieted the anxiety, he being regarded as a friend of the Entente. Baron Sonnino in talking to me about the hard case in which Switzerland finds itself, expressed the hope that Switzerland would not be pushed to the extremity of drawing nearer to Germany and Austria. He appeared to think that this would be a disastrous policy and he said that it would be necessary, he thought, to make certain concessions to Switzerland in the way of permitting her to have certain supplies beyond what are allowed to other neutral countries, because Switzerland's life depends on her procuring these things, and if she does not get them from the Entente powers she will go over nearer to the Central Empires. I get this impression also from Mr. DePlanta,[2] the Swiss Minister, who is an absolute believer in the neutrality of Switzerland. And indeed this is my own conviction, based on what I have learned about the conditions in Switzerland, all of which I have already telegraphed to the Department.

I am, my dear Mr. President, always,

Most sincerely yours,   Thos. Nelson Page

TLS (WP, DLC).

¹ Arthur Hoffmann, a member of the Swiss Federal Council (the Cabinet) and Chief of the Political Department (the Foreign Ministry) had sent a telegram on June 5 via the Swiss Minister to Russia to Robert Grimm, a Swiss socialist then in Petrograd, which indicated that Germany was interested in making a separate peace with Russia. The telegram fell into other hands and was published in Stockholm on June 16. This caused a furor in the Entente nations. The Provisional Government expelled Grimm from Russia. In Switzerland, the affair created great resentment among French-speaking Swiss and even among some of the German Swiss. Hoffmann was forced to resign on June 20. Gustave Ador, a French Swiss, then president of the International Red Cross, was elected to succeed Hoffmann on June 26 and took office on July 1. See the *New York Times*, June 17, 20, 21, 22, 26, and 27, 1917.

² Alfred von Planta.

William Graves Sharp to Robert Lansing

Paris, June 27, 1917.

2238. Your confidential telegram number 2389 of the twenty fifth instant.¹ Your request affords me the opportunity of giving to you my opinion of the Swing telegram² to Colonel House free from the embarrassment which the circumstances under which it was authorized to be sent placed me. Appreciating, however, the possible harm that such statements might produce I briefly cabled Colonel House on the twenty third instant, a warning against accepting such information at its face value. My message also entirely sustained your own conclusions.

A few days after the arrival of Mr. Swing from America, he called on me, and, telling me he was expecting soon to proceed to Switzerland, where he was to represent Colonel House in reporting upon conditions existing there, said that on account of certain information he had gathered here he would like to have the privilege of using the Embassy code to cable to Colonel House. He did not venture any statement as to the nature of this information and brought no letter of introduction. I told him that I preferred not to make the request for such permission suggesting he get in touch with Colonel House.

He evidently later secured this permission through cabling to Colonel House direct. I only saw him the one time and that but for a few minutes. He is a man, I would say, twenty-seven or twenty-eight years of age, and impressed me as a rather familiar type of the young American newspaper correspondent, which profession he said he had followed.

Upon reading his message which he had left to be sent in code, I was greatly surprised at the position he had taken. Greater importance might have been attached to his statements if they had not been so obviously exaggerated and unfounded. His own opinions also were so luridly tinged with the most pronounced socialistic leanings as to carry their own condemnation. In view of the recognized high ideals for which France herself has been fighting, his reference to the revolutionary spirit of those radical socialists as being extraordinarily fine, earnest and idealistic smacks of the ironical, to say the least. The young man had simply been seeing things through red colored glasses and whether by natural selection or otherwise it is certain that he must have obtained his information from socialists of the most radical type. As to whether he has any definite affiliations with any organized socialists in France or other countries I do not know but I would doubt it. There has been evidence within the past few weeks of renewed activities on the part of this small group of administrators [agitators]. A stimulus was given to its revival by the recent return of one of the radical socialistic members of the Chambers from Russia.[3] I understand, however, that as a result of certain charges made by him on the floor of the chamber in the debates that followed the Government received an overwhelming indorsement in the vote of confidence by both Houses of Parliament. In my telegram of the seventh instant, number 2264, I sent copy of resolutions indorsing the declarations of the President of the Council which was passed unanimously by the Senate. There is no doubt in my mind but that that resolution faithfully reflects the sentiments of the mass of the French people.

Candidly agreeing with Colonel House I do not think that any useful purpose could be served by giving authority to Swing, to furnish any more information and possessing the convictions which he expresses I think it would be a mistake for him to be intrusted to go to Switzerland.

Had any of these conditions of inquietude really existed to the extent of which Swing makes a complaint I would not have failed to inform the Department with that fact but such is not the case. Every indication and I have sought to verify my opinion in many ways points to the fact that after nearly three years of a most exhausting struggle the morale of the French people is equal if not above that of any other belligerent in its determination to carry out the war for a final victory. This feeling permeates all classes.

Here and there have been found evidences of German intrigue

to arouse discord particularly among the industrial circles. There was brought to my attention a few days ago by the wife of Mr. Coolidge[4] the case of her cha[u]ffeur who has just recently denounced a Spaniard whose mission seemed to be to incite trouble among the soldiers and strikers. I presume that such instances could be multiplied many times. While it is probably true that in most cases where strikes were commenced higher wages should have been paid and some reforms in length working hours made yet if *any* cases could they have been said to be of a serious character. In the streets of Paris I saw on several occasions the strikes of the modiste and other women workers parading the streets in full swing and must say that they were characterized by most orderly conduct. Continued no longer than three weeks and were in the end satisfactorily adjusted I hear.

While it is true that there are rumors of some dissatisfaction involving mutinous conduct by some of the soldiers at the front yet from a careful investigation from a reliable source it is certain that it was of no threatening magnitude.[5] One cause for complaint was due to the irregularity of the granting of leave of absence from the trenches some of the soldiers being made to serve continuously for a long time. It has been said that in some instances too strict authority men shown by the gendarmes in the localities where soldiers were quartered. Presumably the recent promotion of General Petain to a position of complete authority over the army was for the purpose of bringing about reforms where needed, and it is the general belief that he has fully succeeded in doing such. He has always been very popular with the soldiers.

I have referred to these conditions not because they may be considered as of any moment but to bring to the knowledge of the Department the only possible reasons for stating that there has been anything out of the normal order in France excepting of course conditions accompanying all wars. But taken altogether, and multiplied several times, they would not then justify the statement made by Mr. Swing in his telegram.

There has been from the start, and continues to be, every evidence of a solidarity of interests and unanimity of purpose among all classes of the French people. While undoubtedly the long endured suffering entailed by the prosecution of the war has caused a common and growing desire to see it end as soon as possible, yet such desire must not be confounded in the slightest degree with a lack of detirmination that it must end only by the allied powers being placed in a position to name the terms of peace.

As to the attitude of the French Government, as well as the French people toward the United States, and the position taken by President Wilson, I have never seen anything so remarkable as their manifestation of gratitude, confidence and even affection. The recent reception of General Pershing upon less than three hours notice of the time of his arrival by great throngs of people lining the streets of Paris made up of all classes, whose faces I had a very good opportunity to study, went further than words would go to demonstrate the feelings of the people toward our country.[6] The General has made a most excellent impression in Paris. In both houses of Parliament a few days later I had the opportunity to see a similar enthusiastic reception accorded him. I have also seen great assemblies make remarkable demonstrations over the mention of President Wilson's name. It truly makes one living in France very proud and happy to be an American.

Sharp.

T telegram (SDR, RG 59, 763.72119 So/6½, DNA).

[1] RL to W. G. Sharp, June 25, 1917, T telegram (SDR, RG 59, 763.72119 So/5½, DNA). Lansing requested Sharp's "personal views as to [Raymond Edwards] Swing's extraordinary telegram to Colonel House." He asked specifically if Swing had "socialistic tendencies" or was "in sympathy with the efforts of the socialists in the various countries to have a voice in making peace." He also reported that House had suggested that Swing "be not allowed hereafter to send telegrams of such length" and that "it would be well not to facilitate his traveling about too generally."

[2] Swing's "telegram" to House was embodied in W. G. Sharp to RL, June 13, 1917, T telegram (SDR, RG 59, 763.72119 So/5½, DNA). Swing reported that France was "perilously near revolution," primarily because of the socialists' hatred of "secret treaties." He discussed socialistic unrest in other countries and earnestly recommended that the United States seize the leadership of the forces of democracy and socialism. Actually, there was much truth in Swing's report, for example, about the mutinies in the French army. See n. 5 *infra*.

[3] The Socialist deputy, Marcel Cachin, who had visited Russia in May and reported to the Chamber of Deputies on his visit on June 2. *New York Times*, June 2 and 3, 1917.

[4] That is, Helen Granger Stevens (Mrs. John Gardner) Coolidge.

[5] Following the disastrous campaign of Chemin des Dames in April, which led to the dismissal of General Nivelle as commander of the French armies, widespread incidents of mutiny broke out in those armies and reached a peak in May and early June. There was very little outright violence. For the most part, the rebellious soldiers simply refused to return to the trenches after a period of relief in the rear or refused orders to attack. Most of these incidents took place in the area of the front between Soissons and Auberive, but it was widely feared at the time that most of the French armies were affected. The best modern estimate is that some 30,000 to 40,000 individuals were directly involved. General Pétain dealt with the uprisings with a combination of swift punishment of those leaders who could be identified, genuine efforts both to listen to and act upon the real grievances of the soldiers, and a general policy of avoiding any more bloody offensives for the time being. Many authorities believe that the mutinies were the gravest crisis which the western allies faced during the First World War and say that the German armies might have swept to Paris and to victory had they had more than scattered hints and rumors of these events. However, strict censorship prevented any detailed reports of the uprisings from reaching either the Central Powers or France's allies. The authoritative study of the mutinies, and the only one based upon the extant archival sources, is Guy Pedroncini, *Les Mutineries de 1917* (Paris, 1967).

[6] Pershing and his staff had arrived at Paris in the late afternoon of June

13 and had received a tumultous welcome from Frenchmen who filled the Gare du Nord and lined the route of the Americans' automobile procession to the Hôtel de Crillon. For details, see Frank E. Vandiver, *Black Jack: The Life and Times of John J. Pershing* (2 vols., College Station, Tex., 1977), II, 716-19.

To Thomas Watt Gregory

My dear Gregory: [The White House] 28 June, 1917

I hate to unload on you a document of the sort enclosed,[1] but I want to make the proper answer and I do not know how to do so without a tip from you.

Faithfully yours,   Woodrow Wilson

TLS (Letterpress Books, WP, DLC).

[1] W. E. Chilton to WW, June 26, 1917, TLS (WP, DLC). Chilton called Wilson's attention to a case then pending in the federal district court in New York in which certain coal operators of West Virginia were charged by the government with violation of the Sherman Antitrust Act by meeting in New York in January 1917 to fix the price of high-grade bituminous coal. Chilton did not deny that the operators had in fact agreed to set the price of their product at $3 per ton but argued that this price was well below the going rate for even inferior grades of bituminous coal both at the time of the alleged conspiracy and since. Much of Chilton's sixteen-page letter was an attempt to show that the complex conditions in the coal-producing industry made it absolutely necessary to fix a reasonable price for their grade of coal. Chilton further argued that, regardless of the outcome of the trial, the necessity for the operators to attend the proceedings in New York, to say nothing of their possible imprisonment if convicted, would disrupt the production of coal at a critical time for the war effort and even make it impossible to provide adequate supplies for heating during the coming winter. He suggested that the indicted operators be allowed to plead *nolo contendere* and pay a "reasonable" fine.

To Samuel Huston Thompson, Jr.

My dear Thompson: [The White House] 28 June, 1917

I am sending in the nomination for the Court of the District, but I am not naming you and I want to tell you why.

I need hardly say that it is through no lack of confidence or even admiration, for I hope that you know how entirely I trust you and how warm my personal feeling for you is, but I am doing this out of genuine friendship and after searching my mind and heart pretty thoroughly. I do not believe that it would be doing you any service at all, but a disservice rather, to put you in a judicial position in the District of Columbia, or in any other position, for that matter, which would tend to fix your status for life and narrow your development.

You will probably shrug your shoulders at this and say that, after all, you are the best judge of what your career should be, but the longer I live in Washington, the more I feel disinclined to put men I wish to see succeed in a large way in any permanent official position whatever, and whether I am right or wrong, I wanted you to know that that is the principle I am acting on in this case.

Cordially and faithfully yours, [Woodrow Wilson]

CCL (WP, DLC).

From Walter Hines Page

London, June 28, 1917.

Greatest urgency.

Wholly confidential for the President and the Secretary of State and Secretary of the Treasury.

Mr. Balfour asked me to a conference at seven oclock with him, the Chancellor of the Exchequer[1] and their financial advisers. It was disclosed that financial disaster to all the European Allies is imminent unless the United States Government advances to the British enough money to pay for British purchases in the United States as they fall due.

Bonar Law reports that only half enough has been advanced for June and that the British agents in the United States now have enough money to keep the exchange up for only one day more. If exchange with England fall, exchange with all European Allies also will immediately fall and there will be a general collapse. Balfour understood that in addition to our other loans and our loans to France and Italy, we would advance to England enough to pay for all purchases by the British Government made in the United States. He authorizes me to say that they are now on the brink of a precipice and unless immediate help be given financial collapse will follow. He is sending an explanatory telegram to Spring Rice.

I am convinced that these men are not overstating their case. Unless we come to their rescue we are all in danger of disaster. Great Britain will have to abandon the gold standard.

Page.

T telegram (SDR, RG 59, 841.51/216, DNA).
[1] That is, Andrew Bonar Law.

From Vance Criswell McCormick

Dear Mr President: Harrisburg, Penn. June 28th, 1917

I am sorry to trouble you but would like very much to have your advice. Secretary Lansing has asked me to serve on the

Administrative Committee of the Export Council along with the representatives appointed by Secretaries Redfield and Houston and Mr Hoover. I will, of course, be glad to do this if I can better serve you and the country by giving my efforts in this direction rather than working as I now am as a free lance.

Since the beginning of the war I have been in Washington practically every week and feel that I have been of some assistance by coming in contact with the various Department heads and assisting them in every way possible. Not being officially connected with any of the Departments gives me some advantages, as information and suggestions from disinterested outsiders are often more acceptable than from other sources.

Having no official government position, I have been able to pick up information and get the real sentiment of the country much more accurately and completely than in being confined to any particular kind of work. I have also felt the importance of expending some effort along the lines of arousing loyalty toward the Administration among the members of our party in Washington, and of securing positions there for men in sympathy with your policies to create a wholesome atmosphere and to check in some measure the propaganda being carried on by many of the so-called patriots of the Republican party, who have volunteered their services in Washington and who are doing all they can to discredit the work of the Administration.

In addition to this I have been performing my regular duties as National Chairman and endeavoring to assist in the important legislative matters in Congress, as well as trying to harmonize our disgruntled Senators and Congressmen. This work, of course, is most general and not specific, but I have been and am ready at all times to devote my entire time to the cause, if necessary, and am writing you hoping you will frankly tell me if you feel I can be of more service in the work I am now doing than by taking up the work of the Export Council. If I take up the latter, do you think I should resign from the National Chairmanship, which I would, of course, be perfectly willing to do.

My whole desire is to help you and serve my country and I am ready to take my coat off at any time but I want to place my efforts where they will count the most.

I expect to return to Washington Saturday morning to give Mr Lansing an answer and, if convenient to you, would appreciate a word from you to me at the Shoreham Hotel.

Very sincerely yours,   Vance C. McCormick

TLS (WP, DLC).

From James Thomas Heflin

My dear Mr. President: Washington, D. C. June 28, 1917.

Your letter, suggesting the creation of a standing Committee on Woman Suffrage, has been received and noted.[1] Personally, I believe that each State ought to have the right to say who shall or shall not exercise the privilege of voting, but I realize that in consenting for a Committee on Suffrage to be created, I would not surrender my convictions on the matter of granting votes to women.

After reading your letter several times and thinking over the situation, I have concluded to follow your suggestion and not oppose the creation of a Committee in the House on Woman Suffrage.

Whenever I can serve you, call on me.

With best wishes, I am,

Yours sincerely,   J. Thos. Heflin.

TLS (WP, DLC).
 [1] See WW to J. T. Heflin, June 13, 1917, Vol. 42.

From Franklin Knight Lane

My dear Mr. President: Washington June 28, 1917.

I feel that we are in a rather awkward situation regarding the Bering River coal field, which as you know is forty or fifty miles from the Copper River Railroad. We have withdrawn these coal lands and they cannot be taken up excepting upon leases. Private parties were in there and we ousted them because they had not, as we held, complied with the law. Then a leasing bill was passed and we have had these properties on the market for two years, but manifestly no one will take up any property and develop it. Unless there are transportation facilities given for taking the coal out, a lease, as such, would be valueless. It was principally upon the ground that the men who were in there as claimants had not developed the properties commercially that we cancelled the old claims. Now no one will go in and take up these properties, because we require that they shall develop them commercially and invest a certain amount of money in them. This they cannot do unless they have means of access to the mines and means of taking the coal out to market.

So that we must, it seems to me, if we are going to get the benefit of that coal for our needs on the Pacific Coast, either build ourselves or allow some private parties to build. It will cost between $4,000,000 and $5,000,000 to build, and we would have to build in from a private road, namely, the Copper River, which would be an anomalous condition, a Government railroad tied up with a private concern. I doubt very much if Congress would listen to such a proposition. There is no other harbor than Cordova, so that we have got to go to the Copper River Railroad with whatever line we build from the Bering River.

I talked with you about this matter, and you suggested that an option should be had by the Government upon the railroad if the right of way was granted. This condition makes the proposition unattractive; in fact, they cannot raise the money if the Government has an option on the road. To gain the advantage of the development of the coal field, it seems to me that it would be wise to let private enterprise construct that road and the Interstate Commerce Commission fix the rates. Otherwise we will have to say frankly that the Bering River field is not available for leasing, because there are no transportation facilities, and that the Government neither will at this time build any itself nor permit a right of way to private parties. You undoubtedly appreciate the fact that along the Copper River Road there are many copper properties carrying low grade copper, which can only be developed if a smelter is erected at Cordova. The Morgan people are taking out only the high grade ore in the Kennicott mine, and this they carry to Tacoma. No low grade ore could be transported that far. In Tacoma they smelt with coal from British Columbia. We can develop a smelting industry at Cordova and a number of low grade copper properties, as well as the coal field and the adjacent country, by allowing a line to be built from Copper River to the Bering River field.

Cordially yours,   Franklin K Lane

TLS (WP, DLC).

Sir Cecil Arthur Spring Rice to Arthur James Balfour

[Washington] June 28, 1917.

Private. Count Horodyski has received satisfactory replies from Sec. of State who says President quite concurs, and also today from special Russian Ambr.[1] Latter however says it is necessary to go slow for fear of frightening nascent spirit of democracy. Count rather doubts his sincerity but at all events he said he would do his utmost in order that 500 or 600 Polish officers should be sent over. Count has appointment with Counsellor of State Dept. tomorrow June 29 at which his object is to induce U.S.G. firstly to recognize Poland as independent sovereign state and secondly, consequently to authorize recruitment of Poles just as the other allied Powers are allowed to recruit their nationals.

Count says matter is urgent as he desires to get the officers from Russia and the recruits from this country which he estimates at about 100000 in time to give them 6 weeks training in Canada before the winter—say mid October.

I suggested he should modify this idea slightly and get U.S.G. to take note of proclamation of the new Russian Govt. reaffirming that of the old Imperial Govt. which assured Polish autonomy, and authorize the recruiting in virtue of their declaration. He agreed.

Sec. of State expressed himself in favour of appointing some form of provisional Govt. to which Count is opposed, but he thinks it would be for President of U. S. to approach the C.O. and his principal officers. I suggested instead appointment of a local committee which would recommend names for these officers which President wd. recognize.

It seems as if U.S.G. would like to take a hand in this matter but only if they are pretty certain that it will be a success.

Count does not like to broach matter of German prisoners to U.S.G. for fear of doing too much at one time, but Russian Amb. expressed himself in favour of the scheme.

Hw telegram (FO 115/2302, pp. 244-45, PRO).
1 Boris Aleksandrovich Bakhmet'ev, the newly arrived Ambassador to the United States from the Russian Provisional Government.

Arthur James Balfour to Sir William Wiseman

[London] June 28th 1917.

Following for Wiseman to be decyphered by himself.

Please convey following to House as an urgent personal message from Balfour.

For reasons fully explained to Page here and to Spring Rice in Washington we seem on the edge of a financial disaster which would be worse than a defeat in the field. If we cannot keep up the exchange neither we nor our Allies can pay our dollar debts, we should be driven off the gold basis, and all purchases from United States would immediately cease and the Allies' credit would be shattered. These consequences which would be of incalculable gravity may be upon us on Monday next if nothing effective is done in the meantime. You know I am not an alarmist: but this is really serious. I hope you will do what you can in the proper quarter to avert the calamity.[1]

T telegram (A. J. Balfour Papers, FO 800/209, PRO).
  [1] House sent a copy of this telegram to Wilson. See EMH to WW, June 29, 1917.

To William Charles Adamson

My dear Judge: [The White House] 29 June, 1917
  Thank you for your letter of yesterday.[1]
  May I not suggest this: The proviso referred to has, as you and I both think, no relation to the text or purposes of the bill, but is it not legitimate in order to quiet a misunderstanding to embody it nevertheless? I feel convinced that a failure on the part of your committee to approve it would be subject to a very grave misunderstanding, and that seems to me too high a price to pay.
  In haste
          Cordially and sincerely yours,   Woodrow Wilson

TLS (Letterpress Books, WP, DLC).
  [1] It is missing.

To Robert Lansing, with Enclosure

My dear Mr. Secretary: The White House 29 June, 1917
  I would be very much obliged to you if you would guide me as to what you think I would best do by way of replying to Mr. Carranza's letter enclosed.
          Faithfully yours,   Woodrow Wilson

TLS (SDR, RG 59, 812.001C23/30, DNA).

E N C L O S U R E

Translation

VENUSTIANO CARRANZA,
  President of the United Mexican States,
  To His Excellency, Mr. WOODROW WILSON, President of the United States of America.
Great and Good Friend:
  I have the honor to inform Your Excellency that having been elected by the free vote of my fellow-citizens to the presidency of the republic, I have, on this day, taken possession of my high office with the legal formalities.

In fulfilling this agreeable duty, it is extremely satisfactory to me to express to Your Excellency the earnest desire and firm intention of my government to cultivate and to extend the frank and cordial relations which happily link the United Mexican States with the United States of America over whose destinies Your Excellency presides.

Hoping that Your Excellency entertains the same sentiments with regard to Mexico, I take pleasure in availing of this occasion to express the sincere wishes which I feel for the aggrandizement of the United States of America and for the personal happiness of Your Excellency, at the same time, tendering you the assurances of my highest consideration and especial esteem with which I have the honor to sign myself, Your Excellency's

Loyal and Good Friend,   V. Carranza.[1]

T MS (SDR, RG 59, 812.001C23/30, DNA).
[1] The HwLS is filed with the translation.

To Robert Lansing, with Enclosure

My dear Mr. Secretary: [The White House] 29 June, 1917

Father de Ville[1] left this letter with me in person the other day and I have been puzzled as to the form, or even the propriety of my making the answer. I would very much value your advice.

Cordially and faithfully yours,   [Woodrow Wilson]

CCL (WP, DLC).
[1] The Rev. Jean Baptiste De Ville, sometimes known as John B. Deville. Born in the Austrian Tyrol of a Belgian mother and an Italian father, he was a naturalized citizen of the United States. Before the entrance of the United States into the war, he had served as intermediary between the American Belgian Relief Society and the Roman Catholic Church in Belgium. He had made repeated trips between the United States and Belgium and had brought several hundred refugees to the United States. *New York Times*, March 10, 1918, sect. 7, p. 6.

E N C L O S U R E

From Désiré-Joseph Cardinal Mercier[1]

Mr. President,   Malines, February 9, 1917.

Often, since the commencement of the war, I have had the desire to express to the people of the United States, of whom you are the highest representation, my grateful sentiments. You have been prodigal to us of your sympathy, of your help, of your devotion. At the very moment when you see yourself compelled to break off the diplomatic relations of your country with Germany, you have had still an exquisite thought for our poor country; to the fifty delegates of the C.R.B. you have given the advice not to abandon us as long as the power of occupation left them free to provide for our alimentation. May you be thanked for your magnanimity, Mr. Pr[e]sident, and accept as well, I pray you, the thanks of the entire Belgian nation. Permit me to say that we shall pray to the good God and ask Him to bless your noble country and its very noble President. An American priest, Father de Ville, is kind enough to undertake to deliver this message to you. Please accept, Mr. President, together with the renewed expression of my gratitude, the homage of my very high consideration.

X D.I. Cardinal Mercier, Archbishop of Malines[2]

T MS (WP, DLC).
[1] Cardinal Archbishop of Malines. He had become a symbol of Belgian resistance to the German occupation. His full name was Désiré Félicien François Joseph Mercier.
[2] The ALS is in WP, DLC.

To Newton Diehl Baker

Personal and Confidential.

My dear Mr. Secretary: The White House 29 June, 1917

I am very much distressed about what has been done with regard to agreeing upon a price for coal.[1] The price said to have been agreed upon is clearly too high and I do not think that the government departments would be justified in paying it. It happens to be the particular price upon which charges are at this very time being based by the Department of Justice against the coal dealers.

I am myself personally embarrassed because I had just had conferences with the Federal Trade Commission which made me hopeful that I might be instrumental in bringing about an understanding which would be in every way more fair and reasonable.

I would very much value your counsel upon this matter, and I would appreciate it very much if you and your colleagues of the Council of National Defense would keep me in touch with plans of this sort, because unconsciously we are working at cross purposes.[2]

Cordially and faithfully yours,   Woodrow Wilson

TLS (N. D. Baker Papers, DLC).
[1] See NDB to WW, June 30, 1917, and J. F. Fort to WW, June 30, 1917.
[2] Upon receiving this letter, Baker replied in a lengthy letter stating what he knew of the origins of the coal price-fixing affair and indicating his own distress and disagreement with the action taken in the matter. However, Baker doubted the wisdom of issuing a statement from the Council of National De-

fense to "clarify" the situation. NDB to WW, June 30, 1917, TLS (N. D. Baker Papers, DLC). Baker did not send this letter. Instead, he and Gregory met with Wilson at the White House at 12:30 P.M. on June 30. Ray Stannard Baker later reported what transpired: "The Attorney General and Secretary Baker arrived for a conference with the President on the bituminous coal price fixed by the coal operators' conference on the 28th. Gregory was especially perturbed, for, he said, the price fixed during the conference and approved by Secretary Lane as a member of the Council of National Defense, was actually higher than the coal price which had previously been fixed in secret, and for which he then had pending indictments against many of the coal operators! The President said, with some indignation, that he planned to repudiate, publicly, the price fixed. Baker, realizing that such a move would probably force the resignation of Secretary Lane, suggested that he himself, as head of the Council of National Defense, repudiate the price. The President agreed, and Baker wrote out then and there the statement which he planned to publish. The President approved it, and it was given to the press the same day." Ray Stannard Baker, *Woodrow Wilson: Life and Letters* (8 vols., Garden City, N.Y., 1927-39), VII, 138. The document made public on June 30 is the Enclosure printed with NDB to WW, June 30, 1917.

To James Cannon, Jr.[1]

My dear Doctor Cannon: [The White House] 29 June, 1917

I am very glad to respond to the request of Senator Martin, the Democratic Floor Leader in the Senate, that I give to your Legislative Committee an expression of my opinion with regard to the wisest and most patriotic policy to be pursued towards the Food Administration legislation now pending in the Congress. I regard the immediate passage of the bill as of vital consequence to the safety and defense of the nation. Time is of the essence; and yet it has become evident that heated and protracted debate will delay the passage of the bill indefinitely if the provisions affecting the manufacture of beer and wines are retained and insisted upon.[2] In these circumstances I have not hesitated to say to members of the Senate who have been kind enough to consult me that it would undoubtedly be in the public interest in this very critical matter if the friends of those provisions should consent to their elimination from the present measure. Feeling that your Committee is actuated by the same patriotic motives which inspire me, I am confident that these considerations will seem to you, as they seem to me, to be imperative.

With much respect,

Sincerely yours,   Woodrow Wilson

TLS (Letterpress Books, WP, DLC).

[1] Methodist Episcopal clergyman, President of Blackstone (Virginia) College for Girls, and chairman of the national legislative committee of the Anti-Saloon League of America.

[2] Representative Alben William Barkley, Democrat of Kentucky, had, on June 23, introduced an amendment to the Lever bill which prohibited the use of foods, food materials, or feeds for the production of alcohol or alcoholic beverages. The House accepted the amendment on the same day. *Cong. Record*, 65th Cong., 1st sess., pp. 4161-63, and 4181.

When the bill reached the Senate, some senators opposed to prohibition threatened to prevent passage of the Lever bill altogether unless the amendment was removed. On June 28, Senator Martin summoned the legislative committee of the Anti-Saloon League to his office and informed them that Wilson had asked that they agree to drop the Barkley amendment, at least insofar as it affected the manufacture of beer and wine. The representatives of the League agreed to support such a move, provided that Wilson himself wrote a public letter making the request. See Peter H. Odegard, *Pressure Politics: The Story of the Anti-Saloon League* (New York, 1928), pp. 167-70.

To Thomas James Walsh

My dear Senator: [The White House] 29 June, 1917

Thank you for your letter of June twenty-second.[1] I beg that you will pardon my long delay in replying to it. It has been due to the withdrawal of my attention in other directions.

I feel the pressure of the coal and oil situation as keenly, I think, as even you do and it has been giving me a great deal of concern.

I found that I could not bring myself to agree with the Senators who last session were urging certain concessions to those who have begun operations in the oil fields in a way that makes their legal claims unquestionable[2] because of former executive orders and Acts of Congress, but I am sincerely anxious to meet the situation as promptly and as effectually as possible. I would be very much obliged to you if you would let me see a copy of the bill by which you are proposing to do this without invading the naval reserve.

In haste

Cordially and sincerely yours,   Woodrow Wilson

TLS (Letterpress Books, WP, DLC).
[1] T. J. Walsh to WW, June 22, 1917, Vol. 42.
[2] Wilson dictated "questionable."

To Franklin Knight Lane

My dear Mr. Secretary: [The White House] 29 June, 1917

I have your letter about the awkward situation with regard to the Bering River coal field and find that I cannot form a judgment about it until I have in mind an answer to this question: How soon is it likely that private enterprise would undertake the construction of such a railroad, and in how short a time could they finish it? In other words, is it a proposition which would affect the coal situation on the Pacific Coast during the probable period of the present war?

Cordially and faithfully yours,   Woodrow Wilson

TLS (Letterpress Books, WP, DLC).

From Edward Mandell House

Dear Governor: Magnolia, Massachusetts. June 29, 1917.

Things began to break yesterday afternoon in British quarters. Spring-Rice is at Woods Hole and McAdoo at Buena Vista and the machinery became clogged. As usual, Sir William took hold and is trying today to see what can be done.

Northcliffe received a message from Lloyd-George to come here and advise with me before moving further. He was ready to take the ten o'clock train this morning when I received, through Sir William, the cable from Balfour which I sent you by Lansing. I therefore advised Northcliffe to go to Washington immediately rather than come here, which he has done.

By putting together what I gather from Washington and Sir William, the trouble that has come about concerning finances is largely a matter of misunderstanding, with some fault on both sides.

Sir Richard Crawford tries to work through Administration channels. Lever works partly through Morgan & Company, and it is not certain that the Morgans have not lent a helping hand to this crisis.

The British understood that we would take care of certain Russian obligations they have been carrying. They claim if they had not been under this impression they would have arranged to take care of the matter in a different way.

What they need is $35,000,000. on Monday; $100,000,000. on Thursday and $185,000,000. a month for two months beginning ten days from next Thursday.

This is a staggering amount and indicates the load Great Britain has been carrying for her allies. It seems to me that we should have some definite understanding with England as to what money she will need in the future, and how far she can count upon us.

It seems absurd to be giving her comparatively small amounts, the frequent publication of which make[s] a bad impression on our people. Would they not stand one large amount better than these lesser amounts constantly brought to their attention?

Affectionately yours,   E. M. House

TLS (WP, DLC).

From Sir Richard Frederick Crawford

Very Confidential.

My dear Mr. President: Washington June 29th 1917.

With reference to my letter of the 25th June I now have the honour to transmit the following supplementary information which has been received from London.

The total loss of tonnage (all vessels over 100 tons gross) by war risk from the beginning of the war till *June 20th 1917* was approximately:

	Gross tonnage.
Great Britain	4,300,000
Allies (including the United States of America)	1,343,000
Neutrals	1,531,000
	7,174,000

Of this total the following loss was incurred between the beginning of February and June 20th 1917 (i.e. since the intensive submarine campaign)

	Gross tonnage:
Great Britain	1,800,000
Allies	500,000
Neutrals	628,000
	2,928,000

This gives an average loss by war risk during this period of 636,000 gross tons per month. In addition about 34,000 tons per month may be taken as lost by marine risk, making a total (excluding damage without total loss) of 670,000 tons gross (or 1,117,000 tons dead weight) per month.

The above figures give gross losses without any offset for new building.

As against the loss Great Britain is building at the rate of 100,000 gross tons (or 170,000 tons deadweight) per month and the rest of the world outside America at not more than 40,000 tons gross (or 70,000 tons deadweight) a month altogether.

(The losses given include small coasting vessels which though important do not directly concern the main problem of maintaining overseas communications. Their total tonnage, however, is relatively small and the general results shewn above would be substantially unaffected if they were excluded.)

I may add in conclusion that should any further points for enquiry arise in connection with the information conveyed in the memorandum enclosed in my communication of the 25th instant Mr. Royden and Mr. Salter would be of course at your disposal at any time. I have mentioned this because these gentlemen I understand contemplate returning to England shortly.

With assurances of my highest respect,
I have the honour to be,
My dear Mr. President,
Yours faithfully,   Richard Crawford.

TLS (WP, DLC).

From Walter Hines Page

Dear Mr. President: London 29 June 1917

The financial panic (it's hardly less) that this Gov't has raises the question, Why on earth do the British drift along until they reach a precipice? That's hard to answer. It's their way. They are too proud to acknowledge their predicament even to themselves till events force them to do so. Mr. Balfour informs me that the agreement that he reached in general terms with Mr. McAdoo was this—(1) that our Gov't wd. thenceforth lend to France and Italy (and Russia?) the sums they wd. otherwise have to borrow from England (as they have all the while been borrowing) and (2) in addition lend to England whatever sums shd. be required to pay for British Gov't purchases in the U. S. So much for that. I have no information whether that is Mr. Mc-Adoo's understanding.

Now, Bonar Law assured me at the fearful financial Conference to wh. they invited me that the Treasury Dp't had given Lever, (the English financial agent) only half enough in June to meet the British Govt's bills in the U. S. Since they had reckoned on meeting all such bills from advances made by us, they find themselves unable to go further without our help. They have used all the gold they have in Canada. This, then, is the edge of the precipice. It came out in addition that a few weeks ago, the French came over here and persuaded the British that in addition to the French loan from the U. S. they were obliged to have the British loans to them continued—for how long, I do not know. Bonar Law said, "We simply *had* to do it." The British, therefore, in spite of our help to France still have France on their back and continue to give them money. I know that for a long time the British have felt that the French were not making a sufficient financial effort for themselves. "A Frenchman will lightly give his life for any cause that touches his imagination, but he will die rather than give a franc for any cause." There is a recurring fear here lest France in a moment of war-weariness may make a separate peace.

As things stand today there is a danger of the fall of exchange and (perhaps) the abandonment of specie payments. These British run right into such a crisis before they are willing to confess their plight even to themselves. They are not trying to lie down on us: they are too proud for that. Why they got into this predicament, I do not fully know. I know nothing of what arrangements were made with them except what Mr. Balfour tells me. It seems to me that some definite understanding ought to have been reduced to writing. But here they are in this predicament, wh. I duly reported by telegram

It is unlucky that "crises" come in groups—two or three at once. But the submarine situation is as serious as the financial. I have a better knowledge of that than I have of the financial situation. But in one respect they are alike—the British drive ahead, concealing their losses, their misfortunes and their mistakes till they are on the very brink of disaster: that is their temperament. Into this submarine peril (the Germans are fast winning in this crucial activity—there's no doubt about that) I have gone pretty thoroughly with their naval men and their shipping authorities. Admiral Sims has reachd. the same conclusions that I have reached—independently, from his point of view. The immediate grave danger for the present lies here. If the present rate of destruction of shipping goes on, the war will end before a victory is won. And time is of the essence of the problem; and the place where it will be won is in the waters of the approach to this Kingdom—not anywhere else. The full available destroyer power that can by any method be made available must be concentrated in this area within weeks (not months). There are not in the two navies half destroyers enough: improvised destroyers must be got. There must be enough to provide convoys for every ship that is worth saving. Merely arming them affords the minimum of protection. Armed merchantmen are destroyed every day. Convoyed ships escape—almost all. That is the convincing actual experience.

If we had not come into the war when we did & if we had not begun action and given help with almost miraculous speed, I do not say that the British wd. have been actually beaten (tho' this

may have followd.), but I do say that they wd. have quickly
been on a paper-money basis, thereby bringing down the financial
situation of all the European Allies; and the submarine success
of the Germans wd. or might have caused a premature peace.
They were in worse straits than they ever confessed to themselves. And now we are all in bad straits because of this submarine destruction of shipping. And time is of the essence of the
matter. One sea-going tug now may be worth more than a dozen
ships next year.   Yours very faithfully   Walter H. Page

ALS (WP, DLC).

From Herbert Clark Hoover

Dear Mr. President: Washington June 29, 1917.
   The Food Bill receives such radical alterations so often in
Congress that it seems difficult to determine when intervention
should be made in order to secure a proper formulation of its
critical features. As the bill has so far been amended in the Senate there have been introduced into it some measures which
render the bill nugatory for food administration.[1]
   The most pertinent of these is the practical reduction of the
operations of the Food Administration to the interstate commerce. If this is to stand it would be impossible for us to control
any commodity unless it had some time in its career passed a
state line. It consequently introduces a myriad of difficulties that
render the whole operation hopeless and worthless to undertake.
   Another one of these amendments is in the matter of farmers'
cooperative associations. These associations are very numerous,
especially in the ownership of elevators and have large position
in the handling of the grain crop. If they are to be excepted from
the bill, it is hopeless for us to control the movement of grain and
entirely unfair to private interests.
   Another amendment to the bill practically throws open
speculation to all persons who are not regular dealers in foodstuffs. The most vicious form of speculation is precisely of this
nature.
   The general changes made in the bill in various particulars
and the inclusion of many other commodities of such widely different character, combined with the difficulties which we now
see in necessarily adjusting commercial operations to Government practice, make it desirable to have some new amendments
added to the bill. This is particularly true with regard to the
handling of the $150,000,000 working capital provided in the

bill for the purchase and sale of foodstuffs by the Government. It is impracticable to conduct the essential activities in this direction without conforming to the usages of the trade, and the delays which will arise in closing transactions by the necessity of passing through the Treasury channels under the general laws, will be fatal. This could be solved by the authorization to yourself to create one or more corporations to be used as agencies for the purpose of food administration and the working capital could be subscribed as the whole capital stock to such corporations. This arrangement is not without precedent, as witness the Emergency Shipping Corporation. By such arrangement the different commodities and the different circumstances can be competently handled. It has also the advantage that it would center the limelight on a definite organ of the Government for a definite purpose and would permit of its creation along normal commercial lines, understandable by the entire people with whom it has to deal.

I have had the advantage of advice from Judge Curtis Lindley of San Francisco,[2] Mr. Edward F. Burling[3] of Chicago and we have called into consultation Mr. Joseph Cotton of New York[4] and Mr. Roublee.[5] They have formulated the attached amendments embracing not only the above, but some other matters of less importance.[6]

It may be possible that these amendments should be taken up in conference and I would like to have your advice as to whether they should be presented to Senator Chamberlain at once or whether we should wait until the conference.

I am,   Your obedient servant,   Herbert Hoover

TLS (WP, DLC).

[1] The House of Representatives had passed the Lever bill, with amendments, on June 23. *Cong. Record*, 65th Cong., 1st sess., p. 4190. Senator Gore, chairman of the Senate Committee on Agriculture and Forestry, reported the bill (H.R. 4961) to the Senate on June 27, with different amendments. *Ibid.*, p. 4356. These amendments opened the way for national prohibition of distilled liquors and beer and provided for governmental control, not only of food, feeds, and fuel, but also of iron, steel, copper, lead, farm implements and machinery, fertilizers, and binding-twine materials. The amendments also authorized the government to take over and operate factories, packing houses, oil wells, and mines, to regulate the wages of their employees, and to commandeer supplies of every kind when needed for the army and navy "or any other public use connected with the public defense." Another amendment barred governmental officials and employees, including those in an advisory capacity, from selling or attempting to sell to the government any materials in which they had financial interests. *New York Times*, June 28, 1917. Gore opposed several major provisions of the Lever bill and left its management in the Senate to Chamberlain. For further information on the congressional handling of the Lever bill, see Monroe Lee Billington, *Thomas P. Gore: The Blind Senator from Oklahoma* (Lawrence, Kans., 1967), pp. 95-107, and Seward W. Livermore, *Politics Is Adjourned: Woodrow Wilson and the War Congress, 1917-1918* (Middletown, Conn., 1966), pp. 48-52.

[2] Curtis Holbrook Lindley, lawyer of San Francisco, long-time friend and associate of Hoover, soon to be named chief counsel of the United States Food Administration.

3 That is, Edward Burnham Burling.
4 Joseph Potter Cotton, lawyer of New York, recently counsel to the United States Shipping Board.
5 That is, George Rublee.
6 T MS (WP, DLC). This document set forth a series of rather technical amendments to various sections of the Lever food and fuel bill; each amendment or related group of amendments was followed by a brief paragraph explaining the need for the change or changes. Hoover discusses the most important amendments in this letter.

From William Denman

My dear Mr. President: Washington June 29, 1917.

Some days ago Mr. Stevens[1] insisted upon a vote of the Board on a resolution whereby he sought to place in the General Manager of the Emergency Fleet Corporation the powers of ship construction now resting in the Board of Directors of that Company, under the plan which we devised and which was concurred in by General Goethals at the time that we employed him. Commissioner White[2] was not in Washington when the resolution was presented, and we requested that its consideration be delayed until his return. We had previously urged Mr. Stevens not to force any consideration by the Board which would make a recorded difference on such a delicate matter, but leave it for your personal consideration on our unofficial representation. Mr. Stevens insisted, and his proposed resolution was defeated, Mr. Brent[3] and myself voting against it. Since Commissioner White's return, we have again taken up the question, and the Board has today passed a resolution providing that the construction of vessels for the Government should follow the plan originally devised and concurred in by the General. The vote upon the resolution was as follows: Ayes—Brent, Denman, and White; Noes—Donald[4] and Stevens.

At the time that General Goethals consented to this form of organization, we contemplated the expenditure of some $300,-000,000 on the construction of wooden ships. This, as you will recall it, was under the plan approved by the Council of National Defense, and by yourself upon their recommendation, and upon ours, after a careful study of the problem extending over many weeks, and with the widest consultation with wooden shipbuilders, professional men skilled in woodworking trades, and the lumbermen.

The present plan contemplates an expenditure of $750,000,-000 for both wood and steel. There has also been granted a power to commandeer vessels under construction on our stocks for the purpose of speeding them up. The exercise of this power is merely incidental to the general scheme of construction, and the majority of the Board thinks it should follow the control over the construction.

We do not know what representations were made to you by Mr. Stevens, as he has declined to inform us, but we beg to say that it is not the intention of the majority of the Board to change the General Manager of the Emergency Fleet Corporation, nor to take any steps other than those required to carry out your original plan of creating a large wooden ship fleet as speedily as possible, and to stimulate the construction of steel vessels for the creation of a steel fleet.

Under certain plans, the wooden ship can be constructed more rapidly than steel. Under the plans for wooden ships accepted by General Goethals for his program of wooden ships, they will take as long to construct, if not longer than steel vessels, and are nearly as expensive. The majority of the Board favor obtaining the more rapidly constructed wooden tonnage.

In view, however, of the vast excess in the rate of destruction of tonnage by the submarine in the last four months over any rate of construction of steel and wood in both Great Britain and the United States, we feel that all the wooden ships that can be contracted for should be constructed, of whatever type, even though they may cost as much as steel and take as long or longer to build. We are inclosing a copy of the resolution and a proposed Executive Order[5] which embodies the ideas of the majority of the Board as to the distribution of the powers conferred by Congress, both as to the construction of vessels or the commandeering of uncompleted vessels, and as to the commandeer and control of vessels which are ready for navigation.

Very faithfully yours,   William Denman.

TLS (WP, DLC).
[1] Raymond Bartlett Stevens.
[2] John Barber White.
[3] Theodore Brent.
[4] John A. Donald.
[5] "Resolution of the United States Shipping Board concerning the delegation of power for the construction of ships, and also for the operation and requisitioning of constructed ships," T MS (WP, DLC). The resolution recommended that the President delegate to the Emergency Fleet Corporation all powers over the construction of vessels, the commandeering and completion of vessels already under construction, and the commandeering of materials for construction. Power to purchase or requisition completed vessels and operate and manage all vessels was delegated to the Shipping Board itself. The proposed Executive Order is printed as an Enclosure with WW to W. Denman, July 11, 1917.

From James Cannon, Jr., and Others

Washington, D. C.

Dear Mr. President: June Twenty-ninth 1917.

Your letter of this date addressed to the Legislative Committee of the Anti-Saloon League of America, discussing the provisions of the food conservation bill now pending in the Senate prohibiting the manufacture of food stuffs into beer and wine, and requesting that "the friends of those provisions should consent to their elimination from the present measure," has been received.

We recognize the force of any appeal from the President and Commander-in-chief of the Army and Navy in time of war. While in response to such appeal we believe we could speak for the constituency which we represent, we do not think we should be justified in making final reply to your letter until we shall have had conference with the friends of these provisions in the Senate, where the measure is now pending, and in the House of Representatives, where the measure has already been passed.

We will immediately seek such conference and will follow the same with further reply.

Sincerely and respectfully yours,   James Cannon Jr.
                    P A Baker   A. J. Barton
                    Edwin C. Dinwiddie   Wayne B Wheeler[1]

TLS (WP, DLC).

[1] Those not previously identified in this series were Purley Albert Baker, Methodist minister and general superintendent of the Anti-Saloon League of America; Arthur James Barton, Baptist minister and superintendent of the Anti-Saloon League of Texas; Edwin Courtland Dinwiddie, national legislative superintendent of the Anti-Saloon League of America; and Wayne Bidwell Wheeler, lawyer of Washington and general counsel and secretary of the Anti-Saloon League of America.

From Henry Lee Higginson

Dear Mr. President: Boston. June 29, 1917.

The matter of national prohibition has been in my mind for a long time, and was stirred up by Professor Fisher in early May. Since then I have been talking with many men of experience and wisdom, including Dr. Eliot and President Lowell.

Our one task is to keep every string drawing to carry through this war successfully, and, in order to do it, we should keep everybody united. We ought not to annoy any large parcel of men. I do not want any beer, wine or liquor, and shall be glad to see them all wiped off the face of the earth; but I do believe that a plenty of honest, good men of temperate habits do care for beer and perhaps for light wines, and I do know that a great many farmers have vineyards on which they rely. It seems to me bad policy and even bad morals to forget what we are about,—that is, to put an end to the Prussian methods of government.

It may seem superfluous to write you a line on the subject. No doubt you have your own views; yet I allow myself that privilege, and I am sure most of our people think in that way.

I am, with great respect,

Very truly yours,   H. L. Higginson

TLS (WP, DLC).

From Eugene Semmes Ives[1]

Phoenix, Ariz., June 29, 1917.

I came to Phoenix with several prominent citizens to request Governor Hunt to mediate between miners and copper mining companies, with a view to stop present impending strikes. Unless something is done it is probable that by Tuesday all Arizona copper mines will be substantially shut down. Governor Hunt is now contesting gubernatorial election in courts. His opponent[2] is de facto governor. Under these circumstances he is unwilling to volunteer, but if invited by you, will do his utmost. He unquestionably has more influence with the miners than any man in Arizona and we believe, and he believes, that if so invited, he can induce miners to make most material concessions to withdraw for patriotic reasons all the demands which are most objectionable to the companies, particularly the demand that the companies recognize the unions. I am sure that both senators from Arizona will confirm my statement as to Hunt's influence over the miners.   Eugene S. Ives.

T telegram (WP, DLC).
    [1] Lawyer of Tucson; prominent in Democratic politics, first in New York, later in Arizona; unsuccessful candidate for United States senator from Arizona in the Democratic primary in 1911.
    [2] Thomas Edward Campbell.

To Francis Bowes Sayre

The White House June 30 [1917]

Love affectionate good byes and good wishes from us all.[1] You will be in our thoughts constantly.

Woodrow Wilson.

T telegram (received from Francis B. Sayre).

¹ Sayre was about to sail for France to assist in the organization of recreational and religious activities among American troops on behalf of the Y.M.C.A. See Francis Bowes Sayre, *Glad Adventure* (New York, 1957), pp. 58-63.

From Thomas Watt Gregory

Dear Mr. President: Washington, D. C. June 30, 1917.

I have your letter of the 28th instant transmitting a statement submitted to you by former Senator Chilton, of West Virginia, in relation to the indictment of certain coal operators in the New River and Pocahontas Districts for combining to fix the price of coal. Senator Chilton asks that the defendants be permitted to plead *nolo contendere* and pay a fine.

This case is now on trial in New York. In the opinion of the law officers of the Government the defendants clearly and deliberately entered into a price-fixing combination, which is clearly unlawful. For the Government to compromise with offenders of this type by the acceptance of a money penalty would have a most unfortunate effect, especially in view of the just and widespread complaint on account of high prices. I do not think that the proposition should be entertained for a moment.

Senator Chilton remarks upon the fact that these men were indicted in New York, although they produce no coal there and sell none there. They did, however, enter into the price-fixing combination there and therefore that is the natural jurisdiction. Senator Chilton expresses the fear that if these mine operators must be absent from their places of business for perhaps weeks attending this trial the result may be a diminution of output and general disorganization in the fields in which they operate. The first answer is that the continuous presence of these men at the trial is not required. The Judge would no doubt excuse them from time to time. In the second place, this is a ground which could always be put forward by violators of the law occupying high places in the business world.

Finally, while I know, of course, that Senator Chilton is thoroughly convinced that his theory is well founded, I cannot but doubt that it is.   Sincerely yours,   T. W. Gregory

TLS (WP, DLC).

From Robert Lansing, with Enclosure

My dear Mr. President: Washington June 30, 1917

I enclose a copy of a communication which was read to me by the Japanese Ambassador on June 15th, in which his Government expresses a wish that we should confirm the statement made by Mr. Bryan in March, 1915.

In view of what amounts to a request on the part of that Government I felt that it would be wise to reply and have therefore drafted a communication to be delivered to the Ambassador here, if it meets with your approval.[1]

I also enclose a copy of a telegram received from our Chargé at Tokio in which the word "paramount" appears,[2] to which reference is made in the draft at p. 2a.

Faithfully yours,   Robert Lansing

TLS (SDR, RG 59, 793.94/570, DNA).
[1] See the Enclosure printed with WW to RL, July 3, 1917.
[2] P. Wheeler to RL, June 22, 1917, T telegram (SDR, RG, 59, 893.00.2624, DNA). The relevant portion of this telegram reads as follows: "The draft which the Minister for Foreign Affairs handed me on June 18 with the statement that it was a copy of the memorandum handed on June 15 to the Secretary of State contains the declaration 'Japan possesses paramount interests both political and economic in China.'"

E N C L O S U R E

This the Japanese Amb. read to me
as an oral communication. It is
not to be considered a document.
June 15/17 RL

That Japan has special and close relations, political as well as economic, with China, is well and has long been understood by the American Government. In a note dated March 13, 1915, addressed to Viscount Chinda, my predecessor, by Mr. Bryan,[1] the then Secretary of State, he recognized this state of affairs and declared that the activity of Americans in China had never been political. Reposing confidence in this statement, the Japanese Government has attached no importance to the recent rumor repeatedly finding its way to the press despatches from China to the effect that the American Minister at Pekin was more or less involved in the present political crisis in China. Again, with regard to the recent important representations made by the American Government to the Chinese Government relative to the political situation in China without previously consulting Japan,[2] the Japanese Government does not entertain the slightest doubt as to the fair and unselfish motives of the United States Government. However, it is constrained, much to its regret, to recognize as a fact that, since the Japanese public is specially sensitive toward Chinese problems, this action of the American Government, in conjunction with the rumor aforementioned, has generated in the minds of a certain part of the people a feeling of uneasiness. In such circumstance, the Japanese Government believes that if the United States Government sees its way by some appropriate means to confirming the statement made by Mr. Bryan and clearly reasserting its friendly attitude toward Japan in respect of Chinese problems, it would leave a good impression on the minds of the Japanese public and would certainly contribute in no small measure to the friendly relations between our two nations, and accordingly it now communicates its conviction most frankly to the American Government and desires to be informed of the latter's opinion.

T MS (SDR, RG 59, 793.94/570, DNA).
  1 About this note, see WW to WJB, March 12, 1915, n. 1 (second letter of that date), Vol. 32.
  2 See Sun Yat-sen to WW, June 9, 1917, n. 1, Vol. 42.

From Herbert Clark Hoover

Dear Mr. President: Washington, D. C. 30 June 1917.

I have been asked to attend a meeting tomorrow morning at ten o'clock with those senators who are endeavoring to get the Food Bill through, to discuss the amendments with regard to which I addressed you yesterday. One of the amendments suggested by us embodies more specific power for the creation of corporations to handle the purchase and sale of commodities. The bill as it stands at the present moment authorizes the President to "create and employ any agencies" desired.

Judge Lindley and Judge Burling, who are advising me, believe that this power is sufficient to cover the creation of corporations, if it should become absolutely necessary; and if you believe that this is the case, it would not be necessary for us to inject a new and probably bitter discussion into the bill.

The other amendments proposed by us we find are more or less in accord with the views of the Senators concerned, and I think there will be little difficulty in securing their adoption in the Senate or in conference.

Sincerely yours,   Herbert Hoover

Telephoned Mr. Hoover that the President thought they were right & that the power was sufficient 6/30/17[1]

TLS (WP, DLC).
[1] JPThw.

From William Graves Sharp

My dear Mr. President: [Paris] June 30, 1917

Noticing in one of the recent press despatches that Baron Ishii, formerly Japanese Ambassador to France, was soon to visit the United States at the head of a Commission,[1] I have thought that it might interest you to get a sort of sidelight on him, or advance information about him,—providing he does not meet you in Washington before this letter arrives—derived from my association with him during his stay here in Paris of about a year and a half after I assumed charge of my mission.

Nothing has given me more satisfaction in connection with news coming out of Japan than the fact that Baron Ishii—since his departure, I believe, elevated to the peerage—was to be sent to Washington on such an important Commission.

Appreciating his sterling qualities and his genuine friendship for the United States, I took occasion, soon after his leaving here to become the Minister for Foreign Affairs at Tokio, to write to Secretary Lansing that I was sure our Government would find in him a true friend. Unfortunately, for some cause or other, the entire Ministry resigned within a few months of his return, and I doubt whether he has been very active in Japanese affairs since.

However, with the possibilities which may grow out of the revolutionary troubles in Russia, Japan may yet be compelled to play a much more important role in this war than she has in the past, and I am very glad that, not only on account of her possible relationship to the Russian situation but likewise to our own Government, she is sending over a Commission headed by such a man as Baron Ishii.

I think there has been not a little dis[s]atisfaction in Government circles here over the part that Japan has thus far played, and I have sometimes thought, in my talks with Mr. Cambon,[2] that there had not been the utmost certainty in the mind of the French Government as to the extent of which the Allies could expect her co-operation.

Within the past week, taking a private luncheon with the

former Prime Minister, Mr. Briand,—whom many regard as the best informed statesman in France—he told me that he thought Japan should have promptly informed the Russian revolutionists that no separate peace with Germany by them would be tolerated under a penalty of war, if necessary, with Japan. Naturally, the isolation of this latter country from the scenes of the activities of the war has placed barriers around its effectiveness, though it was a common report here that Japanese guns and gunners had been of very great service in the successful offensive of the Russian Army last year.

In Baron Ishii, I am sure you will find, as I did—and I had with him, of all my colleagues, perhaps the most intimate association—a frank, friendly man, possessed of good sense and the most cordial feelings toward the United States. During the talks I had with him, generally at my home or his, he manifested not only the greatest admiration for the United States but deprecated any possibility of any future trouble between the two countries.

With Japan as an important factor in almost any kind of combination of Powers to secure the permanency of peace after this war, I am greatly pleased that such a Commission is so soon to be sent to Washington, and especially at a time when the situation in China has added to the gravity of the problems of the war.

In this connection I would say that Mr. Hoo Wei Teh, the Chinese Minister to France, formerly Prime Minister of China, has on several occasions manifested to me a great deal of concern as to the attitude of Japan toward China. He is, to say the least, very skeptical of her good intentions.

In closing, may I briefly refer to my recent telegram (No 2238) of the 27th instant, in reference to the message sent over in code by Mr. Swing to Colonel House, which I assume you have read. This telegram set out at such length some phrases of the situation here—which I regret had been described in such an exaggerated and sensational manner by the informant of Colonel House—that I will not at this time write you further of the conditions to which mention was therein made.

Congratulating you upon your recent Flag Day speech, which not only so scathingly indicted the German Government for its offences against America but so clearly analysed its unscrupulous aims in this war,

I am, believe me, my dear Mr. President,
    With high personal respect,
                    Most sincerely yours,   Wm G. Sharp.

TLS (WP, DLC).

[1] The Japanese Ambassador, Aimaro Sato, had, on May 12, conveyed to Lansing a request of his government to send a special mission to the United States to discuss cooperation in the war effort, Japanese immigration to the United States, loans to China, and other far eastern matters. Lansing replied affirmatively on May 15. Sato informed Lansing on June 14 that Viscount Kikujiro Ishii had been appointed to head the delegation. News of the appointment was made public shortly thereafter. See, e.g., the *New York Times*, June 24, 1917, sect. 6, p. 5. As it turned out, the mission did not arrive in San Francisco until August 13 and in Washington until August 22. See Burton F. Beers, *Vain Endeavor: Robert Lansing's Attempts to End the American-Japanese Rivalry* (Durham, N. C., 1962), pp. 102-110, and *FR 1917*, p. 258.

[2] That is, Jules Martin Cambon, general secretary of the French Foreign Ministry.

From John Jacob Cornwell[1]

Charleston, W. Va., June 30, 1917.

Labor conditions in coal fields of southern West Virginia unsatisfactory with sporadic strikes and central disturbances threatened. Absence of operators now in trial in New York tends to greatly disorganize and disturb conditions. If a settlement satisfactory to the government could be effected speedily so as to permit operators to return to the state much trouble can possibly be averted. John J. Cornwell

T telegram (WP, DLC).
[1] Governor of West Virginia.

From Newton Diehl Baker, with Enclosure

Dear Mr. President: Washington. June 30, 1917.

I inclose a copy of a letter which I wrote to Mr. Gifford, Director of the Council of National Defense, with regard to the action of the Committee on Coal Production.

It seemed wiser to write this to Mr. Gifford than to the Attorney General in order to prevent the counsel for the defendants in the New York law suit from claiming that the letter was written to the Attorney General for the purpose of influencing pending litigation.

I trust the last paragraph but one of my letter is sufficiently tactful. Respectfully, Newton D. Baker

TLS (WP, DLC).

ENCLOSURE

Newton Diehl Baker to Walter Sherman Gifford[1]

My dear Mr. Gifford: [Washington] June 30, 1917.

My attention has been called through the newspapers to the action reported to have been taken at Washington, D. C., during the past week by the so-called Committee on Coal Production of the Council of National Defense, in cooperation with certain coal producers, and representatives of coal mining enterprises, with regard to the price of bituminous and anthracite coal.

The facts seem to be that the Coal Production Committee invited to Washington various coal operators and arranged conferences between them, members of the Coal Production Committee and members of the Federal Trade Commission, leading to the adoption of resolutions in favor of an early and accurate determination of the costs involved in the production of bituminous and anthracite coal, as a basis for some future action by some official agency of the government in fixing fair and just prices for these products, should any such agency be given power to do so. Pending such an ascertainment of costs this meeting seems to have adopted a resolution whereby the operators present agreed to sell bituminous coal at a price not higher than $3.00 per ton, and that this obligation should remain in force until some such action had been taken by an authorized governmental agency.

The color which has been given to this meeting and this resolution in the newspapers may well mislead the public into believing that the Council of National Defense has either undertaken itself to fix the price of coal, or to sanction its being fixed by the Coal Production Committee, or that Committee in conjunction with the coal operators. I, therefore, as President of the Council of National Defense, write this to say that the Council of National Defense has no legal power, and claims no legal power, either to fix the price of coal, or to fix a maximum price for coal, or any other product. The Coal Production Committee is a subordinate Committee of the Council of National Defense, purely advisory in its character, formed for the purpose of advising the Council as to steps which might be recommended leading to a stimulation of production and distribution of coal. No power has been even attempted to be delegated to it to consider or deal with the question of price, and any action taken by that Committee, or sanctioned by that Committee, dealing with price, either fixed or maximum, for coal is clearly beyond the legal power of the Coal Production committee and of the Council of National Defense, from which the Committee derives whatever authority it has.

As you are aware the Federal Trade Commission has been directed by the President to ascertain for his information the costs involved in coal production. I am to some extent familiar with the progress made by the Commission. The information I have from that and other sources, I think, justified me in believing that the price of $3.00 suggested, or agreed on, as a maximum, is an exhorbitant, unjust and oppres[s]ive price.

The fact that these conferences were attended by members of the Federal Trade Commission and by members of the Council of National Defense, of course, adds nothing to their legal powers, and I am sure that none of my associates in the Council will dissent from the view I have herein expressed, both on the limitation upon the powers of the Council and the Coal Production Committee, and the effect of the action alleged to have been taken.

I write this for the information of the Coal Production Committee, and for the guidance of all other sub-committees of the Council.   Very truly yours,   [Newton D. Baker]
President of the Council of National
Defense.[2]

CCL (WP, DLC).
[1] Vice-president of the American Telephone & Telegraph Company and Director of the Council of National Defense.
[2] This letter appeared in the newspapers, e.g., the *New York Times*, July 1, 1917.

From John Franklin Fort

Dear Mr. President: Washington June 30, 1917.

Mr. Davies has advised me of his conversation with you last evening over the telephone.

Last night, at the request of Secretary of War Baker, I met him at his office with the Attorney General and the Secretary of Labor, and we went over this whole coal matter. The resolution which the Attorney General feared was passed is not the resolution that was passed. I attended this convention on the first day of its meeting, at which there were 400 operators present, covering all districts east of the Mississippi. Secretary Lane addressed them, as did Secretary Daniels and myself. I think Mr. Davies and I advised you of this fact when we saw you the other day. When I discovered the character of the resolution which the convention first adopted I called the attention of the Attorney General to it and we agreed that it was not proper. I then went before the convention, had it rescind that resolution, and a revised resolution was drafted, under my direction, and presented and adopted by the convention. This is Resolution No. 1, herewith. Resolution No. 2, herewith, was also adopted by the convention.[1]

Resolution No. 1 is a resolution under which the operators agree that the government agencies; namely, the Secretary of the Interior, the Federal Trade Commission, and the committee on coal production of the Advisory Council of National Defence, shall fix the permanent price of coal f.o.b. the mine. Of course, before this can be done the definite costs of the mine operators must be ascertained. That the Federal Trade Commission is now doing, with the approval of Mr. Peabody and the Secretary of the Interior. When those definite costs are ascertained we can then add a reasonably fair profit for coal at the mine and that, added to the costs, will be the permanent price of coal when thus fixed.

You, of course, know the tremendous interest there is in the nation among all classes of coal consumers with relation to the present speculative price of coal. It seemed to be our duty to get something done, and get it done at once, to end this situation, and Resolution No. 2 was adopted for that purpose. Under that resolution the Secretary of the Interior, the Federal Trade Commission, for which I was acting, and the coal production committee were empowered to fix a tentative maximum price (practically an arbitration) which the operators were to agree, and did agree, should be a tentative maximum price for coal f.o.b. the mines. Of course, no one is required to pay this price. The operators are bound in honor not to ask or charge a price in excess of this.

I am also sending you a statement[2] sent to me from the Interior Department of the effect of our action. The government agencies named in Resolution No. 2 fixed these tentative maximum prices themselves; they simply allowed the operators to suggest what they thought they should be, but I think in every case we reduced their suggestion from at least 50 to 75 cents per ton, and fixed a price, practically in all districts, of $3.00 for mine run coal. In some bituminous districts there is what might be called a semi-anthracite coal, which is domestic lump, egg and nut size. For this they were allowed the price of $3.50.

We recognized when we were fixing these prices that they were high, but the motive was to increase production and throw a large amount of coal on the market as rapidly as possible, and then the matter of supply and demand will reduce the maximum tentative price (in our opinion) very much below the maximum tentative price which we named. In any event, it is going to have a most excellent effect.

You will see in the statement of the Department of the Interior, which was prepared for us, the prices which have been ranging f.o.b. the mines for the past sixty days and the reductions which have been effected on the basis of $3.00.

The operators were told by me in their meeting that the permanent price would undoubtedly be a lower price than the tentative price. Secretary Lane approved this course most heartily, and I think you will find that our action will be proven to be the wisest course that it was possible to take under the circumstances. If we had allowed these operators to go home and had done nothing, and left the speculative condition of the market as it was, the situation would have continued deplorable.

We should be able to get the actual costs and fix the permanent price by the 15th or 20th of July. We have a large part of that work already done.

I talked this over in a very serious way with Secretary Lane. We realized the difficult situation, but to end an intolerable condition we did what we could.

Upon all coal furnished to the Government the operators agreed to allow 50 cents per ton reduction under the tentative maximum price fixed. I protected the Navy Department, at Secretary Daniel's request, by announcing to the convention that the Navy coal would be taken by the Navy Department on the basis fixed by Secretary Daniels, which was $2.333 per ton, until after the Federal Trade Commission had ascertained the costs, when Secretary Daniels would himself fix the price of Navy coal, or ask us to do so.

I think it would be a grievous mistake for any suggestion to be made from any official source, pending the ascertainment of the actual costs of the coal and the fixing of a permanent price, disparaging or criticizing the action already taken. So far as I can see or hear, manufacturers and all classes of operators, with the possible exception of the railroads, realize that what we did will be of great benefit in correcting the present situation. If now the railroads will speed up transportation and help the operators get their coal moved, the price must go down to what would at this time be a fair and normal price.

The great trouble has been due to a feeling in the country that there was no coal, and the fear on the part of public utilities, manufacturers, and others that they would not be able to get coal. The operators can afford to mine to the full under the tentative price, and if they can get transportation to market, the supply will more than meet the demand, and the whole situation will be very much benefitted.

With distinguished respect, I am

Yours very sincerely,   John Franklin Fort

TLS (WP, DLC).
    [1] Two T MSS dated June 28, 1917 (WP, DLC). Fort describes them fully.
    [2] T MS dated June 28, 1917 (WP, DLC).

From James Cannon, Jr., and Others

Washington, D. C. June 30, 1917.

We have earnestly considered the statement in your letter of yesterday to the Legislative Committee of the Anti-Saloon League of America, that in the face of the present food crisis you are greatly concerned lest the early passage of the Food Administration legislation now pending in Congress be jeopardized by a heated and protracted debate upon certain sections of the bill relating to the manufacture of foodstuffs into intoxicating liquors.

We are aware of the threats made by the friends of beer and wine in the Senate of an indefinite and protracted filibuster against those provisions of the bill. We beg to assure you that as patriotic Americans, determined to uphold you as Commander in Chief of the Army and Navy in the present war, we will not for our constituency offer any obstruction to the prompt passage of the Food Control bill.

Of course we can not presume to indicate to members of Congress what action they should take in view of this request from the President of the United States. They will doubtless act in accordance with their convictions of duty.

We are glad to note that your request applies only to the pending Food Administration legislation. It will be our purpose to urge the passage of legislation prohibiting the waste of foodstuffs in the manufacture of beer and wines, at the earliest possible date, either in the form of a separate Bill or in connection with other war legislation.

We assure you of our purpose as patriotic American citizens to cooperate in every possible way in the winning of the great war in which our Nation is engaged.

Sincerely and respectfully yours,   James Cannon Jr.

P. A. Baker	W B Wheeler.
General Superintendent.	Ernest H. Cherrington.[1]
Edwin C. Dinwiddie.	A. J..Barton
Legislative Superintendent.	Legislative Committee.

TLS (WP, DLC).

[1] Ernest Hurst Cherrington, leading publicist of the Anti-Saloon League; at this time, managing editor of the Richmond *Virginian*, which Cannon had established in 1909 in order to provide Richmond with a "dry" daily newspaper. Richard L. Watson, Jr., ed., *Bishop Cannon's Own Story: Life as I Have Seen It* (Durham, N. C., 1955), pp. 136-39.

Arthur James Balfour to Sir Cecil Arthur Spring Rice

[London, June 30, 1917]

Most Secret.

Shipping is at the present time being sunk in the danger zone round the British Isles at a rate which exceeds that at which new tonnage of British origin can be turned out. It is to be foreseen that, if losses continue on the present scale, the available tonnage, leaving America's contribution out of account, will ultimately be inadequate to secure the United Kingdom a sufficiency of food stuffs, oil fuel and other essentials.

France and Italy are in a very similar position.

Under the present methods of operation adopted by the enemy submarines, attacks are made almost exclusively by torpedo. The submarine itself remains submerged and is rarely seen unless and until the ship attacked has been actually struck by a torpedo.

The guns carried by merchant vessels serve to keep the submarines below the surface, but are useless against them when submerged.

The expectation is entertained that the convoy system, when in working order and provided that sufficient destroyers are available to form an effective screen, will serve to minimise losses. Progress is also being made with the introduction of new offensive measures, which will it is hoped ultimately result in the destruction of enemy submarines at a rate sufficient to secure the safety of sea communications with the British Isles.

But the method at present in use, viz., the employment of armed small craft in an attempt to prevent the submarines from using their periscopes for fear of an attack by ram or bomb, offers the only remedy for the next few months. The success of this method obviously depends on small craft being available in very large numbers and the critical character of the present situation is due to the fact that the forces of this nature at the disposal of the British Admiralty are not at present adequate for the work of protecting shipping in the danger zone.

It is therefore of the utmost urgency that additional armed small craft should be made available for use in the area near the British and French coasts where the commercial routes converge. Invaluable assistance could be rendered, not only by destroyers, gun-boats and submarines, but also by trawlers, yachts and tugs. But these are needed immediately and, if sent in as large numbers as possible, would, it is hoped, save what is manifestly a critical situation.

The United States is the only allied country able to afford assistance of this kind, and you should lay the situation outlined above before the United States Government, emphasising its serious and urgent nature.

CC telegram (WP, DLC).

Lord Northcliffe to Arthur James Balfour and David Lloyd George

Washington, June 30, 1917.

Personal. Following for Mr. Balfour and Mr. Lloyd George from Lord Northcliffe:

I had thirty minutes very agreeable interview with the President who owing to dispatches from Page and House seemed well acquainted with the situation. The matter is all right over Monday when I am to see McAdoo. The President promised if necessary to take it up with McAdoo personally.

I pointed out that we must have about $200,000,000 regularly each month, that the money is being spent entirely in the United States, that American figures show that 52% of Allied exports from the United States are British, that we have advanced our Allies over $5,000,000,000 in addition to much shipping, big guns and other needs.

In regard to the Russian money, the President said that his Government was unable to get any reply to communications on the subject sent to their Embassy at Petrograd.

The President was as kind to me as he had been on my previous visit.

When I pointed out to him that statements of the French, Italians, and Russians that we were unfairly getting the lion's share were untrue, he said he knew it.

We have much to contend with in the shape of German influence and jealous statements by our Allies.

The President spoke highly of Crawford and Lever.

I am remaining in Washington till Saturday next to take up the questions of oil and steel and other matters. I shall be with Colonel House July 14th, 15th and 16th at Manchester on the Sea, Massachusetts.   Northcliffe.

T telegram (FO 115/2295, pp. 294-95, PRO).

Colville Adrian de Rune Barclay to Robert Lansing

My dear Mr. Secretary: Washington. July 1st 1917.

I am instructed by His Majesty's Principal Secretary of State for Foreign Affairs to call your immediate attention to the financial position of Great Britain in regard to the war inasmuch as it is of an urgent and critical character. It appears, indeed, to Mr. Balfour that the United States Treasury do not realise how perilous the situation truly is,—namely that there is danger that the ability of His Majesty's Government to effect payments in America from today onwards will be in jeopardy.

The effect which will be produced on the progress of the war by a collapse of the exchange will be no less disastrous than a great military reverse, for not only will all commercial relations between the two countries, including the cotton trade, be thrown into complete disorder entailing the stoppage of the entire private export business from the United States, but, further, the basis of financial relations of all the Allies with the rest of the world will be removed, and a general collapse of credit and of all financial confidence will inevitably result.

It is to be remembered that His Majesty's Government have, single-handed, borne the burden for nearly three years, of financing the whole of the Allied Powers, and have never failed to furnish them with the monies which were indispensable to enable them to meet their actual liabilities whether in the United Kingdom or elsewhere.

When Mr. Balfour was here, he discussed the matter thoroughly with the United States Government and left with the full understanding that they would relieve His Majesty's Government definitely of the expenditure, in the United States, of the other Allied Powers calculating from the day on which the United States entered into the war. Up to the present time however His Majesty's Government have borne Russia's entire expenditure in the United States amounting to some $50,000,000 and they have not been informed that this sum will be repaid.

So far as British requirements are concerned His Majesty's

Government have never feared that the United States Government would not give the financial support required. Indeed upon the entry of the United States into the war His Majesty's Government abandoned financial expedients previously contemplated in order that the American market might be free for the Liberty Loan operation. The needs of His Majesty's Government for the six months beginning June 1 were communicated in writing to the Secretary of the Treasury on May 3rd during the presence of Mr. Balfour in Washington and the specific assistance desired for June was indicated in my note to the Secretary of the Treasury of May 29th. It was confidently expected that these needs would be met.

Now, during the month of June the following transactions have taken place. The British Government have received from the United States Government the sum of $150,000,000. They have had to supplement this however by bringing in $125,000,000 in gold, and by the sale of securities in America to the value of $10,000,000 and on the 28th ultimo they were forced to authorise their Financial representative in New York to bring in a further $25,000,000 in gold. Thus you will perceive that, in the course of this month, only about half of the British expenditure in the United States has been met by the United States Government.

The increase in our exchange expenditure during June arose largely from the withdrawals by American banks of their sterling balances in London, presumably to pay for the Liberty Loan. The amount of these withdrawals has already exceeded $100,000,000 during the course of the month. This is in effect a diminution of the amount loaned by the United States.

In view of the practical depletion of our resources in gold and marketable securities I am instructed to present to you a formal request for the following financial assistance. It is desired:

(I) that the commitments which His Majesty's Government has undertaken in this country on behalf of Belgium and Russia may constitute a first charge on the first loans made to these two countries, and may be repaid to Great Britain with the least delay possible:

(II) that an arrangement may be come to immediately between the United States Treasury and the British agents in America defining the amount of assistance which can be granted to His Majesty's Government for the months of July and August and that the first instalment for the month of July ($100,000,000) may be made available by the 4th July at the latest.

(III) that assistance may be given to cover the amount of

our overdraft with New York bankers amounting to about $400,-000,000. It was explained to the Secretary of the Treasury in April and again in my communication of May 3rd that this overdraft had been incurred mainly in order to enable our other Allies to carry on and he agreed that this sum might be included in our application and regarded as a first call on the credits under the loan.

Mr. Balfour desires me to add that the friendly nature of the discussions which he had on these matters with the statesmen of this country did not leave him in any doubt as to the intentions of the United States Government to meet this situation and that the first and third requests which are now put forward merely embody in a formal manner points which he fully understood to express the settled intentions of the United States Government.

In conclusion Mr. Balfour desires me to add that the foregoing urgent requests are presented solely on account of the immediate and grave necessities of the situation which he is convinced have only to be realised by the United States Government for relief to be forthcoming.

I am, my dear Mr. Secretary,
Yours sincerely,
(for the Ambassador) Colville Barclay.

TCL (WP, DLC).

To William Edwin Chilton

My dear Senator: [The White House] 2 July, 1917

The Attorney General and I have given very careful attention to your memorandum of June twenty-sixth. I beg that you will not feel that there was the least impropriety in your submitting it. I want to assure you that it received our most respectful consideration.

The law officers of the Government are of the opinion that the defendants in the New York trial clearly and deliberately entered into a price-fixing combination which was unlawful, and I fear that if the Government were to compromise with offenders of this sort by accepting a money penalty, it would have a most unfortunate effect, especially in view of the widespread and I cannot but believe just complaint of the prevailing high prices.

It does seem no doubt something of a hardship that these gentlemen should be indicted in New York. That, however, was the *situs* of the price-fixing combination and the jurisdiction is determined by that.

I have no doubt that the judge presiding at the trial can minimize the disadvantage of the absence of these gentlemen from the mines by excusing them from time to time inasmuch as their continuous presence at the trial is not required, but I do not see how further than that this disadvantage could be met. I am sure you do not feel that any of us is in the least inclined to do an injustice, and I beg to assure you that we are trying to pursue the most generous as well as the most consistent course.[1]

        Cordially and sincerely yours,   Woodrow Wilson

TLS (Letterpress Books, WP, DLC).
  [1] As it happened, the government rested its case against the Smokeless Coal Operators' Association on July 2; the defense began its case on the same day. Over the next few days, Federal District Court Judge William Irwin Grubb dismissed many of the indictments against individuals and/or companies, either for lack of evidence or because, in his opinion, the government had failed to prove its case against them. The jury found the remaining defendants innocent of the charges on July 12. On July 19, Judge Grubb dismissed the indictments against another group of individuals and companies being tried separately, and the case was closed. See the *New York Times*, July 3, 6, 7, 10, 11, 12, 13, and 20, 1917.

To John Franklin Fort

My dear Governor Fort: [The White House] 2 July, 1917

You may be sure that I am not in the least inclined to criticise the part you played in the conferences which led to a tentative agreement about the price of coal, but I do think that it was unfortunate that the conference attempted to deal with the matter of prices at all, simply because it is open to so much misconstruction when men, like the operators in this instance, seem to take the initiative in determining what price they shall themselves receive and then arrive at a conclusion which exactly coincides with the agreement which certain operators are now under indictment by the Government for making "in restraint of trade." I think that if the conference could have been confined to the objects stated in the first part of one of the resolutions I read, namely, to the means which would most tend to increase production and facilitate distribution of the product, it would have been wholly admirable. Whenever such conferences go beyond that and deal with matters of price, they open themselves to public misconstruction.

I feel confident that as a result of the costs to be ascertained by the Federal Trade Commission some government agency can itself arrive at a conclusion with regard to price and a liberal profit which will seem to the country satisfactory and conclusive.

        Cordially and sincerely yours,   Woodrow Wilson

TLS (Letterpress Books, WP, DLC).

To James Thomas Heflin

My dear Heflin: [The White House] 2 July, 1917

Your very generous letter of June twenty-eighth has given me great pleasure. It was like you to take so public-spirited a view of the matter of the appointment of a standing Committee on Woman Suffrage,[1] and I thank you heartily.

Cordially and sincerely yours,   Woodrow Wilson

TLS (Letterpress Books, WP, DLC).
[1] The House Rules Committee, on September 24, recommended the adoption of H. Res. 12 which created a standing Committee on Woman Suffrage. Following a debate limited to two hours, the House approved the resolution on that date. *Cong. Record*, 65th Cong., 1st sess., pp. 7369-85.

To Vance Criswell McCormick

My dear McCormick: [The White House] 2 July, 1917

I am heartily glad that you are inclined to accept the duties which the Secretary of State suggested to you the other day. I am particularly desirous to have in that place somebody whom I thoroughly know and whom I can thoroughly trust, and when I was discussing it with the Secretary of State I did not feel, and neither did he, that it would be necessary for you to resign the chairmanship of the National Committee. I should be very much distressed to accept any such conclusion as that. The position is only semi-official and seems to me entirely compatible with the inter-election activities of a National Chairman. Your constant presence in Washington, moreover, will make the other things which you have been doing, and which have been so useful, perhaps easier to do than before.

I hope very much that you will accept and that you will find it possible to take this view of the situation.

In haste

Cordially and sincerely yours,   [Woodrow Wilson]

CCL (WP, DLC).

To Josephus Daniels

Confidential.

My dear Mr. Secretary: The White House 2 July, 1917

Here is a suggestion communicated to me by Tumulty from Mr. Arthur Pollen,[1] which I think is worth acting upon. As you and I agreed the other day, the British Admiralty had done absolutely nothing constructive in the use of their navy and I think it is time we were making and insisting upon plans of our own, even if we render some of the more conservative of our own naval advisers uncomfortable. What do you think?

Cordially and faithfully yours,   Woodrow Wilson

TLS (J. Daniels Papers, DLC).

[1] The Bureau of Ordnance was at this time considering the adoption of a range-finder and other fire-control instruments invented by Arthur Pollen. However, it seems most likely that Wilson here referred to a tactical plan put forth by Pollen at about this time. Daniels described it as follows: "Pollen had made statem[en]t . . . that the way to defeat submarines was to make a lane & to have boats that could send torpedoes under water to hit submarines 2,000 yards off. He believed it was the antidote." J. Daniels Diary, July 15, 1917.

To George Wylie Paul Hunt

[The White House] 2 July, 1917

I have been very much concerned to hear of the possible serious misunderstanding between the miners and the operators in the copper mines and I would deem it a very great public service on your part if you would be generous enough to do what you could to act as mediator and conciliator. I know how confidently I can appeal to your public spirit.

Woodrow Wilson.

T telegram (Letterpress Books, WP, DLC).

From George Wylie Paul Hunt

Phoenix, Ariz., July 2, 1917.

Your wire this date received. I deeply appreciate honor and responsibility that acompanies your expression of confidence. Will act immediately upon authorization.

Geo. W. P. Hunt.

T telegram (WP, DLC).

From George Washington Goethals

My dear Mr. President: [Washington] July 2, 1917.

At the request of the Chief Clerk of the United States Shipping Board, I prepared for your information a statement of moneys required for August by the Emergency Fleet Corporation. On June 11th, I forwarded to you a report outlining the program for an emergency fleet, wood and steel.[1] This was supplemented by a memorandum of our conference of June 22nd.[2]

Our plans are now so far matured that we stand ready to let three contracts for the construction and delivery within eighteen months (beginning about five months from date of contract) of about 2,153,000 tons of "fabricated" steel ships of 5,000 to 7,500 tons dead weight capacity each, at an estimated total expense of approximately $350,000,000. These arrangements include contracts for complete machinery. In these contracts, the Government must furnish the steel, which in these figures I compute at $50. a ton.

Aside from, and in addition to the above, the Corporation has already let, or is about to let, contracts for wood and steel construction of about 1,538,000 tons of "standard" ships as distinguished from the above "fabricated" steel ships, which would involve approximately $200,500,000. Of these contracts, 930,-900 tons are wood and composite ships and 607,600 tons are for steel ships. In addition to these figures, the machinery necessary to install in the hulls contracted for, or in prospect of being contracted for, will call for an expenditure of $30,000,000. The total commitments which we have already taken, or are ready to take, therefore, would amount to a total of 3,691,000 tons at a cost of $580,000,000. against the total of $550,000,000. so far made available. As above stated, these contracts will redeem our promises to Congress of 3,000,000 tons in eighteen months.

The form of Executive Order designed to carry out the program recommended has been previously sent to you under date of June 15th.[3]   Very respectfully,   [Geo. W. Goethals]

CCL (G. W. Goethals Papers, DLC).
   [1] See G. W. Goethals to WW, June 11, 1917, Vol. 42.
   [2] G. W. Goethals to WW, June 24, 1917, TCL, enclosing TC of memorandum (G. W. Goethals Papers, DLC). For a summary of the conference of June 22, see W. Saulsbury to WW, June 23, 1917, n. 1, Vol. 42.
   [3] See G. W. Goethals to WW, June 15, 1917, Vol. 42.

From Franklin Knight Lane

My dear Mr. President: Washington July 2, 1917.

In the matter of opening coal mines for the Pacific Coast consumption, concerning which you recently spoke, I find that the nearest tracts of Government mines available for this purpose are in Colorado and Wyoming.

In Colorado two tracts may be mentioned, both on the Denver and Rio Grande Railway. A considerable acreage of good coal lands remains in Government ownership in the Book Cliffs coal field a few miles east of Grand Junction. For example, a tract of 2080 acres near Palisades contains two coal beds with a total average thickness of about eleven feet of good steam coal with a high heating value. The coal ranges in depth from a few feet to 1,000 feet. This Government land is appraised at from $70 to $100 an acre and lies from ½ to 2½ miles from the main railroad line. Grand Junction is 1215 miles from San Francisco and the freight rate on carload lots is $7 per ton.

Another tract which could be selected is near Newcastle, approximately 1290 miles from San Francisco, with a freight rate on coal of $7 per ton. This tract contains 3680 acres and lies from ½ to 4 miles from the railroad. Several workable coal beds outcrop at the surface and range in thickness from 4 to 48 feet. This is a high grade steam coal and the land has been appraised at from $20 to $300 per acre.

In Wyoming, in the well-known Rock Springs coal field, Government-owned coal lands are available close to the Union Pacific railroad. One tract of 1920 acres, for example, might be selected about six miles north of Rock Springs, and within one mile of the Reliance Branch of the Union Pacific Railroad. Here the coal is of high grade steam quality which commands a wide market, and this coal land contains eighteen beds varying in thickness from a little more than two feet to a little less than six feet, with an aggregate thickness of 80 feet. This land has been appraised at from $95 to $465 per acre. Rock Springs is 974 miles from San Francisco and the freight rate on coal is $5.15.   Cordially yours,   Franklin K Lane

TLS (WP, DLC).

From Robert Lansing, with Enclosure

Dear Mr. President: Washington July 2, 1917.

I have received your letter of the 29th of June, enclosing a letter from the Archbishop of Malines which Father de Ville left with you the other day. You invite my suggestions regarding the propriety of an answer.

I think that, in view of Cardinal Mercier's high representative character as Archbishop of Malines (Mechlin), and considering the warm sympathy of the people of the United States with the Belgian people in their great suffering, a simple but cordial acknowledgment by you, in your own handwriting, would be not only appropriate but good policy at this time, when we are sending our boys to the Belgian Front.

I submit a brief acknowledgment which, if approved and signed by you, I might send to Father Jean B. de Ville at the

Belgian Bureau in New York. We have no means of sending it direct to Cardinal Mercier. He may be in Havre.

Faithfully yours,   Robert Lansing.

TLS (WP, DLC).

ENCLOSURE

DRAFT ANSWER

Your Eminence:

I have been deeply touched by your personal communication of February 9, 1917, which recently reached me through the medium of Father de Ville.

The sympathy of the people of the United States for the Belgian people in their sore affliction has been manifested since the outbreak of the war, and this Government has set its seal of approbation upon this national sentiment by sending our chosen forces to the Belgian Front, there to fight the common enemy. I trust that the efforts of the American people toward the material relief of Belgian suffering may soon be resumed under the favorable conditions which would attend the liberation of Belgium from its present heavy yoke of oppression.

With assurances of my high personal consideration, I remain,

Yours faithfully,

T MS (WP, DLC).

From Thomas James Walsh

My dear Mr. President: [Washington] July 2, 1917.

In response to your letter of June 29th, I am sending you herewith a copy of S. 45.[1] You will notice by the first section that it provides for the disposition of lands owned by the United States "and not otherwise reserved." Accordingly lands in the Naval Reserve are left untouched by its provisions. I am also sending a letter received from home today, together with copy of a telegram from Seattle.[2]

I submitted to the committee on Thursday last price lists issued by coal companies supplying people of Montana, showing various increases made from May 1st, 1916, to June 15, 1917, the coal used for domestic consumption jumping through that period from $1.75 per ton to $3.50 per ton. Other grades showed proportionate increases. I find it hard to get anyone to look with any concern on the affairs of the people west of the Missouri River. This bill, as perfected by the Public Lands Committee, ought to be a part of the food control bill. It would open up a practically inexhaustible supply of potash, the price of which has risen from $35. per ton before the war, to $475. now, a perfectly prohibitive price so far as the use of that mineral for fertilizer, the main basis of consumption, is concerned.

I shall be glad to go to talk with you about these matters at any time you may call me.

Very truly yours,   T. J. Walsh

TLS (WP, DLC).
  [1] A new version of the general leasing bill. Walsh explains the principal difference between it and earlier bills. This bill was sent to committee and never emerged.
  [2] L. M. Rheem, secretary and manager of the Helena, Mont., Commercial Club, to T. J. Walsh, June 28, 1917, TLS (WP, DLC), enclosing Seattle Chamber of Commerce and Commercial Club to Helena Commercial Club, June 26, 1917, T telegram (WP, DLC).

From Edward Mandell House, with Enclosure

Dear Governor: Magnolia, Massachusetts. July 2, 1917.

Baruch's right hand man, Frederick Allen[1] of Boston, New York and St Louis, has been here for two days, and has made the enclosed memorandum which he tells me is Baruch's conclusion as well as his own.

Baruch, it seems, does not want to ask you for an interview because of the load you are carrying, and he hopes that I will boil their views down in order that you may have them in condensed form.

I am told from another source that Baruch hopes if you appoint a commission and he is included in it, you will also name Allen and Vance McCormick as the other members.

Allen has had ten years experience as buyer for the Simmons Hardware Company of St Louis. He is now connected with Lee, Higginson & Co. of Boston.

Vance McCormick would know but little about the purchasing end, but he is a man of such char[a]cter that I believe his appointment would be generally approved and would give confidence in the commission.

Baruch and Allen believe that it is necessary to have fairly high prices in order to stimulate a maximum production, and they believe the more favored firms and corporations should be subject to an excess profit tax which would act as a leveling medium. For instance, many copper companies can produce copper below ten cents. Others cannot produce it much below twenty-five cents, therefore, in order to get them all at work a twenty-five cent basis should be maintained, and the excess profit should be taken from the more favored producers. (I name twenty-five cents merely as an illustration as I do not know the actual figures.)

They also claim that high prices would stimulate business and make the flotation of bonds and the carrying on of the war easier. They assert that the United States is the last reservoir of capital and that nothing should be done to depress our industries.

They suggest, in order to get at an excess profit, a three years average be made. (In passing, let me personally say that if this three year average is agreed upon, it should be three years before August 1914 and not three years from April 1917. I mention this because what they have in mind is from 1917 which seems to me unfair as there have been enormous excess profits made since 1914, and unless you use the earlier period the purpose contemplated would not be met.)

There is common agreement that something should be done quickly, for there is much evidence that the delay in having a general purchasing committee is working to the disadvantage of a more vigorous prosecution of the war.

Affectionately yours,   E. M. House

TLS (WP, DLC).
1 Frederic Winthrop Allen, partner in Lee, Higginson & Co. of Boston.

E N C L O S U R E

A Memorandum by Frederic Winthrop Allen

[c. July 2, 1917]
Central Purchasing Commission.
1. Appoint Commission of three
   a) To make all United States purchases
   b) To vise foreign purchases
   c) To control and exercise the decisions of priority.
2. Announce to public either directly, or by letter to Commission, the purposes of the Commission as follows:
   "To win this war we must have maximum production, therefore urge that the Commission establish prices which will produce maximum production—prices sufficiently high to permit the smaller and more disadvantageously situated manufacturers to produce his quota at a generous living profit. Such prices will necessarily bring to larger and more

advantageously situated manufacturers excess profits, but it will be suggested to Congress that these profits be reduced by a progressive excess profit tax, so that he who makes the greater profit will pay the greater tax. Indecision and delay will postpone the day of peace and thereby directly cause an additional loss of life and money. The war is costing ourselves and our Allies many thousands of lives and approximately $100,000,000 a day. While the law of supply and demand was not created by man and may not be repealed by him, many factors affecting its working may be materially changed by governmental action.

Relying upon the patriotism of our business men it is believed that the Commission through suggestion and requests will permit the establishment of satisfactory prices. In this work it is thought that the Federal Trades Commission may be of service to both the Commission and the manufacturers and producers. Priority decisions have been created in the Commission because they are inevitably interwoven with the purchasing of supplies.

TC MS (WP, DLC).

To Newton Diehl Baker, with Enclosures

Personal and Confidential.

My dear Mr. Secretary: The White House 3 July, 1917

The enclosed explains itself. I dare say from what Senator Williams told me personally there is some danger of trouble of a serious nature if this officer[1] is not separated from his present command.

Cordially and faithfully yours,   Woodrow Wilson

1 That is, Col. Young.

ENCLOSURE   I

To John Sharp Williams

My dear Senator: The White House 29 June, 1917

I have conferred with the Secretary of War about the case of Captain Dockery, and I believe that the Lieutenant Colonel referred to will not in fact have command because he is in ill health and likely when he gets better himself to be transferred to some other service.

Cordially and faithfully yours,   Woodrow Wilson

From John Sharp Williams

Personal & Confidential.

My dear Mr. President: [Washington] June 30, 1917.

I just got this letter and return it in order to refresh your memory. You seem to have forgotten that it is a negro regiment as well as a negro colonel.

I send both your letter to me and my letter to you by my secretary, so that you can read them and destroy them, if you choose.

You remember the letter that Captain Dockery wrote to his father? I think it must have impressed you.

I am, with every expression of regard,

Very truly yours,   John Sharp Williams

TLS (N. D. Baker Papers, DLC).

To Josephus Daniels, with Enclosure

My dear Mr. Secretary,   The White House. 3 July, 1917.

If you approve of the enclosed will you not have it forwarded at once through the State Department. Of course if you do not approve I will gladly heed your advice.

Perhaps it would be well to add, for yourself, the experience of the convoy of Pershing's troops in keeping the submarines off.[1]   Faithfully Yours,   Woodrow Wilson

WWTLS (J. Daniels Papers, DLC).

[1] The first convoy of American troop transports sailed from New York on June 14 under the overall command of Rear Admiral Albert Gleaves, recently appointed as commander of convoy operations in the Atlantic. The fourteen transports were divided into four groups, according to their speed. Each group was escorted by a number of cruisers, destroyers, and other armed naval vessels, a total of twenty-three in all. The fastest group arrived at St. Nazaire on June 28; the last on July 2. Although three of the four groups were attacked by German submarines, all arrived at their destination without damage or casualties. One submarine was possibly destroyed by an escorting destroyer. For a good description of the expedition, and especially of the elaborate precautions against enemy attack, see Thomas Goddard Frothingham, *The Naval History of the World War* (3 vols., Cambridge, Mass., 1925-26), III, 131-42.

E N C L O S U R E

FOR ADMIRAL SIMS, Confidential from the President:

From the beginning of the war I have been surprised by nothing so much as the failure of the British Admiralty to use Great

Britain's great naval superiority in any effective way. In the presence of the present submarine emergency they are helpless to the point of panic. Every plan we suggest they reject for some reason of prudence. In my view this is not a time for prudence but for boldness even at the risk of great losses. In most of your despatches you have very properly advised us of the sort of aid and cooperation desired from us by the Admiralty. The trouble is that their plans and methods do not seem to us effective. I would be very much obliged to you if you would report to me, confidentially of course, exactly what the Admiralty have been doing and what they have accomplished and add to the report your own comments and suggestions based upon independent study of the whole situation without regard to the judgments already arrived at on that side of the water. In particular I am not at all satisfied with the conclusions of the Admiralty with regard to the convoying of groups of merchantmen. I do not see how the necessary military supplies and supplies of food and fuel oil are to be delivered at British ports in any other way than under convoy. There will presently not be ships enough or tankers enough and our shipbuilding plans may not begin to yield important results in less than eighteen months. I beg that you will keep these instructions absolutely to yourself and that you will give me such advice as you would give if you were handling an independent navy of your own.

Woodrow Wilson.[1]

WWT MS (WP, DLC).
[1] There is a WWsh draft of this document in WP, DLC.

To Robert Lansing, with Enclosure

My dear Mr. Secretary,   The White House. 3 July, 1917.

As I have just indicated to you, over the telephone, I entirely approve of this. I hope that you will re-read the latter portion of it, however, with a view to making the idea of Japan's *political* influence over China a little more prominent as the thing we have *not* assented to in the sense she evidently has in mind.

Faithfully Yours,   Woodrow Wilson

WWTLS (SDR, RG 59, 793.94/570½, DNA).

E N C L O S U R E

As evidence of the friendly attitude of the United States towards Japan in respect to questions relative to China, the

American Government is pleased to remove any doubts which may arise as to its purposes by reaffirming the statements made in the note of Secretary Bryan to Viscount Chinda, dated March 13, 1915. In that note Secretary Bryan, after reviewing what he termed the

"beginnings of the policy of the United States and other powers interested in the welfare of China for the maintenance of the territorial integrity and administrative entity of China and for equal opportunities in commerce and industries in her behalf,"

and after pointing out in what respects the proposals made by Japan to China in 1915 (in so far as the objects and purposes of those proposals were known and understood by the United States Government at the time) were in derogation of the policy mentioned as well as of the understanding based upon the exchange of notes of November 30, 1908,[1] and the treaty rights of the United States in China, said in conclusion:

"The United States, therefore, could not regard with indifference the assumption of political, military, or economic domination over China by a foreign power, and hopes that Your Excellency's Government will find it consonant with their interests to refrain from pressing upon China an acceptance of proposals which would, if accepted, exclude Americans from equal participation in the economic and industrial development of China and would limit the political independence of that country. * * *

"The United States Government embraces this opportunity to make known that it has viewed the aspirations of Japan in the Far East with that friendship and esteem which have characterized the relations of the two nations in the past. This Government cannot too earnestly impress upon Your Excellency's Government that the United States is not jealous of the prominence of Japan in the East or of the intimate cooperation of China and Japan for their mutual benefit. Nor has the United States any intention of obstructing or embarrassing Japan, or of influencing China in opposition to Japan. On the contrary, the policy of the United States, as set forth in this note, is directed to the maintenance of the independence, integrity and commercial freedom of China and the preservation of legitimate American rights and interests in that Republic."

I desire to direct Your Excellency's attention to the fact that, while Mr. Bryan's note thus expressed the views of the United States in regard to international relations in the Far East, I do not find that it anywhere went to the extent of stating or recognizing that Japan has special and close relations, political as well as economic, with China as a whole, as Your Excellency stated at our interview on June 15th last. Mr. Bryan merely said that the United States recognized that territorial contiguity created special relations between Japan and the districts of Shantung, Southern Manchuria and East Mongolia, but he did not admit that the United States might not in the future be justified in expressing its views in regard to Chino-Japanese relations involving even these districts. This view is borne out by the fact that Mr. Bryan felt justified in his communication of May 11, 1915, in declining to recognize any agreement or understanding entered into then or thereafter between Japan and China impairing the treaty rights of the United States, the political or territorial integrity of China, or the international policy of the open door.

As the official memorandum which Your Excellency handed me on June 15th referred to Japan's interests both political and economic in China as "paramount," and as Mr. Shidahara[2] informed the American Chargé at Tokyo that Your Excellency had telegraphed to your Government that I had expressed myself as quite in accord with the deep sense of the memorandum, I feel that in this restatement of the attitude of the United States Government I ought to make it clear to Your Excellency that I had no intention in our conversation of June 15th to convey the impression that this Government recognized that Japan possessed in China a paramount interest. It was my intention to vary in no way the formal declaration of Mr. Bryan, and, as I recall my language, I did not employ the word "paramount" but spoke of "special" interest in the same sense in which the term was used in the note of March 13, 1915.

The United States has no political ambitions in respect to China, but its historic interest in the welfare of the Chinese people and the territorial and administrative integrity of the Republic, its treaty relations and extensive commerce with China, render it impossible for the United States to be indifferent to matters affecting these interests, which the civil dissension in China, according to reports, threatened to do. As, however, the factional difficulties did not seem to threaten the *status quo* in the region of the Pacific and the principle of equal opportunity, there would seem to have been no necessity under the Agreement of 1908 to communicate to the Japanese Government the intention of the United States Government to express to China its views on the internal dissension in that country and its interest and hope in the composing of the political difficulties, but with the purpose of avoiding any possible misunderstanding on the part of Your Excellency's Government as to the motives of this Government, the subject of the proposed communication to China was promptly brought to the attention of the Japanese Government, notwithstanding the fact that the Japanese proposals of 1915 were made to China several weeks before Japan acquainted the United States with them in accordance with the exchange of notes in 1908. In the case of the Japanese demands growing out of the Cheng Chia Tun trouble,[3] the United States was not informed of the action of Japan until after inquiry had been made by this Government.

In taking the action which has led to the representations by the Japanese Government the United States Government is of the opinion it has departed in no way from its traditional policy towards China or from the views expressed by Mr. Bryan in 1915, in neither of which has the United States claimed the prerogative to control China's political development nor recognized the right or paramount interest of any other country to extend political influence over China.

Department of State
Washington, July 6, 1917.[4]

T telegram (SDR, RG 59, 793.94/570, DNA).
  [1] That is, the Root-Takahira Agreement.
  [2] Kijuro Shidehara, Vice-Minister of Foreign Affairs.
  [3] On August 13, 1916, a clash had occurred between Chinese and Japanese troops stationed at Chengchiatun (or Chengkiatun, now known as Shwangliao), Manchuria. Ten Japanese soldiers were killed and six wounded; four Chinese were killed and nine were wounded. As a result, the Japanese Minister in Peking, on September 2, presented to the Chinese government a list of four demands and four requests. Reports varied as to the exact nature and wording of this document. However, the Japanese demands clearly included the punishment and/or dismissal of the Chinese commander and officers at Chengchiatun allegedly responsible for the incident, orders to be issued to all Chinese soldiers to avoid further clashes with Japanese personnel in Manchuria and Mongolia, and, most important, the right to station Japanese police in areas where significant numbers of Japanese resided. The "requests," which were almost as obligatory as the "demands," included a formal apology from the Chinese Governor General of Manchuria to the Japanese Military Governor of Kwantung, indemnities to be paid to the Japanese, and the employment of Japanese military officers as advisers by all Chinese military academies and by Chinese military units stationed in South Manchuria and eastern Inner Mongolia. Lansing, having read reports of the Japanese diplomatic action in the newspapers, on September 6, 1916, asked Ambassador Guthrie to inquire into the matter. Guthrie reported the general nature of the démarche on September 11 and noted that the Foreign Minister had questioned the right of the United States to "interfere" in the matter.
  The negotiations between China and Japan continued until late January 1917, by which time the Chinese government had agreed only to "reprove" the commanding general of the Chengchiatun area, punish "according to law" the officers responsible for the incident, issue proclamations enjoining Chinese soldiers and civilians to "accord considerate treatment" to Japanese soldiers and civilians, send a representative to apologize to the Japanese consul general and the Military Governor of Kwantung, and pay $500 to a Japanese merchant, one

Yoshimoto. For the American diplomatic reports on the affair, see *FR 1917*, pp. 241-58.

⁴ This is the only copy of this memorandum in the State Department files. Lansing undoubtedly added the final paragraph in response to Wilson's suggestion. Polk, in F. L. Polk to American embassy, Tokyo, July 10, 1917, T telegram (SDR, RG 59, 793.94/570, DNA), summarized the substance of this exchange with the Japanese Ambassador. The State Department instructed the embassy in Tokyo to mail a paraphrase of Polk's telegram to Reinsch for his "confidential information." A. A. Adee to American embassy, Tokyo, July 23, 1917, T telegram (SDR, RG 59, 793.94/570, DNA).

To Franklin Knight Lane

My dear Mr. Secretary: [The White House] 3 July, 1917

Thank you for your memorandum about the coal lands available for producing coal for consumption on the Pacific Coast.

In haste   Faithfully yours,   Woodrow Wilson

TLS (Letterpress Books, WP, DLC).

To James Cannon, Jr.

My dear Doctor Cannon: [The White House] 3 July, 1917

May I not acknowledge the receipt of the letter of June thirtieth, signed by yourself and your associates of the National Legislative Committee of the Anti-Saloon League of America, and express the feeling that the attitude of the Committee is a very admirable proof of their patriotic motives?¹

Sincerely yours,   Woodrow Wilson

TLS (Letterpress Books, WP, DLC).

¹ Following a lengthy debate on July 6 and 7, the Senate agreed to an amendment to the Lever bill, proposed by Senator Joseph T. Robinson of Arkansas, which forbade the use of food, food products, or feeds for the production of distilled beverages. *Cong. Record*, 65th Cong., 1st sess., pp. 4718-63, 4767-92. This amendment replaced the Barkley amendment to the House version of the bill and thus allowed the continued manufacture of beer and wine. However, the conference report on the Lever bill, submitted to the two houses on August 2, while retaining the prohibition on the manufacture of distilled beverages, contained a new provision which gave the President authority to limit or prohibit the production of beer and wine whenever in his judgment such action was essential to an adequate national food supply or to national security and defense. 65th Cong., 1st sess., Senate Doc. No. 70, p. 5. Both houses agreed to this version, and it became part of the Lever Act.

To William Denman

Confidential.

My dear Mr. Chairman: [The White House] 3 July, 1917

I send you the enclosed without comment.¹ I take it for

granted you will not wish what you have suggested[2] in view of this report.

Cordially and sincerely yours,   Woodrow Wilson

TLS (Letterpress Books, WP, DLC).
 [1] That is, G. W. Goethals to WW, July 2, 1917.
 [2] That is, the dismissal of Goethals as head of the Emergency Fleet Corp.

To Frank D. Beattys,[1] with Enclosure

My dear Mr. Beattys: [The White House] 3 July, 1917

I have unavoidably been delayed in replying to your letter of June twenty-seventh,[2] but take pleasure, now that I have found a moment to write it, in sending you the enclosed.

In haste   Sincerely yours,   Woodrow Wilson

TLS (Letterpress Books, WP, DLC).
 [1] Proprietor of Frank D. Beattys & Co., publishers, of New York.
 [2] It is missing.

E N C L O S U R E

I want to give myself the pleasure of prefacing this modest but very significant little book[1] with an expression of my affectionate admiration for an old friend, Professor Rice, its author.[2] The fine spirit of the man everyone who reads it will feel and will take refreshment and stimulation from. It speaks in authentic tones the character of the man I learned to admire in years now too long gone by when I had the privilege of being his colleague; and I have written this in order that I may have an opportunity to avow publicly a very earnestly cherished friendship.

Woodrow Wilson[3]

T MS (Letterpress Books, WP, DLC).
 [1] William North Rice, *Through Darkness to Dawn* (New York, 1917).
 [2] Professor of Geology at Wesleyan University since 1867; he had been a colleague of Wilson's from 1888 to 1890.
 [3] This was printed in facsimile on p. v of *Through Darkness to Dawn*.

To Henry Lee Higginson

My dear Major: [The White House] 3 July, 1917

I was happy in reading your letter of June twenty-ninth to realize how entirely I concurred with you in the judgment you expressed and that I had already been successful in acting upon that judgment.

Cordially and sincerely yours,   Woodrow Wilson

TLS (Letterpress Books, WP, DLC).

To Thomas Watt Gregory

The White House

My dear Mr. Attorney General: 3 July, 1917

Before replying to the enclosed,[1] I will be very much obliged if you would let me know whether the facts as reported are true. Apparently, if true, it was a most unwise thing on Preston's[2] part.

Cordially and faithfully yours,   Woodrow Wilson

TLS (JDR, RG 60, Numerical File No. 186782-20, DNA).
[1] M. J. O'Neil *et al.* to JPT, July 2, 1917, T telegram (JDR, RG 60, Numerical File, No. 186782-20, DNA). About this incident, see TWG to WW, July 19, 1917.
[2] John White Preston, United States attorney for the northern district of California.

To Joseph Patrick Tumulty

Dear Tumulty: [The White House, July 3, 1917]

I would be very much obliged if you would ascertain from Mr. Wadsworth[1] whether these statements[2] are true or not. I quite agree with the senders of the telegram that if this was done it was most ill-advised. I think we must stand up to the last for the right to judge which of our citizens are loyal and which are not.[3]   The President.

TL (WP, DLC).
[1] That is, Eliot Wadsworth, vice-chairman of the central committee of the American Red Cross.
[2] Chairman, Red Cross Finance Committee, Sheboygan, Wisc., to WW, June 28, 1917, T telegram (WP, DLC). He wished to know if it was true that Col. Jefferson Randolph Kean, U.S.A., director-general of the Department of Military Relief of the American Red Cross, had issued a statement suggesting that persons of German, Austrian, Turkish, or Bulgarian parentage or birth be excluded from service in Red Cross units to be sent overseas because of French and British objections to their presence. The chairman of the Sheboygan committee declared that the people of German heritage in his area were unquestionably loyal to the United States and urged Wilson to repudiate the alleged discrimination in Red Cross units. "Who has the right in this country," he asked, "to question American loyalty, when based solely upon the parentage of the citizen?"
[3] Wadsworth replied to Tumulty on July 7, 1917 (TLS [WP, DLC]), and said that the American Red Cross had acted "entirely under orders" in the matter and suggested that William Phillips of the State Department could provide further information. In response to a query from Tumulty, Phillips responded on July 9, 1917 (TLS [WP, DLC]) by enclosing F. L. Polk to WW, July 9, 1917, TLS

(WP, DLC). Polk's letter, written in response to a different query, stressed that the State Department's concern in the matter derived solely from the fact that various Allied nations had formally objected to the presence of persons of German, Austrian, Turkish, or Bulgarian birth or ancestry in Red Cross units sent to their countries to assist either their armies or their civilian populations. The department's suggestion that the Red Cross cease using such persons was meant to apply only to such units and not to units being recruited to serve with the American armies overseas.

To George Wylie Paul Hunt

[The White House] 3 July, 1917

I greatly appreciate your generous and unselfish cooperation.
Woodrow Wilson.

T telegram (Letterpress Books, WP, DLC).

From Josephus Daniels

Dear Mr. President: Washington. July 3, 1917

I think the telegram ought to go, but suggest probably that you have not been informed that the English have recently adopted the policy of convoying merchant ships with cruisers from their side. They have just inaugurated it and we are ready to cooperate with them. Therefore, would it not be best to omit those portions embraced in the parenthesis?[1]

At present the inadequacy of convoy is within the danger zone and the Department is very much impressed with the fact that the British should make greater effort to supply a larger number either of destroyers or small craft for convoy through the danger zone. Apparently they are largely with the main fleet.

The absence of small craft for convoying is even more apparent on the French coast than on the English coast and in the channel. We are attempting to improve this condition on the French coast and by tomorrow will have eight American patrol vessels there for that duty. This will make 43 destroyers and small craft we have sent over for patrol duty. Orders have been given to make ready 27 more to go across.

Will you not please return the telegram with any changes you desire to make in view of the above? I will then send [it] at once.
Faithfully yours,   Josephus Daniels

TLS (WP, DLC).
[1] The sentences beginning "In particular I am not at all satisfied" and ending "important results in less than eighteen months."

To Josephus Daniels, with Enclosure

My dear Mr. Secretary,   The White House. 3 July, 1917.

Thank you for your correction of the enclosed. I have altered it to suit the facts.

Are the British now convoying *groups* of ships or are they trying the vain experiment of convoying individual craft?

The reply to this question does not affect the form of this message, but I should like to know for the guidance of my own thinking.   Faithfully Yours,   Woodrow Wilson

WWTLS (J. Daniels Papers, DLC).

 E N C L O S U R E

FOR ADMIRAL SIMS, CONFIDENTIAL FROM THE PRESIDENT:

From the beginning of the war I have been greatly surprised at the failure of the British Admiralty to use Great Britain's great naval superiority in an effective way. In the presence of the present submarine emergency they are helpless to the point of panic. Every plan we suggest they reject for some reason of prudence. In my view this is not a time for prudence but for boldness even at the cost of great losses. In most of your despatches you have quite properly advised us of the sort of aid and cooperation desired from us by the Admiralty. The trouble is that their plans and methods do not seem to us effective. I would be very much obliged to you if you would report to me, confidentially of course, exactly what the admiralty has been doing and what they have accomplished and add to the report your own comments and suggestions based upon independent study of the whole situation without regard to the judgments already arrived at on that side of the water. The Admiralty was very slow to adopt the practice of convoy and is not now, I judge, supplying convoys on an adequate scale within the danger zone, seeming to prefer to keep its small craft with the fleet. The absence of craft for convoy is even more apparent on the French coast than on the English coast and in the Channel. I do not see how the necessary military supplies and supplies of food and fuel oil are to be delivered at British ports in any other way within the next few months than under adequate convoy. There will presently not be ships or tankers enough and our ship-building plans may not begin to yield important results in less than eighteen months. I beg that you will keep these instructions absolutely to yourself and that you will give me such advice as you would give if you were handling an independent navy of your own.   Woodrow Wilson.[1]

WWT telegram (SDR, RG 59, 763.72/133/21a, DNA).
[1] This was sent as JD to American embassy, London, July 4, 1917, T telegram (SDR, RG 59, 763.72/13321a, DNA).

Three Letters from Newton Diehl Baker

My dear Mr. President: Washington. July 3, 1917.

Confirming our conversation of last night, I beg leave to submit herewith an order which when signed by you will authorize the immediate transfer to the Navy of the ships named therein for troop transports.[1] The suggested order is recommended by the Admiral,[2] the Chief of Staff, the Secretary of the Navy and myself.

The Admiral of the Navy[3] had these ships looked over by an engineer officer of the Navy, and he reports that the repairs now being made are proceeding slowly. The Admiral's judgment is that if these ships be now turned over to the Navy the repairs could be rushed, and the shipping board thus freed from all responsibility in the matter would be enabled to concentrate its energies on the ships which are in the main under its control for commercial uses.

The Secretary of the Navy tells me that there would be no difficulty about these ships bringing back from French ports return cargoes under the direction of the Navy to the extent that such cargoes can be secured without delaying the schedule made out for the transportation of supplies and troops. Should the need for any of these ships at any time grow less for the purpose herein indicated, I understand the Navy and War Departments would be very glad to [t]ransfer them either temporarily or permanently to the shipping board for commercial uses.

This general subject has been discussed with Mr. Denman by all of us. He is not, however, in agreement with us as to the wisdom of making such an order.

                    Respectfully,   Newton D. Baker

[1] Wilson, on June 30, had signed an Executive Order which authorized the United States Shipping Board to take possession of eighty-seven German vessels in American ports. Wilson transferred some of these vessels to the Navy Department on July 11. See WW to W. Denman, July 11, 1917, TLS (Letterpress Books, WP, DLC).
[2] That is, the Chief of Naval Operations, Rear Admiral William Shepherd Benson.
[3] He meant Benson. There was no "Admiral of the Navy" in 1917.

My dear Mr. President: Washington. July 3, 1917.

In order that I may answer definitely the inquiry of the Director of the Council of National Defense[1] as to the effect of my
letter in the matter of coal prices, and the general price-suggesting activities of the subordinate bodies of the Council, I beg leave
to submit for your consideration the following statement:

Questions of price-fixing must be sharply divided into two
general questions. First, the use of the power of the Government to affect the general commercial price of commodities in
the country; and, second, the question of the price to be paid by
the Government for present purchases of supplies needed for
war uses.

The first of these questions looks to a donation of power by
Congress either to the President or some other agency, and
requires an inquiry into the cost of production, beginning with
raw materials and adding proper allowances for the stages intermediate between raw material and finished product. To this
inquiry the Council of National Defense has no present relation.
Should Congress give the President power to fix maximum,
minimum, or sale prices of raw materials or finished products,
the President would doubtless inquire through the Federal Trade
Commission, the Department of Commerce, and perhaps through
the Council of National Defense, for data as to costs and percentages, ultimately leading to the price to be fixed. But as yet
the Council of National Defense has been given no power in the
premises, and any inquiry made by it or any of its subordinate
agencies on this subject must, in the nature of the case, be extra-
legal and purely for the information of the President.

As to the second aspect of price-fixing, affecting purchases
now to be made, with the Nation at war, with the necessity upon
us of making immediate contracts for the increase of manufacturing facilities, for the stimulation of output, for supplies needed
by our troops over seas and in training here, it is impossible
for the Secretary of War to withhold purchases until the larger
aspects of price regulation and control above referred to shall
have been completed and put into operation. It, therefore, becomes necessary to adopt a policy with regard to present purchases, always with the understanding that a particular price
paid for a particular quantity of any commodity is not to be
regarded as establishing that or any other price for subsequent
purchases of the same commodity if in the meantime through
any agency or from any cause conditions shall have changed. The
Council of National Defense through its various committees
ought, therefore, with regard to any projected purchase, to

inquire first as to the sources of supply, disclosing in its inquiry where the commodities can be secured from existing establishments if that be possible, and from created facilities if that be necessary. They ought to recommend terms upon which such purchases can be made, and in so doing they ought to consider as far as practicable the just price, based on such knowledge of costs as can be readily procured by a body which has not the power to compel testimony or administer oaths, and without involving themselves in the intricate economic inquiry of varying costs of production for the same commodity from different producers. Wherever the price recommended by them as fair under all the circumstances is not acceptable to the producer, they should advise the Secretary of War to use the commandeering power given by law, which is based upon the fixing of a just and reasonable price by the Secretary of War. In cases of this kind the Secretary of War would undoubtedly fix what he deems a reasonable price under all the circumstances, and any overplus demanded by the producer would be awarded him by the courts if it should be determined that the price fixed by the Secretary of War was not in fact just and reasonable.

Pursuit of the policy here suggested in ascertaining prices for present purchases will undoubtedly lead to inequalities; it may lead to the payment of larger sums than will hereafter be shown to have been reasonable. That is to say, when the agencies for the determination of the first class of questions have made the necessary inquiries and determined accurately the costs and proper percentages, and disclosed the truly reasonable price, it may well be that it will be found that the War Department has paid higher prices for some commodity bought by it, and it will also appear that a just and reasonable price to one producer would be an excessive price to another more favorably placed, either as to the sources of raw material, perfection of his organization, his accessibility to transportation facilities, or some other advantage. There is no way of equalizing these inequalities except by an excess profits tax. This I understand to be the policy adopted in England, and I personally believe that an excess-profits tax as high as 70 or 80 per cent. will be thoroughly justified and would be the proper method of adjusting these inequalities without depressing production or discouraging capital.

I of course do not mean to suggest that the Council of National Defense has any business at this time considering excess-profit taxes, but would desire to instruct the Director that the price-suggesting function of the Council be limited to the suggestion of a fair and reasonable price for Government purchases as above suggested, with the thought that in the event of disagreement between the producers and the Department, an advance payment might be made, leaving the final price to be paid to future determination. This would seem to be necessary, since we cannot expect private enterprice [enterprise] to finance large Government purchases without a substantial payment, even where the total price is necessarily held for future determination.

Respectfully submitted,   Newton D. Baker

1 That is, Walter S. Gifford.

Dear Mr. President: Washington. July 3, 1917.

Some time ago Mr. Stimson,[1] former Secretary of War, was commissioned as a Major in the Judge Advocate's Corps as a reserve officer because of his general familiarity with military law. He was called into active service here in Washington, and assigned to the War College Division to assist in the legal aspects of military questions.

In order to facilitate the interchange of military information, the British Government has strongly urged that our ordinary military attaché at London be enlarged into a commission of several officers who will keep in touch with all phases of military preparation in England and transmit it for the use of the War College here. This plan is approved by the War College and among the officers they recommend to be added to the present military attaché, Col. Lassiter,[2] is Major Stimson.

I do not feel warranted in sending Major Stimson to London in this capacity without your approval. I think he is a discreet man, with a good deal of valuable experience both as a lawyer and as Secretary of War; but he will be in a sense attached to our Embassy in London. While it is more or less necessary for us to use reserve officers for purposes of this kind in order to free our limited number of regular officers for more active service, I can imagine that there might be objection to sending Major S[t]imson to London. The instructions issued to such a commission in London would, of course, make clear that they had no power beyond collecting and forwarding to the War College information and such suggestions as may be made by the British military authorities for our consideration.

I would be grateful if you would let me know what your feeling is about sending Major Stimson in such capacity.

Respectfully,   Newton D. Baker

TLS (WP, DLC).
1 That is, Henry L. Stimson.
2 William Lassiter.

From William Gibbs McAdoo

Dear Mr. President: Washington July 3, 1917.

I had a most interesting conference with the representatives of the largest life insurance and accident insurance companies in the United States yesterday afternoon. About sixty-five companies were represented. The session was not only illuminating but clarifying. By practically unanimous vote the representatives of the insurance companies approved the principle of indemnification by the Government of its armed forces in the field. The problem is too big for the insurance companies, and if it were not, the premiums they would have to charge in order to protect themselves absolutely against the risk would be extremely high if not excessive. The Government would have to pay these premiums. It would be much better, therefore, if the Government were to carry its own risk.

This is the right solution and the one I have always favored. I believe a thoroughly practical plan can be worked out quickly and that it will receive the overwhelming approval of the country. At the same time, it will tend more to popularize the war, I think, than any single thing that could be done. This consideration is, of course, subordinate to the higher consideration of humanity and justice. Our Government ought to set an example to the world of a just and generous policy toward our soldiers and sailors which will give every man who enters the ranks the assurance, in advance, of protection for his dependents and of compensation for disabilities he may suffer, not as a gratuity but as a part of the consideration for his patriotic service. If this is done, we can eliminate the scandals as well as the inequities and favoritism of our past pension experience, because this can be made a substitute for future pensions and it will, at the same time, prove far more satisfactory to the beneficiaries and far more economical for the Government.

I can progress with this matter rapidly, and I believe it is possible to get action at the present session of Congress (and it ought to be had if possible at this session) if I am allowed to go forward unhampered. After I had, with your approval, issued the call for the conference, I learned that this matter had been under investigation by the Council of National Defense, which had referred it to the Department of Commerce, and also that the Department of Labor had been making an investigation. These investigations have produced information of value, and I desire to have the cooperation of all of these agencies in the work that must be done. As soon as I learned of the activities

to which I have referred, I invited the Secretary of War, the
Secretary of the Navy, and Secretary of Commerce and the
Secretary of Labor to attend the conference or to send repre-
sentatives. They were all represented at the conference except
the Secretary of Labor, who was unable to attend. I also invited
Mr. Gompers, who was out of town. I asked, however, Judge
Mack[1] to attend, as he is the Chairman of the Subcommittee of
the Labor Committee of the Advisory Commission Council of
National Defense, and he has done some work on this matter.
Judge Mack was present.

I enclose for your information copies of letters exchanged
between Mr. Baker and myself.[2] I think there is a cordial desire
to cooperate, but I think it is essential that you should say to
Mr. Baker that I had taken the matter up with your approval and
as a result of your reference to me of a letter from one of the
insurance companies,[3] and that you would be glad if all concerned would cooperate with me in setting this work forward. I
am sure that such a suggestion will put at rest any tendency,
if such exists, on the part of others, to work at cross purposes or
independently in this matter. I cannot go forward with satisfaction or success unless I am permitted to have direction of the
matter.

This insurance is a proper function of the War Risk Insurance
Bureau; it is, again, a matter of finance; therefore it relates
properly to the Treasury, and this is the Department which ought
to administer it. I earnestly hope that you will imediately adopt
the suggestion I have made, and speak to the Secretary of War.
Otherwise, I am afraid that there may be an unnecessary and
unpleasant mix-up, to which I certainly do not wish to become a
party. Having gone to the extent I have already gone, with your
approval, it will be extremely awkward if there should be any
alteration of plan.[4]   Cordially yours,   W G McAdoo

TLS (WP, DLC).
    [1] Julian William Mack, judge of the United States Circuit Court of Appeals
for the second circuit.
    [2] NDB to WGM, June 30, 1917, TCL (WP, DLC), and WGM to NDB, July 2,
1917, CCL (WP, DLC).
    [3] WW to WGM, June 16, 1917, n. 1; WGM to WW, June 23, 1917, both in
Vol. 42.
    [4] See WGM to WW, Aug. 15, 1917.

From Robert Lansing, with Enclosure

My dear Mr. President: Washington July 3, 1917.

I am sending you enclosed a copy of a confidential telegram
just received from London[1] stating that Mr. Balfour is of the

opinion that the United States should, if it chooses, take part in the war conferences which are sometimes held in London and sometimes in Paris or Rome, to discuss subjects of large policy rather than technical military subjects.

Mr. Bakhmetieff has this morning received instructions from his Government to the same effect and is pressing for a reply as to whether the United States will be represented.

I should be very grateful for an indication of your views.

With assurances of respect, etc., I am, my dear Mr. President, Faithfully yours, Robert Lansing.

TLS (WP, DLC).
[1] WHP to RL, July 2, 1917, T telegram (WP, DLC).

From Marie of Rumania

Dear Mr. Wilson   Jassy[1] July 3rd, 1917

I feel the desire to thank you for having sent part of your mission down to our country.

Their coming has filled us with new courage and hope.

It is as woman who has suffered much that I write to you, but as a woman who is at the same time a Queen a Queen who loves her country and who feels that she must appeal to you on its behalf.

None of our misfortunes have discouraged us, we mean to hold out to the bitter end—but to be able to hold out we must still exist—to be able to exist we need your help.

Keep us from starving and give us the means to be able to stick it out!

Excuse me for using such simple words, but I know that your heart will except them. I am also confident in the great heart of your Country knowing that it has ever been on the side of those fighting for a just cause.

Sincerely Yours   Marie

ALS (WP, DLC).
[1] The temporary wartime seat of the Rumanian government.

From Louis Seibold

My dear Mr. President: Washington July 3, 1917.

I thank you sincerely for your recent note.

My chief regret is that the incident should have intruded an additional burden on your already overtaxed shoulders. As you are about the only hero I ever had in politics, I should deeply deplore the loss of your confidence, particularly under the present trying conditions. Loyalty to you is not a virtue; disloyalty merely a crime. One of my chief pleasures in life is in acclaiming the sincerity of your motives and the intelligence of your methods.

I am conscious of dissenting from your views in but one single respect. I mean, of course, the censorship project. That undertaking seemed to me to be premature. I still believe that if the eventualities had been permitted to develop naturally—as they probably will develop—a reasonable and clearly defined censorship will be the inevitable result. I have never been able to associate any thought of you with secrecy.

But even in the censorship incident, Mr. President, I did not credit the inspiration of it to you personally. I regarded it as the ill-advised conception of less discerning officials, actuated by arbitrary considerations of a military character or lacking confidence in their own abilities to adequately perform the functions imposed upon them by the unusual conditions of war.

I am exceedingly sorry that my earnest convictions compelled the performance of a duty and caused you the slightest annoyance. I would rather do something to help than to question any project proposed by you, for, believe me, sir, I have the fullest appreciation of the responsibilities thrust upon you.

It seems to me that the most important consideration to the whole people of the United States is the well-being of its President and his freedom from unnecessary criticism and annoyance. I know that the President of the United States is making more personal sacrifices today than any of his fellow-citizens, subordinates or wards.

If I can serve my country, I report "ready" to respond to the call of its Commander-in-chief, because I hold for him the greatest admiration and personal affection. I know that he is inspired by the loftiest ambitions for the protection of myself and other citizens of our country and I hope that success will crown his every venture.

Sincerely your friend,   Louis Seibold

TLS (WP, DLC).

Two Telegrams from Sir Cecil Arthur Spring Rice
to Arthur James Balfour

Washington 3 July 1917.

personal

Your June 30.[1] Thanks. I am sure that you will not believe that personal or official jealousy exists or could at such a moment weigh with Crawford or myself.

I had a long conversation with House a week ago. It was evident that N's[2] mission here without consent being asked of President has weakened House's position and left a painful impression. I explained to him imperative necessity of sending N at once for purposes of organization of British operations here and urged that N's great influence at home could be utilized to the advantage of British and American good relations. He entirely agreed and said he would be glad to see N at his home. Wiseman was present and conveyed this message to N on his return to N. Y. House also requested the President to see N again which the President was at first reluctant to do and the interview was satisfactory. The difficulty remains that the State Dept would prefer that negotiations should take place through that channel but to this the Secretary of the Treasury may raise objections. The main point is that the necessary communications should reach the President, and this can be done through both the official & unofficial channel.

I am acting in full understanding with N.

I pointed out to President today that it would be to the advantage of everyone that N should be in close touch with the situation here as he was so well qualified to make it known in England.

Hw telegram (FO 115/2295, p. 208, PRO).
[1] A. J. Balfour to C. A. Spring Rice, June 30, 1917, T telegram (FO 115/2295, p. 207, PRO).
[2] Northcliffe's.

Washington 3 July 1917

No. 1867. Sir R C and I were received by President today and communicated to him in writing substance of your telegram No. 2500[1] omitting statement as to our resources in American Securities and Gold which we communicated verbally in strict confidence.

President was very sympathetic and fully realized gravity of the situation.

He said that he had great confidence in S of Treasury in whose hands he had placed the matter and recommended that we should make the fullest & frankest statement to him. (The long interview with S of Treasury is reported separately.)[2]

The USG desired to use financial advances as a means of obtaining military results e.g. from Italy Russia & Japan. For this purpose it was important to have full information as to the general military situation—tonnage submarines, supplies &c. (He agreed that he had received recently full information as to tonnage & submarines)

They also wished to have full particulars (as were provided by the French) as to the needs of the individual nations respectively.

When the information was received and tabulated it would be possible to arrive at a judgement as to the best method of employing the financial resources of the USG

We pointed out the urgent present necessities of G.B. and the supreme importance of meeting present situation. President understood from S of Treasury that the hundred million would be paid over on 5th July. He recommended that we should ascertain from Secretary of Treasury what further information he required as to our financial needs.

Hw telegram (FO 115/2259, pp. 147-48, PRO).
   [1] A. J. Balfour to C. A. Spring Rice, June 29, 1917, T telegram (FO 115/2259, pp. 117-20, PRO).
   [2] C. A. Spring Rice to A. J. Balfour, July 3, 1917, Hw telegram (FO 115/2259, pp. 149-50, PRO)

From George Wylie Paul Hunt

Phoenix, Ariz., July 4, 1917.

Secretary Wilson has mediators in disturbed mining districts, have informed them of my willingness to cooperate and aid all in my power to settle trouble. Am I to receive any further authorization from yourself or Secretary Wilson. Would suggest that conference between mine operators and employees be arranged so that there would be no stoppage of work during period of the war.   Geo. W. P. Hunt.

T telegram (WP, DLC).

From Jean Jules Jusserand

Dear Mr. President,   Washington July 4 1917.

In this day, when American Independence is celebrated with as much enthusiasm in France as in America, the five Academies composing the "Institut de France" have united to send their greetings to the head of the great Sister Republic now taking part with us in the fight for Liberty.

It is my privilege to forward you herewith the text of their telegram just received.[1] I beg to add, as the Representative of France and a life long friend and admirer of this country, my heartfelt congratulations and wishes for its leader who has written his name in history as one of the men whose acts will have proved most influential in the cause of Independence.

I have the honor to be, dear Mr. President
Very Sincerely and respectfully yours   Jusserand

ALS (WP, DLC).
[1] E. Bontroux *et al.* to WW, n.d., ALS (WP, DLC).

From the Diary of Colonel House

July 4, 1917.

Hoover came at 10.30 and remained until half past five. We went over the food situation both from a domestic and international viewpoint. We went into the question of trading with the enemy, trading with neutrals, blockade, and all the ramifications of the food question. Hoover knows the story better than anyone. It is a pity he has so little personal charm, for he could go further than he will with the lack of it.

Cullinan of Texas,[1] who is assisting Hoover, came for a part of the day and joined us at luncheon. Hoover thinks matters are getting into a jam at Washington, and wonders why the President does not take some action. The truth of the matter is, the President does not know things are not going smoothly, because he talks to almost no one excepting his Secretaries and they reassure him. From their viewpoint, things are going well, but viewed outside of departmental circles, they are not. If the President comes through the present situation without serious trouble he will have to be in good luck. I can see how circumstances will carry him through, but I can also see danger lurking on every side. He has the power to hold the situation so well in hand that there could be no danger of failure.

Hoover says he has not seen the President for two weeks and then only for twenty minutes. There are a few men like Hoover who could clear up the situation for him within a week, if he would only sit down with them and work the thing clear through. I tried to get him to do this when war became inevitable after he had sent Bernstorff home. At that time I urged him to let me organize a war machine for him.[2] It is the kind of thing I know how to do, and I have experience gathered from intimate touch with the European belligerents. I assured him that it could be done in a few weeks and in a way to give him entire freedom from details. Our country is rich in the kind of material needed for such an organization and if he would let me select it regardless of party, the result would inure to his credit. He feared I would displace certain members of his Cabinet and he did not wish that done without first trying to work out a satisfactory organization with them. Mrs. Wilson told me the next morning, after I had given him this talk, that he had spent a sleepless night worrying over what I had said.

Among other things I told him that he did not have the kind of ability necessary to organize the country for war. I softened this by saying that the ability to organize was not rare and could be found in plenty, but the ability to frame and force policies of government was rare, and he should confine his time to that. I shook him, but did not entirely convince him that I was right.

Hoover is to put our conclusions in the form of a memorandum, copies of which he is to send to the President and to me.

T MS (E. M. House Papers, CtY).
[1] Joseph Stephen Cullinan, organizer and first president of the Texas Co., at this time president of the American Republics Corp. of Delaware.
[2] House referred to the conversations which he had had with Wilson on March 27 and 28. See the extracts from House's diary printed at those dates in Vol. 41.

A Greeting to the New Russian Ambassador[1]

[*July 5, 1917*]

To the keen satisfaction which I derived from the fact that the Government of the United States was the first to welcome, by its official recognition, the new democracy of Russia to the family of free States, is added the exceptional pleasure which I experience in now receiving from your hand the letters whereby the Provisional Government of Russia accredits you as its Ambassador Extraordinary and Plenipotentiary to the United States, and in according to you formal recognition as the first Ambassador of free Russia to this country.

For the people of Russia the people of the United States have ever entertained friendly feelings, which have now been greatly deepened by the knowledge that, actuated by the same lofty motives, the two Governments and peoples are co-operating to bring to a successful termination the conflict now raging for human liberty and a universal acknowledgment of those principles of right and justice which should direct all Governments. I feel convinced that when this happy day shall come, no small share of the credit will be due to the devoted people of Russia who, overcoming disloyalty from within and intrigue from without, remain steadfast to the cause.

The mission, which it was my pleasure to send to Russia, has already assured the Provisional Government that in this momentous struggle and in the problems that confront and will confront the free Government of Russia, that Government may count on the steadfast friendship of the Government of the United States, and its constant co-operation in all desired appropriate directions.

It only remains for me to give expression to my admiration of the way in which the Provisional Government of Russia are meeting all requirements, to my entire sympathy with them in their noble object to insure to the people of Russia the blessings of freedom and equal rights and opportunity, and to my faith that through their efforts Russia will assume her rightful place among the great free nations of the world.

Printed in the *New York Times*, July 6, 1917.
1 That is, Boris Aleksandrovich Bakhmet'ev.

To Désiré-Joseph Cardinal Mercier

Your Eminence,   The White House 5 July, 1917.

I am deeply touched by your personal communication of the ninth of February, 1917, which recently reached me at the hands of Father de Ville.

The sincere sympathy of the people of the United States for the people of Belgium in their sore affliction has been manifested in many ways since the very outbreak of the war, and this Government has set its seal of approbation upon this national sentiment by sending its chosen forces to the Belgian front, there to fight the common enemy. I trust that the efforts of the American people towards the relief of suffering among the stricken people of Belgium may soon be resumed under the happier auspices which will attend the liberation of Belgium.

With assurances of my high personal consideration,

Faithfully yours,   Woodrow Wilson

TCL (WP, DLC).

To Louis Seibold

My dear Seibold: [The White House] 5 July, 1917

Your letter of the third has touched me very deeply and I cannot deny myself the pleasure of sending you at least a line of very grateful acknowledgment. Such letters keep me in heart and make the labor worth while, even amidst the darkness which seems sometimes to gather about the path. Please always believe that your generous confidence is heartily and even affectionately reciprocated.

Faithfully yours,   Woodrow Wilson

TLS (Letterpress Books, WP, DLC).

Two Letters to Newton Diehl Baker

My dear Mr. Secretary: The White House 5 July, 1917

I have your letter of July third embodying your explanation to the Director of the Council of National Defense of the effect of your letter in the matter of the coal prices upon other price suggestions, and beg to thank you for it. It is a very useful memorandum of our conversation of the other day.

Cordially and faithfully yours,   Woodrow Wilson

Confidential.

My dear Mr. Secretary: The White House 5 July, 1917

I have your letter of July third about the question of assigning Major Stimson, former Secretary of War, to duties in connection with the Embassy in London, and I entirely agree with your judgment that this would in no way be desirable. Major Stimson's attitude has been anything but helpful and I think his influence on the other side would be distinctly bad.

Cordially and sincerely yours,   Woodrow Wilson

TLS (N. D. Baker Papers, DLC).

To Joseph Patrick Tumulty, with Enclosure

Dear Tumulty: [The White House, c. July 5, 1917]

Please say to Mr. Walling that we are making a rigid investigation of this case[1] and he may rest assured everything within the power of the Federal Government will be done to check these outrages.   **The President.**

TL (WP, DLC).

[1] That is, the so-called race riot at East St. Louis, which raged during July 2 and resulted in the death of at least thirty-nine blacks and nine whites. We use the term "so-called race riot" because it was actually a murderous assault by a large group of white people upon the black community. Elliott M. Rudwick, *Race Riot at East St. Louis, July 2, 1917* (Carbondale, Ill., 1964), is the definitive study of this event.

E N C L O S U R E

New London, Conn., July 3, 1917.

Unchecked savagery at East St Louis worse since Civil War, as it was deliberately preparing for whole month and in accord with many American mob precedent and without military excuse it was worse than anything Germans did in Belgium and comparable only to Jewish pogroms of the chear [czar], the pretext of labor invasion from south is invalid. There is no oversupply of labor anywhere in America today, massacre clearly due to effort of the anti-Negro element of the South to check exodus of colored labor which promised to force south to suspend the reign of terror which has ruled there for half a century and to give negroes better pay and to treat them like human beings to check this exodus southern anti-negro editors have been saying that the north treats the negroes worse than the south and have seized upon and magnified every northern incident to prove it. This agitation has spread from St Louis to East St Louis. The reign of terror has passed from the south to the north, doubtless fostered by German spies who have been exposed in several such enterprises. The German plot to prevent conscription of negroes and keep large sections of American troops in America may succeed, even more dangerous is the effect of [on] revolutionary Russia, South America and Japan all the most bitter attacks od [of] Russian untra [ultra] revolutionists and Latin American politicians will seem justified, the Japanese will conclude that they can expect no real friendship from a race mad America, the international and military situation calls for immediate action, there must be swift and severe punishment for the mob, but this will not suffice. There should be an immediate Presidential proclamation that in the present military exigency the full military power of the nation will be used in defense of the lives and liberty of our colored fellow citizens. I send this as a member of the board of directors of the national association of colored people.[1]

William English Walling.

T telegram (WP, DLC).
[1] That is, the National Association for the Advancement of Colored People.

From Joseph Patrick Tumulty

The White House.
Memorandum for the President: July 5, 1917.

Senator Mark Smith asks that the attached telegrams addressed to him[1] be brought to the President's attention. He says they are from some of the leading mine operators in Arizona. Senator Smith says that in his judgment former Governor Hunt is not the kind of man who can adjust the strike differences; that he is persona non grata with most of the operators. The Senator would be glad to talk with the President about this matter if the President cares to see him. The situation is a desperate one.

T MS (WP, DLC).
[1] J. S. Douglas to M. A. Smith, July 4, 1917; W. H. Brophy to M. A. Smith, July 4, 1917; and F. E. Shine to M. A. Smith, July 4, 1917, T telegrams (WP, DLC). All protested against Wilson's appointment of Hunt as mediator in the labor-management dispute in the Arizona copper mines on the ground, principally, that Hunt was prolabor and biased in favor of the strikers.

From Louis Freeland Post

My dear Mr. President: Washington July 5, 1917.

Referring to the strike situation in the copper districts of Arizona and to your telegram to former Governor Hunt and his reply thereto, which have just been referred to me by direction of Mr. Forster, I have, in acordance with your instructions, appointed Governor Hunt as a Commissioner of Conciliation and telegraphed him to cooperate with Mr. McBride, whom Secretary Wilson had assigned to handle the situation in Arizona.

My latest information from Mr. McBride is that the troubles in Arizona are nearly statewide and that he preferred to handle them in a general rather than in a local way. Following out this plan he consulted with the Governor and the State Federation officials before proceeding to Globe. The Department has also instructed Mr. Joseph S. Myers,[1] who was handling a railroad controversy in Houston, Texas, to proceed to Clifton to aid in the general situation. Messrs. McBride and Myers have had considerable experience in controversies in the copper fields of Arizona, the former having successfully negotiated the recent settlement in the Jerome district and the latter was successful in the Clifton-Morenci settlements of a year ago. The appointment of Governor Hunt has gone forward today by telegraph, and I have wired Commissioner McBride to cooperate with him.

Faithfully yours,   Louis F. Post

TLS (WP, DLC).
  [1] Commissioner of Conciliation employed by the Department of Labor on a *per diem* basis.

From William Denman

My dear Mr. President: Washington July 5th, 1917.

We have been carefully analyzing General Goethals' statement that he is about to enter into contracts for

"about 2,153,000 tons of 'fabricated' steel ships of 5,000 to 7,500 tons dead weight capacity each, at an estimated total expense of approximately $350,000,000. These arrangements include contracts for complete machinery. In these contracts, the Government must furnish the steel, which in these figures I compute at $50. a ton."

Several weeks ago I procured for the General a contract for the construction of eight vessels in a yard then unbuilt, at a rate, computing steel at the same price—$50. a ton—of about $137. per dead weight ton. These people estimated that there was a liberal profit at this figure. The fabricated price is $162.50.

I have today learned from Mr. Royden, the British representative sent here by Mr. Balfour, that, with steel at $60 a ton for plates, merchant tonnage was being generally constructed in Great Britain for under $80. a dead weight ton. Our analysis of the figures is not yet complete, but we are certain, from the distance we have gone, that our friends in the steel group have, in the fabricated ship contracts proposed to be entered into, a profit which, in addition to an ordinary profit, would equal a charge for steel at around $100. a ton.

We believe that a further analysis of the figures will show that, under the fabricated system, which, in an order of $350,-000,000 would be developed to its highest efficiency, it is a far cheaper system of constructing vessels than that pursued in the small yard in California where the eight vessels are to be constructed at $137. a ton, assuming steel at $50. a ton.

I yesterday asked General Goethals to send me a statement of the prices that had been paid under the contracts for 2,153,-000 tons of fabricated ships, and he advised me in a written memorandum as follows: "Price not yet settled." It seems to me that a further discussion of this matter between us would be advisable, and that, before any decision is made, I obtain from the General his actual fixed prices. They must be certainly sufficiently fixed in his mind after having advised you, as he did in his letter, that is to say 2,153,000 tons, and estimated an approximate cost of $350,000,000, or $162.50 a ton. The amount at stake in the contracts is a difference of $50,000,000. With this deducted, there would, I feel quite confident on further analysis, be a liberal profit to the firms undertaking the contracts.

The personnel of these firms we have also carefully analyzed, and they are made up of the masters in the steel producing group.   Very faithfully yours,   William Denman

TLS (WP, DLC).

From Robert Lansing

My dear Mr. President: Washington July 5, 1917.

The more I consider the matter the more I am convinced that it would be unwise for Mr. Root or any of the Diplomatic Mission with him to stop in Japan on their return to the United States. We are informed that they are leaving Petrograd about the 9th of this month. The present unrest in the Far East and the possible divergence of views of Mr. Root as to the policy of this Administration in regard to that region seems to me to make it unwise for him to represent the Government. If it is advisable to send a mission to Japan I think we should pursue the course of sending new men directly from the United States.

                    Faithfully yours,   Robert Lansing

TLS (SDR, RG 59, 763.72/5737½, DNA).

To Joseph Patrick Tumulty

Dear Tumulty: [The White House, July 6, 1917]

Please say to this gentleman[1] that I am obliged to avoid interviews at the present time if it is possible to do so consistently with the public business; that he cannot feel more distressed than I do at the terrible things which have recently been happening; and that no suggestion from any quarter is necessary to increase my interest or my purpose to do whatever it is possible to do.   The President.

TL (WP, DLC).

[1] R. M. Bolden to WW, July 4, 1917, TLS (WP, DLC). The Rev. Richard Manuel Bolden was pastor of the Spiritual, Moral and Intellectual Society of the First Emanuel Church, 105 W. 130th St., New York. He had written to request an interview for a committee, including himself, to lay before Wilson "an appeal and prayer in behalf of the colored people of this country."

To Kenneth Douglas McKellar

My dear Senator: [The White House] 6 July, 1917.

May I not take the liberty of asking you if you would not be willing to withdraw the amendment you have proposed to the pending food legislation prohibiting members of the advisory committees of the Council of National Defense from selling to the Government? My reason for making bold to make this request is that the passage and enforcement of such a law would practically break up the instrumentalities we have laboriously created for mobilizing the industries of the country at this crisis.

As a matter of fact, as the actions of the Council are now guided and determined, no one of these gentlemen sells to the Government in any way which gives him control of the terms upon which he shall sell, and we are rapidly throwing such complete safeguards about the whole question of price that it is already impossible for these advisers to obtain an excessive price, if they were disposed to demand it. Among them are the chief business men of the country, upon whose assistance and advice we are dependent and who are giving that assistance and advice in an admirable spirit of patriotism and disinterestedness.

It is because I can assure you of these circumstances and can say that it would be nothing less than a calamity to have these means of cooperation withdrawn from us that I am taking what would otherwise be a very great liberty. I am sure that you know me well enough to know that I would not do anything of this sort except upon grave cause.

I am writing this letter rather than seeking an immediate interview because of the rush of business and because I know that the amendment will probably come up for very early consideration.

With warmest regards,

Cordially and sincerely yours,   Woodrow Wilson

TLS (Letterpress Books, WP, DLC).

To William Cox Redfield

My dear Mr. Secretary: [The White House] 6 July, 1917

I do not believe that you knew of or authorized the enclosed,[1] did you? I know how thoroughly you agreed with me the other day about statements of general policy issuing from any but one source, and statements about a policy of wholesale commandeering from any apparently authoritative source at this moment have the same stimulating effect on ocean freight rates as the reports of heavy sinkings have on the price of war insurance. A mounting freight market is immediately reflected in the market price of ships. The Government is about to become a buyer of a vast tonnage of ships on the stocks and, whether wisely or not, the courts do look at the market in determining what the Government must pay. Our obvious interest is to keep the market down and not stimulate it. I have meant to exercise these powers myself with the utmost prudence and in a way that will be most beneficial to all concerned, and I hope that you will again make efforts to see that statements of no kind regarding the general policy of the Government proceed from your department. Knowing as I do that you concur in the wisdom of this, I do not hesitate to make this request very urgently.

Cordially and sincerely yours,   [Woodrow Wilson]

CCL (WP, DLC).

[1] "Secretary Redfield Warns Shipowners," New York *Journal of Commerce*, July 3, 1917. The opening sentence occasioned Wilson's distress: "Requisition of all United States ships by the Government is the present plan under consideration by officials, it was declared to-day by Secretary of Commerce Redfield." The balance of the article provided background for this alleged statement by Redfield.

To Louis Freeland Post

My dear Mr. Post: [The White House] 6 July, 1917

Thank you sincerely for your letter of yesterday with its information about what is being done in Arizona. I knew that you would be perfectly willing to associate Governor Hunt with Commissioner McBride.

Cordially and sincerely yours,   Woodrow Wilson

TLS (Letterpress Books, WP, DLC).

To William J. Lee[1]

My dear Sir: [The White House] 6 July, 1917

I cannot imagine any circumstances which would justify you in using my name in any connection without my permission.[2] I take the liberty of returning the medal.

Very truly yours,   Woodrow Wilson

TLS (WP, DLC).
   [1] Director of recreation in the Park Department of New York City.
   [2] In his capacity as chairman of the executive committee of Mayor Mitchel's Independence Day Committee, Lee had taken it upon himself to make Wilson the honorary "President of all Games" for the athletic activities to be held in New York on July 4. He sent Wilson a copy of a medal bearing Wilson's likeness which was to be presented to all competitors. W. J. Lee to WW, July 3, 1917, TLS (WP, DLC).

From William Cox Redfield

My dear Mr. President: Washington July 6th, 1917.

In answer to your letter of this date covering the enclosed clipping, let me say first and directly—I did not authorize it. I could hardly have done so because I did not know until your letter came of any policy for wholesale commandeering or general purchase of tonnage on the stocks further than that I recall that authority to that effect was recently given by law. As I write I recall also that Mr. Denman spoke to me of some large transactions of the kind but in the most general way. At the time the article was printed, however, I had no knowledge of those facts and could not have spoken of them. I think the origin, however, of the article is clear from an entirely different matter.

The recent requisitioning of certain ships by the War Department caused serious distress, amounting in one or more cases almost to ruin, to certain large exporting houses who entered serious complaint at once against the continuance of that process without some sort of notice that they might protect themselves against possible disaster as innocent parties. For example, goods are shipped from factories to the exporting houses who pay for them at sight. They cannot get their own funds till they can present ship's bill of lading. If the ship is requisitioned without any notice, the exporter may advance large sums and wait indefinitely for his own funds. The situation thus created is real. It is not a theory but a condition. To meet it the Secretary of War has advised us in a recent case of the desire to requisition one or two other ships and the matter has been taken up by us privately with the parties concerned in an effort to straighten the matter out without harm. It is part of the delicate adjustment incident to war.

Knowing nothing, as I have said, of any Government policy looking toward a general requisitioning or purchase and having in mind only that one or two or more ships might from time to time be suddenly taken, I instructed the Bureau of Foreign and Domestic Commerce to let the exporters know that instead of making contracts as in the peaceful past, they should protect themselves by making their contracts subject to requisitioning so that, for example, they should not make contracts C.I.F.[1] but rather F.O.B. In other words, they should not agree to deliver goods at the foreign port at a fixed price but rather, if possible, deliver them on board vessel New York.

This sort of notice to exporters has long been thought the duty of our commerce service. Long weeks ago they were advised, when the legislation was pending, that export licenses might in the future be required, and this notice has gone far to adjust the exporting world in advance to the possibility of such licenses. They are not, in other words, taken by surprise.

The whole matter will be clear from the enclosed copy of letter of the 3rd to the Shipping Board,[2] which you note bears the date of the article published and says nothing whatever about any general purchase or requisitioning of which, I repeat, at the time I knew nothing.

This notice being given to the Bureau of Foreign and Domestic Commerce, in the way and for the purpose stated, resulted in the publication in Commerce Reports of the 5th (two days later than the article sent) of the enclosed notice.[3] This notice, therefore, could not have been the source of the statement. It was in fact printed without my knowledge. I never saw it until after your letter came although instructions have been given that matters of this kind shall be OK'd by me before printing. I have given further orders today consistent with your letter.

I repeat that no such statement as is credited to me in the first five lines of the clipping (which is the only statement so credited) was ever made by me, and at that time I had no knowledge of the facts.

A clause in your letter, however, requesting me to make efforts to see "that statements of no kind regarding the general policy of the Government proceed from your Department" gives me some concern as to its precise meaning for it is a very broad phrase and taken literally might suspend much of our correspondence. For example, since the "Trading with the enemy" Act[4] was introduced and statements were made before the Committee by Secretary Lansing and myself at your request, numerous letters have come from exporting houses asking what they should or should not do in view of the pending Act. Letters in response to these have been drafted by our Solicitor for my signature. Without my knowledge or approval one of these letters was printed in the Journal of Commerce on June 12th and, I am glad to say, met approval and seems to have done good. It seems necessary to answer these letters with care, explaining what the legislation means and what seems wise to do pending its passage. Indeed it is hardly possible not to answer these letters without giving an impression at once misleading and dangerous while at the same time in some cases permitting practices to go on helpful to our enemies which can readily be stopped. Yet, I suppose, these might be called letters "regarding the general policy of the Government" although, of course, that policy has been officially defined before a Committee of the House of Representatives. My assumption is, therefore, that you refer to original statements of policy or policy not yet developed. In order, however, to be sure, I am withholding some letters, which otherwise would be sent, until I hear further from you.

Yours very truly,   William C. Redfield

TLS (WP, DLC).

¹ That is, cost, insurance, and freight.

² WCR to U. S. Shipping Board, July 3, 1917, TCL (WP, DLC).

³ "Precautions Advisable in Export Contracts," *Commerce Reports*, July 5, 1917. This brief note advised exporters that, since "public necessity" might in the future require the sudden requisition of vessels by the federal government, they should make exporting contracts contingent on their obtaining shipping space and an export permit, where required.

⁴ H.R. 4960, a bill to define, regulate, and punish trading with the enemy, was introduced by William C. Adamson on May 25, 1917. It was reported out of the Committee on Interstate and Foreign Commerce on June 11, 1917. The chief objects of the bill were to recognize and apply concretely the principle and practice of international law interdicting trade in time of war and to conserve and utilize upon a basis of practical justice enemy property found within the jurisdiction of the United States. See 65th Cong., 1st sess., House Report No. 85.

From Josephus Daniels

My dear Mr. President: [Washington] July Sixth, 1917.

I sent the telegram as you directed to Admiral Sims through the State Department in the most confidential code, and I feel certain it will do good.

In reply to your question whether the British are now convoying groups of ships, the fact is that the British are now convoying, particularly the slower ships, in groups of as many as twenty. But the convoy is composed of only one or two cruisers. The convoy is increased by destroyers and small craft, which are constantly operating in the danger zone. We have detailed seven or eight cruisers to co-operate in this service, one such group to be convoyed from New York about the 8th and another about the 10th. So far three groups have been sent over successfully and the plan is to send convoyed groups twice a week from Hampton Roads and also from New York. Ships from the South collect at Hampton Roads—the others collect at New York.

Sincerely yours,   [Josephus Daniels]

CCL (J. Daniels Papers, DLC).

From Arthur Capper

Topeka, Kas., July 6, 1917.

Permit me to express the hope that the Department of Justice will conduct the most searching investigations into conditions at East St. Louis to the end that the persons and influences leading up to the recent race riots may definitely be pointed out. If ever this country needed to use the strongest possible forces against this kind of outrage, that time is the present. With the country entering the world war in the interest of democracy, freedom, a fair chance for every man regardless of color or social position. It is certainly a most humiliating circumstance that in the center of our own nation, in one of the great centers of population, a hundred or more helpless negroes, men and women, were butchered by white men while officers of the law were present. East St. Louis provided the country of the most convincing proofs of the damning effects of liquor.

Arthur Capper,   Governor.

T telegram (JDR, RG 60, Numerical File, No. 186835-13½, DNA).

From Henry Fountain Ashurst

Dear Mr. President:　　　　　　　[Washington] July 6, 1917.

Herewith I hand you a telegram from Hon. Wiley E. Jones,[1] Attorney General of Arizona, in which he points out that in his opinion it would be a grave blunder at this time to withdraw the name of former Governor Hunt as mediator in the strike in Arizona. The Attorney General's view is exactly my own. In my judgment, Governor Hunt's name having been proposed should not now be withdrawn.

I also submit herein telegram from the Arizona State Federation of Labor.[2]　　　　Respectfully,　　Henry F. Ashurst

TLS (WP, DLC).
[1] Wiley Emmet Jones to H. F. Ashurst, July 5, 1917, T telegram (WP, DLC).
[2] T. A. French to H. F. Ashurst, July 6, 1917, T telegram (WP, DLC).

From Newton Diehl Baker

My dear Mr. President:　　　　　Washington. [c. July 6, 1917]

I have just received your letter of July 5th. I had not sent the memorandum embodied in my letter of July 3rd to the Director of the Council of National Defense, but rather intended to submit the whole question to your judgment before writing to the Director on the subject, so that I could have the benefit of your correcting judgment in the matter. In view of our subsequent conversations, I feel quite sure now that I can write to the Director definitely, setting at rest the doubts he felt and also outlining the course of action which the committees of the Council should take.　　　　　Respectfully yours,　　Newton D. Baker

TLS (WP, DLC).

From Walter Hines Page

Dear Mr. President:　　　　　　London, July 6. 1917

A few days ago Mr. Balfour informed me privately and confidentially that he had just submitted to the Cabinet the draft of a treaty, which, if the Cabinet approved, would be proposed to the Governments of the United States, France, and Japan—binding his own Government and these other three to come to the rescue with their navies if an attack shd. be made on any one of them—binding them for (say) four years after the declaration of peace. His main,—I understood, in fact, his sole-aim, is to bind the British Gov't to send its navy to our aid in case we shd. be attacked by Germany or Japan. But, since France & Japan are Great Britain's Allies, he thought it best that they, too, shd. be included in the agreement—or should at least be askd. to join it. If Japan signs such a treaty, all right; and, if not, still all right: the opportunity had been given to her. This in no way to take the place of, nor in any way to affect, any League to Enforce Peace that may hereafter be made, but only to pledge to us now the help of the British fleet during this period, so that we may feel free with regard to Japan or Germany. Mr. Balfour will inform me whenever the Cabinet takes the subject up and then, no doubt, he will request me to inform you.

The recent financial conferences into which the Government here have calld. me wd. soon become somewhat tiresome if they continued them. I have telegraphed quite fully about every one of them. I say "tiresome," because they have so far been expressions of British (more or less) disappointment. In this last Conference about our loan of 400 millions to be advanced out of the Liberty Loan, they seemed to me to squeal before they were hurt, and I told them so. In the preceding Conference about loans to pay for their purchases in the United States, their point seemed to me well taken—on their statement of the case. My misfortune is that I have no information from our Government whereby I can check their statements. Of what agreements (about this or other subjects) were come to with Mr. Balfour I have never been informed. The chief impression made on me by all these financial discussions is—how hard they were pressed and how sorely ridden by their Allies! They had been obliged to finance the whole war and, when we came in, they were financially exceedingly tired. They do not mean "to lie down on us"—there's nothing yellow in them. But help was so welcome that they were (as I intimated to them) not unlikely to produce on us a feeling of a little weariness.

I think each Gov't made a mistake by not making a memorandum of whatever agreement was come to.

Let me tell you, while I think of it, that Admiral Sims is greatly pleased at the direct request that you made yesterday for an extensive survey, made by himself on his own information, of the whole naval situation. He keeps me in his confidence and he does not always nor wholly agree with the British Admiralty. In fact, they have made considerable reorganizations after seeking his advice. They defer to him greatly. Not only did they, during the British Admiral's absence from Queenstown, put him in command of their fleet in those waters as well as our own, but they have now summonsed him before the War Council for his advice and they have consulted him about the forthcoming naval attack on the Belgian Coast and he will go to the meeting of their Admirals about this plan.

I hardly venture a judgment on a technical naval problem. But I have a very clear judgment (and, I think, a sound one) on the British stolidity about the submarine danger. Every naval man knows the peril and every disinterested civilian who knows the facts sees it clearly—it's a plain arithmetical problem—and the situation becomes increasingly worse. Yet the Prime Minister goes to Glasgow and delivers soothing sentences about it, and when last week showed a decrease in the number of ships sunk, probably because many submarines went to attack our transports, the British Government & press boast of the falling off of ship casualties. This stolidity is the same quality that led to the tragedies of Gallipoli and Messopotamia. The British will not confess that any danger awaits them. It is to be hoped that the ingenious aparatus wh. one of our destroyers here is equipped with, to find submarines, will prove its good promise. But this or some other device, quickly got, or a big fleet of anti-submarine craft is necessary to save the war.

So much in criticism. All else, so far as I know, goes well. In the thousand-and-one matters of less importance the Government very heartily plays the game with us here. On July 4, our flag again flew over Westminster.

Very heartily Yours,   Walter H. Page

ALS (WP, DLC).

From the Diary of Josephus Daniels

1917 Friday 6 July

Cabinet—I told what Gen. Wood told Charlotte people: "Two kind of folks learn nothing Dems & D— Fools" President said there were once two professors—one a renegade Southerner[1] who always sneered at the section of his birth and the other a soldier who had served under Grant.[2] The Yankee soldier hated the Southern renegade and would not speak to him. When his father visited W.W.[3] the Southern renegade called & after being introduced asked: Where do you live Dr Wilson? President's father said: "Wilmington, North Carolina.["] "I am thankful to say my foot never touched the soil of that State.["] "If you should visit it, the feeling would be mutual and they would wish you to leave it,["] or words to that effect.

How far shall President fix the distance of saloons from camps

& cantonments? Baker should be left to control. I said 4 or 5 mi—
enough to prevent easy access.

Talk of spies. Greg. thought hysteria.

President who has always believed in convoying, wanted to
know why there should not be a single lane for ships to reach
Britain, with plenty of patrol boats & hydroairplanes so as to
make submarine operations there impossible. I telegraphed to
Sims.

Hw bound diary (J. Daniels Papers, DLC).
    [1] Henry Clay Cameron, about whom see the references in Vol. 13.
    [2] Gen. Joseph Kargé, a flamboyant Polish nationalist, who had fought in the
Polish Revolution of 1848 and with the Union forces in the American Civil
War.
    [3] About this visit, see the entry in Wilson's diary for Sept. 11, 1876, Vol. 1.

To Thomas Watt Gregory

[The White House]
My dear Mr. Attorney General: 7 July, 1917

Do you think we could exercise any jurisdiction in this tragical
matter?[1] I am very anxious to have any instrumentality of the
Government employed that could be effectively employed to
check these disgraceful outrages.

Cordially and faithfully yours,   Woodrow Wilson

TLS (Letterpress Books, WP, DLC).
    [1] The assault against blacks in East St. Louis.

To William Cox Redfield

My dear Mr. Secretary: [The White House] 7 July, 1917

Thank you for your letter of yesterday. I felt quite confident
that the statement to which I called your attention had not been
issued by your authority.

Of course, I realize the necessity in the course of the correspondence of the department of answering questions the
answers to which will disclose either partially or wholly the
policy of the administration with regard to large matters, and I
do not wish to interfere with that at all, but evidently somebody
in the Bureau of Foreign and Domestic Commerce has a taste for
publicity and is apt to create the greatest embarrassments for
the administration by, either directly or indirectly, getting into
print with the announcement of "policies," and I think that it is
imperative to avoid this.

The letters going out from the several bureaux of the department could easily be marked "for information but not for publication," and I would be deeply obliged to you if you would say to Doctor Pratt, the head of the Bureau of Foreign and Domestic Commerce that I shall depend upon him to serve me in this matter so far as his bureau is concerned.

Of course it is going to be hard to work out all these things, but not impossible, and I am sure we will all cooperate in the same spirit.

Cordially and faithfully yours,   Woodrow Wilson

TLS (Letterpress Books, WP, DLC).

To Paul Oscar Husting

My dear Senator: [The White House] 7 July, 1917

Thank you for the memorandum sent you by Mr. Nieman. You may be sure I shall place it where it will "do the most good."

Cordially and faithfully yours,   Woodrow Wilson

TLS (Letterpress Books, WP, DLC).

To Thomas Watt Gregory

My dear Gregory: [The White House] 7 July, 1917

Here is another item for your budget about the activities of some of our fellow-citizens of German extraction.[1]

Faithfully yours,   Woodrow Wilson

TLS (JDR, RG 60, T. W. Gregory Papers, DNA).
[1] The Editors were unable to find this enclosure.

From Herbert Clark Hoover

Dear Mr. President: Washington July 7, 1917.

I am very anxious to bring to your attention a very serious crisis that is daily gathering with respect to wheat and corn owing to the very considerable drain by the neutrals and the apparent holding of grain in the country by someone, possibly their agents.

We are faced with an actual shortage in liquid supplies of such dimensions as to seriously imperil the situation until the new harvest arrives. The flour mills in Minneapolis are practically all closed down owing to their inability to buy wheat, although statistical information shows over 3,000,000 bushels available in that territory. The price of wheat is rising steadily again. Furthermore, the drain of fodder material from the country is going on at a very rapid rate; prices have risen very largely in the past thirty days and one of the many results from this is the forcing of dairymen to sell their cattle for meat as they can no longer, at the ruling prices of dairy products, afford to purchase fodder materials on the present terms. In fact, we are today shipping fodder to European neutrals to maintain the cattle which furnish dairy products to the Germans while our own cattle are being slaughtered because our dairymen can no longer maintain them.

Altogether, I feel greatly disturbed over the situation between now and the flow of the new harvest and there appears to me to be no remedy to our internal situation but immediate embargo. If this is followed by the passage of the Food Bill at an early date, we should be able to then procure liquidation of the held stocks. In any event, the embargo is the most critical portion of the operation.

I remain,   Your obedient servant,   Herbert Hoover

TLS (WP, DLC).

From Newton Diehl Baker

My dear Mr. President: Washington. July 7th, 1917.

Referring to the letter (which I return herewith) addressed to you by Senator Williams and which you enclosed to me in your personal and confidential note of July 3, I beg to state as follows.

The facts appear to be that Captain Dockery has been serving in a regiment the lieutenant-colonel of which is a negro officer,— Lieutenant-Colonel Charles Young. Prior to your note to me Lieutenant-Colonel Young was ordered before a retiring board on the report of the surgeons that he was incapacitated for duty by reason of Bright's Disease. Meanwhile, the Adjutant General of the State of Ohio has urgently requested his services with the colored command of that State. As soon as the proceedings of the retiring board have been completed, and pending final action on them by the War Department, Colonel Young will be directed to report to the Adjutant General of the State of Ohio for the above duty. This, I think, will remove the cause of trouble so far as I now understand it.

The colonel of Captain Dockery's regiment is a white officer as are also the other officers of the regiment.

Cordially yours,   Newton D. Baker

TLS (WP, DLC).

From Robert Russa Moton

Tuskegee Institute,
Dear Mr. President: Alabama, July 7, 1917.

I know how overwhelmed you are at a time like this, but I am sure you will appreciate the spirit in which this is written. I sincerely hope that this letter may be brought to your personal attention. It concerns a matter of the utmost importance.

You must know something of the unrest and discontent among the colored people at this time. Many of them are very much discouraged because they have had little or no opportunity to *volunteer* for service, and at a time when strenuous efforts are being made to secure 70,000 recruits to fill out the Federal Army. Of course, they with others will be "drafted."

The latest matter giving them concern is the matter of Lieutenant Colonel Charles Young's being ordered to the Letterman General Hospital at the Presidio of San Francisco, California. The colored newspapers and the colored people generally are very much concerned about this matter. I am venturing to call some of the newspaper comments to your attention. I am sending these as samples of other comments.[1]

Personally, I very much hope it may be possible to continue Lieutenant Colonel Young in the Regular Army. It will be a very great disappointment to hundreds of thousands of colored people if he should be retired at a time like this, as he himself states that he "has never felt better in his life, and has never enjoyed better health than at present."

If you can, for the reasons I have sought to mention, give this matter some part of your personal attention, I am sure it will be altogether in the right direction, and will mean more to the ten or twelve million Negroes than I need here express—and to the country as well.

Very sincerely yours,   R. R. Moton

TLS (WP, DLC).
[1] Moton enclosed clippings from the *New York Age*, June 28, 1917; the *Chicago Defender*, June 30, 1917; and the Indianapolis *Freeman*, June 30, 1917. All reported on the proposed "retirement" of Lt. Col. Young on grounds of "high blood pressure." An editorial from the *Nashville Globe*, June 29, 1917, commented on the same subject. Finally, an article from the *St. Louis Argus*, June 29, 1917, reported that blacks had no opportunity to volunteer for military service.

From Kenneth Douglas McKellar

My dear Mr. President: [Washington] July 7, 1917.

Mr. Postmaster General Burleson handed me your letter of July 6th., yesterday afternoon.

Evidently, some one has misinformed you about my connection with the amendment in question. I did not introduce it at all. It was put in the Food Bill, as I understand it, by the unanimous vote of the Senate Committee on Agriculture. I did not even know that such an amendment was contemplated until I saw it in the Bill. I am not on that Committee.

On Tuesday last, in the course of a speech that I made in the Senate, I earnestly and vigorously approved this amendment of the Committee, and I believe that the amendment should be passed. The amendment is in direct keeping with Sections 1781, 1782 and 1783 of the Revised statutes, which prohibits Senators, Representatives, and other agents of the government from being interested in any contract with the government. I am rather inclined to think that many members of the Advisory Committees of the Council of National Defense are now violating Section 1783 of the Revised Statutes, to which I call your especial attention, and they are probably already open to indictment under it. Section 1783 is as follows:

"No officer or agent of any banking or other commercial corporation, and no member of any mercantile or trading firm, or person directly or indirectly interested in the pecuniary profits or contracts of such corporation or firm, shall be employed or shall act as an officer or agent of the United States for the transaction of business with such corporation or firm; and every such officer, agent, or member, or person, so interested, who so acts, shall be imprisoned not more than two years, and fined not more than two thousand dollars not less than five hundred dollars."

Mr. President, I am convinced from a personal examination into this matter that many of the members of these committees of the Council of National Defense are interested in contracts which they recommend that the government enter into, their recommendations being final, and I want to urge you, as your friend, believing in you to the very limit, desiring above all things to uphold you and your administration, and desiring that your administration shall not be involved in any charges of wrongdoing or scandal, carefully to examine into the workings of these committees of the Council of National Defense.

It may be that you have heard only one side. There are a

number of Senators and Representatives, who are your warm personal friends, who have investigated this matter, and I hope you will call them in and talk to them before reaching a final conclusion about this amendment.

I am convinced myself that many of the operations of these committees will not bear this scrutiny of investigation, and may I not here and now suggest that instead of these committees of men, who are interested for themselves as well as for the government, you will recommend that Congress establish a separate and independent department to handle the matters of all contracts with the government, that department to be composed of officers and agents who only have to serve one master, and that master the United States. The well know[n] principle of Equity Jurisprudence that a trustee cannot be permitted to contract in his individual capacity with the trust finds [funds] in his hands whether he makes anything out of it or not, is peculiarly applicable to this matter. This principle is a combination of the two Scriptural injunctions that no man can serve two masters and avoid the appearance of evil. Whatever may be the facts, where it is understood that representatives of the government are permitted to do away with competitive bidding, and let contracts directly or indirectly to themselves in their individual or corporate capacities upon a commission, payment going to the corporate or individual entity, the public at large, not being on the inside, will believe that wrong is being done. I am sure that Congress would do whatever you recommended about it, because Congress has every confidence in you.

On May 13th, last, I wrote a letter to Secretary Baker, a copy of which I enclose you.[1] Secretary Baker replied[2] that the information would be given me, but as yet I have not received any information at all on the subject though it has been nearly a month. I had intended, if it were necessary, to put this letter to the Secretary in the Record, to show, as it seemed to me, the necessity for the passage of this amendment about which you have written. In view of your letter to me, however, I shall not take any further steps until I hear from you. Of course, in view of my previous statements and my sincere convictions, I shall be obliged to vote for the amendment.

We have given you the power to commandeer anything that is needed for the Army and Navy, or for the government, and it seems to me, under these circumstances, that this affords additional reasons why the government's agents in buying should not be the same as those who are selling. Under this power you are absolutely independent of the great trusts, the agents of which infest the committees of the Council of National Defense. I am told that they draw their usual salaries from their usual employers. Can it be reasonably expected that in dealing with their employers they will overlook their interests, and look alone to the interests of the government? Their duty to the government requires that they buy at the lowest price possible. Their duty to their company's stockholders, and employers require that they sell at the highest price possible. Therefore, under this system they are obliged to violate their duty to the one or the other.

Mr. President, I want to do whatever is necessary to make this war a success, and I want it to reflect credit on your administration. In my judgment, it is vital that there should be a better understanding on the part of our Legislators in Congress about this contract system. Many of us think it is not run on a proper basis. If we are in error the error should be pointed out to us, and my suggestion is, that the matter should be cleared up by frank and open conference between you and Congressmen as to the best course, after consideration of both sides and all the facts.

With great respect, I am,

Sincerely your friend,   Kenneth McKellar

TLS (WP, DLC).
1 K. D. McKellar to NDB, June (not May) 13, 1917, TCL (WP, DLC).
2 NDB to K. D. McKellar, June 15, 1917, TCL (WP, DLC).

From the Diary of Josephus Daniels

July Saturday 7 1917

Baker had a talk with the President and will call a meeting of the steel committee on Tuesday to tell them he must know the cost of production before price is fixed. If they cannot give right price, he will take over mills and run them and fix reasonable prices. Denman is also to be there.

A Draft of a Statement[1]

July 8, 1917.

In controlling ⟨through⟩ *by* license⟨s⟩ the export of certain ⟨necessary⟩ *indispensable* commodities from the United States, the Government has *first and* chiefly in view ⟨, first of all,⟩ the amelioration of *the* food conditions which have arisen *or are likely to arise* in our country ⟨until the⟩ *before* new crops are harvested. ⟨, for⟩ *Not only is* the conservation of our prime food and fodder ⟨necessities is⟩ *supplies* a matter which vitally concerns our own people ⟨. Also⟩, *but* the retention of an adequate supply of raw materials is essential to our program of military and naval construction and the continuance of our necessary domestic activities. *We shall, therefore, similarly safeguard all our fundamental supplies.*

It is obviously the duty of the United States in liberating any surplus ⟨supply⟩ *products* over ⟨our⟩ *and above our own* domestic needs to ⟨first⟩ consider *first* the necessities of ⟨those⟩ *all the* nations engaged in war against the Central Empires. As to neutral nations ⟨of the World, the⟩ *however, we also recognize our duty. The* Government does not wish to hamper them ⟨, but⟩. On the contrary ⟨to, by⟩ *it wishes and intends, by all* fair and equitable means, *to* cooperate with them in their difficult task of adding from our available surplus*es* to their own domestic supply and of meeting their pressing necessities or deficits. ⟨But⟩ *In* considering the⟨se⟩ deficits of food supplies the Government ⟨obviously will be obliged⟩ *means only to fulfil its obvious obligation* to assure itself that neutrals are husbanding their own resources and that our supplies will not become available, either directly or indirectly, to feed the enemy.[2]

T MS (WP, DLC).

[1] This statement was originally drafted by the Exports Council and sent in RL to WW, July 3, 1917, TLS (WP, DLC). Words in angle brackets deleted by Wilson; words in italics added by him.

[2] This statement in its emended form was given to the press on July 9, 1917.

To Arthur Capper

[The White House] 8 July, 1917

You may be sure that I share your feeling entirely about the tragical and outrageous things that have occurred at East St. Louis. I will take pleasure in seeing if the suggestion conveyed in your telegram of Friday opens the way to any means of control or correction.   Woodrow Wilson

T telegram (Letterpress Books, WP, DLC).

From Edward Mandell House, with Enclosure

Dear Governor: Magnolia, Massachusetts. July 8, 1917.

I am enclosing a cable which I have just received from Balfour. I am sending it in duplicate so you will have a copy of [for] the State Department. No one knows of these negotiations excepting Lansing and Polk, and I would suggest your cautioning Polk about letting them go any further.

Breckinridge Long who is here today is taking this letter.

I cannot see that the solution Balfour suggests would be of much service, excepting that it would prevent Japan from falling into the hands of Germany and forming a combination against us.

In the event of trouble between Japan and ourselves, or other parties to the agreement, they would be forced to be neutral, or if there was war between any of the signatory powers, the others would necessarily be neutral.

That is not quite what we had in mind. I see no reason why our first proposal should not be accepted, and I see no reason why it should offend Japan or any other nation if known. What I suggested was that in view of our diverting government ship-building in our naval yards from the construction of capital battleships to that of vessels suitable for anti-submarine warfare, and the building of a merchant marine in order not to interrupt the supplying of the Allies with necessary materials for the continuation of the war, Great Britain should agree to give us an option on the purchase of such capital battleships as we might wish, to replace those which we discontinued building because of our desire to aid them.

This would not be directed against Japan any more than it would be against France, Italy, Russia or even England herself.

Sir William Wiseman expects to return to England early next week and before going he will spend a day with me here. Will you not let me know your conclusions, so I may discuss the matter with him and let him in turn take it up with his Government?

If the English are afraid of Germany, it seems to me it would be reasonable to include in the agreement a clause by which in the event of war between Germany and England, they might demand the return of these capital battleships.

I take it they desire these negotiations to go on unofficially, in order that there may be no embarrassment with Japan. That is, as soon as they become official, their treaty obligations with Japan might compel them to disclose all negotiations of this nature.   Affectionately yours,   E. M. House

P.S. I do not believe Balfour has taken anyone on this side into his confidence regarding these negotiations excepting Sir William Wiseman. Spring-Rice, I am sure has not been told.

TLS (WP, DLC).

ENCLOSURE

Following from Balfour for House.

Since my return to England the question which you discussed with Drummond of a possible naval agreement between the United States and Great Britain in order to allow of extended building of destroyers and light-craft instead of capital ships already authorized by the United States programme has been carefully considered by the War Cabinet.

In view of submarine menace ADMIRALTY attach the highest importance to building by your Government of maximum number of destroyers and light-craft; indeed, it is not too much to say that this may have a great effect on ultimate result of war. I need hardly tell you that Cabinet were and are profoundly attracted by the idea of any defensive arrangement with the United States. They were clear that, with or without guarantee, popular opinion in this country would undoubtedly force us to go to the assistance of the United States if she were attacked by Japan. At the same time we realize that a private and informal recognition of this would hardly be sufficient to allow the United States Government to forego building capital ships, in view of widespread popular mistrust of Japan's intentions, though in opinion of our Naval authorities the United States has nothing to fear from Japan, since with some important exceptions the United States fleet is much superior to Japan numerically and otherwise. In larger capital ships, both constructed and under construction, with exception of battle cruisers, the United States has already a considerable preponderence. On the other hand their number of fast light cruisers is in the opinion of our naval authorities quite inadequate for operations of a fleet of dimensions of that of the United States, while their superiority in destroyers over Japan is also insufficient. The most urgent requirements of the United States Navy as against Japan are in fact for light cruisers, destroyers, and anti-submarine craft, and, with the exception of the battle cruisers, it would seem a waste of resources for the United States Government to build more capital ships.

The main difficulty of an arrangement between our two countries is that if Great Britain undertakes to give Naval aid to the United States in future possible war Japan will probably consider the agreement is directed against her. We think the spirit of our treaty with Japan would make it incumbent on us to inform her of what we were doing, and we assume the idea of secrecy must be excluded.

Announcement in Japan of such an arrangement must

inevitably raise highly dangerous discussion, and would certainly be interpreted by Japan primarily aimed at blocking her aims in China, in the Pacific and Far East generally, with the result that she might throw herself in the arms of our enemies, in which event a most perilous situation would be created.

I have therefore endeavored to find a formula which would, while overcoming these difficulties, assure the United States of absolute protection at the end of the war either against the German Fleet—which as you recognized is a real peril—against Japan or against both; and only method of so doing appears to be to endeavor to associate Japan from the beginning with the new arrangement. This would have triple effect of allaying Japan's fears, of engaging Japan's support, and of adverting [advertising][1] treaty as a protection against Germany; but, if Japan is brought in and if Germany is marked out as power against whom precautions have to be taken, ought not France to join in, and, if France, also Italy? Russia might perhaps be excluded on grounds of geographical position, though I think this would be a mistake.

I do not know whether you will consider such an arrangement as is here suggested practicable at the present moment, but if so it would seem to afford, besides everything else, a foundation for a maritime league to ensure peace strongly.

The following are actual terms of arrangements I would suggest:

"That, in view of diverting Government ship-building in naval yards of the United States from construction of capital ships to that of vessels suitable for anti-submarine warfare, the Governments of the United States, Great Britain, France, Italy, Russia and Japan engage singly and severally to assist each other against any maritime attack for a period of four years after conclusion of the present war."

Should President like this scheme I am prepared to take any steps he may desire to help in bringing it to fruition. If he sees objection to it I would endeavor to find some acceptable alternative.

T MS (WP, DLC).
[1] Correction from A. J. Balfour to Consul-General Bayley (New York), July 5, 1917, T telegram (A. J. Balfour Papers, FO 800/209, PRO).

From Marcus Aurelius Smith, with Enclosures

PERSONAL.

Dear Mr. President: [Washington] July 8, 1917.

I hand you herewith a telegram from Mr. E. E. Ellinwood,[1] attorney for the Phelps, Dodge people at Bisbee, Arizona. He always knows exactly what he is talking about, and I have no doubt he has touched the real facts involved in the effort to have Hunt appointed as mediator in the mining disturbances in Arizona. If I had had an opportunity to see you before this appointment was made, I should have advised differently, for I feared just exactly what has now happened, knowing as I did the extreme attitude of the two factions in Arizona.

I also inclose telegram from the Mayor of Globe,[2] stating that Hunt is attempting to use his influence to have the Federal troops withdrawn from that District. I see by this morning's dispatches—Sunday—that there has already been fighting at Globe between these foreign strikers and the citizens of the town. Please see that Hunt's activities are somewhat modified, if not entirely dispensed with.

Yours very sincerely,   M. A. Smith

TLS (WP, DLC).
1 Everett E. Ellinwood.
2 G. D. Barclay.

ENCLOSURE I

New York NY Jul 7

President of the United States has been imposed on in the appointment of Hunt in Arizona labor trouble It is purely a political scheme to revive his lost prestige with the purpose to put him in the race for the US Senate in 1920 It is preposterous to appoint as conciliator the very man who is primarily responsible for the labor unrest in Arizona and who was defeated because of that fact and who will be afforded a good opportunity to and who intends to use the office for mediator for his political advantage solely The only effect of such appointment will be to aggravate the situation and prolong the trouble   E E Ellinwood.

ENCLOSURE II

Globe Ariz [July] 7

A statement offered in our evening paper of this date from exgovernor Hunt expressing a desire to use his influence to have federal troops withdrawn from this district which if done should mean destruction of property and the lieves [lives] of citizens endangered by a foreign enemy   G D Barclay

T telegrams (WP, DLC).

To Marcus Aurelius Smith

My dear Senator: [The White House] 9 July, 1917

I am distressed that you should think I have made a mistake in connection with the difficult and trying conditions in Arizona. I hope with all my heart that it will not turn out to be so in the event. The Department of Labor is represented down there by very competent men, and I hope with all my heart that after the first flurries are over some living agreement may be worked out.

Cordially and sincerely yours,   Woodrow Wilson

TLS (Letterpress Books, WP, DLC).

To Joseph Patrick Tumulty, with Enclosure

Dear Tumulty: [The White House, July 9, 1917]

I think that perhaps it would be wise for you to acknowledge this for me, saying in the acknowledgment that it has been brought to my attention and assuring those who sent it that the matters it deals with are having my gravest and most anxious consideration.   The President.

TL (WP, DLC).

ENCLOSURE

Los Angeles, Calif., July 8, 1917.

We, the Forum of Los Angeles, voted the following message to be sent to the President of the United States July 8th, 1917. Honored Sir:

In view of the East St. Louis outbreak, the ruthless slaughtering of unoffending and defenseless negroes; in view of the numberless wrongs perpetrated upon the negroes of this country, from Washington to California; we, the loyal negroes, subjects of this Union, being undismayed and still believin[g] in the deep abiding sense of fair play, found in the hearts of the great American people, having assembled for the purpose of advising among ourselves, what is the best course to be pursued by us under the present circumstances, and what is the best way to preserve our own loyalty and to secure for our race protection in the future. We have decided upon the following message to be telegraphed to the President and to the Congress of the United States of America:

We see and feel the utter hopelessness of ever securing a fair consideration at the hands of the unthinking masses so long as the course pursued by the general government is such that plainly and palpably discriminates. We feel that when the general govermnet [government] tolerates discrimination against its citizens it lowers the value of human life and causes the state governments to follow its example. Then each county and city following the example of the state, so, when the influence of these examples reaches the individual, he has lost that keen sense of justice as is expressed in the opening words of the great Constitution, which says:

"We believe all men are created equal and endowed by their Creator with the inalienable right, among these life, liberty and the pursuit of happiness."

These truths are held as self-evident, but the individual, under the mobs violence, influenced by Federal, state, county and city discriminations, feel that they can, with impunity, trample upon human rights. We hold that there can be no secure establishment of human liberty in this country and no man is safe until the negroe is made secure. We look upon the general government for protection and feel that in the summing up of all things, eternal justice will place no little of the blame for this ruthless discrimination at the hands of our general government.

Hence [Since] the National Government has not called us in vain when its rights and honor were in danger, we ask the Federal government to come now to the rescue of its own citizens and save them from these furious causeless onslaughts, as took place a few days ago in East St. Louis and have taken place in many other portions of this country. It might be thought by some that this is a matter which should be left entirely with the state, but when this country wanted to save itself from a foreign embarrassment, not long ago, it took a strong hand in the school of legislation of the State of California.

Now, while this country is going to the rescue of Ireland from England, of the Armenians from the Turks, of the Belgians from the Germans, we ask you in the name of justice to consider the following request, which registers the sentiments in every negros' breast; that sentiment which must of necessity be found in the breast of every human being whom God has honored and evolved to the plane of human responsibility.

We ask that every form of discrimination in army and navy be removed by law and regulation, whether in private or official ranks, and that all barriers to negroe promotion be taken away for when the progress of the soul is stopped, stagnation ensues. We also ask if all men are created equal and endowed by their Creator, that jim-crowing be made, from this time on, a crime against the nation, whether on railroad, cafes or hotels.

We ask further that legislation be enacted that would place the responsibility for lynching on state, county, town and precinct where such lynching occurs, and that twenty five thousand dollars be piad [paid] to the family of the one lynched, collected by the general government from the state, county, town and precinct. We know that such form of legislation will indictae [indicate] this country's determination and willingness to put down this form of lawlessness.

In view of the fact that our country is asking of us to give up our very lives for civilization against barbarism and to establish world democracy, also to save Europe and this country from German militarism, we feel, as human beings, we could ask for nothing less   only by these methods, can the pursuit of happiness be secured, for back of all loyalty there must be love of country, but if the country will not protect us in the time of need, we feel that it is not humanly possible to nourish our hearts to loyalty by the memory of cold neglect from general government.

Since we are painfully in earnest, we sincerely hope that nothing we have said will give offense to our great President, his Cabinet officers or any of the National legislators, who are alive to human rights. We wish to be regarded as the loyal citizens of this great republic who, in this message, are speaking the only way we know that can perpetuate in us that form of loyalty exhibited by the negroes from the fall of Crispus attacks [Attucks] on the commons of Boston, to the heroes of Carrizal in Mexico.   Julius Stephens, President;
                    J. L. Jarrett, Secretary.

T telegram (WP, DLC).

To Henry Fountain Ashurst

My dear Senator: [The White House] 9 July, 1917

Thank you for your letter of July sixth. I requested Governor Hunt to act as mediator in the strike in Arizona on what I thought was the best advice, and do not feel that I made a mistake, difficult and complex as the situation in the copper mines has turned out to be. I agree with you and with the Attorney General of Arizona that it would certainly not be wise to alter any step I have taken.

　　　　　Cordially and sincerely yours,　Woodrow Wilson

TLS (Letterpress Books, WP, DLC).

To Kenneth Douglas McKellar

My dear Senator: [The White House] 9 July, 1917

Thank you for your frank and full letter of July seventh, which I have read with the greatest interest.

I am sorry to have made a blunder about your authorship of the amendment referred to in my recent letter to you, but, after all, no harm has been done since you so earnestly favor the amendment.

I am afraid I did not make it clear enough in my letter to you just what is taking place. As a matter of fact, under the reorganization of the advisory instrumentalities associated with the Council of National Defense such persons as the amendment refers to are being put very distinctly in the relation which was originally intended. They are, that is, to assist the Council by information and cooperation but are in no way to be connected with either the initiation or the conclusion of contracts. If anything in the law should make it necessary to dispense with their services, the Government would be seriously and perhaps fatally embarrassed, inasmuch as we must in the circumstances have the cooperation, and the active cooperation, of the men who are in actual control of the great business enterprises of the country. I should find myself hampered in a degree which I think you cannot realize if I were deprived of the opportunity to use these gentlemen as they are willing to be used.

They are in no sense agents of the Government and do not wish to be considered as such.

　　　　　Cordially and faithfully yours,　Woodrow Wilson

TLS (Letterpress Books, WP, DLC).

To Robert Russa Moton

My dear Principal Moton: [The White House] 9 July, 1917

I have your letter of July seventh. You may be sure that I am no less deeply interested than yourself in the matters to which you call my attention, and I think you are surely laboring under a misapprehension as to the case of Lieutenant Colonel Charles Young. There is no possible ground in that case for the fear that he is in any way being discriminated against and you may be sure that he will be treated as any other officer would be in similar circumstances. I know that is the disposition of the authorities of the War Department, and it is certainly my own purpose.

Cordially and sincerely yours,   Woodrow Wilson

TLS (Letterpress Books, WP, DLC).

To Frank Lyon Polk, with Enclosure

My dear Mr. Counselor,   The White House. 9 July, 1917.

The attached has made me a little uneasy. We have not asked either the French or the English government to take the Hearst people back into their favour in any degree, have we? I should be most unwilling to do so, indeed would do so in no circumstances; and this despatch leads me to write to ask what you know of the matter.

With warm regard,

Faithfully Yours,   Woodrow Wilson

WWTLS (RSB Coll., DLC).

ENCLOSURE

London. July 6, 1917.

6661. Your 5074 July 3, 4 p.m. must have crossed a telegraphic instruction to the British Ambassador in Washington to the effect that as the attitude of Hearst Press has become markedly less unwholesome since our entry into the war. The British Government were not disposed to grant reinstatement International News Service here unless you request it and they should like in announcing the reinstatement, if it be made, to explain that it was done at the instance of the United States Government.

The information which reached you to the effect that the French Government are willing to restore cable privileges to Bertelli,[1] the Paris correspondent, appears to Foreign Office to conflict with understanding reached within the last few days with the French Authorities who it is understood are of the same mind as themselves.

Foreign Office request Dillon's[2] full name or initials.

Page.

T telegram (WP, DLC).

  [1] Charles Filippo Bertelli.

  [2] Daniel Dillon, correspondent for Hearst's International News Service.

From Frank Lyon Polk

My dear Mr. President: Washington July 9, 1917.

In regard to the attached despatch, I feel very certain that Mr. Lansing never asked the French or the British to take the Hearst people back. He did go so far as to discuss the matter with Mr. Balfour and, I believe, suggested that from the British standpoint it might be worth while to readmit the Hearst service. Great care has always been taken, I am sure, never to make a request or anything like a request.

The War Department permitted a man named Dillon, representative of the International News Service, to go over with the Pershing expedition. The British raised some question about passing his messages after he went over, but when it was explained that Dillon merely went with our expedition and not as a general correspondent abroad, arrangements were made for passing his despatches.   Yours faithfully,   Frank L Polk

TLS (WP, DLC).

From William Gibbs McAdoo

PERSONAL.

Dear Mr. President: Washington July 9, 1917.

The enclosed clipping recites the arrest of Carl Heynen[1] in New York. I am glad to see that this has been done. Our Secret Service has had this man under more or less observation for the past two years. He is one of the most active German agents in this country. He was concerned originally in buying up munitions plants in this country to prevent the manufacture and shipment of supplies to the Allies; was active in Mexico and is even now interested in the Mexican oil fields and has been doing all the mischief he can down there. His counsel are Hayes, Kaufman & Lindheim, of New York City, who represent professionally German interests in this country. They are also attorneys for the New York Evening Mail, which was bought up by German sympathizers and is being published by them.[2]

When Bernstorff was dismissed, Heynen was among those slated to leave the country. He and his pro-German American friends brought pressure upon the State Department to let him remain. This was at the instance of the German Embassy. They even succeeded in getting Henry Morgenthau to intervene with the State Department in Heynen's behalf. I told Mr. Polk at the time that Heynen ought to be sent out of the country, but, to my surprise, he and the Secretary of State decided to let him remain. Mr. Polk was familiar with the facts I am giving you, because he has read the Secret Service reports. I do not mean this as criticism—it is mistaken leniency.

This is typical of what is going on in the country. The German spy system is highly organized and is operating efficiently. I have no hysterical notions about it, but I think it ought to be extirpated with a strong hand. The country is very much aroused about the German spy activities. What you said on this subject in your Flag Day speech made a great impression. I earnestly hope that you will soon take action to make more effective the secret service agencies of the government, so that the dangerous activities of German agents and sympathizers in this country may be more effectively dealt with.

Cordially yours,   W G McAdoo

TLS (WP, DLC).

[1] The clipping was from the Baltimore *Sun*, July 7, 1917. Heynen, arrested in New York on July 6, was a former employee of the Hamburg-America Line and sometime German consul at Mexico City. He had been associated with the propaganda and sabotage activities of Heinrich Albert in New York and elsewhere. See the lengthy discussion of him in "3 Noted Germans Interned for War in Hunt for Spies," *New York Times*, July 7, 1917.

[2] Actually, the German government itself, acting through Hays, Kaufman, and Lindheim, had purchased the New York *Evening Mail* in April 1915. The pro-British Samuel Sidney McClure was brought in as the nominal editor, and the newspaper was held by the S. S. McClure Newspaper Corp. However, effective control of the editorial policy and news content of the paper was in the hands of Edward Aloysius Rumely, the publisher, and it was a principal outlet for German propaganda in the United States until taken over by the United States Alien Property Custodian in July 1918. See David Wayne Hirst, "German Propaganda in the United States, 1914-1917" (Ph.D. dissertation, Northwestern University, 1962), pp. 80-86, and Peter Lyon, *Success Story: The Life and Times of S. S. McClure* (New York, 1963), pp. 354-60, 382-83.

From Joseph Patrick Tumulty, with Enclosure

[The White House] July tenth [1917].

Will the President kindly advise the Secretary as to the reply to be made to this letter?

TL (WP, DLC).

ENCLOSURE

Frank Thilly to Joseph Patrick Tumulty

Dear Mr. Tumulty: Ithaca, New York July 7, 1917.

Professor O. Guerlac[1] and Professor Elie Halévy, both of Paris, France, have decided to write a Life of Woodrow Wilson for the French people.[2] Professor Guerlac is an old friend of mine; he left Cornell University, where he was a member of the Faculty, at the outbreak of the Great War, having been called to the colors by the French government. He served in the army until a few months ago when he was invited to take a position in the French Foreign Office at Paris, a post which he now holds. He is a scholar and writer of ability and a man of fine character, whom all his colleagues here hold in high regard. Monsieur Halévy is the son of the wellknown French author Ludovic Halévy; he occupies a professorship at the Ecole des Sciences Politiques of Paris, and has published a number of able books.

Professor Guerlac has addressed an inquiry to me concerning President Wilson's travels abroad, to which I am unable to give a satisfactory answer, and I am therefore taking the liberty of appealing to you for help. I know that he has been in England and Scotland, but I do not remember having heard of his visiting France or Italy or any other country. Could you give me the information which Professor Guerlac desires, with dates, or refer me to the books where it may be found? I should feel greatly obliged to you for your kind assistance in this matter.

Very sincerely yours,   Frank Thilly

TLS (WP, DLC).
[1] Othon Goepp Guerlac.
[2] Actually, the book, *Le Président Wilson* (Paris, 1918), was written by Élie Halévy's younger brother, Daniel Halévy.

To Joseph Patrick Tumulty

Dear Tumulty: [The White House, July 10, 1917]

Frank Thilly is a very lovable fellow with whom I was once associated at Princeton, and I am very glad to answer his letter. I have spent several summers in England and Scotland but only once visited the Continent. I then visited only France and Italy, going into Italy only so far as Lake Como for a few days there, and in France visiting only Paris and the cathedral towns of Amiens and Cha[r]tres.   The President.

TL (WP, DLC).

From William Gibbs McAdoo

PERSONAL.

Dear Mr. President: [Washington] July 10, 1917.

I enclose memorandum of the proposed arrangement to be entered into, with your approval, under authority of the Act of Congress approved April 24, 1917, between the Secretary of the Treasury and the foreign governments to which we are extending credits under said Act, for the appointment of a Commission in the United States through which all purchases of such foreign governments shall be made.[1] Attached to this agreement is the form of letter I purpose writing to each of the governments concerned, providing for the prompt creation of an Inter-Allied Council, to sit in London or Paris, for the purpose of determining their respective needs and priorities in the markets of the United States, and of making recommendations to me as to the amount of loans that shall be made from time to time to them by the United States.[2] You will observe that our Government, under this plan, is permitted to be represented in an advisory way on such Council, but does not have voting power thereon, although we reserve the right to modify the agreement in this respect if it should become desirable.

The representatives here of Great Britain and France have indicated the probable acceptance by their governments of this arrangement. I am sure that Italy and Russia will follow suit.

With this machinery set up and operating, a more effective coordination of the operations of the European Governments will be brought about, not only in Europe, but in the United States. The quicker this is accomplished, the better for all concerned, because the confusion now existing is extremely hurtful.

The purchasing commission, which is to have its headquarters in Washington, should have as members such men, in my opinion as Mr. Baruch, Mr. Endicott, of Endicott, Johnson & Company, whom you know as one of the most progressive manufacturers of the country and head of the Endicott Johnson Shoe Company which established the eight hour law during the campaign of 1916, and Henry Ford, or some man equally efficient and able. It is very doubtful if Ford would accept such a place, and I have no reason to believe that Endicott would; I mention them as types of men whom I think we should secure for this commission. I think they would be less likely to come unless the purchases of our Government are passed through this commission, because they would naturally feel that the efficiency of the commission and its ability to get results will depend, as in fact it must depend, upon the power of the commission to control inquiries and direct the purchases for our Government as well as for those foreign governments in our own market. If two or three purchasing agencies are established, they will inevitably cross each other's wires, keep the markets excited by independent inquiries and negotiation, and by actually competing with each other in the purchases and deliveries of supplies and materials. This ought not to be permitted, and I earnestly hope that you will not sanction any plan which does not put the whole situation under single and firm control.

My idea has been that if we could agree, in advance of the execution of these European agreements, on the personnel of a suitable purchasing commission, you could name it as the purchasing commission of our own Government, and direct the War, Navy and other purchasing agencies of the United States to proceed through this commission in purchasing supplies and materials for our Government. The same commission could be named in the proposed agreement with the foreign governments and empowered to act for them in the purchase of supplies in our markets, so that the effect would be to have the foreign governments empower a commission of the United States Government to make their purchases in the American market. This would effect a thorough coordination and cooperation.

The crux of this situation, to my mind, is, first, the power to control or to regulate the prices of the leading raw materials and supplies required for the conduct of the war, and that power I hope the Congress will give you in its broadest possible form; and, secondly, the consolidation of the purchases of the foreign governments and our Government in our own market so as to keep prices within a reasonable range, and to secure the most efficient and prompt distribution of supplies among the nations concerned. Unless this is accomplished, I do not hesitate to say that it will be impossible for the United States to finance the requirements of this war. Excessive and extortionate prices mean a drain upon the Treasury of the United States and the resources of the American people which it will be impossible to meet. Such prices reduce the purchasing power of the dollar and make it necessary to increase taxation and multiply bond issues. Even if the Congress should fail to give you broad powers to control or regulate prices of essential supplies and materials, the creation of a strong commission in Washington, through which the purchases of all the foreign governments and our Government must proceed, will tremendously improve the situation. Such a commission can force reductions in prices and exercise a very considerable control over the markets, even though it will be far less effective in this direction than price regulation or control by the Federal Government. If we can establish the commission and get the price regulation powers as well, so much the better.

The present condition, so far as foreign purchases in our markets are concerned, is confusing and in the highest degree unsatisfactory. We should remedy it as quickly as possible. I shall be greatly obliged, therefore, if you will indicate your approval or disapproval of what I have outlined, or suggest any changes or modifications you may think wise or desirable.

Copies of the memorandum of arrangement and the proposed letter, referred to herein, have been sent to the State Department.

Cordially yours,   W G McAdoo

TLS (Letterpress Books, W. G. McAdoo Papers, DLC).

¹ "Memorandum of an arrangement . . . ," T MS (W. G. McAdoo Letterpress Books, DLC). This was a model of the form of agreement to be reached and signed separately with each of the Allied governments. It provided for a commission of three Americans to pass on all Allied purchases in the United States. The commission's expenses and compensation were to be paid by the foreign governments using its services. All requests for materials and supplies were to be communicated to the commission through a designated representative of the government concerned. The commission would then seek bids on goods at the best obtainable prices and terms. The foreign government was not obliged to accept these prices and terms, but it could not, so long as the agreement continued, make purchases in the United States other than through the commission. The agreement might be terminated upon ninety days' notice by either party.

² WGM to——, n.d., TL (W. G. McAdoo Letterpress Books, DLC). This letter proposed to the foreign governments addressed that an Inter-Allied Council be formed to report to the American purchasing commission the needs of all governments concerned and on the transportation requirements for the needed goods. They would also determine among themselves the priorities for the purchase and transportation of the needed materials and supplies and would also make forecasts of their later needs for periods of three, six, and twelve months. These requests and forecasts were needed especially, McAdoo wrote, to assist him in allocating the $3,000,000,000 in loan funds already approved by Congress and any additional funds approved later.

From Joseph Patrick Tumulty

Dear Governor: The White House 10 July 1917.

Senator France of Maryland telephoned me this morning and requested an appointment with the President for himself and a *delegation of negroes* to discuss the East St. Louis situation. I told him you were very busy but that I would get in touch with you.

Now that the effect of this terrible thing is slowly passing away, I am afraid that if you see this delegation the fire will be re-kindled and that a greater impetus will be given to an agitation which is contagious in its effects. I would suggest that you personally reply to Senator Franze, telling him that I communicated his wish to you and that you regret because of the press of matters having to do with the international situation you are so tied down that it will be impossible for you to see him and the delegation at this time, although you will be glad to take it up at a later date; and then say to him practically what you said in the Capper telegram, that you share the feeling of everyone about the tragical and outrageous things that have occurred at East St. Louis, and that you are working through the Department of Justice to find out the real facts of the situation so that there never can again be a repetition.

Or you might use the substance of this letter to Dr. Bolden of New York City:

"The President asks me to acknowledge the receipt of your letter of July 4th,[1] with enclosure, and to say that he is obliged to avoid interviews at the present time if it is possible to do so consistently with the public business. He asks me to assure you that you cannot feel more distressed than he does at the terrible things which have recently been happening, and that no suggestion from any quarter is necessary to increase his interest or his purpose to do whatever it is possible to do."

Sincerely yours,   Tumulty

TLS (WP, DLC).
[1] See WW to JPT, July 6, 1917, n. 1.

From William Gibbs McAdoo

PERSONAL AND IMPORTANT.

Dear Mr. President: Washington July 10, 1917.

I hand you herewith the letter of the British Ambassador addressed to the Secretary of State on the first of July, 1917, in reference to Mr. Balfour's negotiations with the Secretary of the Treasury and certain financial assistance desired by the British Government.[1] I also enclose copy of my proposed letter to the Secretary of State in reply thereto.[2]

I shall be greatly obliged if you will read these letters, taking them into consideration in connection with my previous letter of today containing my proposed reply to the cable of Ambassador Page dated July 5,[3] which I received from the State Department on July 7.   Cordially yours,   W G McAdoo

TLS (WP, DLC).
   [1] C. Barclay to RL, July 1, 1917.
   [2] WGM to RL, July 9, 1917, TLS (SDR, RG 59, 841.51/67, DNA). McAdoo's letter was a point-by-point refutation of almost everything stated in the letter cited in n. 1 above. It was true, McAdoo said, that he had not been aware of the fact that Great Britain would be unable to make payments in the United States, but this was true because he had not received complete and detailed information on British finances. Nor did he have specific information on the amount of loans by Great Britain to her allies. He denied that he had made any specific commitments to Balfour to meet British needs or to relieve them of the burden of expenditures in the United States on behalf of the other Allied powers. He asserted that he had informed Balfour that he could provide no assistance to any of the Allies beyond the $3,000,000,000 in loans authorized by Congress on April 24, 1917. He declared that he had provided prompt assistance to the British in the amount of $400,000,000. He insisted that he could give no assurances for sums necessary to pay off maturing indebtedness of the British government in the United States incurred before America's entrance into the war. In regard to the specific requests in Barclay's letter of July 1, McAdoo declared that he could not make British commitments in the United States on behalf of Belgium and Russia a first charge on loans to those nations without first consulting them on the matter. He had authorized an advance of $100,000,000 to the British government on July 5 and was considering a further loan of $85,000,000 in July. However, he was not yet prepared to make any commitment in regard to the $400,000,000-British overdraft on New York bankers, although he had the matter under consideration.
   [3] WHP to RL and WW, July 5, 1917, T telegram (SDR, RG 59, 841.51/63, DNA). Page reported on a "financial conference" with the Prime Minister, the Chancellor of the Exchequer, the Foreign Secretary, the Governor of the Bank of England, and others, to which he had been summoned on July 4. The conference dealt with the $400,000,000 overdraft mentioned in n. 2 above, which Page said was owed entirely to J. P. Morgan & Co. Balfour and others asserted that they had had repeated assurances from McAdoo that the overdraft would be paid out of the proceeds of the first Liberty Loan. The British officials had got the idea that this meant that the payment would be made on July 2, the day after the close of the Liberty Loan.

From Sir Cecil Arthur Spring Rice

Dear Mr. President: Washington July 10, 1917.

With reference to your letter of the 23rd June and Sir Richard Crawford's replies of the 25th and 29th June, I have pleasure in forwarding you the following further information with regard to losses by war risk each month this year which has now been received from London:

1917.	Total war losses gross tons:	(By British, Allied and Neutral).
JANUARY	354,917	
FEBRUARY	519,080	
MARCH	583,122	
APRIL	835,242	
MAY	580,254	
JUNE	630,000	

This gives a loss of 3½ million tons gross (or about 5,800,000 deadweight) for the 6 months ended June 30th. For the period of the intensive submarine campaign the average monthly loss has been about 630,000 tons gross. To this should be added about 34,000 gross tons a month for loss by marine risk, with a considerable further addition, hard to estimate exactly, for vessels damaged though not lost by war risk and put out of commission for considerable periods.

At the rate of loss of the last few months the wastage through all the above causes, before allowing for new building, should probably be reckoned at about 8,500,000 tons gross per annum or about 14,000,000 tons deadweight.

As against this the present rate of building, outside the United States, may be taken at about

1,200,000	Great Britain
500,000	Other countries
1,700,000	tons gross or
3,000,000	tons d.w.

i.e. only a little over ⅕ of the loss and leaving a net loss of some 6,800,000 tons gross or 11,000,000 tons d.w.

For further information as to the tonnage position I would refer to the memorandum of Messrs. Royden and Salter forwarded with Sir Richard Crawford's letter of the 25th June. In this memorandum detailed reasons are given for suggesting that, in view of the present wastage of shipping and the fact that the Allies have necessarily had to devote their main strength to increasing their armies, navies and munitions (all of which are now dependent upon shipping) America would be making a unique and perhaps decisive contribution to the war if she could concentrate a special effort, for which her industrial and engineering resources qualify her in a peculiar degree, upon building up to the amount of the net wastage shewn above.

(It may be remarked that 12,000,000 tons d.w. in steel ships would represent about 4½ million tons of steel, i.e. not more than about 11% of the total annual steel output of the U. S. A).

Although it is of course outside the immediate scope of your enquiry, I venture to add that it has been abundantly proved that the use of light naval craft is the best available method of defending merchant ships and attacking submarines and that this is a consideration which we must all bear in mind in arranging our programme of ship building.

I have the honour to be with the highest respect,
    Dear Mr. President,
                        Yours faithfully,   Cecil Spring Rice

TLS (WP, DLC).

From the Diary of Josephus Daniels

1917 Tuesday 10 July

Cabinet—WW told President & Mrs. W. went to Pohick to church. Secret service men told he was coming. "President of what?" President of U. S. Dismissed S.S. so children could go home to tell their parents. Preacher told sexton to ring the bell. "Cannot" said sexton. "I must go home & shave." Preacher had to ring bell in rain. Good congregation came out. Service delayed while preacher was trying to find the special prayer to make when the President was present. Couldn't find it. Had to make usual prayer. President enjoyed telling story.

Jean Jules Jusserand to the Foreign Ministry

Washington, s.d. reçu le 10 juilliet 1917

No. 905 Suite à mon télégr. no. 902.

Reçu en audience par le Président, je lui ai exposé les motifs humanitaires et d'intérêt général qui devaient nous faire souhaiter à tous le raccourcissement de la guerre, but que nous aiderait à atteindre la vigoureuse application du blocus. Je lui ai cité les chiffres principaux montrant l'énormité de l'aide reçue en 1916 et depuis par l'Allemagne des pays du Nord.

Le Président, qui a écouté mon exposé avec beaucoup d'attention, me demandant des explications complémentaires sur divers points, m'a dit qu'il était pleinement d'accord sur la nécessité de pareilles mesures. Les agents américains s'occupent présentement d'établir un tableau aussi exact que possible de la quantité de vivre indispensable pour chacun des pays en cause; mais, m'a dit M. Wilson, ce tableau est établi en tenant compte de toutes les sortes de denrées comestibles produites par ces pays.

C'est le total qui nous guidera, sans considération de tel ou tel produit en particulier.

J'ai beaucoup insisté sur l'importance de la saison actuelle et sur l'urgence.

Le Président incline à montrer (moyennant dues précautions) moins de rigueur pour la Norvège qu'on nous représente, a-t-il dit, comme peu éloignée de prendre part à la lutte de notre côté.

Il m'a interrogé avec quelques détails sur la Suisse et je lui ai indiqué que le système adopté donnait à peu près satisfaction, et sur l'Espagne à propos de qui j'ai surtout parlé de la question du charbon.

Je me suis exprimé de même après du Ministre du Commerce et du gérant du Département dEtat, (M. Lansing est absent pour probablement 3 semaines), que j'ai vu ensuite.

Jusserand.

T telegram (Guerre 1914-1918 États-Unis, Vol. 58, pp. 36-37, FFM-Ar).

T R A N S L A T I O N

Washington, no date
received July 10, 1917

No. 905 Continuation of my telegram No. 902.

At an audience with the President, I set forth for him the humanitarian motives and the universal interest that make us all hope to shorten the war, a goal that vigorous application of the blockade will help us to reach. I cited to him the principal figures showing the enormity of the aid that Germany has received in 1916 and afterwards from the northern countries.

The President, who listened very attentively to what I had to say, and asked for supplementary explanations on various points, told me that he fully agreed on the necessity for measures of the type described. American agents were now preparing, as exactly as possible, a chart showing the indispensable quantity of food for each of the countries involved. On the other hand, Mr. Wilson added, this chart is set up to take account of every sort of foodstuff produced by these countries.

It is the total that will guide us, without regard to this or that product in particular.

I placed great emphasis on the importance of the present season and the urgency of the matter.

Assuming proper precautions, the President is inclined to be less rigorous toward Norway, which, he said, is reported to be not far from taking part in the struggle on our side.

He asked me about some details regarding Switzerland, where I said that the system adopted was more or less satisfactory, and regarding Spain, where I spoke mostly about the coal situation.

I said the same afterwards to the Secretary of Commerce and the Acting Secretary of State, whom I saw later. (Mr. Lansing is absent for probably three weeks.)

                                                              Jusserand

To William Denman, with Enclosure

My dear Mr. Chairman: The White House 11 July, 1917

After very mature consideration of the matter and after checking my own judgment as best I could by consultation with others who might be regarded as entirely disinterested and separated from the matter, I have come to the conclusion that the enclosed Executive Order recommended by the Shipping Board is the best solution of a difficult matter, and I have therefore today signed it.   Cordially and sincerely yours,   Woodrow Wilson

TLS (W. Denman Papers, CU).

E N C L O S U R E

EXECUTIVE ORDER.

By virtue of authority vested in me in the section entitled "Emergency Shipping Fund" of an Act of Congress entitled "An Act Making appropriations to supply urgent deficiencies in appropriations for the Military and Naval Establishments on account of war expenses, for the fiscal year ending June thirtieth, nineteen hundred and seventeen, and for other purposes," approved June 15, 1917, I hereby direct that the United States Shipping Board Emergency Fleet Corporation shall have and exercise all power and authority vested in me in said section of said act, in so far as applicable to and in furtherance of the construction of vessels, the purchase or requisitioning of vessels in process of construction, whether on the ways or already launched, or of contracts for the construction of such vessels, and the completion thereof, and all power and authority applicable to and in furtherance of the production, purchase, and requisitioning of materials for ship construction.

And I do further direct that the United States Shipping Board shall have and exercise all powers and authority vested in me in

said section of said act, in so far as applicable to and in further-ance of the taking over of title or possession, by purchase or requisition, of constructed vessels, or parts thereof, or charters therein; and the operation, management and disposition of such vessels, and of all other vessels heretofore or hereafter acquired by the United States. The powers herein delegated to the United States Shipping Board may, in the discretion of said Board, be exercised directly by the said Board or by it through the United States Shipping Board Emergency Fleet Corporation, or through any other corporation organized by it for such purpose.
The White House, 11 July, 1917.

CC MS (W. Denman Papers, CU).

To George Washington Goethals

My dear General Goethals: The White House 11 July, 1917

I have given very mature consideration to the question of how it is best to handle the ship-building programme and have come to the conclusion, after talking the matter over with disin-terested persons who I thought could check my own judgment, that the original arrangement ought not to be disturbed.

This will not in any way hamper your own activities. I find everybody willing and anxious to contribute to the completion of the programme you have entered upon and to the efficiency of the work you are doing, and I know that the directors of the Emergency Fleet Corporation share my desire that you should not in any way be hampered. Therefore, I am signing the Executive Orders requested by the Shipping Board upon purely business considerations.

May I not express the pleasure we all have in dealing with you and cooperating with you in this all-important national service?
        Cordially and sincerely yours,   Woodrow Wilson

TLS (G. W. Goethals Papers, DLC).

From Joseph Patrick Tumulty

[The White House] July eleventh [1917].

Mr. George Creel would like to know how the President wants this query answered.[1]   The Secretary.

TL (WP, DLC).
[1] Albert Johnson, Republican congressman from the State of Washington, to G. Creel, c. July 11, 1917. Johnson inquired about the circulation of the *Official Bulletin* and the number of persons employed by it. White House memorandum, T MS (WP, DLC).

To Joseph Patrick Tumulty

[The White House, c. July 11, 1917]

I would suggest that Creel say that the Committee on Public Information was created by me, that Mr. Creel is my personal representative, and that he feels constrained in the circumstances to refer to all inquiries about the Committee and the work it is doing to me.   The President.

TL (WP, DLC).

To Joseph Irwin France

My dear Senator France: [The White House] 11 July 1917.

Mr. Tumulty has placed in my hands your letter to him of July tenth.[1] I wish very much that it were possible for me to see the delegation of colored citizens of whom you speak. Knowing their errand and wishing in every way possible to promote the safety and welfare of our colored fellow-citizens, I am sure I should listen to their representations with entire sympathy, but, unfortunately, it is imperative for me to conserve my time as much as is practicable, and I write to beg you to assure those who made this request of you that through the Department of Justice, through the Department of Labor, and through every other channel open to me I am doing and will do my utmost to safeguard the interests of the colored people who are, of course, as much entitled to our protection and support as any other citizens of the United States, and that you will request them in view of these assurances to excuse me for the present at any rate from a personal interview.

Cordially and sincerely yours,   Woodrow Wilson

TLS (Letterpress Books, WP, DLC).
  [1] J. I. France to JPT, July 10, 1917, TLS (WP, DLC).

To Thomas Watt Gregory

Strictly Confidential.

The White House

My dear Mr. Attorney General: 11 July, 1917

Some time ago you told me that you thought that the nomination of Mr. Ewing,[1] now head of the Patent Office, afforded the best solution as to the vacant judgeship in New York, and when you stated that conclusion to me I knew of nothing which would have justified my differing with you in it, but I have since become convinced that we can hardly make that appointment wisely, and I want frankly to lay these reasons before you:

First, Mr. Ewing is desired in that office by ex-Senator O'Gorman whose principles in picking out men to recommend for office I have learned thoroughly to distrust.

Second, Mr. Ewing is a Roman Catholic, but not of the genuine and democratic sort we are accustomed to associate in our minds with that church. He is of the class of the privileged and the socially ambitious and, therefore, prefers affiliations which in my view are very unwholesome for a judge.

Moreover, I think it is legitimate to consider the fact, which I now find to be true, that he has been far from being a loyal supporter of the administration, seeming ready at any time to get on some other "band wagon." Some of the details of this I can tell you some time.

I know that you will be interested in all this.

Cordially and faithfully yours,   Woodrow Wilson

TLS (T. W. Gregory Papers, DLC).
¹ Thomas Ewing, formerly a patent lawyer of New York.

From Edward Mandell House

Dear Governor: Magnolia, Massachusetts. July 11, 1917.

Since Balfour's cable I have been keeping in intimate touch with the financial differences between the British Government and the Treasury Department, and I am glad to tell you that everything seems on the road to an amicable adjustment.

I do not believe the fault was with McAdoo, further than his office is not properly organized for the strain that has been put upon it.

I have brought McAdoo and Wiseman in touch, and since Sir William is sympathetic with McAdoo's point of view, I believe another such crisis can be avoided in the future. It will be necessary, however, for the British to send out another financial man. Lever undoubtedly sees things from the Morgan point of view, and I do not blame McAdoo for not wanting to continue relations with him.   Affectionately yours,   E. M. House

TLS (WP, DLC).

From Bernard Mannes Baruch

My dear Mr. President: Washington, D. C. July 11th, 1917.

Yesterday the Advisory Commission was shown for the first time the plan of re-organization as proposed by the Council of National Defense.[1] I do not agree with the re-organization as being a wise one or an improvement upon the present plan.

In view of the fact that you have done me the honor to consult me about it in the past, I deem it my duty to so inform you. In case you desire to hear my further views upon it, I am at your command.

Very sincerely yours,   Bernard M Baruch

TLS (WP, DLC).

[1] That is, the plan described in NDB to WW, June 13, 1917, Vol. 42. It provided, among other things, for a War Industries Board to replace the General Munitions Board. A general description of the plan was printed in the *New York Times*, June 24, 1917. It stated that Baruch was likely to be in charge of raw materials and Julius Rosenwald of finished products. For further information on discussion of the proposed reorganization, see Franklin H. Martin, comp., *Digest of the Proceedings of the Council of National Defense during the World War* (Washington, 1934), pp. 218-35, and Cuff, *The War Industries Board*, pp. 86-112.

From Kenneth Douglas McKellar

My dear Mr. President: [Washington] July 11th, 1917.

Your letter of the 9th received and carefully noted.

I am delighted to know that the advisory instrumentalities associated with the Council of National Defense are going to be reorganized. It is also gratifying to know that these gentlemen are going to be put in the relation which was originally intended under the Act creating this Board. And it is most gratifying to know that they are not to be connected, either with the initiation or the conclusion of contracts.

With this done, Mr. President, they need not fear in the least the proposed prohibitions of Section 3 of the Food Act in question. There is nothing whatever in Section 3 or in the present law that should make it necessary for you to dispense with the services of these men under the conditions stated in your letter. There is nothing whatever in these provisions that prohibits the men who are in actual control of the great business enterprises of the Country from giving you the most cordial, active and unembarrassed cooperation.

As I understand it, these men are all serving the Government now, without hope of gain or profit to themselves and purely for patriotism, and now that their attention has been called to the matter I am quite sure that they will not be any the less co-operative or any the less patriotic, since they have found that they will not be able to make gains or contracts for themselves or their firms or corporations while engaged in this splendid patriotic service.

Personally, it is very gratifying to know that there will be no conduct of the Advisory Board or its Committees in the future of the character which I criticised in my speech of July 3rd. Mr. President, permit me to say that I appreciate to the limit the spirit of fairness to both sides shown in your letter, which is in keeping with what everybody knows is your intense desire to be just in all matters, great or small.

With great respect, I am

Sincerely your friend,   Kenneth McKellar

TLS (WP, DLC).

Richard Crane to Joseph Patrick Tumulty, with Enclosure

My dear Mr. Tumulty: Washington July 11, 1917.

I am enclosing herewith a copy of a telegram which I have just received from my father in Petrograd.

I believe that the President would be interested in seeing this.

Yours very truly,   Richard Crane

TLS (WP, DLC).

ENCLOSURE

Petrograd. July 6, 1917.

1476. Sixth. For Richard Crane. Mr. Mott and I have just made our third journey to Moscow. This time it has been to assist at the election of the New Metropolitan.[1] The election took place in the Church of the Savior and followed the new form through delegates chosen by universal suffrage in the diocese. This form was also a reversion to the practice of the church in the earlier centuries and so was very impressive. The delegates met the day before and voted unanimously to invite Mr. Mott and me to take part in the proceedings on the floor of the church. Before the election Mr. Mott and I were taken behind the alter of the Cathedral and each one given with a very pretty ceremony a rare old ikon from the ikonastaf of the Uspensky Cathedral of the

Kremlin. *Lod* [Old] Russians say that this ceremony is most un-usual. And it is doubtful if it has ever occurred before with people not of the orthodox faith. Mr. Motts visit has made a profound impression on the minds and hearts of the Russian people and will be remembered for a century. Much in it recalled the other visit with President Harper.[2] He returns home with a wider and deeper understanding of the present day Russia and her prob-lems than anyone else who has come here since President Harper. He has seen a great variety of people and the wonderful sympathy and understanding has caused them to speak to him as I have known them to speak to no one else before. On his arrival home he would probably be willing to make a general public statement for the MONITOR.[3] I personally am very happy about his visit and entirely content with the message he takes home. In the general anarchy prevailing in Russian affairs the church gives the note of perfect order not only in its church service but also in its very extensive organization. It is a com-fort to follow the orderly processes of its evolution. Mr. Masaryk is also here. The commis[s]ion bears messages from me. I feel that I should remain somewhat longer as my own work *with* [was] much interrupted by my duties on the commission. The Russian ship is still in the trough of the seas and I should like to see her headed on her new course before leaving if more im-portant things at home do not demand my return. Affectionate messages. Father.   Francis.

T telegram (WP, DLC).
    [1] Archbishop Tikhon (Vasili Ivanovich Belyavin). As a bishop, he had been head of the Russian eparchy in North America, at San Francisco, from 1898 to 1907.
    [2] For a brief account of William Rainey Harper's visit to Russia in 1900, see Paul V. Harper, ed., *The Russia I Believe In: The Memoirs of Samuel N. Harper, 1902-1941* (Chicago, 1945), pp. 6-7.
    [3] *The Christian Science Monitor.*

Frank Lyon Polk to Walter Hines Page

Washington, July 11, 1917.

5129 Your 6599 has been referred to the President and the decision reached that, while Mr. Balfour's cordial invitation is greatly appreciated, this Government is not ready at the present time to take part in the inter-allied war conferences.

Polk Acting.

T telegram (SDR, RG 59, 763.72/5646, DNA).

A Statement to the American People[1]

[July 12, 1917]

My Fellow Countrymen: The government is about to attempt to determine the prices at which it will ask you henceforth to furnish various supplies which are necessary for the prosecution of the war and various materials which will be needed in the industries by which the war must be sustained. We shall of course try to determine them justly and to the best advantage of the nation as a whole; but justice is easier to speak of than to arrive at, and there are some considerations which I hope we shall all keep steadily in mind while this particular problem of justice is being worked out. I therefore take the liberty of stating very candidly my own view of the situation and of the principles which should guide both the government and the mine owners and manufacturers of the country in this difficult matter.

A *just* price must, of course, be paid for everything the government buys. By a just price I mean a price which will sustain the industries concerned in a high state of efficiency, provide a living for those who conduct them, enable them to pay good wages, and make possible the expansions of their enterprises which will from time to time become necessary as the stupendous undertakings of this great war develop. We could not wisely or reasonably do less than pay such prices. They are necessary for the maintenance and development of industry; and the maintenance and development of industry are necessary for the great task we have in hand. But I trust that we shall not surround the matter with a mist of sentiment. Facts are our masters now. We ought not to put the acceptance of such prices on the ground of patriotism. Patriotism has nothing to do with profits in a case like this. Patriotism and profits ought never in the present circumstances be mentioned together.

It is perfectly proper to discuss profits as a matter of business, with a view to maintaining the integrity of capital and the efficiency of labor in these tragical months when the liberty of free men everywhere and of industry itself trembles in the balance; but it would be absurd to discuss them as a motive for helping to serve and save our country. Patriotism leaves profits out of the question. In these days of our supreme trial, when we are sending hundreds of thousands of our young men across the seas to serve a great cause, no true man who stays behind to work for them and sustain them by his labor will ask himself what he is personally going to make out of that labor. No true patriot will permit himself to take toll of their heroism in money or seek to grow rich by the shedding of their blood. He will give as freely and with as unstinted self-sacrifice as they. When they are giving their lives will he not give at least his money?

I hear it insisted that more than a just price, more than a price that will sustain our industries, must be paid; that it is necessary to pay very liberal and unusual profits in order to "stimulate" production; that nothing but pecuniary rewards will do it—rewards paid in money, not in the mere liberation of the world. I take it for granted that those who argue thus do not stop to think what that means. Do they mean that you must be paid, must be bribed, to make your contribution, a contribution that costs you neither a drop of blood nor a tear, when the whole world is in travail and men everywhere depend upon and call to you to bring them out of bondage and make the world a fit place to live in again amidst peace and justice? Do they mean that you will exact a price, drive a bargain, with the men who are enduring the agony of this war on the battlefield, in the trenches, amidst the lurking dangers of the sea, or with the bereaved women and the pitiful children before you will come forward to do your duty and give some part of your life, in easy peaceful fashion, for the things we are fighting for, the things we have pledged our fortunes, our lives, our sacred honor to vindicate and defend—liberty and justice and fair dealing and the peace of nations? Of course you will not. It is inconceivable.

Your patriotism is of the same self-denying stuff as the patriotism of the men dead or maimed on the fields of France or else it is no patriotism at all. Let us never speak, then, of profits and of patriotism in the same sentence, but face facts and meet them. Let us do sound business, but not in the midst of a mist. Many a grievous burden of taxation will be laid on this nation, in this generation and in the next, to pay for this war; let us see to it that for every dollar that is taken from the people's pockets it shall be possible to obtain a dollar's worth of the sound stuffs they need.

Let me turn for a moment to the shipowners of the United States and the other ocean carriers whose example they have followed and ask them if they realize what obstacles, what almost insuperable obstacles, they have been putting in the way of the successful prosecution of this war by the ocean freight rates they have been exacting. They are doing everything that high freight charges can do to make the war a failure, to make it impossible. I do not say that they realize this or intend it. The thing has happened naturally enough, because the commercial processes which we are content to see operate in ordinary times have, without sufficient thought, been continued into a period where they have no proper place.

I am not questioning motives. I am merely stating a fact, and stating it in order that attention may be fixed upon it. The fact is that those who have fixed war freight rates have taken the most effective means in their power to defeat the armies engaged against Germany. When they realize this, we may, I take it for granted, count upon them to reconsider the whole matter. It is high time. Their extra hazards are covered by war-risk insurance.

I know, and you know, what response to this great challenge of duty and of opportunity the nation will expect of you; and I know what response you will make. Those who do not respond, who do not respond in the spirit of those who have gone to give their lives for us on bloody fields far away, may safely be left to be dealt with by opinion and the law, for the law must of course command these things. I am dealing with the matter thus publicly and frankly, not because I have any doubt or fear as to the result, but only in order that in all our thinking and in all our dealings with one another we may move in a perfectly clear air of mutual understanding.

And there is something more that we must add to our thinking. The public is now as much part of the government as are the army and navy themselves; the whole people in all their activities are now mobilized and in service for the accomplishment of the nation's task in this war; it is in such circumstances impossible justly to distinguish between industrial purchases made by the government and industrial purchases made by the managers of individual industries; and it is just as much our duty to sustain the industries of the country, all the industries that contribute to its life, as it is to sustain our forces in the field and on the sea.

We must make the prices to the public the same as the prices to the government. Prices mean the same thing everywhere now. They mean the efficiency or the inefficiency of the nation, whether it is the government that pays them or not. They mean victory or defeat. They mean that America will win her place once for all among the foremost free nations of the world, or that she will sink to defeat and become a second-rate power alike in thought and in action. This is a day of her reckoning, and every man among us must personally face that reckoning along with her.

The case needs no arguing. I assume that I am only expressing your own thoughts—what must be in the mind of every true man when he faces the tragedy and the solemn glory of the present war for the emancipation of mankind. I summon you to a great duty, a great privilege, a shining dignity, and distinction. I shall expect every man who is not a slacker to be at my side throughout this great enterprise. In it no man can win honor who thinks of himself.

Printed in the *Official Bulletin*, I (July 12, 1917), 3, 7.
  [1] There is a WWsh outline, a WWsh draft, and a WWT draft of the following document in WP, DLC.

To Edward Beale McLean

My dear Mr. McLean: [The White House] 12 July, 1917

The Mexican Ambassador has called my attention to an article recently appearing in the Washington Post under the name of "Ryley Grannon" to which he has made a protest to the Secretary of State.[1] This is one of a series of articles of misrepresentation and distortion of fact which have recently appeared in the Post under this name.

I do not believe that you would permit the Post to be used for the embarrassment of the nation, especially now that it is engaged in war, but I am bound in frankness to say that the character of these articles has made me feel that the Post, consciously or unconsciously, is conducting a propaganda for the embarrassment of the nation in its relations with the Allies and in the conduct of its own war against the German Government. I am loath to believe that these misrepresentations have been made by your direction.

I have no desire to suggest any limitation or criticism of the Government, but in view of our friendly talk at the White House shortly after you assumed control of the Post,[2] I do feel free to call your personal attention to this series of misrepresentations by the unknown writer who calls himself Ryley Grannon.
                    Sincerely yours,   Woodrow Wilson

TLS (Letterpress Books, WP, DLC).
  [1] I. Bonillas to RL, July 11, 1917, CCLS (WP, DLC).
  [2] At some time in late 1916 or 1917. McLean became editor of the *Washington Post* in December 1916. The White House and Executive Office diaries do not record their meeting.

To Thomas Watt Gregory

My dear Gregory: [The White House] 12 July, 1917

You may remember that the other day I spoke jestingly at the Cabinet about my perplexity concerning the varying counsels among the several departments having secret service with regard to a correlation of those services. Underneath the jest, of course, lay a very serious difficulty and I am writing now to ask if you would be generous enough to cooperate with the Secretary of the Treasury and Mr. Polk in working out for me a plan for the cooperation of these services into which we can all enter with spirit and effect. I am genuinely in need of counsel in this matter and am sure that you three can compound a plan which will be worth acting upon.

    Cordially and faithfully yours,   Woodrow Wilson

TLS (Letterpress Books, WP, DLC).

From Josephus Daniels, with Enclosure

Dear Mr. President: Washington. July 12. 1917

    I am enclosing a statement dictated by Secretary Baker as a result of our conference with the steel men. They came in good shape. Your statement this morning convinced them as it will hearten the whole country. I think the result is an achievement that must make you happy, for it opens the way to make "profiteering" on the same plane with slackers.

    Sincerely   Josephus Daniels

ALS (WP, DLC).

E N C L O S U R E

WAR DEPARTMENT
WASHINGTON

July 12, 1917

    At the conference this morning between the Committee of the American Iron and Steel Institute and the Secretary of War, the Secretary of the Navy, the Chairman of the Shipping Board, and Mr. Baruch, further discussion was had of the prospective demand upon the steel industry of the country for supplies of various steel products for carrying on the war. The steel men repeated their assurance that their entire product would be available for the need and that they were doing everything possible to stimulate an increased production and speed deliveries. The price to be paid for the iron and steel products furnished was left to be determined after the inquiry by the Federal Trade Commission is completed, with the understanding that the price, when fixed, would insure reasonable profits and be made with reference to the expanding needs of this vital and fundamental industry.

The representatives of the Government assured the Committee of the Steel Institute that it was the intention of the Government to distribute the war requirements over the entire iron and steel producing capacity of the country.

T MS (WP, DLC).

To Josephus Daniels

My dear Daniels: The White House 12 July, 1917

Thank you warmly for your memorandum about the conference with the Committee of the American Iron and Steel Institute. Your letter is indeed gratifying and I am very happy that you should feel as you do about my statement published this morning.

In haste   Faithfully yours,   Woodrow Wilson

TLS (J. Daniels Papers, DLC).

To Newton Diehl Baker

My dear Mr. Secretary: The White House 12 July, 1917

I don't quite understand the enclosed letter from Baruch. Do you happen to know what he objects to in the new plan?[1]

In haste   Faithfully yours,   Woodrow Wilson

TLS (N. D. Baker Papers, DLC).

[1] Baruch, at a meeting of the Council of National Defense and its Advisory Commission on July 13, explained his objections. He said that the proposed W.I.B. had no decision-making authority and that it and the Advisory Commission would continue to be "debating societies." Also "One of the principal things expected is to stop public criticism because of relations of business men. The present plan would only enrage as it looks like an endeavor to fool the people. Better defend and explain relations which are correct If not correct let us stop them." Diary of Bernard M. Baruch, entry for July 13, 1917, Hw bound diary (B. M. Baruch Papers, NjP).

From Joseph Patrick Tumulty, with Enclosure

Dear Governor: The White House. July 12, 1917.

By reason of your absence at the theater and not wishing to disturb you I took up this matter with the Secretary of War, who informed me that he had notified General Parker,[1] at Fort Sam Houston, to send his officers to Arizona to acquaint him—Parker —with the conditions there and to act upon the request of Governor Campbell that troops be sent there at once. The Secretary of War thinks it would be well if you would reply tonight saying that the Secretary of War has notified you of the above instructions to General Parker. The Secretary thinks it would be wise if in your telegram to Governor Campbell you would say that you look with grave apprehension on the efforts being made by the citizens of Arizona to deport wholesale those who are merely accused of being members of the I.W.W. That it is establishing a dangerous precedent for citizens of any state to take the law in their own hands in matters as grave as this. The Secretary also thinks it would be wise for you to urge caution in the matter.

J.P.T.

TL (WP, DLC).
1 Brig. Gen. James Parker, U.S.A., commander of the Southern Department.

E N C L O S U R E

Phoenix, Arizona, July 12, 1917.

Industrial conditions throughout Arizona, due to presence of large numbers of members Industrial Workers of the World, coming from outside the state and agitating their propaganda, are rapidly getting beyond the control of peace officers. There are no state troops under my authority, all Arizona National Guard being in Federal Service, making it impossible for me to use this force for the preservation of peace. At Bisbee today, fifteen hundred citizens rounded up approximately twelve hundred Industrial Workers of the World and other alleged undesirable citizens, deporting them by rail en route to Columbus, New Mexico. At Jerome, similar action was taken by citizens, with result that sixty one similar characters were deported Tuesday enroute to California, being stopped at the California line at Needles, California, and returned to Kingman, Arizona.

I instructed Sheriff at Kingman to release these people, except in cases where legal charges would hold against them. This was done. Citizens in the many mining communities affected, feeling that peace officers cannot afford adequate protection, are acting as hereinbefore stated, meantime praying for federal intervention. I have recommended to General Parker, commanding at Fort Sam Houston, with whom I am in constant telegraphic communication, that troops be immediately dispatched to Bisbee, Kingman, Jerome, Humboldt, Ajo, Ray, Clifton and Morenci, that peace be maintained, important mining industries continued and recurrence of such affairs as at Bisbee and Jerome prevented.

This movement on the part of the I.W.W. is general throughout the western mining states, with particular activity centered at the present time on Arizona copper production, seventy five percent of which is idle today.

It is generally believed that strong pro-German influence is back of this movement, as the I.W.W. appear well financed and are daily getting inton [into] their ranks many aliens, particularly Austrians.

I am unable to ascertain definitely activity of pro-German influence, but the result remains, in so far as copper production is concerned.

I consider the situation in Arizona sufficiently serious to warrant immediate federal intervention and am most anxious to cooperate with such forces as will allay present civic and industrial situation.   Thomas E. Campbell.

T telegram (WP, DLC).

To Thomas Edward Campbell

[The White House] July 12, 1917.

Secretary of War has instructed General Parker to send officers to Arizona at once to report to him conditions there with a view to cooperating in maintenance of order. Meantime may I not respectfully urge the great danger of citizens taking the law in their own hands as you report their having done. I look upon such action with grave apprehension. A very serious responsibility is assumed when such precedents are set.[1]

Woodrow Wilson.

T telegram (Letterpress Books, WP, DLC).
[1] Wilson's message was made available to newspapers in Phoenix on July 13. Also, it was reported at El Paso that Brig. Gen. George Bell, Jr., the district commander, had received orders to provide rations for the men deported from Bisbee. Bell issued orders to bring them from Hermanas to Columbus, N. M., and to provide them with rations until further notice. The men would not be prisoners, Bell said. *New York Times*, July 14, 1917.

From Louis Bernard Whitney[1]

Phoenix, Ariz., July 12, 1917

Fifteen hundred armed members citizens protective league Bisbee, Arizona, made house to house canvas and deported in cattle cars. Those who refused to work in mines eleven hundred ninety three including three women deported. State officials absolutely powerless to act because State troops in Federal service. I implore you to send Federal troops to Bisbee so men will get protection when they return to families. Fear bloodshed if this wrong not redressed by Government. Understand all gunmen Bisbee in employ of mining companies. Arizona in deplorable conditions. Companies refuse to treat with any Federal mediator. Advise.[2]   Louis B. Whitney.

T telegram (WP, DLC).
[1] Assistant Attorney General of Arizona.
[2] Swem recorded this instruction by Wilson: "Please let this gentleman know briefly what is being done." A pencil note indicates that a telegram was sent on July 13. T memorandum by C. L. Swem [July 12, 1917] (WP, DLC). The telegram is missing, but it presumably referred to Wilson's telegram to T. E. Campbell, July 12, and the orders to General Bell.

Two Letters from Frank Lyon Polk

My dear Mr. President: Washington July 12, 1917.

I enclose an interesting despatch from Morgenthau.[1] It was badly mangled in transmission and the cipher experts are still working on it. I hope to have a better copy for you tomorrow. This is the message referred to in the despatch from Frankfurter which I sent you today.[2]

Yours faithfully,   Frank L Polk

July 13 President directed me to express surprise at his evident going beyond instruction, to tell him to proceed to Cairo with Frankfurter.[3]

TLS (F. L. Polk Papers, CtY).
[1] J. E. Willard to RL, July 8, 1917, T telegram (F. L. Polk Papers, CtY). This message, signed "Special Agents" (Morgenthau and Frankfurter), was transmitted as Willard's telegram No. 670 from Madrid. The text, corrected by comparison with the text later received by mail, is printed in FR-WWS 1917, 2, I, 120-22. The two special agents had met in Gibraltar on July 4 and 5 with Chaim Weizmann, representing Great Britain, and Col. E. Weyl, representing France, and had discussed the situation with regard to Turkey. The telegram reported that recent political and military developments and the strong recommendations of their British and French colleagues had led the Americans to believe that the time was "not ripe" for negotiations with Turkey. The telegram also quoted in full a document signed by the four men as a report to their respective governments. It noted that the American representatives had set forth Wilson's views regarding a possible approach to Turkey. The report also summarized the discussions and stated the agreed conclusion that Allied military success had to precede any diplomatic démarches. Weizmann's copy of this report, with minor differences from the American text, is printed in The Letters and Papers of Chaim Weizmann, Series A (7 vols., London, 1968-75), VII, 465-67. This volume gives additional information about the Morgenthau mission, the meeting at Gibraltar, and British and French views on the Turkish and Palestinian questions.
[2] J. E. Willard to RL, July 8, 1917, T telegram (F. L. Polk Papers, CtY). This "extremely confidential" message from Frankfurter to Polk and Brandeis was sent as telegram No. 671 from Madrid. Frankfurter reported that Weizmann had said that the British Foreign Office wanted Zionists, especially Americans, to go to Russia to influence Jewish opinion there. Frankfurter thought that this would be desirable from the American point of view, and he suggested that,

if Wilson approved, he might go to Russia with Lewis Epstein (Eliahu Ze'ev Halevi Lewin-Epstein), a wine importer in New York, and Max Lowenthal, a lawyer, both of whom were with the Morgenthau mission.

3 Polk, in a telegram of July 14, informed Morgenthau that the State Department had been "surprised and disturbed" to learn that he apparently believed that he was authorized to negotiate for a separate peace with Turkey. Polk reminded Morgenthau that his final instruction had been to deal solely with the conditions of Jews in Palestine, and he concluded as follows: "The President requests that you and Frankfurter proceed to Cairo to carry out announced purpose of the mission, and that under no circumstances should you confer, discuss, or carry messages on any subject relating to the international situation in Turkey or bearing upon a separate peace." *FR-WWS 1917*, 2, I, 129. Polk's admonition was transmitted as telegram No. 2446 to Paris.

My dear Mr. President: Washington July 12, 1917.

The representative in Washington of the *de facto* Government of Costa Rica has withdrawn, on instructions from his Government. His withdrawal was the occasion of his addressing to the Secretary of State a communication which you may desire to see.[1]

I am accordingly enclosing a copy thereof herewith, together with a brief summary of the contents of the note.

I am, my dear Mr. President,

Faithfully yours,   Frank L Polk

TLS (WP, DLC).

[1] Lansing, "by the express direction of the President of the United States," on June 9 had instructed the American Chargé in San José, Stewart Johnson, to reaffirm to General Tinoco Wilson's previously expressed determination not to recognize him as President of Costa Rica. Johnson was also instructed to urge Tinoco to retire in the immediate future. Tinoco's agent in Washington, Ricardo Fernández Guardia, on July 4 addressed to Lansing a note which expressed chagrin over his country's failure to maintain friendly relations with the United States and asserted that failure to recognize a government in undisputed control of a country was a form of intervention in that country's internal affairs. The letter quoted Jefferson, Clay, Pierce, and Wilson, himself, to show that Tinoco's regime should be recognized. R. Fernández Guardia to RL, July 4, 1917, printed translation of letter, with attached summary by John Foster Dulles and Edith B. Newman, TI memorandum, both in WP, DLC. Lansing's instructions and a translation of Fernández Guardia's letter are printed in *FR 1917*, pp. 326-27, 332-37.

From Herbert Clark Hoover

Dear Mr. President: Washington July 12, 1917.

Considerable effort will be made in the Senate to secure the substitution of Mr. Gore's amended bill,[1] though I am uncertain as to what the possibilities of success are in this effort. I enclose for your information some notes on Mr. Gore's substitute[2] which have been furnished me by Judge Curtis Lindley who is assisting us on the legal side.

I would like to point out in this matter that Mr. Gore's sub-

stitute extracts absolutely the whole of the teeth from the bill
and renders it impossible for us to control speculation, for it
reduces the hoarding and board of trade provisions to a nullity
and makes it impossible for us to control wasteful practices in
distribution and manufacture and impossible to control extortion
in profits and charges. If the bill should pass Congress in this
form the whole objective of the Food Administration in the sense
of securing for the consumer in this country foodstuffs at a reasonable ratio to the return to the producer, is entirely hopeless.
I may also mention that the form of administration proposed by
Mr. Gore also destroys the whole question of the imaginative
side of leadership of yourself and sense of volunteer service in
the interest of the Nation, which is absolutely critical in order to
amass the devotion of the people. I simply cannot hope to secure
this sort of administration if it is to be controlled by a meticulous
"board" with its impossible mixture of irresponsible executive and
advisory functions. Moreover, at your wish the Food Administration was launched upon this basis and it becomes merely a drive
at yourself personally and to a lesser degree at me.

    I remain,   Your obedient servant,   Herbert Hoover

TLS (WP, DLC).
  1 Following Gore's report of June 27 on the amended Lever bill, H.R. 4961
(described in H. C. Hoover to WW, June 29, 1917), the Oklahoman had introduced a substitute for the entire Lever bill on July 10, with further changes on
July 11. Gore's substitute called for a three- or five-member Board of Food
Administration, instead of the single Food Administrator desired by Wilson.
Gore's substitute also imposed fewer controls and made different provisions
for enforcement. Also, it empowered the President to commandeer stocks of
whisky in bond, when he considered it necessary, and to determine just compensation to the owners of stocks taken over. This provision was not expected
to be adopted, but it was considered likely to open the way for a compromise
on the prohibition issue. *New York Times*, July 11, 1917; *Cong. Record*, 65th
Cong., 1st sess., p. 4902.
  2 This enclosure is missing.

To Thomas Watt Gregory, with Enclosure

                                The White House
My dear Mr. Attorney General: 13 July, 1917
    What do you think of the enclosed? Please do not reply in
writing because I know it would involve profanity!
               Faithfully yours,   Woodrow Wilson

TLS (T. W. Gregory Papers, DLC).

E N C L O S U R E

From Hoke Smith

Dear Mr. President: Washington, D. C. July 12th, 1917.

Your note of the 11th has just been received.[1]

With your multitude of responsibilities in connection with the war, I am unwilling to worry you with smaller matters, and certainly would not have you troubled about minor courtesies.

Without reference to the differences between the Attorney General and Senator Hardwick, and even if Senator Hardwick had desired his nomination, I would object to Judge Thomas[2] for the position of District Court Judge for the Southern District of Georgia.

I regard him as having no special qualifications for the place. He was an active candidate for Congress last year while on the Bench, and an inactive candidate for one or two other places.

He gives too much time on the Bench to his own political ambition, and I lack that confidence in his devotion to the high responsibilities of the office which I think he should possess.[3]

Very respectfully,   Hoke Smith

TLS (T. W. Gregory Papers, DLC).
[1] WW to H. Smith, July 11, 1917, TLS (Letterpress Books, WP, DLC).
[2] William E. Thomas, of Valdosta, Ga., had been solicitor-general of the southern circuit of the Superior Court of Georgia, 1897-1911, and judge of that circuit since 1911.
[3] The Senate rejected the nomination of Thomas on July 12. *Cong. Record*, 65th Cong., 1st sess., p. 5027.

To Thomas Staples Martin

My dear Senator: [The White House] 13 July, 1917

After you and Senator Simmons left me yesterday I applied myself to a very careful study of the bill you left with me,—the bill which, as I understand, is to be introduced as a proposed substitute for the pending Food Administration Bill. Upon examining the bill I was amazed and distressed to find that in practically every important particular it emasculates the original measure, except as regards the provision concerning the use of foodstuffs in liquors. I feel that it would be fatal to pass it or to substitute any part of it except that which I have mentioned for the bill upon the consideration of which the Senate has been engaged. I cannot help believing that it was the intention of whoever framed this bill to rob the proposed legislation of practically all its effective features.[1]

I would not be so unqualified in these statements if I had not scrutinized the bill with the utmost particularity. I have been amazed to find how carefully, and sometimes how subtly, the effective features of the proposed legislation have been eliminated and the whole character of the bill as an administrative measure weakened and rendered unworkable.

I, therefore, hope, my dear Senator, most sincerely that so much of the original bill as concerned Food Administration will be passed by the Senate as finally reported by the committee. Undoubtedly that legislation in its main features is what is expected and I may even say demanded by the country.

May I not also express the earnest hope that the passage of this legislation may be accomplished within the shortest possible time? The delay which has already occurred, and which has arisen out of the opposition of those who are for the most part opposed to the legislation altogether, has caused incalculable injury to the country, and every day of delay adds to the injury and to the embarrassment. The Senate could render no greater public service than by curtailing the process of consideration as much as possible and pressing the bill to a very early passage.

If it were necessary, I could go into the details of the bill section by section which justify my opinion of it, but I feel confident that you yourself will be convinced of the justice of my judgment if you will give the substitute a more detailed examination than you said you had been able to give when I saw you yesterday.

Cordially and sincerely yours,   [Woodrow Wilson]

CCL (WP, DLC).
¹ Gore withdrew his substitute bill on July 21 upon the pretext that most of its provisions had been "transferred into the pending bill upon the installment plan." *Cong. Record*, 65th Cong., 1st sess., p. 5365.

To Kenneth Douglas McKellar

My dear Senator: [The White House] 13 July, 1917

Thank you for your letter of the eleventh.

I am sorry to say that I cannot construe the language of the provision about which we have been having such an interesting correspondence as you interpret it. It is to the effect that nobody connected with the Government or any of its instrumentalities, though even in an advisory capacity, may *procure* a contract. That would make it impossible for us to advise with any of the real producers of the country, for they are the only ones with whom we can possibly make contracts, and it would be impossible to discriminate between their procuring and receiving them if they were in conference with us about the supplies.

I think you will understand how imperatively necessary it is that we should be in constant conference with the committees of the producers in order to ascertain what the supply is, where we can get it, in what quantities and qualities, and when and how fast.

In haste

Cordially and faithfully yours,   Woodrow Wilson

TLS (Letterpress Books, WP, DLC).

To Amos Richards Eno Pinchot

My dear Mr. Pinchot: [The White House] 13 July, 1917

The letter of yesterday signed by yourself, Mr. Eastman, and Mr. Reed has just been laid before me and you may be sure has been read with a great deal of interest and sympathy. I am going to take the matter you present about the paper called The Masses up with the Postmaster General to see just how the case may best and most justly be handled.

You will understand, I am sure, why I would hesitate to make a public statement such as you suggest. It would undoubtedly be taken advantage of by those with whom neither you nor I have been in sympathy at all.

In haste

Cordially and sincerely yours,   Woodrow Wilson

TLS (Letterpress Books, WP, DLC).

To Albert Sidney Burleson, with Enclosure

My dear Burleson: The White House 13 July, 1917

May I not have your advice as to the enclosed? These are very sincere men and I should like to please them.

Cordially and faithfully yours,   Woodrow Wilson

TLS (WP, DLC).

From Max Eastman and Others

My dear President Wilson: New York July 12, 1917.

May we appeal to you for advice and for an expression of opinion upon a serious problem of the time.

A number of the smaller papers and magazines, to some of which we contribute, either editorially or otherwise, have been practically suspended or suppressed by the action of Solicitor Lamar[1] in denying them the use of the mails. Among these publications are the following:

The Jeffersonian, Augusta; The American Socialist, Chicago; The Masses, New York; International Socialist Review, Chicago; Social Revolution, St. Louis; People's Press, Philadelphia; the Socialist News, Cleveland; the Michigan Socialist, Detroit; St. Louis Labor, St. Louis; The Rebel, Halletsville, Texas; Appeal to Reason, Girard, Kan.; Four Lights, New York.

In suppressing the MASSES, in which we are particularly interested, he has refused to make complaint against any specific article appearing in it, but simply declares the "general tenor" of the magazine unmailable under the Espionage Law. This leaves the editors in such uncertainty as to make it practically impossible for them to make up the magazine.

The MASSES has been studious not to publish anything unmailable under the law, because the editors are anxious in this crisis to put their opinions before the public. And what we wish to ask you is, whether you think that free criticism, right or wrong, of the policy of the government ought to be denied at this time the right of public expression.

Is it not of the utmost importance in a democracy that the opposition to the government have a free voice? Can it be necessary, even in war time, for the majority of a republic to throttle the voice of a sincere minority?

This seems to us to be a public question of such importance as to call for an expression of opinion from you. And also, it is to us personally a matter of so much moment that we ask you for personal advice. As friends of yours, and knowing how dear to you is the Anglo-Saxon tradition of intellectual freedom, we would like to feel that you do not sanction the exercise, by an official of the Post Office, of a bureaucratic discretion, which we believe was never intended by the act of Congress.[2]

Yours sincerely,   Max Eastman
Amos Pinchot
John Reed

TLS (WP, DLC).

[1] William Harmong Lamar, Solicitor of the Post Office Department, 1913-1921; a lawyer in the Department of Justice, 1906-1913.

[2] The Masses Publishing Co., on July 3, presented the issue of *The Masses* of August 1917 at the New York Post Office for mailing. It included cartoons and articles against conscription, a cartoon that showed the Liberty Bell in ruins, and a cartoon that depicted Congress as subservient to big business: "Run along, now! We got through with you when you declared war for us." Another cartoon indicated that the purpose of the Root Mission was to make the world safe for capitalism. The August issue also included an editorial by Max Eastman and a poem, "A Tribute," by Josephine Bell, both of which supported the cause of Alexander Berkman and Emma Goldman, who had recently been convicted of conspiracy to resist the draft.

The publishers, on July 5, received from the postmaster of New York, Thomas Gedney Patten, a letter which stated that, according to advice received from the Solicitor of the Post Office Department, the August issue was "unmailable under the Act of June 15, 1917." *The Masses* retained as counsel Gilbert Ernstein Roe, who entered in the United States district court for the southern district of New York a bill in equity to enjoin Patten from excluding the magazine from the mails. At a hearing on July 21, Earl Bryant Barnes, assistant United States district attorney, said that the Post Office Department construed the Espionage Act as giving it power to exclude from the mails anything which might interfere with the successful conduct of the war. He submitted affidavits by Burleson and Lamar which specified four cartoons and four articles as being in violation of the Act, in that they would "cause insubordination, disloyalty, mutiny and refusal of duty" in the army and navy and obstruct recruiting and enlistment. Roe, on the contrary, argued that the Act was not intended to prohibit political criticism or to establish a censorship set up without warrant of law. "What Happened to the August *Masses*," *The Masses*, IX (Sept. 1917), 3; *New York Times*, July 22, 1917.

Judge Learned Hand, in an extended decision on July 24, granted a preliminary injunction against Patten. Hand wrote: "The [Postmaster's] action was based, as I understand it, not so much upon the narrow question whether these four passages actually advocated resistance, though that point was distinctly raised, as upon the doctrine that the general tenor and animus of the paper as a whole were subversive to authority and seditious in effect. I cannot accept this test under the law as it stands at present. The tradition of English-speaking freedom has depended in no small part upon the merely procedural requirement that the state point with exactness to just that conduct which violates the law. It is difficult and often impossible to meet the charge that one's general ethos is treasonable; such a latitude for construction implies a personal latitude in administration which contradicts the normal assumption that law shall be embodied in general propositions capable of some measure of definition." Hand pointed out that he made "no question of the power of Congress to establish a personal censorship of the press under the war power." That question did not arise in this case. 244 Fed. 535.

Hand's decision included descriptions of the cartoons and quotations of the texts to which Patten and his superiors objected. It is reprinted in *The Art and Craft of Judging: The Decisions of Judge Learned Hand*, Hershel Shanks, ed. (New York, 1968), pp. 84-97. See also Kathryn Griffith, *Judge Learned Hand and the Role of the Federal Judiciary* (Norman, Okla., 1973), pp. 132-33, 142-45.

On the day following Hand's decision, United States Circuit Judge Charles Merrill Hough signed at Hanover, N. H., or Windsor, Vt., an order that stayed execution of it and required the parties to appear before him at Windsor on August 2 to show cause why the stay should not be made permanent pending an appeal taken by Patten. *New York Times*, July 27, 1917. Later, on November 2, the United States Court of Appeals, Second Circuit, unanimously reversed Hand's decision. 246 Fed. 24; *New York Times*, Nov. 3, 1917.

From Edward Mandell House

Dear Governor: Magnolia, Massachusetts. July 13, 1917.

I have a letter from Frank Cobb of the World in which he says:

"There is another little matter which I wish I could discuss with you personally. Before long, the President will have to devote some personal attention to the relations between the newspapers and the Administration, which have become intolerably tangled. It is not necessary to assess the responsibility for the situation, but it is very unfortunate both for the Administration and the press and if something could be done to straighten it out, it would have an immense influence on the conduct of the war."

I am sending you this for your information.

Of course, you know there is trouble brewing between the Council of National Defence and the Advisory Commission. It is the intention of the Commission to resign in a body unless some satisfactory understanding is reached within a week from next Monday. It is their purpose, however, to ask you for an audience before taking decisive action.

I believe a little personal direction on your part at this time will smooth out the differences. Hot weather, over-work and like causes are probably at the bottom of the irritation, and a word of encouragement from you should set matters straight.

Affectionately yours,   E. M. House

TLS (WP, DLC).

From John Franklin Fort

My dear Mr. President: Washington July 13, 1917.

I want to join most heartily with all your friends and supporters in admiration of your splendid address to your countrymen, issued yesterday. You seem, not only, to always say the right thing in a most forceful and able way but to say it in a kindly way and at the most timely moment.

Before I came to Washington I used to wonder how it was possible for you to do, so admirably, all the things you did, and since I have been here and have realized more fully the multitude and magnitude of the things you have to do my marvel has increased.

The unquestioned confidence of the American people in you is becoming more and more unbounded every day, and my knowledge of your superb leadership at close observation only increases my personal admiration. I am delighted, and esteem it a great privilege, to be in a position to stand behind you in your great work.

May the Providence that rules over this nation be especially kind to you is the wish of

Your faithful friend,   John Franklin Fort

TLS (WP, DLC).

From Allen Bartlit Pond[1]

Dear Sir: Chicago July 13th, 1917.

The War Committee of the Union League Club of Chicago is considering the advisability and feasibility of undertaking a rather considerable propaganda. It is the judgment of the Committee, based on observation and hearsay, that a very large number of people in this country are still puzzled as to why America might not have kept out of the European war and why, having got into the war, it may not fight a purely defensive war, and are quite at sea with regard to any obligations resting on America to take account of the deep rooted ambition of the German ruling class and the resultant effect upon permanent peace for America in a settlement of what seem to the uninitiated to be purely local European matters. Not only does this puzzle-headedness weaken the American will to make a vigorous offensive, but it leaves the minds of the people who are thus confused open to influence by the energetic and scarcely disguised German propaganda which is being vigorously carried forward, partly under the guise of an open advocacy of the German cause, but much more at the present time covertly, by way of attack on Great Britain and an attempt to lead people to give undue weight to lesser matters that can be temporarily postponed.

It is our theory that not only should there be published the two pamphlets already got out by the Committee on Public Information,[2] so wisely created under your initiative, but that steps should be taken to issue these documents in exceedingly large numbers and send them broadcast gratis throughout the length and breadth of this country; and that an outside volunteer agency, if the Government does not find itself in position to undertake this distribution, might well furnish funds and devise methods of distribution which will tend to give these documents the widest publicity. For example, to have copies of them sent out with the packages purchased from and delivered by mail order concerns, such as Sears, Roebuck & Co., Montgomery Ward and the like, reaching every corner of the country; to have them sent to officials of towns, school officials, library officials, newspaper men, officers of chambers of commerce and the like the country over; to advertise in the newspapers the fact that copies may be obtained on receipt of post card at the distribution base.

Secondly, it is our theory that the documents published by the Government, which will be chiefly if not wholly official documents, should be supplemented by a considerable number of documents containing statements of fact and deductions therefrom, dealing with the basic conditions that Americans must understand in connection with the war and any rational peace that is to ensue at its close, such for example as the following considerations:

The rights of the various European races and nations and the way in which these rights are involved in any peace that is worthy of the name.

Arguments to show why a permanent peace cannot be founded on permanent injustice arising from denial of rights to individual nations or groups of nations when such rights are capable of rational demarcation.

Why America cannot, as you have wisely said, hope to keep out of future wars, no matter where started or by what caused. To point out the nature of that machtpolitik that is the deeprooted creed of the classes that rule Germany and decide for her the question of war or peace. This argument going to show that America must inevitably concern itself, not merely with a peace that defines rights of commerce and life on the high seas, but also with international relations both broadly and in detail, and even in matters that do not to [the] uninitiate appear directly to involve America.

An explanation of how it has come about in the process of social evolution that nations have reached the point where they —no more than the individual—can deny that they are their brother's keeper, and that the time is now here when no great and powerful nation can, without meriting the contempt of all who think rightly, hold itself aloof from outrages inflicted on other nations and by no deed interfere in behalf of righteousness—that it is today inconceivable that a nation of honorable men should be content to be safe in a world made safe by the blood of other people while it does not turn a hand. Documents such as these to be published by the volunteer group and sent broadcast through such agencies as were referred to above in connection with documents published by the Government.

Thirdly, to cause to be prepared boiler-plate matter dealing with all the above topics, in form to be sent out to and used by local papers the country over; the purpose of the entire movement being to build up, so far as possibly can be done, a solidarity of knowledge, sentiment and purpose in the United States and thus to aid as rapidly as may be in the process of making America a nation and not a mere aggregate.

The Committee of the Union League Club will be greatly indebted to you if you will give it your judgment as to the vital importance of such a propaganda as above indicated and your feeling as to the question whether it may or may not best be undertaken by the initiative of proper groups.

With best wishes for your continued health under the tremendous task laid upon you, we are,

Respectfully yours,   The War Committee of

The Union League Club of Chicago

by Allen B. Pond

TLS (WP, DLC).
 [1] Architect of Chicago.
 [2] Committee on Public Information, *The War Message and the Facts Behind It* (Washington, 1917), and *How the War Came to America* (Washington, 1917), the first pamphlets in the War Information Series and the Red, White, and Blue Series, respectively. On the publications program of the Committee on Public Information, see George Creel, *How We Advertised America: The First Telling of the Amazing Story of the Committee on Public Information that Carried the Gospel of Americanism to Every Corner of the Globe* (New York, 1920); James R. Mock and Cedric Larson, *Words That Won the War: The Story of The Committee on Public Information, 1917-1919* (Princeton, N. J., 1939); and Vaughn, *Holding Fast the Inner Lines*, already cited.

From Washington Ellsworth Lindsey[1]

Santa Fe, N. M., July 13, 1917.

Some twelve hundred alleged strikers deported from state of Arizona without authority of law now on side track at Hermanas, New Mexico, have directed local sheriff to peaceably conduct these parties to Columbus and hold in tents of stockade and feed at state expense until federal authority can take charge. Hermanas is a way station without police or accommodations. Arizona guard which accompanied deportation train returning to home jurisdiction. New Mexico is without organized military force, because regiment now in federal service. Request that general government take charge and dispose of matter according to federal law and order. Local sheriff reports liklihood of riot.   W. E. Lindsey.

T telegram (WP, DLC).
 [1] Governor of New Mexico, a Republican.

From George Wylie Paul Hunt and John McBride

Globe, Ariz., July 13, 1917.

Am calling your attention to telegram from William B. Cleary, who was deported from Bisbee, quote. Hermanas, N. M., to Geo. W. P. Hunt, Globe, Ariz. "We were taken to Columbus first then back to Hermanas, where we are now. Gunmen have departed fourteen hundred men stranded here, no food, no shelter, no money to get away on. Suggest you insist that we be brought back to Bisbee with troops, as protection much suffering if men kept here more than a day. (signed) William B. Cleary. End quote. We think that this matter requires the serious and immediate attention by the Government.

Geo. W. P. Hunt,
John McBride, Commissioners of Conciliation.

T telegram (WP, DLC).

From Walter Hines Page

London, July 13, 1917.

6728. CONFIDENTIAL for the President and the Secretary.

With the consent of his Government the First Sea Lord of the Admiralty came to see me yesterday to represent the urgent necessity in his opinion for closer cooperation between the Admiralty and our Navy Board. This is in accordance with the Navy Department's policy as defined in a recent letter from the Secretary of the Navy to the Secretary of State. He said that the Admiralty would warmly welcome the most complete cooperation in order to effect this. He said it is essential that United States naval officers should actually work in the Admiralty in seclusion. Suggested in answer to my question as to how many officers, one captain and one commander for the Operations side of the War Staff; one commander for Convoy section of War Staff; one lieutenant-commander for the anti-submarine Division of War Staff and one lieutenant-commander for material generally.

In the course of our conversation Sir John Jellicoe informed me that in his judgment this is the only method whereby the most complete and efficient cooperation can be secured. He looks forward with keen pleasure to working with officers of the kind we should naturally send. His experience has proved to him the indispensable value of this plan.[1]

T telegram (SDR, RG 59, 763.72/5827, DNA).
[1] Phillips, on July 26, notified Frederick Augustine Sterling, Acting Chief

of the Division of Western European Affairs, Department of State, as follows: "Adm. Benson tells me it has been determined to hold this in abeyance for the present. Better so reply." W. Phillips to F. A. Sterling, July 26, 1917, Hw memorandum (SDR, RG 59, 763.72/5827, DNA).

A Memorandum by Sir William Wiseman

NOTES ON INTERVIEW WITH AJAX [WILSON] FRIDAY, JULY 13TH.

(1). AJAX asked me to come to his study, and there we talked for more than an hour.

He began by asking me to explain to DAMON [BALFOUR] the misunderstanding regarding Morgenthau. Morgenthau was sent to the East for relief work, and instructed that, if opportunity arose to get in touch discreetly with some of the Turkish leaders, he might do so, and sound them on the subject of peace. He appears to have discussed his secret mission with a number of friends here before he left, and on arrival at Gibraltar to have discussed it again with the British Naval officers, who discouraged the idea of his attempting it. He then proceeded to Paris, where he further discussed the proposition. He appears to have given the impression that he was authorised by AJAX to express certain views as to the settlement of Turkey in peace terms. Ajax wished me to assure DAMON that Morgenthau was not authorised to express his views to anyone, or to approach any Turkish leaders officially. AJAX expressed to Morgenthau privately the same views regarding the disposition of Turkey that he explained to DAMON: He had no idea that they would be repeated, and certainly did not authorise Morgenthau to communicate them to anyone.

(2). AJAX then produced a memorandum from CAESAR [HOUSE] regarding the proposed modification of the U. S. shipbuilding programme. AJAX said that he was not familiar with this proposition, and was therefore discussing it somewhat in the dark. In his own words—he was "thinking aloud to me." His observations were approximately as follows:

That in his opinion the war had proved that capital ships were not of much value; that future naval warfare depended on a large number of destroyers and submarines. That with this in view he did not consider the question of U. S. delaying the building of capital ships as very important from a strategic point of view. He explained, however, that when Congress voted money for the Naval programme a specific estimate had to be made of the exact number of the different classes of ships upon which the money was to be spent. It would therefore be unlawful for him to change that programme and alter the number of ships to be built. The only way in which this could be done would be by laying the whole facts before Congress, which would probably be undesirable.

When asked for a suggested solution, he stated that he had always been opposed to allowing merchantmen to cross the Atlantic without convoys; that he was strongly in favor of forcing merchantmen to cross in fleets adequately protected by light naval craft. That he believed some such arrangement was now being put in force: that when the merchantmen reached some point near the British coast, lanes should be formed, strongly guarded by destroyers, through which the merchantmen could pass, and, again, when they were quite close to shore, they should radiate to the various ports. He suggested that if some such scheme could be devised as an American scheme, it would undoubtedly require a larger number of destroyers than the U. S. at present have, but that he could go to Congress with this scheme and ask for an appropriation specifically for this purpose. That, as far as shipbuilding accommodation was concerned, there would be no difficulty in delaying the building of capital ships and to make room for the laying down of destroyers, if necessary. He went on to say that Admiral Sims, who is always considered an original man, had done nothing since his arrival in London but report the views of the British Admiralty.[1] That more than a week ago he had cabled Sims pointing out the submarine menace was as serious as ever, and that the only views reported to him had been those of the British Admiralty, and that he wanted Sims to cable him fully saying what steps he (Sims) would take if he had charge of the whole naval arrangements. Up to the present Sims has not replied, and AJAX assumes that he is studying the matter.

(3). With reference to finance, AJAX expressed his opinion that the recent crisis looked as though it was capable of solution. He urged strongly that more information, both as to actual financial needs and general policy of the Allies, must be given to the U.S.G. He pointed out that there was much confusion and some competition in the demands of the various Allies. Specifically, as far as the British are concerned, he pointed out that there was no one who could speak with sufficient financial authority to discuss the whole situation, both financial and political, with the Secretary of the Treasury. All these things should be remedied as soon as possible. That he was thoroughly in favor of a scheme proposed by the Secretary of the Treasury for a Council in Paris. This council, composed of representatives of the Allies, should determine what was needed in the way of supplies and money from America. It should also determine the urgency of each requisition, and give proper priority. I suggested that such a council should be composed of the Naval and Military commanders, or their representatives, and that the U. S. should be represented on it. AJAX did not seem to have any objection, but thought it would be unnecessary for the U. S. to be represented on it until they had their own portion of the front to look after and a large force in Europe.

(4). AJAX said he was disturbed by a dispatch which he had from Paris stating that the morale of the French troops and the French nation generally was low; and that even the arrival of the American contingent had not materially improved it.

(5). With regard to DAMON's suggestion covering the Naval shipbuilding difficulty by some species of defensive alliance: AJAX stated that in his opinion the Allies had entered during the stress of war into various undertakings among each other which they would find it very difficult, if not impossible, to carry out when the war was over; and he was not in favor of adding to that difficulty. Moreover, he pointed out that while the U. S. was now ready to take her place as a world-power, the strong feeling throughout the country was to play a "lone hand," and not to commit herself to any alliances with any foreign power. With regard to JAPAN, AJAX said that in his opinion a successful attack on the Pacific Coast was absurd owing to the long distance from the Japanese base and the difficulty they would have in obtaining any suitable base on the Pacific Coast. The possibility of their attacking the Phillipines or some outlying possession was, he thought, quite another matter, and presented a possibility which could not be overlooked.

Finally, he assured me that it was his intention to co-operate with Great Britain frankly and whole-heartedly in the common object of bringing the war to a successful conclusion as quickly as possible.[2]

T MS (W. Wiseman Papers, CtY).
[1] E.g., W. S. Sims to JD, May 8, 1917, TLS, and W. S. Sims to JD, May 26, 1917, ALS, both in the J. Daniels Papers, DLC.
[2] W. Wiseman to E. Drummond, July 17, 1917, T telegram (W. Wiseman Papers, CtY), is a brief summary of the foregoing memorandum.

From the Diary of Josephus Daniels

July Friday 13 1917

Cabinet—W.W. said Dr GTW[1] once asked "What do you think of faculty meetings?" "They are a means of grace. If a man can keep his temper during a faculty meeting, he shows he is a Christian"

Baker brought up labor matter and told of Gompers speech.[2] President agreed 8 hour, union labor.

IWW & Socialists, & Peace party[3]

[1] George Tayloe Winston, former President of the University of North Carolina and the University of Texas.

[2] Gompers and Theodore Roosevelt had spoken on July 6 in Carnegie Hall at a meeting arranged by the American Friends of Russian Freedom and other groups to honor the new Russian Ambassador, Boris A. Bakhmet'ev, and his colleagues. Roosevelt prefaced his remarks by denouncing the recent brutal attacks on blacks in East St. Louis and by saying that the United States must put its own house in order before it could really help other countries achieve liberty. He then spoke of some encouraging developments in Russia. Gompers began by saying that he approved of "the general sentiments" of Roosevelt's speech. On the other hand, Gompers went on, it should also be noted that labor leaders and others in East St. Louis had warned that Negroes were being lured there from the South to be used in undermining the conditions of labor. This, Gompers charged, was "on a par with the behavior of the brutal, reactionary and tyrannous forces that existed in Old Russia." Despite this, he concluded, there was a larger degree of freedom and justice in America than in any other country.

To this Roosevelt retorted that not for a moment would he "acquiesce in any apology for the murder of women and children in our own country." He then "strode over to Mr. Gompers and shook his fist under the labor leader's nose." An uproarious scene ensued, with the large audience divided, but Mayor Mitchel at last restored order by reminding everyone that the meeting was being held to honor the Russian guests, whereupon Bakhmet'ev gave his address. *New York Times*, July 7, 1917.

[3] The People's Council of America for Democracy and Peace. Organized in late April and May 1917 by left-wing Socialists and labor leaders and radical peace advocates, this group was explicitly modeled on the Petrograd Soviet and was designed to promote both immediate international peace and radical social reform in the United States. For the most extensive discussion of the composition of the organization and of its short and troubled history, see C. Roland Marchand, *The American Peace Movement and Social Reform, 1898-1918* (Princeton, N. J., 1972), pp. 294-322.

Amos Richards Eno Pinchot to Joseph Patrick Tumulty

New York, July 14, 1917.

Meeting of civil liberties bureau[1] was held yesterday to discuss power of post office department in general and postmasters in particular to suppress newspapers by denial of mail service, meeting at which I presided addressed by Dudley Malone, Fred Howe, Dr. Frank Crane,[2] Max Eastman, Royal Davis of Evening Post, Abraham Cahan of Jewish Daily Forward, John Reed[,] Stoughton Cooley of the Public[3] and others. We received messages of cooperation from John Temple Graves, John P. Gavit, John E. Milholland,[4] John Dewey, Don Seitz of the World, and others. Believe situation grave enough to be called directly to President's attention especially as details of arbitrary suppression of newspapers by local postmasters is arousing strong condemnation of the government. We would like to bring small delegation to talk matter over with President Monday or Tuesday. Can you arrange interview. Answer to Roger Baldwin, Harvard Club, New York.   Amos Pinchot.

T telegram (WP, DLC).
  1 The Civil Liberties Bureau had been organized on July 2 by Roger Nash Baldwin as the successor to the Bureau for Conscientious Objectors, which he had established in May. Baldwin had come in April from St. Louis to New York, where he had become associate director of the American Union Against Militarism. For an account of these organizations, see Donald Johnson, *The Challenge to American Freedoms: World War I and the Rise of the American Civil Liberties Union* (Lexington, Ky., 1963).
  2 Frank Crane, formerly minister of Methodist and Congregational churches and, since 1909, a journalist; editorial writer in New York for the Associated Newspapers syndicate.
  3 *The Public: An International Journal of Fundamental Democracy*, the Single-Tax weekly published in New York, formerly edited by Louis F. Post.
  4 John Elmer Milholland, journalist, inventor, political and social reformer, and father of Inez Milholland Boissevain.

To Joseph Patrick Tumulty

Dear Tumulty: [The White House, c. July 14, 1917]

Please reply to Mr. Pinchot that what he requests is literally impossible the early part of the week, and tell him that I doubt the necessity of the interview inasmuch as I am making a very thorough investigation and will go to the bottom of the matter in any case. Nothing more could be accomplished by their putting themselves to the inconvenience of coming down here.

The President.

TL (WP, DLC).

To John Franklin Fort

My dear Governor: [The White House] 14 July, 1917

Your exceedingly generous letter of yesterday has more than pleased and encouraged me. It has touched me very deeply. Such words of commendation coming from one who sees the inside of things here are particularly grateful to me during these days of difficulties of all sorts, and I shall feel a new energy because of them.

Gratefully and faithfully yours,   Woodrow Wilson

TLS (Letterpress Books, WP, DLC).

Two Letters from Newton Diehl Baker

Dear Mr. President: Washington. July 14, 1917.

I return herewith Mr. Baruch's letter.

At a meeting of the Council of National Defense a day or two ago, we discussed at length the proposed reorganization. Mr. Baruch and Mr. Rosenwald did not believe the plan effective to accomplish its prime purpose which was explained to be the insertion of a disinterested governing board between the business experts and the making of contracts. Mr. Houston, Mr. Willard, Mr. Redfield, Mr. Lane and I all took the other view and we had an earnest discussion. I understand what Mr. Baruch's feeling about it is, although I do not share his feeling and I do not know what remedy he would suggest, if any.

Respectfully,   Newton D. Baker

Dear Mr. President: Washington. July 14, 1917.

A very serious strike took place a few days ago in one of the plants of the International Nickel Company. The Secretary of Labor appointed a conciliation commissioner who reported to me that they had been unable to effect a reconcil[i]ation because the company insisted upon not taking back into its works the men who had been leaders in the precipitation of the strike. The men were willing to abandon all claims upon which the strike had been called. I therefore telegraphed the President of the International Nickel Company[1] that in my judgment it was his duty to compose the strike and go forward with the production of metal in the interest of the country.

I have just learned that within an hour after our telegram left the President of the company threw open its gates and announced that everybody could come back to work.

I send you this memorandum only because it seemed a pleasing evidence of the ability of the Government to get things like this done when they are plainly right.

Respectfully,   Newton D. Baker

TLS (WP, DLC).

[1] Ambrose Monell, who resigned later in 1917 to become a colonel on the staff of Brig. Gen. Benjamin Delahauf Foulois, Signal Corps, the senior American military aviator.

From Josephus Daniels, with Enclosure

Dear Mr. President: Washington. July 14, 1917.

The answer from Admiral Sims to your telegram has just been received by State Department code. In sending it I am also sending his last two letters.[1]

We are doing all that he suggests except his idea of sending the dreadnaughts. There is no reason he advances that would justify placing our last and main reliance in jeopardy. The British battleships outnumber the Germans 2½ to 1, not counting the French and Italian ships. The English are sorely troubled to secure enough oil and supplies for their great fleet. It would require an immense supply of oil and coal to be transported to our fleet and I do not know where we would get the tonnage for this.

As to the sending of smaller craft, we are doing that as rapidly as possible. We have sent 35 destroyers and five more are to leave shortly. This leaves our fleet of 32 battleships with less than 20, and some of them are under overhaul. We have sent two flotillas of converted yachts and are pushing the changing of others so as to help France.

We are building all the destroyers, trawlers, and small craft our facilities, public and private, will permit and enlarging the facilities.

We are now convoying merchant ships and Rear Admiral Wilson[2] is making ready to go over with practically all our cruisers and we hope to send twenty new submarine chasers early in August.

As to building, all stress is being put upon destroyers and small craft. We expect to finish the four dreadnaughts launched in the early fall and winter, but we are holding up upon battle cruiser construction and have given such precedence to all other construction of smaller craft we have not even decided upon the plans for the three dreadnaughts authorized.

We are requisitioning other ships and in conference with oil men for tankers. We are sending our own oil ships over to supply our destroyers with oil.

The suggestion of a War Council in London is along the line of the suggestion of Admiral Mayo that he go over with his staff. Mayo is not nearly so brilliant a man as Sims but if we are to carry out that idea I think Mayo should go. Sims already has a number of officers. Some of the men he mentions are on the way.

You have no doubt observed with satisfaction that they have

all come around to your original proposition that merchant ships should be convoyed. When you proposed it I took it up with our General Board, Benson, Mayo and the English and French Admiral who nearly all took the ground that merchant ships should not be convoyed. That was the attitude of the English Admiralty also. But they have all now adopted it. All wisdom does not come from trained naval officers and your point of view is now accepted. Sims looks for the best results from its adoption.   Sincerely   Josephus Daniels

ALS (WP, DLC).
    [1] One was W. S. Sims to JD, July 6, 1917, CCL (W. S. Sims Papers, DLC). This nine-page letter gave detailed and precise instructions for convoys to follow. The other letter from Sims to Daniels is missing in all collections and record groups.
    [2] Rear Admiral Henry Braid Wilson, U.S.N., Commander of the Patrol Force, Atlantic Fleet.

E N C L O S U R E   I

London, July 11, 1917.

6710, CONFIDENTIAL. Extremely confidential for the President from Admiral Sims:

"Your 5089, July fourth. I have sent by the last mail to the Secretary of the Navy an official paper dated this month giving the present British naval policy, the disposition of the vessels of the fleet and the manner and method of their employment. This will show to what extent the various units of the fleet, particularly destroyers, are being used to oppose submarines, protect shipping and convoys. It is hoped and believed that the convoy system will be successful, it is being applied as extensively as the number of escorting cruisers and destroyers available will permit. The paper shows also that there remains with the main fleet barely enough destroyers and auxillary forces to meet a possible sortie of the German fleet on equal terms. The opposition to submarines and the application of convoy system are rendered possible on the whole because of the British main fleet and its continuous readiness for action in case the German fleet comes out or attempts any operations outside of shelter of its fortifications and mine fields. I am forwarding by next pouch the copy of a letter from the Minister of Shipping[1] to the Prime Minister of June twenty-seventh showing the present shipping situation and forecasting the result of a continuance of present rate of destruction. This shows briefly that this rate is more than three times rate of building. A certain minimum amount of tonnage is required to supply allied countries and their armies. The letter shows that at present rate of destruction this minimum will be reached about next January, this is not an opinion but a matter of arithmetic. It means simply that if this continues the Allies will be forced to make an unsatisfactory peace. The North Sea is mined by the British and German mines for more than a hundred miles north and west of Helgoland up to the three mile limits of Denmark and Holland, over thirty thousand mines, and additional mines are being laid. It is through these neutral waters that almost all submarines have been passing. A sea attack alone upon German ports or any heavily fortified ports could not succeed against the concealed guns of modern defenses. I have just been informed that preparations are now being made for a combined sea and land attack to force back the German right flank and deny them the use of Zeebrugge as a provisioning base, though not yet definitely decided by the War Council. This would have been done long ago but for disagreement between Allies. The German fleet has not left neighborhood of Helgoland for about a year. I am aware of but two plans suggested by our Government for preventing egress of German submarines. These were contained in Navy Department's despatch April seventeenth and May eleventh and were answered in my despatches April eighteenth and May fourteenth respectively. These same suggestions and many similar ones have been and continue to be made by people of all classes since the beginning of the war. I have been shown *studies* of the proposed plans and I consider them impracticable. It is my opinion that the war will be decided by the success or failure of submarines campaign. All operations on land must eventually fail unless the Allies lines of communication can be adequately protected. For this reason and as further described in my various despatches sea war must remain here in the waters surrounding the United Kingdom. The latest intelligence is available here and can be met only by prompt action here. It is wholly impossible to attempt to direct or to properly coordinate operations through the channel of communications, letter or cable, therefore as requested by you if I had complete control of our sea forces, with the success of Allied cause solely in view, I would at once take the following steps:

First. Make immediate preparations to throw into the war area our maximum force. Prepare the fleet immediately for distant service. As the fleet, in case it does move, would require a large force of protective light craft, and as such craft would delay the fleet's movements we should advance to European waters all possible craft of such description either in service or which can be immediately commandeered and put into service. That is, all destroyers, submarines, armed tugs, yachts, light cruisers, revenue cutters, mine layers, mine sweepers, gunboats, trawlers and similar craft.

Second. Such a force while waiting for the fleet to move should be employed to the maximum degree in putting down enemy submarine campaign and in escorting convoys of merchant vessels and troops and would be in a position at all times to fall back on our main fleet if it *were without* these waters.

Third. Prepare maximum number of supply and fuel ships. Establish at once lines of supply to our forces in France and be prepared to support our heavy forces in case they are needed.

Fourth. Concentrate all naval construction on destroyers and light craft and postpone construction of heavy craft, and depend upon the fact, which I believe to be true, that regardless of any future developments we can always count upon the support of the British navy. I have been assured this by important government officials.

Fifth. As far as consistent with the above building program of light craft, particularly destroyers, concentrate all other shipbuilding on merchant tonnage, divert all possible shipping to supplying the Allies.

Sixth. As the convoy system for merchant vessels at present affords better promise than any other means for insuring safety communication lines to military and naval forces on all fronts, we should lend every support possible to insure success. To this end we should cooperate with British authorities in the United States and here who are attempting to carry out convoy system.

Seventh. To carry out the above policy questions of economy should not be allowed to influence military decision and every consideration of the nature of (?) methods of peace should be swept aside. Our entire naval war activities will be wholly dependent efficiency organization, similar in all respects to British squadron, and successful commercial organization[.] I believe the above advice to be in accordance with Government's principles of military warfare. The first step is to establish here London branch of our War Council upon whose advice you can thoroughly depend. Until this is done it will be impossible to insure that the part which the United States takes in this war whether it is won or lost will be that which the future will prove to have been maximum possible. It is quite impracticable for our interest nearly single handed to accumulate all the necessary information and it is not only impracticable but unreasonable to depend upon decisions which must necessarily be based upon incomplete information since such information cannot be efficiently communicated by telegraph or letter. This can be assured if I be given adequate staff but they must be competent officers of the required training and experience. I urgently recommend that they be selected from the younger and most progressive types, preferably War College graduates, men of the type of Knox, Pratt, Twining, McNamee, Cone, Sterling, Pye, King, Cotton, Coffee.[2] I wish to make it perfectly clear that my reports and despatches have been in all cases an independent opinion based upon specific facts and official data which I have collected in the Admiralty, and other government departments. They constitute my own conviction and hence comply with your request for an independent opinion."   Page.

T telegram (SDR, RG 59, 763.72/13324, DNA).
    [1] That is, Sir Joseph Paton Maclay, Bt., Controller of the Ministry of Shipping.
    [2] That is, Commander Dudley Wright Knox, Captain William Veazie Pratt, Captain Nathan Crook Twining, Commander Luke McNamee, Commander Hutchinson Ingham Cone, Commander Yates Stirling, Jr., Lieutenant Commander William Satterlee Pye, Lieutenant Commander Ernest Joseph King, Commander Lyman Atkinson Cotten, and Lieutenant Commander Reuben Burton Coffey. The ranks are as shown in United States Navy Department, *Register of the Commissioned and Warrant Officers of the United States Navy and Marine Corps, January 1, 1917* (Washington, 1917). Twining, who since April had commanded Squadron Two, Patrol Force, Atlantic Fleet, became Sims' chief of staff, effective August 1, 1917.

From Edward Beale McLean

My dear Mr. President: Washington, D. C. July 14, 1917.

Upon my arrival from Atlantic City tonight I find your letter dated July 12, which my secretary informs me was delivered at the Post building today about four thirty P:M. I hasten to reply thereto.

I regret exceedingly that any matter has appeared in the Post which is a cause of embarrassment to you or which might injuriously affect the nation.

It is contrary to my standing orders for injurious matter to be printed, and so far as possible I know there is no intention on the part of the Post staff to deviate from these instructions.

Now that you have courteously called the subject to my attention I shall redouble my efforts to avoid publication of any objectionable matter.

If mistakes should be made, I trust you will attribute them to the unavoidable differences of judgment in the handling of news, and not to any desire to publish that which should not be published.

Permit me to thank you, Mr. President, for calling this subject to my attention, and beleive [believe] me to be

                    sincerely yours,   Edward McLean

TLS (WP, DLC).

From the Diary of Colonel House

                                                    July 14, 1917.

Gordon[1] from Washington, and Sir William from New York, say the dinner at the White House last night was a success. The President, Mrs. Wilson, Gordon, Sir William and Sam Auchincloss[2] were present. Gordon overheard the President and Sir William discussing me at some length. The President said I was wholly detached in my viewpoint and kept it entirely untangled from personal ambition, and, as he expressed it, I "could see things as through a vacuum."

Sir William is in the seventh heaven of pleasurable excitement. The President asked him into his study and talked with him for an hour concerning the naval negotiations which we have in hand with the British government, and which Sir William is coming here to discuss with me on Monday before he sails for England.

He has another cable from the Foreign Office about this asking the status of it. He has replied that he will take it up with me on Monday and will cable further.

The President told Wiseman that it would be necessary for them to send another financial man here other than Lever. I advised this in my letter of a few days ago. I also advised the President not to discuss the naval matter with anyone other than with Lansing, Polk and Sir William. He has neglected, however, to discuss it with the State Department at all which has caused them some chagrin since I told them he would do so.

Frank Polk believes the President has gotten a wrong view concerning the value of capital battleships. I know this to be true, and when I thresh it out further with Wiseman I shall again take it up with the President. There may be something better in the future, but up to now, Great Britain's successful blockade of Germany is maintained because she has a superiority in capital battleships.

Polk says Morganthau's trip has turned out to be a fiasco. When Morganthau spoke to me about it in May, I asked him how many people knew of it. He claimed to have told only Houston, Lane, Adolph Miller, Lansing and the President. My advice to Morganthau then was to undo this part before he left. Instead of that, it seems he told a few more, and that it is known to practically every synagogue in New York. He has also undertaken to speak for the United States as to future peace conditions, which is disturbing the President and the State Department. They are undetermined whether to let him go as far as Palestine and bring him home from there, or to bring him home directly from France. I advised the latter.

[1] Gordon Auchincloss had been appointed as an assistant to the Counselor of the State Department, effective June 11, 1917.
[2] Samuel Sloan Auchincloss, older brother of Gordon, was a member of Auchincloss Brothers, textile commission merchants in New York.

Edward Mandell House to Frank Irving Cobb

Dear Mr. Cobb: Magnolia, Massachusetts. July 15, 1917.

Some weeks ago I asked Sir William Wiseman to suggest to you a challenge from the World to the Berliner Tageblatt to present in each paper the respective views of the Allies and the Central Powers. That is the World to offer an editorial column twice a week in which the German side of the controversy might be presented to the American people, provided the Tageblatt would give the same space in which the American side might be presented for the enlightenment of the German people.

The two papers would at once become a world forum, in which all belligerents and neutrals could form some judgment (1) as to what the quarrel was about and (2) who was in the wrong.

Northcliffe, who is here and to whom I mentioned what I had in mind, thinks it conceivable that such a discussion might lead to peace. He promises to aid in every way we think he can.

If the plan appeals to you, I hope you will come up and talk it out with me, for there are many sides to it, and no move should be made until it has been thought through. The German Government would probably decline to permit such a discussion, but the refusal would hurt their cause and help that of the Allies. Before making any move the President should approve, and his potential aid be invoked.

I am writing you direct because Sir William tells me he did not have an opportunity to present the suggestion because of your absence.   Sincerely yours,   [E. M. House]

For your information and approval.   E.M.H.

CCL (WP, DLC).

Paul Moritz Warburg to Edward Mandell House

Dear Col. House: Hartsdale, New York. July 15, 1917.

I was disappointed to learn last week that you had left New York. I had wished so much to "compare notes" with you, and wish so today more than ever.

I think the turn of things in Germany is most hopeful. Personally I have no doubt that the people through the Reichstag are going to assert their will, which is peace without annexations and indemnities and government by and for the people.[1] I do not understand the present combination; I never heard of Michaelis[2] and do not know whether he is a pro- or a con-Hindenburg. But I am confident that if the people are strong enough to force the government to grant equal suffrage in Prussia[3] and to ship Bethmann-Hollweg, against the dictum of the Kaiser, they will be strong enough to force the rest of the program. Let us hope so, I never hoped for anything quite so much.

Our great opportunity is now coming and I am quite confident the President is not going to miss it, indeed he has been waiting and playing for it right along. The thing that I view with considerable alarm, however, is that the State Department, instead of encouraging the Reichstag against the militarists, is throwing cold water on the impetus of the liberal faction by permitting the thought to be exploited that the fight is a sham battle and that the Reichstag does not amount to anything.

The Reichstag is as dead in earnest as was the Duma, and we should take the same attitude towards it of saying "good for you, boys, we are with you, go on." To say the Reichstag has no power is silly. The Government cannot spend a cent without the grant of the Reichstag and even in the past the will of the people as expressed by it has been the most important legislative instrument even though counter-balanced by the Bundesrath; as in England the same condition prevails through the House of Lords, and with us the two Houses and the President. The Bundesrath will from now on move in the same direction as the House of Lords, that is it will lose importance from year to year. And this will come all by itself as the various states, like Prussia at this time, become governed by diets elected on equal suffrage.

If the influential press in this country is permitted to belittle the fight and success of the German liberal parties (with their strange Catholic bed-fellows) we strengthen the militarists in Germany who will say: "It is no use democratizing because they in the United States don't trust you anyhow and moreover they don't care whether you do democratize. They want to lick and destroy us, that's all."

That will mean that there will be a fight to the finish and that the militarists in Germany, England and France will have their way.

Over-confidence would, of course, be undesirable because it would stop the speed of our preparations which ought to go on at full blast. But we can well say that we are uncertain as to who will win in Germany and therefore must go on in grim earnest and at the same time show the people of Germany that we are with them and wish them to come out on top.

Pardon this letter. I have a day off today and am aching for a chat with you. Tomorrow I have a conference with six Fed. Res. banks and want to get some "dope" about past experiences in handling the Liberty Loan and suggestions as to how best to handle the next slice which—at the rate of expenses—will soon have to be discussed.

Warmest regards from Mrs. Warburg[4] for both Mrs. House and yourself, sorry we see so little of each other.

Very sincerely yours,   Paul M. Warburg.

P.S. The new German Foreign Secretary[5] is, I believe, a modern and liberal man. I remember that my brother[6] thought highly of him and knew him quite well—unless I am mistaken in the man.

TCL (WP, DLC).

[1] A speech on July 6 by Matthias Erzberger, leader of the Center party, had led to a political crisis. Erzberger, pessimistic about Germany's military prospects, had urged the Reichstag to pass a resolution opposing annexations and looking toward a negotiated peace. The resolution reads in part as follows: "The Reichstag declares: as on August 4, 1914, so on the threshold of the fourth year of the war, the word of the speech from the Throne holds good for the German people. 'We are not impelled by lust of conquest.' Germany resorted to arms in order to defend her freedom and independence and the integrity of her territorial possessions. The Reichstag strives for a peace of understanding and the permanent reconciliation of peoples. Forced territorial acquisitions and political, economic, and financial oppressions are irreconcilable with such a peace."

Ludendorff used the situation to force the Emperor to choose between himself and Bethmann Hollweg, who resigned as Chancellor on July 13. Six days later, the Reichstag passed the "Peace Resolution" by a vote of 212 to 126, with the Center party members, Progressives, and Majority Socialists in favor and the Conservatives and National Liberals opposed. The Independent Socialists also opposed the resolution, which they considered not antiannexationist enough. A translation of the resolution is printed in the New York Times, July 21, 1917. For further information, see Arthur Rosenberg, The Birth of the German Republic, 1871-1918, Ian F. D. Morrow, trans. (London, 1931), pp. 153-93, and Klaus Epstein, Matthias Erzberger and the Dilemma of German Democracy (Princeton, N. J., 1959), pp. 182-213.

[2] The Emperor, on July 14, chose Georg Michaelis, Under Secretary of Finance and Food Controller of Prussia, as the new Imperial Chancellor. Michaelis, a political unknown who was acceptable to Hindenburg and Ludendorff, said on July 19 that he would accept the "Peace Resolution" as he interpreted it.

[3] The Emperor's "Easter Message" of April 7, 1917, had promised reform of the Prussian three-class suffrage system after the war; moreover, on July 11, Wil-

liam had instructed Bethmann Hollweg, as Minister-President of Prussia, to draw up, in time for the next elections, a bill providing for equal franchise. London *Times*, July 14, 1917.

4 Nina J. Loeb Warburg.

5 He probably referred to Count Ulrich von Brockdorff-Rantzau, at this time Minister to Denmark. Actually, Richard von Kühlmann, currently Ambassador to Turkey, became State Secretary in the Foreign Office on August 7.

6 Max Moritz Warburg, member of the banking firm of M. M. Warburg and Co. of Hamburg.

To Thomas Watt Gregory

Personal and Confidential.

[The White House]

My dear Mr. Attorney General: 16 July, 1917

The enclosed memorandum[1] was left me the other day by Dudley Malone of New York. I do not know who prepared it, but I take it that it is well founded or Malone would not have sent it to me.

Cordially and sincerely yours,   [Woodrow Wilson]

CCL (WP, DLC).

1 It is missing, but see TWG to WW, July 27, 1917 (second letter of that date).

From Albert Sidney Burleson

My dear Mr. President: Washington, D. C. July 16, 1917.

I return the letter addressed to you under date of the 12th instant by Messrs. Max Eastman, Amos Pinchot and John Reed, with reference to certain publications which it is claimed have been suspended or suppressed by the action of the Solicitor for the Post Office Department.

I beg to state that the publications involved have neither been suppressed nor suspended, but particular issues of them which were unlawful have been refused transmission in the mails, as the law requires.

Certain issues of the publications mentioned in the communication of Messrs. Eastman, Pinchot and Reed were submitted to the Department by postmasters at the post offices where they were deposited in the mails, for a ruling as to their mailability, and upon examining the publications it was found that they were not transmissible in the mails under the provisions of the Espionage Bill, for the reason that they contained matter which would interfere with the operation or success of the military or naval forces of the United States, or would promote the success of its enemies, or would cause insubordination, disloyalty, mutiny, or refusal of duty in the military or naval forces, or would obstruct the recruiting and enlistment service of the United States, or that such matter advocated or urged treason, insurrection or forcible resistance to some law of the United States.

The terms of this law are perfectly plain, and publishers should have no difficulty in avoiding a violation of either the letter or the spirit of the law, but certain of them have not been content with criticism of the policy of the Government, as has been indicated to you, but in their opposition to the war in general and the conscription law in particular have gone far beyond what might properly be termed criticism and have shown a disposition not only in the particular issues on which the Department's action was based, but in previous issues, to obstruct the Government in its conduct of the war in many different ways.

It is needless for me to say that the Post Office Department has not the slightest disposition to suppress free criticism, right or wrong, of the Government, nor has it been the policy of this Department in any way to interfere with the legitimate expression of views which do not coincide with those of the Government, in the matter of the war with Germany or any other matter. The law has been enforced by the Department in an absolutely fair and impartial manner, both as to the smaller papers and magazines and the larger papers and magazines alike, and no bureaucratic discretion has been exercised. Of course, any of these publications which feel that the Department has acted improperly have the courts open to them for the review of any action which may have been taken by the Department under this law. As a matter of fact, the August issue of "The Masses," which is referred to by Messrs. Eastman, Pinchot and Reed as the publication in which they are particularly interested, was submitted to this Department by the Postmaster at New York, and as this issue of the magazine contained matter which the law provides shall not be transmitted in the mails or delivered by any postmaster or letter carrier, the Postmaster at New York was instructed to exclude it from the mails. The publishers have brought suit in the United States District Court for the Southern District of New York to enjoin the Postmaster at New York from carrying out the instructions of the Department, and this matter is now pending in court. This Department is not averse to like action by any publisher who may feel himself aggrieved.

Faithfully yours,   A. S. Burleson

TLS (WP, DLC).

From William Gibbs McAdoo

Dear Mr. President: Washington July 16, 1917.

Thank you for your note[1] expressing approval of the suggestions contained in my letter of July 10th, for the creation of a central purchasing agency or commission through which purchases of supplies for the Allied Governments and for our own Government are to be made.

I sincerely hope that I am correct in my understanding that you approve the plan in full, as I should consider it one of the greatest steps we have yet taken toward a proper organization and control of our own markets, and toward the orderly, efficient and economical purchase of the supplies and materials required for the prosecution of the war. This concentrated control is absolutely essential, and if you have accepted it, I am sure that the results will vindicate the wisdom of your action. The whole thing can be easily accomplished now, whereas it will be very difficult if we set up an intricate and less direct acting piece of machinery that will have to be up-rooted later. Meanwhile, we should have to pay a heavy price for the experience.

You did not say whether you would like me to sound Mr. Endicott about membership in the commission, although I assumed that you meant that I should do so. I write merely for confirmation. I do not want to get a wrong start. What do you think of Henry Ford? If we can get these two men with Mr. Baruch we shall have a commission which will instantly command public confidence. I have spoken to Mr. Brandeis about Mr. Endicott, and he assures me that Endicott is one of the ablest, most vigorous and progressive men he knows; that he has a high conception of public duty and service. I am sure that this task, if it comprises service both to the Allied Governments and to our Government, will appeal to these two men, because each of them, with his business experience, will see at a glance that such a consolidation of purchasing power offers the opportunity for genuine success. Will you please let me know immediately if I shall proceed along these lines?

Cordially yours,   W G McAdoo

P.S. I find that the Allies are continuing to make independent inquiries in our markets in spite of their assurances to me that they would proceed through Mr. Baruch until final arrangements for a Purchasing Commission have been perfected. This emphasizes the need of prompt action.   WGM

TLS (WP, DLC).
[1] It is missing.

From William Kent

My dear Mr. President: Washington July 16, 1917.

Mr. Victor Berger[1] writes me asking me to secure for him, if possible, a brief interview with you. To quote from his letter: "The Socialist parties rank among the greatest political organizations in the world—considering their strength in Russia, Germany, France, England and every other civilized country. By suppressing the Socialist papers, the Socialist movement will simply be compelled to become secretive, vicious and consequently dangerous, while any political party work that is carried on in the open, can never become dangerous in a democracy."

Knowing Mr. Berger intimately as a sensible, able and loyal citizen, representing great numbers of good people, I sincerely hope that you can find time to meet him.

The hope of democracy and of peace rests so largely with the Socialists of the world that it seems to me necessary that a strong sane and honest representative like Mr. Berger should have his day in court.

Mr. Berger has requested that I wire him so that he can come this week if agreeable to you.

Yours truly,   William Kent

TLS (WP, DLC).
    [1] Former Socialist congressman from Wisconsin and editor of the *Milwaukee Leader*.

From Thomas Montgomery Bell[1]

Dear Mr. President: Washington, D. C. July 16, 1917.

I desire to call your attention to the matter of placing raw cotton under the Food Control bill, now being considered by the Senate and to protest against the same.

I cannot conclude that cotton can be classed with wheat, corn and other food stuffs although of course it is a necessity. It will be remembered that in 1914 when the South had no market for cotton and was facing what seemed to be financial disaster, an appeal was made to Congress for Federal aid in the loan of money, to be secured by cotton, and we were met with the proposition that supply and demand should control the price, which the South accepted, and it appears that if the law of supply and demand was right in 1914 it is equally right in 1917.

Your interference in this matter means a great deal to the South and may I ask that you take this matter up with the leaders of the Senate and ask that cotton be not included in the provisions of this bill. If cotton should be included in the bill, I am sure it means a long-drawn out fight when it returns to the House for final consideration.

Very respectfully, Thos. M. Bell

TLS (WP, DLC).
[1] Democratic congressman from Georgia.

From John Singer Sargent

Sir   Boston July 16th 1917

I am informed by cable that you have given a favourable, though not a final answer, to the request of the National Gallery of Ireland that you should sit for your portrait for that Institution, and, being the artist who would have the honour of painting you, I place myself at your disposal.

I hope that some interval in your grave occupations may admit of your favouring me with sittings, and that I may look forward to a communication at the above address, indicating the time and place that will best suit your convenience.

In view of making plans for the summer I would be grateful if I could have an idea of the probable month when you would be most likely to find the time for eight or ten sittings.

Believe me, Sir, Yours respectfully John S. Sargent

ALS (WP, DLC).

From the Diary of Josephus Daniels

1917 Monday 16 July

Cabinet. Grant[1] made Vice Admiral. "I was more foxy than you thought" said the President "in my letter to S ___. His friends would say later 'Sims is original. If he had been given his way, he would have started along lines of such vigor as to win success' Now he has advised only what the English are doing, &c.["]

Report that I.W.W. was so determined to make trouble by burning the wheat & the President had letters wishing protection from I.W.W.'s. It was not deemed an imminent danger.

W.W. had a letter from Mr. Burnett[2] who wanted to deport aliens who did not fight for this country or their own country. Gregory said: Their own countries should be allowed to draft them here. There are many aliens here who ought to serve in the army & who escape military duty

Complaint of partisan sectionalists because many camps have been authorized in the South.

[1] Albert Weston Grant, who since 1915 had commanded the Submarine Force, Atlantic Fleet, was appointed Commander of Battleship Force One, Atlantic Fleet, in July 1917.

[2] John Lawson Burnett, Democratic congressman from Alabama and Chairman of the House Committee on Immigration and Naturalization. His letter is missing.

Two Letters to Newton Diehl Baker

My dear Mr. Chairman: The White House 17 July, 1917

I have, as you know, been giving a great deal of thought to the plan of reorganization submitted to me some time ago by the Council of National Defense.

The more I think of it the more it seems to me that the organization can be still more simplified greatly to its advantage. My suggestion,—a suggestion which I hope you will be kind enough to lay before the Council,—is that the three persons[1] to whom will be entrusted the direction of purchases of raw materials, the purchases of finished products, and the arrangement of priorities of purchase and of shipment shall themselves be members of the War Industries Board, together with Mr. Frayne and representatives of the War and Navy Departments, under the chairmanship of Mr. Scott; that the War Industries Board serve as a clearing house for the determination of the immediate needs of the Government and the sequence of those needs; and that the three officials I have named, those charged, namely, with the purchase of raw materials, with the purchase of finished products, and with the determination of priorities, shall in association with Mr. Hoover in the matter of the purchase of foodstuffs be the executive agency through which all purchases are arranged for. It seems to me that in this way we shall get rid of what might be in danger of being a complicated piece of machinery without in any way interfering with the independence and energy of the three active officials mentioned.

There would then be a free field for these three officials to use the various committees now associated with the Council of National Defense for the fullest information and for any kind of assistance which they can properly render, and it would be within their choice, of course, to employ assistants or lieutenants as systematically as seemed necessary.

I would be obliged if I might have an early opinion from the Council on this suggestion.

Cordially and sincerely yours,   Woodrow Wilson

[1] Bernard M. Baruch, Robert S. Brookings, and Robert Scott Lovett, respectively.

My dear Mr. Secretary: The White House 17 July, 1917

Thank you heartily. You are one of the few persons from whom I receive cheering news and what you tell me about the action of the International Nickel Company is indeed cheering.

Cordially and faithfully yours,   Woodrow Wilson

TLS (N. D. Baker Papers, DLC).

To William Kent

My dear Mr. Kent: The White House 17 July, 1917

I so much respect your judgment that when I find myself differing from you, I question my own conclusion, but I must say to you very frankly that I have no confidence whatever in Victor Berger. His recent actions and utterances have convinced me that he is not to be trusted as in any sense a friend of the Government and I do not think that it would be wise or serve any useful purpose for me to see him personally.

Not all the Socialists of the country by a great deal are of his sort or follow his counsel. Indeed, I have seen very many evidences of late that the bulk of the Socialists in this country have genuine American feeling and in no sense represent the revolutionary temper such as Mr. Berger has shown.

Cordially and faithfully yours,   Woodrow Wilson

TLS (W. Kent Papers, CtY).

To Amos Richards Eno Pinchot

My dear Mr. Pinchot: The White House 17 July, 1917

May I not take the liberty of sending you the enclosed copy of a letter I have just received from the Postmaster General[1] and ask for it your most friendly consideration?

Cordially and sincerely yours,   Woodrow Wilson

TLS (A. Pinchot Papers, DLC).
[1] ASB to WW, July 16, 1917, TCL (A. Pinchot Papers, DLC).

To Allen Bartlit Pond

My dear Mr. Pond: [The White House] 17 July, 1917

May I not acknowledge with much appreciation your letter of July thirteenth about the patriotic plans of the War Committee of the Union League Club of Chicago with regard to undertaking propaganda with a view to making the purposes and circumstances of the war clearer to our fellow-citizens?

You will be interested to know that there are instrumentalities already widely at work for this same purpose and that they are very widespread throughout the country. Committees everywhere are cooperating, and I am happy to believe that the impression that the country is not generally aware of the objects of the war is an erroneous one. In some parts of the country there is very subtle and pervasive agitation against the Government and every possible means should be taken to expose and neutralize that. There are certain agencies at work, for example, in the general region with which the Union League Club would naturally be most in touch which are very determined, very hostile, and very sinister, and I believe that a great deal could be accomplished by the Club if it turned its energies towards meeting those influences directly and running them from cover to their utter destruction. Men like Mr. Nieman of the Milwaukee Journal have been very active and very successful in unearthing these influences and exposing them, and if the Club were willing to counsel and cooperate with him in any way, I think some very noteworthy results might be achieved, greatly to the benefit of the country.

Cordially and sincerely yours,   Woodrow Wilson

TLS (Letterpress Books, WP, DLC).

From Edward Mandell House, with Enclosures

Dear Governor: Magnolia, Massachusetts. July 17, 1917.

Northcliffe has been here several days. Wallace[1] has been taking care of him since our little farmhouse is only large enough for our immediate family.

I never thought to find Northcliffe in such a modest mood. He admits that he has been thrust into a situation of which he knows next to nothing, and he frankly seeks advice. He has discussed with me every phase of the financial controversy in which the two Governments and Morgan & Co. are involved, even letting me read his cables to his Government upon the subject.

McAdoo has promised to come here sometime during the next week, and if I can get an opportunity to talk the matter over with him I think a plan can be worked out, though it is not an easy problem.

I am sending you a list of the participants and the amounts

taken of the loan other than that held by Morgan & Co. Sir William, who was also here yesterday, agrees with me that there is something yet to be disclosed by Morgan & Co., and he is in New York today endeavoring to get at the bottom of it. Northcliffe does not understand enough about banking technique and international finance to be of much value.

In talking of you, he thought you were easily the greatest figure upon the world stage, and he seemed grateful for the courtesies that you had shown him.[2]

In talking with him and Sir William about the person[n]el of the British representatives in this country it was concluded that the situation was an impossible one because of the attitude of Spring-Rice. Sir William and I think it would be far better for Spring-Rice himself if he would ask for a vacation and remain in England while Northcliffe was here. Sir William tells me that Spring-Rice would like to go home, but the Foreign Office do not seem to want it. The probable reason for this is that they are afraid of the criticism which would follow this action. The Northcliffe "baiters" would be certain to attribute the Ambassador's home coming to Northcliffe, and this, I think, is what the Government is trying to avoid. Sir William hopes to straighten it out when he gets there.

I never saw anyone so pleased as Sir William was at being asked to dine with you. He speaks of it with emotion, and declar[e]s it to be the happiest event of his life.

He told me of the discussion which you had regarding the naval negotiations. He says you have a poor opinion of the value of capital battleships, and thought they had not been of much service during this war.

I have a feeling that he misunderstood you, for surely the present control of the seas is solely due to the superiority of the British Fleet in capital ships. No amount of smaller craft could take their place. While they are not effective in submarine warfare yet, submarine warfare is as distinct a phase of sea warfare as air craft are in land warfare. I think it is as true today as it was before the war that the nation having the most potential capital battleships in both size and speed, is the nation that will dominate the sea.

I hope you will insist upon some arrangement with England by which this country may obtain some of their capital ships at the end of the war, in the event we should wish them. The arrangement would be a safe one, for they need not be taken if not desired. I discussed this question thoroughly with Lord

Fisher and other British naval men, and there was no disagreement as far as I can remember.

Affectionately yours,   E. M. House

TLS (WP, DLC).
    [1] That is, Hugh Campbell Wallace.
    [2] Northcliffe paid a courtesy call at the White House on June 16. He saw Wilson again at the White House on June 30.

E N C L O S U R E   I

PARTICIPANTS IN SECURED BRITISH LOANS.

Confidential.   July 13, 1917.

Boston.
  First National Bank $2,000,000
Chicago.
  Continental & Commercial Tr. & Sav. Bnk.   2,000,000
  Corn Exchange National Bank,   250,000
  First Trust & Savings Bank,   1,000,000
  Illinois Trust & Savings Bank,   1,000,000
Cincinnati.
  First National Bank,   300,000
Cleveland.
  Citizens Savings & Trust Co.   1,500,000
  First National Bank,   500,000
New York.
  American Exchange National Bank.   9,000,000
  Astor Trust Co.   350,000
  Bank of New York, N.B.A.   150,000
  Bank of the Manhattan Co.   1,250,000
  Bankers Trust Co.   9,400,000
  Central Trust Co.   5,200,000
  Chase National Bank.   12,500,000
  Chatham & Phoenix Nat. Bank.   300,000
  Columbia Trust Co.   500,000
  Corn Exchange Bank,   2,000,000
  Empire Trust Co.   300,000
  Farmers Loan & Trust Co.   3,000,000
  Fifth Avenue Bank,   300,000
  First National Bank,   45,000,000
  Guaranty Trust Co.   20,000,000
  Hanover National Bank.   1,500,000
  Irving National Bank,   1,000,000
  Liberty National Bank,   11,000,000

Mechanics & Metals National Bank,	4,500,000
National Bank of Commerce,	17,000,000
National City Bank,	30,000,000
National Park Bank,	1,500,000
New York Trust Co.	2,200,000
Title Guarantee & Trust Co.	800,000
Union Trust Co.	500,000
U. S. Steel Corporation,	30,000,000.

Philadelphia.

Central National Bank,	200,000
Commercial Trust Co.	750,000
Corn Exchange Bank,	200,000
Drexel & Co.	3,000,000.
Farmers & Mechanics Nat. Bank,	50,000
Fidelity Trust Co.	1,500,000
First National Bank,	200,000
Fourth Street National Bank,	600,000
Franklin National Bank,	600,000
Girard Trust Co.	50,000
Philadelphia National Bank,	3,000,000
Philadelphia Trust Co.	750,000
Tradesmens National Bank,	50,000

Pittsburg.

Mellon National Bank,	1,000,000
People's National Bank,	250,000
Union Trust Co.	2,500,000

St Louis.

St Louis Union Bank,	500,000
	$233,900,000

T MS (WP, DLC).

E N C L O S U R E   I I

Robert Wickliffe Woolley to Edward Mandell House

Dear Colonel: Washington, D. C. July 14, 1917.

I just want to let you know that the President has once more taken Washington by storm. The manner in which he brought the Steel people to terms and straightened out the shipbuilding controversy has won the unqualified admiration of his bitterest critics.

Mark Sullivan sat down to table with me yesterday and volunteered in most earnest manner the pledge that never again would he criticize the President.

"He has done a number of things in the past which I do not approve," said Sullivan, "but as I look back on them they were little things. He can do big things in a bigger way than any man of modern times and if I can help it, Colliers shall never contain another word of criticism of his official acts. Peter Dunne,[1] who writes many of our editorials, may try to get by with unfriendly matter, but he will not do so, so long as I have the power to stop him. The President's achievements of the last few days have thrilled me."

Sullivan really spoke with all the ardor of a religious convert.

With kindest regards and best wishes, I am,

Cordially yours,   R. W. Woolley.

[1] That is, Finley Peter Dunne.

E N C L O S U R E   I I I

Frank Irving Cobb to Edward Mandell House

Dear Colonel House: New York City. July 17, 1917.

Your suggestion appeals very much to me and I shall take it up with the other people on the World at once. Just as soon as we come to a decision, I will write you. But it seems to me that it ought to be practicable.

With sincere regards,

As ever yours,   Frank I. Cobb.

Two letters which may be of interest.   E.M.H.

TCL (WP, DLC).

From Benjamin Ryan Tillman

Dear Mr. President: Washington. July 17th, 1917.

Pardon me for making this suggestion. My interest in you and the subject must be my excuse for intruding.

The fight between Denman and Goethals has broken out afresh, and it is disgusting the Senate, the House and every sensible man in the United States to see the Democratic Administration at war within its own ranks. We need ships badly. That goes without saying. We can not get them unless this row is settled, and you seem to be the only man who can settle it.

I do not know Denman, nor do I know Goethals, but I have followed the controversy pretty closely in the papers, and Denman to me always seemed to have the best of it. He is right now, and ought to be sustained by you for this reason.

Year before last I was on the Isthmus of Panama and saw Goethal's work. A very great and grand work it was, building the canal, but I learned a good deal about the man himself, and those he worked with in building the canal. I formed the opinion that there had been scores of millions of dollars wastefully spent, and some bad mistakes made. He was an Autocrat who would brook no differences of opinion from any one under him. He had great will power and untiring energy. His make up is dictatorial by nature; his training as an army officer has unfitted him for work with equals on any terms. He recognizes no other man as having the right to an opinion, and however wrong he may be, his will power and prestige compel every one to give him the right of way.

I know nothing about the merits of the controversy between Denman and Goethals as between iron and wooden ships. We need ALL WE CAN GET OF BOTH KINDS AS SOON AS POSSIBLE, and we can not get any at all as long as these two men keep up their controversy. Stop it please. To quote Hamlet: "It is time for them to leave off their damned nonsense and begin."

Another thing. I fear that Goethals who has no conception of economy—no army officer I have met ever had—will cost the treasury several hundred millions of dollars squandered unnecessarily. I also fear the steel trust has got its fingers in his eyes, and will dupe him into making contracts, which will be very much to the detriment of the treasury and cause a scandal.

Please examine into this matter and settle it. The country will be happy to know you have done it, and they know you will settle it RIGHT, BECAUSE THEY HAVE FAITH IN YOU.

By way of additional suggestion I want to remind you that Goethals could not agree with Col. Sibert;[1] he could not agree with Col. Guillard,[2] both of whom did great work on the Isthmus, and he can not agree with anybody who presumes to think for himself. He has been made a fool of by the way Congress had honored him, and got the "big head." For God's sake take him down a button hole or two.

Please forgive me for this bluntness and frankness of an old friend who loves you.　　Sincerely,　B. R. Tillman

TLS (WP, DLC).
[1] Maj. Gen. William Luther Sibert, who had served as a member of the

Isthmian Canal Commission, 1907-1914, was at this time commander of the
1st United States Division, in France.

    [2] That is, Lt. Col. David Dubose Gaillard, not Guillard, who had died in 1913.
The Culebra Cut was renamed the Gaillard Cut in his honor.

From Miles Poindexter

Dear Sir: [Washington] July 17, 1917.

    I enclose herewith letters from Farmers' Union Local No. 5,
of La Crosse, Washington;[1] C. T. Tupper, Spokane, Washington;[2]
Dr. C. A. Hauber, Chewelah, Washington;[3] and telegram from
The Inland Empire Employers' Association, of Spokane, Washington.[4]

    I have had numerous other telegrams and representations
indicating a serious menace in the State of Washington and
adjoining portions of Idaho for sometime and have, in response,
called attention to the desirability of vigorous action by the
State authorities.

    I do not know what has been done, but possibly the Governor
of the state[5] has been in communication with you on the subject.

    In my opinion the whole problem can be solved quickly by
prompt and vigorous action with sufficient force. Military force
is the only influence adequate to the occasion. Even a display of
it will quiet the situation and prevent the carrying out of threats
of destruction of wheat fields, saw mill and other machinery,
and the disloyal and treasonable speeches being made by the
leaders of the I.W.W. organization. In my judgment this is the
only way to deal with the matter in that section at least, and to
make it effective action should be taken promptly. I will appreciate exceedingly your attention to the matter. The enclosed
telegram speaks of federal troops at Leavenworth and Wenatchee.[6] I am not advised as to what has been done in that regard.
Trust that vigorous action will be taken.

                        Very respectfully,   Miles Poindexter

TLS (WP, DLC).

    [1] Farmers Union, Local No. 5, La Crosse, Wash., to M. Poindexter, W. L.
Jones, and William Leroy La Follette, received July 16, 1917, TCL (WP, DLC).
It petitioned the two senators and the congressman to arrange for federal
protection of crops threatened with burning by members of the I.W.W. The
petition concluded: "Will you act or shall we?"

    [2] C. T. Tupper to M. Poindexter, July 3, 1917, TLS (WP, DLC). Tupper, of
Armin and Tupper Mortgage Loan Co. of Spokane, warned of the menace to
crops by the I.W.W., noted that the Governor declined to do anything on the
ground that "people were unduly frightened," and suggested that men subject to
the draft be given brief training and assigned to guard the fields and, if need
be, to harvest the crops.

    [3] C. A. Hauber to M. Poindexter, July 3, 1917, ALS (WP, DLC). Hauber
called for federal protection of the new magnesite industry at Chewelah against
interference by the I.W.W.

4 Employers Association of Inland Empire to M. Poindexter, July 17, 1917, T telegram (WP, DLC). It urged that the Secretary of War officially notify the officers in charge of federal troops at Wenatchee and Leavenworth, Wash., of powers available under the Espionage Act to deal with the critical situation caused by the I.W.W.
5 That is, Ernest Lister, a Democrat.
6 That is, the Employers Association of Inland Empire to M. Poindexter, July 17, 1917.

William Graves Sharp to Robert Lansing

Paris July 17, 1917.

2299. Confidential. Your 2446, fourteenth.[1] Please assure the President that nothing done or said that in the remotest degree exceeds instructions. There is no cause for the President or you to feel disturbed. Under all the circumstances it is most desirable that Frankfurter make a detailed report orally. Frankfurter therefore will return. I shall rest with my wife at Aix les Bains prepared to proceed to Cairo if after hearing report of Frankfurter the President still desires me to go. Morgenthau.   Sharp.

T telegram (WP, DLC).
1 That is, the telegram summarized in F. L. Polk to WW, July 12, 1917 (first letter of that date), n. 3.

A Memorandum by Gilson Gardner

[c. July 17, 1917]

Gilson Gardner, Washington correspondent of the Scripp's newspapers, asked for an appointment for to-day, saying,

"I wish to bring to the President's personal attention, the matter of sending the suffrage pickets to the workhouse.[1] I am informed, and accept the information as accurate, that this entire matter has been handled without President Wilson's personal attention. He does not know the ultimate bad effects which are certain to result when the publicity goes to the country that women of prominence and refinement like Charles A. Dana'd[s] daughter, and the daughter of former Senator and secretary of State Bayard, have been sent to the Washington workhouse for sixty days. I am sure that the President will agree with me as to the political unwisdom of this procedure, and I wish to direct his attention to the fact that the publicity which has gone to the country, resulting from the court action, will tend to place the burden of responsibility on him, unless he personally intervenes at this time, and corrects this great blunder. Merely for the sake of frankness, I will add that my wife is one of those who have gone with the others. I am willing that all allowances be made for this fact, and that my suggestion be weighed entirely on its merits."

T MS (WP, DLC).

1 Sixteen prominent women representing the National Woman's party from various parts of the country were arrested on July 14 for creating a situation conducive to riots while picketing the White House. They included Alison Low Turnbull (Mrs. John Appleton Haven) Hopkins, Florence Bayard (Mrs. William Samuel) Hilles, Matilda Campbell Hall (Mrs. Gilson) Gardner, Eunice Dana (Mrs. John Winters) Brannan, Amelia Himes (Mrs. Robert) Walker, Elizabeth S. White (Mrs. John) Rogers, sister-in-law of Henry L. Stimson, and others. The sixteen posted bond and were released until July 17, when Judge Alexander R. Mullowny of the police court found them guilty and imposed fines of $25 each or sentences of sixty days in the District of Columbia workhouse at Occoquan, Va. As reported in the *Washington Post*, "The ladies tilted their noses at an anti-aircraft angle and frigidly informed him that it would be jail for theirs [them]." They were taken directly to Occoquan, and their experiences as inmates became the subject of long newspaper articles. *Washington Post*, July 15, 18, 19, and 20, 1917; *New York Times*, July 17 and 19, 1917.

Louis Brownlow, then the District commissioner in charge of the police, tells the story of Wilson's reaction to the arrests as follows:

"The women were taken to Occoquan, and the President almost instantly pardoned them. Then he sent for me. I went to the White House about three o'clock on the afternoon of July 19.

"Mr. Wilson was highly indignant. He told me that we had made a fearful blunder, that we never ought to have indulged these women in their desire for arrest and martyrdom, and that he had pardoned them and wanted that to end it. I was obliged to tell him that the women had refused to accept his pardon. He was more indignant than ever when he found that they were still in prison despite his pardon, and his temper was not improved when I told him that the attorney general, Thomas Watt Gregory, had ruled that a pardon wasn't an effective pardon until it was accepted. Later, Mr. Malone persuaded the women to accept the pardon.

"Mr. Wilson let me know in very plain terms that he disapproved of the arrests. I told him that I had acted with great reluctance, that I agreed entirely with him about the utter undesirability of giving these women their accolade of martyrdom, that I furthermore believed their antics were delaying the grant of suffrage, and so on. I also told him that I was responsible for peace and order on the streets of the capital, that the nation was at war, that these riots were being misconstrued in Europe, and that, while my resignation was his for the asking, I could not continue to hold my position and fail to accept full responsibility for policing the city.

"At the end he asked me not to make any further arrests until after notifying him, making it plain that he would never consent and that he wished to be advised if I, knowing his dissent, nevertheless intended to take further action." Louis Brownlow, *A Passion for Anonymity: The Autobiography of Louis Brownlow, Second Half* (Chicago, 1958), pp. 78-79.

To Miles Poindexter

My dear Senator: [The White House] 18 July, 1917

My attention had been called to the serious situation with which your letter of July seventeenth deals and I need hardly assure you that it has given me grave concern and that I have been casting about to see what might be done. I am in correspondence now with the Secretary of War to ascertain if it is possible for us to use the forces of the United States in any way that would be influential.

Cordially and sincerely yours, Woodrow Wilson

TLS (Letterpress Books, WP, DLC).

To Newton Diehl Baker

My dear Mr. Secretary: The White House 18 July, 1917

The enclosed explains itself. I would be very much obliged for your advice as to how wise and how practicable it would seem to you to act upon Senator Poindexter's suggestion as to the use of federal forces.

Cordially and faithfully yours, Woodrow Wilson

TLS (N. D. Baker Papers, DLC).

To John Singer Sargent

My dear Mr. Sargent: [The White House] 18 July, 1917

Thank you very much indeed for your kind letter of July sixteenth.

Apparently it is vain to hope for time for sittings while the Congress is in session and, unfortunately, with the extraordinarily dilatory practices possible in the Senate no man would be rash enough to predict how long the present session will last. I do not see how it can very well continue beyond the first of September, and I had in a general way formed the expectation that I might during that month have a chance to give myself the pleasure of seeing you. I should consider it a privilege to do so, and I am warmly obliged to you for your kind letter.

Cordially and sincerely yours, Woodrow Wilson

TLS (Letterpress Books, WP, DLC).

From William Gibbs McAdoo

Dear Mr. President: Washington July 18, 1917.

The responsibility of lending $3,000,000,000 to foreign governments making war upon the enemies of the United States is a very grave one and I feel the weight of it keenly. At best it is a most difficult and exacting piece of work. In order to discharge it even with measurable intelligence and judgment, it is very necessary for me to be saturated with all available information concerning conditions in Europe and the progress of events. The power our Government has through these loan and credit operations is tremendous and I should like to be in the best possible position at all times to judge how and when that power can be exerted to the best advantage. As things stand today I have little or no knowledge of what is going on in Europe except what I read in the newspapers or can gather from my conversations with representatives of the governments seeking loans from us.

Do you not think that it would be wise and in the public interest for the State Department to send me, in confidence, copies of all telegrams and communications interchanged with the Allied Governments? It seems to me essential that I should have such information, and I am sure that it will be of great value to me in the discharge of my responsibilities. Of course, I do not want dispatches relating to routine or immaterial things. It seems to me that our financial policy can be made doubly potential if the State Department and the Treasury Department work in thorough cooperation. Mr. Lansing has shown always a genuine desire to cooperate and I would not have you infer that this suggestion is occasioned by any doubt on my part that he will continue to do so. I have not spoken to him about this matter, as I would not feel at liberty to make such a request without your approval. If you do approve, will you not kindly advise Mr. Lansing direct?   Cordially yours,   W G McAdoo

TLS (WP, DLC).

Two Letters from William Denman

My dear Mr. President: Washington July 18, 1917.

The editor of a leading paper in Washington has just telephoned me that a very skillful agent of the group that is behind these large ship contracts has examined the correspondence between General Goethals and myself, and told him that he has not a leg to stand on if it is ever published; that this man is now addressing a letter to you, which probably will be signed by the General or some important person, which will endeavor to put the entire matter in your hands. There is strong evidence that this is the program. General Goethals today declined to sit with us this evening, and strongly urged a postponement until tomorrow morning.

Our discussion today made more clear than ever before that the scheme for the control of the Government owned plants and the heavy commissions to be paid for the service that a fifth of the amount would amply cover, was not described in any correspondence between you, and the General, in the written record which we have here, was unconsciously led to admit it.

The evidence today still confirms our opinion that the General is in the hands of those influences which called for the message you gave to the people last week.

In any event, there should be a very substantial modification of the General's program, which in our opinion will give a larger tonnage within the appropriation made by Congress in the time limit of 18 months and complete a larger portion of it at an earlier date.   Very faithfully yours,   William Denman.

P.S. The discussion this afternoon consisted merely of inquiry on our part. If he had resigned abruptly, I should have published the inclosed statement,[1] every line of which I can establish beyond question.

[1] W. Denman, undated T MS (WP, DLC). Denman denied that there was any personal controversy between himself and Goethals, but he said that there were "certain profound differences of opinion" between the General and the Shipping Board on the rapidity of shipbuilding, prices for ships, and the ownership of ships being built in American yards for British and other foreign contractors. Denman mentioned Goethals' opposition to wooden ships, the construction program, the price of steel, the commandeering of iron and steel plants, which Goethals opposed, the disposition of alien tonnage, and the financial terms proposed by Goethals for the construction of two government-owned shipyards.

My dear Mr. President: Washington July 18, 1917.

There have been several letters passed between General Goethals and the Shipping Board, with which I will not burden you. This is simply to suggest that the project he put out last Friday[1] is not by any means described in the previous letters to you, which I looked over. An approval of the previous letters would not be an approval of the project we are now considering.
    Very faithfully yours,   William Denman.

TLS (WP, DLC).
[1] Goethals, in a letter to Denman made public on July 13, had written: "Now that the President has authorized the Emergency Fleet Corporation to exercise the powers granted by Congress to build and commandeer ships, I intend, on Monday, to start ship construction which will complete my shipbuilding program." Goethals went on to say that 348 wooden ships had been contracted for or agreed upon, contracts for 100 more were being negotiated, and contracts for seventy-seven steel ships had been let or agreed upon. He also outlined plans for the construction of standardized ships and the commandeering of ships in yards. Denman replied to Goethals on July 13 that "joint deliberation" of these matters was necessary. Denman on the same day sent copies of Goethals' letter and his own reply to Wilson. W. Denman to WW, July 13, 1917, TLS (WP, DLC), with enclosures: G. W. Goethals to W. Denman, July 13, 1917, TCL, with attached TC of statement (WP, DLC), and W. Denman to G. W. Goethals, July 13, 1917, TCL (WP, DLC). The text of Goethals' letter was printed, e.g., in the *Washington Post*, July 14, 1917.

To William Denman

My dear Denman: The White House 18 July, 1917.

I earnestly request that all publicity in respect of the ship-building and requisition matter be suspended until I can communicate with you further—which I shall do very shortly—but push the work forward, *please*. In haste and preoccupation,

Faithfully Yours,   Woodrow Wilson.

TCL (W. Denman Papers, CU).

From Frank Lyon Polk

My dear Mr. President: Washington July 18, 1917.

In accordance with your direction I sent Morgenthau a despatch stating that the Department was disturbed by his telegram, asking for a full report of what had happened and directing him to proceed to Cairo and to confine himself strictly to the purposes of the mission as announced in the press.[1]

I had a personal note from the British Ambassador yesterday, saying that his Government informs him that Frankfurter, Lewin and Epstein are prepared to go to Russia for the purpose set out in the telegram from Frankfurter to me.[2] The British Ambassador adds that Mr. Balfour thinks it would be an excellent thing, and that if the State Department approves he entirely concurs in the suggestion.

I have not cabled Frankfurter, as I was waiting to hear from Morgenthau. Do you not think it would be a good plan to let Frankfurter come home and keep Morgenthau in France? It could be explained that, owing to the military situation in Palestine, Mr. Morgenthau could not now secure the information which would be necessary for an intelligent report on conditions.

Yours faithfully,   Frank L Polk

TLS (WP, DLC).
[1] See F. L. Polk to WW, July 12, 1917 (first letter of that date), n. 3.
[2] *Ibid.*, n. 2.

From Frank Lyon Polk, with Enclosure

My dear Mr. President: Washington July 18, 1917.

Referring to a conversation which I had the honor to have with you in regard to the sending of a small force of the United States Army to the Eastern Provinces of Cuba, for the purpose of protecting sugar, and other industrial properties, I have the honor to enclose herewith a copy of a cablegram which has been received from the American Minister at Habana, stating that President Menocal has given his approval to the sending of such a force.

I further enclose a copy of a message which has been received by the Navy Department from the Naval Station at Guantanamo, from which it would appear that a further revolutionary outbreak may be feared and that this movement may be backed by Germans.[1]

A copy of a letter addressed to the Secretary of War, requesting him to despatch, at the earliest possible moment, at least one regiment to the Eastern end of Cuba, is also enclosed herewith.[2]

Faithfully yours,   Frank L Polk

TLS (WP, DLC).
[1] Guantánamo, Cuba, to Opnav, July 17, 1917, TC telegram (WP, DLC).
[2] F. L. Polk to NDB, July 18, 1917, CCL (WP, DLC).

E N C L O S U R E

Copy of telegram received from American Minister
at Habana, dated July 14, 1917.

Your July 12, 7 p.m. received midnight July 13th. Saw President at his country place today and presented matter, passing lightly over necessities of such force in Oriente which is now not manifest and stressing wisdom of plan as war measure. He gives his cordial approval.

The President also authorizes me to offer United States sites for training camps in other parts of Cuba if it should be considered desirable to send troops to train in mild winter climate. Should it at any time appear advisable to impress eastern Cuba with fact of presence of United States troops this offer would open the way for tactful commander to arrange for extensive practice marches from Guantanamo station.   Gonzales.

T MS (WP, DLC).

From Herbert Clark Hoover

Dear Mr. President: Washington July 18, 1917.

You are probably aware that a new substitute food bill has been introduced to the Senate this morning by Senator Hollis and some of his friends.[1] I hear from many quarters that this is being represented as the Administration bill and this impression is today being systematically given to the press.

The bill contains many vicious provisions and does not return to the text of the Lever Bill, which should be made the Administration measure. It contains a provision for putting the Food Administration under commission form and it seriously alters the provisions of the bill in many directions already attempted by the Gore substitute.

To my mind it is very important that the Senators who are desirous of getting legislation satisfactory to yourself, and workable from an Administration point of view, should be informed as quickly as possible that this bill does not conform with the desires of the Administration and that great damage is being done by these reports which have been spread that it does so fulfill the requirements.

I am having a memorandum prepared showing the deficiencies of this measure, practically all of which arise by departure from the original Lever bill. Among others, I may mention that practically the flour millers, the refiners, importers, exporters, commission men, and many other food distributors are immune from the action of the bill. The bill also contains a provision which guarantees the price of wheat at $1.75 per bushel without establishing any adequate basis or having given adequate consideration as to whether this is a right or justifiable price or not.

I remain,   Your obedient servant,   Herbert Hoover

TLS (WP, DLC).
   [1] Instead of introducing a substitute bill, Hollis and other senators offered additional amendments to H.R. 4961, the texts of which are printed in 65th Cong., 1st sess., *Journal of the Senate*, pp. 190-97.

Robert Russa Moton to Joseph Patrick Tumulty

Hampton, Va., July 18, 1917.

Is there any objection to my giving President's letter July ninth, to newspapers. He answers therein wisely many questions in minds of negro people. Wire me Hampton Institute, Hampton.   R. R. Moton.

No objection   W.W.

T telegram (WP, DLC).

Walter Hines Page to Frank Lyon Polk

London July 18, 1917.

6767. Confidential. For the Secretary. The allied war conference will meet in Paris July twenty-fifth. British delegates leave London Monday morning. Since the President does not wish to appoint delegates I venture the suggestion that Admiral Sims and General Pershing be permitted to attend the conference as visitors. I am privately informed that this would please the British Government. Discussions of military subjects are likely to occur that it would be advantageous and perhaps necessary for our officers to hear. An invitation will be given to them to sit with the conference if this suggestion commends itself to the President, and be quickly received.[1]   Page.

T telegram (SDR, RG 59, 763.72/5896, DNA).
  [1] See F. L. Polk to WHP, July 20, 1917.

Sir William Wiseman to Sir Eric Drummond

New York 18 July 1917.

Number: 10

Reference to your telegram No.: 5.[1]

(A). I have discussed your telegram, Number 4, with Colonel House, and at his request had information discussed with President Wilson also. Colonel House authorized me to send you the following message: "With reference to the Agreement discussed, I believe that a plan can be found which will meet the wishes of both Governments. In the meantime, the United States will proceed as energetically as possible to build Destroyers and use every other means to meet the U Boat menace."

(B). To message of Colonel House, I add the following as my own observations: President Wilson is willing to use his authority as President to delay building capital ships so as to free yards for light craft; but, with regard to money necessary for the construction of additional Destroyers, President Wilson does not wish to amend the Naval Vote, but would prefer to submit to Congress a request for funds to carry out an American campaign against the U Boat menace. In my opinion, the next step depends upon the general relations between the two countries, which I propose to discuss with you in London.

(C). It is important that no one here should know of my Conferences with President Wilson and Colonel House.

(D). I propose to sail on the "St. Louis" on Saturday, 21 July. My Chief does not know of this and other messages I have for you from President Wilson and Colonel House, and may not therefore have realised the necessity for my crossing now. I have cabled advising him that I think that it would be desirable, and it would facilitate if you tell Colonel Browning, 2 Whitehall

Court, as much as you think desirable or necessary to satisfy him.[2]

(E). If, while I am away, you address cables to me here exactly as you do now, I have made arrangements (? that they) will get to Colonel House promptly. These arrangements are safe, and Colonel House approves.

T telegram (A. J. Balfour Papers, FO 800/209, PRO).
[1] Drummond's telegrams Nos. 4 and 5 are missing, but his telegram No. 6 to Consul General Bayley, New York, July 13, 1917 (A. J. Balfour Papers, FO 800/209, PRO), reads as follows: "Following for Wiseman No. 6. My telegram No. 5. Cabinet are anxious that negotiations as regards modification of capital shipbuilding in order to allow of increased construction of anti-submarine craft should be pressed forward as soon as possible. Admiralty have received information some arrangement may be possible. Its importance cannot easily be exaggerated. Secretary of State would be glad if you would take an opportunity of impressing Cabinet's opinion on Colonel House in whatever way you think best."
[2] Lt. Col. Frederick Henry Browning, a General Staff Officer, 1st Grade, under the Director of Military Intelligence, in the War Office.

To Herbert Clark Hoover

My dear Mr. Hoover: The White House 19 July, 1917

In reply to your letter of yesterday, may I not convey at least this degree of reassurance: I am keeping a very careful watch on the progress of the Food Bill in the Senate and believe that, although the measure will go into conference with many undesirable and perhaps impossible features in it, it will come out of conference with practically the provisions we have all along urged.

It is a tedious and vexatious process but necessary to be endured.

Cordially and sincerely yours,   Woodrow Wilson

TLS (H. Hoover Papers, HPL).

To Thomas Montgomery Bell

My dear Mr. Bell: [The White House] 19 July, 1917

I had not known that raw cotton was being included in the Food Administration Bill. I am obliged to you for calling my attention to the fact, and I shall take pleasure in considering it very carefully.[1]   Very truly yours,   Woodrow Wilson

TLS (Letterpress Books, WP, DLC).
[1] The Lever Act contained no mention of cotton or any other material for fabrics.

To William Denman

Confidential.

My dear Denman: The White House 19 July, 1917

For the same reason that I have stated in the first lines of the enclosed letter to General Goethals,[1] I am not seeking a personal interview of you, because I do not want to lend any further weight to the public impression that there is a row of some sort on. We must work this thing out and work it out along the lines suggested in my letter to General Goethals, a copy of which I take the liberty of enclosing. It follows exactly the lines of several of our conversations and I am sure that the directors of the corporation will do everything in their power to put things upon a clear road.

I wrote you my little penciled note of yesterday because I think it is imperatively necessary that we ignore public impressions of a controversy at present and also for the time being pay little regard to settling the question as to who was right or who was wrong. To keep counsel and do business it seems to me is the only way to clarify the situation.

Very cordially and sincerely yours,   Woodrow Wilson

TLS (W. Denman Papers, CU).
  [1] Wilson enclosed a TC of the next document.

To George Washington Goethals

My dear General Goethals: The White House 19 July, 1917

I am writing you a letter because if I were to ask for a personal interview in the midst of the present elaborate misunderstanding which the newspapers have created it would of course be said that I had sent for you for purposes of discipline, and of course I have no such thought in mind. I merely want to put before you very candidly my conclusions with the hope that you will acquiesce in them.

It is clear that the ship-building programme is subject to the authority and approval of the Emergency Fleet Corporation, both with regard to the programme itself and with regard to the terms of the contracts under which that programme is carried out, and I have no doubt that it is as clear to you as it is to me that the right way to get action harmoniously and at once is to put yourself in the hands of the directors of the Corporation entirely with regard to these matters.

On the other hand, it is equally clear that it is desirable and that the directors of the Corporation desire to concentrate executive authority in respect of the carrying out of the contracts and the execution of the programme in the hands of a single agent.

It is of my personal knowledge that this is the desire and purpose of the directors of the Corporation. Anything that may have happened that might be given a different interpretation has, I am sure, been due only to a misunderstanding and, I dare say, to your very natural desire to push the programme forward with the utmost possible rapidity.

The terms and the conditions of the contract being agreed upon, the way is cleared and I am hoping and expecting that a complete understanding may immediately be arrived at with regard to these matters.

It was not possible in your judgment to procure wooden ships driven by powerful machinery that would be seaworthy in the trans-Atlantic commerce where high speed is desired in order to secure greater possibilities of immunity from submarine atttack; but that we should build wooden ships in considerable numbers for that part of our sea-going trade which will not in all probability be exposed to submarine attack is my very clear judgment, as I believe it is also the judgment of the directors of the Emergency Fleet Corporation. The directors may deem it advisable to carry out the programme for the building of wooden ships in some other way than that which was at first contemplated, as of course they are free to do.

I take the liberty of suggesting that no further resort be had to the public prints, either directly or indirectly. There is nothing insoluble in the present situation unless it is allowed to grow into a public controversy.

With much respect,

Cordially and sincerely yours,   Woodrow Wilson

TLS (G. W. Goethals Papers, DLC).

To Albert Sidney Burleson, with Enclosures

Confidential.

My dear Burleson: The White House 19 July, 1917

Here is a poll proceeding from suffragette sources, of course, of the situation in the House with regard to the suffrage amendment. How nearly do you think it is likely to be accurate?

In haste   Faithfully yours,   Woodrow Wilson

$$3\,|\underline{96} \qquad 3\,|\underline{435}$$
$$32 \qquad\quad 145$$
$$\underline{2} \qquad\quad \underline{2}$$
$$64 \qquad\quad 290^1$$

TLS (A. S. Burleson Papers, DLC).
[1] WWhw.

E N C L O S U R E   I

From John Appleton Haven Hopkins

My dear Mr. President: Washington, July 18, 1917.

Following our interview today and in accordance with your request, I enclose a sheet showing the list of votes in both the House and the Senate which after a careful compilation I believe can be depended upon if you bring the passage of this amendment before them as an administration measure and ask Mr. Webb and Mr. Jones[1] to report their respective bills as they have stated they are prepared to do as soon as you approve this course.

The question of a pardon for the women at the workhouse[2] will undoubtedly relieve this particular situation, but as you said today the picketing will doubtless continue and the only ultimate solution and the only one which will satisfy the critical situation that now exists is the passage of the Anthony amendment.

Realizing the very grave conditions which now prevail throughout the entire United States, I cannot urge upon you too strongly the immense advantage of relieving the tension in the way that has been suggested, but as the situation is becoming very complicated and as there are many wheels within wheels which require our immediate and earnest consideration I venture to ask whether you cannot give me some information as to the course you decide to pursue as quickly as possible. You will of course appreciate that this will be treated confidentially and will be used to the best possible advantage towards accomplishing the objects which we both have in mind.

Very sincerely yours,   J. A. H. Hopkins

TLS (A. S. Burleson Papers, DLC).
[1] That is, Edwin Y. Webb, Democrat of North Carolina, chairman of the House Judiciary Committee, and Andrieus A. Jones, Democrat of New Mexico, chairman of the Senate Committee on Woman Suffrage.
[2] Following his interview with Wilson, Hopkins declared that Wilson had

been "deeply shocked at the whole affair" and, on learning the circumstances, had wanted only to "straighten the matter out." Hopkins gave a much fuller account of his conversation with Wilson in the news report printed at Aug. 13, 1917. Wilson granted pardons on July 19 to the sixteen women held at the work-house in Occoquan. After some discussion, they decided to accept the pardons, and by 6 P.M. they were released and returned to the District of Columbia. *Washington Post*, July 19 and 20, 1917.

ENCLOSURE II

Senate—out of 96 total
    Actually promised 28 Republicans out of 43
                       22 Democrats out of 53
           Total 50
    Leaving   15 Republicans
             31 Democrats
        or 46 from which to draw the necessary 14 if made
an administration measure

House—out of 435 total
    Actually promised 139 Republicans out of 215
                       74 Democrats out of 215
                        4 Independents out of 5
          217   435
    Leaving   76 Republicans
            141 Democrats
            1 Independent
          218 from which to draw the necessary 73 if made
an administration measure

T MS (A. S. Burleson Papers, DLC).

From Helen Hamilton Gardener

My dear Mr. President: Washington, D. C. July 19, 1917
    Mrs Carrie Chapman Catt, who has greatly wanted to confer with you regarding possible future moves in the suffrage work, has held back awaiting a time when you are less burdened than you have been during this extraordinary session of the Congress.
    It was left to me to write you asking for a conference when I thought the time might be ripe, or before you take any farther action in the matter.
    There has been a "war measure" plan in mind for some time past. Mrs Catt hopes to have the opportunity to explain it to you. She is now "booked" in the campaign as speaker in Maine and N. Y. so that, except Saturday of this week (July 21) she has

not an open date when she could come to Washington until August 2.

If you think there is reason to believe it wise for her to see you before August second could you see her on Saturday?

If so, I must wire her at once. If not I trust that you will set a date, pleasing to yourself, on or about August second.

It may not be unwise for me to say, in this connection, that our next annual National Convention is set for Washington the second week in December. It is to be far the largest and most representative of any we have ever had.

Our hope has been to secure your interest and powerful influence at that time—at the opening of the new Congress—for a real drive for the enfranchis[e]ment of twenty million of American women, as a "war measure" and to enable our women to throw, more fully and whole-heartedly, their entire energy into work for their country and for humanity, instead of for their own liberty and independence.

We hope and believe that you will see your way to help us then in the manner we have thought out, if you do not feel that it is wise sooner.

Therefore we have refrained from forcing the matter to your attention while you have been so overwhelmed, and have been meeting with such splendid courage, the immediate demands of the war both here and abroad.

Nevertheless we do not want to be found wanting should you deem the time ripe to act at an earlier date and we think that a conference (wholly without publicity) would be most helpful to us and, we trust, not unwelcome to you.

Awaiting your reply,[1] I have the honor to remain,

                    Yours sincerely,   Helen H. Gardener

Mrs Catt would like for me to be present at the conference if you are willing.

TLS (WP, DLC).
    [1] "Please be kind enough to telephone to Miss Gardener that I will not be in town tomorrow and that I shall hope to see Mrs. Catt on the later date she mentions. The President." T MS (WP, DLC).

From Thomas Watt Gregory

Sir: Washington, D. C. July 19, 1917.

I have the honor to transmit the following information in reply to your letter of July 3, 1917, regarding statement alleged to have been given out by United States Attorney Preston to the San Francisco Examiner.

This matter was first brought to my attention by a telegram

dated June 30th (received in this Department July 2d), from Rev. P. C. Yorke,[1] as follows:

The United States District Attorney Preston has given to the Examiner this morning for publication with his approval an anonymous letter, in which the Catholic chapl[a]ins in the Army and Navy of the United States are accused of betraying the secrets of the United States Government to enemies. He also accuses American citizens, Friends of Irish Freedom, of violation of American laws in demanding that the case of Ireland be considered among those small nationalities entitled to freedom and a democratic form government. Can nothing be done to abate this man's pernicious activities. His personal habits are such as to remove him from all responsibility.

A similar telegram was sent by Rev. Mr. Yorke addressed to the Secretary to the President, the White House, and also to Senator Borah and Senator Phelan and others. Subsequently, telegrams of protest were received from the officers of the Ancient Order of Hibernians and others; and on July 9th, the Department received a long letter from Rev. Mr. Yorke, dated July 2d, transmitting a copy of the San Francisco Examiner.[2]

This Department, on July 3, 1917, wired a copy of the Yorke telegram to the United States Attorney, and instructed him to "wire Department at once whether Yorke's telegram states facts correctly, and wire full report." The United States Attorney transmitted, under date of July 5, 1917, a long telegraphic reply, copy of which is hereto attached,[3] which stated in brief that Yorke was the owner and real editor of the Leader, a paper which had severely denounced the war and the Administration for entering into it, and a copy of which had been denied the use of the mails; that since April there had been many pro-German disloyal meetings taking place in San Francisco under the guise of proclaiming Irish independence; and that at one of these meetings Yorke presided and read a telegram from ex-Senator Works directed against those people who forced us into the war.

The United States Attorney further stated that in view of this condition, he asked the press reporters, on June 30th, to give publicity to Sections 3 and 4, Title I, of the Espionage Act, directed against the promotion of disloyalty and interference with recruiting and enlistment. At the same time he showed the reporters certain fanatical letters addressed to him which previous pro-German-Irish meetings had called forth. The agreement was that he, the United States Attorney, should read proof of the article before publication; but the San Francisco Examiner failed to allow him to do this, and published the letter in question which has been complained of, and which letter was anonymous and was as follows:

Did you attend the big patriotic outpouring at Dreamland Rink last night. If you did you will take due notice that the Irish are in the saddle and that while you may be able to bluff and oppress the Germans the Irish are always ready and able to meet you half way. Your boasted land of the free and home of the brave will have to come over to our thoughts and principles. You have no secrets that we don't have and we have many that you don't have. Our clergy in the Army and Navy keep themselves and their friends fully posted. You notice that our flag still floats over the Kay Are Bee Hall on Mission Street right under your nose and what are you going to do about it. The Shamrock will be the American national flower before the conflict is over. Signed Erin.

The United States Attorney telegraphed that he did not endorse or vouch for the letter, or claim that it was authentic or its contents true; but "intended this among other letters to be proof bad effect this propaganda."

I transmit herewith the full newspaper article, in order that you may see the connection in which the anonymous letter was published. There would appear to be nothing in the article which is objectionable otherwise than the inclusion of the anonymous letter in question.

In addition to the above, the United States Attorney calls attention to an organization known as the "Friends of Irish Freedom," and in a letter dated July 8, 1917, received in this Department July 14, 1917, he presents facts regarding a plot on the part of this organization to bring about the escape of the German Vice Consul, Von Schack,[4] who was convicted in connection with the Bopp conspiracy, and who is now interned on Angel Island in California under the President's Proclamation of April 6, 1917, relative to alien enemies. This plot has apparently been engineered by the man who is nominally the editor of the Rev. Mr. Yorke's newspaper, the Leader. The plot apparently has been to effect the escape of Von Schack and to transport him to Mexico, where he could then deliver secret information which he had for transmission to Germany.[5] This latter matter has not yet been fully developed, and the facts will shortly be laid before the grand jury. It is of the highest degree of importance that the facts here stated by me should not become known to anyone.

I have been informed that the Rev. Mr. Yorke is extremely disloyal, and an active agitator against the war and the Administration, and I believe that Senator Phelan is entirely familiar with his activities.

I transmit herewith a statement which the United States Attorney gave to the press after complaint was made of the original publication,[6] in which statement he explains as follows:

The anonymous letter objected to was not vouched for by me, nor are the contents thereof believed by me to be true. I cited it as the act of a fanatic, which showed the impropriety of many of the utterances of these meetings.

I had not the slightest notion of offending either the religion or patriotism of any American of Irish birth of [or] descent. I have Irish blood in my own veins. I associate daily with Irish and Irish-Americans, both officially and socially. I have sent my daughter to convent schools. I entertain no religious or social prejudices. I am also strictly in favor of free speech within the honest interpretation of that word.

There are a few disloyal people in our midst, and I intend to see that they obey the law. And I take it that all citizens will uphold me in this. Further than this I have no motive whatever.

I was really surprised that the newspapers published the letter. I only desired that it be referred to as the result on the minds of the weak and credulous of some of the utterances that have been made.   Respectfully,   T. W. Gregory

TLS (WP, DLC).

[1] The Rev. Peter Christopher Yorke, born in Galway City, Ireland, in 1864; ordained a priest in the Roman Catholic Church in 1887; rector since 1913 of St. Peter's Church, San Francisco; a regent of the University of California, 1903-1913; and author of various books on religion, liturgy, education, and the family. For an account of his participation in labor questions, journalism, municipal affairs, and numerous controversies, see Joseph S. Brusher, *Consecrated Thunderbolt: Father Yorke of San Francisco* (Hawthorne, N. J., 1973).

[2] Gregory enclosed a clipping from the issue (probably that of June 30) which reported a warning by Preston that the Espionage Act would be "rigidly enforced." The *Examiner* printed the letter signed "Erin" that Gregory quoted later in his letter to Wilson. Preston held, according to the account, that speeches at mass meetings which inspired letters of this sort were clear violations of the Act, because they tended to interfere with military recruiting and enlistment.

[3] J. W. Preston to TWG, July 5, 1917, TC telegram (WP, DLC).

[4] Franz Bopp, German Consul General at San Francisco, Eckhard von Schack, and three employees of the Consulate General were convicted in San Francisco on January 10, 1917, of violating the neutrality laws of the United States. They were accused of having planned to blow up munitions plants, ships, bridges, and trains in the United States and Canada. Two actions were consolidated in the trial. The defendants were charged with conspiring to restrain interstate and foreign commerce and to set afoot a military enterprise to be carried on against the territory of the King of Great Britain and Ireland. Bopp and Schack were sentenced on January 22 to two years in prison and fines of $10,000. *New York Times*, Jan. 11 and 23, 1917. See also Reinhard R. Doerries, *Washington-Berlin 1908/1917: Die Tätigkeit des Botschafters Johann Heinrich Graf von Bernstorff in Washington vor dem Eintritt der Vereinigten Staaten von Amerika in den Ersten Weltkrieg* (Düsseldorf, 1975), pp. 212-14.

⁵ Lawrence De Lacey, an employee of *The Leader*, and D. J. Harnedy, proprietor of a shoe store, were arrested in San Francisco on August 14 in connection with the suspected plot to release Bopp and Schack and spirit them to Mexico. *Washington Post*, Aug. 15, 1917.
⁶ Undated newspaper clipping (WP, DLC).

From Edward Mandell House, with Enclosures

Dear Governor: Magnolia, Mass. July 19, 1917.

I am enclosing you a copy of another letter from Cobb and my reply.

I have but little hope that the German Government will permit such a discussion, but if they do not, their refusal can be used in such a way as to make serious trouble for them within Germany itself.

Quick action, of course, is important and I would appreciate your writing or wiring me your decision.

I will give the matter my personal attention and arrange that nothing is published from our side without the most careful consideration. If any question should arise about which there is doubt, it will be submitted to you.

It seems to me we have an idea that may startle the world and, conceivably, be of great value. There is an ever increasing distrust by the plain people of secret diplomacy, and such a move as this under your sanction would have great influence for good.   Affectionately yours,   E. M. House

P.S. I suggest Northcliffe because of the influence of his publications in England, and Tardieu because he is one of the most brilliant writers on international subjects in the world. Simkovitch would give the liberal Russian touch.

Unless we can break down Germany from within, I am afraid of what may happen in France and Russia before the year ends.

TLS (WP, DLC).

E N C L O S U R E   I

Frank Irving Cobb to Edward Mandell House

Dear Colonel House: New York. July 18, 1917.

The World will be glad to take that matter up and carry it through, if possible. I cannot get away at present to see you, but perhaps we can arrive at some kind of a general understanding by letter. Of course, the thing cannot succeed unless we have the full co-operation of both the United States and German Governments.

I am not sure, in my own mind, how the matter could best be presented to the Tageblatt—whether by direct communication or through the good offices of the Swiss Minister. What is your own opinion about that? We could prepare a formal proposal to the Tageblatt and ask the State Department to have it transmitted by cable or otherwise. If the German Government acquiesced, or even permitted the Tageblatt to receive the communication, the details could then be worked out.

Such a debate would really amount to a preliminary discussion of peace in its ultimate effect and I do not think its value could well be overestimated, if it could be done. There would be little use in undertaking it, however, unless there were assurances from Germany that our side of the case would not be censored, although we might properly have a private agreement as to the limits of the debate.

Will you be good enough to let me know your own views as to the method of carrying it through? I agree with you thoroughly that nothing must be done unless we have the plans completely mapped out and agreed upon.

With sincere regards,

As ever yours,   Frank I. Cobb.

TCL (WP, DLC).

ENCLOSURE   II

Edward Mandell House to Frank Irving Cobb

Dear Mr. Cobb: Magnolia, Massachusetts. July 19, 1917.

I am glad my suggestion regarding making of the World and Tageblatt an international forum appeals to you and your colleagues.

The next step is to get the approval of the President and that I shall try to do at once. Of course we must have the full cooperation of both the United States and German Governments. After the President has given the word to start, we can take up with the State Department the best method of procedure.

It goes without say[ing] that the whole plan must fail unless we have assurances that whatever is written must be published verbatim, although it might be necessary, as you say, to have a private agreement as to the limits of the debate.

My thought is to make it practically an international discussion rather than one between two great newspapers, although the governments would apparently have no part in it.

It might be well to have an advisory council to help select the questions to be argued, and the manner of their presentation and also the replies to the German arguments which would be made. You, of course, to do the actual writing. In this council might be included Northcliffe, Tardieu and perhaps Simkovitch of Columbia. The discussion would immediately take on an international importance hard to estimate.

Pending a reply from the President, will you not let me have any further thoughts that come to you.

Sincerely yours,   [E. M. House]

CCL (WP, DLC).

To William Byron Colver

My dear Colver: [The White House] 20 July, 1917

Thank you for your letter of yesterday.[1] As a matter of fact, I had not sent word that I thought that iron ore (steel, copper, leather and other basic things) might properly be left out of the Food bill, but the facts are these:

These articles were not included in the House bill. They were added in the Senate, and have now been eliminated there because their inclusion would have brought on a long fight and perhaps endangered or indefinitely delayed the passage of the Act itself. Under other laws I feel convinced that power enough has been granted the administration to deal with these articles with some effectiveness, and I am certainly going to use every ounce of power I have.

By the way, in ascertaining the facts upon which we can base a price for steel, it seems to me, as it no doubt seems to you, that we must fix the costs of these several things: First, iron ore; second, coke; third, pig iron; fourth, billets; and then, fifth, the various forms of manufactured steel.

In haste

Cordially and sincerely yours,   [Woodrow Wilson]

CCL (WP, DLC).

[1] It is missing. A covering note said that it had been sent in response to a request by Tumulty. W. B. Colver to JPT, July 19, 1917, ALS (WP, DLC).

To Joseph Patrick Tumulty

Dear Tumulty: [The White House, July 20, 1917]

Please ask Mr. Bell to seek interviews with the Secretary of Labor and the Attorney General about this important matter.[1] These are the men upon whom I shall depend for advice.

Please say to Mr. Bell, if he asks for an interview with me, that I make this suggestion in the interest of the saving of time and that he can rest assured that I have been keeping in close touch with the situation so far as it was possible for me to do so and would be glad to have his suggestions in formulated shape.

                                              The President.

TL (WP, DLC).
[1] George Lewis Bell, an industrial relations expert, was at this time executive officer and attorney of the California State Commission of Immigration and Housing and special representative of the governors of California, Arizona, Nevada, Utah, Idaho, Colorado, Oregon, and Washington. On July 18, he laid before the Council of National Defense a report of the I.W.W.'s activities throughout the West, and, on behalf of the governors and councils of defense of those states, he presented recommendations for federal action to deal with the situation. Martin, *Digest of the Proceedings of the Council of National Defense during the World War*, p. 226. For a general account of anti-I.W.W. measures proposed by Bell and others, see Dubofsky, *We Shall Be All*, pp. 398-422. Bell called on Tumulty with letters of introduction from the governors and requested an interview with Wilson. JPT to WW, July 20, 1917, T memorandum (WP, DLC).

From Leonidas Carstarphen Dyer[1]

My dear Mr. President: Washington, D. C. July 20, 1917.

I beg to call your attention to the enclosed Resolution that I recently introduced[2] touching the massacre of a large number of colored people at East St. Louis, Illinois. I have reliable information that there were more than five hundred of these people, men, women, and children, murdered upon this occasion. The situation there is still very serious, I having just returned to Washington from a trip to St. Louis, Missouri, which is only across the river from East St. Louis, Illinois. I have received very many letters from the business men and other citizens of East St. Louis, begging that the Government take some action at once to relieve the situation. Most of the letters urge that a United States Judge be sent to East St. Louis to call a grand jury for the investigation of this matter, and that there be vigorous prosecutions of those guilty of these horrible crimes. Those who write me say that this is the only certain remedy to prevent a repetition of what happened on July second. I therefore respectfully urge that you bring this matter to the attention of the

Attorney General at once and direct that such action as indicated above be taken. If it is not, I fear the consequences.

Yours very respectfully,   L. C. Dyer

TLS (JDR, RG 60, Numerical File, No. 186835, DNA).
  [1] Republican congressman from St. Louis, Mo.
  [2] H.J. Res. 118, to create a "joint committee from the membership of the Senate Committee on the Judiciary and the House Committee on the Judiciary to investigate the causes that led to the murdering, the lynching, the burning, and the drowning of innocent citizens of the United States at East St. Louis, Ill., on July 2, 1917; whether the Constitution and laws of the United States were violated; and what legislation, if any, is needed to prevent like outrages in the State of Illinois and other States and Territories of the United States." Dyer introduced the resolution on July 9, and it was referred to the House Committee on Rules. *Cong. Record*, 65th Cong., 1st sess., pp. 4879-80. A printed copy of H.J. Res. 118 is enclosed with Dyer's letter.

From Edward Mandell House

Dear Governor: Magnolia, Massachusetts. July 20, 1917.

I have just received the following cable from Balfour:

"Communication of the utmost importance and urgency with regard to financial position was made to the United States Gov-[ernment's] Ambassador today with request that he telegraph it in extenso to State Department. I should be most grateful if you could insure that it receives the personal attention of the President, and for any assistance you can give as matter is really vital. I am sure nothing short of full aid which we ask will avoid a castastrophe [catastrophe]."

I have answered that I would immediately call your attention to the urgency of the matter.

McAdoo intended coming here on Thursday but was detained. He hopes to come next week. I know this question from every angle, and I feel if I could get with McAdoo a plan could be worked out that would be satisfactory.

Affectionately yours,   E. M. House

TLS (WP, DLC).

From Walter Hines Page

Paraphrase of telegram dated July 20, 1917, from the American Ambassador at London.

6779. The long financial statement by the Chancellor of the Exchequer was handed me by Mr. Balfour, who requests me to telegraph for the information of the President and the Secretary of the Treasury. A copy is also being sent by pouch. Greater fear and depression has been caused by the financial situation than has heretofore been felt from any cause since the start of the war. Mr. Bonar Law's memorandum follows.　　　　Page

6780. Mr. Law's Memorandum: Ambassador Page was seen on July 14th by the Chancellor of the Exchequer, who requested Mr. Secretary Balfour to cause the following Note to be sent to Mr. Page in reply:

(1) Mr. McAdoo's statement that "At no time, directly, or indirectly, has the Secretary of the Treasury or anyone connected with his Department promised to pay the Morgan's overdraft," is of course accepted by the Chancellor of the Exchequer. This question of past misunderstandings is, in any event, of small consequence as compared with the question as to whether the financial interests of the Alliance makes this repayment at the present time necessary or advisable. In view, however, of what passed at the Chancellor of the Exchequer's interview with Mr. Page, the Chancellor thinks it right to quote the actual words received by cable from Sir Cecil Spring Rice on April 9th, which were the foundation of what he said on that occasion. Ambassador Spring Rice telegraphed as follows:

"Sir R. Crawford desires the following to be communicated to the Chancellor of the Exchequer. I told the Secretary of the Treasury last night that you appreciated and concurred in his proposals. He was very much gratified and asked me to convey his compliments. I mentioned to him that [the] four considerations referred to in paragraph two of your telegram.

"He agreed that repayment of overdraft on four [hundred] million dollars should be a first call on the loan." (Here follow remarks on three other distinct topics.) (The telegram continues.) "This morning Governor Harding called, at the request of the Secretary, and confirmed the views expressed by the latter on the above points. This evening I went over the matter again with the Counselor of the State Department, who fully concurred that our overdraft should be a first charge."

(2) In Mr. McAdoo's note there are several indications that he desires above all a freer and fuller communication of facts from us. It has never been desired or intended by us to keep from him any reserves as to our financial condition. It has been our preoccupation, on the other hand, to bring home to him the exact nature of that condition. We will answer any specific question. The following figures are presented in the meantime in the belief that they are the figures most closely related to present problems:

(A) It is pointed out by Mr. McAdoo "that America's cooperation cannot mean that America can assume the entire burden of financing the war." The following table of assistance rendered to the European Allies by the United States and the United Kingdom, respectively, since the date of the entry of America into the war exemplifies how much less than this has been expressly asked of it.

Financial assistance from April 1, to July 14, 1917.

United Kingdom advanced to France £50,072,000; advanced to Russia £78,472,000; advanced to Italy £47,760,000; advanced to Belgium £8,035,000, which included the Congo; advanced to minor allies £3,545,000; total £193,849,000.[1]

United States advanced three hundred and ten million.

Nil

One hundred million.

Fifteen million.

$2,000,000. Total $427,000,000, or the equivalent of £90,000,-000.

Roughly, the advances made by the United States equal £90,-000,000 against the advances by the United Kingdom of nearly £194,000,000. $100,000,000. has been promised Russia, but it is understood that no cash installments have as yet been received by her. Total amounts promised for Belgian relief $45,000,000. Total amount promised Serbia three million.

It is gratefully acknowledged by the Chancellor of the Exchequer that the United States Treasury has advanced $686,-000,000, to this country in addition to the sums given to the other Allies, as stated above.

Mr. McAdoo's particular attention is, however, invited to the fact that even since America came into the war the financial assistance afforded by the United Kingdom to the other allies has been more than double the assistance afforded by the United States to them, and that the assistance afforded these other allies by the United Kingdom much exceeds the assistance received from the United States by herself.

(B) The assistance of the United States Treasury has so far been limited to expenditure which the Allies have incurred within the United States, recognizing rightly that this assistance involves a burden which is much less onerous than financial assistance abroad. The United Kingdom have not been able to adopt this attitude with regard to their allies, but have supported the burden of their expenditure in every part of the world. If the Allies had not received this support they could not have obtained

[1] *Sic!*

the supplies of munitions and food which have been essential to their carrying on the war.

The foregoing has been the case to such a degree that up to this time Great Britain is still financing Russia's expenditure in the United States.

(C) Between the first of April 1917, and the fourteenth of July 1917, the total amount of expenditure from the British Exchequer was £825,109,000 of which £131,245,000 was taken care of by loans raised in the United States. These figures both relate to expenditure and income brought to account out of date 14th.

(D) The financial burden upon Great Britain's Exchequer did not begin, however, on April 1st last. The total amount expended between April 1, 1914, and March 31, 1917, amounted to £4,352,798,000, which amount added to the expenditure of £825,109,000 since the 1st of April 1917, gives a total expenditure of £5,161,471,000. It is after having supported an expenditure of this magnitude for three years that Great Britain ventures to appeal to the United States for sympathetic consideration in financial discussion where the excessive urgency of her need and the precarious position in which she is may somewhat lend a tone of insistence to her requests for assistance which under ordinary circumstances would be out of place.

There is attached at the end of this communication, for the information of Mr. McAdoo, a statement which shows precisely how this sum of £5,000,000,000. has been financed up to date. Included under the heading of the ways and means advances are the proceeds of the New York overdraft. There are included in this statement a number of particulars which have not been given to Parliament and the statement is to be regarded as in the case of all the other figures given in this note, as being solely for the confidential information of the Government of the United States.

(E) The statement which follows indicates the expenditure and receipts of the Government of Great Britain in New York City from April one to July 14th, 1917. Payments out of the treasury account in New York for use in the purchase of commodities and interest due $602,000,000.

Purchase of exchange (E.G.) the cost of all purchases of wheat for the Allies is included in this figure inter alia during the greater portion of the period concerned $529,000,000: total $1,131,000,000.

Loans from the Government of the United States $685,000,-000.

British Treasury notes (Sundry munitions contracts) $27,-000,000.

Repayments by Italian and French Governments $134,000,-000.

Gold, $246,000,000.

Sale of securities $58,000,000.; miscellaneous $19,000,000: Total $1,169,000,000.

(F) From the preceding statement it will be noted that gold and securities were realized, during the period in question (mostly during June), to the amount of $304,000,000. The following facts show the impossibility of the continuance on this scale of the United Kingdom to supplement United States Government assistance.

Gold. The United Kingdom have exported to the United States since the war commenced (including gold lately ear-marked for the New York Federal Reserve Bank) the sum of $305,000,-000. in actual gold. All of this has been sent on behalf of the United Kingdom but a considerable portion has been purchased or borrowed from the other allies. In addition to this a fairly substantial amount has been sent to other destinations. This represents a tremendous effort, of which the United States reserves have obtained the benefit.

The United Kingdom now have left in the reserve of the Bank of England about £50,000,000., £28,500,000. in the currency note reserve and an unknown amount estimated at a maximum of £50,000,000. with the joint stock banks. There is in addition a sum of about £10,000,000. at the Treasury's disposal but which is not included in any published reserve. This makes a total of about £140,000,000. There are virtually no Government bonds in circulation. This is about 6% of the United Kingdom's banking liabilities and considerably less than the allotted circulation of the government bonds in the United States.

The amount of this government loan with which we could part and not destroy the confidence upon [which] rests our credit is inconsiderable.

Securities. Before the initiation by the treasury of their official mobilization of dollar securities there were disposed through private channels large amounts, and also by the Bank of England who were engaged systematically in disposing of Dutch Government securities in New York.

The figures which follow have relation only to the treasury's scheme:

Value of securities purchased $770,000,000; value of securities

obtained on deposit as a loan $1,130,000,000. Total $1,900,-
000,000. The above has been disposed of as follows: Sold in
New York, $750,000,000; deposited as security against loans
$600,000,000.; deposited as security against call loan $400,000,-
000.; still in hand $150,000,000.: Total $1,900,000,000. (All
figures approximate.) We have now obtained virtually all the
dollar securities which are available in this country, and in view
of penalties now attached it is considered that the amount of
salable securities held privately is now very small. Only gradual
disposition can be made of the balance in hand and this is not in
any case an important amount.

(3) In short, resources of the United Kingdom which are
available for payments in the United States are exhausted. Unless the Government of the United States can meet fully our expenses in America, including exchange, the entire financial fabric
of the alliance will collapse. This conclusion will be a matter of
days, not months.

The question is one requiring the taking of a large view. If
matters continue on the same basis as they have during the past
few weeks it will not be possible to avoid a financial disaster of
the first magnitude. During August the encouragement of which
our enemy is in so great need will be received by him at the time
in the conflict when perhaps he most needs it.

(4) It is suggested by Mr. McAdoo that the settlement of
joint allied purchasing arrangements must be made before any
promises are made by him of financial support in the month of
August. The Government of Great Britain are at a loss to understand how this statement should be interpreted. They are doing
what they can to promote the establishment of such arrangements and at the end of the month of June prepared a scheme in
detail along lines which they had been given to understand would
commend themselves to the Government of the United States
for submission to the other allies, but the settlement is dependent
upon the progress of events in the United States and the acquiescence of the other allies concerned. His Majesty's Government
will instruct Ambassador Spring Rice to communicate to the
Government of the United States unofficially the details at once
without waiting for replies from the other Allies. The British
Government cannot believe that if these or other natural and
unavoidable causes of delay are operative for reasons which may
be out of their control, financial support will not be forthcoming
and a catastrophe precipitated.

(5) With regard to the concluding statement of Mr. McAdoo

the Chancellor of the Exchequer desires to state that Lord North-cliffe is the duly authorized representative of His Majesty's Government to conduct all financial negotiations on their behalf. It has been suggested by Lord Northcliffe, however, that the Government of the United States would themselves prefer that someone having political experience, such as an ex-member of the cabinet, should be sent to the United States purposely for dealing with the financial situation. Should this be the desire of the Government of the United States the British Government would gladly comply with it.

Exchequer receipts and issues (net) 1914-15, 1915-16, 1916-17, 1917-18, to July 14th)

		RECEIPTS
Balance April 1st, 1914	£	10,435,000
Revenue		
(tax) £1,115,136,000		
(non tax) £ 163,151,000		
	£1,278,287,000	
Treasury Bills (excluding bills bought		
as collateral shown below)	£	647,160,000
3½% War loan (net)	£	189,149,000
4½% War loan	£	592,345,000
4% & 5% War loans	£	944,277,000
3% Exchequer bonds	£	20,449,000
5 & 6% Exchequer bonds (net)	£	546,957,000
War savings certificates	£	85,300,000
War expenditure certificates	£	23,561,000
American loan, 1915	£	50,820,000
Other debt		
In the United States (net)	£	314,213,000
In Canada (including *précis*,		
£20,549,000 Collateral		
treasury bills, net)	£	73,959,000
In Japan		
For French gold	£	10,527,000
For Russian gold	£	53,320,000
Treasury bills	£	60,000,000
(Dutch) £14,819,000		
(Scandinavian		
collateral) £14,760,000	£	29,579,000
Miscellaneous		
(In colonies and loans without		
interest)	£	4,502,000

Ways and Means Advances (never
    contemplated)   £ 226,631,000
Total   £5,161,471,000
ISSUES

National debt services   £ 273,417,000
Other consolidated fund services   £   39,368,000
Supplemental convention services
    (including £60,400,000 for army
    and navy in 1914-15[)]   £ 365,283,000
Votes of Credit   £4,439,467,000
  Expenditures   £5,117,535,000
Exchequer bonds 1910 paid off   £   16,395,000
Miscellaneous issues
    (Old sinking fund account) net   £   2,703,000
Balance July 14, 1917,   £   24,838,000
  Total   £5,161,471,000

Balfour requests that a copy of the memorandum be given to
Spring Rice.   Page

T MS (WP, DLC).

From Samuel Gompers

Sir: Washington, D. C. July 20, 1917.

A number of telegrams have been received by me from several
parts of Arizona, calling attention to the treatment accorded to
the workmen of that state. I quote herein three telegrams as follows:

Phoenix, Arizona,
July 18, 1917.

"Samuel Gompers, President,
    American Federation of Labor,
       A. F. of L. Building, Washington, D. C.

Use your best efforts with President to have all men who were
deported from Bisbee returned to their homes under military
protection. Many American Federation of Labor members with
families were deported. Their wives and children are in want.
Act at once.   W. E. Holm
                                                F. J. Perry

Former Secretaries Warren District Trade Assembly."
Phoenix, Arizona
July 19, 1917.

"Samuel Gompers, President,
    American Federation of Labor,
        A. F. of L. Bldg., Washington, D. C.
Appeal to the President to order men deported from Bisbee returned to their homes with military protection. Many members of American Federation of Labor deported and treated like brutes. Families of deported men suffering with hunger in Bisbee. Quick action is necessary.   Thos. A. French,

Secretary Arizona State Federation of Labor.["]
                                    Phoenix, Arizona.
                                    July 19, 1917.

"Samuel Gompers, President,
    American Federation of Labor,
        A. F. of L. Bldg., Washington, D. C.
Fred W. Brown, Organizer American Federation of Labor, number 7352, a bitter opponent of I.W.W. is among the men deported from Bisbee. Deportation was a general fight on organized labor. We are advised of no action by Federal Government as yet.   Thomas A. French, Secretary.
                        Arizona State Federation of Labor."

The reason I have given these three telegrams is because they are official and from representatives in the labor movement in Phoenix who I know to be trustworthy and truthful.

I assume it is not necessary for me to give any assurance of how utterly out of accord I am with the I.W.W. and any such propaganda; but some of the men deported are said to be law-abiding men engaged in an earnest effort at improvement of their condition. If the men treated as stated have been guilty of any crime, they should be tried in the courts and given the opportunity for defense. There is no law of which I am aware that gives authority to private citizens to undertake to deport from the state any man. If there be lawlessness, it is surely such conduct.

I am fully impressed with your desire not only to see that justice is done but to do justice to all our people alike, regardless of their walk in life, and I respectfully submit this matter to your consideration, confident that you will take such action as the circumstances warrant.
                        Respectfully,   Saml. Gompers.

TLS (WP, DLC).

From Charles William Eliot

Dear Mr. President: Asticou, Maine 20 July 1917

For several years past I have paid a good deal of attention to the industrial warfare; so that what I say here is based on studies which ante-date our going to War with Germany.

It is now obvious that the American trades-unions mean to avail themselves of the necessities of the Government—national, state, and municipal—during the War to strengthen their hold on the chief American industries, such as agriculture, commerce, transportation, and mining. They have no patriotic scruples, and no intention of abandoning or qualifying, even in times of great national anxiety and distress, their two most injurious doctrines —limitation of output and the closed shop.

Now, the experience of all the belligerents demonstrates that war cannot be effectively carried on by a nation whose principal industries are crippled by those two doctrines carried into execution.

You are doubtless aware that our present preparations for war are being crippled in many places and in many trades by the demands of the labor-unions enforced with an unexampled strictness. To be sure, some corporations are successfully resisting the closed shop; but in general owners—persons, firms, or corporations—have been yielding almost without resistance to the demands of the unions, some of which are entirely unreasonable. The points of greatest danger in regard to our efficiency in war seem to be the industries concerned with foods, fuel, munitions, and transportation.

Is it possible for you to avail yourself of the intense interest of the people in the successful prosecution of the War against Germany to procure at once the enactment of the Canadian law for the investigation of industrial disputes, making it applicable to trades concerned with foods, fuel, munitions, and transportation? That Act makes a sudden strike impossible, and gives time for public opinion to assert itself. A more effective measure would be an act prohibiting strikes in all those trades; but it may be doubted whether Congress would adopt so strenuous an enactment even as a War measure.

You have procured great concessions from Capital in the interest of War efficiency; can you not do likewise with Labor, the other combatant in the dangerous industrial warfare?

The tide of public opinion in favor of vigorous prosecution of War against Germany has risen so rapidly of late, and run[s] so strong, that I am beginning to hope that the time may come before long when Congress can be induced to consider the adoption of a permanent military system for the United States, a system which would closely resemble that of Switzerland. We have wisely made the term of voluntary enlistment and the draft to expire at the conclusion of the present War; but we ought to begin soon to provide a permanent army always ready, and always perfectly equipped, but sure to create no professional military class, and not to interfere in any significant measure with either the industries of the country or its system of public instruction. Without an effective army and navy we cannot do our part in the work of enforcing peace in the world. As you have so finely declared, the American people propose not only to stop this War, but to make another such war impossible. The adoption of a military organization closely resembling that of Switzerland by all the nations which accept the function of preventing war will be an indispensable step in that long undertaking. It must precede limitation of armaments, and the abolition of professional, paid armies.

I am, with the highest regard,

Sincerely yours   Charles W. Eliot

TLS (WP, DLC).

From George Washington Goethals

My dear Mr. President: Washington July 20, 1917.

I beg to acknowledge the receipt of your letter of July 19th, and wish to express my appreciation of the considerate manner in which you have stated the conclusions which you have reached.

In the project for the "Rapid Emergency Construction of Small Ships," dated March 20, 1917, and approved by you on April 4th last, it was stated that

"to secure the speed of production, which is all important, we feel that the task of securing and equipping these ships should be put in the hands of one man. Centralized control is essential for rapid and efficient work."

It was on this understanding on my part that I undertook the work at your request. This understanding was subsequently confirmed, not only when I took up the matter with the Shipping Board, but at the hearings before the Sub-Committee of the Committee on Appropriations of the United States Senate, where it was stated that I was to have "absolute and complete authority for the administration on the constructing side; that everything the Board could do would be done, and that it would act on my suggestion and initiative." These assurances were placed much more clearly before the members of the Sub-Committee on Appropriations of the House of Representatives.

The necessity for shipping makes it imperative that results be secured as rapidly as possible. It is results, by whomsoever obtained, which count after all, and nothing should be allowed to interfere with the accomplishment of this end. I have endeavored to establish harmonious relations with the Shipping Board, but regret to state I have not succeeded, and it seems impossible to secure the unison of purpose essential to the success of the work. Believing that a centralization of authority in one man is necessary to carry out the shipbuilding program rapidly and successfully, after mature consideration of the whole subject, I am satisfied that I cannot secure efficient results under the conditions of your letter. I am convinced, therefore, that the best interests of the public welfare would be served if I were replaced by some one on whom full authority can be centered and whose personality will not be a stumbling block. It is my urgent hope that this solution will commend itself to you, and, in order that the work may be delayed as little as possible by a change, if you deem it wise, I shall be glad to continue in charge until my successor can be selected and remain with him until he has a thorough knowledge of the organization that has been built up and is able to familiarize himself with the work that has already been undertaken.

You may be assured of my loyal acquiescence in the directions given in your letter and all future orders.

Very respectfully,   Geo. W. Goethals

TLS (WP, DLC).

From Kenneth Douglas McKellar

My dear Mr. President: [Washington] July 20th, 1917.

I did not write an immediate answer to your last note about the defense advisory boards provision in the Food Bill because I had hoped we would agree on a provision that would be satisfactory all around; but, as you have seen, the Pomerene Amendment, with a proviso that the present law is to remain on the statute books, has been tentatively adopted and I suppose will be ratified by the Senate tomorrow.

This is not exactly what I wanted, as you saw from my previous letters, but I believe it is sufficient to deal with the situation. This, with the publicity that may be given any contracts made in violation of it, I am very hopeful will prevent any contracts between interested committees and the government.

I hope that the Amendment that we have adopted will meet your approval, too, for I regretted exceedingly that I could not look at the matter as you did.

With great respect, I am

Very sincerely yours,   Kenneth McKellar

TLS (WP, DLC).

From Alison Low Turnbull Hopkins

My dear Mr. President: Washington July 20, 1917.

The pardon issued to me by you is accompanied by no explanation. It can have but one of two meanings: either you have satisfied yourself, as you personally stated to Mr. Hopkins, that I violated no law of the country and no ordinance of this City in exercising my right of peaceful petition, and therefore, you, as an act of justice, extended to me your pardon, or you pardoned me to save yourself the embar[r]assment of an acute and distressing political situation. In this case, in thus saving yourself, you have deprived me of my right through appeal, to prove by legal processes, that the police powers of Washington despotically and falsely convicted me on a false charge, in order to save you personal or political embar[r]assment.

As you have not seen fit to tell the public the true reason, I am compelled to resume my peaceful petition for political liberty.[1] If the police arrest me, I shall carry the case to the Supreme Court if necessary. If the police do not arrest me, I shall believe that you do not believe me guilty. This is the only method by which I can release myself from the intolerable and false position in which your unexplained pardon has placed me.

Mr. Hopkins and I repudiate absolutely, the current report that I would accept a pardon which was an act of your "good nature."

In this case, which involves my fundamental constitutional rights, Mr. Hopkins and myself do not desire your presidential benevolence, but American justice.

Furthermore, we do not believe that you would insult *us*, by extending to *me*, your mere "good nature" under these circumstances.

The pardon, without any explanation of your reasons for its issuance, in no way mitigates the injustice inflicted upon me by the violation of my constitutional civil rights.

Respectfully yours,   Alison Turnbull Hopkins.

TLS (WP, DLC).

¹ Late in the afternoon of July 20, Mrs. Hopkins returned to the west gate of the White House. She carried a yellow banner bearing these words: "We ask not pardon for ourselves, but justice for all American women." A crowd gathered, but the police saw to it that she was not molested. A few minutes after she arrived, Wilson and Mrs. Wilson drove through in their automobile. "Seeing Mrs. Hopkins in position," the New York *World* reported, "the President doffed his hat and smiled. Mrs. Wilson joined in the salute and smiled also." At the White House, it was stated informally that the suffragists would be allowed to picket the Executive Mansion if they did so in such a way "as not to create disorder." Big demonstrations that might cause riots would be suppressed by the police. Mrs. Hopkins that same day made public her letter to Wilson. On the following afternoon, twelve militant members of the National Woman's party picketed the White House, without incident, and there were reports that groups opposing the draft planned to follow suit. New York *World*, July 21 and 22, 1917.

From Annie Howe Cothran

Dearest Uncle Woodrow,   [New York, c. July 20, 1917]

We¹ have decided to be married on Thursday the 26th of July and take our vacation together. We will have a very quiet little wedding here in New York and send no invitations. You know how much I should love to have you all here to wish me all the happiness in store for me but I shall not beg you to come for I know what tense, busy, terrible days these are for you. I hope Brothers can be here with me. Brother Geo's coming is doubtful, however.

With all sorts of love to you all & specially your self.

                              Every devotedly   Annie

Write me a line if you can, however.

ALS (WP, DLC).

¹ That is, she and Frank E. Compton of Chicago.

Frank Lyon Polk to Walter Hines Page

                    Washington, July 20, 1917

For the Ambassador.

Your 6767, July eighteenth.

Your suggestion submitted to the President and he feels presence of Admiral Sims and General Pershing, even as visitors, could be misconstrued. All necessary naval and military information can be obtained after the conference. I find this is also the opinion of the War Department.

For your confidential information the President unwilling to be represented by conference of all powers engaged in the war, as we are not at war with Austria, Bulgaria or Turkey. Attendance at the conference also might give the impression to this country that this Government was discussing not only the conduct of the campaign, but the ultimate purposes having to do with peace terms.[1]   Polk Acting.

T telegram (SDR, RG 59, 763.72/5896, DNA).

[1] Pershing and Sims did in fact take part in some of the military meetings at Paris on July 25 and 26. See John J. Pershing, *My Experiences in the World War* (2 vols., New York, 1931), I, 116-19, and David F. Trask, *Captains & Cabinets: Anglo-American Naval Relations, 1917-1918* (Columbia, Mo., 1972), pp. 144-46. Pershing and Sims did not attend the political sessions, but Pershing indicates (p. 117) that he considered it permissible to go to a separate meeting of military leaders. In a letter of July 27, he informed Bliss that General Ferdinand Foch, the new commander in chief of the French armies, had taken advantage of the presence of high military representatives to hold "an informal discussion of military matters of interest." The main subject was "the Russian defection." J. J. Pershing to T. H. Bliss, July 27, 1917, CCL (J. J. Pershing Papers, DLC).

From the Diary of Josephus Daniels

1917 Friday 20 July

Cabinet—President W. spoke of Smoot resolution to send to Congress all about ship contracts.[1] "Why will Democrats pass any old resolution of inquiry a Republican offers?"

Discussed Mr Bell & IWW. His plan was to intern when cases were suspicious, ask the papers to print nothing because it made the IWWs martyrs & try to get better conditions. W.B.W. said mine operators this week refused to meet a committee of mine employes & much of the friction came from unfair treatment. W.W. was willing to have & favored secret service men but not taking over a function of the separate states. He will see Bell before he goes back.[2]

[1] The Senate had agreed on July 19 to Smoot's resolution (S. Res. 106) to request the President to give the Senate "such information as may be in the hands of the Shipping Board to show what contracts have been let or are pending for the construction of ships under the authority of that board, the names of the contractors, the location and capacity of their yards, the price per ton to be paid to them, the nature and amount of any advances to be made to them from Government funds, together with any other information which will indicate the disposition of appropriations already made for the uses of the Shipping Board or which will assist the Senate in the consideration of requests from the said board for further appropriations." *Cong. Record*, 65th Cong., 1st sess., p. 5245.

[2] For an account of their meeting, see the memorandum by George L. Bell printed at July 25, 1917.

To Edward Mandell House

My dear House,   [*U.S.S. Mayflower*] 21 July, 1917.

Frankly, I see some very grave possibilities of danger in your plan for an interchange of views about peace between THE

WORLD and the TAGEBLATT, particularly if Northcliffe and Tardieu are to be made counsellors in the matter. England and France *have not the same views with regard to peace that we have* by any means. When the war is over we can force them to our way of thinking, because by that time they will, among other things, be financially in our hands; but we cannot force them now, and any attempt to speak for them or to speak our common mind would bring on disagreements which would inevitably come to the surface in public and rob the whole thing of its effect. I saw this all too plainly in a conversation with Viviani. If there is to be an interchange of views at all, it ought to be between us and the liberals in Germany, with no one else brought in.

Even at that, how is the State Department, or any other official agency of the Government going to ask that the TAGEBLATT be allowed to print what the WORLD says without any interference by the censor without its appearing that what is proposed is really an interchange of views between the German liberals and this Government? I do not think it possible to keep the hand of the Administration concealed.

It seems to me that these are very real difficulties and disclose some deep dangers. Our real peace terms,—those upon which we shall undoubtedly insist,—are not now acceptable to either France or Italy (leaving Great Britain for the moment out of consideration).

I have delayed writing you about this deeply important matter until I could think it out; and I must say that I have not been able to think myself on to safe ground regarding it. You may have entirely satisfactory replies to make to my objections; but I cannot think of them myself. Will you not write me again. I have thought about it enough now, I think, to promise a prompt reply.

I am writing on the MAYFLOWER, on which Mrs. Wilson and I are seeking a day or two of relief from the madness of Washington. A point is reached now and again when I *must* escape it for a little.

With affectionate messages from us all,

Your grateful Friend,   Woodrow Wilson

WWTLS (E. M. House Papers, CtY).

To Samuel Gompers

My dear Mr. Gompers: U.S.S. MAYFLOWER, 21 July, 1917

Thank you for your letter of July twentieth and the generous confidence which it expresses.

I have been, of course, very much disturbed by the news from Arizona and New Mexico and you may be sure that in consultation with my colleagues of the Cabinet I have been concerting such steps as it was possible to take within the limits of federal authority.

In haste

Cordially and sincerely yours,   Woodrow Wilson

TLS (S. Gompers Corr., AFL-CIO-Ar).

To Joseph Patrick Tumulty, with Enclosure

Dear Tumulty: [*U.S.S. Mayflower*, July 21, 1917]

I would like very much to have a verification of the story about the man being taken through the streets of New York chained. I would need a very specific proof of that, and I would like to know who did it.

Mitchel's administration has done many unwise and unjustifiable things but that ought to be corrected by local opinion, not by federal intervention and I understand that to be what Mr. Villard is chiefly referring to in the latter part of his letter.

He is entirely mistaken about certain papers having been "suppressed." Nothing of the kind occurred. Certain copies of certain newspapers were excluded from the mails because they contained matter explicitly forbidden by law.   The President.

TL (WP, DLC).

E N C L O S U R E

Oswald Garrison Villard to Joseph Patrick Tumulty

My dear Mr. Tumulty: New York July 20th, 1917.

I wonder whether so hard driven a man as yourself realizes the excesses to which certain departments of the Government, with which you are naturally not brought into contact, have gone. You have noticed the protest against the suppression of sixteen newspapers since this war began, not by any authoritative persons but by postmasters or underlings of the Department of Justice. In my judgment that cannot continue without arousing much ill feeling.

On Tuesday of this week fourteen of the interned Germans at Ellis Island were taken through the streets of New York, chained together.[1] I do not know any one of the men who were subjected to this indignity. Some of them may be thoroughly bad men, but two of them are reported to me by responsible people as the most pro-American of all the Germans who have been officially or semi-officially in this country. They are not, I take it, criminal but political offenders. I need not tell you what a wave of anger would pass over the United States if it were known that fourteen interned Americans were dragged through the streets of Berlin, chained and padlocked, and open to photographing. It would, I am sure, cause an outburst of rage. Unfortunately, these excesses of underlings, who seem to have been Prussianized over night in this war for democracy, will be reported in Germany as soon as the war is over, if not before, by those who are victims, and will make it hard indeed to restore friendly relations between the two countries. I need not remind you of the numerous persons illegally punished here in New York who were exercising their constitutional rights to criticize existing laws, and their punishment under what seems a totally unwarranted extension of the crime of disorderly conduct. An utterance from the President on this subject would be of enormous value in restoring a state of mind and conduct worthy of our American citizenship and officialdom.

　　With best wishes, I am,

　　　　　　　　Yours faithfully,　　Oswald Garrison Villard.

TLS (WP, DLC).
　1 Thomas D. McCarthy, the United States Marshal in New York, on Monday, July 16, had transferred fourteen Germans from Ellis Island to military custody at Jersey City for transfer to Fort Oglethorpe, Ga. Some of the men were "looked upon by Federal officials as the most dangerous enemy aliens yet taken into custody." New York *World*, July 17, 1917. Villard wrote to Tumulty on July 26 that McCarthy stated that the prisoners had been handcuffed to officers, but that he, Villard, had no direct proof that the men had also been chained together. O. G. Villard to JPT, July 26, 1917, TLS (WP, DLC).

To Jessie Woodrow Wilson Sayre

My precious Daughter,　　　　　　[*U.S.S. Mayflower*] 21 July, 1917.

　I cannot put into words the thoughts, the loving, wistful thoughts, I have had of you and of the dear little ones since Frank went away; and they have been with me at all sorts of times, amidst all sorts of business and all sorts of public anxieties. Edith and I are on the MAYFLOWER to-day to get away from the madness (it is scarcely less) of washington for a day or two, Not to stop work (that *cannot* stop nowadays), for I had to bring Swem and my papers along, but to escape *people* and their intolerable excitements and demands. This is, therefore, the first time in weeks that I have had any chance at all to turn to my private thoughts and to the dear little girl whom I so dearly love in Nantucket and try to say some of the things that are in my heart.

I know that Helen has written to you and I have tried to keep track of you as best I could; but that is not the real thing,—that does not satisfy my heart. I hope that the visit that Margaret was planning to pay you may come off soon. Helen has gone up to Canada to join Marion Erskine[1] and her little family at a camp somewhere up by Georgian Bay in Canada. She will probably be gone for an indefinite stay. She needs something of the kind. She has been going to lunches and dinners almost every day for months past and must have used up all the strength her nerves contained. Edith and she have been working hard (Edith is working now) on Red Cross supplies and warm things for the sailors. They have made pajamas enough, it seems to me, for a whole hospital! We try to take things light-heartedly and with cool minds, but it is not always possible, and I fear that I notice little signs of its Telling on Edith. As for myself, I am surprisingly well, by all the tests that the doctor can apply, though *very* tired all the time. I am very thankful. I do not see how any but a well man could safely be trusted to decide anything in the present circumstances.

No doubt you heard of Annie Cothran's engagement to Mr. Compton, the Chicago publisher who was for so long Margaret's ardent suitor. To-day I get a letter from her telling us that they mean to be married very quietly next week, on Thursday, the twenty-sixth![2] They had at first planned to be married in September! Such is the ardour of young people, notwithstanding at least one previous misadventure! Really I am very glad about it; for Mr. Compton is said to be a very fine fellow, and this marriage settles a great many anxious questions about Annie and little Josephine. Annie seems to be really in love and, with no too intimate personal oversight of the marriage, such as Sister Annie so mistakenly tried to exercise in the first match, everything has a chance to go as it should.

I believe this is all the family news. My heart goes out to you, my darling Jessie, with unbounded love and solicitude! Please, when you have time, write me how things are going with you, what you hear from Frank, if a real message has had time to get through yet, and all the things, big or little, that you know I want to hear; and I do not know of anything I do *not* want to know about you in your new home.

Edith joins me in warmest love to you all and I send you, for myself, all the love that a father's heart can give to a dear daughter whom he admires as much as he loves.

Your devoted Father

WWTLS (WC, NjP).
  [1] Marion McGraw Bones Brower (Mrs. Albert DeWolf) Erskine, Wilson's first cousin once removed.
  [2] Actually, they were married on July 21. Annie H. Compton and F. E. Compton to WW and EBW, July 21, 1917, T telegram (WP, DLC).

From Asbury Francis Lever

My dear Mr. President: [Washington, July 21, 1917]

I am handing you herewith a copy of the Food Conservation Bill as it passed the Senate. It is my purpose to make an effort to get the measure in conference as soon as possible, with a view to expediting its final passage. I recognize the pressing necessity of its enactment into law at the earliest moment, and will lend my earnest endeavor to hasten action thereon.

I beg to direct your attention to Section 23 of the Bill.[1] This amendment is wholly foreign to the purpose of the measure, which in my opinion should deal alone with food control. Inasmuch as Section 23 is new matter sought to be engrafted on the Bill and has been given but little consideration by me, may I venture to ask from you an expression as to its value?

I would appreciate an early reply from you, which, if I deem it necessary, I would like the privilege of making public.

Sincerely yours,   A. F. Lever

TLS (WP, DLC).
  [1] This section of H.R. 4961 was based upon an amendment offered by Senator Weeks on July 18. It established "The Joint Committee on Expenditures in the Conduct of the War," which was to confer and advise with the President and the heads of the various executive departments, commissions, and voluntary boards or other organizations connected with the conduct of the war, with a view to safeguarding expenditures. The committee was to report to Congress from time to time in its own discretion or when requested to do so. *Cong. Record*, 65th Cong., 1st sess., pp. 5231, 5363.

From Edward Mandell House

Dear Governor: Magnolia, Massachusetts. July 21, 1917.

I have a letter from Frank Trumbull in which he says:

"It may interest you to know that President Stevens[1] of the Cheasapeake & Ohio told me today that Mr. Howe[2] has been appointed Deputy Commissioner of the Tidewater Coal Bureau at a salary of $6000.00 per annum. Mr. Stevens has given him leave of absence from the C & O so he can accept this position. It may, however, outlast the war. He has 'made good'—as you said he would." Affectionately yours, E. M. House

TLS (WP, DLC).
1 George Walter Stevens.
2 Wilson's nephew, J. Wilson Howe.

From John Singer Sargent

Sir   Boston July 21st 1917

Your very kind letter of the 18th gave me great pleasure by showing that you are not disinclined to allow me to paint your portrait for the National Gallery of Ireland. I take note that you think it is doubtful that an opportunity will occur before September.

A letter to this Hotel will always reach me, and with a few days notice, I will appear when you [are] ready for me.

Believe me, Sir, Yours respectfully John S. Sargent

ALS (WP, DLC).

From Thomas Watt Gregory

Sir: Washington, D. C. July 22, 1917.

I have the honor to acknowledge receipt of your letter of the 20th instant enclosing a letter from L. W. Nieman of The Milwaukee Journal and certain newspaper clippings concerning the attitude of the German-American newspapers.[1]

Unfortunately a great many of these papers still print in their news and editorial columns much disloyal matter, but there seems to be no way in most cases in which this can be prevented lawfully. Close attention is being given the matter, with a special view to bringing to bear in proper cases the provisions of Title XII of the recent Espionage Act governing the use of the mails.

Respectfully, T. W. Gregory

TLS (WP, DLC).
1 WW to TWG, July 20, 1917, TLS (Letterpress Books, WP, DLC).

From Amelia Himes Walker

Baltimore, July twenty second [1917].

For my release from an unjust sentence in the District workhouse, I wish to express my gratitude.

When I went to Washington to present my petition to the President, that he should put his great energy to the passage of the Anthony Amendment, I was actuated by the deepest patriotism. How *can* we force the world into democracy, when you do not permit twenty million citizens to have a voice in the government of the United States?

With my thanks for my release, I must protest to the President that more deeply do I desire political liberty for the women who need it. The woman who knows the value of the ballot is the woman who will use it.

I inclose an expressive cartoon which tells the situation at a glance.[1]

Again let me express my gratitude for my speedy return to my family.

I am, sir,   Very truly yours,   Amelia Himes Walker.

ALS (WP, DLC).
[1] The cartoon was on the cover of *The Woman Citizen: The Woman's Journal, Official Organ of the National American Woman Suffrage Association,* I (July 21, 1917), 125. It showed a woman, "United States," wearing a hobble skirt marked "State Constitutions," which prevented her from climbing the hill to "Full Enfranchisement." The caption read: "Her Hobble Skirt Is Out of Date." There is a copy in WP, DLC.

A Statement[1]

[July 23, 1917]

The Bible is the word of life. I beg that you will read it and find this out for yourself,—read, not little snatches here and there, but long passages that will really be the road to the heart of it. You will find it full of real men and women not only but also of the things you have wondered about and been troubled about all your life, as men have been always; and the more you read the more it will become plain to you what things are worth while and what are not, what things make men happy,—loyalty, right dealing, speaking the truth, readiness to give everything for what they think their duty, and, most of all, the wish that they may have the approval of the Christ, who gave everything for them,— and the things that are guaranteed to make men unhappy,— selfishness, cowardice, greed, and everything that is low and mean. When you have read the Bible you will know that it is the Word of God, because you will have found it the key to your own heart, your own happiness, and your own duty.[2]

T MS (WP, DLC).
[1] Prepared for transmission, through Josephus Daniels, to Robert B. Haines, Jr., Secretary of the Scripture Gift Mission, for United States soldiers and sailors.
[2] There is a WWsh draft of this statement in the C. L. Swem Coll., NjP.

To Asbury Francis Lever

My dear Mr. Lever: The White House 23 July, 1917

I am very much obliged to you for your thoughtful courtesy in stating to me the circumstances of the present action on the Food Administration Bill, and I am particularly obliged to you for calling my attention to Section 23. I deem it my duty to express my opinion about that section and its effect upon the whole administration of the war very frankly indeed, since the public interest manifestly demands that I should do so.

Section 23 is not only entirely foreign to the subject matter of the Food Administration Bill in which it is incorporated but would, if enacted into law, render my task of conducting the war practically impossible. I cannot believe that those who proposed this section scrutinized it with care or analyzed the effects which its operation would necessarily have. The constant supervision of executive action which it contemplates would amount to nothing less than an assumption on the part of the legislative body of the executive work of the administration.

There is a very ominous precedent in our history which shows how such a supervision would operate. I refer to the committee on the conduct of the war constituted by the Congress during the administration of Mr. Lincoln. It was the cause of constant and distressing harassment and rendered Mr. Lincoln's task all but impossible.

I am not, I beg you to believe, in any way questioning what might be the motives or the purpose of the members of such a committee; I am ready to assume that they would wish to cooperate in the most patriotic spirit, but cooperation of that kind is not practicable in the circumstances. The responsibility rests upon the administration. There are abundant existing means of investigation and of the effective enforcement of that responsibility. I sincerely hope that upon the reconsideration of this matter both Houses of Congress will see that my objections rest upon indisputable grounds and that I could only interpret the final adoption of Section 23 as arising from a lack of confidence in myself.[1]

Cordially and sincerely yours,   Woodrow Wilson

TLS (A. F. Lever Papers, ScCleU).
[1] The Senate conferees in the conference committee agreed to drop Section 23. See, particularly, Livermore, *Politics is Adjourned: Woodrow Wilson and the War Congress, 1916-1918*, pp. 55-56.

To Louis Wiley

My dear Mr. Wiley: The White House 23 July, 1917

Thank you for sending me the full version of Maximilian Harden's article of June sixteenth, together with a copy of your remarks on press censorship.[1]

The matter of censorship is growing daily more difficult and more important, because there are certain hostile and disloyal elements in the press of the country which are taking advantage of the present situation and are doing the most dangerous and hurtful things.

In haste

Cordially and sincerely yours,   Woodrow Wilson

TLS (L. Wiley Papers, NRU).

[1] Wiley's letter and enclosures are missing. Harden's article, "Der Traum von Stockholm," was originally printed in the Berlin *Die Zukunft*, XCIX (June 16, 1917), 275-302. The title, "The Stockholm Dream," meant that the international socialist meetings there would not lead to peace. The article also dealt with the situation in Russia and Wilson's efforts for a peace of understanding. It suggested that Germany had to be prepared to make concessions regarding Poland and Alsace-Lorraine. A short summary of Harden's article is printed in the *New York Times*, June 29, 1917. *Die Zukunft* was forced to suspend publication for several months following its issue of June 30, 1917. For accounts of the evolution of Harden's views during the war, see Harry F. Young, *Maximilian Harden: Censor Germaniae; The Critic in Opposition from Bismarck to the Rise of Nazism* (The Hague, 1959), pp. 178-218, and B. Uwe Weller, *Maximilian Harden und die "Zukunft"* (Bremen, 1970), pp. 220-66.

To Robert Latham Owen

My dear Senator: [The White House] 23 July, 1917

I did not know until today that an amendment had been attached to the Food Bill providing for a Congressional Committee to sit in the recess and superintend the expenditures of the Executive. I am sure, my dear Senator, that you cannot have reckoned the embarrassment and constant hampering that the existence and activity of such committee would impose on the Executive. It is in substance a reproduction of the sort of committee which distressed Mr. Lincoln so constantly throughout the Civil War, and I hope with all my heart that you may be willing to have the action reconsidered and reversed. I honestly think that it would be impossible for me to conduct the war with success if I am to be placed under daily espionage.

Cordially and sincerely yours,   [Woodrow Wilson]

CCL (WP, DLC).

To Thomas Watt Gregory

My dear Gregory: The White House 23 July, 1917

Will I not be right in saying to Mr. Dyer that this is a matter to which we cannot under the existing law extend our jurisdiction, much as we should like to do so?

Cordially and faithfully yours,   Woodrow Wilson

TLS (JDR, RG 60, Numerical File, No. 186835/34, DNA).

To Lucretia Thatcher Osborn[1]

My dear Mrs. Osborn: [The White House] 23 July, 1917

I thank you sincerely for your thoughtful courtesy in sending me the copy of the Atlantic containing Mr. Olds' article on the disloyalty of the German-American Press.[2] I know only too well the foundations for his statements and you may be sure that the matter has been giving me a great deal of deep concern.

Cordially and sincerely yours,   Woodrow Wilson

TLS (Letterpress Books, WP, DLC).

[1] Mrs. Henry Fairfield Osborn, wife of the eminent paleontologist and an old friend of Wilson.

[2] Frank Perry Olds, "Disloyalty of the German-American Press," *The Atlantic Monthly*, CXX (July 1917), 136-40. It stated that American newspapers in the German language, while they carefully avoided anything that would lay them open to charges of treason, were "spreading a fabric of anti-government lies, anti-Ally calumnies, and anti-war agitations." Olds cited examples of what he found objectionable and concluded as follows: "The Constitution allows free speech. The Constitution does not allow comfort to the enemy. The case of the German-American press is between the two. What are we going to do about it? What *can* we do about it?" Following Olds' article, the editors of *The Atlantic Monthly* proposed "a sane war-time censorship upon enemy propaganda, and a substantial war-time tax on the printed use of the enemy language."

To Joseph R. Wilson, Jr.

Dearest Joe: [The White House] 23 July, 1917

I am ashamed to have overlooked your birthday and thank you with all my heart for your generosity in writing to me.[1] Being ten years ahead of you, I can't feel impressed by your fifty years, but still I shall always try to treat you with moderate respect! I certainly congratulate you on being well in the midst of so much and such hard work. It does my heart good to hear you say that you are.

Can't you, instead of working to get rid of the loneliness, drop over and see us some time if only for an evening and night?[2] Edith and I are all alone. Helen is in Canada with Marion Erskine and her children; Margaret is in Connecticut with her singing teacher; and Nell is seventy miles away at Blue Ridge Summit: so that we have a house empty except for the painters and can always find joy in putting you up for the night.

Edith joins me in most affectionate messages, and I am as always   Your affectionate brother,   Woodrow Wilson

TLS (Letterpress Books, WP, DLC).
  [1] J. R. Wilson, Jr., to WW, July 20, 1917, TLS (WP, DLC).
  [2] Joseph R. Wilson, Jr., came to lunch at the White House on July 28.

From Newton Diehl Baker

Dear Mr. President: Washington. July 23, 1917.

I return the correspondence in your note of the 18th.

I assume that the conclusion you have reached and will express to Mr. Bell, the representative of the Western Governors, will cover the situation so far as Senator Poindexter's suggestion is concerned.

If in your judgment I should go any further than I have gone in directions to the military commanders in this matter, it will give me great pleasure to issue the necessary instructions.[1]

Respectfully yours,   Newton D. Baker

TLS (WP, DLC).
  [1] On July 27, Baker had General Bliss send the following message to the commanding general of the Western Department:
  "It has been reported unofficially to the Secretary of War that, as a result of some labor trouble, Federal troops have been sent to the town of San Jose, California, at the request of the mayor. This report may not be true, but in general connection with the subject the Secretary of War directs that all requests from [for] Federal troops from local authorities be disregarded and the matter be at once referred to the Governor of the State concerned for an expression of his desire. Troops must not be ordered out for any such purpose except on the call of the Governor." T. H. Bliss to H. P. McCain, July 27, 1917, CC MS (T. H. Bliss Papers, DLC).

From Edward Mandell House

Dear Governor: Magnolia, Massachusetts. July 23, 1917.

The Russian Ambassador was here yesterday. He tells me that he has gone the round of Cabinet officers and officials and is at the end of the passage regarding certain matters. He wanted to know whether he had better approach you with these questions. I advised him to again press the proper officials rather than to take his troubles to you. I promised, however, to tell you of them.

His general concern is that he cannot get any shipping or dependable assurance of it. Vladivastock is congested and it will take eight months to haul what it [is] now there, therefore, they need nothing excepting rolling stock to go via the Pacific. If they could get the rolling stock they could relieve the congestion.

He says it is not true that Russia is making demands upon us for railroad equipment looking to after war conditions, but what they ask is needed immediately to conduct the war properly. He declares that Stevens will verify this statement.

As for Archangel, he is unable to get any commitment from Denman, and it is very important to know what they are to get or are not to get so they may arrange accordingly. Something definite is the thing of most importance. Archangel will be closed in October and what is done must needs be done during August and the early part of September. The time is therefore short and means everything to Russia and the Allies.

As to finances, Russia has been given only about one hundred millions—a sum he thinks entirely out of proportion to what has been given the other Allies and out of proportion to Russia's great needs. Unless money can be had he believes the Government cannot last. With it, he believes conditions will steadily improve and a stable democracy will be established.

I am wondering if you cannot say a word to Denman, on the one hand, and McAdoo on the other, and send word to Willard or Felton[1] regarding the necessity for rolling stock. Felton has the matter in direct charge, but is favoring France rather than Russia, I am told.

If the war is to end on the field it seems fairly clear that it cannot end on the Western Front. Have you thought of the advisability of sending some of our troops to Russia via the Pacific? They would have open warfare instead of trench warfare, and would be a steadying force to the Russians.

I do not think we can devote too much attention to the Russian situation, for if that fails us our troubles will be great and many.   Affectionately yours,   E. M. House

TLS (WP, DLC).
[1] Baker had just appointed Samuel Morse Felton, president of the Chicago Great Western Railroad since 1909, as Director General of Military Railways.

From William Denman

My dear Mr. President: Washington July 23, 1917.

I have not burdened you with the stenographic record of the two conferences with General Goethals because they cannot be understood without reference to a number of other documents. Two things, however, are apparent. One is that the General did not know himself any of the essential grand subdivisions of either his commandeering scheme or his scheme for fabricating ships. I am not now referring to mere subordinate technical details, but those which go to the essence of the scheme, both as to basic prices and as to volume of output.

Since our commandeering plan necessarily involves publicity, we are taking no action on it until the interview with you to which you referred in your letter.

The "stalling" process to which I referred in a former letter is still being carried on. It took two days to obtain from the General a two line modification of a sketch of a contract that he gave us on Thursday. He is today treating in a most casual way the delay in obtaining the figures which we called for last week.

> Very faithfully yours,   William Denman.

TLS (WP, DLC).

From Alice Hay Wadsworth[1]

Dear Mr. President: [Washington] July 23, 1917.

As a loyal American citizen and a life long resident of the District of Columbia, I wish to protest against the wilful and persistent disregard for law and order systematically displayed by the members of the National Woman's Party.

Your action in pardoning the sixteen women sentenced to Occoquan was one of clemency and not of Justice. It was a proof of your tolerance and magnanimity and showed your appreciation not so much of woman's rights as of her duties.

The women had been repeatedly warned that further violation of the laws would be punished and they had arrogantly and defiantly courted arrest. They went to Occoquan rather than pay the small fines imposed, simply to gain the notoriety and publicity of such an action, and then with a transparent mental dishonesty that is almost inconceivable in persons of normal intelligence, they advertised their martyrdom to the Cause of Suffrage.

In spite of the obvious justice of their sentence you let them go because their families needed their services—but will their families reap the benefit? Mr. Hopkins warned you that the "picketing would continue." He was right—it has continued.

The American public is good natured and long suffering—that was well proved before we took up the glorious burden of this war, but are not orderly and law-abiding citizens entitled to protection from annoyance? Is it wise to fan the flame of class jealousy by allowing the deportation from the State, (in cat-

tle cars) of undesirable citizens in one section of the country
and permitting women of wealth, family and position to violate
the laws and go unpunished in another? And not only unpunished but actually demanding what they consider a reward
for their misconduct.

Can it be necessary that to preserve peace within our borders
in this time of stress and imperative need for progress, the
machinery of government should be halted that these "flies on
the wheel" may bask in the light of publicity?

They who prattle of "democracy" and strive to force the will of
the few upon the vast majority; they who shout of patriotism
and defame the good name of their country in the hearing of
other nations; they who prate of equal rights but who will not
observe them under the law: Mr. President, are these to be
trusted with the solemn responsibility of Suffrage?

I am submitting this question for your serious consideration, and with great respect, I am

Cordially yours,   Alice H. Wadsworth.[2]

TLS (WP, DLC).
  [1] Mrs. James Wolcott Wadsworth, Jr., president of the National Association
Opposed to Woman Suffrage. She was a daughter of John Hay.
  [2] Wilson made the following comment on this letter: "This is a very awkward
letter to answer. I would be obliged if you would write to Mrs. Wadsworth saying that I have asked you to acknowledge the letter and express my warm appreciation of her sincere and candid letter." WW to JPT, c. July 24, 1917, TL
(WP, DLC).

From Henry Lee Higginson

Dear Mr. President: Boston. July 23, 1917.

May I say a few words about the fixing of prices? Of course,
any decent man sympathizes with keeping the prices within
bounds; but it is a hard matter to arrange.

I have no interest in coal mining, but many of the coal miners
have gone on for years making very small profits or none, and
now they see good times. If the price is marked too low, the output of coal will be less—perhaps much less. The same is true
of copper. The costs to which all these companies are subjected
are much higher than two years ago.

With regard to copper I have inquired yesterday and today.
The laborers are not working well,—rarely work at all on Monday,—and are getting such high wages that they are indifferent to their work. The price of coal to these mines has increased enormously. The copper miners, therefore, cannot see
how much metal does cost. If the price of copper is fixed at
eighteen or nineteen cents, many mines will be closed, and then

will come scarcity of copper; and either the trade of the country or the Government will be pinched.

Some people are busy opening new mines, and they will not do it if the prices are as low as before. If to the present demand by the Government is added the demand by the manufacturers at the same price, one man will buy and another man will wait for lower prices. Presently the second man,—absolutely needing coal, iron or copper for his business,—will ask for them and will have to pay the first man an advance—perhaps a very large advance. Nothing will prevent this but an ample supply.

Something can be done about prices, but I doubt the wisdom of meddling much. The great laws of the world, the laws of supply and demand, overrule any laws made by man, and settle the point. If the Government and the public pay a good price for a thing, many people rush in to manufacture and mine, and then the price falls. We have seen the result on the railroads, which have been crippled, and are, therefore, much less effective than they ought to be, chiefly because the Interstate Commerce Commission has limited the prices. The public will not supply the fresh capital needed.

It will be less difficult to restrain the price of provisions, the most important part of all, because provisions must be consumed within a few months; but too low prices will bring short crops. Just now an enormous quantity of potatoes has been raised, and the price has fallen, and will fall further.

If the farmers who raise livestock can be prevented from selling anything not full grown, a good result may be obtained.

Meanwhile, unless the manufacturers and miners know the course this Government is going to take, they will diminish their operations; and then comes the scarcity. A year and a half ago metal could be shipped to the other side of the water for $8 a ton, and now it is $85 a ton.

One head of a great house said to me the other day,—"If I earn twelve per cent. on my shares and the Government takes six per cent., there is six per cent. left; if I earn fourteen and the Government takes seven, there is seven per cent. left." The amount of it is, as I see it, that the Government must not hamper anything, and this especially applies, because the coal and the copper and the iron are good in the ground. They can wait, and the mine owners will let them be there unless they can get a fair profit. Tax the output; do not interfere with the price. It is very necessary to keep the manufacturers and merchants in good humor and to give them something certain so far as may be, on which they can make their figures. At present everybody is uncertain, and men are doing little as compared with brisk times.

The Liberty Loan drew dollar bills from many small pockets, and therefore the supply of cash is considerably increased. When the last loan is salted away, another loan can come.

Meanwhile, let me say to you that last week we sold some bonds running for a short time, and they were subscribed five times over. They were excellent, and were short. If in the next few months the Government wants money and goes to the banks with short paper, the banks will take it, and by and by the public will be ready for another loan.

As it seems to me, the secret for success in selling is to give the public what it wants; it wants short loans,—what the English call "Exchequer bills."

It is easy enough for men to do nothing, or little. What we need is the largest possible production which can be used; and the Government can help or hinder this matter.

Will you forgive me for putting these views down on paper, and believe me

Very respectfully yours, H. L. Higginson.

TLS (WP, DLC).

From Ben Webb and Others

Columbus, N. M., July 23, 1917.

All the eleven hundred and forty five men deported from Bisbee have been residents of the Warren district long before the strike was called and many of them have homes and families there. We now demand that we be returned immediately to our homes and families under adequate protection. We appreciate and are thankful for the aid given us by the federal government when we were left helpless on the desert and for the shelter and food given us since.

Ben Webb, A. S. Embree, A. D. Kimball
for Executive Committee.

T telegram (WDR, RG 94, AGO-Misc. File, No. 2638715, DNA).

Thomas Watt Gregory to Joseph Patrick Tumulty, with Enclosure

My dear Mr. Tumulty: Washington, D. C. July 23, 1917.

Referring to your letter of July 7, 1917,[1] enclosing a telegram from S. V. Costello,[2] of San Francisco, relative to the arrest of one Henry Rule,[3] as stated in my letter of July 9, 1917,[4] I sent a telegram to the United States Attorney at San Francisco stating that it was the desire of the President that he should express to the judge, through proper channels, the President's hope that leniency be extended to Mr. Rule.

I am in receipt of a letter from the United States Attorney at San Francisco, under date of July 12th, reading as follows:

> Referring to your telegram to me of the ninth instant requesting that I express to Judge Oppenheim[5] of San Francisco the hope that leniency be extended to Henry Rule charged with exclaiming "Hypocrite" when a picture of President Wilson was flashed on the screen of a local theatre, I desire to state that Mr. Costello, attorney for Mr. Rule, called upon me and I gave to him a letter which he delivered to Judge Oppenheim, a copy of which I enclose herewith. Upon this letter, the case against Rule was dismissed.
>
> Yours cordially,   T. W. Gregory

TLS (WP, DLC).
  [1] It is missing.
  [2] Stephen V. Costello, lawyer of San Francisco. His telegram is missing.
  [3] Manager of a hotel in San Francisco.
  [4] TWG to JPT, July 9, 1917, TLS (WP, DLC).
  [5] Maurice L. Oppenheim, judge of the police court of San Francisco.

E N C L O S U R E

John White Preston to Maurice L. Oppenheim

Dear Judge,   [San Francisco] July 9th 1917.

Referring to the case of People vs. Henry Rule, I am directed by the Department of Justice to say to you that it is the wish and hope of President Wilson himself, that leniency may be shown to Rule for the offense charged against him, a statement of the facts of the case having been laid before the President by his attorney, Mr. Costello. The Department of Justice concurs in the view that it would be highly agreeable to it that leniency may be shown.

Respectfully,

Jno. W. Preston United States Attorney.

TCL (WP, DLC).

William Graves Sharp to Robert Lansing

Paris, July 23, 1917.

Urgent. 2321. Confidential and urgent, in sections.
Section one.

Mr. Cambon has asked me to transmit to the Department certain questions which Mr. Ribot, President of the Council, had formulated as likely to be discussed, though unofficially and exclusive of those relative to the Balkans which are the stated object of the conference to be held in Paris Wednesday, twenty-fifth, instant. He had previously asked me to call at the Foreign Office, that he might acquaint me with the contents of a cablegram received from Mr. Jusserand which set forth the reasons of the President for declining to have our government represented at this so-called Balkan conference. I feel sure the President decided very wisely. While expressing disappointment that our government was not to be represented at the conference, Mr. Cambon said that it had occurred to both Mr. Ribot and himself that in lieu of such reports it might be very helpful if they might get some opinion as to the attitude of our government upon questions which, under certain contingencies are liable to arise. He did not indicate at the time the nature of the questions and I did not anticipate they would take form so quickly.

On the following day, however, Mr. Cambon telephoned me that a note had been mailed to me setting out these questions and we thereupon arranged for a meeting at this office. The questions which he asked me to transmit are in substance as follows:

One. The Russian Government has proposed to submit to a future conference the examination of the allied objects of the war. The English, French and its representatives may be called upon on this occasion to examine the expediency of accepting or rejecting this proposition and in case that it should be accepted the objects that the allies ought to maintain in common accord.

Two. A rumor has circulated that Austria was looking for a separate peace and certain indications show that that country is manifestly tired of the war. It may be useful to examine how one should look upon the suggestions which might come from that direction.

Three. The questions concerning Asia Minor have been at several times the objects of agreements between the allies. These agreements can be affected by the very nature of the issue of the war and we should be happy to know the sentiments of your government on the subject.

Four. There is need of caution that persons who make themselves, knowingly or not, the echoes of German intrigues in allied countries spread the report that the military efforts of the United States will be incomplete and tardy. It is essential to combat these harmful rumors and, at the same time in order to regulate the effort that on our front the Anglo-French, Belgian and Italian forces ought to make, to know exactly the expectations of the Government of Washington on the total military concourse that it will be able to lend us and on the different delays that this concourse will necessitate.

Five. Finally it has been learned that the American Government had the thought of leaving to the allies themselves the allotment of the sums that the United States should put at their disposition, and Mr. Cambon added that the French Government would be pleased to know if it would be notified of a proposition in this sense before the conference of Paris twenty-fifth of July for it would be appropriate to be able to deliberate upon it. Concluding his communication to me he said: "Such are the different questions to which it seems to me expedient that you should call the attention of your Government and that you should ask from it precise indications."

Mr. Matsui,[1] the Japanese Ambassador, telephoned me this morning that while his Government had been invited to participate in conference, yet on account of the uncertainty of it doing so, he had cabled at the request of the Foreign Office to find out its position upon certain questions. End of first section.[2]

Sharp.

T telegram (SDR, RG 59, 763.72119/685, DNA).
   [1] Keishiro Matsui.
   [2] Section 2 is W. G. Sharp to RL, July 24, 1917. For Wilson's reply to Ribot's questions, see W. G. Sharp to J. M. Cambon, Aug. 6 and 7, 1917.

Sir Cecil Arthur Spring Rice to the Foreign Office

Washington July 23 1917

Your tel 2859[1]

Counsellor says that several requests have been made by Poles here and he asked Horadowsky to make a definite statement. Statement now received is rather vague. USG is favourable in principle to anything likely to conciliate Poles and favour their demand for national treatment. As regards military force there are difficulties as to a national Polish army under Polish officers as part of the American force, even if Polish contingent is trained in Canada.

Counsellor will submit your telegram to President and inform me later.[2]

Hw telegram (FO 115/2302, p. 263, PRO).
[1] Foreign Office to C. A. Spring Rice, July 21, 1917, T telegram (FO 115/2302, p. 259, PRO).
[2] See the Enclosure printed with F. L. Polk to WW, July 28, 1917.

From the Diary of Josephus Daniels

July Monday 23 1917

Went to Bakers office where talked with the Pres about G & D.[1] It was painful. "I have so many pains—it is like a tooth that hurts—you get pleasure only in pain."

[1] That is, Goethals and Denman.

To William Denman

My dear Mr. Denman: [The White House] 24 July, 1917

I hope and believe that I am interpreting your own best judgment as well as my own when I say that our duty concerning the debates and misunderstandings that have arisen in connection with the shipbuilding programme ought to be settled without regard to our personal preferences or our personal feelings altogether and with the single purpose of doing what will best serve the public interest. No decision we can now arrive at could eliminate the elements of controversy that have crept into almost every question connected with the programme; and I am convinced that the only wise course is to begin afresh,—not upon the programme, for that is already in large part in process of execution, but upon the further execution of it.

I have found both you and General Goethals ready to serve the public at a personal sacrifice. Realizing that the only manner in which the way can be completely cleared for harmonious and effective action is to carry our shipbuilding plans forward from this point through new agencies, General Goethals has put his resignation in my hands; and I have adopted[1] it in the same spirit in which it was tendered,—not as deciding between two men whom I respect and admire, but in order to make invidious decisions unnecessary and let the work be developed without further discussion of what is past. I am taking the liberty of writing to tell you this in the confidence that you will be glad to take the same disinterested and self-forgetting course that General Goethals has taken. When you have done as he has done I am sure that you may count with the utmost confidence upon the ultimate verdict of the people of the country with regard to your magnanimous and unselfish view of public duty and upon winning in the retrospect the same admiration and confidence that I have learned to feel for you.

With much regard and very great appreciation of the large services you have rendered.

Cordially and sincerely yours,   [Woodrow Wilson][2]

CCL (WP, DLC).
[1] Wilson typed "accepted" in his WWT draft of this letter in WP, DLC. Swem made this mistake in copying Wilson's draft.
[2] There is also a WWsh draft of this letter in WP, DLC.

From William Denman

My dear Mr. President: Washington July 24, 1917.

I am wondering whether you are aware that I am under fire in the Hearst papers in California for an alleged personal interest in contracts for timber. The accusation is a brutal one, and absurdly easy to answer, but the suggested action of your letter of July 24th, with which I will of course comply, will have a peculiarly unfortunate significance at this time.

In my own mind, I know that some few of the kind words of your letter are justified, though much of it is merely your kindliness of spirit. I beg of you that you will permit me to have a personal interview with you at the earliest possible date.

Very faithfully yours,   William Denman.

TLS (WP, DLC).

Two Letters to William Denman

My dear Denman: [The White House] 24 July, 1917

You have asked for a personal interview and I want to make a suggestion to you about it. I have learned to have a sincere and warm admiration for your ability and I hope that you have felt my genuine friendship, for it has been very real, and therefore I can say this to you frankly, that I do not think it would be wise for us to have a personal interview at present. It would certainly be misconstrued in ways which I think a moment's reflection will easily reveal to you. It would be taken to mean either that we were still discussing the situation or that there was some difference between us that needed to be straightened out.

I want to serve your interest in every way that I can, and frankness I am sure is one of the ways. There was, as I take it for granted you also think, no other solution for the *impasse* we had arrived at but that which I suggested, and I have confidence that in the end all the merits involved will be clearly revealed.

Cordially and sincerely yours,   [Woodrow Wilson]

My dear Denman: [The White House] 24 July, 1917

I am surprised and indignant to learn of the absurd charges that are being made against you in some of the California papers, and I hope sincerely that if there is any way in which I can be of service to you in exposing their gross injustice you will let me know and I shall be very glad indeed to do anything that I can to express my entire confidence in your ability not only, but in your integrity.

Cordially and sincerely yours,   [Woodrow Wilson]

CCL (WP, DLC).

To George Washington Goethals

My dear General Goethals: The White House 24 July, 1917

Your letter of July twentieth does you great honor. It is conceived in a fine spirit of public duty, such as I have learned to expect of you. This is, as you say, a case where the service of the public is the only thing to be considered. Personal feelings and personal preferences must be resolutely put aside and we must do the thing that is most serviceable.

It is with that thought in mind that I feel constrained to say that I think that you have interpreted your duty rightly.

No impartial determination of the questions at issue can now set the shipbuilding programme promptly and effectively on its way to completion and success. It is best that we take the self-forgetting course you suggest and begin again with a fresh sheet of paper,—begin, not the shipbuilding, but the further administration of the programme. The shipbuilding is, happily, in large part begun and can now readily be pushed to completion, if the air be cleared of the debates that have unfortunately darkened it.

With deep appreciation, therefore, of your generous attitude and with genuine admiration of what you have been able in a short time to acomplish, I accept your resignation, and feel that in doing so I am acting upon your own best judgment as well as my own. I hope that you will feel the same undoubting confidence that I feel that the people of the country, for whom you have rendered great services, will judge you justly and generously in this as in other things, and that all personal misunderstandings and misjudgments that may have been created will pass in a short time entirely away.

With warm regard,

     Cordially and sincerely yours,   Woodrow Wilson[1]

TLS (G. W. Goethals Papers, DLC).
  [1] There is a WWsh and WWT draft of this letter in WP, DLC.

A Press Release

[July 24, 1917]

Desiring to go forward with the ship building programme as rapidly as possible and counting upon the patriotic and disinterested motives which he has learned to associate with the conduct of both Mr. Denman and General Goethals, the President today accepted the resignation of General Goethals and the resignation of Mr. White of the Shipping Board, tendered some weeks ago,[1] and laid the matter before Mr. Denman in the following letter:

           (copy Denman letter)

The President's letter to General Goethals also follows:

           (copy Goethals letter)

In case of Mr. Denman's acquiescence in this action of the President, the name of Mr. Edward N. Hurley will be sent to the Senate as Chairman of the Shipping Board and the name of Mr. Bainbridge Colby of New York to take the place upon the Board made vacant by the acceptance of the resignation of Mr. White. The President will designate Admiral Capps,[2] the well-known and experienced naval constructor, to serve in the stead of General Goethals.

        (Also give out letter from General Goethals)[3]

        (Also give out letter to Mr. White)[4]

T MS (WP, DLC).
  [1] John Barber White to WW, June 28, 1917, ALS (WP, DLC).
  [2] Washington Lee Capps, Chief Constructor of the Navy with the rank of rear admiral.
  [3] G. W. Goethals to WW, July 20, 1917.
  [4] WW to J. B. White, July 24, 1917, CCL (WP, DLC).

Two Letters from William Denman

My dear Mr. President: Washington July 24, 1917.

I beg herewith to tender my resignation as a member of the United States Shipping Board, which I send to you with the deepest appreciation of your sympathy and sustaining hand I have felt during the difficulties which have arisen during the period of my occupancy of that office.

Very affectionately and respectfully yours,
William Denman.

My dear Mr. President: Washington July 24, 1917.

I had no idea that your letter would have been so soon given to the public. Had I known it, I would not have added to the burden of your many cares a matter of personal consideration. I beg of you to forget that the suggestion was made to you. What becomes of the tiny reputation of one man is a matter of insignificance in a World's struggle.

Very faithfully and cordially yours,   William Denman.

TLS (WP, DLC).

To Charles William Eliot

My dear Doctor Eliot: The White House 24 July, 1917

I have your letter of July twentieth. Unhappily, what you suggest about the labor difficulties is practically impossible. I have dealt with this matter so much now that I have a somewhat intimate knowledge of the feeling of Congress and of the possibilities of legislation along those lines, and I am sorry to say that it would be impossible at this session at any rate to obtain any legislation whatever.

You do not overstate the dangers and ominous signs of the times and we are watching the whole thing with anxiety. I dare say that if it develops, a time may come when some sort of legislative action dealing with the matter will be obviously necessary.

In great haste, with warm appreciation,
Sincerely yours,   Woodrow Wilson

TLS (C. W. Eliot Papers, MH-Ar).

From Newton Diehl Baker, with Enclosure

My dear Mr. President: [Washington] July 24, 1917.

I have just received the enclosed confidential letter from General Pershing, which was brought me by one of our officers who has been in Paris on a special mission, and was deemed by General Pershing too confidential to be entrusted to the mails. I am sure you will be interested in the General's observations on the situation in France. May I ask that these letters be returned to me so that I can frame an answer which will be sent by one of our officers leaving for France?

On every hand I hear from returning American military men stories of good nature, tact and good sense on General Pershing's part.   Respectfully yours,   [Newton D. Baker]

CCL (N. D. Baker Papers, DLC).

E N C L O S U R E

John Joseph Pershing to Newton Diehl Baker

Confidential.

Dear Mr. Secretary: Paris, France, July 9, 1917.

I feel it important that I should write you confidentially something of the general situation in France as it appears from certain facts that have come to me since my arrival in Paris. Sometime before our arrival, as you know, the French army had been badly hammered, so much so that its morale dropped to a very low ebb. As a consequence also the people themselves became very much disheartened and gave voice to rather severe criticism of the army management in general. The result of all this was that Nivelle was replaced by Petain as commander in chief.

Dissatisfaction in the army has rather continued to grow and has probably been encouraged by the French civil socialistic element, no doubt influenced by German socialists. It is generally known that several instances of mutiny have occurred among the troops, and that it became necessary recently to execute some of the ring leaders, variously reported to number from thirty to one hundred and twenty. The socialistic element of the Chambre of Deputies itself has subjected the army to criticism that still further served to unsettle the minds of the people, and add to the discontent of the army.

The fact is that France is very tired of this war. The common people openly complain of the heavy taxes, and protest that they are being ground down to enrich government contractors, and possibly officials well up in government service. Prices of food are high, so that the general cost of living weighs heavily upon the civilian population. Coal costs from $80.00 to $90.00 per ton and the supply is very limited. Complaints from families have their effect on the men in ranks, so that the fighting ability of the troops may be seriously impaired by their discontent. The army authorities seem to be gravely concerned, as is indicated by the fact that General Petain, last week, asked me to meet him at the home of a mutual friend for conference.

At this meeting, he told me frankly that affairs were not going well in France, and that unless the government and the people would stand by the army and assist at home, instead of undermining its morale by criticism and fault-finding, he felt that something bordering on revolution might result. Such an outcome, he said, would permit the Germans to dictate the terms of peace instead of the allies. He, of course, feels that our entering the war has brought courage to the nation, but, realizing as he does, that we shall not be in a position to render any material assistance before next spring, he thinks that, in addition to that, some outside pressure might be brought that would check political intrigue among government officials and prevent a further loss of confidence among the people at large.

As you know, of course, politics ordinarily play a very important part in every act of the average French public official and that they are inclined to over-play the game. Of course anything like a revolution in France at this time might not be easy to stop, and the final burden of the war might thus fall upon our shoulders. Realizing the low spirits of the people, I have taken advantage of an occasional opportunity, without appearing to meddle and without talking too much, to speak encouragingly of the splendid stamina of the French people and of the army, and have endeavored to inspire confidence among them in their military organization and its commander.

With this same idea of bolstering up French morale, General Petain has issued a public statement setting forth the reasons why the French are fighting. Before giving it out, he asked me if I would do something to back it up after it was published. I am enclosing a translation of General Petain's article, and my brief comment published the following day.[1]

General Petain believes that perhaps there may come a time when President Wilson, for whom the whole French nation have a sublime admiration, might take some action through the French ambassador at Washington, or otherwise, that would stiffen or may be frighten the French government into a full realization of the seriousness of these matters and of their responsibility in the premises. By this I mean the civil end of the government in whose hands rest so much obligation to support their army commanders.

On the other side of this general view of the subject, our ambassador here holds the opinion, which I have gained from general conversation with him, that all factions in France are working together harmoniously. I should add also that many others hold this same view. Of course they all know of the general complaints and all that, but they do not regard them as indicating anything serious. I have the very highest regard for Mr. Sharp and for what he says, and what I say is in no way a criticism of him. He is in every sense a high-minded, and I believe efficient and conscientious official. But I am writing in order that you may also have the view point of the French Commander-in-Chief, whose views I could not safely mention to anyone else.

It must be stated that our Fourth of July celebration with troops participating has stirred all France, also that, yesterday, the government and the Chambre of Deputies seem to have had a very satisfactory understanding, and the French people are in much better spirits than when General Petain made the above comments on the situation. General Petain, himself, now says that the morale of the army has improved lately. So for the present things look better.

My own opinion is that the army as it stands to-day, can hold on until spring against any probable effort of the enemy, but that poverty and discontent, magnified by the socialistic press, especially should the government fail to continue to back up the army, may so dishearten the people and the army that the latter will lose its morale and disaster follow.

I shall do everything, consistent with my position, to encourage and hearten both people and soldiery. With the Red Cross now under an organization that is working practically under my very general control, much can be done to cheer up the soldier in the trenches and to help his family at home during the coming winter. The Y.M.C.A. is also working with us in its own field toward the same end.

I should very much prefer that all this be held as entirely confidential insofar as my conference with General Petain and my remarks about the ambassador are concerned. For General Petain's sake, as well as my own, no suggestion or recommendation should be made connecting him or me in any way with whatever course that may be considered advisable, should future events seem to suggest action along the lines indicated.

I trust, Mr. Secretary, that you will understand that I am writing you only because I feel that in no other way could I place before you a situation filled with possibilities. In conclusion I would add that I have the utmost confidence in General Petain, and believe that he is a loyal patriot, whose sole aim is to serve and save France.

With high personal esteem and respect, I remain,

Yours very sincerely, [John J. Pershing]

CCL (J. J. Pershing Papers, DLC).

[1] Pétain's article appeared in the French army bulletin on June 27, 1917. He stated that France was fighting to drive the German invaders from French soil and to secure a "firm and complete peace" that would insure that such an "unprovoked" invasion could never again occur. Much of his article dealt with the events that led to hostilities in 1914; he attempted to prove that Germany had been the sole aggressor. The article is summarized in the *New York Times*, June 29, 1917.

Pershing commented on Pétain's article on June 28 as follows: "I have read General Pétain's article with deepest interest. . . . The facts set forth should convince the world of the justice of our great cause. . . . It is quite beyond reason that any one, knowing the truth, should fail to condemn the course pursued by the German Government, and the truth has been clearly pointed out by the distinguished Commander in Chief of the French Army. There must be no peace except a lasting peace. The ideals for which the Allies are contending must be held sacred. France will continue her splendid fight for human rights and human liberties, and fresh examples of heroism by her valiant armies will still further inspire those fighting by her side." *Ibid.*

From Edward Mandell House

Dear Governor: Magnolia, Massachusetts. July 24, 1917.

You can never know how glad I am that you have settled the shipping controversy. It has worried me more than anything recently. I did not write you of the rumors and criticisms that were current, because I felt sure you would act as quickly as you could.

Gavin McNab was here the other day. In talking of Denman he said:

"I consider him intellectually able, very tenacious, not altogether trustworthy, and without any executive ability. He has no political influence in California. I believe his cleverness as a lawyer will give him the advantage over Goethals in any controversy which may arise."

Affectionately yours, E. M. House

TLS (WP, DLC).

From Charles Samuel Jackson

Portland, Oregon, July 24, 1917.

Allow me to congratulate you for your vigorous work in connection with tangle of building of ships. Problem is solved. People are behind you. So would they be with still greater concert if you did same thing to bungling undemocratic progressive peanut political Congress. American people awaiting chance to back you up against chattering procrastinating membership of that time, wealth and life destroying body.   C. S. Jackson.

T telegram (WP, DLC).

William Bauchop Wilson to Joseph Patrick Tumulty

My dear Mr. Tumulty: Washington July 24, 1917.

I am in receipt of your letters of July 22d and 23d, with inclosures, relative to the labor troubles in the Northwest and the President's request for information concerning the matter.

The situation in the State of Washington at present is very critical. There is not only a strike in the lumbering industry but one has recently been precipitated on the street car systems at Seattle and Tacoma. The longshoremen are likely to go out at any moment.

I have detailed Henry M. White,[1] our Commissioner of Immigration at the Port of Seattle, to take charge of the situation as mediator, selecting such assistants as he may deem necessary and recommending them to me for appointment. Mr. White is a lawyer and former State Senator who has the confidence of the organizations affiliated with the American Federation of Labor to a very great extent.

The street car strike seems to have intensified the strike fever throughout the state, and it is not likely that we will be able to do much with the other difficulties until we get that adjusted. I am advised that it was precipitated by the discharge of some motormen and conductors because they belonged to the union. The lines are operated by Stone and Webster, of Boston, Massachusetts, who control the power plants in the vicinity of Seattle. I have telegraphed former Assistant Secretary of the Treasury Andrew J. Peters, of Boston, asking him to bring what influence he can to bear on Stone and Webster to bring about an adjustment.

One of the telegrams I have states that they have fifteen hundred men en route from Chicago to Seattle in three special trains to act as strikebreakers. If that is so, I fear there will be a tremendous clash when they arrive. I wired Inspector in Charge Prentis,[2] of the Immigration Service in Chicago, for a statement as to the truth or falsity of this report, and this morning I am in receipt of a telegram from him in which he says:

"Concerning Secretary's telegram regarding strikebreakers for Seattle, have definite information that effort being made to ship men from Chicago. Hope to secure facts and telegraph further early tomorrow."

I am just in receipt of the following telegram from Mr. Peters:

"Have conferred with Mr. Webster[3] of Stone and Webster. He is taking matter up immediately with his partner who is now in Seattle. Will wire you results later."

I have also been handed a telegram addressed to Ashmun Brown,[4] which reads as follows:

"See Samuel Gompers with the end of organizing logging and timber workers in American Federation of Labor. Mill and camp operators are willing to grant eight hour day to a union affiliated with American Federation. There are ten thousand I.W.W. in state and the timber is dry as powder. Situation extremely serious. Dillon."[5]

Immediately upon receipt of it I telegraphed it to E. P. Marsh,[6] President of the Washington State Federation of Labor, and to Commissioner White of this Department, advising them to get in touch with Dillon and work out an adjustment on this plan, if possible. I also forwarded a copy to Mr. Gompers, with a full statement of the situation, and asked his cooperation looking to an adjustment.

I know of nothing further that can be done at this time.

Sincerely yours,   W B Wilson

TLS (WP, DLC).
[1] Henry Middleton White.
[2] Percy L. Prentis.
[3] Edwin Sibley Webster, electrical engineer, founding partner in the firm of Stone & Webster, builders and managers of electrical utilities.
[4] Ashmun Norris Brown, Washington correspondent of the *Seattle Post-Intelligencer*.
[5] Thomas Joseph Dillon, managing editor of the *Seattle Post-Intelligencer*.
[6] Ernest P. Marsh.

William Graves Sharp to Robert Lansing

Paris. July 24, 1917.

2321. Confidential. Section two. Next to the actual participation of the United States in the war on the side of the Allies, certainly no other one thought has given so much satisfaction to the French Government as that of the prospect of America becoming an important factor in shaping the terms in the ultimate peace convention. At the very time that Lord Northcliffe was quoted as saying in substance, at a banquet in London soon after our entrance into the war, that he could not look with pleasure upon the United States taking part in such convention,[1] Mr. Cambon was telling me at the Foreign Office, with unfeigned delight, of the satisfaction with which France hailed such a participation. All the Allied lesser powers in Europe have voiced the same feeling and with scarcely a single exception the representatives of those countries have at different times expressed to me that view in the warmest terms. Particularly among these latter powers the coming conference has excited much interest and some concern. With the past few days the Minister for Foreign Affairs of the Montenegrin Government[2] came to ask if I would intercede to have my Government represent his country at the conference as he had been told that its desire for participation had not been favorably entertained. He expressed the gravest concern over a future autonomy of Montenegro on account of the ambitions of Servia. My reply that my own government was not to be represented at the confederation (conference) was a sufficient answer to his request. The same day the Chinese Minister[3] came to me to tell me that he looked with much anxiety in regard to the future policy of Japan toward his country though he expressed the conviction that the recent rebellion in China was undoubtedly fomented by German intrigue. He stated that its early suppression served the double purpose of not only restoring stability to the country but prevented the Japanese Government from sending over troops on the plea of protecting its interests in China. Later Mr. Roussos,[4] the new Greek Minister to the United States, who sails this week, came in to pay his respects and during our brief conversation he told me that while matters looked now very favorable for improved conditions in his country yet there were some differences existing between Greece and Italy growing out of the insistence of the latter to control that section of Greece through which (pass) (?) the railroads for the movement of troops, Venezelos requesting that the civil Greek authorities be permitted to exercise control in that territory, not, however, thereby preventing the free use of the railroads to Italian troops.

Yesterday Mr. Vesnitch,[5] the Servian Minister, very highly esteemed by his colleagues, came to my office to tell me that although his government and that of Roumania and Greece had been invited to attend the conference in a consultative capacity,

yet they had been given to understand that it was not expected
that they would have a vote or be permitted to take any other
action in affecting the decision of the conference. He had informed the Foreign Office that it was his intention to offer a
protest to such action and was then awaiting the arrival of the
Minister of the Foreign Office of the Servian Government[6] to
consult him upon what action to take. He in turn expressed to me
much concern over the designs that Italy had toward his country.
I know from previous statements made by him on other occasions
that he has strong convictions as to the dangers and complica-
tions that may grow out of such designs. He showed much
pleasure recently in telling me that he had been notified by his
government that it was planned to send a mission over to
America of which he would be the head.

All my colleagues to whom I have referred, however, have with
one common accord manifested the greatest faith in the good
intentions of France.

I assume that the principal discussion at the conference itself—the object of which has been stated to be the consideration
of the Balkan question—will center around the policy of maintaining the Allied forces at Salonica, concerning wisdom of which
there has been at different time[s] a good deal of doubt and dissatisfaction, chiefly growing out of the difficulties, I understand,
of meeting the burdens which it involves in the employment of a
large tonnage of ships.

It is my belief that France and England are now more in accord upon this matter than at the beginning of the Salonica
movement, though it has been a heavy burden on England for the
reason stated.

Russia will be represented by the Chargé d'Affaires and several officials who have been sent to Paris by the Provisional Government for that purpose. I am informed on good authority however that they have been instructed to only discuss Balkan
affairs as they relate to maintaining the Salonica front.

I have given this general outline of some of the issues which
may be raised and of the attitude of some of the participants in
reference thereto in order to enable the Department to get some
appreciation of the conditions which exist here on the eve of this
conference, which is the first of the Allies to be held since the
advent of the United States into the war and the Russian Revolution.

Personally I believe that its deliberations will be characterized
by great wisdom and harmony, for no matter what differences
may exist among some of the powers or concern as to their

own particular interests, they all recognize the great necessity of presenting a united front with as little division as possible.

Sharp.

T telegram (SDR, RG 59, 763.72/5971, DNA).
 [1] If Northcliffe made such a statement at all, the Editors have been unable to find it.
 [2] Evgenije Popović.
 [3] Hu Wei-te.
 [4] Georges Roussos.
 [5] Milenko R. Vesnić, often spelled as Vesnitch.
 [6] Nikola P. Pašić, often spelled as Pashitch or Pachitch.

To George Washington Goethals

My dear General Goethals: The White House 25 July, 1917

Our crisis is past and I do not believe that anybody concerned need feel apprehensive of the general verdict of opinion when the matter comes to be summed up in retrospect. The whole thing, I dare say, was inevitable, and I have sincerely admired the manly and soldierly qualities you have shown.

I am sure that no suggestion from me is needed that you get into touch with Rear Admiral Capps and put him in your place as completely as is possible in the circumstances.

Cordially and sincerely yours,   Woodrow Wilson

TLS (G. W. Goethals Papers, DLC).

To William Denman

My dear Denman: [The White House] 25 July, 1917

May I not say that you have acted admirably and in perfect accord with the high estimate I had formed of you?

Cordially and sincerely yours,   Woodrow Wilson

TLS (Letterpress Books, WP, DLC).

To Edward Nash Hurley

My dear Hurley: [The White House] 25 July, 1917

You are certainly a soldier and I honor you greatly. I did not have time, as you will understand, at the crisis of the matter just settled to express to you my feeling, but the way you responded to the call I sent you through Tumulty was evidence enough that you understood.

This line is sent merely for my personal gratification, because I want you to know how warmly grateful I am.

Cordially and sincerely yours,   Woodrow Wilson

TLS (Letterpress Books, WP, DLC).

To Washington Lee Capps

My dear Admiral Capps: [The White House] 25 July, 1917

I fear that you have learned rather too informally of the new and exceedingly important duty to which I have taken the liberty to assign you, and if that has caused you any inconvenience I beg to apologize.

I am sure that you will realize the necessity that existed for prompt and definite action, leaving no elements of conjecture in the settlement, and I want you to know that my selection of yourself for the task which it has been necessary that General Goethals should lay down was based upon a very great confidence in your character and ability. I beg that you will accept the assignment as an evidence of my friendship and trust.

I have no doubt that General Goethals will be very glad to confer with you about every phase of the business that will need your attention, and I have this to suggest: I am told that General Goethals has brought into association with him some very energetic and capable men and it may be that you will find it to your advantage to retain them at your own side in this undertaking into which you have been so suddenly thrust.

Cordially and sincerely yours,   Woodrow Wilson

TLS (Letterpress Books, WP, DLC).

To Bainbridge Colby

My dear Mr. Colby: The White House 25 July, 1917

Every time I make any sort of test of your quality my admiration for you is increased and my confidence in you enhanced. The way you responded to the suggestion conveyed to you by Mr. Tumulty the other evening on the telephone is characteristic of you and I look forward with the greatest pleasure and satisfaction to being associated with you here in Washington. I am taking it for granted that the Senate will have the good sense to confirm very promptly the nominations I sent in to it yesterday.

Cordially and sincerely yours,   Woodrow Wilson

TLS (B. Colby Papers, DLC).

To Theodore Brent

My dear Mr. Brent: [The White House] 25 July, 1917

I have your letter of yesterday.[1] It is an additional evidence of the spirit you have always shown and I thank you for it most sincerely.

I beg you to believe that in the action I have taken I was not trying to play arbiter on the merits of any question that has been in debate. I merely felt, as I said to Mr. Denman and General Goethals, that no settlement of the controversy would be a clarification of the situation, and they have responded to that suggestion as generously and in as handsome a spirit as could have been shown by anybody.

At the same time, I believe that I read between the lines of your letter a feeling on your part that you would be happier if released from further service in the Board, and I do not feel at liberty to ask you to remain feeling as intimately identified with the controversy, now happily passed, as you evidently do. I, therefore, accept your resignation without desiring it, and in doing so I want to express my deep appreciation of the conscientious and highly useful service you have rendered the Government and the country.

          Cordially and sincerely yours,   Woodrow Wilson

TLS (Letterpress Books, WP, DLC).
   [1] T. Brent to WW, July 24, 1917, TLS (WP, DLC).

To Julius Kahn

My dear Mr. Kahn: [The White House] 25 July, 1917

Mr. Burleson has told me of the fine spirit you have shown in the matter of cooperating in the Food Bill and I cannot refrain from expressing my very deep appreciation. You have certainly shown a quality of patriotic disinterestedness which has won my sincere admiration.

          Cordially and sincerely yours,   Woodrow Wilson

TLS (Letterpress Books, WP, DLC).

To Dee Richardson[1]

Personal.

My dear Mrs. Richardson: [The White House] 25 July, 1917

Alas, there are only too many cases of the sort that you call my attention to[2] and I feel that it would be a mistake to intervene in regard to them. If the lady to whom you refer is dependent upon her remaining son in any way, of course he can be exempted under the regular rule and should be, but if she is not, I would have no ground upon which to make the exception that would not apply in scores of other cases. I am sure you will understand.

I, of course, appreciate what you say about the picketing but I want to remind you that my first duty is to take pride in myself obeying the law. I fear that what these ladies are doing is doing a very great deal of damage to the cause they are trying to promote. That they are deeply mistaken I believe the whole country thinks, but that should not lead us to irregular action ourselves.

I appreciate very deeply your feeling in the matter and the earnestness with which you have entertained it.

Cordially and sincerely yours, Woodrow Wilson

TLS (Letterpress Books, WP, DLC).
¹ A woman, originally from Missouri, who lived in Washington and had worked, apparently as a clerk, for various congressmen. She often wrote to Wilson, Tumulty, or Thomas W. Brahany to ask for positions for her son, her daughter, and others. She always signed herself simply as "Mrs. Dee Richardson."
² Dee Richardson to WW, July 24, 1917, ALS (WP, DLC). She asked that the one surviving son of another woman be exempted from military service. She also asked Wilson to "put a stop" to the "unamerican" picketing of the White House by suffragists.

From Frank Lyon Polk, with Enclosure

My dear Mr. President: Washington July 25, 1917.

I have the honor to transmit herewith copy in translation of a note received from the French Ambassador at this Capital,¹ in which, under instructions from the President of the Council, Minister of Foreign Affairs, he refers to the proposal to constitute a Society of Nations for the purpose of maintaining peace, and states that Mr. Ribot intends to convene a French commission to examine the question. Ambassador Jusserand requests that this information be communicated to you and states that any suggestions which you may care to offer in the matter will be greatly appreciated by Mr. Ribot.

I should be glad to communicate your reply to Ambassador Jusserand.

I am, my dear Mr. President,
Very sincerely yours, Frank L Polk

TLS (SDR, RG 59, 763.72119/684, DNA).
¹ The TLS is J. J. Jusserand to the Secretary of State, July 20, 1917 (SDR, RG 59, 763.72119/684, DNA).

ENCLOSURE

Translation.

Mr. Secretary of State: Washington, July 20, 1917.

A telegram which I have just received from the President of the Council, Minister of Foreign Affairs of the Republic, states that among the lofty motives which the President of the United States assigned to the entrance of his country in the war that lacerates the world, the French democracy was particularly impressed with the desire manifested by Mr. Wilson that a society of nations be constituted; this, to its mind, would be the best way of maintaining peace.

Mr. Ribot who, as Your Excellency knows, supported that proposition from the Rostrum of the Chamber, is giving his attention to finding out how such a society could be brought into existence and intends to convene a Commission charged with the duty of examining the question.

But before coming to any decision in that respect, the French Government would be glad to have the views of the American Government and of President Wilson in particular, as there is no doubt that his high moral authority will promote an early execution of this grand undertaking.

I should be very thankful to Your Excellency if you would kindly make this wish known to the President and enable me to report to my Government the suggestions he may be pleased to offer. Mr. Ribot tells me he would attach great value to receiving positive information on this matter at the earliest possible date.

Be pleased and accept etc.   Jusserand.

T MS (SDR, RG 59, 763.72119/684, DNA).

From Edward Mandell House, with Enclosure

Dear Governor: Magnolia, Mass. July 25, 1917.

Your letter about the challenge of the WORLD to the TAGEBLATT has come. It was addressed to Manchester instead of Magnolia which delayed it.

I have been conscious of the pitfalls in such a debate, but I believe they can be avoided. Cobb writes me this morning as follows:

"I shall try to work out a general plan embodying my own

theory in that debate and send it to you in a few days. The more I think of it, the more it appeals to me."

When I receive his plan I will write further.

Affectionately yours,   E. M. House

TLS (WP, DLC).

ENCLOSURE

Arthur Hugh Frazier to Edward Mandell House

Dear Mr. House: Paris, France. June 22, 1917.

The arrival of General Pershing produced the result anticipated by the Government which arranged a demonstration in his honour.[1] Public opinion is distinctly more hopeful than a week ago and if our troops arrive in sufficiently large numbers before many months, I believe that a very grave crisis will have been tided over.

What I dread is that the French will expect too much of us and will be disappointed if we do not take over any considerable sector of the front before next year. A revulsion of feeling at this juncture might have serious consequences; for this reason I sincerely hope that the troops will be sent over in as large numbers as possible with the utmost despatch.

I have finally got at the truth of the rumours of insubordination in the army to which I referred vaguely in my last letter. In a certain number of regiments (I cannot say how many) the soldiers voted to elect their officers and to march on Paris. Order and discipline were only restored by the execution of about a dozen ring leaders. Apparently the unrest is under control.

I am slowly beginning to realize what a profound repercussion the Russian revolution has had in France. For instance, in several munition factories the employes wished to elect their foremen, reduce the hours of labour and introduce the so-called English week or Saturday half holiday with Sunday off.

Still, as I said before, the presence of American uniforms in the streets of Paris and elsewhere has done wonders to allay discontent. I think it can safely be asserted that from now on France will lean more and more heavily upon us.

None of the President's state papers has been received with more unanimous praise and enthusiasm than his Flag Day address. The authorities are going to placard a French translation of it all over the country.

I am giving the former Mayor of Colmar, Mr. Daniel Blumenthal, a letter of introduction to you. I am sure you will find him interesting on his subject which is the restoration to France of Alsace-Lorraine.

With kind remembrances, believe me,

Respectfully yours,   Arthur Hugh Frazier.

TCL (WP, DLC).
¹ See W. G. Sharp to RL, June 27, 1917, n. 6.

From Amos Richards Eno Pinchot

My dear Mr. President: New York July 25, 1917.

Let me thank you for sending me the letter of Postmaster General Burleson, written to you on July 16 about the denial of postal service to certain publications.

When I was in Washington, I had a long talk with Mr. Burleson and also a session with Judge Herron.¹ What I tried to bring home to these gentlemen was, that it was exceedingly unwise as well as unjust to deny mail privileges to a newspaper, on the ground that it contains matter objectionable under the third section of the Espionage Law, and at the same time to refuse to specify what parts of the publication were against this law.

I begged the Postmaster to instruct his subordinates, that, whenever denial of the mails is resorted to in the future, the particular ground of this action shall be disclosed to the editor, so that the next time he will be able to make up a paper without danger of being suppressed. Judge Herron quite readily admitted that it was an injustice not to do this, but Mr. Burleson said that he could not even consider the question. He said that a remedy for the situation was amply provided for by the courts.

This, of course, is true only in theory—and not very strong theory at that. For, supposing that after some days or weeks, a court enjoins the Postmaster from denying the mails to a certain issue of a paper, how does this either act as a remedy for the harm that has been done, or guarantee the editor against the repetition of similar action?

Mr. President, I do not like at this time to increase the burdens you are bearing, but I assure you that the course of the Post Office in regard to these Socialist papers, which generally represent the working classes, is certainly not helping the situation or accomplishing what it is intended to.

I remember some years ago, when Albert Beveridge was running for the Senate, I asked him how the newspapers in Indiana were treating him. He replied "Oh, damn the newspapers; what counts is the mouth to mouth talk among the people."

What depressed me most about Mr. Burleson was, not that he did not apparently see the injustice of the course the Department was following in regard to these newspapers, but that he seemed to look at the whole problem with a degree of aloof externalism, which prevented him from realizing the futility of trying to control the spread of a certain set of thoughts by the particular mechanical means the Department has adopted.

Not even the most optimistic officials of the government can fail to see that there is widespread opposition to the war. Especially since the visits of the allied commissions and Lord Northcliffe, the public is beginning to ask, whether we are not being involved in a situation, where we will be asked to fight for things which we are unwilling to fight for. I, for instance, am of French blood; I have always been pro-Ally. I would like to see Alsace-Lorraine returned to France, as Germany's title to it is defective, and so on. But I would be quite unwilling to have my boy's shell-torn body dumped in a ditch in Flanders, in order to help bring about this territorial restoration, no matter how desirable.

I think I am putting it mildly in saying, that the American public will never be interested in the redistribution of the Austro-Italian border according to nationality; that it has no wish to see England own more of Africa than she now possesses; and I do not think the average American cares whether the Turk is driven out of Europe or not. All of these things do not appear to be germane to the general proposition of making the world safe to democracy by preventing the triumph of Prussian militarism.

America's so-called Northcliffe press is engaged in trying to ram home the idea, that we must have no war aims of our own; and that we must generally accept those of the Allies, i.e. England's. We know the international economics which shape the newspapers' policies in this respect; and the people suspect them. What I foresee is, that, unless the impression, that America will accept the Northcliffe theory of the war, is vigorously combated, it will do more in the next month or two to discredit the war and weaken the hand of the administration in prosecuting it, than the whole pacifist and socialist press can accomplish in several years.

On the other hand, Mr. President, I have not the slightest doubt that this situation can be easily remedied. I am entirely confident that, if we formulate a definite body of war aims similar to those of the Russian Council of Soldiers and Workmen, the people will be found solidly behind the war. I have equally little doubt that, until this is brought about, there will be increasing disunion, distrust and a widening breach between the government and the people. Of course, the public attitude toward the war may all be altered when our men begin to be lost in France or on the way across; still, I think it is too soon to predict exactly what direction the emotions aroused by such unfortunate events will take.

To sum up; as I look at the United States at war, I am reminded that St. Paul said "There is a natural body and there is a spiritual body." I think the natural body of the war is being well taken care of by the various agencies of the government, which are raising armies and supplies and sending them to the battlefields. But the spiritual body, the attitude of the people toward the war, is not being so well taken care of. As you know, I was against entering the war, and still believe that we were mistaken in doing so. But, when the war came, I accepted it as a fact. And when the Russian Revolution came, I realized that, whether we were right or wrong in going in, great things for our country and for the world might emerge, if the war were fought by a people consciously united for a great purpose.

With kindest regards and best wishes, I am

Yours, as ever,   Amos Pinchot

P.S. Since writing the above, a friend of mine, a theatrical producer, has just dropped into the office. He tells me that his friend, Somerset Maugham, tells him that he is commissioned by Northcliffe to go to Russia and buy up Russian newspapers.[2] He tells me, also, that it is generally understood that Northcliffe is making a vigorous campaign to get the American newspapers to stand behind the British program. Doubtless you know all about this.

TLS (WP, DLC).

[1] William Collins Herron, an attorney in the Department of Justice.

[2] Actually, Sir William Wiseman sent Maugham to Russia. About this episode, see Fowler, *British-American Relations, 1917-1918*, pp. 109-17.

From Samuel Gompers

Sir: Washington, D. C. July 25, 1917.

In connection with recommendation for appointment to the office of District Attorney of the Southern District of West Virginia, I wish to bring to your attention information that has come into my possession.

For many years I have been in close touch with conditions in

West Virginia because corporation control made the efforts of workers in that State to secure better conditions of life and work a serious battle for liberty. The domination of mining corporations over both industrial and political affairs has resulted in feudal conditions in West Virginia. All efforts of workers to secure improvements of conditions of work and life were opposed by the concentrated opposition of corporations and the activities of their resident managers, and their political and legal agencies. For this reason the appointment of any federal officer in West Virginia has a direct bearing upon the progress of the people in establishing real democracy that they may protect their rights and interest and have opportunity for development.

As you know, in the past, not even federal attorneys and judges have maintained a position of independent administration unsusceptible to influences from the great corporations of the State.

There is now before you for appointment as United States District Attorney of the Southern District of West Virginia, the name of a man who has been associated with the corporations of the State in their efforts to dominate the political agencies of the State in furtherance of private interests,—Mr. George I. Neal.[1] For a number of years Mr. Neal has not devoted his time to service of the higher purposes of the legal profession. He has accepted work as the political representative of corporate interests and has not practiced law in or before the courts. In other words, he has been known as the paid lobbyist of corporations and has before the Legislature of West Virginia persistently urged the enactment of legislative measures for the special benefit of these interests, and has used every means at his command to bring about the defeat of progressive legislation urged for the welfare of workers and the people generally.

Mr. Neal was conspicuously diligent in his efforts to defeat legislation proposed by the workers for the enactment of future legislation to regulate and limit the use of the anti-injunction bill, a measure drafted in conformity with the Federal Clayton Anti-trust Bill. Mr. Neal as a paid representative of the corporations of the State appeared before the Judiciary Committee of the House of Delegates to argue in opposition to the passage of this legislation.

The opinion which his fellow-workers have for Mr. Neal is shown by the fact that when he was candidate for Congress in campaign of 1914, he failed to receive a full party vote of his District by about 1600. In addition to these matters concerning his public activities, of which I know, I am informed that it is common information in the State that Mr. Neal is not regarded as a man worthy of confidence and trust and that he is not a man of his word.   Very respectfully yours,   Saml. Gompers.

TLS (WP, DLC).
[1] George Ira Neal.

A Memorandum by George Lewis Bell

[c. July 25, 1917]

SUGGESTIONS FOR A CONSTRUCTIVE STATE PROGRAM
MADE BY PRESIDENT WILSON TO MR. BELL IN JULY, 1917[1]—
FOR PRESENTATION TO WESTERN GOVERNORS AS NECESSARY
STEPS IN OFFSETTING THE GROWTH OF THE I.W.W.
AND IN REMOVING SOME CAUSES OF DISCONTENT.

I. The Governor to have the Industrial Commission, or the appropriate department, *immediately* make a survey of the working and living conditions in all industries where trouble is likely. If they find any conditions which are objectionable and which could be used as a cause *or pretext* for agitation, they shall report the same to the Governor. The Governor will then call in the employers of such places and ask them, as a patriotic duty, to remedy the conditions AT ONCE. If they fail to respond, the Governor to communicate with Mr. Bell. This in order that Mr. Bell can report the matter to the President. The survey, conference with employers, and everything suggested under this heading to be done without publicity.

II. The Governor to direct his State Board of Health, or other appropriate department, to *immediately* inspect and clean up living and working conditions in labor and construction camps where migratory laborers are employed. (It is from this class that members are recruited and where agitation is easy if there are bad conditions.)

III. The Governor to direct the Immigration Department of the state government, (or if there is no such department one might be created, or special agents could be found,) to send men speaking foreign languages to the places where large bodies of foreign born men are employed. These agents to:

(a) Explain the war situation to these people, and inform them that they will not only not be harmed but will be protected by the state as long as they are peaceful and show no tendency wilfully and treacherously to interfere with industry or the government.

(b) Urge them not to affiliate with any lawless organizations or to take part in any riotous disturbances—otherwise they will be liable to arrest and perhaps deportation.

(c) Urge them to learn English, to take out first papers, and to become American citizens.

(This is acknowledgedly agitation in itself—agitation to offset the active agitation of the organization among these simple, foreign born people. It is from among them that they are recruiting most of their new members.)

IV. The Governor not to call for troops until he feels that they are absolutely necessary, but when he feels they are necessary he should call for them rather than rely on more or less impromptu posses, "home guard committees," etc.

V. This entire program and matter to be kept confidential, and no publicity to be given to any actions taken in carrying it out, until agreed on by all.

(Presented by Mr. Bell on August 11, 1916 [1917], to the governors of California, Oregon, Washington, Idaho, Nevada, Utah and Montana, and unanimously approved and adopted by them.)

T MS (F. Frankfurter Papers, DLC).
1 That is, on July 25, at the White House.

To William Cox Redfield

My dear Mr. Secretary: [The White House] 26 July, 1917

The Trading with the Enemy Bill[1] is now in the hands of the Senate Committee, as I dare say you know, and they are about to report it out. My advice having been sought with regard to certain portions of the measure, I have advised the Committee that all of those provisions of the bill which relate to banks and strictly financial business be placed for administration in the hands of the Secretary of the Treasury.

I did this in order to avoid duplication. The machinery already exists in the Treasury for undertaking this administration, and it would be necessary in any case that that machinery should be used, which would mean a good deal of lost motion unless the responsibility also was placed with the Treasury Department.

I hope that you will feel as I do, that the reasons for this were conclusive.

Cordially and sincerely yours,   Woodrow Wilson[2]

TLS (Letterpress Books, WP, DLC).
1 See WCR to WW, July 6, 1917, n. 4.
2 WW to TWG, July 26, 1917, TLS (Letterpress Books, WP, DLC), is a similar letter.

To Henry Lee Higginson

My dear Major Higginson: [The White House] 26 July, 1917

You may be sure that the difficulties stated in your interesting letter of July twenty-third are very much in my mind and have been from the first. I am not at all confident (as who could be?) that we shall be able to work the thing out discreetly and without deleterious effect upon the business of the country, but we shall at least work with a knowledge of the possible mischief we might do, and letters like your own help me to think the matter through.

I shall be very glad to discuss with the Secretary of the Treasury your suggestion about short-term securities.[1]

Cordially and sincerely yours,   Woodrow Wilson

TLS (Letterpress Books, WP, DLC).
[1] WW to WGM, July 26, 1917, CCL (WP, DLC).

From Charles William Eliot

Dear Mr. President: Asticou, Maine 26 July 1917

I am not surprised that you think it impossible at this session of Congress to obtain any legislation whatever touching the Labor situation. Before we went to War with Germany, I was not expecting Congress, or any State Legislature, to deal effectively with the industrial strife; but since we went to War it has seemed to me possible that this country might do something like what Great Britain did to diminish the reduction in the productiveness of the country's industries which the limited output and the closed shop inevitably bring about. That hope now disappears, at least for the present.

Organized Labor does not produce its worst effects in the factory and machine shop industries. There the machinery sets the pace in some measure, and an incessant supervision over the workmen can be exercised by foremen and superintendents. In the building trades, on the other hand, or in any trade which makes small use of machinery, the limited output policy and the closed shop policy, with uniform wage for all workers, have thoroughly demoralized all the men that belong to unions. They no longer work well during the union number of hours, and they waste and kill time in the most shameless manner. It is impossible that a union carpenter, mason, painter, or plumber should not be personally demoralized by working under union rules and practices in the building trades. Of course the cost of buildings of all sorts has doubled within the last fifteen years, and as to repairs their cost has become so great that to own a house has become for many families an unjustifiable luxury.

You are already encountering not only difficulties which result from the impossible rules of American labor-unions in trades which affect the conduct of the War; but you will soon be struggling, perhaps you are already struggling, with an extreme scarcity of labor which is general all over the country from Maine to southern California. I hope you will be able to find time for taking the best available advice from business men and manufacturers as to the means of coping with these two obstacles to a successful conduct of the War.

Some years ago, I had excellent opportunities for studying the mental and moral processes of Mr. Samuel Gompers. He is an able man; but a patriot had better be very careful how he deals with Mr. Gompers on any matters in which the selfish interests of the labor-unions are concerned.

I am, with high regard,

Sincerely yours   Charles W. Eliot

TLS (WP, DLC).

From Edward Mandell House

Dear Governor: Magnolia, Massachusetts. July 26, 1917.

Dudley Malone was with me last night until nearly twelve o'clock. I will not give you any details for you know his state of mind.[1] I have asked him not to resign at the moment, but he made no definite promise.

He is standing on the brink and I am afraid that his political, domestic and religious affairs are about to crumble. The loss of his friendship, if indeed, it is lost, may cause you to doubt if any can endure. Such a dénouement must bring suspicion upon all, even upon those who wish nothing but an opportunity to serve you and the country well.

Your devoted friend,   E. M. House

TLS (WP, DLC).

[1] Malone had had a heated confrontation with Wilson at the White House in the late afternoon of July 17 over the issues of woman suffrage, in general, and the imprisonment of the White House pickets, in particular. See the extract from the House Diary printed at July 26, 1917, and the *New York Times*, July 18, 1917.

Leonidas Carstarphen Dyer to Rudolph Forster, with Enclosure

My dear Mr. Forster: Washington, D. C. July 26, 1917.

I enclose herewith a letter to the President as per my request to you over the 'phone this morning. I will appreciate it very much if you will present this matter to the President and advise me of his action in the premises.

Very truly yours,   L. C. Dyer

E N C L O S U R E

From Leonidas Carstarphen Dyer

My dear Mr. President: Washington, D. C. July 26, 1917.

I respectfully present to you the request of the National Association of Colored Women of the United States, with a membership of 100,000, for an opportunity to present to you thousands of petitions to you to have the Federal Government investigate the recent riots at East St. Louis, Illinois, at which time more than 500 men, women and children were murdered. If you will grant the audience I will act as the representative of this Association in presenting to you these petitions. I am sure it will only take two or three minutes of your time.[1]

Very truly yours,   L. C. Dyer

TLS (WP, DLC).
[1] "Please say to Mr. Dyer that every channel of inquiry that is open to the Federal Government is already being employed in this matter and that I cannot see what good would come of receiving the delegation he suggests. The President." WW to JPT, c. July 27, 1917, TL (WP, DLC).

Helen Hamilton Gardener to Thomas W. Brahany

My dear Mr. Brahany: Washington, D. C. July 26, 1917

Mrs. Catt now thinks that the proposed Conference with the President might better be left to a later date when the war measures and the Congress will bear less heavily upon him.

You and Mr Tumulty were good enough to say that the exact date might be left open and that if any great stress or suffrage action became imminent we could arrange the date upon application to you.

This is wholly satisfactory to Mrs Catt and she thanks you,

and through you the President, for your always kind appreciation of the situations as they arise.

His serene and tactful handling of the recent "picket crisis"
cleared the air for the time, at least, and makes a conference unnecessary, *we hope*, until the close of this Congress.

Thanking you for your courtesy, I remain,

Yours sincerely,   Helen H. Gardener

TLS (WP, DLC).

Frank Irving Cobb to Edward Mandell House

Dear Colonel House: New York. July 26, 1917.

I can appreciate the President's misgivings, but I think it can
be done without dropping into any of the pitfalls that he foresees.
It is a danger that will have to be avoided. So far as getting the
challenge to The Tageblatt is concerned, I am certain that could
be arranged so it would appear merely to be done by permission
of the United States Government, and not by participation of the
United States Government.

So far as that is concerned, we can make a formal request to
the State Department in any way to endorse or approve of the
proceedings.

It seems to me, also, that the debate should be nominally re-
stricted, in so far as possible, to the issues between the United
States and Germany. On that basis we can get in everything else
that we desire to put into the record.

Very truly yours,   Frank I. Cobb.

TCL (WP, DLC).

Sir Cecil Arthur Spring Rice to Arthur James Balfour, with Enclosure

NO. 427

Sir: Washington July 26th 1917.

I have the honour to transmit herewith a memorandum drawn
up by Messrs Royden and Salter relative to their interview with
the President on the shipping question.

The conflict which has filled a large space in the press between
General Goethals and Mr. Denman, Chairman of the Shipping
Board, has at last resulted in drastic action by the President. The
General thought that he had been placed in full control of the

building operations by a letter which he had received from the President. Mr. Denman, however, had also received a letter which, as he conceived its meaning, fully admitted the powers of control to which he laid claim as Chairman of the Board. To put an end to this state of uncertainty General Goethals seems to have been induced by certain friends to place his resignation at the disposal of the President unless his position were freed from the doubt and uncertainty which as he thought paralyzed his activities. The President unexpectedly accepted his resignation and at the same time addressed a letter to Mr. Denman inviting him to imitate the General's patriotic action. In this manner the dispute was brought to an end by the removal of the disputants.

Mr. Denman who has always been closely connected with German interests on the Pacific, has shown an evident disinclination to take any action likely to serve the cause of the allies. Mr. Tardieu tells me that he has had the gravest complaints to make against the Chairman of the Shipping Board and it is stated, I believe with truth, that the War Office had to insist that the repair of the German ships should be taken in hand by the Navy Department, as the Shipping Board had done nothing. Mr. Royden and Mr. Salter have done everything possible to communicate with the Board, and make known to them the imperative needs of the situation. But Mr. Denman had kept these communications to himself and actually suppressed two important memoranda which had been drawn up by the British delegates. Mr. Denman's anti-ally sympathies were indeed no secret and being in constant communication with the press, the workings of his mind were common property.

The American public became restive under this long inaction and complaints were freely made in the press. The President as usual waited to take action until the public demanded it: and much satisfaction is expressed at what is supposed to be a step towards greater efficiency. Mr. Hurley and Admiral Capps who have taken the places of the retiring disputants are generally believed to be willing and efficient. Further changes are announced in the Board, and it is to be hoped, that a new spirit will be now introduced into it.

It was before these changes took place that I thought it desirable that Mr. Royden and Mr. Salter should seek in a personal audience with the President to lay before him the facts connected with this most vital question. On the announcement of Mr. Denman's dismissal Mr. Polk told me he thought it possible that the President might not wish to receive them. I said that I left the matter entirely in the President's hands and made no request to be received myself. The President, to whom the matter was referred from another quarter, not only received them, but accorded them the rare honour of a prolonged audience in the course of which he expressed himself with great frankness. It is still to be doubted whether he entirely realises the immense importance of this question, but I have no doubt that Mr. Royden and Mr. Salter will now be able, by a frank interchange of views with the new Board, to bring home to the persons chiefly concerned the overpowering necessity of energetic and drastic action.

You will no doubt, should you think it right and proper, take such steps as your experience here has shown to be desirable, to communicate to the press the salient facts, and such considerations as may serve the purpose of arousing public opinion. This, as far as we are concerned here, must be done after consultation with the officials concerned and with the knowledge and consent of the State Department.

I will lose no opportunity of keeping the matter before their attention and I have requested that Mr. Salter might be allowed to stay here a little longer, in order to acquaint himself with such new developments as may now arise.

I have the honour to be,

    With the highest respect, Sir, Your most obedient,

        humble servant,   Cecil Spring Rice

TLS (FO 368/1836, No. 158310, PRO).

ENCLOSURE

NOTE AS TO DISCUSSION OF CERTAIN SHIPPING QUESTIONS BETWEEN PRESIDENT WILSON AND MR. T. ROYDEN AND MR. J. A. SALTER ON JULY 26TH 1917.

President Wilson granted us an audience this afternoon July 26th 1917.

After a brief preliminary conversation he stated that he was glad of the opportunity of discussing with us, before we left America, several of the more important shipping questions on which action was urgently required.

The points on which we laid particular stress were (a) the necessity for shipbuilding by America on a scale much larger than any hitherto indicated and in this connection we explained the extreme importance which Great Britain attached to what America could do if she concentrated her immense resources, (b), the importance, for the immediate future, of America making available (by economizing in civilian consumption and at the expense of trade at present being carried on) American tonnage suitable for trans-atlantic work.

We explained that one of the most striking experiences of Great Britain in the war had been the extent to which (beyond what any experts early in the war had considered possible) we had in fact been able to economize in the use of tonnage by reducing civilian consumption and by subordinating the interests of our trade to those of the war.

We also referred to the desirability of at once making arrangements which would enable America to consider shipping policies continuously in conjunction with the Allies and prevent the evils of competition for neutral tonnage.

We left with the President a memorandum[1] stating the position more fully in regard to each of the above subjects.

The President showed that he was taking an immediate and personal interest in the shipping question and had been giving a great deal of consideration to it.

He referred with regret to the abandonment of the wooden shipbuilding programme and added that there had been much misunderstanding as to its intention which was to use the wooden ships for American coastal and Pacific trade and so release suitable steel vessels now in those employments for trans-atlantic work.

He stated that he recognised the immense importance of building on the largest possible scale but added that so far as he could see building now being carried on by other countries together with the maximum amount that America could build having regard to her existing facilities would not exceed more than half the amount of tonnage being destroyed. (Incidentally he expressed the opinion that the naval policy of the allies ought to be more aggressive, remarking that the defensive had considerable advantages on land but was always at a disadvantage at sea. This was of course outside our province and we offered no comment.)

In connection with the American shipbuilding programme the President referred to the difficulty of obtaining raw materials, ore etc., for the manufacture of steel, the shortage of labour and, in particular, to the difficulties of internal transportation (he remarked that American railways were at present far from adequate for their work). He stated that he had been feeling anxiety as to whether the constant diminution of merchant shipping would prevent the allies carrying on operations in accordance with present programmes over the winter. At this point we remarked that it was our considered view that if building could be arranged so as to give a prospect of relief after the winter the Allies could, with such assistance as America could give with her existing tonnage, continue the war without actual disaster ti [to] their present military programmes through shortage of ships until the early months of next year.

We think we should record a general impression that while the President clearly realises that the position is grave and is anxious to take what action is possible to relieve it he has scar[c]ely at present contemplated, as both practicable and necessary, the degree of drastic action both in extending shipbuilding facilities and in subordinating civilian and trade interests to those of the war which our experience in Great Britain and a dispassionate survey of the shipping position would make us believe to be both possible and urgently required.

In parting from the President we referred to the question of British vessels building in America and the suggestion that they might be taken over by the American government. The President indicated that while he had come to no conclusion in his mind he had been advised that it might be desirable that America should take these vessels over (a) partly in order that they might be treated just like vessels building for the American Government in the arrangements for speeding up, and for the allocation of labour and material, without any complication either as to the extra expenses incurred or as to questions of priority and (b), partly because the use of these vessels might be required for American war purposes or essential imports. We explained the action Great Britain had taken in similar circumstances and pointed out particularly that complete control of the building of the vessels had been in no way inconsistent with their ownership by Great Britain after completion and that no difficulty need arise about the repayment of extra expenses incurred. We also pointed out as regards (b) that it might be hoped that American tonnage might be made available for war purposes by economies in other directions and that some neutral ships might also be forthcoming if, as we hoped, arrangements were made for America and the allies to deal with the questions of the acquisition and allocation of neutral tonnage in co-operation. We stated that a special memorandum on the subject had been sent to the State Department of which we would be pleased to send him a personal copy.[2]

T. Royden
J. A. Salter.
July 26th 1917.[3]

T MS (FO 368/1836, No. 158310, PRO).
[1] T. Royden and J. A. Salter, "Notes as to the More Urgent and Important Outstanding Shipping Problems," July 26, 1917, T MS (WP, DLC).
[2] It is printed as an Enclosure with F. L. Polk to WW, July 27, 1917.
[3] C. A. Spring Rice to the Foreign Office, July 27, 1917, T telegram (FO 368/1836, No. 149164, PRO), is a paraphrase of the foregoing memorandum.

From the Diary of Colonel House

July 26, 1917.

Dudley Malone telephoned from New York asking for an engagement in the late afternoon. As a matter of fact he did the usual Malone act and arrived at twenty minutes after ten o'clock. It was twelve before I got to bed. He brought the Collector of the Port of Boston with him, but considerately left Billings in the open automobile, out of doors in the fog, during the time we talked. It was a distressing interview.

He is ready to quarrel with the President because of his lack of action in the Suffrage movement. He told the story of his interview with the President and it was not a pleasant thing to hear. He feels that the President, and perhaps rightly, could bring about national suffrage almost immediately if he was sincerely for it. The President was inclined to argue the matter and stated that he did not feel it was right to go to Congress and demand it of it. In reply to this, Dudley asked him why he considered it right to demand of Congress practically all of the important legislation he had gotten through. The President made a mistake in giving such a reason, he should have stated the truth.

Whenever the President gives evasive or foolish reasons—reasons I know are not the real ones, I never argue with him as Dudley did, but I simply cease talking. The President understands that I know he is talking nonsense, and my method is far more effective.

Dudley's action has led, I am afraid, to a breach—a breach that will widen as time goes on. It is a pity that a man of Dudley's remarkable talents should not use them to better advantage. He is temperamentally unable to do sustained work. He wishes to resign at once. I urged him not to do so for the present. In demanding my reasons, I thought it would be better for him and better for the President that there should be no apparent breach. He gave me no definite promise.[1]

[1] Malone resigned as Collector of the Port of New York on September 7. See D. F. Malone to WW, Sept. 7, 1917.

To Thomas Davies Jones

My dear Friend: The White House 27 July, 1917

I am afraid you will think me very persistent in asking you to render this, that and the other service of capital importance to the Government, but the fact is that I trust and believe in you so entirely that I am, I must confess, covetous of the privilege of having you at hand here to take counsel with.

Mr. Hurley, as you know, whom I have just asked to serve as Chairman of the Shipping Board, was serving as the representative of the Department of Commerce in the board to which is assigned the very important duty of working out the practical application and operation of the restrictions we are putting on exports, and his transfer leaves a vacancy on that board which I am particularly anxious to have you fill if you feel that you have the freedom and the strength to devote yourself to what I am afraid are rather arduous duties but duties which I dare not entrust to anybody who will not take a look around the horizon in performing them. The Secretary of Commerce has asked me if I would not write to you.

I know that you will make the frankest and most candid response. That is one of the reasons I feel at liberty to make such a request.

Cordially and sincerely yours,   Woodrow Wilson

TLS (Mineral Point, Wisc., Public Library).

To Louis Wiley

My dear Friend: The White House 27 July, 1917

Thank you for your thoughtfulness in sending me the full text of Lloyd George's address on the British War Aims.[1] I had not seen it elsewhere.

In haste   Cordially yours,   Woodrow Wilson

TLS (L. Wiley Papers, NRU).
[1] It is missing in WP, DLC. However, it was the text of a speech which Lloyd George delivered on June 29 on the occasion of his being made a free-man of the City of Glasgow. Among other topics, the Prime Minister had spoken

in general terms of Britain's war aims. The independence of Belgium had to be restored and an indemnity paid to that country. Mesopotamia had to be permanently removed from Turkish control. The future of the German colonies would be determined by the peace conference, and the desires of the colonial peoples would be the dominant consideration. Most important, there would have to be a guarantee against the repetition of the war. This would come either through the destruction of German military power or, better still, the establishment of a democratic government in Germany. A full text of Lloyd George's speech appears in the London *Times*, June 30, 1917. There is a partial text in the *New York Times*, June 30, 1917.

To Charles William Eliot, with Enclosure

My dear Doctor Eliot: The White House 27 July, 1917

I was discussing with the Secretary of Labor the fears expressed in your last letter to me and he has written me a memorandum of which I venture to send you a copy herewith. There are elements of reassurance in it.

In haste
        Cordially and sincerely yours,   Woodrow Wilson

TLS (C. W. Eliot Papers, MH-Ar).

E N C L O S U R E

From William Bauchop Wilson

My dear Mr. President: Washington July 26, 1917.

Referring to the intimation contained in a letter from Dr. Eliot to the effect that the workingmen are taking advantage of the present emergency to compel recognition of their unions, which you mentioned at the Cabinet Tuesday, I have had the records of our Mediation Service examined with a view to securing an approximation of the number of disputes since April 6, 1917, in which the men have included recognition of the union as one of their original demands. The information brought out is interesting and may be of assistance to you in your correspondence with Dr. Eliot.

Number of labor disputes occur[r]ing since April 6, 1917, handled by the Mediation Division of the Department of Labor, 254.

Number of these in which recognition of the union was one of the demands, 58.

Number of cases in which the demand for recognition was withdrawn before adjustment, 9.

Number in which recognition was conceded, 34.

Number of cases still pending, 15.

We have no accurate figures showing the number of workers involved in the fifty-eight strikes where recognition was demanded. Twenty-five thousand would be a large estimate of the number. When you take into consideration that there are approximately thirteen million wage-workers engaged in mining, manufacturing, transportation and building industries, which are the industries in which strikes occur most frequently, you will immediately observe that the percentage demanding recognition of the union is infinitesimal. I may add that by far the largest proportion of cases in which a demand was made for recognition of the union occurred in the mining industry.

Faithfully yours,   W B Wilson

TLS (WP, DLC).

From Frank Lyon Polk, with Enclosure

My dear Mr. President: Washington July 27, 1917.

At the request of the British Ambassador it gives me pleasure to send you enclosed a copy of a note which the Ambassador addressed to the Department under date of July 25th and which was in reply to the Department's note to the Ambassador announcing the resolutions of the Shipping Board as to requisitioning vessels building in United States yards for foreign governments or owners. The British Government consider this a very important communication.

With assurances of respect, etc., I am, my dear Mr. President,   Faithfully yours,   Frank L Polk

TLS (WP, DLC).

ENCLOSURE

Sir Cecil Arthur Spring Rice to Frank Lyon Polk

Sir: Washington, July 25th 1917.

I have the honour to acknowledge the receipt of your note of the 24th instant enclosing a Resolution of the Shipping Board as to requisitioning vessels building in American yards for foreign governments or owners.[1]

As you are aware, this has been the subject of frequent discussion both verbally and in correspondence between your Government and ours.

We had expected in view of the state in which these discussions were left that no actual decision would be arrived at without a further communication with us and we had no idea that the Shipping Board were re-considering the matter with a view to a final decision.

Your note forwarding the Resolution is dated on the day on which the resignations of the Chairman and one of the members of the Board were announced; and I see that it is stated today that the Vice-Chairman also has tendered his resignation.

In the circumstances, I presume that we may expect the new Board will reconsider the matter in the light of the representations which have already been made.

I should be obliged if the following considerations could also be brought to the notice of the Shipping Board:

At the beginning of the war there was a considerable number of vessels building in Great Britain which were the property of Great Britain's allies or of neutral shipowners just as there is now a number of vessels building in the United States which are the property of the British Government.

It was therefore necessary for Great Britain to consider, as America has now had to consider, how she should control the building of such ships in view of the limited supplies of labour and material, and whether in view of the enormous strain upon her mercantile marine imposed by war requirements she would be justified in breaking contracts, and requisitioning the vessels.

It must be remembered that the strain thrown upon the British mercantile marine by the immediate necessities of the war was enormous.

While the vessels in question were still building, half of the British mercantile marine had to be devoted to direct naval and military requirements.

In addition, in view of the inadequate Mercantile Marines of her Allies Great Britain provided some 2,000,000 tons to France, Russia and Italy at rates very much below (and in the case of nearly a million tons at less than one-sixth of) the present market rates.

The strain gradually forced Great Britain to abandon her shipping interests, and to destroy old established lines, till now no ocean-going British vessels are allowed to trade on any route except those which are required, not for trading purposes but for the transport of articles essential to the Empire.

A moment of relaxation

David Lloyd George

Sir William Wiseman

Gen. Tasker H. Bliss in France

Samuel Gompers

The Council of National Defense and the Advisory Commission

The Women's Committee of the Council of National Defense. Dr. Anna Howard Shaw, Chairperson, is in the center.

The Secretary of War draws the first draft number, July 20, 1917

Similarly, civilian consumption had to be cut down to a point involving real hardship to the individual citizen as well as destruction of industries not directly required for war purposes. Before the war, Great Britain imported over 50,000,000 tons for civilian and industrial requirements (including nearly 20,000,000 tons of foodstuffs). This year her imports for civilian requirements will be about 20,000,000 tons including foodstuffs, and this in spite of the fact that she is bound anyhow to import four-fifths of her wheat supply.

At the same time the brunt of the submarine campaign has fallen upon Great Britain whose mercantile marine has lost a larger proportion than that of any of her allies.

Since the war began, over four million tons gross of British tonnage have been destroyed by war risk. Allowing for gains by new building and by seizure of German ships, this still leaves a net loss of 2¼ million gross tons. In contrast to this American tonnage shows an increase (including some half million tons of seized German ships) of nearly 1¾ million gross tons. Excluding as gains in both cases the seized German ships, the war has meant a net *loss* of 2¾ million tons gross to Great Britain and a *gain* of nearly 1¼ million gross tons to America. At the same time America is only beginning to have her mercantile marine drawn upon either for her own military requirements or for providing ships to the Allies.

In the circumstances described above, the action taken by Great Britain was as follows:

In the case of vessels building for Allied countries, she gave unconditional facilities for the completion of the vessels and allowed them to remain under Allied ownership, under the Allied flag and under Allied control, both during the war and afterwards.

Even in the case of mercantile neutral vessels, she did not feel justified in breaking the contracts. All she did was to make an arrangement with the neutral owner under which, in return for facilities for the speedy completion of the vessels, they were chartered (at rates leaving about five times the profit allowed for British ships) for the period of the war and six months after, the vessels being then transferred to the neutral flag and remaining throughout the property of the neutral.

These arrangements both in the case of the Allied ships and the neutral ships were of course in no way inconsistent with the proper control of building by the British Government who arranged for the supply of steel, etc., under the priority system set up on account of the shortage of material. The control of building however was treated as an entirely separate question from that of the control and ownership of vessels after completion.

In conclusion I ought to add that the communications I have received from His Majesty's Government show that they consider the retention of their vessels building in America to be essential to their shipping programme and would learn with great regret that the United States Government intended to break the contracts.

I have the honour to be,

With the highest consideration, Sir,

Your most obedient, humble servant,

Cecil Spring Rice.

TCL (WP, DLC).

[1] F. L. Polk to C. A. Spring Rice, July 24, 1917, TLS, enclosing TC resolution (FO 115/2333, pp. 216-17, PRO).

From Henry Clay Hall

My dear Mr. President: Washington July 27, 1917.

As requested by your letter of the 25th inst.,[1] yesterday received, the Commission will do what it can to ascertain and report to you the capacity of the plants in this country now manufacturing railway cars and railway locomotives, and the extent to which that capacity is being utilized in such manufacture.

Meantime let me say that from the best information which has been available during the last few months the car building plants are and have been working at less than half capacity in the construction of cars, and of those many are for foreign use. Something over 100,000 cars, mostly freight, are now under order from railways for use in the United States, and at least 30,000 for railways in Russia, France and Italy. The reason generally given for reduced production is inability to procure steel and lumber in sufficient quantities, although the selling price of the completed car has increased from 20 to 250 percent in 1917 over 1916, according to kind or type. Some of the plants are said to have been and to be largely engaged in manufacturing shells and other munitions of war. I understand the same to be true of car plants in Canada. So far as I have been able to learn no car plant in this country, whether carrier owned or independent, has been or is working to capacity in the construction of cars.

As to locomotives the situation is somewhat different. The plants are relatively few and are being worked more nearly to capacity in filling orders for locomotives. These orders now include over 2,300 locomotives for railways in the United States, and as of July 1st 1,164 for foreign governments, of which some may have been delivered since, as 318 were due at that time.

I am unable at this writing to indicate even approximately how rapidly these orders are being filled. Locomotives also have greatly increased in price since 1916, the increase varying according to type from 25 to 110 percent.

The increased cost to carriers has naturally tended to restrict orders to some extent.

The principal plants engaged in construction of equipment are being asked by wire for the desired information brought down to date, and the results will be promptly compiled and transmitted to you.

Very sincerely and cordially, Henry C Hall.

TLS (WP, DLC).
[1] WW to H. C. Hall, July 25, 1917, TLS (Letterpress Books, WP, DLC).

Two Letters from Thomas Watt Gregory

Dear Mr. President: Washington, D. C. July 27, 1917.

A reply to your note of the 23d instant wherein you suggest that it will probably be appropriate to say to Congressman Dyer that the recent disturbances at East St. Louis do not present a proper predicate for the exercise of Federal jurisdiction has been necessarily delayed pending a complete investigation both as to the origin and course of events at East St. Louis, and the law applicable to the facts after they had been thus carefully developed.

I have been giving a good deal of thought to this situation and the United States District Attorney at East St. Louis[1] and special agents of this Department have been at work gathering information to enable us to finally determine whether any Federal Statute has been violated. Up to this time no facts have been presented to us which would justify Federal action, though it is conceivable that a condition which would justify it may develop later on.

I am informed that the Attorney General of the State of Illinois[2] has gone to East St. Louis adding his efforts to those of the county and city officials in inaugurating prosecutions under the state laws. The representatives of the Department of Justice are so far as possible lending aid to the state authorities in their efforts to restore tranquility and guard against further outbreaks.

In replying to the letter of Representative Dyer which is herewith returned, I suggest that you do not state flatly that under existing laws the Federal authorities have no jurisdiction, but rather follow the lines of this letter, bearing in mind that it is still barely possible that something may develop which would authorize Federal action. You might also add that the matter had been referred to the Attorney General by you as requested by Mr. Dyer with result above indicated.

Faithfully yours,   T. W. Gregory

1 Charles Adam Karch.
2 Edward Jackson Brundage.

Dear Mr. President: Washington, D. C. July 27, 1917.

I acknowledge receipt of yours of July 16th enclosing memorandum left with you by Mr. Dudley Malone of New York and relating to certain Irish activities.

I am having careful attention given to the matter.

Faithfully yours,   T. W. Gregory

TLS (WP, DLC).

From Richard Crane, with Enclosure

Department of State [c. July 27, 1917]

Perhaps the President would be interested in reading this paraphrase from Mr. Crane, Petrograd.

Richard Crane.

TL (WP, DLC).

Petrograd. July 21, 1917.

1539. For Richard Crane. It has been a difficult week for the Cooper Union Government.[1] Many Jews and other exiles who have lived out of the country for a long time, have been placed suddenly in positions of a large amount of power, on the theory somewhat that they are acquainted with European methods of administration and affairs. They know nothing at all of government administration, and really very little of Europe, and their long exile and their habits of life have entirely put them out of touch with Russia. Amateurs compose the administration, and it is one which is very much open to influences of evil of all kinds, particularly German ones. To understand present day history here, carefully study all stages of the Young Turks movement, including the present center of power outside of the country. Customs or fashions or morals are not changed by revolutions. Human nature continues, and habits persist. Best reports from here by Professor Masaryk, London Times. Charles R. Crane.   Francis.

T telegram (WP, DLC).
    1 That is, a government like a debating society.

From Julius Kahn

My dear Mr. President: Washington July 27, 1917.

I have your kind note of July 25th. I fully appreciate the sentiments you express regarding my stand on various matters during the present crisis.

Let me assure you that I deem it the duty of every patriotic American to forget petty politics and stand by you in your effort to vindicate the country's honor.

Do not hesitate to command me whenever I can be of service.
                    Very sincerely yours,   Julius Kahn

TLS (WP, DLC).

From John McCarthy and Others

Butte, Mont., July 27, 1917.

Metal Mine Workers Union, representing ten thousand miners of Butte, request you to send Miss Jeannette Rankin here as your personal representative, to try and bring industrial peace to this community and some small measure of justice to the miners. We feel that knowing industrial conditions in Butte as Miss Rankin does, that she can bring about a just settlement.
                    Strike Committee, Chairman John McCarthy;
                           Peter Kelly, John O'Brien.

T telegram (WP, DLC).

To Leonidas Carstarphen Dyer

My dear Mr. Dyer: [The White House] 28 July, 1917

I have your letter of yesterday[1] with the accompanying papers which I take the liberty of returning.

The Attorney General and I have been giving a great deal of thought to the situation in East St. Louis, and the United States

District Attorney there as well as special agents of the Department of Justice have been at work gathering information to enable us to determine whether any federal statute has been violated. Up to this time I am bound in candor to say that no facts have been presented to us which would justify federal action, though it is conceivable that a condition which would justify it may develop.

I am informed that the Attorney General of the State of Illinois has gone to East St. Louis to add his efforts to those of the officials of the county and city in pressing prosecutions under the state laws. The representatives of the Department of Justice are so far as possible lending aid to the state authorities in their efforts to restore tranquility and guard against further outbreaks.

I need not tell you how much anxiety the whole matter has given me. It is a very serious thing for the whole nation that anything of the sort that happened in East St. Louis should be possible.

Cordially and sincerely yours,   Woodrow Wilson

TLS (Letterpress Books, WP, DLC).
  ¹ He meant L. C. Dyer to WW, July 20, 1917.

To Henry Clay Hall

My dear Mr. Chairman: [The White House] 28 July, 1917

Thank you very sincerely for your reply of yesterday to my letter of the twenty-fifth. The information you give me is significant and important and I shall await the later information with the greatest interest.

Cordially and sincerely yours,   Woodrow Wilson

TLS (Letterpress Books, WP, DLC).

From Frank Lyon Polk, with Enclosure

My dear Mr. President: Washington July 28, 1917

I am sending you a copy of a memorandum recently handed me by the British Ambassador, stating that the British Government are of the opinion that the efforts of the Polish people to obtain their freedom should be supported in every possible way. In consequence, the British Government propose that all Poles, whether of German, Austrian or Prussian origin, living in the Allied countries, should be granted open recognition as friends and potential allies. The British suggest the establishment of a committee to represent the Polish community in each of the Allied countries.

I should be very grateful if you would kindly indicate whether the plan as outlined in the accompanying memorandum meets with your approval, and, if not, what line you wish me to take in replying to the British Ambassador.

With assurances of respect, etc., I am, my dear Mr. President,
Faithfully yours,   Frank L Polk

TLS (SDR, RG 59, 860C.01/54, DNA).

ENCLOSURE

Washington July 23rd, 1917.
MEMORANDUM.

Intelligence received lately by His Majesty's Government of the progress of events in Poland shows clearly that Germany and her Allies have been greatly concerned by the situation there, and His Majesty's Government are of the opinion that the efforts of the Polish people to obtain their freedom and their independence should be supported in every possible way, and that they should be similarly discouraged from listening to the specious assurances of the enemy of a spurious independence. The feeling that they are being abandoned by the Allies and their prolonged sufferings are calculated otherwise to make them welcome these assurances.

The need for action of the nature indicated would appear to have become all the greater owing to the late changes in the German Government which portend a more rigorous policy in Poland as milder methods must have been unsuccessful.

In consequence His Majesty's Government propose that all Poles whether of German Austrian or Prussian origin, living in the countries of the Allied Powers should be granted open recognition as friends and potential allies.

Such a step would crystallize the idea of a separate and free Polish state and people in the minds of the public in the countries of the Allied Governments, and it would be in the nature of a guarantee to the Polish people themselves that their claims to independence were being backed by the Allies.

As a corollary to such action it would be highly desirable to establish a committee to represent the Polish community in each of the Allied countries. Such a body would be valuable, if recognized by the Government, in affording assistance in case of necessity to the individual members of the communities, of whatever origin they might be, in requesting for them the protection of the Government and in giving guarantees for them, as well as in serving as a means of communication with Polish patriots.

His Majesty's Government are anxious to learn the opinion of the United States Government on this subject.

Cecil Spring Rice

T MS (SDR, RG 59, 860C.01/54, DNA).

From William Phillips

My dear Mr. President: Washington July 28, 1917.

I am sending you enclosed a paraphrase of a telegram[1] received to-day at the British Embassy from the Foreign Office in London which has just been left with me by the Ambassador, in which the British Government asks that the United States send to London one or two representatives to participate in a conference to be held on August 10th to discuss the whole shipping problem.

I should be grateful if you would be so good as to indicate whether or not this Government should be represented at this conference of the allied governments.

With assurances of respect, etc., I am, my dear Mr. President,

Faithfully yours,   William Phillips

July 31, 1917

The President feel[s] that as there is a conference on here, it would be well to settle affairs here first[2]   FLP

TLS (SDR, RG 59, 763.72/6101, DNA).
[1] "Paraphrase of telegram just received by the British Embassy from the Foreign Office in London," T MS (SDR, RG 59, 763.72/6101, DNA).
[2] F. L. Polk to C. A. Spring Rice, Aug. 1, 1917, CCL (SDR, RG 59, 763.72/6101, DNA), conveyed Wilson's message.

Two Letters from Josephus Daniels

CONFIDENTIAL   Aug. 10(?)[1]

My dear Mr. President: Washington [c. July 28, 1917]

There is quoted below for your information two despatches which have just been received from Vice Admiral Sims:

"146. Following is the text of a memorandum prepared at a combined allied military and naval conference in Paris after a statement before the conference by the British Minister of Shipping[2] and a general discussion initiated by the French Chief of Military staff.[3] The memorandum was unanimously agreed to.

"The review of the maritime situation and the very clear explanations given by Mr. Graeme Thomson[4] show that we have to face a total monthly reduction of allied and neutral countries which can be estimated at 500,000 tons for the high seas tonnage. In the first instance Graeme Thomson on behalf of the British Ministry of Shipping is of the opinion it will be possible to meet the requirements of the supply of United Kingdom (limited to those that are absolutely necessary) until October 1918 provided that new construction amounts to 3,000,000 tons from the first of January 1918. For prevention it is essential that the necessary labor should be called back from the British Army and the steel required provided. Mr. Graeme Thomson states that for the period extending to October 1st 1918 the continuous reducing available tonnage will suffice for imperative needs but the people of Great Britain will undoubtedly have to suffer serious privations. It will not be possible to make an increase of imports into allied countries with British tonnage. From November 1918 and with the help of the Americans presuming their ship-building program comes up to expectations we may hope that the total construction will approximately compensate for the losses caused by submarines. It appears from the above that the situation will only begin to improve from November 1918 and that until then the total available tonnage of the allies may be insufficient to cover all their requirements. It is therefore indispensible to establish a general list of available tonnage for each of the allies and to put against it the figure of their requirements. Only then will it be possible to take a decision as to the amount and the nature of the restrictions which will have to be made in the various kinds of traffic. Further, transport of American Army to France has created fresh needs which we have to face. On this particular account, it is indispensible to draw a complete statement of the total allied tonnage, and it is only when this is done that it will be possible to get an idea of the available tonnage if any which can be put at the disposal of the American Army in France; it about seems, on a first examination, that these means will be limited solely to the resources of the American mercantile marine as supplemented by their ship-building program. Members of the meeting consider that is a most important point which must be cleared up without delay and ask that the allied Governments should take at once the necessary measures to that effect; with this end in view a meeting of the representatives of the transport services of the allies should be held in London at the earliest opportunity. 18028.

"147. Following naval and military conferences this week at Paris 136 representatives France Great Britain and U. S.[5] under chairmanship chief of French Army Staff it has been decided to hold allied shipping conference in London August 10th for general exchange of positive information regarding shipping situation present and during next twelve months and upon which allied success fundamentally depends stop No definite information is available as to part which United States may be expected to play either as to relieving critical merchant shipping situation or in increasing military forces in France and particularly as American plans concerning shipping necessary to maintain overseas forces stop French are very much concerned as to military support from America they may rely and plan upon and particularly to demands which such support may make upon their already seriously depleted resources stop At present 585 ships or over one million two hundred thousand tons of British shipping is allocated to supplying France and similarly large amounts to Italy and other European allies stop Naval and military conference clearly established that it will be impossible to increase imports or ships serving France or other continential [continental] allies before November 1918 and even then additional support will be dependant on withdrawing 80000 shipwrights from British army and obtaining necessary materials stop In view of allied war experience as to amount of shipping necessary to maintain overseas forces and possible effects on general allied shipping situation of American primary object maintain her forces the need of coordination of allied effort is considered imperative stop For example withdrawal by America of its present shipping with South America or other countries would immediately place new demands upon other allied shipping which probably could not be met stop Most serious crisis confronting allies and upon which ultimate success will undoubtedly primarily depend is shipping situation as produced by enemies submarine campaign stop All future naval and military policies and operations are dependant thereon stop Early steps towards allied coordination of shipping is considered to be the most vital military necessity of moment stop All measures contemplated cannot be safely considered without sufficiently complete information of American proposed plans stop I am therefore requested by French and British Admiralties in agreement with French and British chiefs to urge United States to send to London by August 10th responsible shipping representatives who will be competent and authorized to discuss above questions with similar representatives France Italy England and United States stop Instructions now enroute through British Ambassador but may be delayed 19028.   SIMS."

Sincerely yours,   Josephus Daniels

TLS (WP, DLC).
  [1] WWhw.
  [2] That is, Sir Joseph Paton Maclay.
  [3] General Foch.
  [4] Director of Transports for the Ministry of Shipping.
  [5] As has been noted, Admiral Sims and General Pershing met informally with the military and naval representatives of the Allies in Paris, July 24-27.

My dear Mr. President: Washington July 28, 1917.

Replying to your letter of the 23d instant in reference to the plan submitted by Mr. Frank J. Sprague[1] for limiting the activities of German submarines in the present war I have to say as follows:

Mr. Sprague's plan, in brief, is to build immediately large numbers of a special type of seakeeping boats of about 145 tons displacement, 159 feet in length, speed of from 20 to 25 knots and cruising radius of 3000 to 3500 miles. These vessels to be armed with one or two 3-inch (14-pdr.) and a few smaller guns, 50 depth bombs and 12 "dwarf" torpedoes of a type much smaller than those now used in our torpedo vessels.

When built these torpedo chasers are to be used, in conjunction with the destroyers and other vessels now employed against submarines, to guard certain "lanes" leading to the principal ports of entry and departure abroad and at home and extending several hundred miles to sea.

All who have given the problem of successfully combating the submarine menace consideration, are convinced of the necessity of large numbers of seakeeping surface vessels to meet it. All agree that the present type of torpedo boat destroyer is the best type for this purpose yet developed, and all would doubtless agree that if a smaller and more quickly constructed type, able to accomplish its work, could be obtained in much less time than can the destroyer, such a type should be produced as soon as possible. Whatever the method adopted for searching out submarines,—patrol, convoy or guarded lanes—larger numbers of small craft than are now available are urgently needed and *time* is of the utmost importance.

  [1] WW to JD, July 23, 1917, CCL (WP, DLC). Frank Julian Sprague, electrical engineer, pioneer in the development of electric railways and electric elevators; a member of the Naval Consulting Board.

It was for these reasons that the Navy Department adopted the 110 foot motor boat of about 66 tons displacement of which 360 are now under construction. It was, however, fully recognized at the time that building these vessels was only justified by the emergency; that they were too small to keep the sea in bad weather or to carry as heavy an armament as the later submarines and, further, that their cruising would have to be confined to such areas as would enable them to quickly reach a port of refuge from bad weather.

The 159 foot boats proposed by Mr. Sprague would be better sea boats, would have greater speed and cruising radius than the 110 foot boats, but even if it should be proved that they could safely keep the sea in Atlantic winter gales it is as certain as any untried thing can be that they could not hold station as "lane" guards under such conditions. A heavy gale would scatter them widely and leave the "lane" unprotected until they could, perhaps after many days, resume their stations. The seagoing submarines of the enemy, ranging from 800 to 2000 or more tons, would ask nothing better than an established and unguarded "lane" with a continuous procession of valuable ships passing along it. They would no longer have to hunt for ships, easy as the task now seems to be, but would soon learn exactly where to go and lie in wait.

These boats, while too small for heavy, offshore work, would still be valuable for inshore patrol. They are, however, too small to meet the larger submarines, armed with 2 or 3 5.9″ guns, which outrange the one or two 3″ guns of the proposed batteries. The destroyers under construction will carry at least 4-4″ guns, or 4-5″ guns, if they can be procured in time; and will have sufficient speed to run down any submarine on the surface. From their greater speed, seakeeping qualities and heavy batteries it is considered that the boats under construction and in contemplation would prove more effective than a much greater number of the proposed boats of the Gardner type.

The proposal to form "sea lanes" to be used to the exclusion of other routes by cargo carriers bound to and from British, French and Italian ports, and patrol these lanes with surface craft, is not new. In various forms the proposition has come before the Department, and has received earnest and careful consideration. The scheme is practically working efficiently at the present moment between Dover and Calais, across the English Channel. It is a practical success there for three reasons:—the distance to be patrolled is very short, only 30 miles; the ends of the sea lane abut on the land, and the number of destroyers and other patrol craft, together with a number of submarines, is relatively great enough, when an important movement takes place across this narrow body of water, to have on each side several lines of protecting vessels, one beyond the other and very closely placed.

The three conditions which make the passage of the English Channel practicable are unfortunately not the conditions which will obtain in the localities where sea lanes are to be used to protect trans-Atlantic traffic. Mr. Sprague proposes to have a sea lane leaving, say, the English coast, projected out into the Atlantic, so closely patrolled by surface craft on either side that cargoes may pass between them in safety. It may be well to state in order some of the difficulties to be overcome in putting this plan into successful operation.

Considering the carrying trade to and from England alone, an investigation of this subject and the testimony of the Senior Naval Officer of the British Commission recently in this country,[2] leads to the conclusion that the immense quantity of stores and munitions received daily in England, and the inadequate railroad transportation facilities there, makes it imperative to keep open several ports, instead of bringing the vast volume of seaborne supplies into one port. So, probably six lanes must be patrolled instead of one—at least to the main lane extending out into the Atlantic.

From all reports received from actual encounters with submarines, it is certain that the periscopes of submerged submarines can not usually be seen under daylight conditions in clear weather a greater distance than 1,000 yards; and this distance decreases to practically zero with failing light, mist, fog, or snow. It would therefore be necessary to have the patrolling vessels spaced not more than one mile (2,000 yards) apart, on each side of the lane in question in clear weather; and at night or in foggy weather, the patrol would be practically blind, so far as sighting periscopes is concerned. In fact, vessels have been torpedoed in open daylight, with destroyers on either beam, and close aboard, by submarines getting within 1,000 yards of the convoy and firing torpedoes without being seen.

Among the difficulties encountered by submarines in prosecuting their work are, first, to find the enemy's cargo carriers; second, to estimate the course and speed of the cargo carriers by tracking; and third, to then approach and fire when within torpedo range, preferably from a position somewhere forward of the beam of the target ship.

2 That is Rear Admiral DeChair.

An easy determination of these usually unknown factors in the problem will be practicable for the enemy by the establishment of the sea lane. The double lines of picket boats between which the cargo carriers must pass will make a search for them unnecessary; the course of the target ship is also known by the direction of the lane; and a few minutes periscope observation of the disposition of picket vessels would give the desired ranges. Then, if anywhere the unavoidable action of the wind and sea had increased the intervals between picket boats, or at night or in bad weather, the submarine could easily approach within torpedoing distance, fire and totally submerge.

The length of the lane depends upon the number of patrol boats available. Assuming only three ports in England open to commerce, London, Bristol and Liverpool, the sea lanes from these ports to the Scilly Islands, the beginning of the sea lane out into the Atlantic, aggregate 150 miles; and assuming patrols placed one mile apart, 300 patrol boats would be required. Patrols must be relieved regularly; it is a liberal assumption that not more than $\frac{2}{3}$ of the force could be kept in position on the lanes —$\frac{1}{3}$ being in port, coaling, overhauling, etc., and getting back to stations. Therefore, the lanes to the ports named would require 450 boats; and the 600 proposed would supply a lane only 50 miles long from the Scilly Islands to the westward. Or, assuming that the British could supply 450 patrols for the three lanes, the 600 to be supplied by the United States would project a lane only 200 miles into the Atlantic.

Unless a patrol could be maintained across the Atlantic, 3,000 miles, the outer end of the lane must always remain the end, practically, of patrol protection; a point perfectly well known to the enemy, located as definitely as the Scilly Islands, as the point upon which submarine attacks were to be concentrated —and from there to other points of attack farther west.

If the boats in sufficient numbers could be obtained, there would still remain the absolute impossibility, recognized by all seamen, of keeping boats of the type proposed on station along a sea lane, in the heavy seas and strong gales to be encountered in the Atlantic, off the British Islands; and patrol boats would themselves be in great danger from submarines, their exact location being known, and as, necessarily, they would be keeping station at low speed.

After disposing of the 600 boats of the type proposed, there would still remain the ports in France, to which most war munitions and troops from this country must go, and also those of Italy, to be protected.

The practicability of building so many vessels, even of small size, in a short time, say twelve months, is gravely doubted and could only be done at all by the cessation of practically all other work in the ship and engine building yards of the country.

We are not prepared for such a programme, however simple, practicable and necessary it may seem to its advocates.

It may well be that in the not distant future, and suddenly, the United States fleet alone will be called upon to meet the enemy fleet in full strength and with this possibility in view we must proceed steadily to strengthen our fleet in all its various military units notwithstanding the immediate and serious peril of the enemy submarine operations. The future protection of our own national interests must be kept prominently to the front in all our plans.

It is a difficult problem. Whatever is done will provoke adverse critic[i]sm from some quarter. The only safe and sane course to pursue is to build as quickly as possible as many anti-submarine craft of approved type as the facilities of the country will permit, using every possible effort, regardless of expense, to increase those facilities and at the same time to proceed with other necessary shipbuilding, both naval and commercial.

We have now 56 torpedo boat destroyers in commission, 66 under contract to be delivered by September, 1918, and 50 more are practically under contract now to be delivered ready for service by January 1, 1919, say 18 months. The Department is endeavoring to arrange for 150 more destroyers to be delivered at the earliest possible date, perhaps in 18 months or two years.

Depth bombs of the character recommended by Mr. Sprague are already in use in our Navy.

The "dwarf" torpedo recommended is a new departure but if an efficient type of such torpedoes can be developed, as seems probable, it will be a valuable addition to the armament of vessels operating against submarines. Certainly it will be productive of greater caution in submarine operations where it is likely to be encountered. This matter is already under consideration by the Department.

As to the use of the "lane" system for minimizing submarine attack the matter had best be left to expert decision. The important thing is to provide the vessels with which to work. A system which might work well under one set of conditions or in a certain locality might not do well under other conditions or in other localities. Whether the patrol, the convoy or the lane systems, any or all, shall be adopted must be decided as experience and special conditions may determine.

I desire to express my great appreciation of Mr. Sprague's paper, the patriotic motives which inspired it and the thought and investigation evidenced throughout. Any recommendations emanating from a man of his ability and experience of affairs are deserving of the highest consideration and are always welcomed by the Department.

Sincerely yours,   Josephus Daniels

TLS (WP, DLC).

From Bainbridge Colby

My dear Mr. President: New York July 28th, 1917

I am deeply sensible of the honor you do me in designating me for the Shipping Board, and I am very grateful to you for the opportunity you give me in this great hour to serve instead of merely to stand and wait.

I have no large idea of my qualifications for this very responsible and difficult post, but at your call I do not feel that I can hesitate even on the score of my own limitations.

I was very happy in the receipt of your letter of July 25th,— a most kind and touching letter,—and I am proud to be its possessor. Even if the Senate should not confirm, the fact of my appointment at your hands and the receipt of such a letter would make the incident, so far as I am concerned, a fully rounded one and an unending source of pride and satisfaction.

With most earnest good wishes,

Sincerely yours,   Bainbridge Colby

TLS (WP, DLC).

From William Cox Redfield, with Enclosures

Dear Mr. President   [Washington] July 28. 1917

To illustrate the attached let me say that within a day or two our solicitor Mr. Thurman[1] in conversation with Mr. Newton,[2] Assistant Secretary of the Treasury told him that he did not see what they wanted with clearances and that every act of the Treasury respecting them was illegal and void. Mr Newton replied "We ought to have them and we've got them."

Clearances are in themselves trifles but the spirit is not one of fellowship   Cordially   William C. Redfield

ALS (WP, DLC).
   [1] That is, Albert Lee Thurman.
   [2] That is, Byron Rufus Newton.

ENCLOSURE I

From William Cox Redfield

Confidential

My dear Mr. President: Washington July 27, 1917.

I have received your letter of the 26th respecting the Trading with the Enemy Bill. Several days ago an amendment to the effect suggested in your letter was submitted to me and I was glad to approve it because it seemed obvious that financial matters affected by the Act should be in the hands of the Secretary of the Treasury. Today before your letter came I was glad to say to the Chairman of the Senate Sub-committee, in response to his inquiry, that I approved this amendment. So far then as your letter goes we are in accord.

I regret, however, to hear that this is not the only matter in which amendments to the bill were suggested by Secretary Mc-Adoo. Senator Ransdell telephoned me, if I understood him correctly, that the Secretary of the Treasury asked to have the bill amended to take the control over clearances out of the Commerce Department and put it in the Treasury Department. He asked my views on this and I protested against it both as to its substance and manner. This is a matter of which you have heard from time to time.

If I may judge from what seemed a casual remark dropped by you at a Cabinet Meeting, this appears a simple thing, taking the apparently obvious form that officers of one department should not give instructions to those of another. If this were all and if the matter affected only clearances, there would be less to say, but this is not all and the matter affects much more than clearances. It was not by accident that after many years of experience and long debate all the legal phases connected with navigation, not merely clearances alone but entries and every thing except revenues, were not only taken from the Treasury Department and placed in the Commerce Department, but a special prohibitory statement was added in the law that the Secretary of the Treasury should not hereafter exercise any of these powers. The Opinions of the Attorneys General in the past are conclusive upon the matter.

From that day to this not in one respect but in many the Collectors have been and are now acting as officers of the Department of Commerce under its instructions daily and guided by its rulings. This has gone on without friction, with the approval of the Collectors, without objection on the part of the Secretaries of the Treasury, and its coming up now is merely the revival of an ancient combat settled fourteen years ago. At that time the Bureau of Navigation, now part of this Department, was in the Treasury Department with the same head it now has. By the law the entire source of authority in the Treasury Department, to wit: the Bureau of Navigation was taken bodily out and has been since then a part of the Commerce Department.

What is involved, therefore, is not clearances alone but the question in substance whether an important bureau of this Department shall be taken out and put back into the place whence it was fourteen years ago removed. Since that time the Bureau of Navigation has been vivified. It has done larger, more effective, work than ever and it never has been as efficient as in the last four years. The intimate, daily relations of the Steamboat Inspection Service, (itself formerly a part of the Treasury Department) and the Bureau of Navigation is such that one could hardly be moved without the other. If the Bureau of Navigation must be altered, I should be forced myself to recommend that the Steamboat Inspection Service went with it. Against either or both changes in whole or in part, both as result of experience and of present conditions, I feel obliged to enter my most respectful and earnest protest.

Before approval is given to what seems so simple and is so far-reaching a change let me ask that the subject be studied not in one phase but in all its relations.

Yours very truly,   William C. Redfield

E N C L O S U R E   I I

From William Cox Redfield

Confidential

My dear Mr. President: Washington July 28th, 1917.

Since dictating the attached Senator Ransdell has confirmed to me the fact that Secretary McAdoo did ask the Committee to make the changes in the bill respecting clearances. The Postmaster General has told me of your wish that clearances should remain in this Department and Senator Ransdell has told me within a brief time that the Senate Sub-committee will not make the change Mr. McAdoo asks, (except as to financial matters on which we concur).

The Senator asks, however, that I send him a statement of my side of the clearance case to be put in the Congressional Record in case the matter should come up on the floor of the Senate. I prefer not to do this. It seems to me no time for departmental friction. I would rather submit without a word to the serious discourtesy which I think the Secretary of the Treasury has shown me than have one word of talk in the Senate about it. To you, however, I may frankly say that while my cares are trivial as compared to your own and those of some of my colleagues, there ought not, I think, to be added to them the necessity of defending the integrity of my Department against the attacks from a colleague.

I cannot carry out Senator Ransdell's request without making it public that all acts of the Treasury Department in the matter of clearances for over two years past have been illegal acts, and this I am quite unwilling to do. I am taking the matter up privately with Mr. Burleson, therefore, asking him to straighten it out with Senator Ransdell, and for myself leave it in your hands for such action as you think fit.

I point out, however, that the Treasury Department is still acting under your Executive Order in control of clearances and that the matter ought to be definitely settled one way or the other.

Yours very truly,   William C. Redfield

TLS (WP, DLC).

To Edward Mandell House

My dear House,   The White House. 29 July, 1917.

Your letter about Dudley, touched with such unmistakable sadness, has filled my heart very full. I know of nothing that has gone more to the quick with me or that has seemed to me more tragical than Dudley's conduct,—which came upon me like a bolt out of the blue. I was stricken by it as I have been by few things in my life. But you may be sure that it did not for a moment affect my utter trust in friends whose qualities I have tested. Dudley was always an individual apart,—not of a type, but a lovable, incalculable compound of all sorts of passions, many of them very beautiful; and now passion has run away with him, and I dare not think what the end will be. Here is one more item of tragedy added to this time of madness, and there is all the more imperative obligation laid upon us to act and judge as if the world were normal, or, rather, since it is not normal

and it would be fatal to assume that it is, to keep our minds cool
and circumspect while others lose their heads. "If you can keep
your head when all about you are losing theirs and blaming it
on you," etc.! We must not let the madness touch us. It is that
sort of strength I pray for all the time. God only can deliver us
from this tragedy!

Your letters are my most welcome visitors, and I ponder and
heed every one of them, so far as they can be made to fit into the
stage of business that has been reached when they get to me.

I am trying to persuade Mac. to run up at the earliest possible
moment and have a conference with you. He is willing and even
anxious to come, but lets "things" stand in the way too easily. Just
now he is, of course, very much absurbed [absorbed] in giving
counsel to the Finance Committee on the Revenue Bill.

All join me in sending most affectionate messages, and I am,
without doubt or misgiving of any kind,

Your affectionate and devoted Friend,

[Woodrow Wilson]

WWTL (E. M. House Papers, CtY).

To William Gibbs McAdoo, with Enclosure

My dear Mac.,   The White House. 29 July, 1917.

I am writing this myself to beg that you will give the most
thoughtful consideration to what Gregory says in this letter. We
must, at all hazards, avoid delay in this important legislation, and
should alter it as conservatively and as little as possible.

I did not know that you had suggested the transfer to the
Treasury of the authority to issue clearances, and I earnestly beg
that you will withdraw the suggestion. I have never agreed with
you about that, and think that the transfer would be a great
mistake. I know that you want me to be perfectly frank with you
about this, as about all things.

Affectionately Yours,   W.W.

WWTLI (W. G. McAdoo Papers, DLC).

ENCLOSURE

From Thomas Watt Gregory

Dear Mr. President: Washington, D. C. July 27, 1917.

I acknowledge receipt of yours of the 26th in which you state that you have advised the Senate Committee having in charge the Trading With The Enemy Bill that all those provisions of the bill which relate to banks and strictly financial matters be placed for administration in the hands of the Secretary of the Treasury, and that you did this in order to avoid duplication, and hoped that I would feel that the reasons for this were conclusive.

As you know, I am leaving Washington tonight and may be away for the better part of a week, and I therefore write this letter to express some general views in regard to this matter.

You will recall the fact that representatives of the Departments of State, Treasury, Commerce and Justice spent many weeks in working out the bill which was passed by the House in practically the same shape in which it was introduced as an administration measure. After this bill had been drafted, copies were furnished to the heads of the four Departments above referred to, and the bill went to Congress with the apparent concurrence of all in its provisions.

For reasons which it would take much time to go into, it was concluded by the representatives of all those Departments mentioned that the administration of this bill should be vested in the Secretary of Commerce, and one of the special reasons for this was that that Department was to be charged with the execution of the details of the Exports Control Act. I have just had a talk with Assistant Attorney General Warren, who has been before the Senate Committee considering this bill for the better part of four days (he having likewise spent several days with the House Committee). I have not seen the amendments to the bill suggested by Secretary McAdoo, nor has Mr. Warren a copy of them. I can therefore only state what I understand to be their general effect. Broadly speaking, they would have the effect of dividing between the Departments of the Treasury and Commerce the duties of the taking over of alien enemy property and its conservation in the hands of the alien property custodian, and would be very far reaching in many respects. In fact, in the opinion of Mr. Warren, it would be better to turn over to the Treasury Department the exclusive control and direction of these activities rather than to divide it as suggested by the amendments. I am reliably informed that a representative of the State Department who participated in the drafting of this bill is very strongly of the opinion that the Department of Commerce should have entire control in accordance with the terms of the bill as originally drafted.

I doubt if you have had an opportunity of considering the bill in connection with the amendments offered, and, as before stated, I have not seen the amendments myself. From what I know of them, however, I feel sure that they involve such substantial changes in the measure and such radical departures from the bill as passed by the House that their adoption would seriously menace the passage of the measure as a whole. From my conversation with Mr. Warren, I conclude that one or two very slight changes in the bill would free the Treasury Department from the embarrassments suggested by the Secretary.

As I understand, the Secretary of the Treasury is fearful that the powers conferred upon the Secretary of Commerce in reference to investigation as to property of alien enemies might, so far as such investigations were conducted relating to property held by banks, be exercised by examiners and investigators other than those of the Treasury Department, thus producing confusion and needless trouble to the banks. All that would be necessary to obviate this difficulty would be an amendment providing that all investigations and reports from banks should be obtained by the Secretary of Commerce through the Secretary of the Treasury or the Federal Reserve Board.

So far as enemies' funds or property may be held by the banks, any conflict which would arise out of an order given by the Secretary of Commerce, under Section 7 (c), to such banks to turn over the funds or property to the alien property custodian for conservation by the Government might be obviated by an amendment which would require that, in case of funds or property held by banks, the order requiring its transfer to the alien property custodian should be issued by the Secretary of Commerce with the concurrence of the Secretary of the Treasury. Even this amendment, however, would not be absolutely necessary, for the bill, as drafted, provides for the turning over of enemies' money or property only "if the Secretary of Commerce, by direction of the President, shall so require"; so that the ultimate authority is now vested by the bill in the President.

Other than these two points, I can see little in this bill which affects the banks or interferes with the power of the Secretary of the Treasury over the banks.

What I have said above refers peculiarly to those amendments which suggest changes in the present bill. So far as the very sweeping amendment is concerned which I understand the Secretary of the Treasury has presented giving to him the power to supervise and control all foreign exchange and foreign credits, I do not understand that the bill, as drafted, confers any such powers on the Secretary of Commerce, so that this proposed section would seem to constitute new and additional legislation, as to the desirability of which I can express no opinion without having read the section itself and given to it very careful thought.

As some action may be taken in the Senate Committee before I return, will you permit me to suggest that you discuss this situation with Postmaster General Burleson? I will ask Mr. Burleson, in the meanwhile, to secure accurate copies of the proposed amendments and to discuss the matter with Assistant Attorney General Warren who is peculiarly familiar with the details of the bill.   Faithfully yours,   T. W. Gregory

TLS (W. G. McAdoo Papers, DLC).

To Annie Howe Cothran Compton, with Enclosure

My dear Annie,   The White House. 29 July, 1917.

I wrote what is on the other sheet last Sunday, when Edith and I were down the river on the MAYFLOWER and before we had received your telegram[1] that the marriage had actually taken place!

We congratulate you with all our hearts! You two are certainly executive persons, and, for my part, I think it a jolly thing to be free to do what your heart so certainly desires. Edith joins me in warmest best wishes.

If I knew where to address this letter (I mean where in New London) I would send it there; but I do not, and so must send it to Chicago. Edith and I sent you the other day a little wrist watch, as a wedding present which I hope you will find awaiting you there in good shape.

With warmest regards and welcome to Mr. Compton and dearest love to Josephine,

Lovingly Yours,   [Woodrow Wilson]

[1] F. E. Compton to WW, July 21, 1917, T telegram (WP, DLC).

ENCLOSURE

To Annie Howe Cothran Compton

Dear Annie,   [*U.S.S. Mayflower*] 22 July, 1917.

We are all very happy in your happiness. The announcement about next Thursday took us by surprise, of course, but we are glad because you evidently are, and we have every reason to admire and trust Mr. Compton. It will not be possible, alas! for us to come to the ceremony, and Helen is in the Canada woods, Margaret at Waterford; but you may be sure that our thoughts will be most affectionately with you. Give our warm regards to Mr. Compton, and keep for yourself the loving thoughts of Edith and   Woodrow Wilson

WWTLS (WP, DLC).

To Joseph Patrick Tumulty

Dear Tumulty: [The White House, c. July 30, 1917]

Please say to Mr. Brisbane orally that I think it would be very unwise for me to discuss these questions now in any informal way.[1] They are full of dynamite, particularly because the various nations that are fighting Germany have to be by one influence or another brought together upon them.   The President.

TL (WP, DLC).
  [1] This was written in response to A. Brisbane to JPT, July 26, 1917, TLS (WP, DLC). Brisbane wrote that he had, that day, printed in the *Washington Times* a "communication" from William Randolph Hearst in which Hearst set forth his views on a peace settlement. Hearst favored a settlement "without indemnity or annexation." Brisbane asked whether the Wilson administration would care to have "some man well known" write a reply to Hearst for publication in the *Times*.

To Joseph Patrick Tumulty, with Enclosure

Dear Tumulty: [The White House, July 30, 1917]

I wish you would discuss this with the Attorney General. Mr. Nieman seems to think that there is something we can do, whereas there is nothing we can do in addition to what we are doing. Anybody is entitled to make a campaign against the draft law provided they don't stand in the way of the administration of it by any overt acts or improper influences.

The President.

TL (WP, DLC).

ENCLOSURE

Lucius William Nieman to Joseph Patrick Tumulty

My dear Mr. Tumulty: Milwaukee July 27, 1917.

Enclosed please find news article from The Journal of July 27, which should, and I believe will, make the administration sit up and take notice.[1] You will recollect that when I was in Washington a few weeks ago, I called attention to the fact that the German language newspapers have been carrying on a campaign based on the point marked in blue pencil.[2] In this state the Socialists are very active, aided by German alliance men and La Follette politicians.

A report which I have not as yet been able to verify is that La Follette is coming here to make a campaign against the draft law. So far the government has taken no steps in this part of the country, at least, to make an example of traitors, and until it does, things will probably go from bad to worse, until there will be very serious trouble, for which the president will be held responsible. Senator Husting will be here Monday on his way to Washington, and I will tell him as much as I can, with the trust that he will pass it on to you. I appreciate that the administration never does anything that Husting advises, but I hope that it won't prejudice the case here for him to describe it.   Yours very truly,   L. W. Nieman.

TLS (WP, DLC).

[1] "Against Service Abroad," *Milwaukee Journal*, July 27, 1917. The article reported on a meeting in New Ulm, Minnesota, of over 5,000 persons opposed to the war and to conscription. The theme of the meeting had been that no one outside the regular army should be sent abroad to fight against his will. Some of the speakers proposed to make a test case of the constitutionality of the selective-service law.

[2] The marked paragraph quoted one of the speakers at the meeting as saying that there would be ample time in the nine or ten months before any draftees would be ready to go overseas to develop an effective opposition to their being sent abroad against their will.

Two Letters from William Gibbs McAdoo

Dear "Governor":   Washington July 30, 1917.

I presume that the report in yesterday morning's paper about the organization of the Purchasing Commission through the Council of National Defense is accurate.[1] Of course, I accept loyally your decision and shall do all I can to help, but I must confess that I am genuinely discouraged that such a complicated piece of machinery has been set up.

You are insisting, and I think properly, on a single-headed Food Commission. I have all along felt that the reasons were equally, if not more convincing, for a single-headed Purchasing Commission. A commission of three, charged with the duty of acting for our Government as well as for the foreign governments, seemed to me to be the most we could have for efficiency and quick action. Such a commission would have had the prestige and power to do great work which would have been reflected in decreased demands on the Treasury. I fear that a separate foreign commission will be a sort of side-show under present conditions, commanding small respect and having little power or influence. It will be regarded as a thing apart, with an entirely different status and intended to differ in treatment so far as prices are concerned. If the commission appointed to purchase for our Government had been identical with that appointed to purchase for the foreign governments, it would have been difficult to draw the line as to what inquiries and prices were being made for foreign account and what for the account of the United States, and the chances of securing equally favorable prices and treatment for foreign orders with those of our own Government would have been greatly improved.

However, I think the foreign Purchasing Commission should be appointed in any case, and it will be an improvement on the present condition to some extent, at least. Before going further with it, I should like very much to have your suggestions as to how you think it can be best related to the new piece of machinery. I hesitate to press the matter further until I have the benefit of your views and suggestions.

Affectionately yours,   W G McAdoo

1 This was an announcement of the establishment of a War Industries Board of seven members to oversee all war-related purchases by the United States Government. The Council of National Defense also established a Central Purchasing Commission, composed of three members of the W.I.B. (and Herbert Hoover, whenever food purchases were involved), to do the actual purchasing. The announcement made no mention of purchases by the Allied governments in the United States. *New York Times*, July 29, 1917.

Dear Mr. President: Washington July 30, 1917.

I am just in receipt of your letter of the 29th instant, enclosing the Attorney General's letter of the 27th, in reference to the "trading with the enemy" bill. The amendments I suggested to the bill are strictly those I discussed with you with the single exception to which I shall refer later. The day before I submitted the amendments to the Senate Committee I sent them to Mr. Warren, who was present the next day when I discussed these amendments with the Senate Committee. The Attorney General is laboring under a number of misapprehensions about the scope of the proposed amendments. I can't imagine how he gets them, since what he says about Mr. Warren's attitude does not in all respects coincide with what Mr. Warren said before the Committee in my presence.

I have not sought to change the status of the custodian of alien property, except to require him to submit duplicate reports to the Secretary of the Treasury of all stocks, bonds and securities of a financial character that may come into his hands. It was suggested to the Committee that it might be better if he should turn over to the Secretary of the Treasury all such securities, just as he turns over all money under the Act, and while I said that that might be better, I did not insist upon it; in fact, I do not think it material.

The amendment giving the Secretary of the Treasury power to supervise and control foreign exchange and foreign credits is not in the bill as it passed the House. This has been the subject of very thorough consideration by me and the Federal Reserve Board, and I feel that it is of vital importance to the financial situation in this country during the period of the war that such powers shall be conferred upon the Secretary of the Treasury.

The Attorney General says as to the desirability (of this amendment), "I can express no opinion without having read the section itself and given it very careful thought." I had not understood that you desired the opinion of the Attorney General upon the policy involved in this amendment. As it relates wholly to financial matters I had supposed that the opinion of the head of this Department and the Federal Reserve Board would be looked to.

Mr. Warren stated to the Committee that this bill as originally drawn gave jurisdiction to the Secretary of the Treasury and not to the Secretary of Commerce. It was subsequently changed, as I understand it, at the instance of the Secretary of Commerce. I distinctly stated to the Committee that I wished to make no changes in the bill, except to preserve the jurisdiction of the Treasury Department over financial matters, and my testimony will so show. I am sure you will agree with me that as to financial policies and financial matters the views of this Department, always subject to your approval, ought to prevail as against the views of other Departments, which are charged with no responsibilities in respect thereto.

I have not sought to transfer to the Treasury Department

"authority to issue clearances," and I can't imagine how you got such an impression.

The bill as it passed the House provides that the Collectors of Customs shall refuse clearances, their action to be subject to review by the Secretary of Commerce. In other words, an independent power is conferred upon the Collectors of Customs —my subordinates—subject to review by the Secretary of Commerce, who undertakes to transmit orders to the Collectors of Customs independently of the head of the Department, frequently causing confusion and irritation. It is not only bad administration, but bad practice. The amendment I suggested was as follows:

"Provided that all instructions to Collectors of Customs or other customs officers in the enforcement of the provisions of this act or other provisions of law shall be issued by the Secretary of the Treasury."

This merely means that when the Secretary of Commerce wishes to give instructions to Collectors of Customs he shall, in the proper and orderly way, transmit them to the Secretary of the Treasury, who will then direct the Collectors of Customs to carry out the orders and instructions of the Secretary of Commerce.

No man can serve two masters. We find that our subordinates are instructed sometimes by bureaus of the Secretary of Commerce direct, and at other times through the Treasury Department. Collectors of Customs frequently have to inquire of the Treasury Department whether they shall carry out the instructions of the Secretary of Commerce and for further information, and again, we sometimes find that if a Collector is jacked up for not having done his duty, he claims he was busy carrying out the orders of the Secretary of Commerce, and when we jack him up because he hasn't carried out the orders of the Secretary of Commerce, he claims he was too busy carrying out the orders of the Treasury Department. If all orders proceed through the Treasury Department, which is the proper procedure, these difficulties will not arise. It is merely for the sake of good administration that I have suggested this amendment. It does not in any way interfere with the Secretary of Commerce; on the contrary, it will facilitate the carrying out by Collectors of Customs of the orders and regulations promulgated by him.

As to difficulties about passing the bill with the amendments I have proposed: There is not the slightest difficult[y] about passing the bill with these amendments. I think I can say that unequivocally. There certainly will be none if the Attorney General and the Secretary of Commerce assist in carrying out your policies and do not raise objections or put impediments in the way.   Cordially yours,   W G McAdoo

TLS (WP, DLC).

From Leonidas Carstarphen Dyer

My dear Mr. President: Washington, D. C. July 30, 1917.

At this time there seems to be going on through this Country a campaign of slanderous attacks upon citizens of this Country of German birth and ancestry. I find this particularly so as regards the City of St. Louis, Missouri which, in part, I represent in the House of Representatives. A number of instances have come to my mind where men have lost their positions in the Government Service there because of some statement charged to them reflecting upon their loyalty to this Country. It is easy at this time to find people who will bear false witness against men of German birth in this Country. I am quite sure that injustice is often the result of these attacks. I have had a number of complaints regarding this matter but have not dared impose upon your time with them. I only do so now to ask you if you will not write me a letter that I may give to the press that will voice your judgment as to the loyalty of the people of this Country of German birth and ancestry and who are citizens of the United States. It would help wonderfully to make a better feeling on the part of the people in the sections of the Country that have large parts of their citizenship composed of men and women of German birth and ancestry. I am sure that these people are as loyal to the Government as any of those of other nationality.

As an evidence of this fact I cite you to my record in this Congress. I have voted to carry out every recommendation that you have made to the 65th Congress touching the war. I know that I voice the sentiments of the people of my District, a large part of which is composed of women and men of German birth and ancestry. As another evidence of the fact that something ought to be done regarding the matter indicated in my letter is a letter that I have just received from Otto Sassman of St. Louis, Missouri.[1] I can not believe that a man with his record as stated in his letter would be guilty of disloyalty to the United States, and I ask you to have this matter investigated and that something be done to prevent so great an injustice being done other like citizens.

I also enclose a clipping from the St. Louis Daily Globe-Democrat of July 26th showing the effort being made by some people to create the impression that men of German birth and German ancestry are not loyal citizens.[2] I feel that this matter is of great importance and that unless some of the Officials of the Federal Government show more judgment and discretion in the future than they have in some instances in the past that there will be created a feeling of dissatisfaction, unrest, and perhaps disloyalty in some quarters. Its hard for men and women to be faithful and loyal in every way when they are continually being criticised, misrepresented and even charged with disloyalty to the Government. I feel that if you will write a letter at this time to the effect that you have every confidence in the loyalty and patriotic purposes of the people in this Country of German birth and ancestry who are citizens of the United States it would help very greatly to make a better feeling in every way and at the same time help us in the great struggle we are engaged to put an end to the militarism and autocratic Government of Germany. In other words we need the help of all the people of our Country and none of them should be alienated by the mistakes of Government Officials.   Respectfully yours,   L. C. Dyer

TLS (WP, DLC).

[1] It is missing. Otto Sassman, a clerk in the Railway Mail Service, was dismissed on July 25 for alleged remarks disloyal to the United States. See ASB to WW, Aug. 6, 1917.

[2] "Carl Anschuetz Says Selph Made Himself Obnoxious at Inn," St. Louis *Globe-Democrat*, July 26, 1917. The article contained statements by Carl Anschuetz, proprietor of the Mission Inn of St. Louis, and Colin M. Selph, postmaster of that city, which concerned an incident in which Selph had demanded that the inn's orchestra play "America." Selph admitted that he had accused Anschuetz and the conductor of disloyalty because of the allegedly unsatisfactory way in which they had complied with his demand.

From Newton Diehl Baker

My dear Mr. President: Washington. July 30, 1917.

In reply to your note concerning the use of sweet potatoes in the army,[1] I beg to submit the following in connection with the attached communication of July 23, 1917, from the Members of the Georgia Delegation in Congress, relative to placing sweet potatoes on the list of supplies authorized to be purchased by the Quartermaster Corps for use of the Army.[2]

The Army ration was adopted after very full and careful consideration, consultation with scientific and medical experts, and as far as known is giving entire satisfaction. Heretofore there has been very little demand for sweet potatoes for issue to troops of the regular army, and this vegetable has been confined to cans and only intended for sales and not for issue to troops, so that there has not been any fresh, but only the canned variety of sweet potatoes authorized.

But under present conditions, it is realized that there will be a large number of troops from the South who like and prefer sweet potatoes to Irish potatoes. In view of this I have decided to authorize the purchase and issue, when practicable, of sweet potatoes to troops who prefer them. I shall also authorize the issue of bacon instead of fresh meat, and corn meal and hominy in the place of bread where troops prefer this change, which those from the South are likely to do.

Faithfully yours,   Newton D. Baker

TLS (WP, DLC).
  [1] WW to NDB, July 25, 1917, TLS (Letterpress Books, WP, DLC).
  [2] F. Park *et al.* to WW, July 23, 1917, TLS (WP, DLC).

From Thomas Davies Jones

My dear Mr. President: Chicago July 30, 1917.

I have your letter of the 27th instant.

I cannot hesitate a moment to agree to accept the appointment which you suggest, if made. You are entitled to the services of any American who in your judgment can render service. I certainly have the "freedom" and my only hesitation is on the other ground which you suggest, namely "strength." I have a deceptive amount of high Welsh color, but my stock of vitality has never been really up to reasonable requirements but whatever strength I have is fairly subject to your call.

I do not know whether this appointment if made will require confirmation by the senate. I recognize the importance of time and I shall hold myself prepared to respond to a very early call. There are certain matters which I want to set in order before leaving; and for that reason I shall be grateful for as early notice as possible of the conclusion of the matter and of the time when I shall be expected to take up the work.

Faithfully yours,   Thomas D. Jones.

TLS (WP, DLC).

From William Dudley Haywood[1]

Chicago, Ills., July 30, 1917.

General strike of metal miners of Michigan has been declared; Minnesota next. Harvest workers of North and South Dakota

will follow unless miners at Columbus, New Mexico, are returned to their homes and families at Bisbee, Arizona.

Wm. D. Haywood.

Copy sent to the Attorney General.

T telegram (WP, DLC).
[1] Principal founder, secretary-treasurer, and *de facto* head of the Industrial Workers of the World.

The Foreign Office to Sir Cecil Arthur Spring Rice

[London] July 30 [1917]

Urgent. 2985

Please communicate following message from Chancellor of the Exchequer to McAcdoo.

Begins. "The Memorandum which was handed to Mr. Page on the 20th July last at the instance of the Chancellor of the Exchequer[1] stated in Clause 3 that "unless the United States Government can meet in full our expenses in America, *including exchange*, the whole financial fabric of the Alliance will collapse. This conclusion will be a matter not of months but of days."

That Memorandum was intended to set forth for the information of the United States Government the extent of the financial effort which His Majesty's Government have already made, and the approaching exhaustion of their resources. It did not deal with the question of exchange in particular. As, however, this form of assistance is at the same time most vital to His Majesty's Government and most difficult to render clear to the Government of the United States, it is dealt with here.

(1) The growth of the existing system for supporting the exchange.

(2) The cost of it.

(3) The consequences of withdrawing it.

(4) It is pointed out that His Majesty's Government must now learn how far the United States Government will be able to give them the necessary support. A point has now been reached when a definite decision must be taken within the next few days and His Majesty's Government trust that the Government of the United States will agree with them as to the necessity of putting an end to the present state of uncertainty.

(1) At the commencement of the War the balance of trade with America was in favour of this Country. That is to say, there were on balance purchasers of sterling in New York. We were

[1] It is printed in WHP to WW, July 20, 1917.

able, therefore, to finance our war purchases from America, as also from the rest of the world, by the sale of sterling exchange. In the summer of 1915 large amounts of dollars were required to finance advance payments on shell and rifle contracts placed for the Russian Government, with the result that the British Treasury were no longer able to provide themselves with all the dollars they required by the sale of sterling in New York as hitherto. A break in the exchange took place, and it became necessary in the course of the autumn of 1915 for the British Treasury to finance their munition purchases by other means than by the sale of sterling in New York. By the beginning of 1916 they had to go a step further and to come to the support of the commercial exchange by making a standing offer through their Agents in New York to purchase sterling from all comers at a fixed minimum rate of 4.7676.

The Anglo-French Loan of 1915, the mobilisation of dollar securities for sale and collateral security of loans and the export of gold to the United States were the chief sources of the funds required for these two purposes.

This arrangement provided a direct means for the conversion of sterling into dollars, by which British purchasers of American goods could reckon on financing them at a fixed rate, while the Allies and Dominions who received sterling credits could turn them into dollars to meet their American payments. Indirectly also it stabilised in some degree all the other foreign exchanges, since sterling could, if necessary, be converted into any other foreign currency by first purchasing dollars and then using these dollars to obtain the foreign currency required.

As time went on this system developed into one by which the nervous centre of the Allied financial system was as much in New York as in London. While gold was occasionally exported to other destinations, the bulk of it was reserved for America. By furnishing America with unprecedented quantities of specie we ourselves provided the basis of the credit she required to finance her sales to us.

As [At] first the adverse balance was relatively small. In fact, up to April, 1916, we were still able to supplement our other resources by the sale on balance of a certain amount of sterling. From May, 1916, the balance has been progressively adverse.

In November and December, 1916, we were faced with the first serious exchange crisis since the summer of 1915. As shown in a table below, the average weekly requirements for the support of the exchange amounted in December, 1916, to $44,600,000.

Since that date high prices, increased expenditure, the growing exhaustion of the Allies, the depletion of British financial reserves in all parts of the world and the progressive destruction of our export trade by diversion of man power into other channels have combined to raise the figures, taking one month with another, far beyond those of 1916.

The past seven months have accordingly required a lavish employment of our ultimate liquid reserves. The conclusion of the third year of War finds us with these reserves at a level which will be entirely exhausted in a few weeks if the present drain on them is to continue.

(2) The appended table shows the average weekly expenditure of the British Treasury in the United States for each month since April, 1916, the first column representing the purchase of commodities and the transfer of dollars to Allies, and the second the support afforded to the dollar exchanges. While the figures in the second column have fluctuated widely, it will be seen that the average weekly requirements during the past three months have worked out at rather more than $40,000,000.

Average weekly expenditure in the
United States of America.

Month	Treasury Account.	Exchange Committee.	Total.
1916.	$000	$000	$000
April	26,969	5,156*	21,813
May	33,033	9,824	42,857
June	35,377	12,608	47,985
July	20,225	5,592	25,817
August	36,267	14,348	50,615
September	37,300	14,073	51,373
October	46,958	19,712	66,670
November	33,588	31,728	65,316
December	34,313	44,600	78,913
1917			
January	31,112	12,125	43,237
February	41,826	35,051	76,877
March	61,856	11,952	73,808
April	42,152	16,717	58,869
May	39,558	40,402	79,960
June	38,072	61,275	99,347
July (3 weeks to 21st)	49,919	21,606	71,525

* sale of sterling.

The fluctuations are mainly due to the movement of American banking funds to and from London. It is obvious that when American bankers are increasing their London balances, the exchange benefits and, conversely, that when they are withdrawing balances the normal burden on the exchange is aggravated. In the course of the present year cash balances and bills held on American account in London have been as high as £53,500,000 (April 14th) and as low as £22,500,000 (June 23).

Allowing for the fact that the figures of the past three months have been abnormally inflated by the withdrawal of American balances and that they include the cost of Allied wheat purchases which will be paid for in future otherwise, the average cost of supporting exchange, assuming that American balances in London remain stationary, is not likely to be less than $25,000,000 a week or $100,000,000 a month.

(3) The above summary of past events will have shown what a central place the support of the dollar exchange has come to take in the financial system of the Alliance. The funds which we have placed at the disposal of the Allies and the Dominions have been mainly sterling, the purchasing power of which, in all parts of the world, has been maintained by this means.

To estimate the consequences of withdrawing support from the sterling exchange in New York, we must consider the purposes now served by supporting it. The following analysis refers in each case to the balance unprovided for after allowing for America's ordinary trade obligations to ourselves and the Allies.

(a) Exports on private account from America to this Country for commodities not yet under Government control of which cotton is chief.

(b) Similar purchases by the Allies who have not yet controlled so many commodities as we have.

(c) Purchases from America by the British Dominions and by India, only a small part of whose trade is under Government control.

(d) The cost of neutral exchange arbitraged over New York, that is to say, those Allied purchases in neutral markets which are being financed at present out of the resources of the United States.

Of these the United States Government will probably wish to enquire most closely into the magnitude and character of (d). The amount involved is fairly substantial but we have no reliable information on which to estimate it.

If the policy of supporting the exchange were to be abandoned to-morrow, the collapse not only of the Allied exchanges on New

York, but also of their exchanges on all neutral countries is to be expected. The Allies and all parts of the Empire, except Canada, would be affected equally. It is likely that exchange quotations would not only fall heavily but would become nominal,—that is to say, there would, for the moment, be no exchange offering at any price and business would be at a standstill.

The consequences of such a state of affairs are partly material and partly psychological.

(i)   On the *material* side exporters from the United States to the United Kingdom, other Allied countries, Australasia, India and South Africa would be unable to sell their sterling bills on London. New business would be interrupted at the source, and vessels would be delayed in port by reason of shippers being unable to obtain delivery of goods without paying for them.

From the American point of view this would involve a breakdown for the time being of the mechanism of a great part of her export trade, the paralysis of business and the congestion of her ports. From the point of view of this Country and of the other Allies it would represent the cessation for the time being of supplies, such as cotton, which, while still left in private hands, are nevertheless essential to the conduct of the War. It must be remembered that practically no trade takes place except in commodities of national importance, considerations of freight, quite apart from finance, having already cut off the greater part of what is dispensable.

At the same time American bankers would see their London assets locked up for the period of the war at least and also heavily depreciated.

How long this state of affairs would last would depend upon the success of our remedial measures. The initial disorganisation must be distinguished from the permanent results. It is possible that even the initial disturbance would be somewhat less serious than indicated above. But whatever the degree of intial disturbance, the eventual result, if the estimate of $100,000,000 a month is correct would be that the foreign purchases of the Alliance would have to be diminished by at least this amount monthly.

This sum, however, would not represent the whole effect. The destruction of British Credit abroad would cut us off from certain sources of income which we now possess. So long as existing foreign balances in London remained immobilised, we could not expect foreign countries to increase them. At present we pay in sterling for numerous foreign purchases. Difficulties of freight and supply prevent the neutral countries from spending this sterling forthwith. In the meantime they leave it in London, and payment is thus deferred.

Allowing, therefore, for losses arising out of the injury to our credit, the economies we should have to effect would largely exceed the $100,000,000 monthly.

Pending reorganisation of trade and finance the loss would, as pointed out above, extend beyond this to commodities which, after things had settled down, we might hope to pay for.

On the material side, therefore, the breakdown of the exchanges must gravely impair our capacity to carry on the war. But by itself it need not prove disastrous. We could, if necessary, effect economies on the scale indicated above and still carry on.

(ii) Turning to the *psychological* consequences, the results would be plainly disastrous. The open abandonment of the support of the exchanges is a step which would be interpreted in all circles as indicative of deep-seated distress. Not only would our credit have been impaired in all neutral centres but vague doubts would have been awakened which might spread far beyond their origin.

Chief of all there is the effect on the mind of the enemy. There are doubtless officials in Berlin whose duty it is to watch and report upon our financial position and embarrassments. They must suspect our growing financial difficulties and can make a good guess at our position just as we can with their food difficulties. But there is a world of difference between a shrewd guess and a piece of tangible evidence.

The encouragement and corroboration of their hopes which they would discover in our abandonment of the exchanges would, therefore, be enormous. Germany would have at last received a second hope added to that of the submarine on which to base her policy of endurance. It would be said, whether it is true or not, that with the collapse of their exchanges the Alliance cannot endure six months more.

We have openly attached hitherto the utmost importance to the position of our exchanges. We have constantly proclaimed to the world that it is the corner stone of our policy. To point out the depreciation of the German exchanges and the stability of our own has been a favourite form of propaganda in all parts of the world. We have urged the neutral world month after month that this is to be taken as the criterion of financial strength. It would be imprudent to believe that all this can be swept on one side without a far-reaching reaction.

(4) The Memorandum handed to Mr. Page on the 20th July

will have shown to the Government of the United States to what a low level our liquid reserves have now fallen. In the event of the exchanges being allowed to fall and of our having to undertake the reorganisation of our affairs thus made necessary, we must do so with a certain amount of liquid resources still in hand. We cannot therefore deplete them further and must look to the United States Government for the future.

We must therefore know if possible immediately whether the Government of the United States can give us the financial assistance we need.

In asking this we do not overlook that we are asking them to moderate two conditions which they have hitherto regarded as essential.

In the first place to provide funds for the exchange is to defray uncontrolled expenditure for undefined purposes. We can only say that we have already extended the sphere of Government control far beyond what would have been believed possible a short time back. But the complexity of the world's trade is too great to allow the whole of it to become amenable to a centralised control. This limited continuance of private commerce is represented financially by the commercial exchange.

In the second place the support of the exchanges involves in part the employment of American funds to finance the purchases of the Allies outside America. America must be the judge of how great a burden she can support. At the present stage of the conflict her resources are greater than ours. She has not only her own pre-war resources but more than £200,000,000 additional in actual gold with which the Allies have furnished her in the past three years. It is necessary for the Allies to make purchases in neutral countries in excess of what they are themselves able to finance. Within comparatively narrow limits they look to the United States to augment these resources out of her exports of goods and of gold to neutral countries so far as her capacity allows. She cannot render a more valuable service.

His Majesty's Government trust most earnestly that they may learn within a few days' time the general attitude of the Government of the United States to this most vital question. This is necessary because it is only by the assistance of the United States Government that the support of the exchange can be continued and at any moment the demand for exchange in New York may be so great that our representatives there may be compelled to cease to support it if they cannot rely upon funds from United States Government for the purpose. If any further information is desired it will be at once supplied and Lord Northcliffe who is familiar with the whole situation would gladly discuss it with you." Ends.

Tel. no. 2986

My immed. prec. tel. has been repeated to New York for Lord Northcliffe.

T telegram (FO 371/3115, No. 150751, pp. 378-84, PRO).

From Louis Wiley

Personal.

Dear Mr. President: [New York] July 31st, 1917.

Acknowledging your letter of July 23d: I observe your reference to hostile and disloyal elements in the press. I hope an example can be made soon of some flagrant offender by indictment by a United States Grand Jury and prosecution and trial under the law of treason.

I think the censorship rules promulgated this morning are excellent.[1] While the Chairman on Public Information is perhaps not an ideal censor, I think the attitude of some newspapers toward him is unjust and unreasonable. If the time ever comes when you conclude that the present plan does not work well, may I venture to suggest another: a committee of four consisting of one representative from the State Department, one from the War Department, and one from the Navy Department with a newspaper man of recognized standing,—for example— Chester S. Lord, former managing editor of The New York Sun, now retired, or Frank B. Noyes, of the Associated Press?[2]

Always sincerely yours, Louis Wiley

TLS (WP, DLC).
    [1] The Committee on Public Information on July 30 issued a new set of "specific requests" to the press concerning the voluntary censorship of news. The new rules, like those which they superseded, dealt entirely with information about the military and naval forces and the convoys and merchant shipping of the United States and her "associates." The "requests" are printed in full in the *New York Times*, July 31, 1917.
    [2] That is, Chester Sanders Lord and Frank Bret Noyes.

From Roland Sletor Morris

My dear Mr. President: Philadelphia July 31, 1917.

I have just learned unofficially that you have nominated me for the responsible position of Ambassador to Japan. Entirely apart from any action which the Senate may take I am writing now to express to you my deep and lasting appreciation of the honor which this evidence of your confidence has conferred on me. I do pray that should the Senate act favorably I may prove myself worthy of the confidence and equal to this opportunity of service which you have given me. I can imagine no greater happiness than to be associated with your administration at this time and to try and help when you are carrying such heavy burdens of responsibility. If confirmed by the Senate I pledge to you and our country the best service of which I am capable.

Faithfully yours,   Roland S. Morris

TLS (WP, DLC).

From Herbert Bayard Swope[1]

My dear Mr. President: New York July 31, 1917.

Let me express, through my congratulations, the admiration I feel for your courage and wisdom in standing firmly against the specious reform that sought, under the cloak of war legislation, to place a vicious restriction upon the rights of the public in the form of absolute, nation-wide prohibition. I think it is the highest form of political morality to oppose a measure that is characterized by fanatical clamor, which does not hesitate to impugn the motives of opposition no matter how honest that opposition may be. And fanaticism is never more clamorous than when it centers on a question of public conduct. In such circumstances it was difficult to justify one's attitude, but your attitude was so well based, so fair, so far-seeing that it commanded the respect and support of every intelligent mind.

There is no doubt that your efforts destroyed what would have become a source of perilous discontent had the workers been denied the right of using beer and light wines. In my visits to the war regions I have noticed that in not one of the belligerents in whose lands I travelled (Great Britain, France, Russia, Germany and Austria), has brewing and the vinting of wines been prohibited. It is another matter with distilled liquors; it is my opinion that they should be prohibited here and abroad.

Your bold and just decision had a reaction other than merely giving to those who like beers and wines the right to have their making continue—it created a feeling of confidence among the masses that you are vigilant in protecting their interests and faithful to the trust they have placed in you as their friend. Viewed from that standpoint, it produced an effect highly favorable at this moment when fullest public confidence in the Executive is quite essential to winning a war that promises to be as desperately fought and as prolonged as the one we are waging.

You have given me, in common with your other friends, a new cause of pride in their friendship.

With sincere regard,

Faithfully,   Herbert Bayard Swope

TLS (WP, DLC).
[1] At this time city editor of the New York *World*.

Frank Lyon Polk to William Graves Sharp

Washington, July 31, 1917

2501 Your 2321.

Question number three refers to agreements between Allies concerning Asia Minor. Department has no information regarding these agreements and would be glad to be informed of their nature in order that it may be in a position to answer the inquiry.

Polk

T telegram (SDR, RG 59, 763.72119/685, DNA).

Sir Cecil Arthur Spring Rice to the Foreign Office

Paraphrase of Washington telegram to F.O. No. 2224 of July 31st.

MOST CONFIDENTIAL.

We have communicated your telegram No 2985 to Mr AcAdoo who told us that he was now engaged in preparing a demand on Congress for extra credits and would find it hard to explain payments to sustain exchange. (There are some very hostile members on the Congressional Committees.) Moreover he was doubtful if the existing Act of Congress would justify such payments. He hoped in a month or two to have means at his disposal. But the present moment was a critical one and he would find it very difficult to justify his action to Congress. He asked us to ascertain immediately for how long we could go on sustaining exchange. I quoted your words and urged that Congress would easily understand the true nature of the eventuality you foresee should there be an entire cessation of trade. He promised to give the matter his most careful consideration and meanwhile begged me to explain to you the difficulty of his political situation for the next month, after which he hoped to be in a position to be able to give more effectual assistance. Crosby asked if it could not be demonstrated more clearly that British exchange really meant

Allied exchange as Great Britain does business for all the Allies. From the point of view of Congress this last point is of considerable importance.

T MS (FO 115/2260, p. 26, PRO).

From the Diary of Josephus Daniels

July Tuesday 31 1917

Cabinet–Discussed I.W.W. Haywood had sent telegram to President that unless IWW were returned to Bixby, Arizona, from which they had been driven out, strikes would occur in Western mines. Then he sent another,[1] that unless this were done, other strikes would take place. Presdt was indignant, but said what Haywood desires is to be a martyr. What shall I do? Referred to Gregory & Wilson.

1 It is missing.

To Leonidas Carstarphen Dyer

My dear Mr. Dyer: [The White House] 1 August, 1917

Your letters of yesterday[1] and the day before have struck a responsive chord in my mind. I have been made aware from various sources of the unfortunate position in which a very large number of our loyal fellow-citizens are placed because of their German origin or affiliations.

I am sure that they need no further assurance from me of my confidence in the entire integrity and loyalty of the great body of our fellow-citizens of German blood. You know that not once but many times in my public addresses I have expressed this confidence. I do not like to make another occasion to express it simply because it would seem to indicate on my part a doubt as to whether the country had believed my previous assurances to be sincere. May I not very respectfully suggest that it would be easy to make use of the passages I have referred to from my former addresses to do something, I hope not a little, to offset the evil influences that are at work?

Cordially and sincerely yours,   Woodrow Wilson[2]

TLS (Letterpress Books, WP, DLC).
    1 Dyer's letter of July 31 is missing. A White House memorandum reveals that it enclosed a letter from G. H. Marquard, Jr., to L. C. Dyer, n.d., on behalf of Otto Sassman. The Marquard letter was referred to Burleson for his consideration. See ASB to WW, Aug. 6, 1917.
    2 Wilson's letter was printed, e.g., in the *New York Times*, Aug. 4, 1917.

To William Gibbs McAdoo, with Enclosure

My dear Mac: The White House 1 August, 1917

I am sure you will read the enclosed letter of Major Higginson's with interest. Everything that he writes bears a remarkable impress of his personality.

Cordially and faithfully yours, Woodrow Wilson

TLS (W. G. McAdoo Papers, DLC).

ENCLOSURE

From Henry Lee Higginson

Dear Mr. President: Boston. July 30, 1917.

May I trouble you once more in reply to your kind letter of the 26th of July?

Liberty bonds are 99.40, or a trifle more than one-half per cent. below par, at which they were placed. It would be very hard to sell a new loan at the present time. Midsummer is always a bad time for business, and people are out of spirits because they are uncertain. I just asked an excellent judge of the investment market about a new issue of Liberty Bonds, and he replied that it should not come before October. The banks will certainly take freely three or four months paper.

If the question of the loan is settled, and no effort to fix prices beyond a minimum price is made, people will feel much better, business will be more active, and then it will be easier to do anything. When people are out of spirits or doubtful, as now, they hold their money, wait, and criticise everything. I should go to the banks and get what money was needed, which could be done; I should let the world know that prices were not to be fixed, and then people would begin to be active. When a corporation has made a great deal of money out of its business, you can under the present laws tax that company very largely, and have the same result as if you fixed the prices low.

The labor unrest is great, and manufacturers and miners are doubtful about their future. Relieve the apprehensions, encourage people to a considerable degree of prosperity, and you can get what you want.

It is very little that I know, but I am sure of these facts.

Yours respectfully, H. L. Higginson.

TLS (W. G. McAdoo Papers, DLC).

To Henry Lee Higginson

My dear Major Higginson: [The White House] 1 August, 1917

I have time for only a line of acknowledgment of your letter of July thirtieth but you may be sure I appreciate it and value the statement of facts which it contains.

          Cordially and sincerely yours,   Woodrow Wilson

P.S. Thank you for your little note about Mr. Allen.[1]   W.W.

TLS (Letterpress Books, WP, DLC).
    [1] H. L. Higginson to WW, c. July 30, 1917, ALS (W. G. McAdoo Papers, DLC). He recommended Frederic Winthrop Allen as "an excellent advisor & a man of unusual ability" who would be available for governmental service at any time.

To Jessie Woodrow Bones Brower

My dear, dear Cousin: [The White House] 1 August, 1917

Please never feel that you are imposing[1] upon me by acquiescing in such requests as that of Judge Thomas.[2] I have just dictated an answer[3] to his letter.

I am glad and I must admit surprised to say that Edith and I are both very well. The house seems very empty without either Margaret or Helen in it and the pleasure of living in it is anything but increased by the odors of oil and paint which now fill the hallways, because of work being done in some of the rooms, but on the whole we are getting on very well indeed. My sense of humor occasionally comes to my relief and enables me to see the comedy of what is going on amongst the prima donnas by whom we are surrounded; and although it is true that the labor is overwhelming in its kind and sometimes threatens to crush me to earth, it is not, fortunately, overwhelming in amount and I do manage every day when the sun is not too savage to get in a game of golf, and then Edith and I succeed in getting a little ride of an hour or an hour and a half late in the afternoon or after dinner.

I dare say Helen has written to you from the Canadian camp. She seems to be perfectly delighted with it and with everything connected with it and exceedingly happy to get to see Marion and the little ones.

Our thoughts often go out to you, my dear cousin. I hope you are keeping well. You may be sure that we think of you with deep and genuine affection.

    Always   Your devoted cousin,   [Woodrow Wilson]

CCL (WP, DLC).
    [1] Jessie W. B. Brower to WW [July 29, 1917], ALS (WP, DLC).

2 Actually Thomas Taylor, Jr., judge of the circuit court of Cook County, Ill. His letter is missing.

3 WW to T. Taylor, Jr., Aug. 1, 1917, TLS (Letterpress Books, WP, DLC).

From Herbert Clark Hoover

Dear Mr. President: Washington August 1, 1917.

Senator Chamberlain has asked me to convey to you the following message.

He states that he thinks the section in the food control bill providing for the joint Congressional Committee can be eliminated in conference, provided it is agreed that it shall be raised as a joint resolution. He further believes that the joint resolution can be defeated on the floor of the Senate, and that if this course has your approval, he feels that he could win over one or two more votes on the conference committee to this program. He would like to have some indication of your feelings in the matter.

I remain,   Your obedient servant,   Herbert Hoover

TLS (WP, DLC).

From Jeannette Rankin

My dear Mr. President: Washington, D. C. August 1, 1917.

I have just received a letter from the Metal Mine Workers' Union of Butte, containing resolutions adopted by the Union at a recent meeting. Thinking you may be interested, I append a copy of these resolutions.

"Metal Mine Workers' Union
Butte, Montana July 25, 1917.

Whereas:

Some time ago several hundred miners, citizens of the United States were forcibly torn from their homes and loved ones by the hired thugs and gunmen of the Mining Companies of Bisbee, Arizona, and,

Whereas:

These members of the working class are at present camped on the burning desert of New Mexico, and,

Whereas:

We have authentic information that these people are in dire need of the necessities of life and have no change of clothing, and,

Whereas:

The Mining Companies of the entire western country are working in conjunction to eliminate from their employ those of the working class who have the manhood to voice a protest against unbearable conditions, and,

Whereas:

The men deported from Bisbee have been branded by the corporations and the public press as agitators and outlaws and will be denied employment on that account; therefore be it Resolved,

That we, the miners of Butte, in mass assembled, do demand and urge that you, as President of the United States, give these people immediate relief and take such further action as will enable them to return unmolested to their homes and families, and be it further Resolved,

That a copy of these resolutions be sent to the President of the United States, to the Secretary of Labor and Representatives in Congress from Montana, and a copy handed to the local press.   Press Committee, M.M.W.U.

G. E. BOYLE"

Respectfully,   Jeannette Rankin[1]

TLS (WP, DLC).

[1] "Please acknowledge this letter and say that I was already in receipt of these telegrams. The President." WW to JPT, c. Aug. 3, 1917, TL (WP, DLC).

From William Green

Indianapolis, Indiana, August 1, 1917.

Some time ago members United Mine Workers were working under contract with Victor American Coal Company, which continues for at least one year at Gallup, New Mexico. This company sold mine and immediately new concern discharged members our union and evicted them from their homes. We furnished tents for them and they were living peaceably therein. Yesterday Sheriff and company forcibly loaded eighty members our union on cars and deported them. We will not countenance this outrage. Demand Federal Government intervene and provide these men be returned to their homes. Unless this is done I will favor strike of coal miners United States until this outrage is righted. Please advise quickly what will be done.

Wm. Green, International Secretary-Treasurer,
United Mine Workers of America.

T telegram (WP, DLC).

From Marguerite Godham[1]

Butte, Montana, August 1, 1917.

This morning at four o'clock an executive board member of the I.W.W., a cripple, Frank Little, was taken from his bed by members of gun men in the employ of the Anaconda Copper Company, shot and hanged. The cause of democracy can only be advanced by the Federal Government taking charge of the copper mines.   Marguerite Godham.

T telegram (WP, DLC).
1 Member of the Good Government Club of Butte, Mont.

From Newton Diehl Baker

My dear Mr. President: Washington. August 1st, 1917.

The Council of National Defense met today, and had a joint session with the War Industries Board.[1] Apparently the organization is now being perfected, and such disposition as there was to have misunderstanding about its functions, and the relations of the members to one another, and to their work, have been cleared away.

After the joint meeting it was suggested by some of the members of the Council that in all likelihood the War Industries Board would consider it a great compliment if you could receive them, and greet them for a very few minutes at an early date. As I shall be out of the City from Friday morning until Tuesday, I beg leave to suggest that if there is a time when it will be convenient for you to receive the Board that you cause Secretary Daniels to be notified of the time so that he can get the members together and bring them over to present to you.[2]

I think, from such observation as I have been able to make of the new members, that the Board is going to be a very strong and effective body, and that in a very little while its harmony will be complete.   Respectfully yours,   Newton D. Baker

TLS (WP, DLC).
1 The members were Frank A. Scott, chairman, Bernard M. Baruch, Robert S. Brookings, Robert S. Lovett, Hugh Frayne, Lt. Col. Palmer E. Pierce, and Admiral Frank F. Fletcher.
2 Wilson received Daniels and the members of the W.I.B. during the afternoon of August 6.

From Joseph Patrick Tumulty, with Enclosure

Dear Governor: The White House. 1 August 1917.

The request for some statement on our part with reference to the East St. Louis affair will not down. This morning a delegation of twenty representative negroes called here and presented this resolution, containing a statement as to their grievances. Until some statement is issued by you deprecating these terrible things, I am afraid the pressure will grow greater and greater.

Sincerely yours,   Tumulty

TLS (WP, DLC).

E N C L O S U R E

We, the Committee of the Negro Silent Protest Parade, in which 1500 colored men, women and children took part last Saturday in New York, come to present to you and through you to the President and Congress a petition for redress of certain grievances. We come representing not only the Negro Silent Protest Parade, but the colored people of greater New York, and the sentiments and aspirations and sorrowes too of the entire Negro Population of the United States.

We come representing Twelve Million Citizens whose devotion and loyalty to the nation have never been questioned. Twelve Million Citizens, Twelve Million Citizens, who, where [when] the present storm broke over our land, took their unqualified stand side by side with the original American stocks that landed at Plymouth Rock and at Jamestown.

We feel that in coming to you, we are well within our rights. The right given by birth, the right given by labor and the right given by loyalty. We feel further that it is especially fitting that we come at this time when the heart of the nation is so deeply touched by the cause of demorcracy and of humanity.

We come asking that the President use his great powers to have granted to us some redress for the grievances set forth in our petition, and we come further praying that the President may find it in his heart to speak some public word that will give hope and courage to our people, thus using his great personal and moral influence in our behalf.

And to these ends, I have the honor to read and respectfully present the following petition:

TO THE PRESIDENT AND CONGRESS OF THE UNITED STATES:

We, the committee of the Negro Silent Protest Parade, representing the colored people of Greater New York and the sentiment of the people of Negro descent throughout this land, come to you to present a petition for redress of grievances.

In the last thirty-one years 2,867 colored men and women have been lynched by mobs without trial. Less than a half dozen persons out of the tens of thousands involved have received any punishment whatsoever for these crimes, and not a single one has been punished for murder. In addition to this, mobs have harried and murdered colored citizens time and time again with impunity, culminating in the latest atrocity at East St. Louis where nearly a hundred innocent, hard working citizens were done to death in broad daylight for seeking to earn an honest living.

We believe that this spirit of lawlessness is doing untold injury to our country and we submit that the record proves that the states are either unwilling or unable to put down lynching and mob violence.

We ask, therefore, that lynching and mob violence be made a national crime punishable by the laws of the United States and that this be done by federal enactment, or if necessary, by constitutional amendment. We believe that there can be found in recent legislation abundant precedent for action of this sort, and whether this be true or not, no nation that seeks to fight the battles of civilization can afford to march in blood-smeared garments.

We ask, therefore, immediate action by the Congress and the President of the United States.

CC MS (WP, DLC).

To Joseph Patrick Tumulty

Dear Tumulty: [The White House, August 1, 1917]

I wish very much that you would think this over and tell me just what form and occasion you think such a statement ought to take. I want to make it if it can be made naturally and with the likelihood that it will be effective.   The President.

TL (WP, DLC).

To Frank Lyon Polk

My dear Mr. Counselor.   The White House. 2 August, 1917.

I like this suggestion,[1] which I have thought over as carefully as possible in the circumstances, and would be very much obliged if the Department would get in confidential touch with such sincere and representative Poles as Mr. Paderewski, for example, and ascertain their views as to the practicability of carrying it out.   Faithfully Yours,   W.W.

WWTLI (SDR, RG 59, 860C.01/54, DNA).
  [1] F. L. Polk to WW, July 28, 1917, and its Enclosure.

To John Sharp Williams

My dear Senator: The White House 2 August, 1917

I am sorry you are committing yourself not to run again for public office.[1] I am sure you know what an irreparable loss I feel your withdrawal from public life would be, and I hope that before your present term runs out you will think differently.

With warmest regard,
            Faithfully yours,   Woodrow Wilson

TLS (J. S. Williams Papers, DLC).
  [1] In the course of a speech in the Senate on August 1, Williams had mentioned in passing that he never expected to be a candidate for office again. *Cong. Record*, 65th Cong., 1st sess., p. 5662, and *Washington Post*, Aug. 2, 1917.

To Josephus Daniels, with Enclosure

My dear Daniels: The White House 2 August, 1917

Here is a suggestion for the new Operations organization which I am sure you will welcome along with the rest.
            Faithfully yours,   Woodrow Wilson

TLS (J. Daniels Papers, DLC).

ENCLOSURE

THE NAVY.   The White House. 29 July, 1917.

A Department of Operations relieved of routine by deputation to some other instrumentality and charged with the development of actual operations at sea (with the freest possible choice as to those operations) and with the equipment, readiness, and disposal of the fighting force of the Navy in carrying out the operations decided on.

    Benson, perhaps, a suitable head, but too prudent, too unimaginative, too early in training to do the necessary bold thinking and planning. Should, therefore, be associated in counsel and action with much younger men,—men of the new school and training, few of whom have passed and some of whom have not yet reached the rank of Commander.

The General Board to be tactfully but altogether relegated to the function of advice upon large questions of general policy, judiciously selected, which it will not be detrimental to the success of the war to treat with the deliberateness of conservative debate. It will almost inevitably get a move on it if stimulated by the reorganized Department of Operations.

Such energy and despatch in the purchase of supplies as the new organization of the advisory instrumentalities of the Council of National Defence will make easily practicable. To this end the two most energtic and sensible men in the army and navy should be placed on the War Supplies Board.

WWT MS (J. Daniels Papers, DLC).

To Joseph Patrick Tumulty

Dear Tumulty: [The White House, Aug. 2, 1917]

    Please remind Miss Rankin that requests for troops should come directly from the Governor of Montana and assure her that if any such request comes it will receive immediate attention. I would be very much obliged to her if she would in the meantime discuss the labor situation in Montana with the Attorney General and the Secretary of Labor. This would in any case be necessary because I would seek their advice.[1]

The President.

TL (WP, DLC).
  [1] JPT to Jeannette Rankin, Aug. 2, 1917, CCL (WP, DLC), is a paraphrase of Wilson's letter to Tumulty. Miss Rankin had spoken about a request for troops in a telephone call to the White House.

To Frank Lyon Polk, with Enclosure

My dear Mr. Counselor,   The White House. 2 August, 1917.

    I entirely concur in the suggestions of the enclosed memorandum,[1] and hope that the plan will be carried out.

I think that it would be a great mistake to cut such relief altogether off, and I think the measures and methods here suggested will afford sufficient safeguards.

Faithfully Yours,   W.W.

WWTLI (SDR, RG 59, 861.48/512, DNA).
1 "Memorandum regarding sending relief into Poland, Turkey and Serbia," July 27, 1917, T MS (SDR, RG 59, 861.48/512, DNA).

E N C L O S U R E

From Frank Lyon Polk

My dear Mr. President: Washington July 27, 1917.

I venture to enclose herewith a memorandum in regard to the general policy of sending relief to persons other than enemy subjects in Poland, Turkey and Serbia. Great pressure is being brought to bear on the Department by the Poles, Jews and Serbians in this country to send individual remittances and funds to be used for general relief in these various countries.

The first question to be decided, therefore, is whether we shall allow limited relief to go through to these countries or whether we shall discontinue it altogether. If we decide to permit limited relief we must be certain that: (1) there are proper guarantees of distribution, and (2) the amounts to be distributed are reasonable.

There appears to be two sides to this important question. The British Government takes the view that these funds ultimately increase the resources of the enemy and therefore should be discontinued. The other side of the picture shows the Poles looking to the Allies for assistance; and if an announcement is made that in future no assistance will be coming to them they will be obliged to turn wholly to the Germans for help, and the Germans would be able to make use of the fact that the Poles had been deserted by the Allies.

Relief in Turkey does not present so many difficulties. In the first place we are not at war with Turkey, and in the second place the Allied Governments are interested in the welfare of the Armenian and Syrian populations.

I should be very grateful if you would be so kind as to indicate whether we should adopt the policy of limited distribution or whether we should discontinue the sending of relief altogether.

With assurances of respect, etc., I am, my dear Mr. President,

Faithfully yours,   Frank L. Polk

TLS (SDR, RG 59, 861.48/512, DNA).

To Edward John King[1]

My dear Mr. King: [The White House] 2 August, 1917

I very much value your kind letter of July thirty-first and thank you for it sincerely.[2] I believe that the matter of the Committee on War Expenditures is slowly working itself out and I am very happy to feel that I can count upon the support of the House in resisting the effort to put this millstone around my neck, as you very properly characterize it.

Cordially and sincerely yours,   Woodrow Wilson

TLS (Letterpress Books, WP, DLC).
  [1] Republican congressman from Illinois.
  [2] It is missing.

To Roland Sletor Morris

My dear Morris: [The White House] 2 August, 1917

You may be sure it gave me great pleasure to nominate you for the post in Japan and I shall look forward with the greatest confidence to your service there. I have not yet heard and do not think I shall hear of any difficulty in the Senate.[1]

Cordially and sincerely yours,   [Woodrow Wilson]

CCL (WP, DLC).
  [1] In fact, the Senate had confirmed Morris' nomination on August 1.

To Thomas Davies Jones

The White House Aug 2/17

Delighted and grateful that you are coming Please come as soon as you can conveniently arrange your affairs

Woodrow Wilson

T telegram (Mineral Point, Wisc., Public Library).

From Walter Hines Page

London, Aug. 2, 1917.

CONFIDENTIAL FOR THE SECRETARY AND PRESIDENT ONLY.

Mr. Balfour has gone over with me the telegram he sent July thirty to Spring-Rice for McAdoo about exchange.[1] He represents the position as most perilous. He hopes that the President has seen it and will cause a reply to be sent at earliest possible time.   Page.

T telegram (SDR, RG 59, 841.51/75, DNA).
  [1] That is, the Foreign Office to C. A. Spring Rice, July 30, 1917.

From Robert Latham Owen

My dear Mr. President: [Washington] August 2, 1917.

In reply to your favor relative to the proposed Joint Committee of Congress,[1] which I offered as a substitute for the Weeks' Amendment, I have the honor to state—

The Weeks Amendment provided for a—

"Joint Committee *on the Conduct* of the War."

It was proposed that this Committee should "*make a special study of the problems arising out of the war.*"

I objected to this Committee because of its ill-defined powers and because the problems of the conduct of the war should be left to the Executive Department, and I insisted that the duty of such Committee should be confined to safeguarding expenditures merely by the force of publicity.

Upon my suggestion Senator Weeks amended his first draft (Cong. Rec. 5902) by inserting the words—"including safeguarding expenditures," but leaving the powers of the Committee still as above quoted. This was not acceptable to me. I therefore submitted as a substitute an amendment providing for a "Joint Committee on *Expenditures* in the Conduct of the War."

We already have committees on expenditures for the different departments of the government, as you know, but they are not ordinarily active.

In the substitute which I proposed, the following authority was given to the proposed committee:

"It shall be the duty of said Committee *to keep itself advised with regard to the expenditure of all appropriations* bearing on the conduct of the war made by Congress *and the contracts relating thereto* made by officers of the executive departments, and *it shall be the duty of the executive departments, on request, to keep said Committee fully advised as to such expenditures and contracts.*"

The Committee was authorized to confer and advise with the President and the various officers of the executive departments,

"*with a view to safeguarding expenditures*, and to *report to Congress from time to time* in its own discretion, or when requested to do so by either branch of Congress."

Congress will appropriate probably during the current year in the neighborhood of twenty thousand millions of dollars,—a sum so gigantic as to stagger the human understanding. These expenditures you will try to safeguard by having your Cabinet Officers pursue a prudent policy, but the expenditures and the contracts will be made by men in various degrees subordinate to the Cabinet Officers.

It will be impossible for you, and it will be impossible for the members of your cabinet, charged as they are with the duties of this war, to completely safeguard these expenditures.

These subordinate officers will be subjected to the influence of the most skilled traders in the world. Already the press is full of a propaganda that the six hundred and forty millions we appropriated for aviation will provide twenty-two thousand aeroplanes. The money appropriated should easily provide over one hundred thousand aeroplanes, if the government makes these planes and allows a fair manufacturer's profit for the making. The Wall Street Journal announces that the Curtis Manufacturing Company will have contracts covering two hundred millions of dollars, and the stock of this company is going through a bull movement on this announcement.

I believe in generosity in dealing with our manufacturing companies, but I do not believe in ninety-five dollar steel, nor in twenty-five thousand dollar prices for aeroplanes. If these appropriations are not very rigidly safeguarded, the cost of this war to the American people, through taxes, will be increased by billions of dollars.

The American people are willing, in my judgment, to pay the full cost of protecting their liberties through this war, but I feel a sense of intense anxiety to protect them as far as humanly possible.

The psychological effect of constant publicity with regard to these expenditures and these contracts, will assist in a very powerful manner your subordinate officers charged with the responsibility of making these contracts, and it was for this reason that I believed such a Committee, charged with the duty of keeping advised as to these expenditures and as to these contracts, and keeping Congress advised, would save the country hundreds of millions of dollars.

I do not believe, and I cannot conceive, how such a committee would embarrass or hamper you, much less that such a committee auditing these accounts can be justly designated as a Committee of "daily espionage."

This Committee, as proposed, was to consist of a majority from each House, of your party associates and supporters. I should expect from the Republicans a sincere and devoted cooperation.

The Republicans in both Houses have shown a gallant and patriotic spirit in holding up your hands in this war, and I believe that the principle which you announced on the 26th of February, last, in your appeal to Congress for authority and power, is a sound principle. You then said, in addressing Congress—

"We are jointly the servants of the people, and must act together and in their spirit."

You have constantly urged—

"Common Counsel."

In this doctrine I believe.

I regret that you should take a different view of the value of this Committee, which I believe is essential to safeguarding the Administration and the Treasury of the United States in protecting the enormous expenditures we are about to make.

I feel a deep sense of responsibility for the taxes which Congress is voting on the people,[2] and a great anxiety to see the expenditure of these taxes safeguarded.

I need not assure you, because you know well, that I am extremely anxious to protect the welfare and success of the Administration.

I am always more than happy to serve the Administration in any way in my power, at any time, and have uniformally done so.

I am informed the Conference Committee has agreed to omit this amendment from the Food Control Bill, which I think is desirable to do, for the reason that the Food Bill should not be delayed a moment and this matter can be more deliberately considered independently.

I am quite familiar with the Ben Wade Committee on the Conduct of the Civil War, '61-'65. It was a Committee on the *Conduct of the War*, and divided the responsibility, which I thought, and think, very ill advised.

It was a Committee hostile to the President of the United States. It was a Committee which summoned Generals from the field, and its purposes were entirely different from safeguarding the expenditures.

The proposed Committee was to be a Committee of your own party associates, friendly and sympathetic, confined strictly to safeguarding expenditures, and with a publicity that would be a necessary corollary to their functions.

I hope whatever is done in regard to this matter, that you will cause constant publicity to be given to these contracts, that they may be subject to public scrutiny.

With sentiments of the greatest respect, I remain

Very cordially and sincerely, yours,   Robt. L. Owen

My absence from the city will explain my inability to answer more promptly.   Yours Faithfully   R.L.O.

TLS (WP, DLC).
 1 WW to R. L. Owen, July 23, 1917.
 2 Immediately after the entry of the United States into the war, McAdoo
had asked Congress to provide $3.5 billion to put the country on a wartime basis
and to finance the war for one year from the date of the appropriation. Both
Wilson and McAdoo favored raising as much as possible of the cost of the war
through taxation. On April 15, 1917, McAdoo submitted to the appropriate
congressional committees detailed suggestions as to new sources of revenue by
which approximately one half of the required sum could be raised. Although
the House, on May 23, approved McAdoo's tax plan without major changes by
a vote of 329 to seventy-six, debate in the Senate dragged on throughout the
summer. In the meantime, it became clear that McAdoo's earlier estimate had
been far too modest, and that at least $15 billion was needed. On September 10,
the Senate, by a vote of sixty-nine to four, finally passed a revenue bill of its
own that was designed to raise $2.4 billion. The final measure, as agreed upon
by the conference committee and signed by Wilson on October 3, 1917, was
estimated to bring new revenues totaling $2.5 billion. It reduced income tax
exemptions by one half to two thirds and imposed a normal tax of 2 per cent
on all personal incomes over the exemptions and a supplementary tax of 2 per
cent on all incomes over $3,000 for single persons and $4,000 for married persons. The new act also sharply increased the surtax on large incomes. Whereas
the Revenue Act of 1916 had levied a surtax ranging from 1 per cent on incomes
over $20,000 to 13 per cent on those over $2 million, the Revenue Act of 1917
provided for an additional surtax that began at 1 per cent on incomes over
$5,000 and rose to 50 per cent on incomes in excess of $1 million. As a result,
the maximum tax rate became 67 per cent through the accumulation of the
normal tax of 2 per cent, the supplementary tax of 2 per cent, the old surtax
of 13 per cent, and the new surtax of 50 per cent. Business taxes were increased
by 4 per cent in addition to the existing 2 per cent. Furthermore, a progressive
excess-profits tax was levied on profits higher than 7-9 per cent of the invested
capital used in a particular business in the period from 1911 to 1913. The rates
of the excess-profits tax ranged from 20 per cent to 60 per cent. Estate taxes
were imposed at the rate of .5 per cent on estates valued below $50,000 to 10
per cent on those valued above $10 million. Moreover, the act increased the long-
established taxes on alcoholic beverages and tobacco and imposed new excise
taxes on luxury goods such as jewelry, cosmetics, automobiles, etc. It also raised
the postal rates and instituted a zone system for second-class mail at increased
charges. On the whole, the new taxes on wealth amounted to about 74 per
cent of the entire additional revenue, the taxes on luxurious or harmful consumption to approximately 13 per cent. For a detailed discussion, see Charles
Gilbert, *American Financing of World War I* (Westport, Conn., 1970), pp.
75-101, and Sidney Ratner, *American Taxation: Its History as a Social Force
in Democracy* (New York, 1942), pp. 372-83. There are no documents relating
to the Revenue Act of 1917 in the Wilson Papers.

From Joseph Patrick Tumulty

Dear Governor: The White House. 2 August 1917.

   In the little talk I had with you some months ago, you did
not seem to be very enthusiastic about Hall Caine;[1] but I am
sending to you for your perusal this very interesting article from
the New York Times of today[2] in which he discusses the impossibility of "full reparation," etc.

   Note what he says: *"But neither France nor England entered
upon this war to readjust bad settlements of former conflicts, and
the experiences of the past three years must teach us that our
newest and greatest ally, America, will go out of it without counting old scores, on the first day we can make a righteous peace*

secure. Security! Security! Security! That is all America will ask for."   Sincerely yours,   Tumulty

TLS (WP, DLC).
¹ Thomas Henry Hall Caine, known as Hall Caine, popular British novelist, who had devoted himself since the beginning of the war to British propaganda in the United States. He had written hundreds of articles published in a syndicate of American newspapers, most notably the *New York Times*.
² Hall Caine, "Caine Has No Hope of Punitive Peace," *New York Times*, Aug. 2, 1917. Caine argued that full restitution of all war losses was impossible, that it was both hopeless and unjust to attempt to make Germany pay the full cost of the war, that it was impossible to apportion the guilt of the war among the nations involved, and that peace conferences were futile. He concluded that the ultimate lesson of the war was that modern warfare threatened to annihilate the human race. Hence, the "free democracies" had to fight on until militarism was destroyed.

From William Green

Indianapolis, Indiana, August 2, 1917.

Am anxiously waiting reply to my telegram of yesterday requesting Federal Government return members United Mine Workers of America deported from Gallup, New Mexico, to their homes. The men were not industrial workers of the world but instead members United Mine Workers of America, affiliated with the American Federation of Labor. Important prompt action is taken because men deported are denied rights guaranteed American citizens. Will Federal Government provide for return of these deported men to their homes immediately.

                                                        Wm. Green.

T telegram (WP, DLC).

From Samuel Gompers

Sir: Washington, D. C. August 2, 1917.

A short while ago I wrote you enclosing telegrams from representative labor men of Arizona protesting against actions of violance committed against the miners of that state, and I urged that the rights of those miners be protected. Since then other communications have come to me both from Arizona and other sections of the United States. Unrest exists among the miners in this country in a greater degree than has been manifested in many years.

The men working in the coal mines in this country are performing a service that is indispensable both to our own government and to our allies in the war which we are now waging. These miners have been generally patriotic and have been trying to do their part in the nation's work. The general organization has entered into an agreement with the mine operators in the organized districts and continuous production of coal is ensured in those districts so long as the contracts are carried out. But in districts where employers refuse to deal with representatives of the miners and where miners presentation of claims for higher wages and better conditions are arbitrarily refused, not only is the output of the mine stopped but there has been stimulated a spirit that will not promote the best interests of our nation, our government, and the necessities of our allies.

This morning I received the following telegram from Mr. Wm. Green, International Secretary-Treasurer of the United Mine Workers of America, and member of the Executive Council of the American Federation of Labor. The telegram explains the feeling that exists among the miners; that the rights of the workers, the common people of this country, must be maintained or we lose democracy and human freedom in our country:

Indianapolis, Ind., Aug. 1, 1917.

"Mr. Samuel Gompers,

    A. F. of L. Bldg. Washington, D. C.

Have sent following telegram to President Wilson and Secretary Wilson. Ask you interest yourself in this matter. Some time ago members United Mine Workers were working under contracts with Victor American Coal Co which continues for at least one year at Gallup New Mexico. This Company sold mine and immediately new concern discharged members our union and evicted them from their homes. We furnished tents for them and they were living peaceably therein. Yesterday Sheriff and company forcibly loaded eighty members our union in cars and deported them. We will not countenance this outrage. Demand federal government intervene and provide these men be returned to their homes. Unless this is done quickly I will favor strike of coal miners United States until this outrage is righted. Please advise quickly what will be done.

(signed) Wm. Green,
International Secretary Treasurer United Mine
Workers of America."

Those of us who have the best interests of this nation at heart can not expect the miners of this country to quietly submit to such illegal acts as occurred in Arizona and New Mexico. Therefore, I feel that I ought to urge upon you the necessity of some action to put an end to such illegal policies and outrages against the working men of this country. In addition to the telegram of Mr. Green,. I also received a telegram from the Secretary of the Montana State Metal Trades Council which is as follows:

Aug. 2, 1917

"Samuel Gompers,
     A. F. of L. Bldg. Washington, D. C.
We respectfully request and urge a speedy investigation of the lynching of Frank H. Little in this city this morning and believe it to the best interests of organized labor and the U. S. government that this be considered at once.
          MONTANA STATE METAL TRADES COUNCIL
                 C. O. EDWARDS, SEC'Y."

Permit me to add my personal request that a speedy investigation be made of the lynching of Mr. Little and official information be given to the people of the United States. These events arouse within me a very great anxiety for the consequences if our government does not take immediate steps to maintain justice and constitutional rights to all of our citizens.
          Very respectfully,   Saml. Gompers.

TLS (WP, DLC).

From Winston Churchill

My dear Mr. President: Washington, D. C. August 2, 1917.

I was indeed very grateful to you for your kind reception of me the other day,[1] and for your appreciation of the spirit of my errand. I feel that I have done my duty under the circumstances, and that there is no further use for my remaining in Washington. I therefore expect to leave here Saturday for New England, and I am hoping to go abroad next month.

My object in going abroad, and especially in going to England, is to study the situation there in relation to the issues and democratic problems of the war as set forth by you in your various proclamations, and also as sketched by you in our conversation. I am going to try to interpret these issues both to the American and British people,[2] for I am and have been heartily in sympathy with them.[3]

With best wishes I remain,
          Sincerely yours,   Winston Churchill

TLS (WP, DLC).
     [1] Wilson saw Churchill (the American novelist and Wilson's friend) at the White House on July 25.

[2] He did so in *A Traveller in War-time* (New York, 1918).

[3] Wilson had asked Churchill, a graduate of the United States Naval Academy (Class of 1894) to survey the Anglo-American naval establishments in the British Isles. See WW to W. Churchill, Aug. 3, 1917, and Churchill's report: W. Churchill to WW, Oct. 22, 1917, printed as an Enclosure with WW to JD, Nov. 12, 1917.

William Graves Sharp to Robert Lansing

Paris. Aug. 2, 1917.

Confidential. 2353.

Your telegram No. 2501, July 31, 4 P.M. In a talk with Mr. Cambon this morning I learned of a most interesting and rather complicated situation as it bears upon the question of allied future interests in Asia-Minor. It develops that prior to the entrance of Italy into the war England, France and Russia had entered into an alliance or at least had an understanding as to their respective interests in that country. The interests and aims of England in the Valley of the Euphrates were tentatively defined, also those of Russia in Armenia, and those of France in Syria where she has valuable properties and many people of French nationality or allegiance. Besides she had in a way for several centuries protected Christianity in that country. This agreement naturally was based upon the collapse and practical dissipation of Turkish dominion in the countries named. Mr. Cambon however, expressed it as his belief that England and France would not feel willing now to support Russia in her control of affairs, stating that that country ought to be autonomous and free from outside control.

When, however, Italy joined the Allies she at once manifested a desire to assert her rights in the participation of a future exercise of power and possible acquisition of territory in the eastern mediterranean which has not been well received by either France or England. As a matter of fact Sonnino,[1] the Italian Premier, has been in London since the adjournment of the conference here last week in consultation with Lloyd George on these questions as they affect these different interests in Asia Minor and surrounding territory. Mr. Cambon said that Sonnino was pressing Italy's claim very persistently but that he thought that it was too early to enter into a definite agreement and I inferred that he also voiced the views of England in expressing that opinion. I have gathered from time to time that the contentions of Italy have been a bone of contention to harmonious action with the other Allied powers and Mr. Cambon made no concealment of the fact that Servia had previously cause for concern and dissatisfaction on account of the ambitions of Italy as briefly referred to in my number 2321, second section, July twenty-fourth. The subject mentioned in Mr. Cambon's third question and to which your telegram number 2501 refers, has to do with the situation which I have thus briefly set forth.

Mr. Cambon added that naturally the questions were submitted to our Government in order that it might be made * the questions which confronted the Allied powers for solution sooner or later. As I have stated in my number 2352 August 2, 6 P.M.[2] Mr. Cambon frankly said to me that on account of the enormous nature of one or two of these subjects of contention he was really glad that our Government was not represented at the conference.

Sharp

* Apparent omission.

T telegram (WP, DLC).
    [1] Baron Sidney Sonnino. He was the Foreign Minister, not the Prime Minister, of Italy at this time.
    [2] W. G. Sharp to RL, Aug. 2, 1917, T telegram (SDR, RG 59, 763.72/6160, DNA).

Sir William Wiseman to Edward Mandell House

[London] 2.8.17.

Following for HOUSE: I have just had long conference with DAMON [BALFOUR]. He says your help in the whole situation and particularly in recent difficulties was the factor which saved a very great disaster.[1] He is intensely grateful to you and anxious to use all his influence to do anything to improve and facilitate relations between the two Governments. I explained the need for the fullest information and frankest exchange of views. After further discussion as to best methods I will cable you again. A very full memorandum on submarine situation has been prepared by War Cabinet. It gives all the important information we have in our possession. We discussed the best way to communicate this and decided to cable the memorandum in full to NORTHCLIFFE to-night with instructions to present it to you and take your judgment as to whether it would be better for you to forward it direct to AJAX [WILSON] or for him to present it formally to AJAX.[2] I shall see this memorandum to-morrow and am told it states the position as very serious, but offers suggestions for further measures which may solve the problem. I have also seen HORACE PLUNKETT. He feels a solution must be reached by Convention[3] at almost any cost and is happy to know that you and AJAX will follow developments with interest and sympathy. He will keep me constantly posted and I shall inform you in confidence of everything. In future cables SYNTAX will mean the man we lunched with at your house at MAGNOLIA recently.[4]

Wiseman.

T telegram (W. Wiseman Papers, CtY).

[1] Balfour referred to a recent series of conferences among McAdoo, Northcliffe, Tardieu, and others in which McAdoo had given assurances that he would meet the immediate exchange crisis by, among other things, having the United States Treasury advance to the British the sum of $185,000,000. C. A. Spring Rice to the Foreign Office, Aug. 2, 1917, T telegram (FO 115/2260, pp. 46-47, PRO); A. J. Balfour to the British Embassy (paraphrase), Aug. 2, 1917, T telegram (FO 115/2260, p. 55, PRO). As subsequent documents will reveal, McAdoo was using the threat of withholding further additional credits in order to force the Allies to establish an Inter-Allied Purchasing Commission in London.

There is no evidence, either in the House Diary or elsewhere, that House had had any hand in effecting this temporary solution of the exchange crisis.

[2] It is printed as an Enclosure with C. A. Spring Rice to WW, Aug. 6, 1917.

[3] The so-called Irish Convention, about which see n. 1 to H. Plunkett to EMH, June 1, 1917, printed as an Enclosure with EMH to WW, June 19, 1917, Vol. 42.

[4] Lord Northcliffe.

To Robert Latham Owen

My dear Senator Owen: [The White House] 3 August, 1917

I thank you sincerely for your full and detailed reply to my letter about the Joint Committee of Congress. My own feeling is this, that the creation of such a committee would produce very much such a situation as I have just tried to cure and I think succeeded in curing in the case of the shipbuilding contracts. In such a case there would be, on the one hand, the Executive entrusted with the expenditures of moneys and the making of contracts and, on the other hand, a body, a committee, which would have no authority in the matter and the function only of criticism and publicity, a function not dissimilar to that which the Shipping Board recently performed with regard to the contracts entered into for the ships. Differences of judgment are always possible in such cases and would almost certainly arise, and there would be no immediate means of settling any differences of opinion. Resort would be to Congress and the result, if there were any result, legislative action with regard to executive matters. I cannot help but believing that this would simply be an arrangement that would produce discussion and not efficiency.

It is not as if there were not already existing means by which Congress can keep itself apprised of the expenditures of the Government, and I want to assure you that in connection with every spending agency of the Government we are at present interested in nothing so much as in providing instrumentalities which will prevent excessive prices and unreasonable contracts. I have very much at heart the economical and efficient expenditure of the vast sums of money which must be spent for the conduct of this war and I feel that the whole thing should be managed with the daily care of a responsible administrative agency.

May I not say how glad I am always to exchange opinions upon matters of such consequence and to express my own with the greatest candor as well as with the greatest respect? I have realized throughout that your own personal desire in this case was certainly not to be obstructive in any way but rather to be helpful.

Cordially and sincerely yours,   Woodrow Wilson

TLS (Letterpress Books, WP, DLC).

To Winston Churchill

My dear Mr. Churchill: [The White House] 3 August, 1917

This is a line to send you my warm good wishes for your journey and to hope for you a safe return. It naturally makes one a little nervous to see one's friends cross the ocean.

I took up the matters about which we talked the other day with the head of the department[1] and think I have things in course to carry out the essential purpose you had in mind.

With best wishes,

Cordially and sincerely yours,   [Woodrow Wilson]

CCL (WP, DLC).
[1] That is, Josephus Daniels.

From André Tardieu

My dear Mr. President,   Washington, D. C., 3rd August, 1917.

The Chairman of the Shipping Board has advised me last night that a ship would be put at the disposal of the C.R.B.[1] for the transportation to Rotterdam of the wheat which is so urgently needed for the subsistance of the French invaded provinces.

I know that this boat has been tended to us on your very kind intervention, and I beg to express to you respectfully the most sincere and hearty thanks of the people to whom this wheat will mean the possibility of existence for some time.

You are too well aware of the conditions over there for me to say that any further relief will not merely bring comfort to my countrymen, but furnish them only with the first necessities of life. The existence of these unfortunate people depends entirely on the tonnage which can be placed in the future at the disposal of the C.R.B.

I am,

With much respect,

Yours sincerely,   André Tardieu

TLS (WP, DLC).
  [1] The Commission for Relief in Belgium.

From Joseph Patrick Tumulty

Dear Governor: The White House. 3 August 1917.

I take pleasure in calling your attention to these two editorials on the negro question, one from the New York Sun and the other from the New York Evening Post.[1]

I think you ought to make a statement in the form of a reply to these resolutions, expressing your feeling of deep disapproval of the terrible things that have been happening in East St. Louis and elsewhere, evidencing a disregard not only of fundamental rights of the citizenship of these unfortunate people but a disregard of the principles of humanity. "America cannot countenance these things without advertising to the world the fact that she is not a sincere believer in the principles of democracy. Every agency of the Federal government will be used to prevent a recurrence of these terrible happenings."

Sincerely yours,   Tumulty

TLS (WP, DLC).
  [1] "Why Woodrow Wilson Will Stand By His Colored Fellow Citizens," New York *Sun*, Aug. 3, 1917, and an untitled editorial in the New York *Evening Post*, Aug. 2, 1917. The first editorial quoted the full text of WW to A. Walters, Oct. 21, 1912, Vol. 25, and suggested that this document indicated that Wilson would support the petitions of blacks for equal protection under the laws. However, it urged the President to speak out on the issue promptly. In contrast, the editorial from the *Evening Post* expressed great skepticism that Wilson would say anything on the issue and said that only an actual statement by Wilson would dispel that doubt about his willingness to take a stand on behalf of blacks.

Frank Lyon Polk to Jean Jules Jusserand

Excellency: [Washington] August 3, 1917.

I did not fail to communicate to the President, upon its receipt, your note of the 20th ultimo, stating that Mr. Ribot, President of the Council, Minister of Foreign Affairs of the French Republic, is giving his attention to finding out how a Society of Nations could be brought into existence, and that it is his intention to convene a commission charged with the duty of examining the question, but that, before coming to any decision in that respect, the French Government would be glad to have the views of President Wilson with regard to the undertaking.[1]

Noting the intention of Mr. Ribot to assemble at some early date a commission to consider the feasibility, the form, and the objects of a Society of Nations, the President, in response to Mr. Ribot's gracious wish for an expression of his opinion, expresses the fear that such a commission, if constituted at this time, would be premature and unnecessarily introduce new subjects of discussion and perhaps of difference of view among the nations associated against Germany. The President's own idea has been that such a society of nations would of necessity be an evolution rather than a creation by formal convention. It has been his hope and expectation that the war would result in certain definite covenants and guarantees entered into by the free nations of the world for the purpose of safeguarding their own security and the general peace of the world and that in the very process of carrying these covenants into execution from time to time a machinery and practice of cooperation would naturally spring up which would in the end produce something which would in effect be a regularly constituted and employed concert of nations. To begin with a discussion of how such a concert or society should be constituted, under the presidency of which nation, with what common force and under what common command, etc., etc., would be likely to produce jealousies and difficulties which need not be faced now.

Accept, Excellency, the renewed assurances of my highest consideration.   [F. L. Polk]

CCL (SDR, RG 59, 763.72119/684, DNA).
    [1] From this point on (except for the last paragraph), Polk quotes the text of a WWT MS, which Wilson sent to the State Department on about August 1. There is a WWsh draft of this document in WP, DLC. The WWT draft is missing, but the copy in SDR, RG 59, 763.72119/684, DNA, bears the following Hw comment by Polk: "Aug 1, 1917 Ans. prepared by President FLP."

Sir Horace Plunkett to Arthur James Balfour

My dear Arthur   [Dublin] 3rd August 1917.

The matter about which I wanted to see you in London can be dealt with quite as well by correspondence. Sir Francis Hopwood[1] and I are very anxious to be kept informed of any news from the United States which throws light upon the effect the Irish question (which is now largely the Convention) may have upon Anglo-American relations. This, as you know, I regard as a matter of supreme importance to the future peace of the world.

Last night, just as I was leaving for the train, I got a telephone message from Sir William Wiseman, who had arrived from New York, that he wanted to see me. We managed to get ten minutes together at Euston, and he brought me a verbal request from President Wilson—who had assumed that I should be a member of the Convention—that I should find some way of keeping him informed of its proceedings, in which he said he would be deeply interested.

I gathered from what your Private Secretary told me on Wednesday night that the latest cables from Spring Rice indicated a decline of the extreme Sinn Feinism which had appeared in the United States, and that now the Irish question was of less urgency out there than several others.

I rather doubt this myself, but Wiseman's judgment on the point would be well worth consideration. I saw a great deal of him when I was in the States and I formed a very high opinion of him which is shared by House. I should, therefore, be very glad if you could authorise John Buchan[2] or some other member of the F.O. staff to give me the information about the Irish situation in the States which my ordinary correspondents do not send me for fear of the Censor.   Yours ever,   Horace Plunkett

TLS (A. J. Balfour Papers, FO 800/211, PRO).
    [1] Sir Francis John Stephens Hopwood, a career civil servant, at this time secretary to the Irish Convention.
    [2] At this time Director of Information for the British government.

From the Diary of Josephus Daniels

1917 Friday 3 August

The President told this: Some years ago he went to a stomach specialist Dr Janaway,[1] who said "What I am about to do, you will find very uncomfortable, but not intolerable." Tried to get doctor to talk, but he was very economical in conversation. A Princeton foot-ball player went to see Dr. J. who gave prescription. The coach could read only word & it was "strychnine." He said: "Don't take it. Dr. J. is a Yale man and he may be trying to poison you." He did unbend then. Discussed labor troubles. Case of owner of coal mine who sent men to other State. Decided to get Judge Covington[2] to go to Governors of certain Western states & urge them to see law enforced; if not, in war Federal government must find a way.

¹ Actually Francis Delafield, M.D., of New York. See Edwin A. Weinstein, *Woodrow Wilson: A Medical and Psychological Biography* (Princeton, N. J., 1981), p. 126.
² James Harry Covington, Chief Justice of the Supreme Court of the District of Columbia. There will be many subsequent documents relating to the Covington mission.

From Frank Lyon Polk, with Enclosures

My dear Mr. President: Washington August 4, 1917.

This important despatch came in from Peking this afternoon. I send it over with the answers attached. In view of the urgency, I thought something should be done at once and I felt that we were being conservative. You will notice that no reference is made to the loan from the Japanese referred to in the telegram from Reinsch. If the Japanese offer us participation it will present an interesting question.

Yours faithfully,   Frank L Polk

TLS (WP, DLC).

E N C L O S U R E   I

Peking. Aug. 3, 1917.

Strictly Confidential. The Prime Minister[1] has just informed me that the Cabinet has come to a decision to declare war against Germany and that acting President Feng[2] has been formally notified of this step and approves of it. Before the decision is carried out various preparations, arrang[e]ments, remain to be completed.

The adoption of this policy is prompted by a desire to strengthen China internationally as well as particularly the present Government against internal opposition which would probably, after the declaration of war, be treated as treasonable negligence. It is probable that parliamentary radicals of the south will resist the declaration. While they may appeal to general theory and while the party in power is strongly militarist yet specifically the case for the defunct parliament seems weak inasmuch as it was dissolved by the same authority that had reinstituted it in 1916 and a general national demand for its reinstitution is lacking. However, it is to be hoped that professions in favor of representative institutions made by the present Government will be lived up to.

General Feng upon his arrival yesterday formally requested Li[3] to resume the presidency. The latter declined. Feng therefore remains acting President for the unexpired term. The present administration represents strong elements of political, military, financial organization; political antagonisms of Tuan against Feng[,] Chin Pu Tang[4] against (?)s[5] may be alleviated by war action. But whether national union can be completely upheld against the opposition of certain provinces inclined to espouse the cause of parliament is doubtful though the Government seems to rely on war power and Allied support to accomplish this.

The Japanese have advanced yen ten millions for urgent needs of the Government; participation will be offered other members of consortium.

Urgent.

Please instruct whether you desire me to participate in conferences of Allied representatives concerning any action affecting the war. If your decision is affirmative communication would seem advisable to France whose representative[6] at present acts as dean of the Allied Ministers and who not only does not consider the United States to be an Ally but has explicitly stated to me that our note of June fourth[7] to the Chinese Government absolves him and his colleagues from any obligation to consult the views of our Government in regard to China questions.

Reinsch.

T telegram (WP, DLC).

[1] Tuan Ch'i-jui.

[2] Feng Kuo-chang.

[3] Li Yüan-hung.

[4] That is, the Progressive party, led by Liang Ch'i-ch'ao.

[5] Reinsch must have written Kuomintang, that is, the Nationalist party, to which both Tuan and Liang were opposed.

[6] Alexandre Robert Conty, who was about to be recalled at the request of the Chinese government for his alleged rudeness and undiplomatic behavior.

[7] See Sun Yat-sen to WW, June 9, 1917, n. 1, Vol. 42.

E N C L O S U R E   I I

Amlegation, Peking (China)   August 4, 1917.

Your telegram of August 3, 2 a.m. You are instructed to be guided by the policy of this government as expressed in its note of June 4 to China, but if war is declared express satisfaction of this government in the support thus given to its course. The

Department is amazed by your statement that of the attitude of the French Minister and is satisfied that it does not reflect that of his government. Nevertheless the Department does not deem it advisable at the moment for you to participate in conferences of allied ministers concerning war matters. However, should any matter arise in which they and you deem concurrent action by this government desirable you may request instructions.

Acting

E N C L O S U R E   I I I

Amembassy, Paris (France)   August 4, 1917.

American Minister at Peking in telegram just received states that the French Representative there, who is the Dean of the allied Ministers, not only does not consider the United States to be an ally but has explicitly stated to him that our note of June 4 to the Chinese Government absolves him and his colleagues from any obligation to consult the views of our government in regard to China questions. The Department does not understand this to be the attitude of the French Government as set forth in your telegram number 2190 June 17, 1917.[1] Please bring this matter to the attention of the Foreign Office.   Acting

TC telegram (WP, DLC).

[1] W. G. Sharp to RL, June 17, 1917, T telegram (SDR, RG 59, 893.00/2620, DNA). This was a translation of a communication to Sharp from the French Foreign Ministry which reaffirmed France's desire to join with the United States in urging the Chinese government to make every effort to reestablish domestic order and harmony as a necessary prelude to Chinese participation in the war against Germany. France held to this position despite the fact that Japan and Great Britain had dissociated themselves from the proposed action.

From Edward Mandell House

Dear Governor: Magnolia, Mass. August 4, 1917.

Hapgood sends a letter in which Josiah Wedgewood of London says:

"I was glad to get the lives of Lincoln and Washington. Between ourselves I think Wilson is as much the greater man than Lincoln as Lincoln was to Washington. You do turn out some wonderful specimens of the race."

You will remember Wedgewood as the man who outlined his idea of a peace settlement and which rather appealed to you at the time.[1]

Sir William Wiseman has reached London. He crossed on the

St Louis and they were shelled by a submarine for an hour on Sunday. I asked him to urge his government to send the latest inside facts concerning the submarine situation, and I also asked him to let us know about the Irish settlement.

He says that "the War Cabinet have prepared a full memorandum upon the submarine situation and will cable it to Northcliffe for your information. The memorandum states that the situation is serious, but offers suggestion for fusion measures which may solve the problem."

He has seen Plunkett, who is Chairman of the Irish Convention, and Plunkett tells him that he feels "a solution must be reached at almost any cost." He is interested to know that you are following developments with interest and sympathy. Sir Horace has promised to keep Wiseman confidentially posted.

I have a letter from Richard Washburn Child from Tokyo July 13th in which he says:

"Japan is at the parting of the ways. She must follow the spirit of our civilization or that of Germany. A sympathetic, but firm and frank attitude now will help her solve her perplexities in the right way. I fear this, though, as well as the stern realities about China are being missed by our representatives in the Far East."

Child will be back about the middle of August.

Captain Gherardi of our Navy, formerly Naval Attache at Berlin, and the most capable man we had abroad during the war, writes that, in his opinion, "The war off the enemy coast (since it is impracticable to get to the coast line) is the war which will stop the submarine, and the appliances to be used are the net, the mine, the destroyer, the trawler and, when the enemy comes out, the big ships. The British should be forced to work to big plans. I have considerable faith in some of our people who are over there if they will not let themselves be dazzled by the past reputation of the British Navy. The British are great sailors, but for planning ahead, they have as yet to make a passable reputation."   Affectionately yours, E. M. House

TLS (WP, DLC).
¹ Wedgwood's memorandum is printed as an Enclosure with EMH to WW, Dec. 29, 1916, Vol. 40.

From Edward Mandell House, with Enclosure

Dear Governor: Magnolia, Massachusetts. August 4, 1917.

Sir Charles Gordon (a Canadian and Northcliffe's right hand man)¹ took lunch with me the other day. His government has placed the question of purchasing almost wholly in his hands.

He is exceedingly anxious that this government announce its policy regarding prices and where the Allied Governments will come in. He tells me there is an immediate necessity for steel, and while his government is paying in England 2½ cents per pound, the only rate the Cunard Company could get from the U. S. Steel Corporation was 8 cents, and this was a special favor. They refused to give the British Government any quotation whatever although they had given our government a rate of 3.60.

The profits of the Steel Corporation as shown by their last statement are colossal and, unless a restraining hand is laid upon them, there will be no limit.

I am merely writing this for your information.

Affectionately yours,   E. M. House

TLS (WP, DLC).
¹ Sir Charles Blair Gordon, a Montreal industrialist, banker, and financial expert who was vice-chairman of the British War Mission to the United States.

ENCLOSURE

Frank Irving Cobb to Edward Mandell House

Dear Colonel House: New York. August 2, 1917.

You must pardon the delay in sending you a copy of the draft of the challenge to The Tageblatt. The weather is too much for me; when I finish my regular work, there is no energy left. I shall get it out for you in a day or two.

In the meantime, may I again renew my suggestion that this would be a proper occasion for the President to straighten out the censorship tangle in Washington. Privately, Creel is hopelessly discredited. Personally, I like him very much but that does not change the situation. The newspaper correspondents distrust him. They have no respect for him. They are suspicious of everything that he gives out, and, therefore, are steadily working at cross purposes with the Government. It would be much better to separate the censorship and the publicity, which can be easily done. If an army officer and navy officer are put in charge of the censorship of news, no trouble will be experienced, in my opinion.* So far as I can find out, the correspondents and the news editors are perfectly willing to rely upon the judgment of army and navy officers in these matters but, the moment Creel enters into the situation, there is trouble.

I am writing this to you in strict confidence. I haven't said anything to the President about it, but I think you ought to know it.
Sincerely yours,   Frank I. Cobb.

* Why would this not be a good solution?   E.M.H.

TCL (WP, DLC).

From Franklin Knight Lane

My dear Mr. President: Washington August 4, 1917.

In connection with the coal situation, I have thought that you might come to the conclusion that it was wise for the Government to own its own coal mines in West Virginia and have had a preliminary examination made of the New River and Pocahontas fields, from which I am sure that lands containing the character of coal which the Navy needs can be bought for approximately $100 an acre. Our people think, however, that for an immediate supply, it would be much better to purchase a property already developed.

The Government could make itself entirely independent in the matter of coal by the purchase of the Virginian Railway, which runs from Norfolk into West Virginia. This road is owned by the heirs of H. H. Rogers[1] and could, I believe, be bought at its cost or at a valuation placed upon it by the Interstate Commerce Commission. I have taken no steps to ascertain definite figures as to either of these propositions, but will be pleased to do so at any time you think it is desirable. The figures of the Interstate Commerce Commission would indicate that the Virginian railroad is already paying operating expenses and interest upon its cost.

There are still great bodies of coal lands removed from the railroad and they can be had for a much less figure than that given above.   Cordially yours,   Franklin K Lane

TLS (WP, DLC).
[1] Henry Huttleston Rogers (1840-1909), a leading figure in the Standard Oil Co., the United States Steel Corp., Edward H. Harriman's railroad operations, and in numerous other financial and industrial enterprises. The Virginian Railway was the last of his ventures and was unusual in that it was financed solely out of his own funds.

From Charles Lee Swem, with Enclosure

Mr. President: [The White House, c. Aug. 4, 1917]

I saw the Secretary of Labor regarding the attached telegram.

The Secretary asks me to say that he has determined upon two mediators to send to Alabama to see what can be done. He has also taken the matter up with the Coal Production Committee. He knows of nothing further that can be done in the situation at the present time.

If it becomes apparent that a shut-down of the mines in Alabama is likely to ensue, the Secretary will take up the matter further with the President. C. L. Swem

TLS (WP, DLC).

ENCLOSURE

Indianapolis, Indiana, August 4, 1917.

Two hundred sixty six delegates in convention assembled in Birmingham, Alabama, representing twenty two thousand six hundred seventy eight members, United Mine Workers of America of State of Alabama, appeal to Government to assist in bringing about conference with coal operators of that State for the purpose of affecting satisfactory settlement of existing differences. Operators so far have refused to meet miners representatives. Convention decided that unless operators agreed to discuss differences on or before August fifteenth the miners of the entire State of Alabama will cease work on August twentieth. International Organization trusts you will use your good offices to bring about joint conference between miners and operators in Alabama and thus prevent threatened strike.

Wm. Green, Secretary Treasurer,
John H. White, President,
Frank J. Hayes, Vice President,
United Mine Workers of America.

T telegram (WP, DLC).

From John Sharp Williams

Personal

My Dear Mr. President: [Washington] August 4, 1917.

I would not have run for the Senate this last time if I had had any real opposition of a respectable character; but I could not very well refuse to take the place when Mississippi had nominated and elected me unanimously. That would have looked like slapping my mother in the face when she offered to kiss me.

My mind was made up from the 3d of August 1915, when I wrote you to that effect from Cedar Grove Plantation that I did not have that amount of political influence that would justify a man in remaining in public life.[1] When a man can't help his friends it is time he ceased asking them to help him.

That, however, was never my main reason for retiring: I am tired of it; am getting too old to enjoy debating and quarreling. I have a perfect horror of "lagging superfluous upon the stage." I will never lose interest in the study and attempted solution of National and International questions; but I will be 68 years old at the end of my term to which I have just been elected. Two great Mississippians—Genl. Walthall and George, and one above the average, as Senators go,—Money,[2]—all three—set the example of retiring in time—voluntarily,—when there was no sacrifice of public interests and when everybody knew that each one of them could be reelected without opposition as I can be.

One of the blessed good things about a democracy is that a nation in which it prevails needs nobody so badly that his rerirement [retirement] is "an irreparable loss."

Many pleasant things have occurred in my public service and among them nothing pleasanter than the recollection of the fact that I have tried to be of loyal service to you while you were trying to be of loyal service to the United States, and to the cause of Freedom and Democracy and representative institutions throughout the world.

I am, with every expression of regard,

Very truly yours,   John Sharp Williams

TLS (WP, DLC).
[1] See WW to J. S. Williams, Aug. 6, 1915, Vol. 34.
[2] Edward Cary Walthall, James Zachariah George, and Hernando De Soto Money.

From the British Embassy, with Enclosure

Washington August 5, 1917.

Annexed is a telegram from the British Ambassador at Petrograd[1] making certain suggestions as to the transport problem in Russia. Mr. Balfour's personal opinion is that the importance of this problem cannot be exaggerated and that it is extremely improbable that the Russians will be able to solve it without foreign assistance. There are however two main difficulties. The first is diplomatic. It will be very difficult to induce the Russian Government to agree to accept the foreign control which foreign help necessarily involves if it is to be effective. The second difficulty is practical. To afford the necessary assistance railway experts are required, rolling stock and locomotives as well as skilled workmen. The European Allies could probably provide a certain number of experts in railway management but they have no locomotives rolling stock or skilled workmen to spare. They cannot provide for their own war needs in railway material and artisans. For instance, Great Britain finds it very difficult at present to carry on at home the increased traffic necessitated by the war and has had to provide for France rails rolling stock engines and skilled labour in addition to her own requirements at home.

Under these circumstances Mr. Balfour thinks that the United States can find a great field for war work of the highest importance without interfering with those efforts which they are now making in many other directions.

The course suggested by the British Ambassador is that the Allies should offer joint assistance. But if this scheme is carried out the procedure will be slow and probably inefficient if it takes the form of an attempt to solve the Russian transport question made collectively by England, the United States, France and Italy. The United States has already given Russia assistance of the greatest value in the shape of engines, rolling stock and railway experts. If America were to pursue this policy of helping Russia to reorganise her transport system conceived on the broadest lines it is probable that the effect on the future of the war would be of transcendent importance. There can be no doubt as to the magnitude of the difficulties to be encountered. In any case they could only be surmounted gradually. If however the task is to be accomplished at all the United States is the country which can perform it. Its importance would certainly justify a great effort. Any diplomatic assistance which is in our power would of course be freely given. Mr. Balfour believes that a certain number of officers accustomed to military railway work could be supplied from Great Britain and also a limited number of civilians trained in the ordinary work of railway administration. Great Britain would be glad to place under American direction such officers and civilians should their services be desired.

T MS (WP, DLC).
¹ That is, Sir George William Buchanan.

August 5, 1917.

The British Ambassador in Petrograd saw the Russian Minister for Foreign Affairs[1] on August 1 and found him somewhat more despondent as to the state of affairs on the fighting line in Roumania. He feared that it might be necessary to evacuate at all events a portion of Moldavia, though he again promised that the Russian armies would do all in their power to check the Germans on that front.

He further informed Sir G. Buchanan that the Ministry would proceed to Moscow on August 4 in order to be present at a large political meeting which was to be held on August 5, & that three of the Moscow school of politicians appeared to be inclined to join the Ministry but beyond this he had no precise news concerning the political crisis. But, apart from this question altogether, there are such vast difficulties of every kind besetting the Russian Government that it would be vain to look to them for any help in the military way, in the course of the current year. When the Ambassador told the Minister that this was the case, and that the real fact was that the Russian army would be quite unable to take any offensive action before the early part of 1918, the latter could not but admit that this was true.

Sir G. Buchanan is entirely at a loss to see how the Russian army is to be kept in existence, & to be properly supplied, especially with winter clothing which he understands is lacking in a very great degree, though he is of opinion that with strict discipline it might be remodelled and brought into a condition fit for resuming the offensive well before the end of the present year. It is his opinion, and he has several times mentioned it to the Foreign Minister, that the right course to pursue is to establish compulsory military service, to recall as many troops as possible to work behind the lines, and to leave at the front only that number as is absolutely indispensable for the purpose of maintaining the defensive. He considers that the real reason underlying the whole of the disastrous situation is the deplorable state into which the means of transportation have fallen. For instance when Kerensky[2] returned to Petrograd from the front, the train broke down four times and fresh engines had to be procured. The tracks, the engines and the rolling stock are all alike used up: the Russian Government with its own resources will never be able to reestablish them, and the aid which the United States Government have agreed to give, will fall far short of what is necessary. The Russian Government have great hopes of the result of their action in placing the railroads under a purely military organization: this undoubtedly is a wise measure but it is not adequate, alone, to meet the situation. Suitable workshops are necessary, and skilled labour for repair work, but it is very questionable whether this latter can be found in large enough numbers, and it is equally doubtful whether there are any men in the Ministry of Communications who have the ability to organize on a large enough scale.

The only suggestion which the Ambassador has to offer is that the Entente Powers should succour the Russian Government by the despatch of a considerable body of men skilled in every department of railroad administration together with a number of efficient employees. He is, however, uncertain to what degree this idea would be welcome to the Russians, whilst it would be necessary for the Allies, in the event of their being prepared to put it forward, to define accurately the lines of the work which was to be taken in hand. A not unsuitable point of contact might perhaps be found in the communication recently sent to the British Bondholders: the reply might contain the suggestion of helping in the task of setting the railroads anew in good order.

Hw MS (WP, DLC).
  1 That is, Mikhail Ivanovich Tereshchenko.
  2 Prime Minister since July 21.

From James Duval Phelan

My dear Mr. President: [Washington] August 6, 1917.

Would it not consolidate the war sentiment and give encouragement to a large number of our fellow citizens to nominate Theodore Roosevelt for a Brigadier Generalship? He has all his sons in action, and it may react on the Administration if he is not given an opportunity to serve. He will be subordinate to the Major Generals in the field, and, I do not believe in this crisis, can be a disturbing element.

                              Respectfully,   James D Phelan

This is wholly spontaneous.

TLS (WP, DLC).

From J. L. Donnelly and Thomas A. French

Clifton, Ariz., Aug. 6, 1917.

The Sixth Annual Convention of the Arizona State Federation of Labor now in session, desires to know if you intend to act in restoring law and order in Cochise County, Arizona, and return to their homes the deported men of Bisbee. Are we to assume that Phelps Dodge interests are superior to the principles of democracy. We await an answer, in convention at Clifton, Arizona. By order of Arizona, State Federation Labor, in convention assembled.   J. L. Donnelly, President,
Thos. A. French,   Secretary.

T telegram (WP, DLC).

From Josephus Daniels

Dear Mr. President: Washington. Aug. 6, 1917.

In the absence of the Secretary of War I will come to the White House with the War Industries Board at three o'clock this afternoon. After your bugle blast, the Committee of the Steel and Iron Institute agreed that all their product should be controlled by the Government and prices should be the same to the allies as to our Government. They now claim that they did not so understand it and one of the concerns is quoting shipplate to Great Britain at 8 cents. We are paying .0290. It seems to me that the first thing for the War Industries Board to do is to take this up. The steel companies should give fair prices to all or we should take them over. They are playing for delay and making contracts at high prices.   Sincerely,   Josephus Daniels

ALS (WP, DLC).

From Albert Sidney Burleson

My dear Mr. President: Washington, D. C. August 6, 1917.

I desire to acknowledge the receipt of your favor of the 3rd instant, transmitting a letter written by G. H. Markquard, Jr., of St. Louis, in behalf of Otto Sassmann, who was removed for disloyalty.[1]

For your information I beg to say that Sassmann was removed on the testimony of several clerks whom the Superintendent of the Railway Mail Service[2] certifies to the Department as being "persons known to me to be entirely trustworthy and reliable and who are at all times reluctant to cause any trouble to their fellows that is unwarranted."

According to the evidence before the Department, just prior to the declaration of war, Sassmann said he "would not shoot a German soldier," that he "would shoot an American officer first." This was said to be in reply to a question whether he would enlist in the event of war, and if he would not what he would do in the event he were drafted. Subsequently to the war, according to the evidence furnished, he said to a clerk who had asked him whether he would loan him money if he got an appointment into the officers' reserve camp, Sassmann replied, "I wouldn't lend you a dam'd cent if you had to go to Germany to fight, but if they came over here I would lend you every cent I had. I don't believe we are right in going over there to fight them." The testimony of another clerk was that on another occasion Sassmann said he would not fight against the German Government.

Still another clerk testified that, subsequent to the declaration of war by the United States Government, and while he was talking to a friend at the supper table on the subject of the war and the high cost of living, Sassmann "spoke up and said the United States was working for the Allies—God damn the Allies! To hell with them is my sentiments!"

Superintendent MacFarland of the Railway Mail Service, who is in charge of the Division, and has long enjoyed the reputation of being a cautious and conservative Superintendent, states, in his recommendation for the removal of Clerk Sassmann:

"I further believe that clerk Sassmann is a dangerous man: also that his traitorous expressions represent his earnest sentiments. He is sullen, morose and high-tempered and I feel that the secret service authorities should be apprised of his attitude. However, I shall do nothing to that end without your instructions."   Sincerely yours,   A. S. Burleson

TLS (WP, DLC).
    [1] See WW to L. C. Dyer, Aug. 1, 1917, n. 1. Wilson's letter of August 3 is missing.
    [2] William Ira Denning.

From Cecil Arthur Spring Rice, with Enclosure

Dear Mr President   Washington 6 Aug 1917

I enclose a memorandum drawn up by the War Cabinet for your personal information. It gives all available facts & figures as to the submarine situation and points out that the part which your government can play in dealing with the menace is absolutely vital to the successful prosecution of the war. I remain; with the deepest respect

Your most obedient humble servant   Cecil Spring Rice

ALS (WP, DLC).

ENCLOSURE

MEMORANDUM

The accompanying memorandum on the submarine situation has been specially prepared and approved by the War Cabinet. It is drawn up for the President's personal information. It is of great importance that no part of it should be made public, and it must be treated as strictly confidential.

Washington August 5, 1917.

T MS (WP, DLC).

[London] 4 August 1917.

SECRET. My telegram personal and secret of today.

Memorandum on submarine situation.

True index to success or failure of submarine campaign in future will be balance between merchant vessels sunk and merchant vessels put into commission for measures we have taken for shortening voyages better loading quicker turning round use of interned German shipping diversion of allied and neutral ships from coastal or non-war traffic & other methods of making improved use of existing resources which have enabled us to keep up tonnage entrances since February despite losses will have soon had their full effect. Effect of submarine in restricting sea borne supplies of allies will be then accurately shown by relative figures of loss and gain. Figures given in gross since February are as follows.

1917 February. British.

313,000. Allied and neutral 219,000. Total 532,000.

March	342,000.	346,000.	588,000.
April	541,000.	324,000.	865,000.
May	352,000.	242,000.	594,000.
June	396,000.	258,000.	653,000.
July	(—on basis of first 29 days July)		
	321,000	(on basis of losses February to June)	
		268,000	579,000.
Total	2,264,000	1,547,000	3,811,000

In addition there are a number of vessels damaged by torpedo or mine. For first six months of 1917 figures were as follows

1917. First three months. British. Allied and Neutral.

194,000.

154,000.

348,000.

Second three months   264,000.   158,000.   422,000.

Of these damaged ships about 50% may be considered as permanently out of commission for the duration of the war owing to places in which they are beached etc. Following tables give actual losses on basis of experience first six months unrestricted submarine campaign.

On basis of February-July 1917. Per month.
British 380,000.

per annum		per month	per annum
4,600,000.	Allied	260,000.	3,100,000
			and neutral.

	per month	per annum	
Totals	640,000.	7,700,000.	On basis of

May June July 1917.   Per month 360,000.   Per annum 4,300,000.

250,000.   3,000,000.

610,000.   7,300,000.

Please see annexed table

Looking at the position as a whole and taking into account exceptional character of April figures and Irrevocable loss from ships damaged but not sunk average total monthly losses cannot at present be taken at less than 650,000 tons a month of which 500,000 a month is ocean going tonnage.

When we come to consider whether this rate of loss is likely to rise or fall in future factors are so numerous and so incalculable that any estimate must be more or less of a guess. Submarine war is a contest in which both sides are continually improving their weapons and their methods. Results therefore are bound to fluctuate and relative success and failure depend on continuous energy and resource not merely upon sea but in building and invention on land.

But certain broad facts begin to stand out. It has never been found practicable to prevent German submarines from using many points of entry into the North sea nor, as experience in channel and Dardanelles has shown, has it been possible to close exits there-from though passage is being made steadily more dangerous. So long as this remains the case enemy submarines will not be deprived of power of successful offence. But there are now nearly 3,000 vessels whose sole duty it is to protect merchant shipping from loss by direct attack or strewing of mines. Our operations have already forced them to rely almost entirely on submerged attack by torpedo but how effective this wholly hidden attack can be is seen from the fact that during April and May and June 75% of the merchantmen sunk did not see either submarine or periscope before being struck. Further there is no doubt that German submarine resources are increasing. Best opinion considers they complete two to three submarines a week. It is quite impossible to frame any accurate estimate of their losses. Results of engagements are most difficult to judge certainties being but a fraction of probabilities and probabilities of the possibilities and possibilities of the encounters. Estimates of their losses from other sources than direct attack are obviously even less trustworthy But the conclusion arrived at is that the number of sinkings will not equal the number of new submarines turned out.

On the other hand methods and instruments for hampering movements of submarines and for attacking them when detected are steadily increasing. It is extremely likely that moral[e] of German submarine service is declining under the continuous and increasing strain of the anti-submarine attack. As regards protection of merchant vessels that the submarines have now to rely very largely on submerged attack by depriving them of their gun armament has diminished their efficiency and shortened period for which they can remain at sea. Extension of convoy system as more patrols and escort vessels become available will also it is hoped make successful attack more difficult. Winter season ought also to have some effect. Good results have also followed from the special courses for training merchant captains how to evade submarines and to handle their ships in the event of an attack. As many Captains and mates as possible are being put through these courses. As regards speed it is considered highly desirable that a sea-going speed of at least 13 knots should be attained in all new construction in order that there may be no doubt that an enemy submarine cannot when submerged overhaul surface craft and thereby use favourable pos[i]tion for attack. It must be borne in mind that the submerged provisional speed of the new submarines is constantly increasing and it may be taken that at present they obtain a submerged speed of between 11 and 12 knots.

To sum up it is obviously impossible to form anything approaching a trustworthy forecast of the future but so far as an estimate is of value as a general guide it is estimated that

On basis of Feb–July 1917.

	per month	per annum
British	380,000	4,600,000
Allied and neutral	260,000	3,100,000
Totals	640,000	7,700,000

On the basis of May, June, July, 1917

	per month	per annum
British	360,000	4,300,000
Allied and neutral	250,000	3,000,000
Totals	610,000	7,300,000

CC telegram (WP, DLC).

From Frank Lyon Polk, with Enclosure

PERSONAL and CONFIDENTIAL

My dear Mr. President: Washington August 6, 1917.

I take the liberty of forwarding to you herewith the translation of the text of a code message from Edmundo Martinez[1] to General Carranza transmitted for him by Ambassador Bonillas, as I believe you will be interested in reading his account of his interview[2] with you.

I understand that Martinez' friends have been talking of the interview, and the impression is being given that Martinez, on account of his alleged close relation with Carranza, is the man with whom this Department should deal.

Yours faithfully,   Frank L Polk

TLS (WP, DLC).
[1] See the index references to him in Vol. 34 of this series.
[2] At the White House on July 18.

ENCLOSURE

CONFIDENTIAL MEMORANDUM

August 4, 1917

SUBJECT: Cipher message dated July 19, 1917,
from Bonillas, Washington, D. C., to
Venustiano Carranza, Mexico City.

Translation of Spanish decipherment.

I have the honor to transmit to you the following telegram (ninety-two): President Wilson wishes me to recount to you the interview he honored me with when he received me. As I told you in Mexico I touched on all the points at interest. President Wilson replied by saying that he holds you in high esteem and that he hopes that you may have the best of results from your government. To prove his sincerity, he promises to lift the embargo on arms, and if you desire it, he will assist in the coining of money. You should present a claim against the journalist Hearst and General Otis of California.[1] He has assured me that he will put into effect a prompt and effective remedy for the evil doings of these gentlemen. He says that you should not be concerned with the fact that they know it, as that will have no effect on him politically, for they display hostility and secret animosity. He desires at the same time to bring about closer relations with you personally, as well as with the government, and is desirous of an understanding. He declares himself disposed to assist you in everything possible, and to assure you of his admiration. He has assured me on his word of honor that no one could ever change the opinion he has of you. He has spoken much of our ambassador, Mr. Bonillas, and of his effective labors here. He frequently invites him to call on him, and to accompany me. He hopes you will extend him your esteem. I send you details by letter. He anticipates a disposition favoring the raising of the sum you desire. I salute you and the family. Affectionately.

Edmundo Martinez.

TC telegram (photostat in RSB Coll., DLC).
    [1] Harrison Gray Otis, publisher of the *Los Angeles Times*. He had died on July 30.

William Graves Sharp to Jules Martin Cambon

Mr. Ambassador,   Paris, August 6th, 1917.

I am charged by the President to express his thanks for your kindness in submitting the questions which were contained in your Note of the 21st ultimo, and to acquaint you with the following replies: . . .[1]

A number of errors in the transmission of the telegram from Washington, which forms the subject of this letter, have made it impossible, in several instances, to present accurately, pending receipt of corrections, the President's views.

I have the honor to be, Mr. Ambassador, with expressions of my high esteem,   Yours very sincerely,   Wm. G. Sharp

TLS (Guerre 1914-1918, États-Unis, Vol. 508, pp. 135-36, FFM-Ar).
    [1] See W. G. Sharp to J. M. Cambon, Aug. 7, 1917.

From the Diary of Josephus Daniels

August Monday 6 1917

Called with War Industries Board to see the President and discussed their duties. He said it had been reported to him the steel trust had agreed to sell to the allies & our country at the same price & that they now were trying to make a dif price. In fact America furnishes the money for allies who need it just now more than we do & it should be at the same price.

To Newton Diehl Baker, with Enclosure

My dear Mr. Secretary: The White House 7 August, 1917

Here is the letter to the soldiers. I hope that you will approve of the change of address with which it opens.

Cordially and faithfully yours,   Woodrow Wilson

TLS (N. D. Baker Papers, DLC).

E N C L O S U R E

To the Soldiers of the National Army:

The White House 7 August, 1917

You are undertaking a great duty. The heart of the whole country is with you. Everything that you do will be watched with the deepest interest and with the deepest solicitude not only by those who are near and dear to you, but by the whole nation besides. For this great war draws us all closer together, makes us all comrades and brothers, as all true Americans felt themselves to be when we first made good our national independence. The eyes of all the world will be upon you, because you are in some special sense the soldiers of freedom. Let it be your pride, therefore, to show all men everywhere not only what good soldiers you are, but also what good men you are, keeping yourselves fit and straight in everything and pure and clean through and through. Let us set for ourselves a standard so high that it will be a glory to live up to it and then let us live up to it and add a new laurel to the crown of America. My affectionate confidence goes with you in every battle and every test. God keep and guide you!

Woodrow Wilson.[1]

TL (Letterpress Books, WP, DLC).
[1] This statement appeared in the *Official Bulletin*, I (Sept. 4, 1917), 1.

To Frank Lyon Polk

My dear Mr. Counsellor: The White House 7 August, 1917

This is an amazing document. I need not tell you that Mr. Martinez's account of the interview is wrong in almost every particular. I did not say that I held Mr. Carranza in high esteem, though, of course, I did say that he had our confidence and that I would wish for the best results from his administration. I did not promise to lift the embargo on arms or to assist in the coinage of money, though I did express the hope that both these things could be done. I remember expressing my opinion very frankly and emphatically about Hearst, but I of course did not promise to "put into effect a prompt and effective remedy for the evil doings" of Hearst or anybody else. The sentence "He has assured me on his word of honor that no one could ever change the opinion he has of you" is ridiculous. I do not remember mentioning Mr. Bonillas at all, and as you know, I do not frequently invite him to call and have never invited Mr. Martinez to accompany him.

I have taken the liberty of having a copy of this extraordinary document struck off and am going to send it to Mr. Gompers, who brought Martinez to see me.

Faithfully yours,   Woodrow Wilson

TLS (F. L. Polk Papers, CtY).

To Albert Sidney Burleson, with Enclosure

My dear Burleson: The White House 7 August, 1917

Pearson's has been represented to me as being one of the magazines most fair to the administration. I cannot imagine who has been doing what Mr. Ricker[1] speaks of, but I am sure you will wish to have the matter investigated.

Faithfully yours,   Woodrow Wilson

TLS (A. S. Burleson Papers, DLC).
[1] Allen W. Ricker, publisher of *Pearson's Magazine*.

E N C L O S U R E

From Allen W. Ricker

Mr. President: New York August 3rd, 1917.

I wish to call your attention to the fact that during the last sixty days my personal mail has been interfered with by the Post Office Department. Letters addressed to me from the People's Council, while I was on a trip in the west, were not delivered at all, and in one specific case a letter reached my address two weeks after it was mailed from New York City. Letters have come to PEARSON'S MAGAZINE bearing evidence of the fact that they have been unsealed, contents read and the letters resealed. The United States mails have become so uncertain that I have had to resort to sending my regular business mail in plain envelopes with the hope that in this way they might pass through the mails undisturbed.

I wish to protest to you as the responsible head of the Government against this illegal interference with my mail. I can think of nothing worse than a secret censorship. I would much prefer to have every piece of mail matter sent out from this office openly examined by a Government Agent and either approved or disapproved, than to have to submit to a secret, stealthy and sneaking censorship.

I want to assure you that I am a part of no secret cabal or intrigue against the Government of the United States. What I do and what I say I am more than willing to do or say in the open.

I cannot believe that you approve this policy of the Post Office Department. Surely you must understand the ultimate effect on a democratic people of interference with rights which they have always regarded as sacred. A political graveyard is being prepared in the public mind for a long list of men holding office in Washington.   Very truly yours,   A. W. Ricker

TLS (WP, DLC).

To Albert Sidney Burleson, with Enclosure

My dear Burleson: [The White House] 7 August, 1917

I don't like even to acknowledge messages like the enclosed without first sending you a copy. I don't even know what the People's Council of America is. Perhaps you do.

Always   Faithfully yours,   Woodrow Wilson

TLS (Letterpress Books, WP, DLC).

ENCLOSURE

Dear Mr. President: Philadelphia, Pa., Aug. 4, 1917.

The Philadelphia branch of the People's Council of America wishes to register its strongest protest against the assaults on a free press that have been committed by officials of the Post Office Department in defiant violation of the principles on which our republic was founded. Newspapers have been barred from the mails in this and other cities whose only known offense is that of daring to criticize the policies of the government and to demand redress of grievances as provided by the constitution. As if ashamed of their acts and afraid to justify them in public, the Post Office officials of whom we complain, have sought in every way to conceal their offense from public knowledge and have refused either to give notice that the newspapers has [have] been barred from the mails or to explain why they had been barred. This autocratic policy insults the memory of our revolutionary forefathers, tramples under foot the supposed guarantees of liberty which they bequeathed us, and strikes at the root of that democracy for which American youths have been conscripted to fight and die in foreign lands. As journalists and American citizens, we members of the People's Council of America, assembled in regular meeting, appeal to you to make the United States safe for democracy by breaking the hold of unAmerican bureaucrats on the threat of America's press.

W. I. Irvine, Paul Hanna,
Publicity committee.[1]

T telegram (WP, DLC).
[1] Irvine cannot be identified. Paul Hanna was a journalist of radical persuasion who was soon to become the Washington correspondent of the *New York Call*, a Socialist daily.

To Samuel Gompers

Personal and Confidential.

My dear Mr. Gompers: The White House 7 August, 1917

I have been both surprised and chagrined at receiving the enclosed. I must beg that you will receive it in entire confidence, but I must say I am not a little chagrined that Mr. Martinez should have given so distorted an account of my interview with him. Having been yourself present, you can see how far he has departed from the literal facts. Is not this an interesting instance of misplaced confidence in Mr. Martinez?

Cordially and sincerely yours,   Woodrow Wilson

TLS (S. Gompers Corr., AFL-CIO-Ar).

To Robert Lansing, with Enclosure

Personal and Confidential.

My dear Mr. Secretary: The White House 7 August, 1917

I dare say you have already acted upon the enclosed, but I take the liberty of suggesting that Mr. Fletcher's suggestion made in this telegram be complied with.

In haste

Cordially and faithfully yours,   Woodrow Wilson

TLS (SDR, RG 59, 812.00/21183½, DNA).

E N C L O S U R E

Mexico City. Aug. 2, 1917.

352. Confidential.

In my interview with the President this morning he informed me that he had received offers from two bankers to lend him the money recently authorized by the Congress to be borrowed, see Embassy's telegrams 293, 294 and 303, and that he believed satisfactory terms could be made if the United States Government did not veto such a loan. I explained to him the interest which our Government has at present in the matter of foreign loans placed in our markets, but stated that I did not believe there was any disposition on the part of the United States Government to place any obstacles in the way of Mexico securing financial assistance. I suggest that I be authorized to say to President Carranza that the United States Government will not oppose his borrowing, if he can in our market, up to the amount authorized by his Congress. I think it is important for me to be able to say this now, as there is some danger that the bankers, not finding the business attractive, may seek to place the responsibility for failure of the negotiations upon our Government. Personally I do not believe he can secure loan from private sources but he intends to try and it is important that he should know that our Government does not oppose his effort so that if he fails he will know the real reason.   Fletcher.[1]

T telegram (SDR, RG 59, 812.51/312, DNA).

[1] Lansing replied to Fletcher as follows: "You may state to General Carranza that this government will not veto loan from the bankers of the United States to the Mexican Government. It would be well, however, in discussing the matter with him to suggest as your opinion that the chances of the Mexican Government obtaining such a loan from any bankers are slight unless they are prepared to give some guaranty in regard to general financial reforms and recognition of valid vested interests, and also that there should be some distinct

understanding that the money would be paid to Mexico in installments." RL to H. P. Fletcher, Aug. 8, 1917, T telegram (SDR, RG 59, 812.51/312, DNA). The reader will note that Lansing added, apparently on his own authority, the portion beginning "It would be well, however."

To William Gibbs McAdoo

My dear Mr. Secretary: The White House 7 August, 1917

I have examined the enclosed papers[1] very carefully and take pleasure in returning them with my entire approval.

Faithfully yours,   Woodrow Wilson

TLS (W. G. McAdoo Papers, DLC).
[1] WGM to WW, July 31, 1917, TLS; two "Exhibits" enclosed in McAdoo's letter, T MS; E. F. Sweet to L. S. Rowe, July 30, 1917, TLS; a summary of Sweet's letter, T MS; and J. W. Mack, "Comments on Mr. Sweet's letter," T MS, all in the W. G. McAdoo Papers, DLC. McAdoo's letter described in some detail the proposed plan of war-risk insurance for persons serving in the armed forces of the United States, which McAdoo was about to submit to Congress. Sweet's letter and Mack's "Comments" dealt with specific controversial details of the plan. For a similar summary of the features of the insurance plan, see William G. McAdoo, *Crowded Years: The Reminiscences of William G. McAdoo* (Boston and New York, 1931), pp. 428-32.

To André Tardieu

[The White House]

My dear Mr. Commissioner: 7 August, 1917

May I not thank you for your gracious letter of the third of August and say how gratified I am that it has been possible for the Shipping Board to make the arrangements you desired about transportation?

Cordially and sincerely yours,   Woodrow Wilson

TLS (Letterpress Books, WP, DLC).

To Franklin Knight Lane

My dear Mr. Secretary: [The White House] 7 August, 1917

Thank you for your letter of the fourth about the coal properties in West Virginia. I dare say it would require legislation to carry out the policy. I wonder whether in your judgment such legislation would have a chance of passing?

In haste   Faithfully yours,   Woodrow Wilson

P.S. I have had some further doubts about Strong's appointment[1] and have been holding it up to think about it a little further.

TLS (Letterpress Books, WP, DLC).

¹ John Franklin Alexander Strong, whose reappointment as territorial governor of Alaska was under consideration at this time. As it turned out, Wilson did not reappoint him. See Keith W. Olson, *Biography of a Progressive: Franklin K. Lane, 1864-1921* (Westport, Conn., 1979), pp. 81-83.

To William Dennison Stephens

[The White House]
My dear Governor Stephens: 7 August, 1917

The bearer of this letter is Judge J. Harry Covington, the Chief Justice of the Supreme Court of the District of Columbia, whom I have taken the liberty of sending to you as my personal representative to consult with you with the utmost freedom and in the most confidential way regarding the labor situation in your state and the means to be employed, either by the State Government or the Federal Government, to produce the greatest possible degree of order and efficiency in this critical time when every laborer counts.

I am sure that after you know Judge Covington he will need no commendation from me. I need only say that he has my entire confidence and that I am glad to call him my personal friend.

Cordially and sincerely yours,   Woodrow Wilson

TLS (Letterpress Books, WP, DLC).

To Allen W. Ricker

My dear Mr. Ricker: [The White House] 7 August, 1917

Your letter of August third calls my attention to a very serious matter and I shall, of course, take pleasure in looking into it at once.   Sincerely yours,   Woodrow Wilson

TLS (Letterpress Books, WP, DLC).

Frank Lyon Polk to Joseph Patrick Tumulty, with Enclosure

My dear Mr. Secretary: [Washington] August 7, 1917.

Yesterday I gave the President a despatch from Mr. Balfour on the railroad situation in Russia with a confidential report from the British Ambassador in Petrograd. Today the attached supplementary report from the Ambassador in Petrograd was sent the Department by the British Embassy.

The President might care to read this and put it with the other papers which I suppose eventually will be sent to the Council of National Defense. Frank L. Polk

TLS (WP, DLC).

E N C L O S U R E

August 6, 1917.

H. M. Ambassador in Petrograd has learnt, since sending his previous messages, that the Russian Government requested the commission of Railroad experts sent by the United States Government to despatch 100 skilled men to supervise repair work, as well as eighty five traffic managers to introduce American methods on a very large section of the railways in Siberia.

The state of affairs is serious: during the first half of the present year the number of cars loaded has diminished by nearly three quarters of a million from the corresponding period in last year: the number of engines under repair is increasing by two per cent per week: political meetings are so much in vogue that from the repair shops alone 6000 men are present continually at them, neglecting their proper tasks.

Sir G. Buchanan considers that by no method could the difficulty be more easily solved than if, with the approval of the Russian Government, the U. S. Government were to undertake the entire task of repairing the rolling stock and of establishing on a fresh basis the administration of the traffic. If this is impossible, the only other means would be to split up the Russian railroads into sections of which each one would be taken in hand by one of the Allies. The Ambassador understands that a conference on transport questions is being held in Paris, and he suggests that this body might discuss the problem of the most appropriate manner in which to reorganize the Russian railroads, and, particularly, to ensure the satisfactory operations of the railroad running to the Murman coast during the coming winter.

Hw MS (WP, DLC).

William Graves Sharp to Jules Martin Cambon

Dear Mr. Ambassador, Paris, August 7th 1917

Referring to the communication which I had the honor to place in your hands yesterday afternoon, relative to certain questions enumerated in your note of the 21st ultimo, I beg to quote again the answers to those questions, being now able to give you the full text after receipt of corrections of the telegram containing these answers:[1]

"1. If the Russian Government is to be considered in complete control of the domestic situation or perhaps to have sufficient control to allow us to assume that its cooperative action could be relied upon and if it should propose a conference with an aim to formulate in common the objects of the war against Germany, the President does not see how such a suggestion could be wisely rejected. The democratic feeling of the period is demanding more and more audibly and more and more insistently that some sort of a statement be made by the Allied Governments which will give the unmistakable assurance that aggrandizement is not the object of this war but that on the contrary it is the freedom of the peoples and the lasting security of the independent units into which they have formed themselves against every form of aggression whether by physical force or exclusive and oppressive economic arrangements. It is the hope of the President that this issue can be squarely and candidly met.

2. The President believes that if only the Austrian people could be definitely satisfied upon these points the present movement in Austria looking towards a peace would become practically irresistible. As to the acceptance or rejection of any particular offers on the part of Austria or of any overtures from her, that would naturally have to depend upon their form and their apparent purpose.

3. As to agreements relative to Asia Minor, the President feels that it would be at present an exceedingly difficult task to reconcile the people of the United States or the opinion of the world in general to the conclusion of peace, with any terms that would mean arrangements in that part of Asia looking towards the convenience or benefit of any particular nation or nations rather than merely for the benefit and protection of the peoples there upon the same footing as peoples in any other part of the world. The sentiment of the entire world in which we all share is aggressively democratic and we all wish to go out and meet it more than half way.

4. The Department of War, the President is sure, will be glad to give an answer to this question at the earliest possible

moment. It is likely that such a reply will be communicated to the French Government through General Pershing.

5. The President hopes that the Governments of France and her Allies will find it practicable and possible at an early date to arrange for such a common agency as was suggested by the Treasury Department with a view to determining from time to time how the allotments from the sums loaned to them by the United States Government shall be made. This seems to the President to be a pressing necessity."

I have the honor to be, Mr. Ambassador, with expressions of my high esteem,

Yours very sincerely,   Wm. G. Sharp.

TLS (Guerre 1914-1918, États-Unis, Vol. 508, pp. 145-46, FFM-Ar).
[1] There is a WWsh draft of these answers in WP, DLC. The WWT draft has not survived, undoubtedly because Wilson burned it; and there is no copy of the telegram from Polk to Sharp or of Sharp to Cambon in the State Department files. Wilson conferred with Polk at 4:15 P.M. on August 6 in the White House. He probably gave Polk his WWT draft then and asked him to return it to him and to make no copy.
We know that Wilson had completed his WWT draft by August 1. Polk, in a "PERSONAL and strictly CONFIDENTIAL" letter to Baker, said that Wilson had received a dispatch from Sharp stating that the Foreign Ministry was eager to obtain the President's views on certain subjects and had submitted five questions; that three of the questions were "diplomatic," one was "financial," and one, the fourth, "had to do with military matters." Polk then repeated the fourth question and Wilson's reply. F. L. Polk to NDB, Aug. 1, 1917, TL (N. D. Baker Papers, DLC).

From the Diary of Josephus Daniels

1917 Tuesday 7 August

Cabinet—Furnishing engines & men to Russia. Depended upon money. Very difficult to get statement of exact & most pressing needs. Rus Am "Please let us have $165 mill dollars. If this is not done it will cause misunderstanding." No particulars. Must have detailed list & secure treasury loan before can determine what can be advanced. English Ambassador wrote to WW gloomily about rr's in Russia, but President did not think he knew much about it. . . .

At Cabinet—Burleson wanted something done with Tom Watson whose articles against the draft were printed in Socialist papers.[1] "We cannot go after all the DFs[2] They know Tom Watson is a fool. We have better things to do[."]

[1] Watson, in his weekly periodical, *The Jeffersonian*, had been carrying on a campaign against conscription and had also been encouraging resistance to enlistment of troops for foreign service. See C. Vann Woodward, *Tom Watson: Agrarian Rebel* (New York, 1938), pp. 455-58.
[2] Damn fools.

From the Diary of Colonel House

August 7, 1917.

McAdoo came from Washington to spend the day and to review the situation, and talk regarding international finances. He spent a large part of the time complaining that the President would not give him sufficient authority to properly discharge his duties as Secretary of the Treasury. There is much in what he says, and yet I can well understand the President's feeling when McAdoo tells him that it is essential for the proper conduct of his office to see all the foreign despatches to the State Department in order that he may have a clear survey of international political affairs and better know how to apportion loans to the Allies. Another day he goes to the President with a demand for representation on the Embargo Board, giving the same reason. The day after he appears with a demand to be placed in control of the Shipping Board, because there must be coordination between the lending of money to the Allies and the purchasing of their supplies, and facilitating the transport of these supplies to Europe. Another day he demands the control of the Purchasing Board, and for the same reason, that is, he cannot properly apportion money unless he is informed as to what is being bought.

When you sum up, it means he would be in complete control of the Government. He even went further and thought the Secretaries of the Army and Navy should report to him in order that he might correct any duplication which they or the Allies might have in mind. He makes a plausible argument; for, in a way, he ought to know something of the entire situation in order to act intelligently, but, taking his demands as a whole, it would leave him as arbiter not only of the United States but of the European nations as well.

He complained that this lack of authority was ruining his health. That he could not work with a brake placed upon him in so many directions. He complained, too, of the President's unwillingness to face any sort of friction or trouble. This trait, McAdoo said, has grown of late rather than diminished. It is a fact that the President does try to evade issues among his subordinates. I have seen him grow grey in the face when I would suggest the need of action that would entail the facing of a disagreeable situation concerning his official family. McAdoo attributes his growing tendancy in this direction to Mrs. Wilson.

McAdoo grumbled at the lack of coordination in the Cabinet. He declares the President never consults any of them about critical situations, and never makes plans for the Cabinet to work to[gether] as a whole. This, I think, is a just criticism. He asked how much the President consulted me. I evaded this in the usual way. He said he knew of no one who had his ear. He thought perhaps Baker had it more than any other member of the Cabinet. The President seldom goes to the Executive Offices, and Tumulty, McAdoo says, knows absolutely nothing of what is going on.

McAdoo said he offered to resign because he thought perhaps his being the President's son-in-law embarrassed him at times, not only with other members of the Cabinet, but with the public. Matters are constantly coming up in which the President has to make decisions between members of the Cabinet and in which McAdoo is involved. He thinks it is embarrassing to the President to decide in his favor, because there is always a latent suspicion that family relationship has something to do with it.

He maintains that he is not a candidate for President. This, however, is contrary to general belief in and out of Washington. He spent so much time talking of his personal relations with the President and members of the Cabinet, that we were not able to discuss the international financial situation as thoroughly as I had hoped. However, I was able to give him my view as to what had best be done in dealing with the Allied demand for loans. I urged him to let the money go, when it had to go, in a spirit that would create satisfaction and gratitude rather than to give it grudgingly, leaving a feeling of resentment. The English, naturally, desire to maintain the pound sterling, but McAdoo would like to see the dollar become the world standard of value, although he did not say so.

To Newton Diehl Baker, with Enclosure

My dear Mr. Secretary: The White House 8 August, 1917

I assume that the statement of fact contained in the enclosed is erroneous, but in any case I would very much appreciate your advice as to what answer I should make to the message if any.[1]

Faithfully yours, Woodrow Wilson

TLS (N. D. Baker Papers, DLC).
[1] See NDB to WW, Aug. 17, 1917.

ENCLOSURE

Chicago, Ills., Aug. 7, 1917.

Report here that War Department has issued order that no negro National Guard regiment shall be allowed to attend training camps in the south because of prejudice of southerners. We protest against any order by the government based upon race discrimination. Our soldiers have enlisted and are being drafted and will fight and die if need be for this country and universal democracy. We demand the same treatment and training all United States soldiers regardless of race and color. Let our government stand for one country, one flag, one duty for all citizens and for real democracy in our own country as well as democracy in Europe.

> Edward H. Wright, Assistant Corp. Counsel,
>   Chicago, Ills;
> Louis B. Anderson, Alderman,
>   Second Ward, Chicago;
> Benjamin H. Lucas, Representative
>   Fiftieth General Assembly Illinois;
> Robert F. Abbott, Editor,
>   Chicago Defender;
> Major R. R. Jackson, Representative,
>   Fiftieth Assembly, Illinois;
> S. D. Turner, Editor, Illinois.[1]

T telegram (WP, DLC).

[1] Edward H. Wright was a leading black Republican politician in Chicago; Louis Bernard Anderson, Republican, was a lawyer of Chicago; Benjamin H. Lucas, Republican, was an insurance broker in Chicago; Robert Sengstacke Abbott was the founder, publisher, and editor of the *Chicago Defender*, already a leading black newspaper; Robert R. Jackson, Republican, was proprietor of a large printing establishment in Chicago; and Sheadrick Bond Turner was editor of the Chicago *Illinois Idea* and a former Republican representative in the Illinois General Assembly.

To James Duval Phelan

My dear Senator: [The White House] 8 August, 1917

I am going to take the liberty of speaking to you orally some time about the suggestion contained in your letter of August sixth. I would have to write you a long letter to put down the interesting things which I can tell you in a few minutes orally.

> Cordially and sincerely yours,   Woodrow Wilson

TLS (Letterpress Books, WP, DLC).

To Samuel Gompers

My dear Mr. Gompers: The White House 8 August, 1917

I don't like to trouble you with any larger correspondence than you have, but I would very much like your advice as to how I should answer the enclosed.[1] I am loath to believe that genuine representatives of the Federation of Labor would send me a message containing so unjust and offensive an intimation.

Cordially and sincerely yours, Woodrow Wilson

TLS (S. Gompers Corr., AFL-CIO-Ar).
[1] J. L. Donnelly and T. A. French to WW, Aug. 6, 1917.

From Joseph Patrick Tumulty

Dear Governor: [The White House, Aug. 8, 1917]

Mr. Taft was suddenly taken ill yesterday at Clay Center, Kansas. He has been making speeches all over the country backing up the Government. Don't you think you could send him a telegram of sympathy? The Secretary.

TL (WP, DLC).

To William Howard Taft

The White House Aug 8 1917

Have been very much distressed to learn of your illness Hope that it is not serious and that you are rapidly coming to feel like yourself again Cordially and sincerely.

Woodrow Wilson

T telegram (W. H. Taft Papers, DLC).

To George Earle Chamberlain

My dear Senator: [The White House] 8 August, 1917

I cannot write you upon another subject without giving myself the pleasure of saying how thoroughly justified I think you were in your remarks of the day before yesterday in the Senate[1] and how sincerely glad I am that you made them. It is time that we put an end in the most emphatic way to the sort of tactics that have been indulged in.

Cordially and sincerely yours, Woodrow Wilson

TLS (Letterpress Books, WP, DLC).
¹ Wilson referred to a bitter exchange between Chamberlain and Thomas P. Gore on August 6. Chamberlain branded Gore as an obstructionist for his opposition to the Lever bill and to other administration measures such as the selective-draft bill. Gore heatedly denied the charge. *Cong. Record*, 65th Cong., 1st sess., pp. 5833-36. See also Billington, *Thomas P. Gore*, pp. 95-101.

From Albert Sidney Burleson, with Enclosure

My dear Mr. President: Washington August 8, 1917.

Referring to the telegram of Messrs. W. I. Irvine and Paul Hanna, Publicity Committee of the Philadelphia Branch of the People's Council, dated August 4, 1917, which you sent me, I enclose a memorandum of the Solicitor for this Department with respect to the organization represented by these parties.

Faithfully yours,   A. S. Burleson

E N C L O S U R E

William Harmong Lamar to Albert Sidney Burleson

                                              Washington
Memorandum for the Postmaster General: August 8, 1917.

Referring to the telegram dated Philadelphia, Pennsylvania, August 4, 1917, addressed to the President, signed by W. I. Irvine and Paul Hanna, Publicity Committee, representing the Philadelphia branch of the People's Council of America, I will say that this organization was organized in New York some weeks ago and is rapidly establishing branches throughout the country. It claims to be modeled along the lines of the Workmen's and Soldiers' organization in Russia and to be organized for the purpose of cooperating with that organization and peace organizations throughout the world to bring about a conclusion of the present war. Copies of some of the literature sent out by this organization are attached, in which appear: "Every organization or group of people" in any city or vicinity "likely to be interested," including "trade unions, socialist locals, branches of the Consumers' League, single tax leagues, peace societies, church and civic clubs, mother's clubs, parent and teachers' associations, etc.," are urged to connect themselves with the People's Council, each of such organizations to be entitled to representation in the Council. In one of the pieces of literature sent out by the organization is found the following:

"The People's Council will be a 'people's power' body in constant operation. It will be a clearing-house for the democratic forces of the country. It will maintain central headquarters with a permanent office staff. It will conduct a publicity bureau. It will uphold the rights of labor. It will be a stronghold of defense for our fundamental American rights of free speech, free press, peaceful assembly and the right to petition the government. It may take a nation-wide unofficial referendum on such questions as conscription and America's concrete peace terms.

"It is hoped that our own People's Council will voice the peace will of America as unmistakably and effectively as the Council of the Workmen's and Soldiers' delegates is speaking for Russia. * * *

"You can become a constituent-at-large by signing the attached blank and sending it to the office. Or, you can get your organization to elect a delegate to the Council, thus becoming a group constituent. Or, you can do both. Better still, you can start the ball rolling for local People's Councils such as have already sprung up in several cities."

Every class of people opposed to the Government in this war appear to be very rapidly connecting themselves with this organization, with the hope that it will be the great force to paralyze the activities of the Government in this war. It appears to be supported by the German propaganda and by every shade of opinion from the extreme anarchist type to the Women's Peace Party, and in my opinion is doing and will continue to do incalculable harm. From the communications of postmasters it appears that its literature is being circulated from one end of the country to the other, and it seems to have back of it unlimited money. It has the active cooperation of the Americal [American] League Against Militarism, which also seems to be supplied with unlimited money and is doing great harm.

Attached also will be found articles from the New York Tribune of August 6th and 8th, showing the nation-wide operations of various elements which are hostile to the Government in this war.[1] From the matter that is daily submitted to this office from various sections of the country I can say that the statements contained in these articles are in no way exaggerated, and it would take many such articles to convey an adequate idea of the operations of the elements in this country hostile to the Government in the present war.

In conclusion, allow me to say that the literature of the various publications and organizations connected with the People's Council throughout the country contain so much falsehood and misinformation, both with respect to the law and the facts, that I am of the opinion unless some general means is adopted to get before the people correct information with regard to the various matters discussed in the publications and circulars now being sent broadcast throughout the land that a most unfortunate condition will result. W H Lamar

TLS (WP, DLC).
[1] They are missing; however, they were "Enemies Within: How the Honorable Institution of Free Speech in the United States Has Fallen Into the Hands of Disloyalists," *New York Tribune*, Aug. 6, 1917, and "Enemies Within: To What Extremes of Disloyalty the Socialist Party Has Committed Itself," *ibid.*, Aug. 8, 1917.

From Albert Sidney Burleson

My dear Mr. President: Washington, D. C. August 8, 1917.

Referring to the communication of Mr. A. W. Ricker, Publisher of Pearson's Magazine, addressed to you and dated the 3d instant, I wish to say:

First, that no complaint has been made to me against Pearson's Magazine and it has not been the subject of investigation by this Department. I can see no reason why any one connected with the postal service should have tampered with the mail of that Magazine or the mail of any one connected with it.

The law makes it an offense to open sealed letters, and this law is rigidly enforced by this Department against every one connected with the service. An investigation has been ordered upon the complaint made by Mr. Ricker to you, and if there has been a violation of the law, as asserted by him, every effort will be made to ascertain and punish the guilty party.[1]

Second. The Act of June 15, 1917, (Espionage Law), provides that matter therein declared to be nonmailable "shall not be conveyed in the mails or delivered from any post office or by any letter carrier." As a result, immediately upon the passage of that Act, this Department became flooded with specimens of matter thought by the various postmasters to be nonmailable, with a request for instructions with respect thereto.

The classification and treatment of these complaints, and the consideration necessarily given as to the scope of the law, which is still being tested in the courts, caused some delay in the handling of certain classes of matter submitted to the Department, including the literature being sent out by the People's Council at

New York, and I assume that the delayed matter addressed to Pearson's Magazine was a part of that which was held in the New York City post office under the circumstances stated.

I will say in this connection that I think the postmaster at New York was fully justified in asking for instructions with respect to the literature of the People's Council, and while it is at present being permitted to go through the mails on account of the questions raised as to the effect of the law, it is doing much harm to the Government in the present crisis of the country. The decisions of the courts may make it clear that such matter comes within the class made nonmailable by the Espionage Law.

Third. As to the delay complained of by Mr. George Savage of Aguanga, California, to Mr. Ricker, of a letter addressed by the latter to the former, I can see no reason for this occurrence, and have ordered the matter investigated to ascertain the cause of the delay.   Very truly yours,   A. S. Burleson

TLS (WP, DLC).
[1] See the memorandum printed at Aug. 15, 1917.

From John Franklin Fort

My dear Mr. President: Washington August 8, 1917.

I suppose by Saturday, possibly before, the food act will become a law and the provision therein with relation to coal[1] will become operative if you elect to put it into operation. This, in my opinion, presents the most important, not to say difficult, problem that has ever been presented to the Chief Executive or any administrative board of the Nation.

I greatly fear the results of the operation of these mines. It is a much more difficult problem, it seems to me, than any of us imagine. There are six thousand mines. I am writing this letter with this in view: I believe that this matter is of sufficient importance to be handled by you personally. I feel that if I could give you a list of about a dozen, or more if you prefer, of the leading bituminous operaters of the United States, whom you could have meet you and put the matter up to them in the way that you could, the result would be an agreement by them to comply with your expressed wish and with the price that you might agree with them should become operative. This, I feel very sure, would result in every operator in the United States complying with that price and operating his mine thereunder. It would also avoid any possible dissatisfaction which the operators might have if not conferred with.

You once made the statement as to the referendum, that it was useful as a "gun behind the door." That was a statement that will stick for all time with regard to this class of legislation, and with this law in your power to enforce, I am convinced that these gentlemen, seeing the situation, will be ready to meet any reasonable suggestion which you would make, and you will not make any suggestions which are not reasonable.

Of course, I would esteem it a great compliment if I could be present should you decide to talk to the operators, and I might be useful to you in my knowledge of the past course of action of these gentlemen.

If you desire to put the matter upon us we will do the best we can and endeavor to accomplish the result which you would much more readily, I believe, accomplish. The great honor and compliment of treating with you will have a splendid effect upon these men. The most serious offendors for the past five months in the coal matter have been the middlemen. The operators themselves have been disposed to be fair, speaking generally; of course, there have been exceptions. But in the present state of affairs, if an accommodation can be reached, and a fair price fixed, and these gentlemen will speed up production and act in good faith, as they undoubtedly would if agreeing with you, I cannot but believe that it would be much better than any arbitrary action on the part of this Commission or any other agency, in fixing a price and endeavoring to operate the mines.

My only purpose in writing you is to be helpful, and if I can aid in any way in any plan which will result, through an adjustment, in bringing about the result which we all so much desire and for which you are so earnestly striving in all directions, I shall be glad. Time is the essence of this matter because we have but a short time before fall and cold weather.

I think I can be able to hand you the costs of many mines in several districts by the first of next week, and with those costs in hand you could get a fair idea of what will be an average cost at practically all of the mines except a few exceptional ones; and then to add to this cost, in the language of the act of Congress, "a just and reasonable profit" might bring about a solution that could only redound to the credit of the Administration.

I would like to be at home over Saturday, and will try to be back Monday evening, possibly Monday morning. If you wish me to, it will be a pleasure for me to give you any information or personal aid that I can render, and I earnestly hope that you will devise some method by which you will act personally, or through some agency, to endeavor to bring about an adjustment with the operators after a conference and without any arbitrary action.

With distinguished respect, believe me

Yours most sincerely, John Franklin Fort

TLS (WP, DLC).

1 The relevant portion of Section 25 of the Lever Food and Fuel Act reads as follows:

"That the President of the United States shall be, and he is hereby, authorized and empowered, whenever and wherever in his judgment necessary for the efficient prosecution of the war, to fix the price of coal and coke, wherever and whenever sold, either by producer or dealer, to establish rules for the regulation of and to regulate the method of production, sale, shipment, distribution, apportionment, or storage thereof among dealers and consumers, domestic or foreign; said authority and power may be exercised by him in each case through the agency of the Federal Trade Commission during the war or for such part of the said time as in his judgment may be necessary.

"That if, in the opinion of the President, any such producer or dealer fails or neglects to conform to such prices or regulations, or to conduct his business efficiently under the regulations and control of the President as aforesaid, or conducts it in a manner prejudicial to the public interest, then the President is hereby authorized and empowered in every such case to requisition and take over the plant, business, and all appurtenances thereof belonging to such producer or dealer as a going concern, and to operate or cause the same to be operated in such manner and through such agency as he may direct during the period of the war or for such part of said time as in his judgment may be necessary." 40 *Statutes at Large* 284.

From Franklin Knight Lane

My dear Mr. President: Washington August 8, 1917.

As to the purchase of coal properties, I do not think you will have to ask Congress for leave. You can buy them outright, as you would buy any other piece of land for army purposes, or you can buy them, agreeing to pay so much royalty up to the amount of the purchase price.

Faithfully and cordially yours, Franklin K. Lane

TLS (WP, DLC).

From William Howard Taft

Clay Center, Kansas, August 8, 1917.

Thank you for your kind telegram and inquiry. I am better and hope to be out in a few days. Wm. H. Taft.

T telegram (WP, DLC).

To John Franklin Fort

My dear Governor: [The White House] 9 August, 1917

Thank you warmly for your letter of yesterday. It makes a deep impression on me and I will consider its suggestion about the matter of handling the coal prices and the coal production very seriously.

I am very happy to know that you are going to let me have the facts now in your possession so soon.

Cordially and sincerely yours,   Woodrow Wilson

TLS (Letterpress Books, WP, DLC).

To Clarence Seward Darrow

My dear Mr. Darrow: [The White House] 9 August, 1917

I agree with Mr. Kent that you could probably do a great deal of good by speaking on the East Side of New York and, as we agreed in our recent conversation,[1] that is a place where wise work is very urgently needed.

You may be sure I will try to work out with the Postmaster General some course with regard to the circulation of the Socialistic papers that will be in conformity with law and good sense.

In haste   Sincerely yours,   Woodrow Wilson

TLS (Letterpress Books, WP, DLC).
[1] At the White House on August 1. William Kent was also present.

From Edward Mandell House, with Enclosures

Dear Governor: Magnolia, Massachusetts. August 9, 1917.

Here is a letter from Walter Lippman[n] enclosing the suggestion of Norman Angell.

The suggestion is not a bad one if properly modified, and is worthy, I think, of some consideration. It is along the line of my two other letters of today.

I do not agree with his thought as to the Parliamentary delegates, although his reason for this is good. The purpose could be reached, however, in another way without having the clumsy machinery which a second body would entail.

Affectionately yours,   E. M. House

TLS (WP, DLC).

ENCLOSURE I

Walter Lippmann to Edward Mandell House

Dear Colonel House: Washington. August 6, 1917.

At Norman Angell's request I am forwarding you the enclosed memorandum, which I hope you will consider carefully, and if possible communicate to the President.

The argument strikes me as absolutely sound, and if in the next few weeks the President should come out publicly with such a proposal, it would inspire the world, and unite this country absolutely. America would fight with a new zest if such a vision were before its eyes.

I long to have a talk with you, and I trust you will soon be taking a trip to Europe.

Sincerely yours,   Walter Lippmann.

TCL (WP, DLC).

ENCLOSURE II

MEMORANDUM OF ALLIED DIPLOMATIC STRATEGY

A Proposal

The proposal here made does not call for peace negotiations with the enemy; nor for making him an "offer" in any diplomatic sense; it does not deny the necessity or desirability of "a fight to a finish"; is in no sense a plea for an early termination of the war, or an incomplete or patched up peace. *What this proposal is Not.*

The proposal is as much a factor of the successful conduct of the war itself as munitions or men or money. It is on that ground only, in so far as this memorandum is concerned, that it is urged. *It is a necessary war measure.*

The proposal here made is the calling now, during the war, of a Conference, or Congress, or Parliament of the Allies, of a special composition for the following object: *Outline of Proposal.*

To frame the international arrangements for mutual protection by which after the war the nations of the Alliance—and ultimately those of the world—are to be assured military security, national independence, and economic rights (access to raw materials and markets, equality of opportunity in undeveloped territory like Africa, Asia and South America, access to the sea for states that have insufficient, or no, ports, etc.); some plan for a League of Nations, such as that forecast by Mr. Wilson and approved by the other leading Allied statesmen.

A mere declaration of intention to be guided in the future by idealistic principles in international affairs will of course serve no end whatsoever. What is needed is the elaboration of a scheme sufficiently concrete to strike the imagination of the German public and to make it evident to them that the Allies have a positive and permanent international policy in this respect, that their present Alliance will be continued after the war, and that all hope of its going to pieces must be set aside.

Incidentally, of course, unless the Alliance *can* take that form during the war, the Germans will achieve their ends after the conclusion of peace.(*) If the Alliance is merely a war alliance, destined, like war alliances of the past, to fall to pieces when war is over, Germany has only to make any terms whatsoever to secure peace, let the inevitable disagreements of the settlement disintegrate one Alliance, and then once more impose her policy. An Alliance which is to last into peace must be based upon peace ends, and—in this particular case—secure the peace co-operation of Russia and America by appealing to the special aspirations, economic and idealistic, of those countries.

The point of this memorandum is to urge that the Allies are depriving themselves of, and presenting to the enemy, a great military asset affecting the actual conduct of the war by the failure to do now what will finally have to be done in any case.

The Conference—or Congress—for reasons indicated later, should be of a special composition, namely:

> The Congress to consist of two bodies, a smaller one composed, as in international Congresses of the past, of the delegates or nominees of the governments participating, and a larger body representing proportionately the component parties of the respective parliaments.

> The smaller body should act as the initiating and drafting committee, their proposals being subject to amendment, approval or rejection by the larger body before being finally ratified by the constituent states of the Congress.

(*) The assumption common at the beginning of the war was that it did not much matter what political situation followed victory, since the destruction of Germany would be so complete, and the balance of power against her so overwhelming, that she would be ruled out as a factor in the future politics of Europe. But the disintegration of Russia, the uncertainties of its future, the problem of the submarine and of man-power in France, have fundamentally altered the situation and make the political outcome of the war mainly dependent upon the solidarity of the Alliance after its conclusion.

The Conference would not deal at all with territorial readjustment, but concentrate solely on the problem of guarantees and security, the future League of Nations.

The immediate object of the proposal is to drive a wedge between the peoples and governments of the Central Empires by making it impossible for those governments to present this war to their peoples as a defensive war;(*) by showing those peoples that the policy of the Allies offers ultimately better chances for their security and welfare than would a Prussian success. Our present diplomacy chains the German people to their government and makes revolutionary or anti-governmental movements in Germany impossible. *Immediate Object*

The Conference, which, on account of the new belligerents that have recently entered the war would be much larger and more impressive than the Paris Economic Conference of last year, would of course sit for weeks or even months, with full reports in the neutral press, arrangements being made for those reports to reach liberal and Socialist minorities in Germany and Austria. Thus, although the Conference would make no formal communication to the Central Powers its decisions would in fact be equivalent to the notification that if the peoples of Germany would democratise themselves, reform their government and discard its aggressive elements, they would not as nations be destroyed or injured. While in effect asking them to put an end to their "militarism" the entente powers would in exchange be offering an alternative means to national security. It is obvious that until some such offer is made in some form there is not the faintest hope that the German peoples will take any step likely to weaken the military power of their government. *Method*

The peoples, as distinct from the governing classes, are not so much interested in territorial adjustments as in security. The Germans, like all peoples are driven by vague fears of what defeat or weakening of their power would involve.

At present they simply do not know what fate would be in store for them, how their country would be protected, what its future chances would be, if they should weaken their military power. *The Present Diplomatic Situation.*

Such a diplomatic situation plays powerfully into the hands of the enemy governments.

(*) An able official in the Foreign Office said the other day: "Every German is animated by the incredible belief that he is fighting to save his country from absolute extinction. If we could get that idea out of their heads it would be worth a dozen army corps." The present proposal is a suggestion to that end.

The Paris Economic Conference, combined with our perpetual talk of "the destruction of German militarism" (a phrase we do not define) is enabling the enemy governments to create the kind of morale which is the very hardest to weaken—the morale founded in the impression of a whole people that they are fighting against absolute national extinction. We have enabled the Prussian government to say to its people:

"If you lose you will be deprived of all means of defending yourselves. The destruction of German militarism really means that in future you will be at the mercy of your enemies who will close all markets, all sources of raw material against you. You are fighting for the right to defend yourselves—the most elementary form of political freedom—and for that commercial opportunity in the future which will be necessary if your children are to earn their livelihood."*

Thus Mr. Asquith, in demanding "the destruction of German militarism" without any definition of what he means by it, enables Bethmann-Hollweg to retort in the Reichstag (April 6, 1916), "Mr. Asquith's primary condition means that Germany is to be rendered helpless again as in centuries past, exposed by her neighbour's lust for power * * * * That is what our foes understand by the destruction of Prussian militarism."

Curiously enough it is Mr. Gerard, the American ambassador to Germany, who gives a hint of the power of the instrument which we thus deliver into the hands of the enemy. Mr. Gerard in his book, "My Four Years in Germany" says:

"We are engaged in war against a people whose counrry [country] was for so many centuries a theatre of devastating wars that fear is bred into the very marrow of their souls, making them ready to submit their lives and fortunes to an autocracy which for centuries has ground their faces, but which has promised them as the result of the war * * * security."

That fear is not only a great military asset to the German government, enabling them to maintain that morale which more than one great soldier has declared to be seventy-five per cent of the whole military factor, but it is a political asset also. It enables the Prussians successfully to check any nascent revolu-

* In the interview with Bethmann-Hollweg which Mr. Swope published in the New York World the German spokesman says: "There can be no doubt as to what Germany is fighting for. It can be reduced to a one-word formula—existence * * * * We ask and fight for the right to live and to earn our living."

tion in Germany. "It is all very well," said Vorwarts[1] recently, "to talk of the German people rebelling against their government, but the truth is that if they did the Entente armies would be in Cologne in a week." Our refusal to define what we mean by our talk of the destruction of German militarism, our failure to formulate any plan to which Germans can look as a means of national defence, in substitution for the military power of Prussia, does in fact, turn this, for Germans, into a defensive war; and stiffens enormously enemy resistance.

But even if the German public saw the truth, what could they do, since they have no power?

Does public opinion in Germany matter?

Now we admit, by our commercial blockade policy, that the attitude of the population as a whole has a great military importance. We know that the fighting forces will suffer last by the blockade, because the civilians will be pinched to keep them going. But we also know that if the pinch is severe enough it will have important effects on enemy populations and through them on the government. That expectation is justified. In a war in which the factory, the mine and the railroad are as important as the army, civilian morale is as important as military. If the civilian population got the idea that their hardships were not only unnecessary but were on behalf of a war contrary to national welfare, the effect would be enormous, even in Germany. We know that more fatigue and a sense of grievance in small matters greatly affects output and efficiency. If popular feeling get beyond that point the decline in output, the decline of efficiency would almost certainly be marked. Actual health would suffer; women would become rebellious; strikes would occur (as they have done); collisions between soldiery and workers (as they have done); soldiers would refuse to shoot work-people (as they have begun to); all this would get worse. "Sabotage" would spring up here and there; shells would be increasingly defective; explosions would take place; the civilian unrest would affect the trenches; more officers would be shot; submarines would begin sailing into Allied harbours without their officers; more naval officers would follow the example of Prince Henry and refuse to sink merchant ships;[2] loans would not be well subscribed; the government would get scared and make wrong decisions; the financial and industrial interests would increasingly want the

---

[1] *Vorwärts*, the Social-Democratic daily of Berlin.

[2] The Editors have not discovered the basis for this statement. A dispatch in 1915 from Amsterdam to the London *Daily Express* reported that Prince Henry of Prussia had asked the Emperor's permission to take part in the submarine blockade. Henry, brother of William II, had until recently been in command of the Baltic Fleet. *New York Times*, Feb. 18, 1915.

thing brought to an end; opinion would become more and more divided, ministerial changes would become more frequent, while of course it would be increasingly difficult in these circumstances to keep Austria, Bulgaria and Turkey in line. If smothered revolt of this kind began to show itself in Germany it would almost certainly be followed by Czech and Slav movements of a like kind. More than once that sort of disorganization has threatened in Austria (in one case half a million men actually did desert to the Russians) and would have matured if certain advances made by Czechs and Slavs to the Allied governments had been encouraged.

Commercial classes also concerned.

One of the tendencies of late in Germany is for certain of the commercial classes to make common cause with the Socialists and Liberals. The exporting merchants and shipping interests, those interested in overseas trade generally, see that their position at the end of the war will be impossible if Germany—however "victorious"—is to be isolated and discriminated against. Mitteleuropa is no sort of compensation for the entire loss of Germany's former overseas trade. It will take a generation, perhaps several generations, to build up in Turkey or the Near East a trade corresponding to what they will have lost; and it may never be built up, as the Mitteleuropa scheme is full of pitfalls. The commercial classes have shown marked uneasiness in this respect of late, and are beginning to see that a military result which, however successful according to the map, ended in shutting them out from seven-eights of the world, would be disastrous.

Government disturbed at Unrest.

That the German government is disturbed at the possibility of a changing public opinion is obvious. With a military situation which on the surface (owing to the Russian collapse and maintenance of U-boat sinkings) is in favour of Germany, we find popular discontent and parliamentary opposition growing, and the government, instead of meeting it with repression, meeting it with soft words. The attitude of the new Chancellor[3] is one of apology. The government goes on making concessions. (Like definite undertakings not to hold another election in Prussia without electoral reform) Scheidemann, despite immense petting by the government, declares himself opposed to U-boat warfare and comes back from Stockholm in very chastened mood.

Our object to accelerate it.

There can be no reasonable doubt that the Allies have it within their power greatly to accelerate this popular movement both in Germany and in Austria. Let this Conference by its published decisions say in effect to the Socialists and Liberals:

If you throw out your militarists and democratise your

---

[3] That is, Georg Michaelis.

country, restore your conquests, drop aggression, and limit your armaments, the Western democracies will give public undertakings, ratified by their parliaments not to dismember or attack or injure the reformed Germany.

And let the Congress say in effect to the Commercial Classes of Germany:

If you will drop your "expansion by military conquest," surrender your schemes of Mitteleuropa, agree with us not to engage in certain forms of commercial competition, and the world will be open to you once more.

And of course the Conference should make plain the alternative and their power to enforce it in terms which amount to this:

But so long as your government and policy is what it is you will be excluded from access to seven-eights of the world, from nearly all the great areas of future economic opportunity. *Time against us.* For, whatever your military situation, the Allies are now, and will be at the end of the war, in a position to enforce this policy. Even assuming that you could during the next year or two of the war retain your present conquests, your military "victory" would deprive you of far more than it would give.

But the weapon that we might use is getting blunter. If several years more of war *compel* Germany to become self-sufficing, commercial blockade or isolation will have lost its efficacy. She will not need the outside world. Refusal, for instance, of access to raw materials would become less terrifying. Turkish cotton, wool pulp cellulose, synthetic rubber, are so many weapons lost to us.

So with the military situation. Russian chaos places the situation in more than one sense in Germany's hands. She may in the future find a situation in which she can bargain with a military chief in Russia; secure a certain policy in return for not attacking. It makes a pro-German dictator still a possibility in Russia. *Effect of Conference on Russia and America.* Germany could even use a Russian military restoration—controlled by herself—to terrify once more her own Socialists. We should have lost the political and diplomatic advantage of a weak Russia and the military advantage of a strong one.

The Conference here proposed is in effect what Russia has been urging. The serious discussion of a League of Democratic Nations, of a real international organization, for the maintenance of peace, as the major war aim of the Allies, is precisely the sort of thing which would help a Russian statesman to keep his country in the war. Had the Russian demand of two months since for a new formulation of war aims,[4] been met by a plan of

---

[4] A public statement by Tereshchenko on May 19. He declared that he would work for an early general peace "without annexations or indemnities,"

this kind, and Russian idealism stirred by the spectacle of such a congress, one may doubt whether the opposition to the war on the part of the extremists would either have been so strong or have net [met] with such popular response. Interest in such an effort might have kept Russia in the war.

The same demand for a restatement of war aims is now being voiced in all sorts of quarters in America. Such a scheme as this would appeal to what is perhaps the most powerful single political sentiment in America. To talk about the independence of the Tczecho-Slovaks or Italy's rights to the Trentino or the future of Bosnia-Herzegovina, stirs no American pulse. To say that these are the things for which America is fighting is a sure way ultimately of making the war, and—which is perhaps just as important—America's future participation in European alliances, unpopular. But to say that America is fighting for the federalism of the world, and its future organization for peace and freedom; and to show the existence of a concrete policy or plan to that end, is to appeal to the most vivid of American political traditions and impulses. If the proposed transfers of territory are part of that plan and necessary to it, America will accept them. Otherwise, sooner or later, she will refuse to support them.

American feeling on this subject should be enlisted before the nationalist cry of "Keep out of Europe" has developed, and been adopted by a possibly powerful political party.

NOTE ON PROPOSED COMPOSITION OF CONFERENCE.

The proposal to have the Conference composed in part only of governmental delegates, and in part of delegates representing parliamentary parties, is prompted mainly for this reason: If the Allies employ that method as between themselves, they will be in a position to insist, when they come to deal with Germany at the end of the war, that she be represented in that way at the congress of the settlement. That would make German Socialists and Liberals, not governmental delegates and Prussians, the predominant element of German representation. And of course we should have enlisted German democratic support of the plan. We should, by this fact, have democratized Germany in her international relations. And it is those relations, of course, with which we are concerned.

The principle would also, in the same way, give to Austrian representation not purely a governmental or Hapsburg charac-

---

but one that would include "a realization of their ideal" for the people of Alsace-Lorraine. For the text, see *FR 1918, Russia*, I, 75-77.

ter, but would ensure a fair representation of the subject nationalities of the Central Empires. The publicity given to their case would be a powerful plea in their fight for autonomy.

Machinery of this kind is of course most cumbersome and quite impossible where rapid decisions are wanted. But in the case of neither of these congresses would rapidity of decision be the chief need. In the one case the main object would be to get certain pronouncements of policy home to the German democrats, and for that purpose a long conference might be desirable. At the close of the war a long period of "provisional settlement" which can be modified, would probably be a good thing. In any case, rapidity of settlement would not, in that case either, be the main need.

T MS (WP, DLC).

From Edward Mandell House, with Enclosure

Dear Governor: Magnolia, Massachusetts. August 9, 1917.

I have just received from London a copy of G. Lowes Dickinson's "The Choice Before Us." In speaking of your speech to the Senate of January 22nd he says:

"The whole speech should be carefully studied; it is perhaps *the most important international document of all history*, and it bears in the most direct way on a kind of peace that is possible and desirable after the war."

The letter from Bernard Ridder is interesting. I believe he is right when he says "There is no adequate realization in Germany today of the enormous preparations being made in our country."

I believe, furthermore, that where the Allies have fallen down is in their lack of publicity work in neutral countries and in the Central Powers.

Northcliffe sent me a letter yesterday from Stanley Washburn, in which Washburn said that Germany was spending millions in Russia in this way, and the Allies were doing practically nothing to offset it.

Bertron writes that "the only way to hold Russia and utilize her enormous latent power effectively is through very thorough and extensive publicity. This we have been strongly urging upon Washington but, up to the time of our departure, nothing definite had been done. The reverses that the Russians have had might have been avoided had we been able to get to work immediately on our arrival in Petrograd with sufficient educational literature to reach the army and people."

If an infinitesimal part of the money spent upon war preparations was spent in explaining the issues and aims of this country,
a different story could probably be told.

Affectionately yours,   E. M. House

TLS (WP, DLC).

ENCLOSURE

Bernard Herman Ridder[1] to Edward Mandell House

Dear Colonel House: New York City. August 7, 1917.

The appointment of Dr. von Kuehlmann may prove to be the
first step in the direction of giving the liberal elements in Germany a voice in the control of the Government.

The process of hastening this desirable result is one that might,
under favorable circumstances, be accelerated by pressure from
Americans of German ancestry.

If we can credit newspaper statements of German editors
brought to us by the cable, there is no adequate realization in
Germany today of the enormous preparations being made in our
country. If this situation could be brought home to them more
fully, the necessary democratization of Germany might receive a
decided impulse forward.

Would it be useful in this connection to send a small group of
men of German ancestry, such as Professor Kuno Francke,
Charles Nagel, of St Louis, J. G. Schmidlapp; Walter Lippmann,
Jacob Schiff or others of their calibre to Copenhagen to confer
not alone with Scheidemann and other socialist and liberal
leaders, but to possibly meet Dr. von Kuehlmann and strengthen
his hand in the internal situation in Germany?

The splendid attitude which the Administration has taken in
its treatment of German subjects, has made a powerful impression, not only in this country but abroad. It was a wise and far-
sighted point of view to take, and will bear its fruit in good time.
The recent letter of the President, emphasizing his confidence in
Americans of German ancestry, fell upon grateful ears. There is
much for us to be thankful about.

Yours very sincerely,   Bernard H. Ridder.

TCL (WP, DLC).

[1] He had succeeded his father, Herman Ridder, who had died in 1915, as
president of the *New Yorker Staats-Zeitung*.

From Edward Mandell House, with Enclosure

Dear Governor: Magnolia, Massachusetts. August 9, 1917.

I am enclosing copies of Cobb's challenge to the Tageblatt. Surely, there could be no objection to putting it in this mild form. Will you not advise me what answer to make.

If this is once started, we could easily get into Germany the knowledge of our preparations as Ridder Suggests. We could also give the Germans as a whole a sense of security which they do not now feel. The whole military propaganda in the Central Powers is directed at the fear of dismemberment and economic ruin. If the German people could be brought to realize that their integrity would be better safe-guarded by such a peace as we have in mind than it would be by the continued reliance upon great armaments, the militarists arguments would break down.

If we want to win this war it seems to me essential that we must do something different from what the Allies have done in the past three years.   Affectionately yours,   E. M. House

TLS (WP, DLC).

E N C L O S U R E

Frank Irving Cobb to Theodor Wolff

New York, August 8, 17.

It is no less important, in the stress of war than in the controversies of peace, that there should be a common agreement as to the issues involved, whatever differences there may be as to the relation of these issues to the aims and objects of government. No such agreement exists as between the German people and the American people. They are at war, but Americans are unable to understand why the German Government adopted a line of policy which forced the United States into the war; nor do the German people understand why the American people should have considered these German policies casus belli.

Believing that a frank discussion of the issues is one of the great duties that journalism owes to the general welfare, The World hereby challenges The Tageblatt to a full and free debate on the questions that have divided the United States and Germany, each newspaper to print the case presented by the other, as well as its own case, under arrangements to be agreed upon later in respect to detail. It seems to The World that such a debate might have a permanent value in the way of clarifying the issues and crystallizing public sentiment in the two countries.

Trusting that it will seem expedient for the Tageblatt to accept this challenge in the spirit in which it is offered,

Most Respectfully,   The New York World.

TCL (WP, DLC).

From Alfred B. Cosey[1]

My dear Mr. President: East Orange, N. J. Aug. 9th., 1917.

Representatives of the Colored People, and their Associations of the Northern and Eastern States, respectfully ask an interview, from 3 to 5 minutes, for a delegation of FOUR; all of whom were introduced to Hon. Joseph P. Tumulty, your private Secretary, on August 1st., 1917, while at the White House; namely Mrs. Walker, Rev. Dr. T. Cullen, chairman of delegation of August 1st, 1917, Rev. Dr. L. Martin, Secretary of Delegation, whose face appeared familiar to Mr. Tumulty on August 1st.,[2] and your humble servant. Our Mission is very worthy and important. We sincerely believe you will appreciate it.

In the name of GOD, and SUFFERING HUMANITY in all parts of the World, Mr. President see us, representing YOUR SUFFERING COUNTRYMEN, FOR 5 MINUTES, on Wednesday the 22nd., day of August, 1917; at such hour as suit[s] your convenience. I hand you herewith a newspaper clipping which will explain itself.[3] We will thank you for an early reply.[4]

I have the honor to be

very sincerely yours,   Alfred B. Cosey

TLS (WP. DLC).

[1] Lawyer of Newark and a leading black Democrat in New Jersey.

[2] A committee which represented several thousand blacks had marched down Fifth Avenue on July 28. They had called on August 1 at the White House to present a petition asking for action by the President and Congress to make lynching and mob violence "a national crime punishable by the laws of the United States." *Washington Post*, Aug. 2, 1917. The petition was signed, *inter alia*, by Sarah Walker, the Rev. Adam Clayton Powell, pastor of the Abyssinian Baptist Church of New York, the Rev. Dr. Frederick Asbury Cullen, the Rev. Dr. Charles Douglas Martin, and Cosey. Committee of the Negro Silent Protest Parade to the President and the Congress of the United States, July 28, 1917, HwS MS (WP, DLC). Dr. Cullen was pastor of the Salem Methodist Episcopal Church of New York. For accounts of the parade and the signs carried in it, see the *New York Times* and the New York *World*, both of July 29, 1917, and "The Negro Silent Parade," *The Crisis*, XIV (Sept. 1917), 241-44.

[3] New York *Globe*, Aug. [7?], 1917, clipping (WP, DLC). It said that Cosey had denied recent reports that Wilson had refused to see the committee because they were Negroes. Cosey had also said that Tumulty had told them that Wilson was very busy conferring about the Lever bill but could see them on the following day. The committee could not stay over.

[4] Wilson saw the group at the White House on August 14. The latter issued

a statement afterward in which they said that Wilson had promised that everything possible would be done by the federal government to punish persons guilty of violence against blacks and to prevent similar offenses in the future. The statement also said that Wilson had said that he had been shocked by the riot at East St. Louis and assured the delegates of his sympathy for their efforts to prevent recurrences. *Washington Post*, Aug. 17, 1917.

From Allen W. Ricker

Mr. President: New York August 9th, 1917.

I thank you for your very prompt and courteous reply to my letter of complaint against the Post Office Department in relation to interference with first class mail matter.

A number of us are preparing an exhibit which may be used as proof of my charges. I dislike to annoy you with what must seem to you a petty matter. I would rather be a booster than a knocker but the attitude of Government Officials toward those of us who do not approve of the present war has about blasted the last atom of patriotism out of us.

This magazine has contributed its former president and his son[1] to the army,—both of them volunteers. If the Post Office Officials were as broadminded in their attitude as we have been here, there would not now be so many rebellious Americans in this country.   Very truly yours,   A W Ricker

TLS (WP, DLC).
[1] Arthur W. Little, printer and publisher, was serving as a major in the 15th New York Infantry (later the 369th U. S. Infantry). His sons were Winslow Little and Arthur W. Little, Jr.

From Robert Lansing

PERSONAL AND CONFIDENTIAL:

My dear Mr. President: Washington August 9, 1917.

I enclose herewith two letters—one of June 18th and one of June 29th,—from Stanley Washburn at Petrograd, and dealing with the general subject of publicity in Russia.[1]
                    Faithfully yours,   Robert Lansing

TLS (WP, DLC).
[1] See WW to RL, Aug. 14, 1917 (third letter of that date), n. 1.

From Newton Diehl Baker

Dear Mr. President,   Washington. August 9, 1917.

The enclosed statement[1] represents, I believe, the more or less united judgment of the War Industries Board, as to the proper policy for them to pursue in the matter of price adjustment.

I wonder if you would have time to glance it over and see whether you would feel disposed to let me say to them that, if they proceed along these lines, it will meet with your approval?

The Board is of course dealing with a very intricate situation, and one which does not permit them at the outset to wait until ultimate prices can be fixed with complete certainty. If, however, they could feel that action tending in the direction discussed in this memorandum was thoroughly in harmony with your desire, I think they could from the very beginning make rapid progress in settling some price controversies and giving a sense of assurance to the business men with whom they have to deal on the subject.   Respectfully yours,   Newton D. Baker

TLS (WP, DLC).
[1] It is printed as an Enclosure with WW to NDB, Aug. 16, 1917 (first letter of that date).

From Newton Diehl Baker

Dear Mr President: Washington. August 9, 1917

I am handing you copies of Gen Scott's observations in Russia and Roumania on the chance of your wanting to glance over them if you take a week end sail[1]
          Respectfully yours,   Newton D. Baker

ALS (N. D. Baker Papers, DLC).
[1] Scott had prepared two lengthy reports, each with several appendices, on board U.S.S. Buffalo, on the return voyage from Vladivostok to Seattle. The reports were addressed to the Secretary of War, but on July 30 Scott gave copies to Root, who included them with the report of the Special Mission. E. Root et al. to the Secretary of State, August 1917, TLS (SDR, RG 59, 763.72/6430½, DNA).
Scott's first report, dated July 25, stated that the two main factors in the military situation in Russia were the "mental and moral state brought about in the privates and non-commissioned officers by the Revolution" and the "inadequacy of the railway rolling stock and the inefficiency of the railway management . . . now disastrously complicated and intensified by the effect of the Revolution upon all railroad employees." After reviewing his discussions and observations in Russia, Scott concluded that the risk that the United States should be willing to take to keep Russia in the war "ought to be gauged by the importance of the results flowing from her defection." In the circumstances, Scott recommended lending Russia $1 billion and sending "all the cars and engines we can," if this would prevent Russia "from making peace this winter with Germany."
Scott's second report, dated July 30, described his brief visit to Jassy, the temporary capital of Rumania, and analyzed the country's military situation and its possible contributions to the Allied cause. Scott recommended that, if the United States decided to lend money and provide supplies to keep Russia in the war, it should do the same for Rumania, whose fifteen divisions were important strategically as well as for the morale of the Russian troops fighting alongside them.

From Richard Heath Dabney

Dear Woodrow: [Charlottesville, Va.] 9 Aug., 1917.

I congratulate you on the passage of the Food Control bill,[1] and should like to "larrup" the obstructionists who have so long delayed it.

Your firm and resolute stand in the conduct of the war, and your refusal to dally with the sham pacifism of the Kaiser & his aiders & abettors have delighted your friends.

In a letter to the N. Y. Times I have recently paid my respects to the self-labeled "People's Council,"[2] a bunch of people comprising probably some sincere dreamers and some cowards and traitors. I enclose a copy, thinking that possibly you might find time to glance through it.

Since the end of our session I have made twelve speeches in different parts of the State, endeavoring to explain the seriousness & necessity of the war, urging subscription to Liberty Bonds, to the Red Cross Fund, etc.

By the way, I am glad to hear that the Government is reorganizing the Red Cross work. For, from all I can hear & read, it sadly needs reorganization. People all over the country are exasperated at the absurd and petty rules & regulations as to how garments, bandages, etc. are to be made. The Fund for the French Wounded, to which I have also subscribed frequently, is far more sensibly managed.   Faithfully,   R. H. Dabney.

ALS (WP, DLC).
  [1] The report of the conference on the Lever bill (H.R. 4961) was approved by the House of Representatives on August 3 and by the Senate on August 8. *Cong. Record*, 65th Cong., 1st sess., pp. 5767-68, 5927. Wilson approved and signed the bill on August 10. 40 *Statutes at Large* 276.
  [2] R. H. Dabney, "A Deaf Ear for the People's Council: Their Pacific Program Would Leave the World a Prey to Prussianism," *New York Times*, Aug. 1, 1917, clipping, WP, DLC.

To George Creel

My dear Creel: [The White House] 10 August, 1917

I am the worst possible subject for moving pictures and I hope you will let me off from having my picture taken when signing the Food Bill. Indeed, I am to sign it very hastily this afternoon because I must go down the river on an official errand,[1] and dare not postpone putting the bill into operation.

        Cordially and sincerely yours,   [Woodrow Wilson]

CCL (WP, DLC).
  [1] To address the officers of the Atlantic Fleet near Norfolk. His address is printed at August 11.

To Arthur Brisbane[1]

My dear Mr. Brisbane: [The White House] 10 August, 1917

Of course I shall be glad to see Raemaekers,[2] whose work I have greatly admired. Won't you ask him to come in at the office at 2:15 next Tuesday just before Cabinet?

Cordially and sincerely yours,   Woodrow Wilson

TLS (Letterpress Books, WP, DLC).
  [1] He had recently bought the Washington *Times* from Frank A. Munsey.
  [2] Louis Raemaekers, a Dutch political cartoonist and artist, noted for his anti-German cartoons. Wilson saw him on August 29.

To Frank Lyon Polk

Dear Mr. Secretary,   The White House [c. Aug. 10, 1917].

I have read these papers[1] with the greatest interest and return them for your files.   W.W.

ALI (SDR, RG 59, 763.72/6430½, DNA).
  [1] Wilson had received Root and the members of the Special Mission at the White House for an hour or more during the afternoon of August 8. Root had probably presented the report of the mission, E. Root *et al.* to the Secretary of State, August 1917, TLS (SDR, RG 59, 763.72/6430½, DNA), to Wilson at this time. The report described the mission's trip, activities in Russia, and meetings of members with various officials of the Russian government; emphasized the seriousness of the problem of transportation in Russia; reported that the Provisional Government had no intention of making a separate peace; and described the extensive German propaganda in Russia and the internal political situation. The report said that the Russian people had "the qualities of character which will make it possible to restore discipline and coherent and intelligently directed action, both in military and civil life, notwithstanding the temporary distressing conditions already described." Finally, the members urged the extension of all possible aid to Russia. This report is printed in *FR 1918, Russia*, I, 131-53.

From Samuel Gompers

Sir: Washington, D. C. August 10, 1917.

Late yesterday afternoon, as I was about to attend a meeting of the Council of National Defense, your letter of the 8th instant, together with copy of telegram, was handed me. After my return from the meeting I sent the following telegram:

Washington, D. C.
August 9, 1917.

"Mr. J. L. Donnelly, President,
    Convention Arizona State Federation of Labor,
        Clifton, Arizona.
Accept and convey to the officers and delegates of your State Federation Convention the fraternal greetings of the organized

labor movement of our country. You may rest assured that every officer of the Federal Government is doing and will do all that lies in their power to see that the great wrong done the deported men shall be righted and they given an opportunity to return to their homes. In this all may count upon my assistance. In this crucial hour of our Nation's life when freedom and democracy are hanging in the balance and for which all free-men must contend it behooves us all to do our level best in the great cause of labor and for the great principles for which the government and the people of the United States are in this world's struggle.

(signed)   Samuel Gompers."

I quite agree with you that the tone and the intimation in the telegram you received are harsh, and particularly so when those who know you know your high sense of justice and consuming purpose to protect the rights and the needs of our people.

But sir, is it not right that we sometimes place ourselves in the position of others and take into account their feelings and their indignant resentment of a terrible outrage? You know that the men in the American trade union movement have nothing in common with the so-called I.W.W.; that as a matter of fact they are as antoganistic to the American Federation of Labor, if not more so, than to any other institution in the world. They are opposed to the constructive policy and methods employed by the American trade union movement for the protection and promotion of the rights, interests, and welfare of the workers. So I am justified in saying, that there is nothing in common between the I.W.W. and the American Federation of Labor.

And yet, when we have seen what we have seen, that hundreds of men, citizens of Arizona, nearly all of them law-abiding, rounded up by a group of capitalistic anarchists who have not only taken the law into their own hands but went far beyond any warrant of law and at the point of guns and bayonets driven into cattle cars, deported from their home, city, and state, into a foreign state, carried in such condition for days without food, or drink, or care, or opportunity for rest and left stranded among strangers and their wives and children at home suffering the anxiety of husband and father ruthlessly and without warrant of law abducted from them; when a man in another state is taken from his abode and put to death by another group of capitalistic anarchists, it is no wonder that men will feel deeply at such treatment, at such brutality, with murder in their hearts and carry it into execution and that when expressing themselves honest American citizens, workmen, union men in conventions assembled, will express themselves in terms forceful even though it may be inconsiderate.

Advice reaches me that the State Federation Convention held at Clifton, Arizona, appointed a committee which proceeded toward Bisbee authorized and directed to make an investigation of the outrageous, unlawful deportation and to report to the convention. When that committee were within a few miles of Bisbee they were halted by a group of the character of persons I have mentioned and warned that their entrance into the city would be prevented and if they attempted to enter it would be at the peril of their lives. Of course, the committee could not attempt to proceed further and so returned to Clifton and reported to the convention.

In many parts of the North-west the employers of labor encouraged the so-called I.W.W. for the purpose of breaking up the bona fide trade unions belonging to the American Federation of Labor. The[y] sewed the wind which made for the results which we have witnessed. I wish I could present a picture to you of the situation that exists in several other places of our country, of employers who are taking advantage of the present war situation; employers who have used the soldiers of our government to force the workers into compliance with the employers' wishes; employers who, under the pretext they have contracts for government work have said that unless the workmen yield they will be imprisoned or interned during the war; of employers who have misinterpreted your own declaration and the declaration of the Council of National Defense, that standards of labor should be maintained, into an insistence that no change will be permitted; that notwithstanding the greater profits which employers have been reaping from government contracts insist that the workers shall not share in the slightest but in fact accept lower standards; of employers who have insisted that the labor laws protecting women and children shall be let down and the workers shall be employed for any length of time to suit the employers' convenience; of the legislatures of West Virginia and of Maryland which so recently passed compulsory labor laws.[1] But, sir, neither you nor I have the time to read or to write the details of all this great wrong which in one form or another is being pressed upon the rights, interests, welfare, and safety of the workers of the United States.

A few of the government departments are helping in the effort for the mobilization of the good-will of the workers. With them my associates and I are helping to work out a solution of the various labor problems, but some of the departments and other agencies of the government are either ignoring the situation and in some instances are positively hostile.

It may be said as a truism that either the government and the employers generally will have to deal with the representatives of the bona fide organized constructive labor movement of the country or they will have the alternative of being forced to take the consequences of the so-called I.W.W. with all that it implies. Repression will beget repression and resentment and the repressions and the resentments will find expression in ways which we now know not of.

It is most difficult for me to advise you as to how the telegram from Messrs. Donnelly and French shall be answered, except as this letter may present a thought upon which an answer could be based; to assume a conciliatory attitude; to express the thought that in this republic of American law and order the regular process of law must be maintained; that the rights of the people must be maintained. The commonest, meanest criminal, whose whole life has been one of criminality, if discovered to be guilty of another crime, is charged with the offense by the duly constituted authorities; he is placed on trial, confronted by a jury of his peers, and given an opportunity of lawful defense. A workman, or a group of workmen who, however mistaken or wantonly and illy designed their purpose and course may be, is entitled to the same protection. Only then, can an orderly government be maintained.

I regret that I could not get this letter to you before this.
        Very respectfully yours,   Saml. Gompers.

TLS (WP, DLC).
    ¹ The Maryland act, which took effect on June 28, 1917, stipulated that all able-bodied men between eighteen and fifty not usefully employed might in time of war be required to register and to work in some public or private employment. A provision that the act was not to apply to persons temporarily unemployed, by reason of a difference with their employers, prevented the use of the act to conscript strikers and force them to work.
    The West Virginia act, which went into effect on August 17, 1917, provided that every able-bodied male resident between sixteen and sixty must habitually and regularly engage in some useful occupation or employment from which he might produce or earn enough to support himself and his legal dependents. Until six months after the end of the war with Germany, any such person who failed to do so for at least thirty-six hours a week would be deemed a vagrant and be subject to a fine or sixty days' labor on the roads or on other public works.
    These acts were known as "lazy men's laws." *American Labor Legislation Review*, VII (Sept. 1917), 551, 554-56. In Maryland, the general observation was that "the number of visible idlers has greatly decreased since the law went on the statute books." Maryland State Board of Labor and Statistics, *Twenty-sixth Annual Report*, 1917 (Baltimore, 1917), p. 181.

From Lillian D. Wald and Others, with Enclosure

Dear Mr. President: New York Office August 10th, 1917.

In accordance with your request through Mr. Tumulty of July 3rd, in answer to our telegram of July 2nd, we submit herewith legal evidence of certain distinct violations of constitutional rights in different parts of the country since the declaration of war.

We present evidence covering only a few recent cases. But this evidence we believe will suffice to convince you that civil liberty in America is seriously threatened under pressure of the war.

May we suggest once more that a public statement from you would tend at once to put a stop to these invasions of established rights at the hands of over-zealous officials?

We are not pleading for those who desire to obstruct the war or embarrass the government. We plead for those whose minds and hearts like yours long for a world order in which all peoples may be really free. They seek it in a common understanding among the people and between the peoples of the warring nations. They express it in discussion of terms of peace, the basis and meaning of democracy, and the war policies of the nation. May we not hope that the ultimate victory for the freedom of mankind is to be won not upon the battlefield but in a new understanding between the peoples, through agitation and discussion?

For this immediate high purpose, as well as for the vindication of constitutional rights on principle, we ask a statement from you now, which will make it easier for public opinion in America to play its part during the war.

Recalling your words in reply to our first appeal to you on this matter:—

"I will have the matter in mind and will act, I hope, at the right time in the spirit of your suggestion."[1]—

we look to you to speak the word which will make every man in public office throughout this country feel the high obligation resting upon him to uphold the liberties guaranteed by the constitution.

Very respectfully yours,   Lillian D. Wald.
                                  Crystal Eastman.
                                  Roger Baldwin.
                                  L. Hollingsworth Wood.

For the American Union Against Militarism.

TLS (WP, DLC).
    [1] That is, in WW to Lillian D. Wald, April 28, 1917, Vol. 42.

ENCLOSURE

Memorandum on Invasion of Constitutional Rights,
Presented by American Union Against Militarism, Aug. 13, 1917

The evidence herewith presented covers the denial of established rights:

1st. By arbitrary denial of the right of free speech and assemblage by local officials.

2nd. By illegal arrest and search by local police and federal authorities

3rd. By lawless assumption of power by members of the military forces.

4th. Through unfounded complaints of overzealous federal district attorneys.

5th. By arbitrary action of postmasters in denying the use of the mails.

1. Free speech and assemblage.

We have the record of eight indictments for crimes ranging from treason and conspiracy to simple misdemeanor for the sole offense of criticizing the government's war policies, or agitating for peace. (These cases have occurred in Philadelphia, Ohio, Chicago, Michigan, Indianapolis, New York City, Pittsburgh and Seattle.)

In Philadelphia 13 persons were recently arrested and charged with treason for distributing a leaflet entitled "Long Live the Constitution of the United States," which dealt in a lawful way with the constitutionality of conscription. See Exhibit A.[1]

In one city (Indianapolis) an ordinance has been passed, making it a misdemeanor, punishable by a heavy fine "To speak disrespectfully of the President or the government of the U. S.," or to have in one's possession literature which comments disrespectfully upon officials or the government; and prohibiting the publication of any matter which might prompt workers to demand better conditions of work or hours of labor in industrial establishments during the war. See Exhibit B.

Two historic meeting places for free speech in New York City have been closed to meetings on peace or war policies, namely, Carnegie Hall and Cooper Union.

One man in New York City was arrested for distributing leaflets which contained only quotations from the Constitution and Declaration of Independence. He was sentenced to 90 days in jail, but later released by a superior court. See Exhibit C.

A postoffice employee in St. Paul, Minn. was discharged after years of faithful service solely because he went on the bonds of three old friends charged with failing to register under the conscription act.

2. *Unlawful arrest, search and seizure.*

The evidence presented shows that federal district attorneys, United States marshals, local prosecuting officials and the police have acted in gross violation of the law in making arrests for opposition to war policies and agitation for peace. In many cities men and women have been arrested without warrant, their private papers unlawfully seized, and the opportunity denied them to secure bail or counsel for hours at a time. See Exhibit D.

In Chicago recently a meeting called to discuss the problem of the conscientious objector, presided over by a distinguished woman, was virtually broken up by federal secret service men, who arrested many present without reason, taking them to the federal building, where they were held for hours, being released the next day on order of the federal district attorney, who apologized for the conduct of the men. See Exhibit E.

3. *Assumption of power by the military.*

The most striking single instance of violence on the part of the military was the breaking up of the Peace Parade in Boston on Sunday, July 1st, by soldiers and sailors. Probably no more extreme violation of citizens' rights at the hands of men in the uniform of the United States has ever taken place in our history. Beginning at the statue of Abraham Lincoln in Park Square, sailors and soldiers followed this parade with the deliberate intention of breaking it up; they tore banners from the hands of women, they beat and injured men and women; later they forcibly entered the Socialist Party headquarters, destroyed property and burned many valuable papers and much literature. The police did nothing throughout this performance to protect the citizens' rights. See Exhibit F.

Less flagrant cases of violence on the part of soldiers and sailors in connection with peace meetings have been reported from all parts of the country. The New York cases were called to the attention of the War Department by local officials and citizens' organizations. Although the War Department has issued orders forbidding soldiers to interfere with peace meetings, the trouble has not ceased. We have the report of an eye-witness that a meeting in the interest of peace and democracy was broken up in Seattle on August 1st by soldiers of the United States.

Soldiers and sailors at many so-called peace meetings have held and searched men for registration cards. Those unable to produce them they have turned over to the police, who have detained them indefinitely until they could produce either the cards or some evidence of the date of birth. Men both above and below the registration age have thus been unlawfully held for hours in many places without any charge being lodged against them, and yet without the right to secure counsel or bail.

4. Activities of over-zealous district attorneys.

We have records of some 12 cases of men and women unlawfully arrested and held on authority of federal district attorneys. Most of the charges made are unfounded in fact and are evidently intended merely as a means of suppressing the activities of persons whom the district attorneys regard as a menace to the conduct of the war. These charges range from treason and conspiracy to violations of the espionage act. For example, in Grand Rapids, Michigan 12 citizens were indicted for distributing literature opposing conscription, before the passage of the espionage act, and under charges so general as to be insusceptible of proof. In Syracuse, New York, a young man who wrote on his registration blank in the state military census that he was opposed to participation in this war was proceeded against by the Federal District Attorney under the Espionage Act for obstructing the recruiting and enlistment service. See Exhibit G

5. Arbitrary action by postoffice officials.

Seventeen issues of various publications have been held and declared non-mailable by the postoffice department under the Espionage Act, although the Department of Justice declined to recognize any of these publications as indictable under the same Act. In some cases the identical matter which caused the suppression of these publications appeared in other publications without interference.

Furthermore, the postoffice department has summoned the editor[s] of several of these publications to show cause why their second class mailing privileges should not be withdrawn on the ground that the "continuity of publication has been broken," knowing full well that the break in continuity of publication was caused solely by its own act in suppressing an issue. Denial of second class privilege would mean the total suppression of the papers. It is inconceivable that the postoffice department will be allowed to proceed to such manifest tyranny, unchecked.

Private sealed first class mail has been held up by the Postoffice department for six weeks at a time, without notice. An extreme instance was the holding for weeks of two thousand circular letters mailed by the American Union Against Militarism

—which contained no reference to the war or conscription, but discussed the growing danger to free press and criticized the administration of the post office department. The fact that all these letters were finally declared "mailable" and allowed to proceed to their destination, makes it clear that the difficulty is due not to the treasonable character of the mail but to the misguided zeal of officious department heads. See Exhibit H.

T MS (WP, DLC).
¹ Three of the exhibits mentioned in this memorandum (C, G, and H) are missing in WP, DLC. The remaining exhibits consist mainly of affidavits showing the highhanded methods of local federal authorities and are well described by Miss Wald and her co-signers. The exhibits are not attached to this letter but can be found among a group of documents entitled "Exhibits submitted by the American Union Against Militarism in support of charges of alleged invasion of constitutional rights," under the date of July 1917 in Series 12, WP, DLC.

From Franklin Knight Lane

My dear Mr. President: Washington August 10, 1917.

As I will not have an opportunity to see you for a few days, perhaps you will pardon me for giving you the gist of my talk with various members of the Commission to Russia, especially my talk with Mr. Mott and with Mr. Russell.

I believe that from our standpoint the immediate need is a great program of education through moving pictures, speeches, Y.M.C.A.'s, etc. as to what the United States is and why it is in the war. Mr. Mott has outlined his own views on this matter to me and I have talked them over with Stanley Washburn, who knows Russia very well, and he concurs in them.

The second greatest matter of help is the improvement of the facilities upon the Siberian railroad. Mr. Willard, who has kept in touch with John F. Stevens, says that he is ready to provide men to go to Vladivostok to set up the locomotives, and that nothing is immediately needed to carry on this work excepting credit for Russia in our markets with which to buy equipment. The ships are available to carry from our coast to theirs.

          Cordially and faithfully yours,   Franklin K Lane

TLS (WP, DLC).

From Edward Mandell House

Dear Governor: Magnolia, Massachusetts. August 10, 1917.

Dudley Malone was here today. He seems in quite a different frame of mind, and I think is genuinely sorry for the happenings of some weeks ago. He spoke of you with his old time affection. My fear now is that he and McAdoo will have trouble because they dislike one another so heartily.

I talked the financial situation out with McAdoo when he was here Tuesday. I think it can be satisfactorily adjusted. Northcliffe comes for tomorrow and Sunday and I will be able to see how nearly the English position coincides with McAdoo's.

The English, of course, want to maintain the pound sterling, and I see a disposition on the part of McAdoo, Harding and others to substitute the dollar as the standard of value throughout the world. This, I am afraid, will finally come to be the crux of the difference between the two nations, and if we are not careful, it will make for trouble.

I cautioned McAdoo to give, when he had to give, with a glad hand for, in any other way, we will lose both money and good will. As long as we have money to lend those wishing to borrow will be agreeable, but when the bottom of the barrel is reached, it may be a different story. It is their turn now to be pleasant—later it will be ours in order to collect what they owe.

I remember, during one of the old time panics, a very rich man was asked by a friend of mine whether he was not terribly worried. He replied "No, I am not at all worried, but the banks that are carrying me are."

Affectionately yours,   E. M. House

P.S. While Woolley is not the ideal man for the Interstate Commerce Commission, yet he seems the best in sight from the South where one of the appointments belongs, and I hope you will feel that it is possible to appoint him. I believe he will make a creditable record.

The railroads are extremely anxious for you to name one very big man, if you can find one to accept. They seem to think that Rublee is of that calibre. I am surprised to know they would be satisfied with his appointment for he is of the Brandeis school.

TLS (WP, DLC).

From Edward Mandell House, with Enclosure

Dear Governor: Magnolia, Massachusetts. August 10, 1917.

I have just received the enclosed cable from Sir William Wiseman. It is a message which they evidently do not care to send through their Embassy and yet they wish your views regarding the questions asked.

It seems a little inconsistent to want us to deny the French the right to recruit from the Poles and yet give them the right to recruit from our own citizens. My feeling is that we should have a Polish division in our own army as the American Poles desire. It would undoubtedly have a profound influence on the Poles in both the German and Austrian armies.

In a message received from Sir William yesterday he tells me that he has persuaded his government that it is necessary to keep you fully informed regarding what is going on in the Allied countries and armies. He has worked out a plan for this which I think will be satisfactory.   Affectionately yours,   E. M. House

TLS (WP, DLC).

ENCLOSURE

London, August 9, 1917.

Mr. Balfour attaches much political importance to the question of a Polish army to form part of the United States forces as the Central Powers are alarmed by the idea of a Polish National Army, formation of which would seriously affect, not only their position in occupied Polish territory, but also, the Poles in the German and Austrian armies.

Mr. Balfour believes the best solution is that a Polish army should form part of the United States forces. We understand the French have sent a message through General [Archinard][1] to Tardieu asking that he should obtain permission to recruit Poles in America for the French-Polish Army. Polish leaders here in close touch with Paderewski consider this highly undesirable. Count Haredeski (?) [Horodyski] one of the chief Polish leaders will leave here for New York in about a week. I think it would be well to await his arrival before adopting the French scheme.

From secret information reaching H. M. Government, morale of the French armies and provinces is in weak state, although somewhat improved by the arrival of General Pershing and American division. The French are about at the end of their man power, and something should be done to strengthen their capacity for endurance during coming winter. Would it be possible to allow American citizens, outside of draft law, to enlist in the French Army and would any considerable number be available?

Naturally the request must come from the French themselves, though if the President is prepared to consider the principle favorably, a medium assistance might be given. We could give the French a hint to lay their position frankly before him and ask his assistance. They are, of course, reluctant to expose even to us their real position. William Wiseman.

TC telegram (WP, DLC).
  ¹ Corrections from W. Wiseman to EMH, Aug. 9, 1917, T telegram (W. Wiseman Papers, CtY). General Louis Archinard was a member of the French Superior Council of War of the War Ministry.

An Address to the Officers of the Atlantic Fleet[1]

August 11, 1917

Admiral Mayo and gentlemen: I have not come here with malice prepense to make a speech, but I have come here to have a look at you and to say some things that perhaps may be intimately said and, even though the company is large, said in confidence. Of course, the whole circumstance of the modern time is extraordinary, and I feel that, just because the circumstances are extraordinary, there is an opportunity to see to it that the action is extraordinary. One of the deprivations which any man in authority experiences is that he cannot come into constant and intimate touch with the men with whom he is associated and necessarily associated in action.

Most of my life has been spent in contact with young men and, though I would not admit it to them at the time, I have learned a great deal more from them than they ever learned from me. I have had most of my thinking stimulated by questions being put to me which I could not answer, and I have had a great many of my preconceived conceptions absolutely destroyed by men who had not given half the study to the subject that I myself had given. The fact of the matter is that almost every profession is pushed forward by the men who do not belong to it and know nothing about it, because they ask the ignorant questions which it would not occur to the professional man to ask at all because he supposes that they have been answered, whereas it may be that most of them had not been answered at all. The naiveté of the point of view, the whole approach of the mind that has had nothing to do with the question, creates an entirely different atmosphere. There is many a question asked you about the navy which seems to you so simple-minded when you hear it that you laugh, and then you find you cannot answer it. It never occurred to you that anybody could ask that question before, it is so simple.

¹ Wilson, accompanied by Daniels, spoke aboard *U.S.S. Pennsylvania*, flagship of the Atlantic Fleet, near Norfolk.

Now, the point that is constantly in my mind, gentlemen, is this: this is an unprecedented war and, therefore, it is a war in one sense for amateurs. Nobody ever before conducted a war like this and, therefore, nobody can pretend to be a professional in a war like this. Here are two great navies, not to speak of the others associated with us—our own and the British—outnumbering by a very great margin the navy to which we are opposed, and yet casting about for a way in which to use our superiority and our strength, because of the novelty of the instruments used, because of the unprecedented character of the war. Because, as I said just now, nobody ever before fought a war like this, in the way that this is being fought at sea—or on land either, for that matter. The experienced soldier—experienced in previous wars— is a back number so far as his experience is concerned; not so far as his intelligence is concerned. His experience does not count, because he never fought a war as this is being fought, and, therefore, he is an amateur along with the rest of us. Now, somebody has got to think this war out. Somebody has got to think out the way, not only to fight the submarine, but to do something different from what we are doing.

We are hunting hornets all over the farm and letting the nest alone. None of us knows how to go to the nest and crush it, and yet I despair of hunting for hornets all over the sea when I know where the nest is and know that the nest is breeding hornets as fast as I can find them. I am willing, for my part, and I know you are willing, because I know the stuff you are made of—I am willing to sacrifice half the navy Great Britain and we together have to crush that nest, because if we crush it, the war is won. I have come here to say that I do not care where it comes from; I do not care whether it comes from the youngest officer or the oldest. But I want the officers of this navy to have the distinction of saying how this war is going to be won. The Secretary of the Navy and I have just been talking over plans for putting the planning machinery of the navy at the disposal of the brains of the navy and not stopping to ask what rank that brain has, because, as I have said before, and want to repeat, so far as experience in this kind of war is concerned, we are all of the same rank. I am not saying that I do not expect the admirals to tell us what to do, but I am saying that I want the youngest and most modest youngster in the service to tell us what we ought to do if he knows what it is. I am willing to make any sacrifice for that. I mean any sacrifice of time or anything else. I am ready to put myself at the disposal of any officer in the navy who thinks he knows how to run this war. I won't undertake to tell you whether he does or not, because I know I cannot, but I will undertake to put him in communication with those who can find out whether his idea will work or not. I have the authority to do that, and I will do it with the greatest pleasure.

The idea that is in my mind all the time is that we are comrades in this thing. I was talking the other day with some commercial men about certain questions which seemed to affect their material interest in this war, and I said: "I can't imagine a man thinking about those things. If we don't win this war, your material interest won't make any difference. The prices you are charging are a matter of indifference with regard to the results of this war because if we don't win it, you won't have the chance to charge any price. And I can't imagine a man in the present circumstances of the world sitting down and thinking about his own interest or the interest of anybody personally associated with him as compared with the interest of the world." I cannot say it too often to any audience: we are fighting a thing, not a people. The most extraordinary circumstance of modern history is the way in which the German people have been subordinated to the German system of authority, and how they have accepted their thinking from authority as well as their action from authority. Now, we do not intend to let that method of action and of thinking be imposed upon the rest of the world. Knowing, as some of us do, the fine quality of the German people, we are sorry that it was ever imposed upon them, and we are anxious to see that they have their glad emancipation, but we intend to see to it that no other people suffers a like limitation and subordination. We went into this war because this system touched us. These people that stopped at nothing paid no attention to our rights, destroyed the lives of our people, invaded the dignity of our sovereignty, tried to make intrigues against us in the minds of our own people, and the thing was intolerable. We had to strike, but, thank God, we were striking, not only for ourselves, but for everybody else that loves liberty under God's heaven, and, therefore, we are in some peculiar sense the trustees of liberty.

I wish that I could think and had the brains to think in the terms of marine warfare, because I would feel then that I was figuring out the future history of the political freedom of mankind. I do not see how any man can look at the flag of the United States and fail having his mind crowded with reminiscences of the number of unselfish men, seeking no object of their own, the advantage of no dynasty, the advantage of no group of privileged people, but the advantage of his fellow men, who have died under the folds of that beautiful emblem. I wonder if men who do die under it realize the distinction they have. There is no comparison between dying in your bed in quiet times for nothing in particular and dying under that emblem of the might and destiny and pride of a great free people. There is distinction in the privilege, and I, for my part, am sorry to play so peaceful a part in the business as I myself am obliged to play. And I conceive it a privilege to come and look at you men who have the other thing to do and ask you to come and tell me or tell anybody you want to tell how this thing can be better done; and we will thank God that we have got men of originative brains among us.

Thus we have got to throw tradition to the wind. Now, as I have said, gentlemen, I take it for granted that nothing that I say here will be repeated, and therefore I am going to say this: Every time we have suggested anything to the British Admiralty, the reply has come back that virtually amounted to this, that it had never been done that way. And I felt like saying: "Well, nothing was ever done so systematically as nothing is being done now. Therefore, I should like to see something unusual happen, something that was never done before. And, inasmuch as the things that are being done to you were never done before, don't you think it is worthwhile to try something that was never done before against those who are doing them to you." There is not any other way to win, and the whole principle of this war is the kind of thing that ought to hearten and stimulate America. America has always boasted that she could find men to do anything. She is the prize amateur nation of the world. Germany is the prize professional nation of the world. Now, when it comes to doing new things, and doing them well, I will back the amateur against the professional every time, because the professional does it out of the book, and the amateur does it with his eyes open upon a new world and with a new set of circumstances. He knows so little about it that he is fool enough to try the right thing. The men that do not know the danger are the rashest men, and I have several times ventured to make this suggestion to the men about me in both arms of the service: please leave out of your vocabulary altogether the word "prudent." Do not stop to think about what is prudent for a moment. Do the thing that is audacious to the utmost point of risk and daring, because that is exactly the thing that the other side does not understand. And you will win by the audacity of method when you cannot win by circumspection and prudence. I think that there are willing ears to hear this in the American navy and the American army because that is the kind of folks we are. We get tired of the old ways and covet the new ones.

So, gentlemen, besides coming down here to give you my personal greeting and to say how absolutely I rely on you and believe in you, I have come down here to say also that I depend on you, depend on you for brains as well as training and courage and discipline. You are doing your job admirably, the job that you have been taught to do. Now let us do something that we were never taught to do, and do it just as well as we are doing the older and more habitual things, and do not let anybody ever put one thought of discouragement into your minds. I do not know what is the matter with the newspapers of the United States! I suppose they have to vary the tune from time to time just to relieve their minds, but every now and then a wave of the most absurd discouragement and pessimism goes through the country, and we hear nothing except of the unusual advantages and equipment and sagacity and preparation and all the other wonderful things of the German army and navy. My comment is always the very familiar comment, "Rats!" They are working under infinite disadvantages. They not only have no more brains than we have, but they have a different and less serviceable kind of brains than we have, if we will use the brains we have got. I am not discouraged for a moment, particularly because we have not even begun and, without saying anything in disparagement of those with whom we are associated in the war, I do expect things to begin when we begin. If they do not, American history will have changed its course; the American army and navy will have changed their character. There will have to come a new tradition into a service which does not do new and audacious and successful things.

I am very much obliged to you for having given me this opportunity to see you, and I hope you will also give me the pleasure of shaking hands with each one of you. I would not like to go away without that, and if you ever want me again for anything in particular—because I am a busy man and cannot come for anything that is not particular—send for me and I will come.

Printed in *Address of President Wilson to the Officers of the Atlantic Fleet* . . . (Washington, 1920), with corrections from a reading of the CLSsh notes in the C. L. Swem Coll., NjP.

To Jacques A. Berst

My dear Mr. Berst: The White House August 11, 1917.

I refer to my letter of June 4th and to your reply thereto of June 9th, regarding the motion picture play "Patria."[1]

Through the courtesy of Mr. Granville S. Macfarland, an opportunity was given for a representative of the Department of

State and of the Japanese Embassy to view the entire film. It was found that the modifications of the original film were entirely inadequate; for instance, the leading Japanese conspirator has been converted into a Mexican conspirator, but the producer neglected to remove his Japanese kimono and substitute therefor suitable Mexican dress. The servants remain Japanese, both in appearance and in the manner of their dress, and the interior fittings in a number of scenes are entirely Japanese. Towards the end of the picture the Japanese conspirator is shown in Mexico in the uniform of a Japanese officer, along with other officers in Japanese uniforms. Several regiments of Japanese soldiers in the regulation Japanese army uniform, with Japanese flags in evidence, are shown in the act of invading this country from Mexico in cooperation with Mexican troops.

I understand that you are willing to modify the film still further and if so, it would seem desirable to omit all those scenes in which anything Japanese appears, particularly those showing the Japanese and Mexican armies invading the United States, pillaging homes, kidnapping women and committing all sorts of other offenses.

I trust that this will be found possible, and if not, I again venture to ask whether you are not prepared to withdraw the film entirely from exhibition.

Sincerely yours,   Woodrow Wilson[2]

TCL (Letterpress Books, WP, DLC).
    [1] See WW to J. A. Berst, June 4, 1917, and WW to F. L. Polk, June 9, 1917, n. 1, both in Vol. 42.
    [2] This letter virtually repeated F. L. Polk to WW, Aug. 11, 1917, TLS (WP, DLC).

From William Kent

My dear Mr. President: Washington August 11, 1917.

I wish to thank you for the engagement for Wednesday at 3 o'clock. An advance memorandum may be servic[e]able.

Miss Helen Todd[1] is anxious to go on the stump on the same sort of mission as Mr. Darrow, and I believe would be equally efficient.

Senator Borah stated to her that he would be glad to join in enlightening the Western part of the country as to the needs of backing this war for democracy. He, however, feels that a definite statement of America's part and policy should be made by you, as a text, if he is to go in to back the Administration. I am satisfied I understand your position and that you are definitely determined not to take over the old feuds and squabbles of our Allies, or their territorial ambitions, and that you do not regard the war from our standpoint as a punitive expedition.

I talked with Secretary Houston the other evening and he thought it might be well for you to collate what you have said in the past and to express the American policy anew in clear and unmistakable terms.

I would not for a moment presume to advise you in this connection. I merely wish to say that such a statement would secure cooperation which would otherwise not be obtainable. I am aware of the delicacy of international relations and also realize the supreme importance of being clearly understood at home.

I am informed that Senator Borah would appreciate a request from you to call. While I disagree with Senator Borah on many things, I know his vigor, clarity of mind, and power of expression. It would be worth much to have him preaching the war gospel in the West where it is as badly needed as it is in the Ghettos.

I have heard that Mr. Gompers has been expressing some violent views concerning war until Germany is crushed. I know this is not your view and is not the view of the country, and I only speak from hearsay. But if he is correctly quoted by Miss Todd, damage may be done.

These are some of the matters I wish to take up with you and if in your judgment you would like to see Miss Todd and Senator Borah, I believe a meeting with them, together or separately, and I believe better together, might be of great use.[2]

Yours truly,   William Kent

TLS (WP, DLC).
[1] Helen Todd, a leader of the movement for woman suffrage in New York, had called on Wilson at the White House on July 20 as a representative of the women of the East Side of New York.
[2] Wilson saw Miss Todd again on August 20. There is no record of a meeting between Wilson and Borah during this period.

From Franklin Potts Glass

My dear Friend: [Birmingham, Ala.] August 11, 1917.

Please permit me to call your personal attention to the fact that a strike of the 25,000 coal miners of this district is called for the 20th instant.

I have tried steadily for two weeks through the columns of The News to prevent this development. But the Operators' Association has finally and positively refused to meet the Union leaders in any sort of a conference.

Wages have been voluntarily advanced in this district three times in the past year, and there is little ground for a strike in conditions. The chief purpose of the Union leaders is to force recognition, and that the Operators firmly refuse.

As I understand the new law, you have ample power to interpose and stop the paralysis this strike would cause. Please consider the data from the columns of The News herewith enclosed,[1] and take such steps as you deem wise before August 20th.

With the steadiest confidence in your ability to steer the ship of State in all these troublous times, and prayers for your health, I am, as ever,   Sincerely yours,   Frank P. Glass

TLS (WP, DLC).
    [1] "The Threatened Miners' Strike: Is there Any Justification?" *Birmingham News*, Aug. 3, 1917; "Miners Reply to Recent Editorial in News' Columns," *ibid.*, Aug. 7, 1917; "The Miners' Position: Organizer Harrison's Card," *ibid.*, Aug. 8, 1917; "Coal Operators Answer Editorial in News' Columns," *ibid.*, Aug. 9, 1917; and "The Coal Impasse Persists: The Government May Interpose," *ibid.*, Aug. 10, 1917, clippings, all in WP, DLC.

From Thomas Deitz McKeown[1]

                                    Washington, D. C.
Sir: August eleventh, Nineteen Seventeen.

No doubt your attention has been called to the recent outbreak and resistance to the selective draft in my Congressional district, especially in Seminole and Pontotoc counties, Oklahoma.[2]

I am pleased to inform you that for the present the insurrection has been put down and overcomed by the loyal and patriotic citizens and the civil officers of the counties affected.

You will pardon me for intruding upon your time, but I desire to call your attention to the splendid exhibition of courage shown by Mr. Bob Duncan, sheriff of Pontotoc County, who lives at Ada, Oklahoma. I desire to quote from a letter written me by Honorable James A. Long, a lawyer of Holdenville, Oklahoma, who describes the exploit of this sheriff, which broke the back of the resisters in Seminole County, which reads as follows:

    "Bob Duncan of Ada, the Sheriff of your home County, lead thirty-tow [two] men up a hill against a hundred and twenty-five armed W.C.U's,[3] on top of a hill protected by rocks and trees, an ideal place for defense, and routed the rebels on the hill by his show of determination. Not a shot was fired. The appearance of the thirty-two cooly advancing in open order up the hill among the trees and bushes so astonished the rebels that they fled in disorder never again to halt or organize for resistance. There was no band or flag to cheer Duncan and his men, but law and justice and a common country. It was a brave act, and will live to show the kind of men who make up the majority of your constituents. The thirty-two were volunteers called for from a posse of forty-two hastily assembled from both counties: Pontotoc and Hughes."

Brave peace officers who uphold the majesty of the law of the country merits the approval of good men every where.

Hoping that you will pardon me for trespassing upon your valuable time, but I felt that you should know the situation.

With much respect, I have the honor to remain,

Your obedient servant,   Tom D. McKeown

TLS (WP, DLC).
  1 Democratic congressman from Oklahoma.
  2 About this, the so-called Green Corn Rebellion, see James R. Green, *Grass-Roots Socialism: Radical Movements in the Southwest, 1895-1943* (Baton Rouge, La., 1978), pp. 358-68; H. C. Peterson and Gilbert C. Fite, *Opponents of War, 1917-1918* (Madison, Wisc., 1957), pp. 40-41, and Charles C. Bush, "The Green Corn Rebellion" (master's thesis, University of Oklahoma, 1932), pp. 18-68.
  3 That is, members of the Working Class Union, an organization of poor tenants and sharecroppers, connected indirectly with the I.W.W.

From Newton Diehl Baker

Dear Mr. President: Washington. August 12, 1917

The inclosed letters[1] were sent to General Bliss by General Pershing under seal by the hands of Felix Frankfurter who has just returned to this country. They are of the most confidential character, and I send them in order that you may glance them over if you have not already been apprised through the State Department of the subjects considered and the decisions suggested.

I ask your particular attention to the suggestion with regard to the Russian transportation system.

Respectfully yours,   Newton D. Baker

TLS (N. D. Baker Papers, DLC).
  1 Only one of these has been found: J. J. Pershing to T. H. Bliss, July 27, 1917, CCL (J. J. Pershing Papers, DLC). In this letter, Pershing expressed his great concern about the need for stricter conservation of shipping and better protection against German submarines. He enclosed a translation of an article, "What Military Aid May the Entente Expect From the United States?", from the *Nouvelliste* of Geneva, July 7, 1917. The article pointed out the shipping problems which the Allies faced. T MS (J. J. Pershing Papers, DLC).

A News Report

QUOTES WILSON'S VIEWS.

Hopkins Tells of Interview Regarding Suffrage Pickets.

J. A. H. Hopkins, National Progressive Commiteeman of Morristown, N. J., sent to the newspapers yesterday copies of letters which he had mailed to members of Congress, giving details of matters he called to the attention of President Wilson in an interview at the White House a few days before the sixteen militant suffragists were pardoned from the Washington Workhouse for picketing the Executive Mansion. Mrs. J. A. H. Hopkins was one of these prisoners.

"At the outset of our interview," Mr. Hopkins wrote, "I stated that, while he was the champion of democracy at home, and while we were engaged in a war having for its object the establishment of democracy abroad, practically every act of the Congress and Administration since war was declared had been of an autocratic character. As evidence of this I cited several illustrations."

Mr. Hopkins says he told the President that because of the situation the entire country was in a state of unrest. He then told the President, he says, that the arrest of the suffragists was "outrageous and farcical." Mr. Hopkins gives the reply of the President in these words:

"The President stated to me that he had never at any time objected to the pickets, nor had they annoyed him. He accepted my statement, and took it as his own, that the sixteen pickets had not violated any law or any ordinance and were absolutely guiltless. He criticised the Judge's introduction of the Russian banner into the trial as quite out of place, and volunteered the statement that he, the President, did not consider this banner was either treasonable or seditious.

"He (the President) finally asked me what I thought should be done, and when I told him that a pardon had been suggested he immediately called my attention to the fact that this would only be a temporary measure of relief and did not at all solve the real problem, which he agreed could only be solved by the passage of the Susan B. Anthony amendment. He told me, however, that he could not add to the war program unless he considered additional measures were necessary as war measures, and that if he did so it would be forcing legislation, which, however, he was justified in doing if an emergency existed."

Mr. Hopkins wrote that his purpose in calling these matters

to the attention of the members of the Congress was to urge them to maintain democracy at home and refute the charge that the legislative branch of the Federal Government had become a mere "rubber stamp."

Printed in the *New York Times*, Aug. 13, 1917.

To Frederick Dozier Gardner[1]

My dear Governor: [The White House] 13 August, 1917

Your letter of August ninth[2] brought with it great cheer, and I thank you for it very warmly indeed. I have been so unfortunate as not to receive the support of one of the Senators from Missouri[3] but I have never at any time doubted the spirit or the purpose of the people of the State. I wish I might convey to them through you some expression of my entire confidence and reliance.

Cordially and sincerely yours,   Woodrow Wilson

TLS (Letterpress Books, WP, DLC).
    [1] Governor of Missouri.
    [2] It is missing.
    [3] Senator Reed, who had opposed various war measures, including the draft, the Lever bill, and especially Hoover's appointment as Food Administrator. Reed had also supported the Weeks amendment to establish a congressional joint committee on the conduct of the war.

To Richard Heath Dabney

My dear Heath: The White House 13 August, 1917

It is always a refreshment to hear from you and I am very grateful to you for your letter of the ninth.

I am very glad you have been "paying your respects" to the People's Council. It is for the most part a bad and mischievous lot.

In haste   Affectionately yours,   Woodrow Wilson

TLS (Wilson-Dabney Corr., ViU).

To William Bauchop Wilson

My dear Mr. Secretary: [The White House] 13 August, 1917

I dare say you know of the threatened strike referred to in Mr. Glass' letter enclosed. I would be very much obliged to you for some advice as to how to answer Mr. Glass's letter.

Cordially and sincerely yours,   [Woodrow Wilson]

CCL (WP, DLC).

From Robert Lansing, with Enclosure

PERSONAL AND PRIVATE:

My dear Mr. President: Washington August 13, 1917.

Sir Cecil came to see me Saturday evening and handed me the enclosed appeal by the Pope to the belligerents which he said would soon be issued.

My own impression is that this statement of peace terms emanates from Austria-Hungary and is probably sanctioned by the German Government. It is undoubtedly preliminary to the Stockholm Conference.

Faithfully yours,   Robert Lansing

TLS (R. Lansing Papers, NjP).

E N C L O S U R E

Following telegram received from British Representative at the Vatican.

Appeal of the Pope to belligerent Governments is a document of nearly 4 pages print. Following is the substance of chief points in it.

After speaking of his own attitude in the past and his desire to work for good of all without regard for persons, without distinction of nationality, religion, the Pope refers to the continuation of the war and its horrors and asks whether Europe is not tending to its own suicide. No longer confining himself to general terms he wishes to put forward concrete practical proposal and to propose as the basis of a just and durable peace the consideration by belligerent Governments of the following points. He leaves to the Governments the care of stating more precisely and completing these points.

Fundamental point is that moral force of law is to take the place of material force of arms. There should be simultaneous and reciprocal reduction of armaments. Armies are to be replaced by Arbitration.

Once supremacy of law is established there should be no obstacle to means of communication between the people but there must be true liberty and common enjoyment of the seas.

As regards reparation and war indemnities, Pope sees no other solution than as a general principle complete and reciprocal condonation, justified by immense benefits of disarmament. Continuation of carnage for economic reasons would be incomprehensible. If there are special reasons in certain cases let them be weighed with equity and justice.

There must be suitable restitution of territory actually occupied. Thus on the part of Germany there must be total evacuation of Belgium with guarantee of full political and military and economic independence as regards every Power. Equally there must be evacuation of French territory and restitution by other belligerents of the German Colonies.

As regards territorial questions, such as those between Italy and Austria, or Germany and France, parties should examine them in a conciliatory spirit, keeping in view what the Pope has said respecting aspirations of the peoples.

Same spirit of equity and justice should be directed to examination of other territorial and political questions, especially those relative to Armenia, Balkans States and territory of ancient Kingdom of Poland whose noble tradition and suffering should conciliate the sympathies of nations.

Pope concludes by appealing to Governments to terminate a struggle which appears more or less a useless massacre.

T MS (R. Lansing Papers, NjP).

From Robert Lansing, with Enclosure

My dear Mr. President: Washington August 13, 1917.

In a conversation which I had with Mr. Root at luncheon on the 9th he asked me if I had seen the address issued by the Stevens Commission. I said that I had not. The following day he sent me a copy which I enclose.

I fear Mr. Stevens is assuming an authority and giving the Commission a diplomatic character which neither possess. I call your particular attention to the portion of the address marked in red,[1] by which he *pledges* the United States to do certain things, a pledge he had no power to make.

The pledge having been given I think that it would be unwise to repudiate it as the Russian people and Russian Government might misconstrue any repudiation of the Commission's promise. At the same time it would seem advisable I think for Stevens to be told, preferably by you as the Commission is not a diplomatic one, that he has no authority to carry on negotiations or enter into agreements for the United States.

Faithfully yours,   Robert Lansing.

TLS (WP, DLC).

[1] In the fifth paragraph, from "this Commission has cabled the Administration at Washington" to the end of the paragraph.

Message to the People of Russia
from the United States Railway Commission.

Petrograd, 4 July 1917.

The United States Railway Advisory Commission is accredited by the State Department of the United States to its ally Russia. The object of the Commission is, as has been stated, to advise with and to assist in every practicable way in the handling of the grave transportation problems which the war against a common enemy has thrust upon the railways of Russia. It seems fitting that upon this, the anniversary of our natal day of Independence, this Commission should convey to the people of Russia a message declaring not only its purpose but also something as to what it has accomplished and which it is believed will cheer the nation and convince it that the United States stands shoulder to shoulder with its great ally in the prosecution to a successful conclusion of the war against the venomous enemy of democratic freedom.

The Commission has been in Russia about five weeks. During this time it has met with the officials of the Russian Railways and has discussed fully and freely the various problems confronting the railways. It has been met everywhere and at all times with the utmost spirit of cordiality and cooperation on the part of those officials. It has found, what was no surprise to it, that as masters of technique the Russian railway officials have no superiors in the world. It has found that in many ways their practices are among the best and that from a basic standpoint the Russian railways are intrinsically sound—backed as they are by the enormous latent resources and the vast population of this wonderful country. At the same time, it believes that a judicious mingling of the best Russian and American railway practices will be of great benefit to the railways of Russia, and in this belief your officials are in hearty accord and have given their approval to the following suggestions made by this Commission.

An improved system of train operation, a better divisional organization, whereby closer supervision can be maintained, and a revision of engine runs whereby a greater capacity of each engine and car can be obtained, resulting in an improvement in the movement of traffic. The construction of locomotive erecting shops at Vladivostok where the immense number of locomotives coming from the United States can be erected and put into service much more speedily than has been the practice heretofore.

The working day and night of all locomotive repair shops so that the great number of out of repair locomotives may be reduced and that they may be put into service where they are so urgently needed. That the 'per diem' rate, or charges of one railway against another for the use of cars, be doubled, and that also the charge for holding cars for loading or unloading be doubled. This to insure prompt handling and release of cars in a reasonable time. That a Supply Department under a General Storekeeper be installed, who shall be responsible for the maintenance and distribution of the vast amount of material and supplies needed for the operation and maintenance of the roads, the duties of such officer to include the reclamation of worn material and the reissuing of such as may be found serviceable.

But the great imperative immediate necessity which confronts the railways of Russia to enable them not only to maintain its armies at the front, but also to support in comfort its civil population, who equally with its soldiers are fighting the great battle for freedom, is a great increase in the number of locomotives and freight cars. On this point the Commission are entirely in accord with the railway officials and with the Russian people. To the end that this absolutely necessary want shall be supplied as quickly as can be done, this Commission has cabled the Administration at Washington advising the immediate construction of 2500 locomotives and 40,000 freight cars to be added to the equipment of the Russian railways. This means, of course, an extension of credit by the United States to Russia of some 750,-000,000 millions of roubles. This matter has no commercial aspect for the Commission has pledged what to it is dearer than family or life itself, the good faith and honor of its country.

The Commission has under further consideration the furnishing of raw material, tools and shop machinery to any extent that may be found advisable after careful consideration with the Russian officials, and stands ready to aid its advice and counsel in any and all matters it may be requested.

In closing it desires to express its hearty appreciation of the aid given it by the efficient Minister of Ways of Communication[1] and his staff of able assistants. It knows that in their hands the future of the Russian railways is secure and it believes with the aid and material assistance which the United States is giving to its great Ally, that Russia will continue to sustain its part in the desperate struggle for freedom which is now convulsing the World.

The United States Railway Advisory Commission
                                            To Russia.

T MS (SDR, RG 59, 861.77/151½, DNA).
¹ Nikolai Vissarionovich Nekrasov.

From Robert Lansing, with Enclosure

My dear Mr. President: Washington August 13, 1917.

I enclose to you a brief report by Felix Frankfurter on the general situation in France, which I think that you will find as interesting as I did.

This morning I had an hour's talk with Frankfurter, which was most enlightening. I believe that you should see him and hear the story.[1]

It is important that I should have an interview with you at your earliest convenience not only on this matter but on several other subjects, concerning which I ought to know your wishes and the policies to be pursued. I have delayed asking an interview until I was familiar with the latest information in the Department, but I am ready now.[2]

Faithfully yours,   Robert Lansing.

TLS (WP, DLC).
¹ Wilson did not see Frankfurter.
² Wilson conferred with Lansing at 8 P.M. on August 17.

E N C L O S U R E

Felix Frankfurter to Robert Lansing

My dear Mr. Secretary: On Board S. S. Espagne, Aug. 7, 1917.

This report is made in response to the telegraphic instructions of Acting Secretary Polk under date of July 19 to "study and make a report for the information of the Department of the present situation in France."

A preliminary word as to the extent and manner of the study is pertinent. From the first day of our arrival in Paris—throughout my stay I was, fortunately, accompanied by Mr. Max Lowenthal, whose critical faculties and imaginative industry were a most important help. I followed events and pursued inquiry with the present study in view, so that the whole of my stay in Paris, including the ten days preceding the receipt of the Department's wire, was in fact devoted to the study requested. This anticipation enabled me to leave Paris in less than a week's time after the receipt of the Department's instructions. Altogether we were in France from July 12 to July 29. This entire period was passed in Paris, except one day at the cantonments of the United States troops at Gondrecourt and Demange-aux-eaux, and the nearby hospital base at Bazoilles, and one day at Bordeaux, whence we sailed on July 30.

Throughout I kept in mind the dangers against generalizing about any people, particularly in war time, and particularly the French. I was also mindful that Paris, however controlling in French life, is not wholly France; that the feelings of those at the front and those at home are not wholly the same; that the people may think differently from the politicians.

Therefore, as to all phases I sought a quantitative judgment, and sought to test individual feelings, doubts and opinions by evidence weighty both in extent and authoritativeness, and by rigorous questioning, to shake down opinions to their residual foundation of facts. In this attitude we touched a wide variety of French life through typical representatives. We talked with French army officers of long service at the front as well as on the staff, army surgeons, French officials, English and American diplomatic officials resident in France during different periods of the war, English and American army officers, French and American journalists of different shades of opinion, members of the Chamber of Deputies, bankers, lawyers, business men, and "just people." I purposely abstained, because the circumstances made it wise, from interviews with cabinet members.

1. *Sources of unrest in French morale.*

That France is tired is surely by this time a platitude. One hears it everywhere, from everybody. In addition to this pervasive feeling of general tiredness there are a few basic facts which have profoundly affected French morale, and are still potent. The outstanding single fact is the enormous loss of lives. Whatever may be the authoritative figures (probably known in the War Department at Washington), the conservative estimates generally accepted in France place the loss in dead and permanently disabled at over 2,000,000. Much more important than the gross total is the widespread conviction among the French that France cannot afford to lose many more. This feeling has been much reinforced since the spring offensive. It is the universal testimony that a veritably tragic shudder went through France when the whole nation came to believe, largely as a result of the letters written home from the front, that 100,000 men were sacrificed through an offensive futile in result and generally regarded as unwise in conception.[1] This heavy blow came on top of an abnormally severe winter, bringing widely felt hardships, especially through want of coal. Other economic conditions, the rising high cost of living and a growing popular belief that wealth is largely immune from the costs of the war, also fed the flame of unrest.

These are the main factors. There are minor elements which serve as items of aggravation, such as the infrequency of furloughs for the men at the front (recently corrected by General Petain), and the resentment aroused in soldiers on leave by the sufferings of their families. All these enervating factors gained collective strength from the disheartening losses of the spring offensive, and together they undoubtedly intensified the French feeling of unrest into a state of deep depression.

This widespread feeling of war weariness and of decreasing hope has become manifest in several noticeable directions. In a subtle yet persistent way it has been availed of by peace propagandists to such a degree that the growing number of pacifist publications became the subject of interpellations in a secret session of the Senate. The most sinister effect, and the one most uncertain as to its future importance, has been the recrudescence of Caillaux.[2] For some time he had been working under cover. Latterly he has come into the open, the financial policies of the government having given Caillaux's conceded financial ability the opportunity for an effective reappearance. Making the most conservative discounts, allowing for all the personal and political feeling against him, it cannot be gainsaid that Caillaux is attaining a growing power in French political life. His interests are associated with the presence of M. Malvy[3] in the Ribot cabinet. His importance is attested by the fact that in secret session the government recently confessed itself dependent upon the Caillaux group as represented by M. Malvy, for its supporting bloc. It does not seem at all likely that Caillaux will himself come into power for the present or that, in office, he would open peace negotiations immediately. But he is distinctly associated with early peace

[1] That is, in the "Nivelle offensive," about which see the Enclosure with RL to WW, May 10, 1917, n. 2, Vol. 42.

[2] Joseph Caillaux, a leader of the Radicals and Radical-Socialists, had been President of the French Council of Ministers in 1911 and 1912 and Minister of Finance in 1913 and 1914.

[3] Louis Jean Malvy, a Radical Socialist deputy since 1906, had been Minister of the Interior since 1914.

aims. In private conversation he asserts that reasonable terms of peace could now be made. More than that, Caillaux is playing on a vague, though probably growing, suspicion, of England's advantage as against France, from continuance of the war. Caillaux frankly avows hostility to England.

2. *Effect on French morale of America's entrance into the war.*

The arrival of American troops and the belief that the United States will largely take over France's burden have oxygized France and greatly checked the peace tendencies of the spring. America's participation is the note of hope in the press, men at the front speak about it with eager persistence, it served as the most effective answer by Ribot to the attack, in secret session, against the government's conduct of the war. For the present the expectation that America will soon be at the front is the fact that envelops one in France. Their hopes in us are surely touching; their hopes have no less the seeds of danger. For the expectations aroused are too exuberant and dangerously vague. If American troops in great numbers will not be in France by the end of the year, if the winter should again be a hard one, if the Russian situation should become worse instead of better, the diverse elements of impatience may well give Caillaux and his friends their opportunity.

3. *France's war aims in their bearing upon France's stability.*

There is then at present, thanks supremely to the American intervention, a decided strengthening of spirit. But what is the native foundation of the endurance of the French fighting spirit? Apart from disciplined obedience, what inner cause holds them in the fight? The presence of Germans on French soil is surely the controlling answer. That is enough to assure France's persistence under normal conditions. But there is a growing feeling, which unusual hardship, as time passes, may raise to a dangerous degree, that in any event French soil will be restored to France. German occupation, then, furnishes no unequivocal affirmative aim of the war. There is Alsace-Lorraine; but one is astounded to find among responsible French opinion the feeling that Alsace-Lorraine may not be worth fighting for much longer. Particularly to southern and western Frenchmen do Alsace and Lorraine seem rather remote. These are feelings not now in the ascendant, but they are feelings entertained with sufficient depth and to a sufficient extent to be kept in mind as important in any evaluation of the present and future forces of wartime France.

There is hardly a trace in France of the larger aim which brought the United States into the war, or at least animates our prosecution of it, namely, to have issue from the war not only the failure of German aggression, but the frustration, through an international partnership, a league of nations, of any future aggression. The program is not discussed in the Chamber of Deputies, it is not made the subject of speeches by the government, the press is silent about it. The important exception is M. Leon Bourgeois.[4] Otherwise the scheme of a league to enforce peace is regarded as too "utopian"—the impatient adjective one hears from practically all to whom the subject is mentioned. They are, they say, too busy with the war to indulge in "philosophizing." It is too vague, they contend; they do not understand it. M. Bourgeois is trying to direct attention to it; he is urging upon his colleagues the appointment of a committee for its study. However, the strong impression left on one's mind is that Bourgeois is, as yet, a voice crying in the wilderness.

4. *Scope of America's activity in France.*

The evident danger to the realization of America's war aims, because of an inadequate comprehension of these aims in France, makes indispensable a consideration no less of the larger aspects of the French state of mind than of the people's fighting morale. The diagnosis of existing French opinion which discloses a grave impediment to the accomplishment of that which is behind our material contributions also discloses that this source of danger can be counteracted, and some of the means by which this can be done. The basic necessity for such action, and the directions it can effectively take, are among the most impelling aspects of the French situation.

Very little impetus can be expected to come out of France itself for a sympathetic and cooperating understanding by the French of the war purposes of the United States. They have hardly, if at all, broken through the surface crust of the popular mind. They have not been accorded more than the beginning of a serious discussion, even in that narrowly limited section which has given them any thought at all. The portions of the President's speeches dealing with a sound future world organization, which in the United States is deemed the very condition of our war

---

[4] Léon Victor Auguste Bourgeois had been Premier in 1895 and 1896, had held various other ministerial posts, and was a delegate to the peace conferences at The Hague in 1895, 1899, and 1907.

participation, are either unknown in France, or deemed aspiring rhetoric.

The need of community of purposes between the two republics is obvious. The conclusion is no less inevitable that, in the present state of the French mind, we must take thought how we can be best assured of French understanding and belief in such purposes. We ourselves must build towards an opinion in France for a league of nations, or we may later be without supporting knowledge in our French allies for such a claim by us. Fortunately the means seem ready to hand for making the purposes of the United States, which are conceived to be the world's purposes, a reality in France. French conditions make clear that some such course can be safely undertaken by the United States, with every solicitude for French susceptibilities. For the outstanding facts in France to-day, so far as the United States is concerned, are the great leverage this country now has in France, and the commanding authority enjoyed by President Wilson. The problem is how this leverage and this authority may be exercised.

5. *Recommendations.*

The following may be suggested:

(1) There is a new need for reciprocal knowledge between France and the United States. Its satisfaction requires America to know the currents of French life and to make known in France the ways of the United States far better than has been heretofore the case. At present we lack the best instruments for knowledge. One way of attaining this end may be by stationing in Paris someone thoroughly saturated with the President's general outlook, who would keep in discreet and effective contact with French public men and opinion. Such a person would accumulate a valuable fund of knowledge. More than that, however,—great, very great influence could be exerted by one whose sole business this task would be, someone thoroughly competent to estimate international affairs, and not diverted by the time-absorbing details of ordinary ambassadorial work.

(2) But Paris is not only the key to France; it is one of the most important centres of allied intercourse. Inasmuch as the recent non-participation of the United States in the Balkan Conferences was not deemed the application of a general principle, some comment may not be amiss as to the presence of a United States representative in future allied conferences. The danger from American participation in these intermediate meetings, the immunity which the United States enjoys by keeping an entirely

free hand until the final settlement, are of course patent. On the other hand, great advantages would accrue to the United States if its representatives could be present at such conferences merely as listeners, and not in any wise to bind the United States:

(a) It would make the United States more familiar with the point of view, the mental habits of the men who subsequently will be at the Peace Conference. There would thus come the important asset of personal knowledge of fellow negotiators;

(b) While nothing in law or diplomacy can be done to bind the United States at these conferences, yet currents of views are exchanged, hopes are aroused, suspicions are generated or allayed, which will leave marked influence upon eventual peace negotiations. By its presence the United States would have knowledge of all these subtle yet serious influences. In addition, our mere presence might have a restraining effect and serve as a source of confidence, particularly with the small nations. There is an element of pathos, not without significance, in the recent plea of Montenegro for our intervention at the Balkan Conferences.

(3) France is at work, through committees, in the preparation of material for the Peace Conference. We should equip ourselves with like knowledge. Competent persons should be set to work on the various questions that are bound to come up, so that all the material which is pertinent will be at hand for our commissioners. Of course, a good deal of this material we have, but is it in an organized form and directed to the specific objective here suggested?

(4) It should be possible to get more details and more continuous publicity in France about the war preparations of the United States. It would influence, for one thing, the maintenance of the French spirit. Besides, it might do valuable service in impressing upon the German prisoners present in France in great numbers the importance of America's participation. At present Michaelis' avowed indifference represents very accurately the German feeling—certainly the feeling of the German prisoners— as to America's impotence. The French papers spread among these prisoners, to convince them of the effectiveness of America's contribution, might make them conveyers of that intelligence into hundreds of thousands of homes in Germany.

Respectfully submitted,   Felix Frankfurter.

TLS (SDR, RG 59, 851.00/26½a, DNA).

From Samuel Gompers, with Enclosure

PERSONAL and CONFIDENTIAL.

Dear Sir: Washington, D. C. August 13, 1917

Your letter of the 7th instant and enclosure came duly to hand. I am astounded at what you have recited and at what Mr. Martinez in his communication conveyed to President Carranza.

The information came to me also in another way, and I deemed it best to communicate with Mr. Martinez from that angle.

Enclosed you will please find a copy of the letter which I have just written and mailed to him.

It is fair to assume that I shall hear from him, and when I do I shall be glad to advise you thereof.

May I suggest this thought? I firmly believe that there was no evil intent on Mr. Martinez' part. He evidently, in his guileless way exaggerated the importance of his "achievements" and was too impetuous to permit time for you to work out a solution of the problem. I feel confident that understanding his breach and misrepresentation, that will have no effect upon your course to the detriment of President Carranza and Mexico.

Very truly yours,   Saml. Gompers.

TLS (WP, DLC).

E N C L O S U R E

Samuel Gompers to Edmundo E. Martínez

Dear Sir: Washington, D. C. August 13, 1917

It is difficult for me to determine how to begin writing this letter to you. I am so much astonished and disappointed in what I am informed you have transmitted to President Carranza of Mexico.

A few days ago I met a gentleman who informed me that you had been talking fully and freely to several persons, and relating to them the interview you had with President Wilson when I was present. He informed me that you discussed with several persons the official report which you communicated to Mr. Carranza; that you stated that President Wilson promised to remove the embargo on arms to him, and that he would assist in the coining of Mexican money in the United States; that he asked you in turn

[to] ask Mr. Carranza to present a claim against Mr. Hearst and Mr. Otis.

Now you know quite well that President Wilson made no such statements or promises, and if you have communicated to President Carranza statements that such promises were made, they only misrepresent President Wilson and can only mislead President Carranza.

It is difficult to recount our half-hour's interview in a letter, yet I am impelled to say that my inference and understanding of the conference is this: that President Wilson listened interestedly and sympathetically to what you had to say, to the message you conveyed to him from Mr. Carranza, and that he, the President, stated that he would take into consideration the subject matter of removing the embargo on arms to Mr. Carranza; that the question of Mr. Carranza having sent a commission to the United States to have Mexican gold coined into money in the mints of the United States was entirely a piece of news to him, and that he would make inquiry into it; if there had been any injustice done Mr. Carranza he would see that it was removed.

President Wilson also expressed his appreciation of the difficult position in which Mr. Carranza finds himself, and that he understands what you declared, that he, Mr. Carranza is not a Pro-Kaiser man, but Pro-American, and Pro-Pan American. He said further that any prejudiced reports circulated in the United States were not likely to change his good opinion of Mr. Carranza.

You may possibly imagine my chagrin upon being informed by a casual acquaintance that you had not only made exaggerated statements for which there is but a very slight, if any, foundation in fact, and as the confidential diplomatic representative of President Carranza in the United States you had not only discussed these matters in general talk, but had communicated them in an official document to the President of Mexico.

I am afraid you have done your country very great injury and if this information which I have recited comes at all to the attention of the President of the United States, I am wondering whether he will ever again consent to meet with you, either directly, through me, or in any other way.

If called upon, how I shall be enabled to explain this to President Wilson is beyond my understanding.

Very truly yours,   Saml. Gompers

TCLS (WP, DLC).

From Edward Mandell House, with Enclosures

Dear Governor: Magnolia, Mass. August 13, 1917.

Enclosed are some cables from Sir William. Balfour is evidently very much concerned regarding the Pope's appeal and I hope you will feel that you can give him your private opinion as he requests.

The cable relating to Spring-Rice and Northcliffe tells of a situation which we already know. I agree with Sir William that Sir Cecil should be asked home for conference and then kept until Northcliffe leaves. It is impossible for the two of them to work in harmony. The British Government cannot do as they please with Northcliffe, therefore, Sir Cecil must be the one to be momentarily eliminated.

Northcliffe, who has been here for several days, continues to show a disposition to be useful and as agreeable as possible. He shows me all his confidential cables and is amenable to advice. I am surprised at his attitude and hope it will continue.

Northcliffe also suggests that Lloyd-George visit America. I discouraged it by telling him that he should be reserved for an occasion when he would be very much needed. Will you not also advise me concerning your wishes in regard to such a visit.

Affectionately yours,   E. M. House

TLS (WP, DLC).

E N C L O S U R E   I

No. 737.   London, August 11, 1917.

Observations from Horace Plunkett on first meeting of the Convention for the confidential information of the President.

Convention has very wide powers to draw up a constitution for Ireland within the Empire. There were greater difficulties in bringing convention together than are generally realized. Success in electing chairman with businesslike opening is hopeful beginning, and has already had good effect in Ireland. Moreover, Convention yesterday elected standing committee, approved rule procedure, planned method enquiry with complete unanimity and good-will. Belfast and Cork have both invited delegates, who agreed to meet in Belfast in September and Cork later. Proceedings hitherto unexpectedly successful. Following refused to take part: SINN FEINERS, because main object of their leaders is to destroy present "nation" party, and some of their extremists insist on nothing less than an independent republic. It is possible that many supporters of the party are more reasonable than their leaders. Undoubtedly they begin to feel convention gaining ground, not only in Ireland but estimation of world outside. The O'Brienites,[1] who are comparatively unimportant, because they insist on the conclusion of the Convention being put to an Irish referendum and the Government feels that it would be a mistake thus to tie the hands of the Convention before they start.

The extreme labour party, because they are also controlled by advanced socialists.

It is impossible to judge how far the Convention represents the Irish people but it is generally felt to be representative of a large majority including political, agricultural, commercial and labour interests, in fact all except extremists.

The Catholic Church is strongly represented. Leaders, who in the past have been bitterly opposed, are meeting for the first time. The greatest difficulty will probably come from Ulster because the Convention is undoubtedly against partition and Ulster may insist. General determination of Convention is to keep on until they reach some conclusion, which may take several months.

Will forward you similar confidential reports at each stage of the proceedings.   William Wiseman.

[1] That is, the followers of William O'Brien (1852-1928), Irish journalist and M.P. who, although formerly a radical nationalist, at this time advocated a combination of all elements of the population of Ireland in a spirit of mutual tolerance and patriotic goodwill.

E N C L O S U R E   I I

No. 741.   London, August 11, 1917.

I should appreciate your opinion on my telegram No. 730 of the 7th[1] as soon as possible.

Feeling here is that as Northcliffe has been appointed he must be given all support. It is realized that the position between Northcliffe and Spring-Rice is impossible.

In general, I believe H. M. Government is prepared to accept all my suggestions which are, of course, precisely those we discussed.

Please give Lord Northcliffe my regards and tell him H. M. Government is beginning to appreciate the immense importance of the United States Government in the game.

William Wiseman.

¹ W. Wiseman to EMH, No. 730, Aug. 7, 1917, T telegram (E. M. House Papers, CtY), which conveyed the British government's desire to keep Wilson better informed about the war and the needs of the Allies. To this end, the British government suggested that it might be well to send "an official of the highest standing" to discuss financial problems with McAdoo and "distinguished" naval and military liaison officers to maintain direct contact with Wilson and the War and Navy departments.

E N C L O S U R E   I I I

No. 742.   London, August 11, 1917.

Mr. Balfour has just received through British representative at Vatican an appeal from the Pope in favor of peace addressed to belligerent governments. Full text of the appeal has not yet been received but from cabled summary it is clear that it will raise many questions of difficulty. What answer, if any, should be returned will have to be very carefully considered, and Mr. Balfour hopes the President will be inclined to let him know privately what his views on the subject are.

William Wiseman.

E N C L O S U R E   I V

No. 747.   London, August 12, 1917.

I have now seen most people of importance including the King, Premier, Chancellor of Exchequer. I found general feeling that Spring-Rice has proved unsatisfactory and therefore the tendency is to support Northcliffe. They do not realize that a man of his temperament is always dangerous.

British Government understands, though reluctant to admit, the most powerful position of the United States Government. British Government trusts the President and will give him all information willingly but certainly did not understand the necessity of keeping him frankly informed, of their weakness as well as strength.

Lloyd-George is anxious to write periodically to the President through you. Lloyd-George is also considering the possibility of visiting America in the Autumn. Some people feel that Northcliffe should be Ambassador, but I have opposed this idea and have suggested Spring-Rice should be called here for conference and his next man left in charge, and that Lord Reading should be sent at once as Financial Representative.

British Government is not strengthened by trouble over * * *

The cable was unintelligeable at this point. He probably refers to the trouble with Henderson over the Stockholm conference.[1]

T MSS (WP, DLC).
[1] EMHhw.

Three Letters from Newton Diehl Baker

(CONFIDENTIAL)

My dear Mr. President: Washington. August 13, 1917

It seemed to me that in the matter of Mr. Swem you ought not to give yourself any further concern about so obviously proper a case. I have therefore directed the Judge Advocate General to prepare the necessary papers for my signature, and I will present them to the local board and procure his exemption, just as I am doing in the case of Walter Lippmann, who is acting for me with wonderful intelligence and understanding in all kinds of labor disputes and controversies. This note is only to inform you that the matter is attended to and needs no further consideration at your hands.   Respectfully yours,   Newton D. Baker

TLS (C. L. Swem Coll., NjP).

My dear Mr President   Washington. Aug 13, 1917

I am sure you will be glad to read the enclosed.[1] It seems to, me not only an astonishingly clear restatement of some old, but also to state some new thoughts most admirably
                    Respectfully yours,   Newton D. Baker

ALS (WP, DLC).
[1] A reprint of Walter Lippmann, "The World Conflict in Its Relation to American Democracy," *The Annals of the American Academy of Political and Social Science*, LXXII (July 1917), 1-10. Lippmann said that Germany had struck at the very basis of the international order when it invaded Belgium. The German proclamation of the submarine blockade had forced the United States to choose between the Allies and the Central Powers. The German bid for complete victory had "abolished neutrality in the world" and forced the entry of the United States into the war, and this, together with the Russian Revolution, had greatly stimulated the movement for a world federation to reestablish international law and maintain peace. The war was "dissolving into a stupendous revolution." The whole world was passionately turning toward democracy as the only principle upon which peace could be secured. There were two ways in which peace could be achieved. The first was "political revolution in Germany and Austria-Hungary." If this happened, then peace could be made through negotiation. The other way to peace was by "the definite defeat of every item in the program of aggression." The United States was fighting only for a "union of liberal peoples . . . determined to erect a larger and more modern system of international law upon a federation of the world." Lippmann then concluded: "If we are strong enough and wise enough to win this victory, to reject all the poison of hatred abroad and intolerance at home, we shall have made a nation to which free men will turn with love and

gratitude. For ourselves we shall stand committed as never before to the realization of democracy in America. We who have gone to war to insure democracy in the world will have raised an aspiration here that will not end with the overthrow of the Prussian autocracy. We shall turn with fresh interests to our own tyrannies—to our Colorado mines, our autocratic steel industries, our sweatshops and our slums. We shall call that man un-American and no patriot who prates of liberty in Europe and resists it at home. A force is loose in America as well. Our own reactionaries will not assuage it with their Billy Sundays or control through lawyers and politicians of the Old Guard."

Dear Mr. President: Washington. August 13, 1917

I return herewith the letters[1] which Senator John Sharp Williams inclosed to you. I think there is a very great deal in Dr. Egbert's[2] suggestion. I do not know Dr. Egbert, but I think one of the most striking facts in history was the adherence of the Russian Army to the revolution, due to the fact, it is stated, that the Zemtsvo Union[3] was sympathetic with the revolutionary cause and that to the Russian soldier Zemtsvo Union was the only representative in Russia with the humane and saving graces which the Red Cross represents.

My own strong judgment is that Mr. Davison and his associates of the War Council ought to be urged to put forth very great efforts in Russia, and if you concur in this view, it will give me pleasure to take the matter up with him at once and see just how the efforts they are now making there can be multiplied helpfully.   Respectfully yours,   Newton D. Baker

TLS (WP, DLC).

[1] E. H. Egbert to J. S. Williams, Aug. 7, 1917, TLS (WP, DLC), and G. Bakhméteff to E. H. Egbert, July 4, 1917, ALS (WP, DLC).

[2] Edward H. Egbert, M.D., a surgeon of Washington, had served, beginning in 1915, as chief surgeon of the American Red Cross hospital at Kiev. Some of his activities are described in Malcolm C. Grow, *Surgeon Grow: An American in the Russian Fighting* (New York, 1918). Wilson saw Egbert at the White House on September 5.

[3] The All-Russian Union of Zemstvos for the Relief of the Sick and Wounded, under the presidency of Prince L'vov, was first organized by the Zemstvo of Moscow during the Russo-Japanese War and was joined by many other local governments in Russia. For a brief account of its work in the European war, see A. J. Sack, "The Zemstvos and the Red Cross in Russia," *The Red Cross Magazine: The Official Publication of the American Red Cross*, XII (Aug. 1917), 280-85. See also Hugh Seton-Watson, *The Russian Empire, 1801-1917* (Oxford, 1967), pp. 698-99.

From the White House Staff

       The White House.

Memorandum for the President: August 13, 1917.

Senator Owen asks for an appointment with the President as soon as it can be arranged to discuss the La Follette and King peace resolutions.[1]

T MS (WP, DLC).

¹ Senator La Follette, on August 11, had submitted a concurrent resolution (S. Con. Res. 11) that took note of various declarations by the Russian, German, and British governments which indicated a willingness to adopt Wilson's doctrine of a "peace without victory" as the only peace that could endure. The resolution called attention to published statements and undisclosed agreements of the Allies for punitive damages and territorial conquests and noted the demand by the American people for a definite statement of the war aims of the United States Government. The resolution then affirmed the full authority of Congress to determine and to declare definitely the objects and purposes for which the United States should continue to participate in the European war. The resolution further declared that the United States would not contribute to a prolongation of the war "to annex new territory, either in Europe or outside of Europe, nor to enforce the payment of indemnities to recover the expenses of the war," but that Congress would favor the creation of a common fund to restore the most devastated areas. Finally, the resolution called for "a public restatement of the allied peace terms, based on a disavowal of any advantages, either in the way of indemnities, territorial acquisitions, commercial privileges, or economic prerogatives, by means of which one nation shall strengthen its power abroad at the expense of another nation, as wholly incompatible with the establishment of a durable peace in the world." *Cong. Record*, 65th Cong., 1st sess., pp. 5956-57.

William Henry King was a Democratic senator from Utah. His resolution (S. Res. 114), also submitted on August 11, was quite different. He offered it in view of "the untimely talk of peace" and also to counter La Follette's resolution. King's resolution listed numerous offenses by Germany and concluded as follows: "Now, therefore, be it *Resolved by the Senate of the United States*, That the Government of the United States will not make peace until its purposes and principles as declared by the President in his address to Congress of the 2d of April shall have been acknowledged and acomplished; and that for this cause the Government of the United States will wage war and employ its military, moral, and economic resources until German trespasses against American rights have been suppressed and the honor and sovereignty of America shall have been vindicated, and until the German Government shall have acknowledged and expiated its crimes and shall seek the terms upon which it may be admitted to the community of the civilized and enlightened States, which have made common cause to vindicate the rights of nations and secure the blessings of justice and civilization, and for these purposes, to establish and maintain the peace of the world." *Ibid.*, p. 5957. Wilson saw Owen on August 15. The La Follette and King resolutions had both been tabled on August 11.

Walter Stowell Rogers to George Creel

Dear Mr. Creel: Woods Hole, Mass., August 13, 1917.

I have just reread the interview with Charles Edward Russell in the New York Times of last Sunday. One paragraph especially appeals to me:

"Observe, now, the really critical point today is the security of the Russian line on the eastern front; take note next of the great fact almost universally overlooked in this country that the security of that Russian line depends solely upon the state of mind of the masses of the Russian people. Then, if you convince the masses of the people that the United States is not really in this war, that it will not prosecute it with vigor and resolution, that it is divided in its councils, that it is really seeking peace, you have done more to make that Russian line melt away than the Kaiser could do with ten million men and ten times as much artillery as he has now."

Just the other day I talked with an experienced observer recently returned from Russia. He said he had talked with a great many Russians and that their expressed opinion was that the United States had made fabulous sums out of the war and now had entered into it to be in position to share the spoils. Not a single Russian that he had spoken with was familiar with the events and the line of thought that had led to our participation in the war. This tragic situation is only partly due to German propaganda; it is still more due to our own blindness and to our inability or unwillingness to realize that we have no case unless our case reaches the attention of the masses of the world. The Russians are not to blame. We state our case in Washington; then innocently expect the Moscow papers to have the story the next day! "Papers everywhere, please copy," seems to be our motto.

It can not be said too often or too loudly that this war is being fought out in the minds of great masses of people as truly as it is being fought out on the battle fields of Europe. Stating our case, convincing the world that we mean business and that we stand for the common rights of men, is just as important a piece of work as that being done by our war and navy departments or by Hoover. We may lose the war or only partially achieve what we are struggling for, if we do not get our grievances and our ideas to the world.

Presenting our case to the world is no small job, it requires the same high degree of brains, technical skill and energy as goes into the actual prosecution of the war in its military aspects.

I am aghast at the situation. Take my own case. I went to China and Japan to learn what people there thought of us and to acquaint myself with Oriental newspaper and press association methods. I found that something drastic ought to be done at once to checkmate unfriendly propaganda and to get the American case presented. China was drifting into chaos. China needed news and truth from America. None was forthcoming—only German, Japanese and British selfishly directed propaganda. The American Minister clearly saw the situation and desired me to impress on Washington the urgency.

I reported to Col. House. He sent me to the State Department. Now I have been about the world and have had considerable journalistic, political and commercial experience. I think I qualify as a trained investigator. Mr. Lansing was too busy to see me. I have been home three months, have been in and out of the Department any number of times, but have not talked with the Secretary yet. I went to the Bureau of Far Eastern Affairs. The Chief of the Bureau[1] inquired about the weather, hotels and railroads, but asked me not a single question regarding conditions. I then turned to Mr. Polk, who gave me ten minutes and agreed to give consideration to certain suggestions. I then turned to Mr. Patchin, head of the Bureau of Information. We had several short talks. Mr. Patchin thought that possibly I wanted a job under him! Patchin partially has the idea, but is not a great person and has no independent authority.

Consider just two questions: What would be the situation now had the President's communications to the belligerents been actually printed textually throughout the world? We are making an appeal to the good sense and honor of the world, but most of the world has never had a chance to read our state papers!

One of these days a peace conference will be held. Will America be looked upon by South America, the Orient and Russia (not to mention the rest) as standing unselfishly for human rights? Or will America be considered merely as a butt-in-sky with a greedy appetite? Our standing at the peace conference, the measure of our influence, will depend largely upon what the world believes of us.

Of course, German propaganda will try to muss everything up, scatter dust about and blind the eyes. Of course, Japanese propaganda will not forget Nipponese aspirations. As to British propaganda—the late cock-of-the-walk is out to regain its lost prestige; for seventy-five years the British dominated the Orient because of the belief that they could lick the world any afternoon; now the British are not going to let the world believe that we are playing a decisive role and that we are the upholders of liberty. We preach our own message—democracy's story—or it isn't told.

I believe the President perceives this situation. I believe we have no greater problem or obligation. Personally I do not believe this task can be handled by the State Department; the Department is not suitably manned or organized. A year ago last June I went to Mr. Lansing and told him of the South American service inaugurated by the United Press—I knew all about it as, in a sense, it was my scheme—and suggested that the Department take advantage of this new service to explain systematically our attitude and actions. The Secretary told me in so many words that it was not one of the functions of the Department to see that the American case was presented to the peoples of other countries.

The President or the Department carefully prepares a statement intended to clarify a situation or to make us friends—the dissemination of that statement is not a matter of official concern! The dissemination is as important as the document. I thought we wrote documents and prepared statements with a view to getting results and not merely for filing purposes in official archives! I have never been a diplomat.

I see no signs of the Department getting the big idea. Certain things are being done grudgingly and parsimoniously. It is laugh-stuff to find the Department felicitating itself upon the idea of sending a million post cards to Russia—and a moving picture film too for good measure. From any big view of the task, such things are merely incidental details.

We have got to organize to spread the teachings and the purposes of our democracy and to show that democracy is a real thing that can have character and direction.

The undertaking is huge. One can not map out a policy, submit blue-prints or accurate estimates of cost. It is a new job which must be done under war-time conditions.

Would that the President might give this opportunity to some experienced man, make him virtually independent of the State Department and turn him loose to do his best?

To me our conversation with the President[2] was not entirely satisfactory. The conversation went off into details. The President was tired. The problem of world wide publicity requires a broad consideration and then the leaving of details to experts.

In conclusion let me emphasize the vital necessity for our democracy to become articulate throughout the world.

Sincerely,   Walter S Rogers.

TLS (WP, DLC).
[1] That is, Edward T. Williams.
[2] Creel saw Wilson at the White House on August 2, and it seems likely that Rogers was also present at this meeting.

Three Letters to Robert Lansing

My dear Mr. Secretary: The White House 14 August, 1917

Mr. Root had called my attention already to the extraordinary action of Mr. Stevens but I thank you for sending me a full copy of Mr. Stevens' proclamation which I herewith return.

Will you not be kind enough to have the following cable sent to Mr. Stevens:

"The President appreciates very highly what Mr. Stevens and his associates are doing in Russia but thinks it wise to remind

Mr. Stevens that it is important that the impression should not be created that he and his associates represent or speak for the Government of the United States. As the President explained to the Commission before they started, they were sent abroad merely to put themselves at the service of the Russian Government. Any assurances conveyed to the Russian people, therefore, as if authoritatively by the Commission would be a very grave mistake. The President does not wish in this way to discredit assurances already given but merely to convey a very friendly caution for the future."

Cordially and sincerely yours,   Woodrow Wilson

TLS (SDR, RG 59, 861.77/151½, DNA).

My dear Mr. Secretary: The White House 14 August, 1917

Thank you very much for this report of Frankfurter's. I had already had a copy of it and had read it with a great deal of interest.

Cordially and faithfully yours,   Woodrow Wilson

TLS (SDR, RG 59, 851.00/27½, DNA).

My dear Mr. Secretary: The White House 14 August, 1917

Thank you for having let me see the enclosed.[1] It is a matter I very carefully discussed with the mission itself.

Cordially and faithfully yours,   Woodrow Wilson

TLS (SDR, RG 59, 763.72/6504½, DNA).
[1] S. Washburn to RL, June 18 and June 29, 1917, TLS (SDR, RG 59, 763.72/6504½, DNA). These two letters were from Washburn as assistant secretary of the Root Mission. In the first letter, Washburn asked Lansing to explain to Wilson that, for reasons of health, he could not take over the management of the publicity campaign in Russia. Washburn then reported that, from any angle, the one outstanding fact was that the Russian people did not want to fight. They were "gentle, kindhearted and docile with the best of instincts but slow of comprehension." For this reason, propaganda and publicity were the only "medicines" that could be used with any certainty. It was not clear whether they could reach the heart of Russia in time to affect current operations. There was now "no real State and no real authority," and everything was "nebulous and extremely misty." A "direct and dignified appeal to the people with rational publicity and explanation of our motives" gave the best hope, but, in any case, progress would be slow. Ultimately, Russia would get "a good government and a decent constitution." It was clear to Washburn, however, that Russia could not be hurried and that Americans had to exercise the same patience that they would exercise toward children, with the same optimism as to the ultimate outcome as they had in "a child of good instincts." Washburn also noted that the condition of Rumania was "extremely pathetic" and that the Queen had asked him to see to it that "little Roumania" was not forgotten.

In his second letter, Washburn gave his opinion, in which he said General Brusilov concurred, that the "greatest moral asset" for the Russian army was the depiction of the United States and the American people "as the most sincere and genuine" of all their allies. Brusilov had approved all sorts of publicity, including the use of speakers, pamphlets, and eight or ten motion picture out-fits that would travel constantly to tell the troops of America's resources and its intention to support Russia "to the end of the war." Brusilov had said that he would give his full backing to these plans for "spreading the American idea in the Russian army." The war was costing the United States forty or fifty mil-lion dollars a day, and Washburn thought that there should be no hesitancy to spend a few millions during the next year, if needed, "to improve the morale and discipline of one of our vital Allies whose retirement or permanent depres-sion in strength" might well prolong the war by an additional year or two. As an investment for the future, the mission was circulating selections from Root's speeches, and it planned to distribute half a million copies of Wilson's message to the Russian people. (Wilson's message to the Russian Provisional Government, printed at May 22, 1917, Vol. 42.)

To John Wingate Weeks

My dear Senator Weeks: [The White House] 14 August, 1917

I have your letter of August eleventh[1] and, while I sympathize to a very great extent with your point about the drafting of aliens, I cannot believe that you mean exactly what you say with regard to our treaty obligations,—"whatever may be our treaties with foreign countries on this subject, it is absolutely essential in my judgment that some action should be taken which will in-clude the alien population of the draft age in the draft." I assume, of course, that you mean that some diplomatic action should be taken to clear the way. That matter is already interesting the Department of State and I have no doubt will be pressed as fast as the circumstances permit.

Your point with regard to the drafting of men with families is undoubtedly well taken and I have reason to believe that it is very much in the mind at any rate of most of the drafting boards. I shall take pleasure in calling the attention of the War Depart-ment again to it.   Sincerely yours,   Woodrow Wilson

TLS (Letterpress Books, WP, DLC).
[1] It is missing, but see NDB to WW, Aug. 18, 1917 (third letter of that date).

To J. L. Donnelly

My dear Sir: [The White House] 14 August, 1917

In reply to your telegram of August sixth let me say that I am fully alive to the very serious situation existing in Arizona and that, while the matters to which you refer lie almost if not entirely within the jurisdiction of the state and not of the fed-eral government, I have been actively endeavoring to do every-thing in my power to see that the situation was dealt with in conformity with the real spirit of America in which law and order and the regular processes of law must of course be maintained and the rights of the people safeguarded.

Sincerely yours,   Woodrow Wilson

TLS (Letterpress Books, WP, DLC).

To Vira Boarman Whitehouse[1]

[The White House]

My dear Mrs. Whitehouse: 14 August, 1917

I learn with sincere pleasure of your impression of a growing sentiment in the State of New York in favor of woman suffrage and I shall look forward with the greatest interest to the results of the state conference which you are planning to hold in Saratoga the latter part of this month.[2] May I not express the hope that that conference will lead to a very widespread interest in your campaign and that your efforts will be crowned with the most substantial and satisfactory success?

Cordially and sincerely yours,   Woodrow Wilson

TLS (Letterpress Books, WP, DLC).
  [1] Mrs. Norman de R. Whitehouse, "chairman" of the New York State Woman Suffrage party. Her husband, a partner in Whitehouse & Co., brokers, was treasurer of the Men's League for Woman Suffrage, a section of the New York State Woman Suffrage party.
  [2] Vira B. Whitehouse to WW, Aug. 10, 1917, TLS (WP, DLC). She wrote, at House's suggestion, to ask Wilson for "a friendly statement" to her party, to be used in promoting an amendment for woman suffrage to be voted on in the New York election on November 6.

To Hamilton Vreeland, Jr.[1]

My dear Mr. Vreeland: [The White House] 14 August, 1917

I am genuinely obliged to you for your thoughtful kindness in sending me a copy of your Hugo Grotius.[2] He is a man in whom I have long been interested and whose works I have in some degree studied, and I hope I shall be able to appreciate what you have written about him with the more intelligence on that account.   Cordially and sincerely yours,   Woodrow Wilson

TLS (Letterpress Books, WP, DLC).
  [1] Hamilton Vreeland, Jr., Princeton 1913, had earned M.A., LL.B., and Ph.D. degrees at Columbia University.
  [2] H. Vreeland, Jr., *Hugo Grotius, the Father of the Modern Science of International Law* (New York, 1917), is in the Wilson Library, DLC.

From Walter Hines Page

My dear Mr. President: London. 14, Aug. 1917

No suggestion or proposal has been received here with a heartier welcome than your proposal to send Admiral Mayo and other naval officers for a conference here about the naval situation.[1] Mr. Balfour welcomed it eagerly and the Admiralty is equally pleased. I ought to add that Admiral Sims, too, is particularly pleased.

Since the war began the Admiralty has of course hoped that the German fleet wd. come out for a fight. The Jutland battle was a bitter disappointment because it was not conclusive; and since then, as before, the British naval programme has been defensive. The Admiralty opinion, which, as I understand, is unanimous among naval officers, is that the German naval bases (in Germany) are impregnable. Mines, submarines, and the biggest concealed guns in the world are supposed to make any sea attack a foolhardy failure. In front the Germans have Heligoland and they have an open backdoor into the Baltic.

I don't know how sound this reasoning is; but I do know that its soundness has at every stage of the war been questioned—somewhat timidly, but still questioned. There has been an undercurrent of doubt. The several changes that have been made in the personnel of the Admiralty have seemed to have a thought of some change of the defensive programme in mind. The one method of attack that one ever hears discussed openly is by aircraft. For that, the British have never had enough machines to spare. Morever it seems to be too far from the German naval bases to any British aircraft base, unless sea planes can be used from the North Sea.

But there seems to be no doubt of the open-mindedness of the Government to any suggestion.

The most pressing naval question—the most pressing question of the whole war—continues to be the submarines. They have found no "antidote." The "mystery" ships catch a few—I do not know how many, but not enough to discourage the Germans. A few more are destroyed by other methods; but the problem of catching them at their exit is unsolved. They make their way along the territorial waters of Denmark and Holland and come out to sea wherever they find it safe. I have gone over many maps, charts, and diagrams on which the presence of submarines in British waters and at sea are indicated; and the one thing that seems to be conclusively proved is that the convoy is the best means so far put into practice to increase safety. The future of the world seems to me to hang on the answer to this question: Can the war be won in spite of the submarines? Can a great American army be brought over and its large subsequent supply-fleet be sufficiently safeguarded? As matters now go, three large British ships are sunk a day. How many are sunk of other nationalities, I do not know. At this rate, the Allies can hold out long enough to win provided our armies and supplies can come over—convoyed, of course—with reasonable safety. But in the course of time the present rate of ship-destruction will greatly weaken the Allied endurance.

British opinion is that the war must be won on the battle-field—that the German armies must be beaten by arms and by economic pressure in Germany; that the German naval bases are untakeable; that the submarines must be endured. And it is universally understood that American intervention is all that saved or can save the Allied cause. France will be practically exhausted by the end of this year as an offensive power; Italy counts for little except to keep a certain number of Austrian troops engaged; Russia, as a fighting force, probably will not recover in time. The probability that is generally accepted is that the war, unless Germany collap[s]e during the next six months by reason of economic exhaustion or by the falling-away of Austria or Turkey or both, will become a war between Germany and the English-speaking nations, all which except the United States are already partially exhausted.

The waste in the war caused by the failures of the European Allies to work together with complete unity is one of the most pitiful aspects of the conflict. The recently begun offensive by the British on the northern French coast, now interrupted for the moment by heavy rains, ought to have been undertaken long ago. But the French withheld their consent because (as the British military authorities say) a certain section of French opinion feared, or pretended to fear that the British wd. keep these coast towns & cities if they were permitted to retake them from the Germans! It is reported, too, that the Belgians objected. The Belgian army now holds 3,000 yards of the whole trench-line: that's all; and the British have so little confidence in them that they keep all the time in easy reach enough reserves to hold this 3000 yards if the Germans shd. attack it. This jealousy and distrust runs more or less through all the dealings of the continental allies with one another. It's a sad tale.

Mr. Balfour tells me that he has information that you have no fear of an attack from Japan at any early time after peace is declared and that you, therefore, regard any such treaty or agreement as he sent House as unnecessary. He (Mr. Balfour) shares your conclusion; and there is not a shadow of a doubt but, if such an attack shd. be made, Great Britain wd. come to our rescue. Lloyd George, by the way, wishd. himself, I hear, to send you a telegram direct on this subject, but his associates preferred to have the matter reach you in the most informal way possible, at first.   Yours Sincerely,   Walter H. Page.

ALS (WP, DLC).
¹ Mayo was about to sail to attend an allied naval conference in London in September. In addition, Wilson and Daniels had instructed Mayo to press upon the British Admiralty the necessity of prompt action in the matter of laying an antisubmarine mine barrage between the coasts of Scotland and Norway. Not until about October 22, 1917, did the Admiralty approve the plan. See Josephus Daniels, *The Wilson Era—Years of War and Afterward, 1917-1923* (Chapel Hill, N. C., 1946), pp. 87-89.

From Arthur Wilson Page

Garden City, L. I., N. Y.
Dear Mr. President: August 14, 1917.

The World's Work is going to issue a number devoted to an appreciation of France. I know, of course, that under the present circumstances things from your pen must be of great rarity, but I hope that in this particular cause it is not improper to ask for two or three hundred words to begin this number with. I should not even suggest this at this time except that it might have a certain bearing on our relations with France, but, of course, you know much better than I whether such a thing would be wise or not.   Very sincerely yours,   Arthur W. Page

TLS (WP, DLC).

A Translation of a Letter from Baron Moncheur to Baron Charles de Broqueville¹

Mr. Minister: Washington, August 14, 1917.

The President received me yesterday in an audience by permission in a most pleasing manner. I conducted the interview along the lines indicated in the written instructions which were given me before my departure for the United States.

I began by indicating the fundamental demands upon which

¹ Belgian Prime Minister since June 1911 and Foreign Minister since July 30, 1917.

Belgium will insist, at the time of the peace negotiations, that is to say:

1. Reestablishment of Belgium in the integrity of its territory, with complete and absolute independence in the political order as well as in the economic realm.

2. Reparation by the enemy for the harm which he has done us, the extent of which I pointed out to Mr. Wilson in detail.

The President having conceded these two points without comment, I passed on to our other desiderata.

First, the question of Luxembourg, to which my questioner did not appear completely a stranger. I explained carefully the motives which justify our wish to see the Grand Duchy returned to Belgium, in case it should be decided at the time of the peace negotiations that the territory cannot continue to exist as an independent state.

Mr. Wilson showed himself in accord in principle; he asked me only whether it was certain that the citizens of the Grand Duchy would prefer to be reunited to Belgium rather than to another country. "As a matter of fact," he added, "you know that I firmly believe in the principle that one should not dispose of any state against its will, the small no more than the great. I think, moreover, that, if one wishes to make a lasting peace, it is necessary to provoke as little discontent as possible."

I then explained that the immense majority of the Luxemburgers would favor a return to Belgium in the event of their loss of independence. I recalled, in this connection, the enthusiastic welcome given to our Sovereign on the occasion of his official visit to Luxembourg before the war.

I then approached the question of the Escaut[2], which I explained briefly on the basis of the memorandum of Baron Beyens.[3] I concluded by saying that the government of the King wished the question to be settled diplomatically during the peace negotiations in such a way as to insure to Antwerp the free use of the river in time of peace and likewise in time of war, and thus to guarantee to Belgium the right to use the Escaut at all times for its military and naval operations, and those of its allies.

The President found this claim quite justified: "I could the less oppose it," he added, "since I declare myself a firm partisan of the theory that all countries have the right to demand free access to the sea."

[2] That is, the Escaut, or Schelde (Scheldt), River, the outlet to the North Sea for the international port of Antwerp. The use of the river had long been a subject of contention between the Belgians and the Dutch, since the latter controlled both sides of most of its estuary.

[3] Baron Eugène van Beyens, Belgian Foreign Minister from January 21, 1916, to July 30, 1917.

I passed then to another subject and, when I said to Mr. Wilson that we had firmly decided to rid ourselves of the neutrality which was formerly put upon us, he appeared a little surprised, but, after my explanations, he well understood that we wished to reject a regime the inconvenience of which had not been compensated for by any effective protection.

I believed that the moment had then come to call the serious attention of the President to the examination of the measures to be taken to preserve from all risk the future existence of Belgium after the war. I noted the great dangers to which her particular situation and its importance from an economic, as well as a political point of view, expose it. The peril would be especially great if the outcome of the struggle should leave in existence a still strong Germany.

Mr. Wilson then developed a plan which he has proposed to the republics of South America and which he would like to see adopted by the nations of the Entente. They would agree mutually to lend aid to each other in case one of them should be attacked. "Thus," said Mr. Wilson to me, "by virtue of this pact, Belgium would have to assist France if she was attacked by Germany, and, reciprocally, France and the other countries which had signed the pact would have to come to the aid of your country if she was the victim of aggression." "There would be here," he added, "a strong guarantee for Belgium, because Germany would never dare to attack it again if she knew that she would thus risk finding herself at war with all the members of the defensive alliance of which it was a part." I thought I understood, although the President did not say it expressly, that it would be his intention to have the United States eventually enter into this combination. The President sees also another guarantee of future peace in the political regime which, according to him, will be automatically established in Germany if she does not emerge victorious from the war.

According to him, it is scarcely probable that the Hohenzollerns will be dethroned, but, under the pressure of the democratic reaction which cannot help but be produced in Germany if the war is not a success, the internal political regime will be profoundly modified. The people will refuse to be launched upon a new adventure which could cause the nation sufferings as terrible as those which afflict it now. "There would be, there," he added, "a guarantee much more serious, in my opinion, than all the declarations which could be obtained from Germany and written in the peace treaty. The Hohenzollern autocracy is the fruit of the policy of Bismarck; it did not exist before 1866 when a group of little states existed in Germany, and it was only after 1870 that it attained its full development. But after the disasters occasioned by the present war, public opinion will get the upper hand."

I am giving you the views of the President, Mr. Minister, just as he laid them out to me.

If the defensive alliance of which I have spoken above should be made, it would be necessary, according to him, to set up in a European city an International Bureau of Information composed of eminent men who are not suspicious of each other. The useful information concerning the alliance would be centered in this bureau; one could resolve certain difficulties there, arising either between the allies, or perhaps between the allies and other countries. This organization could thus take on the character of what he calls a "clearing office," without, however, becoming in any way a court of arbitration.

Mr. Wilson believes that his combination, consisting of a pact for mutual defense, would be much more practical than a "League of Nations," which would be very difficult to organize since all countries, the smallest ones as well as the largest, would wish to take part there on the same footing.

We then talked of ways of combating the political system of *Mitteleuropa*. The President believed that, even as a democratic regime will be instituted in the German Empire after the war, the races forming the Austro-Hungarian agglomeration would wish to be emancipated. The Dual Monarchy would continue to exist, but each people of the confederation would have liberal autonomy. "That will be the greatest obstacle to the consolidation of the *Mitteleuropa* bloc, for the many non-German elements of the Austro-Hungarian Empire will act as a check upon the German policy of the country and prevent Vienna from submitting docilely to Berlin's orders. They will be hostile, also, to the whole idea of a new war."

On the question of annexations, in the event of an Entente victory, the President said to me that he did not yet have any well-defined idea. He thinks that question depends upon the circumstances at the end of the war, and especially upon the magnitude of the victory.

Concerning the restitution of Alsace-Lorraine, he believes, after receiving certain information from Europe, that the moderates and one part of the center party of France do not desire their return to the mother country enough to make it a condition *sine qua non* of peace.

Also, a politician who had just come from Alsace told him that many elements there made clear their desire for the reestablishment of French domination, but that it would, however, be dangerous to submit the question to a referendum.

In summary, I believe that the President would not oppose the restitution of the provinces lost by France if the victory of the Allies is crushing enough to impose it, but that, in the contrary case, it is his opinion that this sacrifice ought not to be required of Germany, if at this price it is possible to arrive at a satisfactory peace from other points of view.

Mr. Wilson spoke incidentally of the question of the Near East. "Turkey, that mass of different races, is a veritable hornet's nest, which keeps Europe always in alarm. It is necessary to find a remedy there, but the solution of the problem has not yet been found."

The President did not want to formulate his opinion on the opportunity which might come to expel the Turks from Europe, but he said that, in all events, the Straits ought to become an international way, and that by virtue of the principle that no nation ought to be deprived of an opening to the sea.

We then left the subject of foreign affairs and, speaking of my trip to the United States, I recalled the words of a number of political leaders, among others the Governor of Massachusetts,[4] who, in welcoming the Belgian mission, had expressed the hope and even the conviction that, if it would be possible to obtain from Germany *complete* reparation for the damages caused to Belgium, the United States would consider it a duty and an honor to make good what is lacking. I asked the President his views on this subject.

He replied that it would be difficult for the United States to act in this way, as a government. It would be criticized by the people if it undertook to pay, even in part, the amount falling to the Germans to pay. But he expressed the conviction that private initiative would contribute large gifts for the economic "reconstruction" of Belgium.

I objected that these gifts would not suffice for such an immense task, and I asked if the American government could not, when the time came, enter into certain combination loans, or even give its guarantee to these loans. Mr. Wilson admitted this idea in principle; but he added that it was preferable not to bring the question up right now, that it should be ignored during the war, and that one could not foresee what would be the situation of the American Treasury at the end of hostilities. . . .[5]

The President, in saying farewell, begged me to convey to the

[4] Samuel Walker McCall, Republican.
[5] Here Moncheur reports on conversations with House and Lansing.

King his warm regards for His Majesty's well-being and the success of His armies.

With high respect and regard.   Baron Moncheur.

T MS (WC, NjP); translation of TCL enclosed in T. N. Page to WW, Oct. 15, 1917, TLS (WP, DLC).

From the Diary of Josephus Daniels

August Tuesday 14 1917

At Cabinet discussed building destroyers. Shall we build merchant ships or destroyers? McAdoo rather thought the first. W said much would depend upon how long the war would last. We are building 117 & the proposed 150 could not be secured until 1919 & later. Then it would be a top-heavy Navy whereas the merchant ships would get in trade & that was the chief need. Decided to confer with Taylor[1] & report

Benson indignant at NL statement[2]

Went to see W about the charge of the Naval League & showed the statement and letter. Time for silence has ended. Speak out.[3] He would, if necessary, demand investigation & examination.

[1] That is, Rear Admiral David Watson Taylor.

[2] The Navy League, on August 14, had issued in Washington a statement that it had learned "from an official source" that an explosion on July 9 in a powder magazine at Mare Island Navy Yard, Vallejo, California, had been "the result of a criminal conspiracy." The league expressed fear "that vigorous investigation of the case" had been "hampered or prevented because of influence exerted by powerful labor interests." *New York Times*, Aug. 15, 1917.

[3] Daniels wrote on August 14 to Robert Means Thompson, president of the Navy League, that, in view of the "false and slanderous statement" given out by the league, he and the other active officials of the organization should resign. Thompson replied by offering a "sporting proposition": if Daniels would resign, so would he. *New York Times*, Aug. 15 and 16, 1917.

Daniels received the report of a special board of investigation on August 22 and made it public three days later. The board found that the explosion was due to "the deliberate act of some person or persons unknown," and it denied that it had been hampered in its investigation. At the same time, the Navy Department also made public a telegram from Commander Mark St. C. Ellis, inspector of ordnance of Mare Island, as follows: "The public statements that investigation was blocked by labor here are not true. Such imputations slander the brave and heroic labor men here who risked their lives to save this plant in successfully fighting the fire. The Board of Investigation was not hampered by the laboring men, but was assisted by every employe here wholeheartedly." *New York Times*, Aug. 23 and 26, 1917.

The Navy League announced on August 30 that it accepted the board's report and regretted its earlier suggestion that the investigation was being hampered by the Navy Department under the influence of powerful labor interests. The league also expressed regret that it had not made it clear "that it was not speaking of the standard labor unions, but of 'the Germanized I.W.W.'" *New York Times*, Aug. 31, 1917.

From Edward Mandell House

Dear Governor: Magnolia, Massachusetts. August 15, 1917.

I am wondering how you will think it best to answer the Pope's peace proposal.

It seems to me that the situation is full of danger as well as hope. France may succumb this winter. Russia is so eager to get at her internal problems that she will soon, almost certainly, insist upon peace on a basis of the status quo ante.

It is more important, I think, that Russia should weld herself into a virile republic than it is that Germany should be beaten to her knees. If internal disorder reach a point in Russia where Germany can intervene, it is conceivable that in the future she may be able to dominate Russia both politically and economically. Then the clock of progress would indeed be set back.

With Russia firmly established in democracy, German autocracy would be compelled to yield to a representative government within a very few years.

On a basis of the status quo ante, the Entente could aid Austria in emancipating herself from Prussia. Turkey could be sustained as an independent nation under the condition that Constantinople and the Straits have some sort of internationalization. This would settle the question of a division of Asia Minor between England, Russia, France and Italy—a division which is pregnant with future trouble. Turkey would be inclined towards the Entente today if it were not that she prefers being a German province, rather than to be dismembered as proposed by the Allies.

The submarine seems to me to be the crux of the situation. We cannot safely undertake to maintain an army in France unless the submarine menace is overcome. France nearly collapsed last winter from the lack of fuel and other essentials. If, with a diminished world tonnage, we add to the strain upon it the maintenance of a large army in France, the French and Italians will be in a worse plight regarding coal and other necessities than they were last winter. Will they bear the strain? I doubt it, if Germany will offer them the status quo ante, plus some sort of adjustment of Alsace and Lorraine which will enable a French government to go before the people with such an offer.

The war in America is not popular. It will become increasingly unpopular as time goes on. If a peace could be made this winter, the United States would be at the apex of power. If it continues for a year or more our resources will begin to show depletion, and we will never again be in a [*sic*] such a position as now to dictate a just peace.

And this leads me to hope that you will answer the Pope's proposal in some such way as to leave the door open, and to throw the onus on Prussia. This, I think, can be done if you will say that the peace terms of America are well known, but that it is useless to discuss the question until those of the Prussian militarists are also known, and further that it is hardly fair to ask the people of the allied countries to discuss terms with a military autocracy—an autocracy that does not represent the opinion of the people for whom they speak. If the people of the Central Powers had a voice in the settlement, it is probable an overwhelming majority would be found willing to make a peace acceptable to the other peoples of the world—a peace founded upon international amity and justice.

I believe an occasion has presented itself for you to make a notable utterance, and one which may conceivably lead to great results.   Affectionately yours,   E. M. House

TLS (WP, DLC).

From Michael Francis Doyle

Confidential

                                        Philadelphia, Pa.,
Dear President Wilson: August 15th, 1917.

In view of the peace proposals issued yesterday by His Holiness, Pope Benedict XV, it is important that I should convey to you the following information at once.

I am sure that he was largely guided in his proposals by Archbishop Cerretti[1] who two weeks ago assumed the office of Secretary of the Congregation of Extraordinary Foreign Affairs at the Vatican. Archbishop Cerretti was formerly Auditor of the Apostolic Legation in Washington. This position corresponds with that of Counsellor in European diplomatic circles. He was appointed Apostolic Delegate to Australia about three years ago, and was recently summoned to his new duties in Rome, and passed through the United States on his return. He reached Washington on June 23rd, and was there several days the following week. I visited him on June 24th and on June 30th he came to Philadelphia where we dined and spent the evening together. We have been very close friends for years, and I think he has confidence in my judgment. He was unable to remain in this country longer than necessary to make steamship arrangements as he was needed at Rome. He sailed under the protection of the Spanish Government and arrived about three weeks ago.

Archbishop Cerretti is a great admirer of our country and its institutions, and it is my thought that his opinions of the United States have a greater weight with the Pope than any other official at the Vatican. He is a man of sound judgment and cheerful disposition. He had a diplomatic training and has a broad knowledge of international affairs. His inclinations are pro-German. He has no sympathy with England. He desires the freedom of the seas and favors disarmament. He spoke in warmest manner of your efforts for peace and regretted our subsequent participation in the war. He was in this country in the summer of 1915 on his way to Australia, and I saw much of him then, and noticed his strong pro-German sympathies. He told me in June last that he expected to take an important part in peace prosposals [proposals], and he thought the Pope should move boldly for peace, out-lining terms, etc. He will shortly be elevated to Cardinal, and to my mind he represents the predominent influence at the Vatican to-day. I spoke to Senator Phelan of the importance of having him meet Secretary Lansing; but his stay was too brief to have it arranged.

In view of the fact that his views will have so much influence in shaping the policy of the Vatican I think it is my duty to convey these facts to you, thinking possibly they might be of value at this particular time.

Faithfully yours,   Michael Francis Doyle

TLS (WP, DLC).
[1] The Most Rev. Bonaventura Cerretti.

From Robert Lansing, with Enclosures

My dear Mr. President: Washington August 15, 1917.

I have received a note from the Russian Ambassador transcribing a communication from the Minister of Foreign Affairs of Russia to the Government of the United States,[1] a translation of which I beg to enclose, together with a draft reply to the Russian Ambassador, which I will sign if you approve.

Faithfully yours,   Robert Lansing

TLS (WP, DLC).
[1] C. Onou to RL, Aug. 3, 1917, TLS (SDR, RG 59, 763.72/6203, DNA).

ENCLOSURE I

FREE TRANSLATION. Washington August 3rd, 1917.

"At a moment when new and grave misfortunes are striking Russia we consider it our duty to give to our Allies, who have shared with us the burden of trials in the past, a firm and decisive expression of our point of view regarding the pursuance of the war. The greatness of the task of the Russian Revolution has determined the amplitude of the commotion which it caused in the life of the state. Reorganization in the face of the enemy of our entire governmental system could not be effected without serious perturbations. Nevertheless, Russia, convinced that there were no other means of salvation, has pursued in accord with the Allies a common action on the front.

Fully conscious of the difficulties of the task, Russia has assumed the burden of conducting active military operations during reconstruction of the army and of the government. The offensive of our army, which was necessitated by the strategical situation, encountered insurmountable obstacles both on the front and in the interior of the country. The criminal propaganda of irresponsible elements was used by enemy agents and provoked mutiny in Petrograd.[1] At the same time part of the troops on the front, seduced by the same propaganda, forgot their duty to the country and facilitated the enemy piercing our front.

The Russian people, stirred by these events, has manifested its unshakable will through the Government created by the revolution. The revolt was crushed, its originators brought to justice. All necessary steps have been taken at the front for restoring the combative strength of the army.

The government intends to bring to a successful end the task of consolidating a power capable to resist against all dangers and to guide the country in the path of the revolutionary regeneration. Russia will not suffer herself to be deterred by any difficulty in carrying out the irrevocable decision to pursue the war to the final triumph of the principles proclaimed by the Russian Revolution.

In the presence of the threat of the enemy the country and the army will contin[u]e with renewed courage the great labor of restoration and, on the threshold of the fourth year of the war, of preparation for the coming campaign.

We firmly believe that the Russian citizens will combine all efforts to fulfil the sacred task of defending their beloved country and that the enthusiasm which lighted in their hearts the flame of faith in the triumph of liberty will direct the whole invincible force of the revolution against the enemy who threatens the country.

We know that our liberty as well as all mankinds' is dependent on the issues of that struggle.

The new trials which crime and treason have inposed [imposed] on us can only enforce, still more, the conscience that the Russian people has of the necessity of consecrating, in a supreme effort, all forces and the whole of its resources for the salvation of the country. Strengthened by this conscience we are convinced that the retreat of our armies will be only temporary and that it will not prevent them, after being reconstructed and regenerated, to renew, when the hour will strike, their march forward in the name of the defense of the country and liberty, and that they will victoriously complete the great work for which they were compelled to take up arms."

T MS (SDR, RG 59, 763.72/6203, DNA).

1 A reference to the events which have come to be known collectively as "the July Days." Radical elements of the army and navy and various workers' groups, dissatisfied with the progress of the revolution under the Provisional Government, took part in confused and often violent demonstrations in Petrograd and other cities on July 16 and 17. They demanded that the Soviets seize the supreme power. However, the tide turned against the demonstrators on July 18 when several units of the army loyal to the Provisional Government arrived in Petrograd. The rebellion, such as it was, rapidly disintegrated. The Bolsheviks, who had reluctantly assumed leadership of the demonstrations, hoping to keep them in bounds, had to go underground for a time. Lenin fled into temporary exile in Finland, while Trotsky was arrested. See William Henry Chamberlin, *The Russian Revolution, 1917-1921* (2 vols., New York, 1935), I, 166-91.

E N C L O S U R E   I I

Robert Lansing to Boris Aleksandrovich Bakhmet'ev

Excellency: Washington August 15, 1917.

I have the honor to acknowledge the receipt of your note of the third instant in which you transcribe a communication from the Minister of Foreign Affairs of Russia to the Government of the United States.

A translation of that communication has been furnished to the President, who, in full appreciation of the vast task confronting the Provisional Government of Russia in the reconstruction of that country and the reorganization of its forces, and of the energy with which that Government is endeavoring, in the face of disloyalty and enemy-inspired propaganda, to uphold the good faith of Russia, welcomes the assurance now given by the Provisional Government of Russia of its intention, of which the President has had no doubt, of being deterred by no difficulty in pursuing the war to a final triumph. No less gratifying to the President is the announcement, by that Government that, like the United States, Russia consecrates all its forces and all its resources to this end. With this tenacity of purpose moving all the Allied Governments, there can be no doubt of the outcome of the conflict now raging.

I ask you to be so good as to give to your Government renewed expression of the President's deep sympathy with them in the burden they have assumed and in the obstacles they have encountered, and are encountering, and his confidence that, inspired and impelled by their patriotic efforts and guidance, there will emerge from the present conflict a regenerated Russia founded upon those great principles of democracy, freedom and equality, right and justice.

Accept, Excellency, the renewed assurances of my highest consideration.   (Signed) Robert Lansing.[1]

CCL (SDR, RG 59, 763.72/6203, DNA).
[1] Wilson must have approved this letter since it was sent at once.

From Henry Noble Hall

[Washington]
My dear Mr. President,   Wednesday; Aug. 15, 1917

In placing before you the following facts I am actuated solely by the belief that you would wish me so to do. I happened to be present this afternoon at the popular demonstration before the Woman Suffrage Headquarters and a little later in front of the White House.[1] As an interested spectator but quite innocent bystander I had the experience of being threatened with a blackjack by a plain clothes policeman—James A. Springmann—whose identity I was able to establish through the courtesy of a police Captain on duty. Perhaps I may be permitted to suggest that it would be wise on the part of the officials charged with the maintenance of public order if only uniformed men were used in dealing with these demonstrations so that the public might be able to at once recognize the representatives of authority.

May I not also take the liberty of expressing to you my genuine concern that if these demonstrations are allowed to develop into scuffles with the police it will only be a question of time when from accident or the design of some misguided person blood will flow. The temper of the crowd was directed exclusively against the seditious and despicable banners carried by the women, and not in any way against their persons. Indeed I saw several instances of chivalrous regard for the women, several men interposing themselves to receive blows which would otherwise have fallen upon the suffragettes.

Among the crowd were many women and men of mature years who openly applauded the tearing down of banners by the younger element. Frequently I heard the sentiment expressed that women who are capable of parading some of the most obnoxious banners must either be traitors or degenerates. If it is not thought that banners referring to the President of the United States and Commander in Chief of the Army and Navy as "Kaiser Wilson" at a time when this country is at war with Germany are calculated to give aid and encouragement to the enemy, it does seem that an indignant public should be allowed to deal with such banners according to the dictates of their patriotism without police interference. To-day it was not the public that was protected, it was the women who held up to ridicule and contempt the President of the United States.

I have the honor to be, my dear Mr. President
Faithfully and obediently yours   Henry N. Hall

TLS (WP, DLC).
1 About the events of August 14 and 15, when crowds, which included servicemen, violently attacked the demonstrators representing the National Woman's party, see C. A. Lindbergh to WW, Aug. 27, 1917, printed as an Enclosure with WW to NDB, Sept. 1, 1917.

From George Creel

Memorandum to The President:

Dear Mr. President: [Washington] August 15, 1917.
About six weeks ago I asked Mr. Lansing what his attitude would be toward a series of articles by Brand Whitlock. I have a very clear memory that he said that the more Whitlock wrote, the better. As a consequence, I took up the matter with several magazines. Brand is my dear friend, and out of a very clear knowledge of his circumstances, I tried to make an arrangement which would not only give us the desired publicity, but which would, at the same time, guarantee him a return in money that would lift him above all worry. Everybody's magazine made the best offer, and Mr. Howard D. Wheeler[1] is now in town, ready to make the trip to France to complete arrangements with Mr.

Whitlock. The magazine stands ready to give the Whitlock articles a circulation without regard to profit, feeling, as I feel, that their publication at the present time will arouse America and steel our determination.

Mr. Lansing, however, just informed Mr. Wheeler that he does not wish Mr. Whitlock to write, as it would establish a bad precedent. This stops me completely. If the Secretary does not recall our former understanding, I cannot insist upon it. At the same time I feel strongly that Whitlock should write a story of Belgium, and that from his pen would flow inspiration and high resolve. It is just the sort of thing that we need. Is it not possible for you to indicate to Mr. Lansing that it might be well to make an exception in the case of Mr. Whitlock, giving him permission to write as he will? His articles, of course, could be submitted to the State Department for visé.

Respectfully   George Creel

TLS (WP, DLC).
1 Howard Duryee Wheeler, editor of *Everybody's Magazine* of New York.

From William Gibbs McAdoo

Dear "Governor":   Washington August 15, 1917.

I enclose a short statement in reference to the bill for insurance of our soldiers and sailors which I am giving out for release on Sunday, next.1 I hope you may have time to glance at it. I feel very much encouraged about the prospects of prompt passage of this important legislation, and hope you will, a little later on, make a statement to the country expressing strongly your approval of the measure. I will suggest an appropriate time.

Affectionately yours,   W G McAdoo

TLS (WP, DLC).
1 *Family allowance, indemnity, and insurance for our soldiers and sailors—the duty of a just government*, printed press release (WP, DLC).

From Raymond Blaine Fosdick

My dear Mr. President: Washington August 15, 1917.

I am turning to you for a little help in connection with the work of our Commission on Training Camp Activities. At the very beginning of our plans, we asked the Playground and Recreation Association of America to assume responsibility for organizing the community work in the vicinity of the military camps. I was especially anxious that the soldiers on leave from camp should find the towns to which they naturally turned in their leisure hours fully organized along recreational and relaxational lines. The instinctive desire of the soldier with an hour's free time "to go to town" is something that had to be definitely prepared for, and the Playground and Recreation Association has been of immense assistance in welding all the activities of the communities in the neighborhood of our military camps—including the Y.W.C.A., the lodges, the churches, the Chambers of Commerce, and many other bodies—into a composite program along healthy recreational lines.

We already have sixty-six representatives in sixty-six different communities near the military camps. Our procedure in each case has been to get the Mayor of the city to appoint a local committee and under its direction swimming pools and soldiers' clubs have been opened, dances arranged and many other activities undertaken. In other words, we are trying to compete with the evil forces which must be eliminated from the environment of the soldier's life.

Needless to say, this work is expensive. We estimate that for one year it is going to cost $2,500,000 to put this program through. This seems a staggering sum, but it must be remembered that $2,000,000 will be raised by the communities themselves. Our idea is to make each community feel its responsibility for work of this kind among the soldiers.

There remains $500,000 of overhead expenses and the salaries of our representatives still to be provided, and I am confident that a word from you to Mr. Joseph Lee, the President of the Playground and Recreation Association, and also a member of our Commission, would greatly facilitate the raising of this sum. I am enclosing a tentative letter addressed to Mr. Lee. If it would be no impropriety for you to sign it or some letter similar to it, I am sure that the difficulty with which we are now faced would quickly disappear.[1] Secretary Baker is thoroughly cognizant of our plans along this line.

With warm personal regards,

Cordially yours,   Raymond B. Fosdick

TLS (WP, DLC).

[1] Wilson used Fosdick's draft as WW to J. Lee, Aug. 16, 1917, TLS (Letterpress Books, WP, DLC).

A Memorandum by George M. Sutton[1]

Washington August 15, 1917.

MEMORANDUM FOR THE POSTMASTER GENERAL:

A copy of a letter of Mr. A. M. Ricker, publisher of Pearson's magazine, New York City, dated August 3, 1917, addressed to the President, was sent to the department by Senator Henry L. Myers. On August 8, 1917, letters were written to the President and to Senator Myers concerning the matter, and the papers referred to this office by the Solicitor for investigation. The papers were transmitted to the Inspector in Charge at New York,[2] the same day, and the report of Inspectors Doran and Ashe,[3] dated August 14, 1917, relative thereto has been received.

Mr. Ricker complained that

"letters addressed to him from the People's Council of America while on a trip in the west were not delivered at all; that in one specific case a letter reached his address two weeks after it had been mailed from New York, N. Y.; that letters have come to Pearson's bearing evidence of having been opened and resealed, and that the United States mails have become so uncertain that he is compelled to send his regular business mail in plain envelopes in order that they may pass through the mails undisturbed."

He was interviewed and stated that the specific letter to which he referred was one mailed by the People's Council of America addressed to him at Shannon City, Iowa; that the letter bore a New York postmark two weeks after the date of mailing, and that it had been opened and endorsed "Opened by mistake." Mr. Ricker further stated that the letter had *probably been opened at his sister's home*[4] to where it was addressed and that he had destroyed the envelope. He made *no mention* of the non-receipt of other letters mailed by the People's Council of America. With reference to the charge that letters for Pearson's magazine had been delivered bearing evidence of having been opened and resealed, Mr. Ricker stated that shortly after the receipt of the letter which was forwarded to him from Shannon City, Iowa, a number of letters addressed to Pearson's were received which he believed had been tampered with. However, the envelopes of these letters were destroyed, and he admitted that *his suspicions* may have been *without foundation*; also that he had *no complaint* to make concerning mail for Pearson's magazine, which had been *delivered for years without delay and in good condition*. The inspectors state Mr. Ricker, who is a *member of the Executive Committee* of the People's Council of America, appeared to be uncertain relative to mail for Pearson's but considered the complaints of the People's Council of America as personal and grievous. Mr. Ricker informed the inspectors that the attitude of the Post Office Department in the case of *the "Masses"* proved to him that persons who disagreed with the policy of the administration would be subject to *unjust treatment* at the hands of this department. He doubted the inspector's sincerity in the investigation, and stated that he *never expected* that any action would be taken on his complaint to the President. The inspectors recommend that the matter be closed for the reason that the complainant has no complaint to make with reference to the mail for Pearson's magazine.

Mr. Louis P. Lochner, Executive Secretary of the People's Council of America, 2 West 13th Street, New York, New York, complained to the department to the effect that matter mailed by the Council between June 12 and 28, 1917, containing for the most part checks in payment of salaries and expenses of their representatives were not delivered; that duplicate checks were mailed and that *subsequently* the original letters were received by the addresses. Mr. Lochner *declined to give* the inspectors the envelopes of some of these letters which were sent to him for the reason that a member of the Congressional Committee, now investigating charges of alleged tampering with mail matter, had requested him to retain them for the use of that Committee.[5] The People's Council of America, formerly known as the *Emergency Peace Federation* and the *American Neutral Conference Committee*, is closely affiliated with the *American Union against militarism*, the *Four Lights* and OTHER organizations of a similar character. Certain mail sent by the People's Council of America was held in New York City until a ruling could be obtained from the Solicitor for the Post Office Department as to its mailability. The nature of the circulars was ascertained by the examination of unsealed matter. The Solicitor advised that the matter *should be dispatched*. The inspectors state that from time to time sealed letters and circulars dispatched by the People's Council of America, and organizations affiliated with it, have been held up, and where the letters were unsealed they were forwarded to the assistant postmaster by the superintendents of the various stations in New York City. It is stated that approximately four thousand letters and three thousand circulars have been thus withheld from dispatch. On July 26, 1917, the superintendent at Station O received instructions from the assistant postmaster at New York, New York, to dispatch all sealed matter mailed by the People's Council of America, and the superintendent did as directed the same afternoon, being compelled to work clerks overtime to get the matter out. The letters upon which the complaint of Mr. Lochner is based bear the return card of the People's Council of America, or of Room 714, 2 West 13th Street, and the inspectors believe, by reason of the postmark which they bear, that they were among the mail held by Station O acting upon the instructions from the assistant postmaster with reference to the treatment of suspected treasonable matter.

Geo. M. Sutton, Chief Inspector.

TS MS (WP, DLC).
    1 Chief Inspector of the Post Office Department.
    2 William E. Cochran.
    3 James J. Doran and John E. Ashe, Post Office Inspectors in New York.
    4 All emphases in this letter Wilson's.
    5 Representative Meyer London, on July 10, had introduced H. Res. 115 which called upon the Postmaster General to furnish to Congress information as to what, if any, periodicals the Post Office Department had barred from the mails under the terms of the Espionage Act. Burleson, on July 21, wrote to John Austin Moon, chairman of the House Committee on the Post Office, to which the resolution had been referred. Burleson recommended that H. Res. 115 be reported adversely to the House. He admitted that certain issues of several periodicals had been barred from the mails but declared that it was incompatible with the public interest to provide any more specific information on the subject to Congress. Moreover, any publisher who objected to the rulings of the Post Office Department had a right to take his case to the courts, as *The Masses* had already done. On July 23, the committee, in reporting adversely on the resolution, commented that the courts offered a means of redress for any injustice that might be done. Moon stated to the press that the committee had no power to compel Burleson to furnish the information and also no power to alter the practices of the Post Office Department, even if the information was forthcoming. *New York Times*, July 24, 1917. London attempted to bring up his resolution in the House on July 30 and 31, but on both occasions an objection by another member prevented its consideration. Thomas W. Hardwick introduced a similar resolution (S. Res. 119) in the Senate on August 17, but no action was taken upon it. On August 22, Burleson's correspondence on the matter with members of both houses, together with the House report against London's resolution, were ordered printed in the *Congressional Record*. See *Cong. Record*, 65th Cong., 1st sess., pp. 4931, 5407, 5569, 5634, 6109, 6257-59.

Walter Hines Page to Robert Lansing

London. Aug. 15, 1917.

6959. I received this morning from the Foreign Office a note informing me That His Holiness the Pope has requested His Majesty the King to forward to the heads of those States with whom the Holy See is not in diplomatic relations the accompanying document addressed to the heads of the Belligerent States by His Holiness containing certain proposals for general peace.

Following is the full text:

(French translation)

To the Rulers of the Belligerent peoples:

From the beginning of our pontificate, in the midst of the horrors of the awful war let loose on Europe, we have had of all things three in mind: To maintain perfect impartiality towards all the Belligerents as becomes Him who is the Common Father and loves all His children with equal affection, continually to endeavor to do them all as much good as possible without exception of person, without distinction of nationality or religion as is dictated to us by the universal law of charity as well as by the supreme spiritual charge with which we have been instructed by Christ, finally as also required by our mission of peace, to omit nothing as far as it lay in our power that could contribute to expedite the end of these calamities by endeavoring to bring the peoples and the leaders to more moderate resolutions to the serene deliberation of peace, of a "just and lasting" peace.

Whoever has watched our endeavors in these three grievous years that have just elapsed could easily see that while we remained ever true to our resolution of absolute impartiality and beneficent action, we never ceased to urge the belligerent peoples and Governments again to be brothers, although all that we did to reach this very noble goal was not made public.

About the end of the first year of the war we addressed to the contending nations the most earnest exhortations and in addition pointed to the path that would lead to a stable peace honorable to all. Unfortunately our appeal was not heeded and the war was fiercely carried on for two years more with all its horrors. It became even more cruel and spread over land and sea and even to the air, and desolation and death were seen to fall upon defenseless cities, peaceful villages and their innocent populations. And now, no one can imagine how much the general suffering would increase and become worse if other months or, still worse, other years were added to this sanguinary triennium. Is this civilized world to be turned into a field of death and is Europe, so glorious and flourishing, to rush, as carried by a universal folly, to the abyss and take a hand in its own suicide?

In so distressing a situation, in the presence of so grave a menace, we, who have no personal political aim, who listen to the suggestions or interests of none of the belligerents, but are solely actuated by the sense of our supreme duty as the common father of the faithful, by the solicitations of our children who implore our intervention and peace-bearing word, uttering the very voice of humanity and reason, we again call for peace and we renew a pressing appeal to those who have in their hands the destinies of the nations. But no longer confining ourselves to general terms, as we were led to do by circumstances in the past, we will now come to more concrete and practical proposals and invite the Governments of the belligerent peoples to arrive at an agreement on the following points which seem to offer the bases of a just and lasting peace, leaving it with them to make them more precise and complete.

First, the fundamental point must be that the material force of arms give way to the moral force of right whence a just agreement of all upon the simultaneous and reciprocal decrease of armaments, according to rules and guarantees to be established, in the necessary and sufficient measure for the maintenance of public order in every State; then, taking the place of arms, the institution of arbitration with its high pacifying function, according to rules to be drawn in concert and under sanctions to be determined against any State which would decline either to refer international questions to arbitration or to accept its awards.

When supremacy of right is thus established, let every obstacle to ways of communication of the peoples be removed by insuring through rules to be also determined the true freedom and community of the seas, which, on the one hand, would eliminate many causes of conflict, and, on the other hand, would open to all new sources of prosperity and progress.

As for the damages to be repaid and the cost of the war, we see no other way of solving the question than by setting up the general principle of entire and reciprocal condonation which would be justified by the immense benefit to be derived from the disarmament, all the more as one could not understand that such carnage could go on for mere economic reasons. If certain particular reasons stand against this in certain cases, let them be weighed in justice and equity.

But these specific agreements with the immense advantages that flow from them are not possible unless territory now occupied is reciprocally restituted. Therefore, on the part of Germany, total evacuation of Belgium with guarantees of its entire political, military and economic independence toward any power whatever; evacuation also of the French territory; on the part of the other belligerents, a similar restitution of the German Colonies.

As regards territorial questions, as for instance those that are disputed by Italy and Austria, by Germany and France, there is reason to hope that in consideration of the immense advantages of durable peace with disarmament, the contending parties will examine in a conciliatory spirit, taking into account as far as it is just and possible, as we have said formerly, the aspirations of the population, and if occasion arises adjusting private interests to the general good of the great human society.

The same spirit of equity and justice must guide the examination of the other territorial and political questions, notably, those relative to Armenia, the Balkan States and the territories forming part of the old kingdom of Poland for which, in particular, its noble historical traditions and the suffering particularly undergone during the present war, must win, with justice, the sympathies of the nations.

These, we believe, are the main bases upon which must rest the future reorganization of the peoples. They are such as to make the recurrence of such conflicts impossible and open the way for the solution of the economic question which is so important for the future and the material welfare of all the belligerent States. And so, in presenting them to you who, at this tragic hour, guide the destinies of the belligerent nations we indulge a gratifying hope, that they will be accepted and that we shall thus see an early termination of the terrible struggle which has more and more the appearance of a useless massacre. Everybody acknowledges on the other hand that on both sides the honor of arms is safe. Do not then turn a deaf ear to our prayer, accept the paternal invitation which we extend to you in the name of the divine Redeemer, Prince of Peace. Bear in mind your very grave responsibility to God and Man; on your decision depend the quiet and joy of numberless families, the lives of thousands of young men, the happiness, in a word, of the peoples to whom it is your imperative duty to secure this boon. May the Lord inspire you with decisions conformable to His very holy will. May heaven grant that in winning the applause of your contemporaries you will also earn from the future generations the great title of pacificators.

As for us, closely united in prayer and penitence with all the faithful souls who yearn for peace, we implore for you of the divine spirit enlight[en]ment and guidance. Given at the Vatican, August 1, 1917. Benedictus P.M.XV.   Page.

T telegram (SDR, RG 59, 763.72119/726, DNA).

From the Diary of Colonel House

August 15, 1917.

Frank Polk took lunch with us and spent the better part of the day. We went over every phase of the international situation and departmental affairs. He does not think the President appreciates Lansing. The President told Polk while he was acting Secretary of State during Lansing's absence, that Lansing could not write clearly; that he always had to do the work himself. Both

Polk and I think this is an unfair criticism, and that Lansing writes unusually clearly. What he lacks, in my opinion, is imagination, the diplomatic touch and a spiritual outlook. He is practical, has a legal mind, and desires to do things largely by precedent.

Polk believes the Secretary has no jealousy toward me, although he realizes I have the full confidence of the President and he has not.

Polk believes the President is practically running both the Navy and Army himself, because he is constantly visiting these departments or sending for Daniels or Baker. He deprecates, as we all do, the President's lack of administrative ability. He cannot seem to arrange affairs so they may be expedited, nor can he get the fullest service from his advisers. Polk, while acting Secretary, sent the President an important letter on Tuesday. Not hearing from him, he called up the White House on Friday to find that he had not even read it. In the meantime, the Senate Committee on Foreign Affairs, who had been awaiting the President's leadership in the matter, decided it for themselves leaving the President to follow. This is typical.

Polk says he gets misinformation from men like Denman and others and it is difficult to put him straight. He has no fear of the President's judgment if he has all the facts before him.

He believes Lane has entirely lost the President's confidence and wonders why. McAdoo thought Baker had more influence with the President than any member of the Cabinet, but Polk thinks that Houston and Wilson are listened to with more attention.

I gave Polk my views of the Pope's peace proposal, and talked at length of the war situation as it appeared to me. I was glad to have him agree. I believe I talked him out of the position he had—a position, indeed, which I am sure Lansing holds. Polk says that Gordon is indispensible, and is already of more value to him than Billy Phillips, First Assistant Secretary of State.

My letter to the President concerning the Pope's peace proposal is the important document of the day. I know I am running counter to the advice of Lansing, Phillips and others in the State Department. I feel, too, I am running counter to the President's own judgment, nevertheless, I am willing to stand upon it for I am sure I have a more complete picture of the situation than either the President or Lansing. I simply saturate myself, in every way possible, with facts relating to the present status of the war. I see ten people to their one, and I read, perhaps, ten documents to their one. Not only that, my knowledge of the situation in the belligerent countries from personal observation since the war began gives me, I feel, a better opportunity than they have to form a correct judgment.

Notes for a Reply to Benedict XV

PAPAL PLAN.

[c. Aug. 16, 1917]

Status quo ante bellum

PLUS

Condonation, disarmament, general arbitration.

Freedom of the seas

French territorial claims ⎫ Conciliatory adjust-
Italian territorial claims ⎪ ment, taking into
Balkan question ⎬ consideration aspira-
Reconstitution of Poland ⎭ tions of populations.

Appreciation of motives which prompted the appeal.

It may be taken for granted that he is equally solicitous that the foundations should be laid for permanent peace and that the peace proposed should not be a mere temporary cessation of arms *The appeal itself expresses this solicitude*

Can be discussed only in view of causes and objects (These to be carefully stated).

The objects may be summed up in one: to deliver the free countries of the world from the menace of a vast military establishment controlled by an irresponsible government which acknowledges no obligation or restriction either of treaty or of international practice and long established principle,—which in this terrible war has brushed aside every consideration of humanity even. It is none of our business how the German people got under the control of such a government or were kept under the domination of its power and its purposes, but it is our business to see to it that the history of the world is no longer left to their handling.

To deal with such a power by way of peace would involve

a) a recuperation of its power and renewal of its policy,

b) a permanent hostile combination against the German people, whereas, in different circumstances the other nations of the world would wish to deprive them of nothing that the rest of the peoples of the world enjoyed, and

c) an abandonment of Russia to intrigue, interference, and counter revolution through the subtle and malign influences which such a power is now known industriously to build up.

Responsible statesmen [k]now everywhere, I believe that no peace can rest securely upon vindictive action towards any people or upon political or economic discriminations meant to benefit some and cripple or embarrass others. It can rest only upon the equal rights of peoples, great and small, upon freedom and security and an equal participation by all in the economic opportunities of the world,—the German people with the rest, if the German people will accept equality and not seek domination.[1]

WWT MS (WP, DLC).
[1] There is a WWsh draft of this outline in WP, DLC.

To Edward Mandell House

My dear House,   The White House. 16 August, 1917.

I do not know that I shall make any reply at all to the Pope's proposals, but I am glad to let Mr. Balfour know what it would be were I to make one,—as it is possible I may be led by circumstances to do.

Appreciation should, of course, be expressed of the humane purpose of the Pope and a general sympathy with his desire to see the end of this terrible war come on terms honourable to all concerned; but these objections should be stated:

(1) That no intimation is conveyed that the terms suggested meet the views of any of the belligerents and that to discuss them would be a blind adventure;

(2) That such terms constitute no settlement but only a return to the *status quo ante* and would leave affairs in the same attitude that furnished a pretext for the war; and

(3) That the absolute disregard alike of all formal obligations of treaty and all accepted principles of international law which the autocratic regime still dominant in Germany has shown in the whole action of this war has made it impossible for other governments to accept its assurances on anything, least of all on the terms upon which peace will be maintained. The present German Imperial Government is morally bankrupt; no one will accept or credit its pledges; and the world will be upon quicksand in regard to all international covenants which include Germany until it can believe that it is dealing with a responsible government.

I see no other possible answer.

I am rushing this through my type-writer (and through my mind, too, for that matter,) on a desperately busy day, and may not have expreesed [expressed] my conclusions happily, but I am in no uncertainty as to their substance.

All unite in affectionate messages. I devour and profit by all your letters, and am

Your devoted and grateful friend,   Woodrow Wilson[1]

WWTLS (E. M. House Papers, CtY).
  [1] There is a WWsh draft of this letter in WP, DLC.

To Newton Diehl Baker, with Enclosure

My dear Mr. Secretary: The White House 16 August, 1917

Thank you for the enclosed memorandum.

I do not feel that the power to determine prices can be *lodged* with the War Industries Board but I do feel that they ought to play a very important function of advice in the matter and I mean to associate myself as closely as I can with them and to be guided by them as much as possible in this important matter.

Cordially and sincerely yours,   Woodrow Wilson

TLS (N. D. Baker Papers, DLC).

E N C L O S U R E

Washington. August 9, 1917

PROPOSED POWERS OF WAR INDUSTRIES BOARD.

Business is suffering throughout the country today because of uncertainty as to Government policy with respect to prices and taxation. In this respect the business loss is serious, but even more serious is the bad effect on the spirit of manufacturers who would be willing, and glad, to work and make sacrifices for the benefit of the Government in its emergency if they felt sure of fair and equal treatment, based on a definite Government policy. Equality of treatment of the different manufacturers is at least as important in keeping up the spirit of willingness to serve the Government as the actual amount of profits that they may be permitted to make.

Under present conditions contractors supplying the various needs of the Government are not treated with equality and are not dealt with consistently on any established principle. Prices of important commodities are soaring out of all reason simply because *price* is the only available way to determine distribution under present conditions. This situation creates disturbance in business, but, worse than that, it creates resentment against the making of undue profits and will, in the long run, make much more difficult the attainment of complete cooperation on the part of business men and labor.

No one department can remedy the situation. The remedy must be sought through cooperation of the War Department, Navy Department, Shipping Board, and any other agency having large purchases to make. The Council of National Defense is especially limited in its powers, by statute, and the Congress itself has neither the facilities nor the desire to undertake the fixing of prices. There is no place that the responsibility of price fixing can be more reasonably lodged than with the War Industries Board, and there is no time like the present time for taking this action, both because of the very urgent national need and because of the occasion afforded by the organization of the new Board.

The question is broader than that of fixing prices for U. S. Government purchases. The allies and the public must also be considered. This position has been definitely taken by the President in his address on the subject of War Profits.[1] If the Government simply drives the best possible bargain for itself and does not concern itself with the needs of the allies and the public, the effect of such action, by using up a large percentage of the country's capacity, would probably be to force even higher prices on the allies and the public. This will lead to unfairness among manufacturers because those manufacturing for the Government will be unduly penalized and the resultant high prices will be disturbing with respect to business and unconscionable, from a national viewpoint, with respect to purchases for the allies.

With the cooperation of the Secretary of War, the Secretary of the Navy and the Shipping Board, and the approval of the President, the War Industries Board could actually control all prices paid by the United States, and, as a practical matter, could control prices generally by request, on patriotic grounds publicly endorsed by the President, that no one quote or pay prices in excess of those fixed by the Board. This could be further enforced by the hint that those quoting higher prices in their private trade would have their capacity entirely used on Government orders so that their private customers would be obliged to look elsewhere.

In fixing prices the principle would necessarily be to make a high enough price to secure the amount of production necessary in the case of any particular product. The Board, with its expert advisers, can make as accurate a guess about this as can be made and can, from time to time, revise prices where errors become apparent. This idea is not inconsistent with the President's reference to certain problems with respect to cost of production to the Federal Trade Commission. Any results of the studies of the Federal Trade Commission on this subject would be serviceable data to assist the War Industries Board in fixing prices, whereas a knowledge of the cost of production, unaccompanied by the other facts which would be known to the War Industries Board, would not enable the Federal Trade Commission fairly to fix prices.

Prices fixed on the basis of securing the necessary production will in many cases yield unreasonably large profits to the industries best organized. Unreasonably large profits ought not to be permitted during the war, but neither the executive departments nor the War Industries Board has machinery to discriminate between the different manufacturers paying a lower price to the more efficient manufacturers. The situation can, however, be handled very easily and simply by Congress by the enactment of an adequate excess profits tax law. It would seem desirable for this Board, after securing the approval of the President, the Secretary of War, the Secretary of the Navy and the Shipping Board, to meet with members of the Finance Committee of the Senate and the Ways and Means Committee of the House, before the final passage of the Revenue Bill, with a view to securing their cooperation in the rounding out of a complete plan.

It would be futile to attempt the fixing of prices until the Board is prepared to carry out a complete system of priorities and delivery so as to be able to assure manufacturers who accept the fixed reduced prices that their products are actually going to be used for the military and economic needs essential to the successful prosecution of the war. It is not fair to ask a producer to abide by a fixed price so long as there is any chance of a speculator getting control of any part of the product.

The suggestions here made do not necessitate any change in existing law. In view of the urgency of the national need of immediate action in the situation, it is submitted that immediate action ought to be taken along these lines. Legislation may be desirable and even necessary later, but can best be suggested as the result of experience in the attempt above outlined. There need be no fear that the number of mistakes made by the War Industries Board would be sufficient to make the situation any worse than that which we are drifting into by failure to grapple with the problem at all.

T MS (N. D. Baker Papers, DLC).
1 That is, Wilson's appeal to the American people, printed at July 12, 1917.

To Newton Diehl Baker

My dear Mr. Secretary: The White House 16 August, 1917

Here again I am at a loss what to say in reply to this communication from the Friends' Reconstruction Unit.[1] I suppose that it will be impossible for us formally to accept this as an exemption, but just what should I say, do you think?

Faithfully yours,   Woodrow Wilson

TLS (WDR, RG 94, AGO-Misc. File, No. 2638715, DNA).
[1] Rufus M. Jones to WW, Aug. 15, 1917, TLS (WDR, RG 94, AGO-Misc. File, No. 2638715, DNA), about a recently organized Friends' Reconstruction Unit for relief and reconstruction work in the devastated war zones of northern France. Jones asked if participation in such work was, for Quakers, a satisfactory alternative to combat service. See also NDB to WW, Aug. 27, 1917. Rufus Matthew Jones, Litt.D., was a minister of the Society of Friends; Professor of Philosophy at Haverford College; chairman of the American Friends Service Committee, European Relief; and a distinguished lecturer and author on historical, social, and religious subjects.

To Newton Diehl Baker, with Enclosure

My dear Mr. Secretary: The White House 16 August, 1917

I am sincerely regretful that I should have to send you so many things from my correspondence, but I do not know how else to handle them without falling out of cooperation with you. Perhaps you have had so many of a similar sort to the ones enclosed that you will be able to suggest a reply with your eyes shut.

In haste

Cordially and faithfully yours,   Woodrow Wilson

TLS (N. D. Baker Papers, DLC).

E N C L O S U R E

New York, Aug. 15, 1917.

Our people in New York appreciate the compliment paid to their loyalty and courage by the selection of our Irish Catholic regiment, the Sixty-Ninth New York, amongst the first to go to the front. I speak the mind of all then [of them] by requesting that a commanding officer who will represent that character of the appointment of Captain Haskell[1] would be eminently satisfactory.   John Cardinal Farley.

T telegram (WP, DLC).
[1] William Nafew Haskell, U.S.A. See NDB to WW, Aug. 18, 1917 (first letter of that date). Haskell was assigned to the field artillery in the National Army in August.

To Arthur Wilson Page

My dear Mr. Page: The White House 16 August, 1917

I am very sorry but it is literally impossible for me to do what you request in your letter of August fourteenth; and, besides, may I not without the least touch of personal feeling say that I do not feel that the World's Work has been at all fair in its criticism, particularly of the administration of the Navy Department, having permitted things to be published which were just as far as possible from the truth? I say this in all frankness because I know you would want me to speak in no other way.

Sincerely yours,   Woodrow Wilson

TLS (W. H. Page Papers, MH).

To Herbert Clark Hoover

My dear Mr. Hoover: The White House 16 August, 1917

It certainly was a very unusual and stimulating exhibition of patriotism given by the grain dealers and elevator men with whom you consulted the other day[1] and I hope that you will have an opportunity of conveying to them an expression of my admiration and appreciation. I am sure the whole country will feel as I do about it.

Cordially and sincerely yours,   Woodrow Wilson

TLS (H. Hoover Papers, HPL).
    [1] H. C. Hoover to WW, Aug. 15, 1917, TLS (WP, DLC). Hoover reported that a group of some 120 grain dealers and elevator operators, with whom he had conferred about the Food Administration's plan for the control of the wheat and rye business of the country, had wholeheartedly approved the plan, despite the fact that it meant that some of them would be put out of business for the duration of the war. Moreover, some fifteen members of the group had agreed to serve without compensation as administrators of the program.

To Robert Lansing

My dear Mr. Secretary: The White House 16 August, 1917

My attention has just been called to a plan which Mr. Brand Whitlock had of writing some articles about Belgium. My own judgment is that he had better be allowed to do it. I realize the awkwardness of the precedent but, after all, this is not a time when precedents are likely to be formed because everything is in such an exceptional state, and I have the instinctive feeling that what Whitlock would write would be very safe and admirable.[1]

Cordially and sincerely yours,   Woodrow Wilson

TLS (R. Lansing Papers, DLC).

¹ A series of articles, all with the general title, "Belgium," appeared in *Everybody's Magazine* from February 1918 to January 1919. They were a serialization of the book which Whitlock published as *Belgium: A Personal Narrative* (2 vols., New York, 1919).

To Ernest Lister

[The White House]
My dear Governor Lister: August 16, 1917.

The bearer of this letter is Judge J. Harry Covington, the Chief Justice of the Supreme Court of the District of Columbia, whom I have taken the liberty of sending to you as my personal representative to consult with you with the utmost freedom and in the most confidential way regarding the labor situation in your state and the means to be employed, either by the State Government or the Federal Government, to produce the greatest possible degree of ardor and efficiency in this critical time when every laborer counts.

I am sure that after you know Judge Covington he will need no commendation from me. I need only say that he has my entire confidence and that I am glad to call him my personal friend.

Cordially and sincerely yours,   Woodrow Wilson

TLS (Letterpress Books, WP, DLC).

Two Telegrams from George Lewis Bell

San Francisco, Calif., August 16, 1917.

Confidential. Governor Alexander, Idaho, wires he has been formally notified by James Rowan, Secretary, I.W.W., Spokane that [there] will be general strike harvest fields, fruit industries and construction work in all Northwest August twenty if all members organization not released from jails, also Governor Stewart, Montana, wires situation in Butte again very tense. May I respectfully suggest War Department might make secret investigation and patriotic appeal to both sides there as we suggested in program submitted to you.   George Bell.

San Francisco, Calif., August 16, 1917.

Confidential. At conference seven Western Governors Portland Saturday was decided to send all information concerning I.W.W.

activities to me in order to have centralized clearing house to keep Federal Government informed and to get assistance when necessary. Three other Governors will probably join. I reported at conference concerning my interview with you on July twenty fifth. Governor[s] determined on renewed State efforts along lines suggested in your interview. Understand Judge Covington now in West as your representative this matter. Could you wire me when he will be in San Francisco.   Geo. L. Bell.

T telegrams (WP, DLC).

From William Kent

Dear Mr. President: Washington August 16, 1917.

I do not know how I came to mistake the hour of seeing you on Wednesday, but it got in my head that it was 3.30, and as I wrote you, I was preparing to get there ahead of time. I have never felt more humiliated than when I found I had not only wasted your time but failed to see you. Not having heard a reply to the note I left at the White House office, I shall carry out my plan of starting West at 1.48 today. As suggested in that letter, I am greatly anxious that you should give Miss Todd another chance to be heard. She is in position to be of great service, but, in common with others, must have a definite text.

I was greatly disturbed by the statement made by a member of your Cabinet which appeared in the noon edition of the Washington Times.[1] I know who made the statement, because he had used the same language and the same argument to me prior to its appearance in the paper. I am hoping it will do no harm, because I doubt whether people will believe that the person talking this way occupied the position that he does. I am much discouraged by finding such a general desire to "get even" with Germany. If the disposition of getting even is carried out to its logical conclusion, how far back shall we date the beginning of the grievances which must be evened up, and what earthly chance is there for termination of the war short of extinction? Your "peace without victory" talk was after all the keynote. We cannot exterminate the Germans, but if we can pull the teeth and trim the claws of the Junker crowd by terms insisted on as preliminary to negotiations, this troubled world may get a rest before the extermination process goes much further, and I, for my part, cannot believe but that the German people can be made to realize two things: First, that they cannot carry out their object of conquest; and second, that the rest of the world does not demand their destruction, either as individuals of [or] as a nation.

I believe it would be a terrible mistake if the Pope's request is ignored by the United States, even if it is turned down by the rest of the Allies. It seems to me that with any Teutonic encouragement of his program, the end of the string is placed in Allied hands, and connection should not be cut off peremptorily, but every encouragement given to following it up while elaborating on the requirements that would go to make the world safe from a recurrence of Junker action.

I do not wish my boys killed, or anyone else's boys killed, because England desires to keep Germany's African colonies.

The Alsace-Lorraine row long ante-dates 1871, and American blood should not be shed for that purpose, and so with other long-time grudges.

I am terribly afraid lest, in certain quarters, there may grow up an ambition to try out our army, and to force the sacrifice of American lives simply because we have been training men for a necessary emergency. I should not speak thus excepting for the ideas that are given me by many different people, in whom I should not have expectee [expected] an inherently pugnacious and war-like tone, and what I regard as the impossible demands of others. You have declared, and all of us have believed, that our fight is not with the German people, and we cannot logically believe that reprisals will fall with those whose leadership has led Germany astray.

I fully appreciate the tremendous difficulties that will come from our refusal to coincide in the ambitions of the Allies, but it is of the greatest importance to set up a standard to which our own American people will rally. It is important, but of much less importance, to take a seemingly easy road of coinciding with the ambitions of the Allies. The same argument holds as holds in the "Signaling" system of Whist.[2] All authorities agree that the best thing is for partners to understand each others' hands, even if the opponents are thereby notified. This country would be solid for the war if great definite ideals were reiterated, coupled with a definite statement of peace without victory in the sense of the destruction of the German nation or of the German people.

Mr. Hohler, of the British Embassy, told me that England proposed to smash Germany, and gave as his reason, "that otherwise England would be untrue to its dead." Germany might well say the same thing. I only mention this as showing the *impasse* that is being created. If Germany were small or weak, Germany might be smashed, but I am convinced that this result will never be achieved, and it would be much better for the world if, through encouraging the hope of peace and reassuring the German people that they would not be smashed, that they, in their weariness, in their disappointed hopes, should see the futility of it, and be assured that the United States, at least, is not plotting or desiring their destruction, but only assurance against a recurrence of the mania of conquest.

Pardon this statement, which I believe expresses the views that you hold. You have complimented me by expressing some confidence in my judgment. My only reason for making this statement is that I believe in my acquaintance and correspondence, which has been purely American, I have been able to accumulate what I believe to be the views of a vast number of every-day people, and of many exceptional ones.

My letter sent you prior to the missed engagement expressed the hope that you could meet Miss Todd, who is extremely anxious to get to work, but who is at a loss for a sufficiently definite text. She is a woman of remarkable ability and great influence, and is heart and soul in the cause of having the Administration's views of the situation understood by the American people in the Ghettos, out and up. I urgently request that she be given an early opportunity to be heard. It is my intention to be gone for a month, unless you may desire my earlier return. I can be reached through this office,[3] and shall give Miss Todd's address to your secretary.   Yours truly,   William Kent

This letter is written in haste but the thought is not one of hasty conclusions.   WK

TLS (WP, DLC).
[1] The noon edition of the *Washington Times* is not extant; the statement does not appear in the only extant edition.
[2] That is, bidding one's hand. Whist was a forerunner of bridge.
[3] The United States Tariff Commission.

From Edward Mandell House, with Enclosure

Dear Governor: Magnolia, Mass. August 16, 1917.

Here is a letter from Lord Bryce which is interesting because of its broad outlook.

A writer in the last Contemporary Review says:

"In the address to the Senate of January 22nd which, it may be, *posterity will rank higher than all other utterances of our times*, the President said—'is the present war a struggle for a just and secure peace, or only for a new balance of power, etc.' "

                    Affectionately yours,   E. M. House

TLS (WP, DLC).

E N C L O S U R E

James Viscount Bryce to Edward Mandell House

My dear Colonel House: London. July 28, 1917.

It was a great pleasure to receive your letter as it has been a great pleasure to see with what alacrity and heartiness your people have responded to the President's call, and what splendid energy and foresight he has been displaying.

Congress, with some lapses, has on the whole done better than one expected, doubtless owing to his personal influence. You would be amused were you with us in England, to see how those who were complaining and carping a year ago and would hardly listen when one explained his position and the need for carrying the whole people with him, now extolling his cautious wisdom in awaiting the right moment.

What you say about the German Government is perfectly true. Their peace talk, vague as it is, like this last speech of Michaelis,[1] is mere playing to their disappointed people, to keep them quiet, not a bona fide wish for peace on any terms but the old ones. They are not to be taken seriously till they intimate a willingness to leave Belgium as free as before the war and to compensate her.

They still fear their own jingoes too much to offer that. Defeat would mean the collapse of the Junker caste, so they will fight so long as they can hope for a draw.

But it is quite true that many foolish things have been said here—and some also in France—not only by the press but by statesmen who ought to have known better. Our great aim ought to be to reassure the German people and get them to understand that we don't wish to harm them or dismember Germany, but to rid the world of an aggressive militarism which gives the world no rest or peace.

I also agree with you that it is not the Emperor we should strike at, but the military caste that rule him and drive him into war.

France, as you know, is in evil case, her man power at a low ebb. Little need be expected from Russia for some time. Prospects would be dark but for your entrance into the war. But you and we will pull things through. Your American influence will be most usefully exerted in discountenancing ideas of a trade war against Germany—a pernicious scheme—and in making also Germans and Russians understand that our aims are unselfish. That will help to undermine the Junker ascendancy.

Believe me,   Sincerely yours,   Bryce.

P.S. Nothing would have a better effect than if some American regiments were to march through London. I dont know why this has not been done; perhaps in order that Germans may not know when your soldiers are crossing. But the risk is very slight. So far as we know, we have not lost troops in the Channel crossing these three years and the extremely slight, if any, risk seems worth taking for the sake of the advantages. Your soldiers would have a wonderful reception here which would tell powerfully in the way of moral effect both here and in Germany.

TCL (WP, DLC).

1 The newly appointed German Imperial Chancellor, Georg Michaelis, had addressed the Reichstag briefly on July 19. On the subject of peace, he declared that Germany would not continue the war a single day for the sake of "violent conquests" if she could obtain "an honorable peace." "The Germans," he continued, "wish to conclude peace as combatants who have successfully accomplished their purpose and proved themselves invincible first. A condition of peace is the inviolability of Germany's territory. No parley is possible with the enemy demanding the cession of German soil. We must, by means of understanding and in a spirit of give and take, guarantee conditions of the existence of the German Empire upon the continent and overseas. We must . . . prevent nations from being plunged into further enmity through economic blockades and provide a safeguard that the league in arms of our opponents does not develop into an economic offensive alliance against us. . . . We cannot again offer peace. . . . The Government feels that, if our enemies abandon their lust for conquest and their aims at subjugation and wish to enter into negotiations, we shall listen honestly and readily to what they have to say to us. Until then we must hold out calmly and patiently." An English translation of Michaelis' speech is printed in the *New York Times*, July 21, 1917.

From Cleveland Langston Moffett[1]

My dear Mr. President: New York City August 16, 1917.

As a trustee of The American Defense Society and an American citizen, I appeal to you for enlightenment as to what constitutes treason of speech.

As you may know, I protested, Monday evening, August 15th, when, on Broadway, New York, an obviously pro-German orator denounced Great Britain as "the most degraded and despicable nation on earth." I again protested when this orator declared that George Washington and Benjamin Franklin, were no better than the German spy and convicted traitor, Roger Casement. I would also protest and I am sure all real Americans would join me in protesting to the last drop of their blood if they heard a statement reported to The American Defense Society by a credible witness as having been made on Broadway and 35th Street on Wednesday evening, August 8th, by a pro-Irish agitator: "We soon will start a Revolution in this country, and the first man we will get will be the greatest traitor in the land—Woodrow Wilson."

I am anxious to know whether I did right or wrong in making the protest I did. At any rate, I was arrested on the charge of "interfering with a lawful meeting" and was brought before a magistrate who gave me an honorable dismissal, congratulated me on my patriotic action, and said that the police ought to have arrested the orator. But the next day, when I was summoned to appear before a high New York police official, this gentleman very courteously but officially told me that I had done wrong, that I had broken the law, although he intimated privately that under similar circumstances he might have acted in the same way.

On behalf of thousands of American citizens who desire to do their patriotic duty, but are uncertain as to what their duty is, I earnestly ask: Was the magistrate correct in his ruling, or was the police official correct?

It seems to me, that, with disloyalty working in various high and low places, (not much disloyalty, thank God, but some) the time has come when Americans, including the police, must be told clearly what is treason and what is not treason. What is sedition and what is not sedition? How far can a street speaker go in attacking and insulting our allies, our flag, our most sacred traditions? Are there no limits to the right of free speech? If the Constitution of the United States guarantees to orators a certain wide latitude in time of peace, does that latitude obtain in time of war, when it may constitute a menace to the safety of the nation?

I respectfully submit, inasmuch as we have entered this war for the loftiest reasons, for the welfare of humanity, that we must regard loyalty to our allies as a sacred duty and disloyalty to our allies as not less treasonable than disloyalty to the Stars and Stripes. Those who are not against Germany are for Germany—there is no middle ground. Any American who assails the enemies of Germany assails America itself. All Germans know this. All Americans should know it. It does not matter whether we love England or hate her—I myself am half Irish and sympathize with Irish wrongs—that is not the question now, *the question is whether this nation is going to fight or die!*

It seems to me an abomination that young Americans, some of them wearing the uniform of the United States Army, the uniform of the United States Navy, as they stroll along the streets of our American cities, find themselves, night after night, in seditious gatherings, in anti-British gatherings that are tolerated in various American communities; and listen, perforce, to disloyal, poisonous, un-American utterances that are apparently approved by our uniformed police, who stand idly by, unless some patriot protests, whereupon they arrest and censure him. Is not that intolerable?

I submit, Mr. President, that this is a very grave state of affairs and I make bold to urge that you define clearly what constitutes treason and sedition and that you deal vigorously with these well attested evils of disloyal street-speaking all over the land by such means, legislative or other, as may commend themselves to your wise judgment. In bringing this matter to your attention, and in publicly protesting as I did, in New York City, I had only one desire: to serve America and to further the great work of World Regeneration toward which you are so ably and fearlessly leading us.

Very sincerely,   Cleveland Moffett

P.S. In view of the imminence of this sedition danger, I am taking the liberty of giving a copy of this letter to the press.[2]

TLS (WP, DLC).
   [1] Free-lance journalist and author of plays and fiction.
   [2] Moffett's letter was published, *inter alia*, in the *New York Times*, Aug. 17, 1917. Wilson wrote to Tumulty about this letter as follows: "Doctor Moffett is so much on the warpath that I don't like to put a letter of mine in his hands at once. I would be very much obliged if you would tell him I have read his letter with interest and concern and have referred the matter to the Department of Justice, who I am sure will act in any cases which the law can reach." WW to JPT, c. Aug. 23, 1917, TL (WP, DLC). Moffett did not hold a doctor's degree of any kind.

From Jacques A. Berst

Sir: New York August 16, 1917.

I acknowledge your favor of the 11th instant, which was received by me at 10.45 o'clock A.M., on the 15th instant.

I have advised the International Film Service, the producing owner of the film "Patria" of your demand and have requested that company to inform me whether it will be possible for it to eliminate the objectionable features which your letter describes without the utter destruction of the film property.

The International Film Service has informed me that it has called an immediate conference of its officers, some of whom are on vacation, and that, as soon as the conference is had, it will answer my queries concerning the elimination of the features to which your letter calls attention.

I will greatly appreciate your consideration if you will suspend judgment with respect to the film "Patria" until I have obtained the information which I have asked from the producing owner, and until I am able as the distributor of the film to answer the question contained in your letter concerning its withdrawal, if the eliminations suggested cannot be made.

Respectfully,   J. A. Berst

TLS (WP, DLC).

From Allen Schoolcraft Hulbert

Dear Mr. Wilson: Hollywood California Aug. 16th 1917

Some time ago I offered myself for the aviation branch of the service but was rejected on account of my eyes. I selected that branch because with my knowledge of gasoline engines I thought I would be most useful.

On June 5th I registered, was drafted, passed the physical examination and told to be ready to report at a concentration camp between September 1st and 5th. If I do this it means the entire loss of the only paying investment I have, which is raising hogs. Upon being ordered away the business will go to smash leaving us without resources except what I would get in the Army.

Reports are current out here that we have a comfortable income. This report like others, is untrue. You are the only friend who can help and guide me in this crisis. I hate like——to take up your time with my troubles but I don't honestly know what to do.

I am studying gasoline motors under G E Ruckstall S.A.E.[1] Ruckstall is really a genius and would be most useful in testing and inspecting motors to be used in air-planes.

The life of aviators and motors rests largely upon the perfection of material used and assembling of the engine. Ruckstall and I feel competent to do this work. Also, with authority and the co-operation of cities, I can produce pork at a low cost. Will you help me to get work along either of these lines?

If you wish I will go to Washington to tell you in detail my plans.

Mother still suffers from her broken foot and I am getting about again after six weeks in bed at home and in the hospital with rheumatism.

We have taken a little house for a few weeks in the foot-hills— the air is fine. I have a small car of the vintage of 1913 that I use in my ranch work and also serves as a pleasure car on Saturday after-noons and Sunday.

With kindest regards to Mrs Wilson and the rest of your family.

I am,   Very sincerely yours   Allen S. Hulbert

P.S. Because of our financial condition I asked for exemption but was denied   A.S.H.

ALS (WP, DLC).
[1] That is, the Society of Automotive Engineers. Ruckstall cannot be further identified.

From the Diary of Josephus Daniels

August Thursday 16 1917

Called with Benson, Mayo and Jackson[1] to see the President. He spoke of absolute necessity of finding & ending the hornet's nest, & destroying the poison or removing the cork. He impressed upon them the need of an offensive and reiterated his view that we cannot win the war by merely hunting submarines when they have gotten into the great ocean. Mayo said he hoped the President would not expect too much. No, but he expected plans by which America could lead & be the senior partner in a successful naval campaign. He was ready to make great ventures for a chance to win but of course wished no policy that would mean suicide.

[1] Captain Richard Harrison Jackson, U.S.N., newly appointed representative of the Navy Department to the Ministry of Marine in Paris. Mayo and Jackson were about to sail to attend the Allied naval conference in London in September.

Two Letters to Thomas Watt Gregory

[The White House]
My dear Mr. Attorney General: 17 August, 1917

Will you not be kind enough to have the enclosed carefully examined by somebody to see whether the allegations contained in these papers are successfully made out?[1] The people who sign the letter which is on top of the other documents are people whom I personally esteem, but I am not always sure that they know what they are talking about.

Cordially and faithfully yours,   Woodrow Wilson

[1] Lillian D. Wald *et al.* to WW, Aug. 10, 1917.

[The White House]

My dear Mr. Attorney General   17 August, 1917

Do you think that any answer to Doctor Cleveland Moffett's letter which is enclosed is feasible? I mean any wise and sensible answer. I would be very much obliged to you for your advice.

Cordially and faithfully yours,   Woodrow Wilson

TLS (Letterpress Books, WP, DLC).

To Robert Scott Lovett

My dear Judge: [The White House] 17 August, 1917

In accordance with our conversation of yesterday, I am writing you this to request and authorize you to undertake the direction in my name of industrial shipments under the authority conferred upon me by the Act of Congress approved August 10, 1917, entitled "An Act to amend the Act to regulate commerce, as amended, and for other purposes," in the following terms:

"That during the continuance of the war in which the United States is now engaged the President is authorized, if he finds it necessary for the national defense and security, to direct that such traffic or such shipments of commodities as, in his judgment, may be essential to the national defense and security shall have preference or priority in transportation by any common carrier by railroad, water, or otherwise. He may give these directions at and for such times as he may determine, and may modify, change, suspend, or annul them, and for any such purpose he is hereby authorized to issue orders direct, or through such person or persons as he may designate for the purpose or through the Interstate Commerce Commission. Officials of the United States, when so designated, shall receive no compensation for their services rendered hereunder," etc.

May I not express my appreciation of the public spirit with which you have consented to undertake this difficult and delicate work, and may I not say that I hope you will feel at liberty to consult me at any time concerning the questions that arise? I shall deem it a duty as well as a pleasure to be accessible for counsel in the matter.

Cordially and sincerely yours,   Woodrow Wilson

TLS (Letterpress Books, WP, DLC).

To Michael Francis Doyle

My dear Mr. Doyle: [The White House] 17 August, 1917

Just a hasty line to thank you for the interesting information brought me by your letter of August fifteenth.

Sincerely yours, Woodrow Wilson

TLS (Letterpress Books, WP, DLC).

To Samuel Gompers

My dear Mr. Gompers: The White House 17 August, 1917

I am very much obliged to you for your letter of August thirteenth. You may be sure that Mr. Martinez's indiscretions will not have the least influence upon my attitude or action in relation to Mr. Carranza and Mexican affairs.

Sincerely yours, Woodrow Wilson

TLS (S. Gompers Corr., AFL-CIO-Ar).

To Rudolph Forster

Dear Forster: [The White House, Aug. 17, 1917]

I do not know that Judge Covington left his itinerary with us or that it is possible to ascertain just where he is. If it should be, I would be very much obliged if you would send him a message advising him to get into communication with Mr. Bell.

The President.

TL (WP, DLC).

From Lucius Eugene Pinkham, with Enclosure

Honolulu, T. H.
Seventeenth of August
Nineteen hundred and seventeen.

Her Majesty, Ex-Queen Liliuokalani of the late Kingdom of Hawaii desires to express her practical and abiding sympathy with the National Red Cross work and the cause of liberty and humanity.

With the light of life at times almost extinguished by the infirmities of old age, the heart and thoughtfulness of Her Majesty is an example worthy of note and public recognition.

Most sincerely Lucius E. Pinkham
Governor of Hawaii

TLS (WP, DLC).

ENCLOSURE

Liliuokalani to Lucius Eugene Pinkham

[Honolulu] August seventeenth,
Nineteen seventeen.

In response to the call for aid and relief and as an expression of my full sympathy with the work of the National Red Cross in the cause of liberty and humanity, it affords me pleasure in handing you for transmission to the proper authorities in Washington, the inclosed donation to the War Relief Fund, with the announcement that the contribution will be renewed monthly to the close of the year.

With assurances of my personal regard and esteem,

Very sincerely,   Liliuokalani

HwLS (WP, DLC).

From William Bauchop Wilson

My dear Mr. President: Washington August 17, 1917.

Referring to your letter of the 13th instant, inclosing a communication from Frank P. Glass, I have asked the Alabama operators and miners to meet me in separate conferences in Birmingham on Thursday, the 23d. The representatives of the miners have advised them to continue at work pending the result of these conferences. A statement of these facts to Mr. Glass would seem to be sufficient answer for the present.

I am returning the communication from Mr. Glass and the clippings herewith.   Faithfully yours,   W B Wilson

TLS (WP, DLC).

From Newton Diehl Baker, with Enclosure

My dear Mr. President,   Washington. August 17, 1917.

I return herewith the telegram enclosed in your note of August 8th. There was an original intention not to send certain of the colored troops to the South, for the reason that it was feared that embarrassing difficulties would arise in places of public entertainment from the demands of these troops, who are associated with white contingents in the Northern States, and are accustomed to a situation which they are sure not to find in the neighborhood of the Southern Camps.

I have felt, however, on reconsideration of the subject, that it is quite impossible to separate these organized brigades and divisions on the color basis, and have therefore directed that the attempt be not made, but that the commanders of these camps exercise discretion and judgment to prevent any difficulty from arising from this cause.

In general I have a feeling that this is not the time to raise the race issue question, and I am trying to preserve the custom of the Army, which has been to organize colored people into separate organizations, without permitting myself to inquire whether ultimately any different course of action will be taken.

I have said to colored men who came to call upon me with regard to this and related questions, that after we have succeeded in the great objective of this war would be a more appropriate time to raise questions of changing existing army customs than now. For this reason, I respectfully suggest that your reply to this telegram be non-committal, not because I now have any reason for not denying the statement made, but because it seems to me better to have a free hand to meet any conditions which may arise when we try the experiment of having colored men in some of these Southern camps. I enclose a suggested telegram which I hope will satis[f]y the situation.

Yours very respectfully,   Newton D. Baker

TLS (WP, DLC).

E N C L O S U R E

I acknowledge receipt of telegram signed jointly by you and others with regard to negro National Guard regiments. The Secretary of War assures me that the so-called separate battalions will in some cases be trained in the camps to which you refer. Purely military considerations will control the training of all troops and the location, from time to time, of various units may be changed. The reason will in all cases, however, be military and not the one suggested by the rumor to which you refer.[1]

CC MS (WP, DLC).
[1] This was sent as WW to E. H. Wright, Aug. 21, 1917, T telegram (Letterpress Books, WP, DLC).

From Edward Mandell House

Dear Governor: Magnolia, Mass. August 17, 1917.

I am so impressed with the importance of the situation that I am troubling you again.

I doubt whether you know how thoroughly I am saturated with information from the other side. By seeing the number of people I see, and by reading as closely as I do, I feel that I have a picture that is fairly accurate.

I believe you have an opportunity to take the peace negotiations out of the hands of the Pope and hold them in your own. Governmental Germany realizes that no one excepting you is in a position to enforce peace terms. The Allies must succumb to your judgment and Germany is not much better off. Badly as the Allied cause is going, Germany is in a worse condition. It is a race now of endurance with Germany as likely to go under first as either of the Entente powers.

Germany and Austria are a seething mass of discontent. The Russian revolution has shown the people their power, and it has put the fear of God in to the hearts of the Imper[i]alists.

A statement from you regarding the aims of this country would bring about almost revolution in Germany in the event the existing government dared to oppose them. The mistake has been made over and over again in the Allied countries, in doing and saying the things that best helped the militarists. The German people are told, and believe, that the Allies desire not only to dismember them, but to make it economically impossible to live after the war. They are therefore welded together with their backs to the wall.

A statement from you setting forth the real issues would have an enormous effect, and would probably bring about such an upheaval in Germany as we desire. While the submarine campaign gives them hope, it is a deferred hope, and the Government, not less than the people, are fearful what may happen in the interim. What is needed, it seems to me, is a firm tone, full of determination, but yet breathing a spirit of liberalism and justice, that will make the people of the Central Powers feel safe in your hands. You could say again that our people had entered this fight with fixed purpose and high courage, and would continue to fight until a new order of liberty and justice for all people was brought about, and some agreement reached by which such another war could never again occur.

You can make a statement that will not only be the undoing

of autocratic Germany, but one that will strengthen the hands of the Russian liberals in their purpose to mold their country into a mighty republic.

I pray that you may not lose this great opportunity.

Affectionately yours,   E. M. House

TLS (WP, DLC).

From John Denis Joseph Moore[1]

Dear Mr. President: New York August 17th, 1917.

As Secretary of the FRIENDS OF IRISH FREEDOM, an organization that contains among its members some of America's most distinguished citizens, it becomes my duty to correct any misapprehensions you may have received about the work of this organization from erroneous statements in a letter addressed to you by Cleveland H. Moffett of this city, or, by false accounts of street meetings published in the public press.

No member of the Friends of Irish Freedom ever made the statement asserted by a Mr. Butterfield,[2] either publicly or privately. No such statement or similar statement was ever made at any public meeting. Our organization would not sanction, tolerate or permit such a wild and absurd suggestion, and you must realize that no citizen would listen in silence to such utterances upon our public streets.

Realizing that our speakers have been most careful in their utterances the men who are now endeavoring to deprive them of their constitutional rights invented this statement as they have deliberately twisted and garbled others. I therefore ask you to accept no statements of such character unless we are given the opportunity eithet [either] to verify or deny them.

Our speakers have pleaded for Ireland's freedom—have discussed America's history as it refers to Great Britain—have told the story of Irelands history—and have compared Casement, Pearse[3] and others to Washington and the patriots of "76."

We have drawn inspiration from your address to the Senate and we have repeatedly praised you for it. We have taken hope from the announced aims of the allies and the United States as to the rights of small nations, and above all, we have been encouraged by your personal attendance upon the unveiling of Emmett's statue in Washington,[4] an act on your part that we feel indicates your devotion to Emmett's principles and your sympathy for the revolutionary effort he made to establish them.

We join with Mr. Moffett in seeking a declaration that shall guide us as to our rights. We stand on the American constitution. We believe our rights of free speech and public assemblage to be inalienable. We are anxious to know whether one citizen or band of citizens can create disorders at perfectly orderly meetings to get themselves arrested for the obvious purpose of posing as martyrs in the defense of foreign nations to suppress facts of history that are indefensible in America.

We want to know also whether the President of the United States devoted as he is to humanity and democracy, sanctions such utterances as have been made by Theodore Roosevelt, Elihu Root, Cleveland H. Moffett, that citizens should be hung or shot at sunrise, in view of what happened to Frank Little at Butte, to the negroes of East St. Louis and to the I.W.W.'s of Arizona, all of which have made your burdens heavier and your task more difficult.

We charge, Mr. President, that the American Defense Society, the Vigilantes, Theodore Roosevelt, Elihu Root, Cleveland H. Moffet[t], and other[s] are banded together in a conspiracy to promote riots and incite citizens to hanging and shooting.

It is not Mr. Moffett who needs protection but ourselves. We have naught but humble people supporting us whilst they have the great newspapers great money powers and privileges with public opinion that we do not enjoy.

For the sake of orderly government we demand protection. We have broken no law—we shall break no law. We are seeking to arouse a public opinion in America that if responded to by Great Britain, may enure as much to Great Britain and the United States as to Ireland herself.

Respectfully,   John D Moore.[5]

TLS (WP, DLC).
[1] Consulting engineer of New York.
[2] One John L. Butterfield of 412 East 10th Street, New York, had had a stenographic report made of a speech delivered at 37th Street and Broadway on August 10. A portion of this report was quoted in the New York Times, August 16, 1917, as follows: "I asked if they did not believe in first whipping Germany, to which one man replied that they certainly did not; that Germany has always been our friend, and that they wanted to see England whipped first. He followed that by saying that America had never been a friend of Ireland anyway, that the country was full of traitors to the cause of freedom, and that 'what we soon will do will be to start a revolution in this country, and the first man we will get will be the greatest traitor of the land, Woodrow Wilson.'"
[3] Padraic (or Patrick) Henry Pearse, Irish literary and revolutionary figure, who was executed by the English for his leadership of the Easter Rising in Dublin.
[4] Wilson had attended, but did not speak at, the dedication of a statue of the Irish patriot, Robert Emmet, at the New National Museum on June 28. Senator James D. Phelan was the principal speaker. Washington Post, June 29, 1917.
[5] Wilson wrote to Tumulty about this letter as follows: "Would you be kind

enough to handle this letter for me and express to Mr. Moore my gratification that he is able to correct the impressions of which he speaks." WW to JPT, c. Aug. 21, 1917, TL (WP, DLC).

From Waddill Catchings

New York, August 17, 1917.

At the request of the department of labor we have submitted to the Secretary of Labor a short statement of our position with relation to the threatened coal strike in Alabama. May we make this further statement to you: We accept without reservation the policy outlined by the Secretary of Labor in his statement of April twenty third, nineteen seventeen,[1] while we have declined to meet with the United Mine Workers of American on the ground that the meeting itself would be a recognition of a union which has been organized in our district only since June third of this year and the demand for this recognition is in violation of the policy outlined by Secretary Wilson. We have offered to accept Secretary Wilson's decision on any question of wages, working conditions and living conditions. We have therefore gone further than a mere conference and have already agreed to accept the Secretary's decision and immediately to grant any demands regarded by him as just. We wish to say to you that if you think we should act otherwise and will first grant us a hearing we will then act in any manner that you may think best in the interest of the country in these times.

Sloss Sheffield Steel and Iron Co,
Waddill Catchings, President.

T telegram (WP, DLC).

[1] The Council of Naional Defense on April 21 had issued a statement to the press about labor and standards of living during the war. Prepared under the direction of Samuel Gompers, the statement urged that no "arbitrary" changes in wages or working conditions be sought by either management or labor for the duration of the war. Any difficulties that arose should be settled by negotiation or mediation without stoppage of work. The Council reserved the right to suggest changes in working conditions or hours but denied any intention to set wage rates.

At a conference of labor leaders held in Washington on April 23, William B. Wilson reiterated the main points of the Council's statement but also added one of his own concerning the question of union recognition. "My feeling," he said, "is that in the present emergency the employer has no right to interfere with you in your efforts to organize the workers into unions, just as you have no right to interfere with capitalists organizing capital into corporations. If you can get a condition where efforts to organize the workers are not interfered with and where a scale of wages is recognized that maintains the present standard of living, it occurs to me that for the time being no stoppage of work should take place for the purpose of forcing recognition of the union. Of course, that would not interfere with the employers and yourselves entering into any arrangement for recognition that might be mutually agreeable." *Monthly Review of the U. S. Bureau of Labor Statistics*, IV (June 1917), 807-809.

From the Diary of Josephus Daniels

1917 Friday 17 August

Cabinet—WW: Should all German newspapers be excluded? Should they be compelled to print in parallel columns translation in English? Baker gave strong reasons against such course. WBW thought comparatively few saw the G. papers & there was more danger from English papers. Burleson thought great danger from the new Peace organization that was calling convention in September to try to compel statement of peace terms.[1] He thought there should be drastic action, but the President asked What? Better let them show their impotence than by suppression as long as they keep within the law.

Redfield indignant at action of Export Commission[2] Went to the President and threatened to resign

[1] The People's Council of America for Democracy and Peace proposed to hold a national convention to perfect its organization and plan of action in Minneapolis on September 1. However, Governor Joseph Alfred Arner Burnquist of Minnesota announced on August 28 that the organization would not be allowed to meet in his state. Feelers for meeting sites in North Dakota and Wisconsin were rebuffed. Finally, Mayor William Hale Thompson of Chicago allowed the group to meet in that city on September 1 and 2. Governor Frank O. Lowden of Illinois sent National Guard troops to break up the meeting on September 2, but the organization had finished its business and adjourned before they arrived. See Marchand, *The American Peace Movement and Social Reform*, p. 315; Peterson and Fite, *Opponents of War, 1917-1918*, pp. 76-78; and William T. Hutchinson, *Lowden of Illinois: The Life of Frank O. Lowden* (2 vols., Chicago, 1957), I, 378-80.

[2] Redfield objected to an Executive Order proposed by the Exports Council (of which he was a member) which would turn over to the Exports Administrative Board the administration of export licenses. See WCR to WW, Aug. 18, 1917 (both letters of that date); WW to WCR, Aug. 21, 1917 (second letter of that date); and WCR to WW, Aug. 22, 1917. See also the *New York Times*, Aug. 23, 1917.

To Araminta Cooper Kern

[The White House] August 18, 1917.

I have learned of Senator Kern's death[1] with deep personal grief and feel that I am expressing a universal sentiment when I say that the country will recognize in his death a national loss. A great public servant is lost to the nation. Will you not permit me to extend to you my heartfelt personal sympathy.

Woodrow Wilson.

T telegram (Letterpress Books, WP, DLC).
[1] He had died of tuberculosis on August 17.

From Amos Lawrence Lowell

New York, Aug. 18, 1917.

The Executive Committee of the League to Enforce Peace, in session here to-day, adopted the following resolution:

Although the peace proposals of His Holiness, Pope Benedict support the principle of a league of nations to enforce peace and in that respect are welcome, the executive committee of the League to Enforce Peace feels that a league of nations which will guarantee the future security of the world, can be made effective only by the abolition of the Prussian military autocracy. At whatever cost peace made with such a government could not, as President Wilson has clearly pointed out, establish conditions of mutual trust and security. The League to Enforce Peace therefore urges the vigorous prosecution of the war until Prussian militarism is destroyed, either by allied force or by the uprising of a German democracy.

A. Lawrence Lowell,   Chairman.

T telegram (WP, DLC).

From Samuel Gompers

Sir: Washington, D. C. August 18, 1917.

Herein I beg to submit to you the petition and memoranda of Mr. John Walker, President of the Illinois State Federation of Labor, Mr. John Fitzpatrick, and Mr. Edward Nockels, President and Secretary of the Chicago Federation of Labor.[1]

In connection therewith, I beg to submit that, knowing so much of the circumstances in the cases recited, I earnestly join with the petitioners signed to the document in asking that you may view the application with sympathetic approval and action.[2]

Respectfully,   Saml. Gompers.

TLS (WP, DLC).

[1] J. H. Walker, J. Fitzpatrick, and E. N. Nockels to WW, Aug. 18, 1917, TLS (WP, DLC). This letter was a petition for pardons for Frank Ryan, Michael J. Young, and Eugene A. Clancy, about whom see S. Gompers to WW, Dec. 5, 1916, and its Enclosures, Vol. 40. Gompers, Walker, Fitzpatrick, and Nockels had had an interview with Wilson about the matter on August 17.

[2] Wilson took no action in these cases at this time. However, when the matter was brought before him again in April 1918, he commuted Ryan's sentence to expire at once. Nothing was done in the cases of Young and Clancy, presumably because their prison terms then had less than two and six months, respectively, to run.

Three Letters from Newton Diehl Baker

(CONFIDENTIAL)

Dear Mr. President: Washington. August 18, 1917

I return the telegram from Cardinal Farley with a suggested reply.[1]

The 69th New York National Guard regiment is locally known as "the Irish 69th." At the time it went to the Mexican border, its Colonel, Connolly,[2] was found disqualified physically, and every sort of suggestion was made that his physical disqualifications, which were very serious and disabling, ought to be waived in deference to the fact that he was one of the men of the 69th of their own kind, and so forth. Captain Haskell, a Regular Army officer, was assigned to take his place, and evidently proved very acceptable to the men in the regiment.

When the National Army was authorized, it became necessary to adopt a policy with regard to the assignment of Regular Army officers to National Guard regiments, and as the National Guard had been on the border and had a lot of training while the National Army would be composed entirely of green men, it was deemed necessary to trust to the National Guard to supply its own officers and reserve the full number of Regular Army officers available for the greater need of the National Army. It therefore became impossible to retain Captain Haskell with the 69th. I have had personal calls and letters from a great number of people on the subject, including letters from Governor Glynn, Dudley Malone, Cardinal Farley and others, but as it was impossible to break the precedent without embarrassing the whole military situation, I transferred Colonel Hine[3] of the New York National Guard to the command of this regiment. For some reason I could not bring myself to select deliberately an Irish Catholic, although Colonel Hine may be both, for ought I know; but it seems to me that a preference on either of those grounds is almost as bad as a prejudice on either of those grounds. My previous experience with the 69th, however, leads me to believe that it will be easily reconciled to their new Colonel, now that the choice is made.

Respectfully yours,   Newton D. Baker

[1] WW to J. Card. Farley, Aug. 21, 1917.
[2] Louis D. Conley, associated with the Conley Foil Co. of New York.
[3] Charles De Lano Hine, railroad expert and former officer in the regular army.

(CONFIDENTIAL)

Dear Mr. President: Washington. August 18, 1917

Mr. F. A. Scott, Chairman of the War Industries Board, called on me this morning about some of the work of the Board, and incidentally remarked: "Judge Lovett is an enormous addition to the strength of the Board; if something should happen to all the rest of us, we would still have a War Industries Board with him left."

I thought you would be interested to have this evidence of harmony in the Board, and appreciation of Judge Lovett's talents.
                    Respectfully yours,   Newton D. Baker

My dear Mr. President: Washington, D. C. August 18, 1917.

On August 11 Senator Weeks wrote you a letter in which the following language appears

"The other suggestion I wish to bring to your attention is that relating to the drafting of men with families, except in the case where the marriage has been entered into for the purpose of escaping the draft. This is economically an unsound policy and it is unwise from the standpoint of a successful prosecution of the war to take married men as long as there are a sufficient number of single men of the draft age to meet the government's requirements."

On August 13 you wrote me saying that you had told Senator Weeks that you had reason to believe that the various draft boards had his point already very much in mind.

In principle the draft boards have in mind the point raised by Senator Weeks. But the language employed by him in describing the cases to which he refers is broader than the language of the Selective Service Law and includes a class of cases in which there is no authority in that law to make exemptions.

I refer to the case where there is a family relationship between the drafted man and those in behalf of whom exemption is claimed, but where there is no condition of dependency in fact.

The Selective Service Law authorizes the President to exclude or discharge from selective draft

"those in a status with respect to *persons dependent upon them for support* which renders their exclusion or discharge advisable."

When the Bill was in the Senate, Mr. Smith of Georgia intro-

ducte [introduced], on April 28, 1917, the following amendment to this language

"and in making selection for active service, married men
shall be relieved as far as practicable."

After deliberation the Senate rejected the amendment.

The issue is sharply this: *Shall married men be exempted
because they are married, or shall they be exempted only because others are dependent upon them for support?* I state the
question for the sake of clearness and not because I think there
remains in us any authority for deciding it. I shall not, at this
moment, enter the merits of the case because I conceive that the
decision on the merits of the case was made in Congress on
April 28 when it was deliberately proposed to give the President
authority to exempt married men as such and when the proposal
was deliberately rejected leaving authority to exclude or discharge from draft only those upon whom other persons were
dependent for support and making the issue one of dependency
and not at all one of relationship.

All registrants stand in equality before the law except as the
law decrees inequality. The law decrees inequality only in those
cases where the President is empowered to authorize exemptions
and where local boards have actually allowed them in the facts
of a particular case. Among those cases are not found married
men as such, and it would therefore be illegal to promulgate a
rule authorizing the exemption of a man because he is married
without reference to whether we are able to find the added reason for exemption that his family is dependent upon him for
support.

It may be true that it would have been a wiser thing from an
economical as well as from a sentimental standpoint if Congress
had decreed that all single men must be taken for the army before a single married man should go. But whether it were wiser
or not is now beyond inquiry and Congress addressed itself to
the question and gave us a law to execute which did not permit a
a reopening of that issue.

I will say this, however, the Regulations, prescribed in your
name on May 18, 1917, provide for the exemption or discharge
of

(a) Any married man whose wife or child is dependent upon
his labor for support;

(b) Any son of a widow dependent upon his labor for support;

(c) Any son of aged or infirm parent or parents dependent
upon him for support;

(d) Any father of a motherless child or children under sixteen years of age dependent upon his labor for support;

(e) Any brother of a child or children under sixteen years of age with neither father nor mother and who are dependent upon his labor for support.

You will observe that the letter and the spirit of the law has been followed and that the right has been clearly given to persons whose families are dependent upon them for support to claim and receive exemption.

It is true that the claims for exemption under the dependency clauses have outrun all statistics. It is true that local boards have been instructed to look carefully into the fact of dependency in deciding each claim, and have been cautioned that, upon the care with which they weed out unmeritorious claims, depends the fate of the present regulations. They have been asked to protect those whom the present generous clauses of the Regulations were designed to protect against the unwarranted claims of hundreds who have attempted to misuse those clauses. If any local board has held to service any man within the classes described by Regulations as subject to exemption, or if any married man whose family is dependent upon him for support, has been held to service, the Law and Regulations have been violated and the case can be corrected upon appeal.

The fact that dependency *is* the determinative issue completely answers Senator Week's suggestion of economic unsoundness in a policy that takes some married men for war. This leaves us to face only his second suggestion that it is "unwise from the standpoint of a successful proscecution [prosecution] of the war to take married men as long as there are a sufficient number of single men of the draft age to meet the government's requirements."

He means, of course, that we are neglecting a chance to reduce the shock of bereavement and the pain of separation that makes war harder for the people to bear. But when I remember that for every wife's husband we release from service, we must take another mother's son, I wonder if he offers us much encouragement in making war popular. Even if it were possible for us to do what the Senate deliberately refused to do and change the rule to exempt married men as such regardless of dependency, should we not, on the very next day, hear the opposing argument from the mothers of at least half our unselected registrants?   Very truly yours,   Newton D. Baker

TLS (WP, DLC).

From William Cox Redfield

My dear Mr. President: Washington August 18, 1917.

As you have under consideration an Executive Order turning over to the Exports Administrative Board the administration of the matter of export licenses, with authority, as the draft of the order reads "to administer and execute the same and to grant or refuse export licenses thereunder," may I suggest, after conference with the Solicitor of this Department, the importance of considering in this connection the pending Trading with the Enemy Bill before that shall go too far?

It appears to me that in the event of the Executive Order being signed and the Trading with the Enemy Bill becoming a law in substantially its present form, there would be a possible conflict of authority. It would appear that a firm might be licensed to act under the Trading with the Enemy law whose export shipments could be refused license under the Executive Order, or vice versa.   Yours very truly,   William C. Redfield

TLS (WP, DLC).

From William Cox Redfield, with Enclosure

My dear Mr. President: Washington August 18, 1917.

In view of the pending Executive Order recommended by the Exports Council, the Solicitor of this Department called my attention to the law concerning the appointment of commissions, councils, boards, etc. At my request he put the matter in writing. A copy of his letter of this date is enclosed for such consideration as you may deem wise to give it.

In addition to the suggestions contained in the letter, it will be noted that the statute not only prohibits the expenditure of money but further prohibits the employment of any of the employees of any executive department.

                    Yours very truly,   William C. Redfield

TLS (WP, DLC).

ENCLOSURE

Albert Lee Thurman to William Cox Redfield

My dear Mr. Secretary: Washington, August 18, 1917.

The following provision appears in 35 Statutes at Large on page 1027 in the Act of March 4, 1909, making appropriations for sundry civil expenses of the Government for the fiscal year ending June 30, 1910, and for other purposes:

"Sec. 9. That hereafter no part of the public moneys, or of any appropriation heretofore or hereafter made by Congress, shall be used for the payment of compensation or expenses of any commission, council, board, or other similar body, or any members thereof, or for expenses in connection with any work, or the results of any work or action of any commission, council, board, or other similar body, unless the creation of the same shall be or shall have been authorized by law; nor shall there be employed by detail, hereafter or heretofore made, or otherwise personal services from any executive department or other government establishment in connection with any such commission, council, board, or other similar body."

In view of the fact that the board proposed is to be created by an executive order and not having been authorized by law, it is exceedingly doubtful, to say the least, if any part of the public moneys may be used for any expenses connected with its work.   Respectfully,   A. L. Thurman.

TCL (WP, DLC).

From John Franklin Fort

My dear Mr. President: Washington August 18, 1917.

I am writing you this letter because for the past three days I have been slightly indisposed, and I am fearful that worse may come. I have never before, that I can recall, gone through a full summer without any let-up, and I am not as young as I once was. The doctor yesterday told me that I must 'pull up' a little and take at least a week off to get normal and avoid possible difficulty; being careful of my diet in the mean time. I am therefore going to my Spring Lake cottage for the week and will not be here until Monday the 27th, but my absence will make no difference in your getting cost sheets. You will get some today.

In the letter I wrote you on August 8 I said I thought we

could hand you the costs of many mines this present week, but we were not able to get them until last night, at 9 p.m. By Monday I am assured that we shall have sixty Navy mines completed. The economists go at these things so thoroughly that it is frequently difficult to get them to appreciate that time is of more importance than detailed accuracy.

I saw the Navy coal cost sheets Thursday, and the lowest cost, as they figured, in any mine, as I recall, was $1.01, and others ran $1.34, $1.55, $1.70 and, I think, one or two as high as $2.00. I question whether they are allowing sufficient for either depletion or depreciation, but if not this would probably not exceed 5 cents additional per ton for either, or possibly both. But you can judge this for yourself or from the Commission's report.

I still adhere to my personal view of your fixing the 'maximum price' for coal (by districts) and announce it yourself; it will be accepted and give satisfaction if you do. A fair price and a speed up of production is what is wanted, and I do trust that you will not find it necessary to put upon us any part of the work of coal operation or distribution. Let us keep to our legitimate functions and serve the public along the lines of your admirable advice to Congress suggesting this Commission. The Commission should not get into controversial fields if it is to do its work and hold public confidence. We have a vast amount of cost finding still left, and much delayed regular complaint work (some of it behind over two years) yet to be done.

I pray daily for your health and strength which, as I see it, means so much for the country.

I am leaving for Spring Lake, New Jersey, at eleven o'clock today.   Faithfully yours,   John Franklin Fort

TLS (WP, DLC).

Robert Lansing to All Diplomatic Missions in Allied Countries

CONFIDENTIAL.

Washington, August 18th 1917

Please ascertain as promptly as possible the views of the Government to which you are accredited in regard to the Pope's recent peace communication. The above information is desired by the President. Cable reply, which will be treated as strictly confidential.   Lansing

T telegram (SDR, RG 59, 763.72119/737a, DNA).

From the Diary of Colonel House

August 18, 1917.

Secretary and Mrs. Lane and Major and Mrs. Stanley Washburn lunched with us. After lunch I had a long talk with Lane. We reviewed what was going on in administration circles. I am sorry the President does not consult Lane more frequently. He has real ability, perhaps the best all round ability of any member of the Cabinet, and yet, outside of his departmental duties, these abilities are seldom or never used.

I discussed with him the Pope's peace proposal and was glad to find him sympathetic with the vvew [view] I gave the President in my letters of the 15th and 17th.[1] These letters are important and I particularly call attention to them.

The President's letter of the 16th which came last night is on the same subject and shows that his mind is not running parallel with mine. His letter is in answer to an inquiry which Balfour made by cable to me through Wiseman. The President did not answer it sooner because the text of the Pope's message did not arrive until Thursday. This message must have reached London, or an intimation of it, nearly a week earlier. I cannot understand why there was so much delay in its coming through to us. I have asked the State Department two or three times a day whether it was in.

The President, I feel, has taken a wrong position and I am as certain as I ever am these days that he will make a colossal blunder if he treats the note lightly and shuts the door abruptly. I wish I could be with him. I feel it something of a tragedy to be heat bound at this moment. I trust the President will decide the question wisely in the end and I shall not borrow trouble. . . .

I am sending a cable to Mr. Balfour today stating the President's position and intimating my disagreement with it. The matter is of such importance that I thought it well to caution him.

[1] "I had lunch yesterday with Col House who asked me what I thought should be done as to the Pope's appeal for Peace. I told him I thought it should be taken seriously. He agreed and asked what the president should say; I answered that inasmuch as all the evidence pointed to the conclusion that the German Centerists and Austria were responsible for this appeal that we could not afford to have them feel that we were for a policy of annihilation—for this would be playing the War Partys game & would place the burden on us of continuing the war. And this we could neither afford at home or abroad. This opportunity should be seized, I said, to make plain not so much our terms of peace but the things in Germany that seemed to make peace difficult, Germany's attitude toward the world, the spirit against which we are fighting; that we wished peace, that we had been patient to the limit, that we had come in in the hope that we could destroy the idea in the German mind that it could impose its authority and system by force upon an unwilling world; that we

were not opposed to talking peace provided at the outset and as a sine qua non the Central Powers would assume that Government by the Soldier was not a possibility in the 20th century." FKL to RL [Aug. 19, 1917], ALS (R. Lansing Papers, DLC).

From Edward Mandell House

Dear Governor: Magnolia, Mass. August 19, 1917.

The Russian Ambassador is with me today. He is very much disturbed over the Pope's peace overture and how you will reply to it.

He believes that success or failure in Russia may depend upon your answer. He takes the same view as I do except that he feels more keenly on account of its effect upon, not only Russia but the present government there. He believes if it is treated lightly and not in a spirit of liberalism, it will immediately split Russia and will probably cause the downfall of the present ministry.

I asked him why he had not conveyed this view to you. His reply was that he hesitated to impose himself upon you unless you sent for him. He is returning to Washington tonight, but has to leave again tomorrow night in order to be present at the exercises in Boston which are being arranged for him on Tuesday. He will be in Washington again Wednesday morning.

His Government think the Allies have made a mistake in refusing passports to the Stockholm Conference. If, in addition to doing this, they brush aside the Pope's overtures, he considers it inevitable that there will be a schism, not only in Russia, but probably in other countries as well.

He would like for you to take the lead and let Russia follow. He hopes you may be willing to say that the United States will treat with the German people at any time they are in a position to name their own representatives. He thinks that is the crux of the situation.

At first, he thought it well to speak of the Kaiser. I explained why this was not advisable and he agreed. He then suggested the military caste as the offenders and, again, I cautioned against this. The German people have for more than a century been taught to believe that their greatest duty to the Fatherland was to offer their services in a military way, and they cannot understand just what we mean by "militarism" as applied to Germany and not to France, Russia and other countries. They can and do understand what we mean by representative government, and they are eager for it.

I have pointed out to such Germans as I have met that the

worst thing that could happen to Germany would be a peace along the lines of the status quo ante, with the present form of government in control. All the hate and bitterness that the war has engendered would cling to them, and it would express itself in trade warfare and in all kinds of social and economic directions. With a representative government, they could return to the brotherhood of nations declaring that the fault had not been theirs. In this way, they would make a certain reparation which would come near leading to forgiveness.

I believe you are facing one of the great crisis that the world has known, but I feel confident that you will meet it with that fine spirit of courage and democracy which has become synonymous with your name.

Affectionately yours,   E. M. House

TLS (WP, DLC).

From Robert Lansing

PERSONAL AND CONFIDENTIAL:

My dear Mr. President: Washington August 20, 1917.

After a careful analysis of the Pope's appeal to the belligerents I am of the opinion that it practically goes no further than the German peace proposal of last December, that is, it amounts merely to an invitation to negotiate. The chief difference lies in a preliminary agreement to restore Belgian independence in exchange for the restoration of Germany's colonies, to erect an independent state out of "*part* of the old kingdom of Poland" (meaning, probably, Russian Poland), and a general condoning of the wrongs committed, though in particular cases a modification according to "justice and equity." Everything else, even the sovereignty of the Balkan States, is left to negotiation.

Belgian independence and the recreation of Poland were at the time of the German proposal in December considered to be essential to any restoration of peace, so that the only new basis suggested is the waiving by all parties of the losses sustained by them respectively. Except in East Prussia, Galicia and Bukowina (territories which have been reconquered) the Central Powers have not suffered from invasion and hostile occupation. They have little to forgive.

On the other hand neutral Belgium has been grievously outraged and her people impoverished, brutally treated, even enslaved. Would it be just to deny the Belgians the right to claim full reparation for all they have lost through three years of German occupation? Serbia and Montenegro have, from all we can learn, been treated with equal, if not with greater harshness. Are they not entitled to be indemnified for all that they have endured? Roumania also has suffered though in a less degree.

Is the enormous damage done by the German invaders in northern France not even to be paid in part, though much of the damage was the result of wantoness? Is the lawless destruction of hundreds of merchant vessels by German submarines to be condoned?

If I read the Pope's appeal aright, all these questions are to be answered in the affirmative. It is carrying the Christian doctrine of forgiveness a long way, since the burden falls very heavily on one side and very lightly on the other. The suggestion is lacking in justice and reciprocity.

The effort of the German Government through its December note was to induce the Allied Powers to meet the Central Alliance in conference to negotiate on the basis of the *status quo ante bellum*. And that is all that the Pope's appeal does, except that Russian Poland is to be given independence. With slight changes of territory here and there amounting to a rectification of boundaries, I do not see that there is to be any material change from the political conditions which existed prior to the war and which resulted in the war.

As to the methods of insuring a continuance of peace, which are suggested for negotiation, their adoption depends largely upon the trustworthiness of the signatories to the peace treaty. In view of the violation of Belgian neutrality, the disregard of human rights, the promises broken by the German Government, I do not see how it is possible to rely upon the good faith of that Government as it is now constituted. It would be folly to expect it to change its character or to abandon its cherished ambitions. To make peace by accepting guarantees from the military rulers of Germany would only be to postpone the struggle not to end it.

I think it unnecessary to consider the motives which inspired the Pope's appeal or the influences which induced him to make it at this particular time, when the military tide of the Central Powers is at the flood, when the submarine warfare appears to be most menacing, when the power of the United States is just beginning to be exerted, when Russia has not yet gained her equilibrium, when a vigorous peace propaganda in this country and other countries is being pressed and when the socialistic bodies are being employed, as at Stockholm, to demand an end of the war. I would only say that the Pope, probably unwittingly or out of compassion for Austria-Hungary, has become in this matter the agent of Germany.

In a word then the Pope's appeal appears to me to be but a renewal of the German proposal to negotiate and a suggestion of a peace based on the *status quo ante*. The proposal to negotiate has already been declined by the Allies. The suggested basis must of course be rejected by all.

Faithfully yours,   Robert Lansing.

TLS (WP, DLC).

From Robert Lansing, with Enclosure

PERSONAL AND CONFIDENTIAL:

My dear Mr. President: Washington August 20, 1917.

I received yesterday the enclosed letter from the French Ambassador. As it asks for your views in relation to the appeal of the Pope will you kindly indicate to me what answer I shall make to Monsieur Jusserand?

Faithfully yours,   Robert Lansing.

TLS (WP, DLC).

E N C L O S U R E

Jean Jules Jusserand to Robert Lansing

My dear Mr. Secretary,   Washington Aug. 18, 1917

As I told you when I saw you this morning my Government would like to know whether, in the opinion of the President, the Pope's note, drawn up, as it seems to have been under inimical influences, demands an answer.

If the President thought it better to send one, my Government consider it would be appropriate to concert as to what should be said, so that a similar attitude be observed by those who fight on the same side of the trench.

I should be much obliged if you would enable me to inform my Government of the President's views in the matter.

Believe me, dear Mr. Secretary

Very sincerely yours,   Jusserand[1]

TCL (WP, DLC).
 [1] The ALS is in SDR, RG 59, 763.72119/768½, DNA.

From George Creel, with Enclosure

Dear Mr. President: [Washington] June [Aug.] 20, 1917.

I have digested the report of the Root Commission to Russia,[1] as requested by you, and return it herewith, together with my own views on the various recommendations. When I see you tomorrow, I hope to have a more definite plan for presentation and discussion.   Respectfully,   [George Creel]

TCL (G. Creel Papers, DLC).

[1] A supplemental report submitted to Wilson about August 15 and entitled *Plans for American Cooperation to Preserve and Strengthen the Morale of the Civil Population and the Army of Russia* (Washington, 1917). A copy is in WP, DLC.

ENCLOSURE

I.

Suggested budget for twelve months for the establishment of a modern news service to furnish news to all periodicals in Russia:

Salaries

Manager	$ 8,000
Two assistants at $4,000	8,000
Assistant in America	4,000
Five Russian writers and translators at $2,500	12,500
Traveling expenses	3,000
Cable service, 1,000 words a day at 32 cents a word (approx.)	125,000
Printing sheets to go to all periodicals in Russia	100,000
Postage, at least	25,000
	$285,500

This is a good idea, but the amount estimated is inadequate. It presupposes that the necessary material is already available and that the one "Assistant in America" will only have to put it on the wire. This is not true. Machinery will have to be created on this side as well as in Russia. Further, no financial provision is made for telegraphing the material throughout Russia. In addition to day by day cable-telegraph service, a news feature service must be established, as many stories will have to be written in response to specific demands.

In order that a high class news service and feature service may be put in instant operation, I figure that the budget for 12 months should be placed at $500,000.00.

II.

Preparation and distribution of pamphlets and leaflets: $250,-000 to $500,000

I do not think that this idea has any merit at all. The British tried it and have only muddled the situation. Let us rather concentrate upon a daily news and an effective feature service.

III.

Film Service
  Salaries

Manager	$ 5,000
Assistant	3,000
Five traveling men at $2,000	10,000
Traveling expenses	12,000
Film outfits for 200 centers	100,000
Cost of films	100,000
Parcel postage	25,000
	$255,000

This is a proper and necessary activity. It should be handled, however, through the War Co-operation Committee of the Motion Picture Industry. These men can supply every need out of their archives, and should also be in a position to take charge of the distribution throughout Russia.

IV.

Special advertising, particularly by means of illustrated colored posters:
  Salaries

Expert advertising man	$ 5,000
Assistant	3,000
Traveling expenses	3,000
Printing, from $100,000 to	200,000
	$211,000

This is a half-baked suggestion. Posters, aside from their enormous expense, are only effective when of the highest class. For four months I have been trying to get some effective posters from the artists of America and I have not yet seen a single one that appeals to me as the real thing. It would take twice the amount to handle such a campaign, also a good many months to get it ready, and the returns are small and uncertain.

V.

The employment of five hundred Russians to influence Russian opinion by means of public speaking:

Salaries

Director of Bureau and Assistant ....$	5,000
100 men at $1,000	100,000
Traveling expenses	100,000
Traveling expenses for 400 volunteer speakers who will give part time	200,000
	$405,000

This suggestion is interesting in theory but mighty dangerous in practice. Who is to select the 500 speakers? How are they to be trained? How is double dealing to be guarded against? In order to determine the effectiveness of the campaign and to see that the 500 were not betraying the bureau, a large force of inspectors would have to be created.

VI.

Headquarters in Petrograd.

Rent of various offices .... $	3,500
Office equipment	2,500
Stenographers (6 from America, 12 from Russia)	25,000
Mailing and other clerks (10)	10,000
Accountant and assistant	5,000
Miscellaneous office expenses	5,000
	$51,000

With regard to this item, the news service and feature service will establish themselves in their own offices and the film service can easily make arrangements for quarters with them. Rentals and office forces are properly expenses that should be taken care of out of the specific appropriations.

VII.

Helping certain Russian Agencies, such as the Soldiers' Newspaper ($10,000) $250,000.00

It may be well to give $10,000.00 to the Soldiers' Newspaper, so that it may have greater efficiency. It is not well, however, to devote any sum of money to making subsidies to any portion of the Russian press.

VIII.

Emergency Fund to Provide for Increased Service as well as for Unforeseen Demands $250,000
I see no reason for any such emergency fund. When money is appropriated the tendency is to spend it. Better to have the specific appropriations large enough to take care of all legitimate expenses, then hold the disbursers to that amount.

IX.

To strengthen the morale of the Army it is recommended that the sum of $3,305,000.00 be spent in installing the Young Men's Christian Association plan, that is, specialization in the physical, mental, social and moral betterment of the men. The money is to be spent on the employment of seven hundred secretaries, their traveling expenses, the purchase or refitting of 200 buildings and their equipment, etc.

Based on an estimate of 7,200,000 now in the Russian Army, even the huge amount mentioned would provide only one building for every 36,000 soldiers, and one secretary for every 10,200 soldiers. It would take months to get such an organization into the field. It is also to be considered that the Russians may not take kindly to the Y.M.C.A.

X.

What we do in Russia must be done well and done quickly. For this reason I suggest the following organization and expenditures:

News Service and Feature Service $500,000.00
Film Service 300,000.00
Soldiers' Newspaper 10,000.00
$810,000.00

With regard to administration, I do not think that the State Department should have anything to do with it at all. The work lies entirely within the province of the Committee on Public Information, and would be merely an extension of activities already under way. I have not included Russia in my foreign campaign out of a desire to learn the findings of the Root Commission, but with its work concluded, I see no reason for further delay.

While not yet ready to present a detailed plan, it is my thought to ask Charles Edward Russell to act for the Committee in Russia. He knows more about the Russian situation than any other, and in addition to his sympathy and understanding, he is one of the best newspapermen in the country and a writer of rare ability.   Respectfully submitted,   George Creel

TS MS (G. Creel Papers, DLC).

From William Lea Chambers

Bainbridge, Georgia, August 20, 1917.

I have just now been shown copy of a telegram dated August 15th addressed to Senator Hollis by Stone, Shea, Sheppard and Dodge, chief executives acting for the four organizations in engine and train service, requesting the Senator to present to you the subject matter of the controversy between train employees and the Georgia, Florida, and Alabama Railroad. Assuming that the Senator has brought the matter to your attention I have decided that it was my duty to report the situation to you by wire instead of waiting until I reached Washington.

The controversy began early in February of this year growing out of the discharge of an engineer and the demand of his brotherhood supported by the others for his reinstatement. Period. The situation at that time threatened to interrupt the business of the railroad to the serious detriment of the public interest, and the services of the board of mediation being requested by the employees were tendered to the railroad and were declined. period.

The Board of Mediation however, never withdrew from the controversy and on the 16th day of July the employees notified the railroad company that unless their demands, which also included a revision of their schedule and an increase of wages, were granted within forty eight hours they would take a strike vote. Period. The railroad officials claim that the employees also notified them that they would strike at the expiration of that time, but this statement is denied by the employees. Period.

Instead of granting the demands of the employees or invoking the services of the Board of Mediation, the tender of which was still open to them, the railroad company sued for an injunction in the superior court of Decatur County, and a temporary restraining order was issued by the judge of the court restraining the employees, and the executive officials representing them, from striking or taking a strike vote or in any way interfering with the operation of trains reporting to their national organization or any other person, corporation or thing, that any strike has been called or is in effect among employees of the railroad, and this temporary order has been made permanent. The judge subsequently modified this injunction in following words: "The men or defendants have a right to resign or quit the service of the plaintiff, but not by concerted action to violate this injunction as granted originally" End quote.

Immediately upon the issuance of the temporary injunction the representative officials of the brotherhoods by wire notified the board of mediation of the status, and the board thereupon again renewed the tender and urged the acceptance of its services by all parties to the controversy. I assume that they informed their chief executives. Period. Since then the defendants have been cited for contempt which proceeding is still pending. Period. I came from Washington to Bainbridge and have been here for a week, and have been endeavoring to bring about a settlement with the full knowledge, approval, and I may say, sympathy of the judge who issued the injunction. The employees have placed their whole controversy in my hands and are ready to mediate through the board of mediation or to arbitrate.

The railroad company declined mediation before I left Washington and my efforts have failed to secure their consent. The company takes the position that the tender of the board services by the commissioners is is [sic] not a tender from the board itself within the meaning of the acts of congress, and secondly, that the board of mediation cannot within the terms of the act of congress tender its services in this case because the persons claiming to be employees of the railroad are not actually at the time engaged in any capacity of train operation or train service. All the efforts of the board of mediation has been exhausted, of which I have felt compelled to advise the employees and their representatives and being enjoined by the court from taking a strike vote or striking, which they contend is a denial of their fundamental right to enforce their demands in the premises, the employees contend that this involves the welfare of their organizations, and I am advised by them that the four executives named at the beginning of this message will convoke in Washington at an early date the six hundred odd general chairmen, a similar body to that assembled there a year ago, the significance of which, and the possible effects of which, you will appreciate.

I am leaving here tonight and will arrive in Washington Wednesday forenoon with a complete record of the case unless you wire me to remain here.   W. L. Chambers

T telegram (WP, DLC).

From Newton Diehl Baker, with Enclosure

Dear Mr. President: Washington. August 20, 1917

Walter Lippmann is attached to my office. He makes me memoranda on many things. This one, I venture to submit to your thought only because you know how thoughtful he is
                         Respectfully   Newton D. Baker

ALS (WP, DLC).

E N C L O S U R E

MEMORANDUM for the Secretary of War: Washington.

Reply to the Pope's proposal.

[1.] We are conducting the war on the assumption that there is a distinction between the German government and German people. The question is: Why have the German people supported this government in the past and why do they continue to? Among the elements which bound the German people to their government in the past are the following:

1. The memory of centuries of oppression and poverty which preceded German unity. Germany was the battleground of Europe.

2. The splendor and prosperity which followed Bismarck's triumph.

3. The fear of imperial Russia.

4. The fear that Germany's access to raw materials would be cut by the British fleet.

On the basis of these memories, hopes, and fears a government and educational system has grown up which makes the German people obedient by playing on these motives. The military, financial, aristocratic and large agrarian class maintains its position because it is associated with the fundamental ideas of national security, economic opportunity, human pride.

If the German people are to be weaned from their governing class they must be made to believe that they can be safe, prosperous, and respected without dependence upon their government as its exists. Unless this is done they will continue to regard as their sole means of defence what we regard as an engine of aggression. The mistake of Allied diplomacy has been due to a failure to see that Prussian militarism which looks so dangerous to us looks to the German people like their best defence against a circle of enemies. They hold the handle of the spear which is pointed at us.

In the last year or so another motive has arisen which binds the people to the government—the yearning for peace. The German government has very shrewdly identified itself with that yearning, and the Allies, through the Paris conference and their reply to President Wilson last December, have very unwisely presented themselves to the German people as implacable enemies intent upon imposing a humiliating peace. It is clear by now that the majority of the German people accept the formula of "no annexations and no indemnities," that this formula is in their opinion a disavowal of aggression, and that the Allies disdain of the formula is convincing proof to them that whatever the origins of the war they are now in fact engaged in a war of national defence.

2. From the American point of view the obstacle to peace is our distrust of the German government. We are not interested in particular territorial settlements; we are interested in the *method of settlement*. "The world made safe for democracy" means concretely not a specific form of government for Germany, not a specific drawing of strategic and nationalist frontiers, but a binding assurance that the future method of settlement between the powers shall be by a civil procedure. We are at war with the German procedure, and we hesitate to negotiate now because we do not see adequate guaranties for the future that the procedure will be different.

3. So long as those guaranties do not exist the nations aligned against Germany are compelled to rely for their safety upon maintaining a balance of power against Germany. The machinery of peace, i.e., a League of Nations accompanied by reduction of armament, cannot be set in motion until Germany becomes, in the President's words, "a fit partner."

4. By a fit partner we understand a Germany in which control of foreign policy and of the military machine has passed to the representatives of the people. We go on the assumption that it is possible to deal in good faith with a democracy.

5. But the progress of democracy in Germany is arrested by the conviction of the German people that a radical change in the midst of war will have results similar to those in Russia, i.e., that it will render them defenceless.

6. *This is the vicious circle which it may be possible to begin breaking by the reply to the Pope.*

Suppose the argument ran as follows:

The American people share his noble desire to see an end of the agony, but they desire even more to end the possibility of its repetition. They believe in the establishment of a League of Peace and reduction of armaments and equal opportunities for all nationalities. They are convinced, however, upon Germany's record in Belgium and in regard to the submarine that it does not respect treaties. The American people, therefore, desire to know what guaranties there are that a negotiation undertaken now would be binding. This is the essential point for which we fight. If those guaranties are forthcoming, the United States will not countenance economic war after the war, will accept Germany as a partner in the League, and as a member of such a league would be prepared to guarantee the German people in the future against aggression.

7. It would be unwise, I think, to specify the terms of territorial settlement for several reasons: Because they are secondary not only from the American point of view but from the world point of view; because it is essential to focus on the method of peace rather than the terms of peace; because such a reply really represents our share in the war. Keeps us clear of entanglements, justifies a continuation of the war if it is rejected, and yet leaves the door sufficiently ajar so that the President cannot be accused either by Germany or by the American people of prolonging the war.

T MS (W. Lippmann Papers, CtY).

From Newton Diehl Baker

Dear Mr President: Washington. Aug 20, 1917

The enclosed was written by General Crowder.[1]

Would it not be wise to avoid the possibility of your letter to Senator Weeks having an unequal effect in different districts by writing me some such letter as the enclosed?

Respectfully,   Newton D. Baker

ALS (WP, DLC).
[1] NDB to WW, Aug. 18, 1917 (third letter of that date).

To Newton Diehl Baker

My dear Mr. Secretary: [The White House] August 20, 1917.

I have your letter of the 18th with regard to the suggestion made by Senator Weeks in relation to the drafting of men with families and particularly married men for military service.

In my reply to the letter of Senator Weeks, I expressed my sympathy with the view that we ought as far as practicable to raise this new National Army without creating the hardships necessarily entailed when the head of a family is taken and my hope that for the most part those accepted in the first call would be found to be men who had not yet assumed such relations. The selective service law makes the fact of dependents, rather than the fact of marriage, the basis for exemption, and there are, undoubtedly, many cases within the age limits fixed by law of men who are married and yet whose accumulations or other economic surroundings are such that no dependency of the wife exists in fact. Plainly, the law does not contemplate exemption for this class of men. The regulation promulgated on May 18, 1917, should be regarded as controlling in these cases, and the orders issued under that regulation directing exemption boards to establish the fact of dependents in addition to the fact of marriage ought not to be abrogated.

Very truly yours,   Woodrow Wilson.[1]

TL (Letterpress Books, WP, DLC).
  [1] Baker's draft is missing; however, this letter undoubtedly repeated it.

From the White House Staff

The White House.

Memorandum for the President: August 20, 1917.

Mr. Vance McCormick telephoned to request that the President be advised that he is ready to report on the matter which the President asked him to look into (the exports administrative matter). Mr. McCormick asks when the President could see him about this matter.[1]

T MS (WP, DLC).
  [1] Wilson saw McCormick at the White House at 12:30 P.M. on August 21.

Helen Todd to Rudolph Forster, with Enclosure

My dear Mr. Forster: Washington, D. C. August 20, 1917.

When I saw you last Friday you asked me to give you a memorandum relating to the subject which I wished to discuss with the President. At that time I felt it would be unnecessary to see President Wilson provided Mr. Kent would be here to do so. I am very grateful, indeed, for the appointment which the President has given me for today, and am sending him the letter which I wrote to Mr. Creel, and also the one which I gave to Mr. Kent to present at his interview with President Wilson. It may save the President's time to glance over these before I arrive.[1]

Sincerely yours,   Helen Todd.

TLS (WP, DLC).
[1] She saw Wilson at 2:45 P.M. on August 20.

E N C L O S U R E

From Helen Todd

Dear Mr. President: Washington, D. C. August 18, 1917.

A few weeks ago you were kind enough to give me an interview[1] at which I represented a group of mothers of the working class. My object in seeing you was to bring to your attention the suffering that was being caused on the East Side, New York, arising from fear and distrust regarding the motives for this war. This, as I pointed out, arose because of lack of any adequate presentation of the great spirit of this war, in terms which the working women can understand, and also because of a most energetic propaganda for the purpose of convincing them of the cruelty and ugliness back of the necessity of war.

You did me the honor to believe that I could be of service in making the issues of the war clearer to the women and referred me to Mr. Creel to perfect plans in that direction. Mr. Creel referred me to Mr. Gompers, and at Mr. Creel's request I came down to see Mr. Gompers regarding the details of this propaganda.

The result of my conference with Mr. Gompers will be seen in the letter to Mr. Creel, copy of which I enclose.[2] In response to this letter Mr. Creel tells me that Mr. Gompers is in entire control of all speakers who will be sent out to form public opinion on the war, and that he, Mr. Creel, feels he must uphold Mr. Gompers in the stand he has taken, viz: to discuss no terms of peace and to continue the war to its finish, its finish being, according to Mr. Gompers, "until the German Emperor and his war party are forced by the Allies to abdicate," regardless of how long it may take or at what price of human life it may be gained.

Mr. President, Mr. Gompers says that we are "willing to pay the price," but he cannot speak for the masses of the millions of mothers of this country. They are not members of the American Federation of Labor, they are in their homes, bearing, nursing, and rearing their children, and they are furnishing the flesh and blood that goes into this war. Mr. Gompers is not paying the price, although he says he is willing to do so, he could not do so. He is sitting in a very beautiful office with hammocks and roof garden to rest in and seems to be entirely out of touch, not only with the suffering, but with the intelligence of the women of this country. He either could not conceal his impatience and contempt for the point of view of which I was a representative, and which was the same that I expressed to you, or else he made no effort to do so. I cannot but feel that to go before women with no finer or more constructive message than Mr. Gompers furnishes would be a grave mistake. I feel, too, Mr. President, that every business interest has been listened to with respect from time to time here in Washington. The business of the majority of women is bearing and rearing the boys who go to the front. Why should not their point of view be listened to with at least as much consideration as if they were the breeders of cattle or creators of steel rails. Why should we, who represent a large body of women, feel when we go to Mr. Gompers that our wishes are unworthy of consideration or discussion?

I met this same attitude in Mr. Charles Edward Russel[l], whom I met by accident in the hotel where I am stopping. Being an old friend I spoke to Mr. Russell about this matter, as I am speaking to you. His anger and contempt were far greater than Mr. Gompers'. He said that any woman who wished to discuss terms of peace at this time was a traitor to her country, that all of us belonged in the German camp, and that he had come to believe that women had no feeling for democracy, and that I was only disturbing and harassing you by trying to see you.

Mr. President, if this is true and the endeavor to bring before you the point of view of the average woman is not of service to you, you have only to let me know.

I was West during the last Presidential campaign and I saw the entire machinery of the Republican party swept away like a straw before the Western woman's vote. As one of the

Republican leaders said to me, "You can't talk to those women, they don't listen or reason, they just sit and say, 'He kept us out of war.'" I was in almost every voting state at that time and I have never seen so great faith and loyalty to any man expressed as in the overwhelming vote of women for you. The men believed that it was the phrase "He kept us out of war," that won you this devotion of women. I, who have studied the situation very carefully, know that this great woman's vote was caused by the fear that we would have to get into war, and the women desired as the head of our Government in such a crisis, the man who had expressed the opinions as to peace, justice, and humanity, which you had made public. Women fear above all things the passion of men when aroused to consider it their duty to conquer and punish. They felt in you a greater capacity for "love and fine thinking," and voted for you.

This same trust has reached to the women of the East Side of New York, and they have asked me to see you and try to explain to you how they feel about this war. It is because of this great and beautiful trust of women in you that I am staying in Washington, refusing to believe that Mr. Gompers' and Mr. Russell's view or the expression of some of the members of your Administration, reflect your attitude toward this war.

I am asking for this interview only that I may bring before you the fact that a great body of women who have followed you loyally in agreeing to any sacrifice which their country requires, now believe that the time has come when America's terms of peace should be considered and stated in terms which all women can understand. Already the youth of the old world has been a blood sacrifice for the sins of European Governments. Must we add to that the life blood and youth of our own land? Since we cannot exterminate the German nation and would not if we could, we must eventually have recourse to arbitration. Can you not, Mr. President, open the door to this opportunity, and avert years of slaughter by re-affirming your former statement of "peace without victory," and offering to the world America's terms of a just and lasting peace?

Yours sincerely,   Helen Todd.

TLS (WP, DLC).
¹ On July 20.
² Helen Todd to G. Creel, Aug. 10, 1917, TCL (WP, DLC).

From Frank Park[1]

My dear Mr. President: Washington, D. C. August 20, 1917.

Each day the mails bring to me communications from men engaged in farming in southern Georgia asking that I appeal to you to permit their sons who have been called under the draft law to remain on their farms (where it is shown to local Boards that they are actually cultivating crops) until October 1st, in order to enable them to complete their work.

As you know, the negroes, on whom southern farmers have to depend for labor, have been coming North for many months leaving our people practically dependent upon their own efforts in the gathering of their crops.

Our people are not protesting against the drafting of their sons for Army service, but merely ask that they be given time to harvest their crops and thereby prevent what would otherwise result in a great loss to them.

May I not ask that you speak to the Provost Marshal regarding this matter?   Sincerely yours,   Frank Park.

TLS (WP, DLC).
[1] Democratic congressman from Georgia.

ADDENDA

To George McLean Harper

My dear Harper,   Princeton, 8 Jan'y, 1903

I read last night your generous review of my *History* in the *Book Buyer*,[1] and I thank you for it with all my heart. It is delightful to be so praised and so discriminatingly criticised. I do not think what I said of the Ku Klux a defence,[2]—I meant it, rather, for an intimate explanation,—and with regard to that particular matter I am an original, contemporary authority,—nor do I think it fine drawn. To me it seems mere matter of fact like the rest. But such matters are subordinate, and I will not trouble you with a new argument for the terrifiers. The rest of your criticism I quite assent to, and the whole of the article gave me the greatest pleasure.

I can't close without saying how much I have admired your recent critical work and the progress of your style, which has been remarkable and delightful. It has become distinguished and is full of the most enjoyable felicities. I congratulate you.

    Always   Faithfully Yours,   Woodrow Wilson

ALS (WC, NjP).
 [1] Printed at Jan. 1, 1903, Vol. 14.
 [2] Harper had called it a "fine-spun argument in palliation of the Ku-Klux movement."

To Smith W. Wilson[1]

My dear Mr. Wilson: Princeton, N. J. March 20th, 1907.

I referred your letter about your son[2] to the Secretary of our Committee on Examinations and Standing, and I am glad to report as a result of my inquiry, that there is no impression that your son has acquired any bad habits at all, or that he can be said to be neglecting his work.

At the same time, his instructors report that he has not been working very hard. I do not think that there is any ground for anxiety, and I hope that if you will counsel your son to pay a little closer attention to his studies, it will probably bring his average up.

Of course, it is very difficult to compare work at a school[3] with work at a college, for many boys who did well at school do much less well at a university, because of the increased difficulty of the studies and the almost entire change in methods of instruction. I sincerely hope that in a little while your son will have struck the pace, and that you will feel that you are rewarded for sending him here.

With sincere regard,

Very truly yours,   Woodrow Wilson

TLS (WC, NjP).
1 Of Clearfield, Pa.
2 Cedric Frederick Wilson, Princeton 1911.
3 Cedric Frederick Wilson had attended the Lawrenceville School.

INDEX

NOTE ON THE INDEX

THE alphabetically arranged analytical table of contents at the front of the volume eliminates duplication, in both contents and index, of references to certain documents, such as letters. Letters are listed in the contents alphabetically by name, and chronologically within each name by page. The subject matter of all letters is, of course, indexed. The Editorial Notes and Wilson's writings are listed in the contents chronologically by page. In addition, the subject matter of both categories is indexed. The index covers all references to books and articles mentioned in text or notes. Footnotes are indexed. Page references to footnotes which place a comma between the page number and "n" cite both text and footnote, thus: "624,n3." On the other hand, absence of the comma indicates reference to the footnote only, thus: "55n2"—the page number denoting where the footnote appears.

The index supplies the fullest known form of names and, for the Wilson and Axson families, relationships as far down as cousin. Persons referred to by nicknames or shortened forms of names can be identified by reference to entries for these forms of the names.

Two cumulative contents-index volumes are now in print: Volume 13, which covers Volumes 1-12, and Volume 26, which covers Volumes 14-25. Volume 39, which covers Volumes 27-38, is in preparation.

INDEX

WITHDRAWN